lessons about controversial as well as non-controversial aspects of substantive criminal law. It is a tour de force that will delight and educate everyone."

Morris B. Hoffman, *District Judge (ret.), State of Colorado; Member, John D. and Catherine T. MacArthur Foundation Research Network on Law and Neuroscience; author of* The Punisher's Brain: The Evolution of Judge and Jury

"Based on immense, wide-ranging erudition and sparkling creativity, Paul Robinson's *American Criminal Law* is a fascinating introduction like no other. Using unconventional but insightful materials, the text will challenge students to consider the genuine principles and concerns that animate American criminal law. It will without doubt create the most interesting course imaginable, generating fascinating discussions with unforgettable examples. If I were teaching the course, it is unthinkable that I would choose another text. The book is a triumph."

Stephen J. Morse, *Ferdinand Wakeman Hubbell Professor of Law and Professor of Psychology & Law in Psychiatry, University of Pennsylvania*

"*American Criminal Law* presents the principles and competing interests in criminal law in a manner particularly appropriate for undergraduate students. The authors' leveraging of students' innate interest in crime – through the use of illustrating cases – coupled with their innovative pedagogical approach, makes this an ideal text for courses in a range of programs."

Raymond V. Carman, Jr, PhD, *Department of Political Science, SUNY College at Plattsburgh*

"*American Criminal Law* offers a very clever approach to teaching this area of law. By focusing on concepts and patters of application – rather than the typical doctrine of a casebook – this text is better suited than most at helping students to become better thinkers about criminal law."

Keith Richotte, Jr, JD, LLM, PhD, *Associate Professor of American Studies, University of North Carolina at Chapel Hill and Associate Justice of the Turtle Mountain Tribal Court of Appeals*

American Criminal Law

This coursebook offers an exciting new approach to teaching criminal law to graduate and undergraduate students, and indeed to the general public. Each well-organized and student-friendly chapter offers historical context, tells the story of a principal historic case, provides a modern case that contrasts with the historic, explains the legal issue at the heart of both cases, includes a unique mapping feature describing the range of positions on the issue among the states today, examines a key policy question on the topic, and provides an aftermath that reports the final chapter to the historic and modern case stories.

By embedding sophisticated legal doctrine and analysis in real-world storytelling, the book provides a uniquely effective approach to teaching American criminal law in programs on criminal justice, political science, public policy, history, philosophy, and a range of other fields.

Paul H. Robinson is one of the world's leading criminal law scholars. A prolific writer and lecturer, Robinson has published articles in virtually all of the top law reviews, lectured in more than 100 cities in 33 states and 27 countries, and had his writings appear in 13 languages. A former federal prosecutor and counsel for the U.S. Senate Subcommittee on Criminal Laws and Procedures, he was the lone dissenter when the U.S. Sentencing Commission promulgated the current federal sentencing guidelines. He is the author or editor of 17 books, including the standard lawyer's reference on criminal law defenses, three monographs on criminal law theory, a highly regarded criminal law treatise, and an innovative case studies course book.

Sarah M. Robinson is a former sergeant in the U.S. Army and a practiced social worker. She currently works as an author and researcher.

American Criminal Law

Its People, Principles, and Evolution

Paul H. Robinson
Sarah M. Robinson

Routledge
Taylor & Francis Group

NEW YORK AND LONDON

Cover image: © suprun / Getty Images

First published 2023
by Routledge
605 Third Avenue, New York, NY 10158

and by Routledge
4 Park Square, Milton Park, Abingdon, Oxon, OX14 4RN

Routledge is an imprint of the Taylor & Francis Group, an informa business

Library of Congress Cataloging-in-Publication Data
Names: Robinson, Paul H., 1948– author. | Robinson, Sarah M., author.
Title: American criminal law: its people, principles, and evolution /
Paul H. Robinson, Sarah M. Robinson.
Description: New York, NY: Routledge, 2022. | Includes bibliographical
references and index.
Identifiers: LCCN 2021060014 (print) | LCCN 2021060015 (ebook) |
ISBN 9781032191867 (hardback) | ISBN 9781032191850 (paperback) |
ISBN 9781003258025 (ebook)
Subjects: LCSH: Criminal law—United States. | LCGFT: Textbooks.
Classification: LCC KF9219.85 .R63 2022 (print) | LCC KF9219.85 (ebook) |
DDC 345.73—dc23/eng/20220524
LC record available at https://lccn.loc.gov/2021060014
LC ebook record available at https://lccn.loc.gov/2021060015

ISBN: 978-1-032-19186-7 (hbk)
ISBN: 978-1-032-19185-0 (pbk)
ISBN: 978-1-003-25802-5 (ebk)

DOI: 10.4324/9781003258025

Typeset in Sabon
by codeMantra

Access the Support Material: www.routledge.com/9781032191850

To my students, who have taught me so much.
    – PHR

To Judy (1938–1975), Bob (1939–1966), Jane (1943–1985), and John Andrews (1946–2021), a generation of devoted citizens.
    – SMR

Contents

Contents

Contents

Chronological Table of Principal Cases

Figure Sources

1.1 https://www.elespanol.com/cultura/historia/20200209/todas-mentiras-creido-segunda-guerra-mundial/465204310_0.html.

1.2 AP, https://www.google.com/search?q=tri+state+crematory&hl=en&tbm=isch&sxsrf=AOaemvK-vqiFqHDdWWlEmGnwi3uVAwDZvQ%3A1638805168097&source=hp&biw=840&bih=906&ei=sC6uYZWoA6TB0PEP87mPgAY&iflsig=ALs-wAMAAAAYa48wKReMoOZSom6wyJTRv2Sk_cyyFyO&oq=tri+state+crematoriu&gs_lcp=CgNpbWcQARgAMgYIABAKEBg6CggjEO8DEOoCECc6BwgjEO8DECc6BQgAEIAEOgglABCxAxCDAToLCAAQgAQQsQMQgwE6CAgAEIAEELEDUOsNWL44YJ9XaAFwAHgAgAGMAYgB2wiSAQQxOS4xmAEAoAEBqgELZ3dzLXdpei1pbWWwAQo&sclient=img#imgrc=m5K8WC4xaQ9h9M.

2.1 Jim Bourdier, https://outlet.historicimages.com/search?type=product&q=thomas+moran.

2.3 https://www.gettyimages.com/detail/news-photo/habitual-criminal-under-texas-state-law-bill-rummel-sits-in-news-photo/515125908.

3.1 https://forensicfairy.tumblr.com/post/168468304985/ian-brady-and-myra-hindley-were-serial-killers.

4.1 https://bostonghosts.com/the-parkman-webster-murder/.

4.2 Jamison Wieser, https://www.flickr.com/photos/51035647214@N01/3331340675.

5.1 https://www.alamy.com/vintage-photo-circa-1924-showing-members-of-the-ku-klux-klan-attending-a-wedding-with-small-children-dressed-in-klan-robes-and-hoods-image448989756.html?pv=1&stamp=2&imageid=EA3C446C-5F2B-4D5C-8465-193BB0262936&p=353586&n=0&orientation=0&pn=1&searchtype=0&IsFromSearch=1&srch=foo%3dbar%26st%3d0%26pn%3d1%26ps%3d100%26sortby%3d2%26resultview%3dsortbyPopular%26npgs%3d0%26qt%3dkkk%2520wedding%26qt_raw%3dkkk%2520wedding%26lic%3d3%26mr%3d0%26pr%3d0%26ot%3d0%26creative%3d%26ag%3d0%26hc%3d0%26pc%3d%26blackwhite%3d1%26cutout%3d%26tbar%3d1%26et%3d0x000000000000000000000%26vp%3d0%26loc%3d0%26imgt%3d0%26dtfr%3d%26dtto%3d%26size%3d0xFF%26archive%3d1%26groupid%3d%26pseudoid%3d%26a%3d%26cdid%3d%26cdsrt%3d%26name%3d%26qn%3d%26apalib%3d%26apalic%3d%26lightbox%3d%26gname%3d%26gtype%3d%26xstx%3d0%26simid%3d%26saveQry%3d%26editorial%3d1%26nu%3d%26t%3d%26edo

ptin%3d%26customgeoip%3dUS%26cap%3d1%26cbstore%3d1%26vd %3d0%26lb%3d%26fi%3d2%26edrf%3d0%26ispremium%3d1%26flip %3d0%26pl%3d.

5.2 Courtesy of the Megan Meier Foundation, https://www.meganmeier foundation.org/.

6.1 https://commons.wikimedia.org/wiki/File:JustineJuliette1797xxv.jpg.

6.2 https://www.pinterest.com/pin/463659724123614376/.

7.1 https://www.etsy.com/listing/837357523/1900-1916-street-scene-fairbanks-alaska?gpla=1&gao=1&&utm_source=google&utm_medium=cpc&utm_campaign=shopping_us_c-art_and_collectibles-photography-black_and_white&utm_custom1=_k_CjwKCAiAhreNBhAYEiwAFGGKPI7ZNGDKFtJ Z4qkoDrynl_ShY5wlO_wOTPXL1WZZ9_GRh9vYfyqAABoCosQQAvD_ BwE_k_&utm_content=go_12573353456_119955064056_507602434727_ aud- 1184785539978:pla-352876712070_c__837357523_116731203&utm_ custom2=12573353456&gclid=CjwKCAiAhreNBhAYEiwAFGGKPI7ZNGDKF tJZ4qkoDrynl_ShY5wlO_wOTPXL1WZZ9_GRh9vYfyqAABoCosQQAvD_ BwE.

7.3 Courtesy of the Lammers family.

7.5 FBI, https://patch.com/new-hampshire/nashua/more-details-on-va-police-chief-from-nashua-charged-ia4231643a3.

8.1 https://historymartinez.wordpress.com/2017/01/12/august-spiesto-arms-we-call-you-to-arms-haymarket-riots-1886-primary-source-analysis/.

8.2 http://www.redrocknews.com/2021/09/05/enjoy-labor-day-summers-last-hurrah/.

8.4 Boston City Archives, https://search.creativecommons.org/photos/ d9b86294-a8ab-4419-8dd4-740b2dd7bdaa.

9.1 https://www.historyonthenet.com/an-alternate-history-of-the-lincoln-assassination-plot.

9.2 Ivan-balvan, https://www.istockphoto.com/photo/social-advertising-on-the-topic-of-drug-addiction-gm855368316-140716433.

10.1 https://ar.wikipedia.org/wiki/%D9%87%D9%8A%D8%AA%D9%8A_%D 8%AC%D8%B1%D9%8A%D9%86.

10.3 https://www.oregonlive.com/oregon-city/2017/03/followers_of_christ_ investigat.html.

11.1 https://emadion.it/en/homicides/cannibals/the-cannibals-of-the-mignonette/.

11.3 https://dewiki.de/Lexikon/Daschner-Prozess.

12.1 https://www.wilgafney.com/2020/11/29/jesus-and-hagar-the-form-of-a-slave/.

12.3 https://www.google.com/search?q=shooting+bernhard+goetz&hl=en&sx srf=AOaemvINweNGgbtkfG2KdvaRvRKZDGoeLw:1638809110072&source =lnms&tbm=isch&sa=X&ved=2ahUKEwimwvDWz8_0AhWpk4kEHaplB dQQ_AUoAnoECAIQBA&biw=840&bih=906&dpr=1#imgrc=gPG0kEVYrbP diM.

13.1 https://explorethearchive.com/things-you-didnt-know-about-wyatt-earp-and-the-gunfight-at-the-ok-corral.

13.4 https://tri-statedefender.com/elton-hymon-an-unsung-hero/02/22/.

14.1 https://americaincontext.com/2014/10/01/james-a-garfield-national-historic-site-mentor-oh/.

14.4 https://www.nbcnews.com/news/us-news/john-hinckley-freed-mental-hospital-35-years-after-reagan-assassination-n646076.

15.1 https://shield-files.fandom.com/wiki/Billy_le_Kid.

15.3 Courtesy of the Pittman family.

16.1 https://historycollection.co/5-nazi-war-criminals-attempted-escape-justice-south-america/5/.

16.3 https://www.nytimes.com/2018/03/12/obituaries/oskar-groning-the-bookkeeper-of-auschwitz-is-dead-at-96.html.

17.1 https://www.worldhistoryedu.com/9-things-that-you-probably-did-not-know-about-mary-queen-of-scots/.

17.4 https://www.motorproyect.com/2015/03/lo-demas-es-historia-delorean-dmc-12.html.

18.1 https://www.latimes.com/nation/nationnow/la-na-johnstown-flood-dam-safety-20140530-story.html.

18.4 LUM3NfromPixabay,https://pixabay.com/photos/dog-hybrid-mixed-breed-dog-816296/?download.

19.1 https://www.alamy.com/stock-photo-american-rock-and-roll-singer-and-musician-elvis-presley-pictured-84666167.html?pv=1&stamp=2&imageid=5B224FC7-D5F8-475D-90C8-084C4262990D&p=62486&n=0&orientation=0&pn=1&searchtype=0&IsFromSearch=1&srch=foo%3dbar%26st%3d0%26pn%3d1%26ps%3d100%26sortby%3d2%26resultview%3dsortbyPopular%26npgs%3d0%26qt%3delvis%2520army%26qt_raw%3delvis%2520army%26lic%3d3%26mr%3d0%26pr%3d0%26ot%3d0%26creative%3d%26ag%3d0%26hc%3d0%26pc%3d%26blackwhite%3d1%26cutout%3d%26tbar%3d1%26et%3d0x000000000000000000000%26vp%3d0%26loc%3d0%26imgt%3d0%26dtfr%3d%26dtto%3d%26size%3d0xFF%26archive%3d1%26groupid%3d%26pseudoid%3d%26a%3d%26cdid%3d%26cdsrt%3d%26name%3d%26qn%3d%26apalib%3d%26apalic%3d%26lightbox%3d%26gname%3d%26gtype%3d%26xstx%3d0%26simid%3d%26saveQry%3d%26editorial%3d1%26nu%3d%26t%3d%26edoptin%3d%26customgeoip%3dUS%26cap%3d1%26cbstore%3d1%26vd%3d0%26lb%3d%26fi%3d2%26edrf%3d0%26ispremium%3d1%26flip%3d0%26pl%3d.

19.3 https://www.alamy.com/stock-photo-david-letterman-010882-32378036.html?pv=1&stamp=2&imageid=D894084B-A9A7-463D-91E3-FA99499E0473&p=96039&n=0&orientation=0&pn=1&searchtype=0&IsFromSearch=1&srch=foo%3dbar%26st%3d0%26pn%3d1%26ps%3d100%26sortby%3d2%26resultview%3dsortbyPopular%26npgs%3d0%26qt%3ddavid%2520letterman%26qt_raw%3ddavid%2520letterman%26lic%3d3%26mr%3d0%26pr%3d0%26ot%3d0%26creative%3d%26ag%3d0%26hc%3d0%26pc%3d%26blackwhite%3d1%26cutout%3d%26tbar%3d1%26et%3d0x000000000000000000000%26vp%3d0%26loc%3d0%26imgt%3d0%26dtfr%3d%26dtto%3d%26size%3d0xFF%26archive%3d1%26groupid%3d%26pseudoid%3d%26a%3d%26cdid%3d%26cdsrt%3d%26name%3d%26qn%3d%26apalib%3d%26apalic%3d%26lightbox%3d%26gname%3

3d%26gtype%3d%26xstx%3d0%26simid%3d%26saveQry%3d%26edito
rial%3d1%26nu%3d%26t%3d%26edoptin%3d%26customgeoip%3dUS
%26cap%3d1%26cbstore%3d1%26vd%3d0%26lb%3d%26fi%3d2%26e
drf%3d0%26ispremium%3d1%26flip%3d0%26pl%3d.

20.1 https://www.soulfulrecords.co.uk/ike%20and%20tina%20turner%20
a%20fool%20for%20you%20sp.

20.4 https://www.denverpost.com/2016/06/01/cody-latimers-girlfriend-
allegedly-slapped-him-before-both-she-and-the-broncos-wideout-were-
arrested/.

21.1 https://musicboxtheatre.com/events/the-indestructible-bette-davis.

21.3 https://www.nydailynews.com/entertainment/gossip/sandra-bullock-
alleged-stalker-stand-trial-article-1.2179894.

22.3 Courtesy of the Anderson family.

23.1 https://www.reddit.com/r/OldSchoolCool/comments/jt3nft/frank_
sinatra_1938/.

24.1 https://i0.wp.com/reynolds-news.com/wp-content/uploads/2019/09/fanny-
hil.jpg?resize=388%2C590&ssl=1.

24.2 https://search.creativecommons.org/photos/d4ba9d30-949b-4404-8b2e-
4bad2acd981a.

25.1 https://timothyrhaslett.files.wordpress.com/2015/05/untitled-32.jpeg.

25.2 https://extra.globo.com/noticias/mundo/adolescente-americano-
processado-por-fotos-nu-em-seu-celular-17563220.html.

26.1 https://fishki.net/1814500-podborka-ljubopytnyh-istoricheskih-faktov.
html.

26.3 https://www.fulcrum7.com/news/2020/4/19/amish-sam-is-coming-home.

27.1 https://thevaulthorseracing.wordpress.com/2014/04/.

27.3 https://zi.media/@yidianzixun/post/aJGazX.

28.1 https://www.loc.gov/item/2003656591/.

28.3 https://wpmarchione.com/2017/05/19/annexation-embraced-brightons-
1873-acceptance-of-boston/.

29.1 https://www.posterazzi.com/joseph-bonanno-wanted-poster-issued-
by-the-new-york-police-after-his-alleged-kidnapping-in-1964-by-fellow-
gangsters-history-item-varevchisl019ec257/.

30.1 https://historica.fandom.com/wiki/Aaron_Burr?file=Aaron_Burr_statue.jpg.

30.3 https://www.heraldtribune.com/news/20051001/police-arrest-man-as-person-
of-interest-in-disappearance.

31.1 http://garysworldblog.blogspot.com/2008/02/hatfield-mccoy-feud_8123.
html.

31.4 https://en.wikipedia.org/wiki/Kiki_Camarena#/media/File:Enrique-
camarena1.jpg.

Preface

History gives us an enormous grab bag of interesting cases that show how criminal law has changed and is continuing to change. This volume uses these cases as an introduction to American criminal law. It is not meant to be a workman's handbook for criminal justice system participants but rather a travel brochure for anyone interested in the life and evolution of criminal law and society.

To ordinary people, criminal law is about doing justice, and avoiding injustice, and there exist some core values that are universally held and not likely to ever change: people ought to be protected from unprovoked aggression; causing personal injury, all other things being equal, is more condemnable than damaging property; the more intentional the wrongdoing the greater the punishment deserved; even intangible interests of societal institutions can deserve criminal law protection; and so on.

At the same time, out from these core principles, people can and do disagree about a variety of things, such as the propriety of criminalizing certain conduct or how the law ought to define the conditions under which an actor deserves punishment: should downloading music without a license be a crime (and not just a civil violation)? Should mental illness that creates a compulsion to engage in conduct that the actor knows is wrong provide an excuse? Should polygamy be an offense? Should accomplices be punished the same as the perpetrator? People disagree. Indeed, a broader historical perspective suggests that even many of the questions that seem entirely settled for us today were at one time entirely unsettled or even settled with a very different answer: adultery, blasphemy, and same-sex intercourse, for example, were at one time serious criminal offenses, while slavery, intercourse by an adult with a 15-year-old, and gross environmental pollution at one time were not.

The nature of societal change is such that it never stops. Generations from now people will look back on our present society and roll their eyes – or scowl in disgust – at something we now criminalize that they have come to see as wholly acceptable or at something we fail to criminalize that they have come to see as highly condemnable. This suggests that we ought to have some greater humility about our views, for we can be sure that some future generation will mock us for some aspect of them.

A related theme of this volume is not just the unending evolution of law and societal values but also a demonstration that there is a good deal of diversity among criminal law rules in present society. People regularly speak of "American criminal law" – as in the title of this volume – but in fact there is no such thing as the American criminal law rule. Instead, there are 52 American jurisdictions – the 50 states, the District of Columbia, and the federal system – each of which has its own criminal code. And, as the chapters in this volume repeatedly demonstrate, there exists an enormous amount of variation among the jurisdictions on a wide variety of criminal law issues.

These points of disagreement often mark issues that may be ripe for reform. That is, a larger historical evolutionary shift may first reveal itself in our present disagreement among jurisdictions. Examining these current differences can be as interesting as examining the differences between the historical and the present legal rules.

The larger point here is that the topics and case studies selected for this volume are not meant to be comprehensive or representative but rather interesting and thought-provoking. As it happens, the volume ends up covering essentially all of the most important offenses and principles of liability, but it is not organized around that goal. Its focus is on the criminal law principles and offenses that can tell us the most about the nature of criminal law, our judgments of justice, and our societal values.

Trigger warning: people do terrible things to one another, and most of those terrible things fall within the purview of criminal law. The fact that these are all real cases with a detailed narrative can make them all the more upsetting. Sometimes, the greater shock is that a previous generation was so accepting of what we now see as so abhorrent.

Criminal law is one of the most interesting perspectives on the human adventure. It requires us to examine how we want people to act, what we will do when they act improperly, and how we decide what we can reasonably expect of people. And to do this, we must assess what makes a successful society, what citizen protections and obligations a society should enforce, as well as the principles of justice that the community shares. What could be more interesting!

We hope this volume can get you thinking about these issues. Have fun!

– PHR & SMR

PART I

Liability Principles

This volume is divided into parts that mirror the way modern criminal codes are constructed. Part I concerns general principles of criminal liability. Part II concerns general defenses to criminal liability. Taken together, these issues make up what is referred to as the *General Part* of the criminal code. The *Special Part* of the criminal code is the collection of specific offense definitions, the subject of Part III of this volume. In a homicide case, for example, the Special Part of the code will have definitions for all the different homicide offenses; those rules are *special* to those offenses. The General Part then addresses issues common to all crimes, such as the rules of complicity and attempt, the definitions of offense culpability requirements, as well as general defenses that might be available, such as self-defense or insanity.

This first part of the book, concerning Liability Principles, examines the general criminal law rules required to establish liability, with separate chapters on the requirements for culpability, causation, the role of consent, as well as liability for attempt, complicity, conspiracy, and omission (Chapters 5–10). It also uses the homicide offense to illustrate generally how offense grades and mitigations work (Chapters 3 and 4).

Perhaps most importantly, this first part begins by explaining the unique form and function of criminal law. The *form* of criminal law – typically codified by the legislature with a good deal of detail, rather than left to decisions by appellate courts – is the product of what is called the *legality principle* (Chapter 1). The *function* of criminal law – whether it is meant to do justice or to prevent future crime – is governed by what are called the *distributive principles* of criminal liability and punishment (Chapter 2).

DOI: 10.4324/9781003258025-1

Chapter 1

Legality

Hitler's Warmaking

1939. Superman, the good guy with the red cape, appears for the first time in his very own comic book, entitled Superman #1. The Beer Barrel Polka reaches #1 on the pop charts but musical tastes are changing; Frank Sinatra makes his first record only weeks later. The department store Montgomery Ward gives America Rudolph the Red-Nosed Reindeer. But these pleasantries occur under a darkening cloud. The world is on the eve of war. Japan attempts to prevent British support for Chiang Kai-shek by blockading China's Tientsin region. President Roosevelt asks Hitler and Mussolini, who have embraced their "Pact of Steel," for assurances they will not invade the United States. Britain begins conscription and the evacuation of children from London.

Adolf Hitler – 1939

While much of the Western World basks in the glamour of the Roaring 20s, Germany is reeling from a devastating loss in World War I and the painful conditions imposed on it by the Treaty of Versailles.[1] By 1921, Hitler, an ambitious soldier with a knack for stirring oration, has taken control of the National Socialist German Workers Party – otherwise known as the Nazi Party. His vitriolic speeches begin attracting the attention of more and more Germans. Support for the party swells. One of the thousands of Germans who joins after hearing a Hitler speech is a successful air force pilot named Hermann Göring. Hitler is immediately impressed with Göring and makes him the head of the *Sturmabteilung*, the paramilitary wing of the Nazi Party known as the SA. The SA is responsible for maintaining security at Nazi rallies and disrupting meetings of opposing political parties.

Through an unlikely set of events, by 1933 Germany is under one-man rule, political opposition has been eliminated, and the country has exceeded the limits on their military forces imposed by the Treaty of Versailles. Hitler is made Chancellor of

DOI: 10.4324/9781003258025-2

Germany and Göring is appointed Minister of Prussia, effectively becoming Hitler's second in command. Hitler and Göring obtain unchecked access to state finances, massively increase the army, establish an air force, remilitarize the Rhineland area, and establish an alliance with Italy's fascist government.

In 1938, Germany announces the Anschluss with Austria, which makes Austria an annex of Germany.[2] After this, Germany begins to devour Europe. When Hitler sets his covetous eye on Poland, he is aware that Britain and Poland have a Mutual Assistance Treaty. To invade Poland is to bring Britain and Germany to war, and yet on September 1, 1939, the assault on Poland begins. Two days later, Britain and its allies declare war on Germany.

Faced with little or no resistance, the invading Germans begin "eliminating the Polish political, religious, and intellectual leadership."[3] Once in control of the country, the slaughter does not abate. By the end of World War II, over six million Polish citizens have perished.

German General Alferd Jodl, who served in World War I, impresses Hitler, who makes him the Chief of Operations Staff of the Armed Forces (Oberkommando der Wehrmacht, or OKW). In this role, Jodl oversees the invasions of Norway, Finland, and France and additionally orders that several kinds of prisoners be shot upon capture. For the duration of WWII, Göring, Jodl, and another general named Wilhelm Keitel are part of Hitler's inner circle.

After the invasion of Poland, Hitler moves to invade Denmark, Norway, France, Belgium, Luxembourg, and the Netherlands. General Keitel signs the orders for these invasions after Hitler states that he will "ignore the neutrality of Belgium and the Netherlands."[4] Jodl also helps to arrange the invasions of Greece and Yugoslavia.

As the Germans prepare to invade the Soviet Union, Jodl signs the so-called Commissar Order, which directs that political commissars identified among captured troops be summarily executed. Keitel issues his own decrees: for every German soldier who is killed, 50–100 communists should be put to death, and captured allies are to be tortured and killed, not taken prisoner.[5]

Figure 1.1 Hitler salutes parading troops in Warsaw, Poland, 1939

Hermann Göring is feared throughout Germany and is responsible for the slaughter of millions of civilians. He is involved in the direction of many of the day-to-day horrors perpetrated by the Nazis. Nazi film footage shows the reality of these policies, including for example films in which "naked women are forced into a ditch, then made to lie down as German soldiers – smiling for the camera – shoot them."[6]

Long before the war ends, the world becomes aware of many of the evils being perpetrated by the Nazis. In December 1942, the allied leaders publish "the first joint declaration officially noting the mass murder of European Jewry and resolving to prosecute those responsible for violence against civilian populations."[7]

The Allies eventually overwhelm the German military. After committing mass atrocities and invading a dozen countries, Nazi government signs the articles of surrender on May 8, 1945. General Keitel signs the documents of surrender because Hitler had previously committed suicide.

After the war, representatives of various allied powers and Nazi-occupied countries organize an international tribunal to charge individuals with war crimes. The American War Department creates a plan that "would try responsible Nazi leaders in court" and identifies "atrocities and waging a war of aggression as war crimes."[8] The ensuing proceedings, which become known as the Nuremberg trials, seek to punish surviving Nazi officials, including Keitel, Jodl, and Göring. The counts brought in the first trial at Nuremberg include "crimes against peace," such as "planning, preparing, starting, and waging aggressive war."[9]

The defense for the Nazi leaders frequently points out that the crime of aggressive warmaking did not exist at the time of the conduct charged to constitute the offense. They have some support from legal scholars around the globe who express skepticism about the newly created crime. Harlan Stone, Chief Justice of the U.S. Supreme Court at the time, calls the trials a "sanctimonious fraud" and a "high-grade lynching party."[10] Associate Supreme Court Justice William O. Douglas feels that the trial is an abuse of power, which confuses "power for principle."[11] Justice Douglas also points to the reactionary nature of the trials, arguing that the trials are using "law created *ex post* facto to suit the passion and clamor of the time."[12]

The Tribunal, however, argues that "[w]ar is essentially an evil thing. Its consequences are not confined to the belligerent states alone, but affect the whole world. To initiate a war of aggression . . . is the supreme international crime." U.S. Supreme Court Justice Robert Jackson, who is chief prosecutor for the U.S. at the war-crimes trial, argues that the laws against wars of aggression are not ex post facto laws, because they involve behavior that humans have always agreed is criminal. "What we propose is to punish acts which have been regarded as criminal since the time of Cain and have been so written in every civilized code," he says. "The wrongs which we seek to condemn and punish have been so calculated, so malignant, and so devastating that civilization cannot tolerate their being ignored because it cannot survive their being repeated."[13]

Göring hardly puts up a defense. He is unrepentant and offers no apologies. To defend himself, Jodl and Keitel invoke the doctrine of superior orders, arguing that they only acted on orders from above and therefore cannot be found guilty in the same way as the person who gave the orders. However, the tribunal bars this defense because "participation in such crimes as these has never been required of any soldier and [he] cannot now shield himself behind a mythical requirement of soldierly obedience."[14] In the closing arguments, Jackson says, "If you were to say of these men that they are not guilty, it would be as true to say that there has been no war, there are no slain, there has been no crime."[15]

The Legality Principle

Criminal law serves to protect people from the most serious wrongs and also holds the greatest power we give to government to intrude in people's lives, even imposing imprisonment or death. For these reasons, it is thought to be particularly important that criminal law be just, fair, and effective, and that the definition of offenses, defenses, and the principles of liability and punishment be the product of the most democratic of the branches, the legislative branch.

Specifically, the criminal law should make clear to people beforehand exactly what conduct is prohibited, required, or tolerated, upon threat of criminal punishment. And when there is a violation of the rules of conduct, criminal liability and punishment ought to be imposed consistently and uniformly for all defendants. It ought to depend on what the offender has done and his or her culpability, not upon the particular decision-maker who considers the case.[16] In elegant Latin, the idea is captured in the phrase "nullum crimen sine lege, nulla poena sine lege," meaning roughly "no crime without law, nor punishment without law."

For all these reasons, the criminal law commits itself to what is called *the legality principle*, which requires that criminal offenses and liability rules be defined and announced by the legislature with clarity and precision beforehand, and that the rules be specific and unambiguous enough to provide clear notice and uniformity in application.[17] As a historical matter,

> the ideal of a political society in which law limits and guides the exertion of power by representatives of the state dates from the beginnings of systematic thought, and was given expression even in the popular literature of the ancient Greeks. A character in a play by Euripides informs us that nothing is more hostile to a city than a despot. But, he continues, "when the laws are written down, rich and poor alike have equal justice, and it is open to the weaker to use the same language to the prosperous when he is reviled by him, and the weaker prevails over the stronger if he has justice on his side."

This early appreciation of the legality principle survived the dark ages.

> [O]ne discovers Bracton in the thirteenth century asserting that even the King rules sub Deo et lege, under God and the law. . . . Most thoughtful members of western societies freely endorse the aspirations given expression in the legality ideal, although many doubt the possibility of their full and satisfactory realization in the actual circumstances of social and political life.[18]

It is in furtherance of the legality principle ideals that every American state has enacted a criminal code that sets down in writing most of the criminal law rules needed to define offenses and adjudicate cases.

It was this legality principle of long tradition that was tested so severely by the controversy in the Nuremberg trials about whether aggressive warmaking could be a crime even though it had not previously been written down and officially recognized as one. At Nuremberg, the tribunal would seem to have cut corners on the legality principle. Has that kind of compromising continued in American criminal law? Consider a more modern case.

Ray Brent Marsh – 1997

Noble, Georgia is an unincorporated cluster of houses off Highway 27, just south of the Tennessee border.[19] The Marsh family are long-time residents of the area who own the Tri-State Crematory, a family business started by the well-regarded Tommy Ray Marsh in 1982.[20]

In 1996, Tommy Ray's declining health has confined him to a wheelchair, so his son Ray Brent takes over the business. Brent was a star sprinter and co-captain of the football team at LaFayette High School, and he was a linebacker at University of Tennessee at Chattanooga. Now he is the Treasurer at New Home Missionary Baptist Church, where his mother sings in the choir.[21] He and his wife Vanessa recently had a baby girl.[22] Like his parents, he lives on the crematory grounds.[23]

Funeral directors are happy to continue working with Tri-State after Brent takes over, and business holds strong. The company has prompt service, and the family has a good reputation.[24]

On the surface, the business seems to be doing well. But after a year in charge of the business, the younger Marsh begins running into financial difficulties. In August 1997, the cremation machine stops working. Marsh orders a $152 starter-motor part. For the past 13 years, the family has declined service visits from the equipment company, so the service representatives are not surprised when Marsh says that no one needs to come to install the new part – he will do it himself.

Despite his best efforts, Marsh is unable to fix the machine. With financial pressure building, he decides to continue to accept bodies for cremation. Unable to burn the bodies, he begins hiding them in the grove behind the crematory. The grove is already littered with dryers, broken chairs, six derelict cars, and a house trailer – a few hidden bodies will blend right in.

Marsh continues to be prompt in arriving to pick up each body, obtaining the transit permit and the family's authorization, and accepting their payment. He always insists on doing pickups and returning the "ashes" himself, often the next day. Unable to return the cremated remains, Marsh delivers a mix of cement chips and limestone.

Marsh lets notices, papers, and bills, often unopened, pile up in the office and tucks them into corners around his home. Soon, the few bodies in his backyard turn into a few dozen. Still, from the outside things seem normal, though the locals later comment that they have not seen any smoke in a long time. Marsh doesn't abuse or injure the bodies; he just dumps them in the grove and ignores them. Although he treats the bodies "like trash,"[25] Marsh becomes more careful about external paperwork required by industry regulations.

By now, hundreds of bodies litter the grove. Some are stacked like cordwood in sheds; others are half buried around the grove. The earliest ones are little more than skeletons, having decomposed for several years. Some were once buried and embalmed, and now are half dug up, perhaps to be stacked later.[26] Some are still dressed in their formal wear; others are wrapped in hospital sheets and still have a toe tag. More than 20 bodies are stuffed into a cement box designed to hold one coffin. There are at least four cement vaults hiding hundreds of corpses.

On February 15, 2002, a woman walking her dog finds a human skull near Tri-State Crematory. Once the police begin to investigate, it becomes clear that there is a serious problem. Georgia Governor Roy Barnes declares a state of emergency, in what is now called the "The Walker County Incident," making state funds available to the small community for cleanup efforts.[27] By February 24, almost 300 bodies have been found.

Figure 1.2 Woman weeping in front of the courthouse during Marsh trial

The families of those who were supposed to be cremated are devastated. The outrage is so great that the police have Marsh wear a bulletproof vest for court hearings. The governor meets with more than a hundred families who dealt with Tri-State, and agrees that the state will pay the cost of identifying the bodies and returning their real ashes.[28] He vows to use the full powers of the state for investigation and prosecution.[29] The local sheriff says what is on the minds of many Walker Country residents: "The Marshes are good folks. I don't know what went wrong."[30] The funeral directors who trusted Marsh reel – some funeral homes are even threatened with civil suits for giving Marsh their business. By the end of the $8.5 million excavation, 339 bodies are found.[31]

Everyone believes that Marsh should be brought to justice. However, Georgia law makes it a crime only when a person "defaces" a dead body.[32] "Defacing" involves some kind of physical intrusion of the body, the courts decide. Marsh never cut or crushed or disfigured the bodies in any way. He just tossed them out. Everyone, including Marsh, probably assumed that his treatment of the bodies was criminal (even apart from the monetary fraud), and there is little disagreement that it should be. But to adhere to the *legality principle* – to avoid *ex post* facto application of an offense that did not exist at the time of the conduct – Marsh cannot be held criminally liable for his abuse of the bodies.

In other words, in situations other than the extreme Nuremberg case of aggressive warmaking, American criminal law takes the legality principle very seriously, even when it clearly frustrates liability and punishment of a *blameworthy* offender.

Legality in the States

To be clear, the *legality principle* is not itself a legal rule but rather an umbrella concept under which huddle a variety of doctrines including, for example, the constitutional prohibitions against vague statutes and *ex post facto* laws, as well as the traditional judicial practice of interpreting any ambiguity in the definition of a criminal offense in a way favorable to the defendant – called "the rule of strict construction" or "the rule of lenity." Further, most modern American criminal codes explicitly abolish common-law offenses (that is, offenses created by judges) and allow prosecution only for offenses codified by the legislature.[33] The *Model Penal Code* contains a provision explicitly stating this, which is quoted in the margin. (The Model Penal Code, which we will cite and quote regularly, was promulgated by the American Law Institute – the national academy for law in the United States – and served as the basis for the recodification of three-quarters of the state criminal codes, with some states closely following its provisions and others introducing a range of variations on its provisions.)

The effect of the doctrines embodied in the legality principle is to bar criminal liability, even for conduct that is seriously wrongful and even if the actor believed it was a crime, if the conduct had not in fact previously been defined as an offense by the legislature. Thus, for example, a Soviet spy visiting the U.S. who secretly takes photographs of military installations believing it to be a crime as it is back home cannot be held criminally liable if such conduct has not in fact been clearly criminalized. Similarly, crematorium operator Marsh, who simply throws the dead bodies in the woods behind his shop, cannot be held criminally liable unless there exists an abuse of corpse offense that unambiguously covers his specific kind of conduct.[34]

While all American jurisdictions commit themselves to the legality principle, there is some variation among the states in how aggressively they adhere to the principle. The map below presents four different approaches found in American jurisdictions.[35]

Thirty-four American jurisdictions, those in the darkest shading on the map, adhere strictly to the legality principle: in order to be criminally prosecuted for an offense the offense must have been previously formally and fully codified by the legislature. Georgia is one of the states in this group, so it is perhaps no surprise that Marsh gets a defense to his abuse of corpse. The state's statute did not strictly cover his conduct. Hitler and his henchmen also would escape criminal liability for aggressive warmaking under this strict form of the legality principle.

In three jurisdictions, those with medium shading on the map – Indiana, Virginia, and West Virginia – a legislative codification of the offense is required but need not be full and complete. For example, the criminal code may formally recognize the offense and set a maximum punishment for it but leave the definition of one or more elements of the offense for resolution by the judicial branch. No criminal liability for Hitler for aggressive warmaking in these states either because they require, at very least, that the criminal code officially recognize the existence of the offense.

All Offenses Defined by Statute.

(1) No conduct constitutes an offense unless it is a crime or violation under this Code or another statute of this State.

Model Penal Code §1.05

Figure 1.3

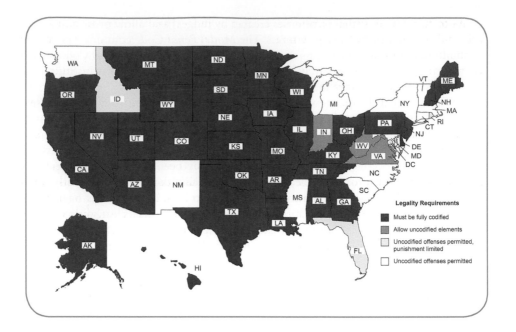

Figure 1.4

In four jurisdictions, those in the lightest shading on the map – District of Columbia, Florida, Idaho, and Rhode Island – common-law offenses may be prosecuted, that is, offenses that have never been codified by the legislature but exist only by virtue of their creation by judges, usually during the "Common-Law" period, when the King's judges, rather than Parliament, created and defined crimes. Such common-law – judge made – offenses were carried over into American criminal law upon American independence.

However, while the legislatures in these states authorize the prosecution of common-law offenses, they put a limit on the amount of punishment that can be imposed for such offenses. Thus, Hitler could be prosecuted for aggressive warmaking (if it were held to be an uncodified offense recognized by the courts) but in Idaho, for example, the offense would be subject to a maximum penalty of five years. The remaining 11 jurisdictions, those with no shading on the map, permit prosecution for uncodified or *common-law* offenses without any explicit punishment ceiling for such offenses.

The Strengths and Weaknesses of a Commitment to the Legality Principle

Given the important rationales behind the *legality principle*, such as providing fair notice of criminalized conduct, promoting uniformity in application of the criminal law, and reserving the criminalization decision for the legislature rather than delegating it *de facto* to the courts,[36] one may wonder about the 18 jurisdictions in the last three groups that allow some, or in some cases a lot, of corner-cutting of the legality principle.

As to fair notice, for example, it is hard enough to expect citizens to consult the criminal code in order to know what the law demands of them, but it borders on silly to think that fair notice has been given when citizens must go read a series of judicial opinions to determine the criminal law's demands. To take this view is essentially to give up on the idea that criminal law should provide fair notice. Such callousness makes the criminal law somewhat hypocritical when it also enforces its traditional rule that "ignorance or mistake of law is no excuse." (Of course, the unfairness of prosecution without a clear prior offense is undermined to some extent if the defendant, like Marsh, mistakenly believes that his conduct is criminal.)

One might seek to excuse these legality corner-cutters on the grounds that it is simply too difficult to draft a criminal code that is fully comprehensive. This would have been a plausible argument until 1962, when the American Law Institute promulgated the *Model Penal Code*, which demonstrated that a jurisdiction really could comprehensively codify all offenses and all liability rules in a clear, concise, and coherent manner. What's more, the effectiveness of this modern codification form has now been proven many times over, as three-quarters of the states re-codified their criminal law during the 1960s and 1970s using the approach of the Model Code. Further, the drafting advances of the Model Code have over the past several decades been further improved,[37] to the point where it is now almost inexplicable, if not irresponsible, for jurisdictions to continue to tolerate the prosecution of uncodified common-law offenses.

What may help explain the continuing legality principle corner-cutting by the 18 jurisdictions is the fact that a large number of these states are the one-quarter of the states that never enacted a modern criminal code during the Model Penal Code recodification wave in the 1960s and the 1970s. But if one cares about fairness and effectiveness in imposing criminal liability and punishment, these jurisdictions (which most shamefully include federal criminal law) ought to join the 21st century by enacting a modern criminal code that rejects the prosecution of uncodified offenses.

However, it has been argued that while there are admittedly important virtues to the legality principle, the principle also has the potential for some serious failures of justice. Most prominently, any defense from criminal liability based upon the legality principle is one that may seem indifferent to the *blameworthiness* of the offender and the punishment he or she deserves. Nothing in the classic legality principle takes account of how serious the offense is or how blameworthy the offender may be.

In many cases, even in serious cases like Marsh's, one might defend the failure of justice caused by the legality principle on the grounds that it promotes a greater good, specifically demonstrating the criminal law's commitment to the protections that all of us enjoy from unfair government overreach. Indeed, one might argue that it is only the government's demonstrated restraint in forgoing punishment of an offender like Marsh that makes its announced commitment to the legality principle credible. Once people see Marsh escape the punishment he deserves, they can take some real comfort that the legality principle is not just legal window-dressing but a genuine restraint on governmental power.

But this line of argument may have an important exception: most people would probably find it appalling if Hitler and his henchmen were to escape liability or have limited punishment because the technical requirements of the legality principle were not satisfied with regard to their aggressive warmaking. No doubt this explains why the Nuremberg Tribunal decided to overlook the legality problems when it charged and convicted the Nazi leaders. The evilness of Hitler's conduct was so overwhelming – his aggressive warmaking resulted in the death or misery of a significant portion of the people on earth – that they may not be willing to tolerate a failure of justice simply to promote a matter of principle. Legality is important, they might argue, but it is not the only important interest in our world.

Aftermaths

The trials for the defeated Nazi leaders begin just six months after Germany surrenders and last for ten months. In unrelenting detail, the truth about the aggressive warmaking is exposed. Göring, Keitel, and Jodl are all found guilty on four counts each (aggressive warmaking plus other war crimes) and sentenced to death. The night before the execution, Göring commits suicide by taking cyanide that had been smuggled to him. Keitel, Jodl, and nine other Nazi leaders are hung a few hours later in the early morning of October 16, 1946.

By virtue of the work and writings of the tribunal, aggressive warmaking becomes a recognized offense under international law, a significant change. Another benefit of the tribunal is that the trials keep the world focused on the effects of the war. As a result, the United States creates the Marshall Plan, which does much to alleviate the post-war suffering of citizens in Germany and across Europe. Many people credit the success of the Marshall Plan with helping to avoid further European military conflict and helping to sow the seeds for what is now the European Union.

For Ray Marsh, although he cannot be prosecuted for his most serious offense, abuse of hundreds of dead bodies, he is convicted of financial fraud and given a sentence of 12 years. He is made to serve his entire sentence even though financial frauds at the time commonly yielded sentences of under two years.[38] In other words, while the *legality principle* does provide a defense for his mistreatment of the bodies, it is not lost on the immediate participants that a significant failure of justice would occur if Marsh were to receive a sentence of only two years. One may wonder, however, whether it is a desirable practice for the criminal justice system to essentially punish Marsh for conduct for which he has not been convicted. Marsh is released in 2016.

Chapter Glossary

Blameworthy/Blameworthiness: The degree to which an individual deserves blame or disapproval for a mistake or for something that has gone wrong.[39]

Common Law: Common law is law that is derived from judicial decisions instead of from statutes. American courts originally fashioned common-law rules based on English common law but eventually matured to the point of relying upon their own precedent.[40]

De Facto: Latin for "in fact." Often used in place of "actual" to show that the court will treat as a fact authority being exercised or an entity acting as if it had authority, even though the legal requirements have not been met.[41]

Ex post Facto: Ex post facto is most typically used to refer to a criminal statute that punishes actions retroactively, thereby criminalizing conduct that was legal when originally performed. Two clauses in the United States Constitution prohibit ex post facto laws: Art. 1, § 9 prohibits Congress from passing any laws that apply ex post facto. Art. 1, § 10 prohibits the states from passing any laws that apply ex post facto.[42]

Legality Principle: It declares that no crime and punishment can exist without a legal base. It is also known as nullum crimen, nulla poena sine lege, which is Latin for no crime, no punishment without law. A person shall not be convicted or punished for an act that is not in violation of existing law or that was not criminalized by law at the time it was committed.[43]

Model Penal Code: A criminal code proposed by the American Law Institute in 1962 after a ten-year drafting project and adopted as the basis for criminal law revision by three-quarters of the states.[44]

Notes

1. This narrative is drawn from the following sources: 'Holocaust Encyclopedia: Polish Victims,' *United States Holocaust Memorial Museum*, 13 June 2019, https://www.ushmm.org/wlc/en/article.php?ModuleId=10005473; United Nations, *Historical Review of Developments Relating to Aggression*, 2003, http://legal.un.org/cod/books/HistoricalReview-Aggression.pdf; G.M. Gilbert, *Nuremberg Diary* (Boston: De Capo Press, 1995); 'World War II in Europe', *The History Place*, 1997, 13 June 2019, http://www.historyplace.com/worldwar2/timeline/nurem.htm; Douglas Linder, 'The Nuremberg Trials: An Account,' *Famous Trials*, 2017, http://www.famous-trials.com/nuremberg/1901-home.
2. 'Judgement: Goerin,' The Avalon Project, Lillian Goldman Law Library Yale University, 2008, http://avalon.law.yale.edu/imt/judgoeri.asp.
3. 'Holocaust Encyclopedia: Polish Victims.'
4. 'Judgement: Goerin.'
5. 'World War II in Europe.'
6. Linder, 'Nuremberg Trials.'
7. History.com editors, 'Nuremberg Trials,' *History*, 7 June 2019, http://www.history.com/topics/world-war-ii/nuremberg-trials.
8. Linder, 'Nuremberg Trials.'
9. 'World War II in Europe.'
10. 'World War II in Europe.'
11. Roza Pati, *Due Process and International Terrorism: An International Legal Analysis* (Leiden, Netherlands: Martinus Nijhoff Publishing, 2009), 132.
12. Pati, *Due Process*, 132.
13. Linder, 'Nuremberg Trials.'
14. 'Nuremberg Trials.'
15. Linder, 'Nuremberg Trials.'
16. Paul H. Robinson and Michael T. Cahill, *Criminal Law*, 2nd ed. (New York: Wolters Kluwer, 2016) pp. 66–68.
17. John Calvin Jeffries, 'Legality, Vagueness, and the Construction of Penal Statutes.' *Virginia Law Review 71*, no. 2 (1985): pp. 189–245, doi:10.2307/1073017.
18. Francis A. Allen, 'A Crisis of Legality in the Criminal Law – Reflections on the Rule of Law.' *Mercer Law Review 42* (1991): pp. 811–813.
19. This narrative is drawn from the following sources: Erin McClam, 'The Living Remain Strangers in a Town of Uncremated Dead; Georgia's Community Is Really a Strip of Road,' *The Record*, 3 March 2002; Sara Rimer, 'Dazed by Crematory Scandal, Undertakers' Trust Is Shaken,' *New York Times*, 21 February 2002, 14; David Firestone and Michael Moss, 'More Corpses Are Discovered Near Crematory,' *New*

York Times, 18 February 2002, https://www.nytimes.com/2002/02/18/us/more-corpses-are-discovered-near-crematory.html?mtrref=www.google.com&gwh=29756 6A6849BD8585226E16DEF802601&gwt; Sara Rimer, 'Crematory Owners' Family Asks Why,' *New York Times*, 24 February 2002, https://www.nytimes.com/2002/02/ 24/us/crematory-owners-family-asks-why.html?mtrref=www.google.com&gwh=84B B61970DE61E20209B25FF6F6D91A4&gwt; Sue Anne Pressley, 'Crematory Questions Stir Anguish – GA. Town Shaken as Body Count Rises,' *Washington Post – Boston Globe*, 24 February 2002; Michael Pearson, 'Crematory Investigation: Why Didn't Tri-State Just Cremate the Bodies?' *Atlanta Journal and Constitution*, 24 February 2002; Bill Poovey, 'Cemeteries Forced to Help Find Answers to Crematory Secrets,' *AP*, 3 March 2002; Norman Arey, 'Tri-State Probe Not Any Closer to Explanation,' *Atlanta Journal and Constitution*, 2 June 2002; Duane Stanford and Micheal Pearson, 'Gruesome Toll Worsens, Funeral Home Licenses in Jeopardy,' *Atlanta Journal and Constitution*, 19 February 2002; Richmond Eustis, 'Questions Grow with Body Count,' *Fulton County Daily Report*, 19 February 2002.

20. Firestone and Moss, 'More Corpses.'
21. Firestone and Moss, 'More Corpses.'
22. Rimer, 'Crematory Owners' Family Asks Why.'
23. Sue Anne Pressley, 'Crematory Questions Stir Anguish – GA. Town Shaken as Body Count Rises,' *Washington Post – Boston Globe*, 24 February 2002.
24. Pearson, 'Crematory Investigation.'
25. Poovey, 'Cemeteries Forced to Help.'
26. Pearson, 'Crematory Investigation.'
27. Firestone and Moss, 'More Corpses.'
28. Firestone and Moss, 'More Corpses.'
29. Firestone and Moss, 'More Corpses.'
30. Poovey, 'Cemeteries Forced to Help.'
31. Arey, 'Tri-State Probe.'
32. Code of Georgia §31-21-44.1(a) (1), Abuse of a Dead Body.
33. Paul H. Robinson, 'Fair Notice and Fair Adjudication: Two Kinds of Legality,' *Faculty Scholarship at Penn Law, 601* (2005). https://scholarship.law.upenn.edu/faculty_ scholarship/601; Markus Duber, 'The Legality Principle in American German Criminal Law: An Essay in Comparative Legal History,' *Comparative Studies in Continental and Anglo-American Legal History, 31* (2013): pp. 365, 372.
34. Paul H. Robinson and Michael T. Cahill, *Law Without Justice: Why Criminal Law Doesn't Give People What They Deserve*, Chapter 5 (Oxford: Oxford University Press, 2005).
35. The map is taken from Paul H. Robinson and Tyler Scot Williams, *Mapping American Criminal Law: Variations Across the 50 States*, Chapter 4 (Westport: Prager, 2018). All supporting authorities are available from that source.
36. Robinson and Cahill, *Criminal Law.*
37. Paul H. Robinson, Matthew Kussmaul, and Muhammad Sarahne, 'How Criminal Code Drafting Form Can Restrain Prosecutorial and Legislative Excesses: Consolidated Offense Drafting.' *Harvard Journal on Legislation* (2020); Paul H. Robinson, Matthew Kussmaul, Ilya Rudyak, and Research Group, 'Criminal Law,' *Report of the Delaware Criminal Law Recodification Project*, 8 July 2017, and *Report of the Delaware Criminal Law Recodification Project to the Delaware General Assembly's Criminal Justice Improvement Committee*, 2017; University of Pennsylvania Law School, Public Law Research Paper No. 17–19, https://ssrn.com/abstract=2950728; Paul H. Robinson, *Final Report of the Kentucky Penal Code Revision Project*, 1 July 2003, and *Final Report of the Kentucky Penal Code Revision Project*, 2003, https://ssrn.

com/abstract=1526674; Paul H. Robinson and Michael T. Cahill, *Final Report of the Illinois Criminal Code Rewrite and Reform Commission*, 2003; Paul H. Robinson, University of Pennsylvania Law School, Public Law Research Paper No. 09-40, https://ssrn.com/abstract=1523384; Paul H. Robinson, 'Vol. 1 Final Report of the Maldivian Penal Law & Sentencing Codification Project: Text of Draft Code' and 'Vol. 2 Official Commentary,' January 2006; Penn Law School, Public Law Research Paper No. 09-38, https://ssrn.com/abstract=1522222 or http://dx.doi.org/10.2139/ssrn.1522222.

38. 'Six Defendants Sentenced for Wide-Ranging Bank Fraud and Identity Theft Scheme,' *US Department of Justice*, 10 January 2017, https://www.justice.gov/usao-ndga/pr/six-defendants-sentenced-wide-ranging-bank-fraud-and-identity-theft-scheme.

39. *Blameworthiness*, Black's Law Dictionary (11th ed. 2019).

40. *Common Law*, Legal Information Institute, Cornell University, https://www.law.cornell.edu/wex/commonlaw.

41. *De Facto*, law.com, https://dictionary.law.com/Default.aspx?selected=455.

42. *Legality Principle*, Legal Information Institute, https://www.law.cornell.edu/wex/expostfacto.

43. https://lawtimesjournal.in/principle-of-legality/.

44. *Model Penal Code*, Black's; *Model Penal Code: Official Draft and Explanatory Notes: Complete Text of Model Penal Code as Adopted at the 1962 Annual Meeting of the American Law Institute at Washington, DC*, 24 May 1962. Philadelphia, PA (1985).

Chapter 2

Punishment Theory

The Prince of Pickpockets

1906. Mahatma Gandhi begins his crusade against colonial abuses, coining the term "Satyagraha" for his non-violent movement. The Wright Brothers, a pair of bicycle mechanics from Dayton, Ohio, patent the first airplane. As the American government seems uninterested in flight, the brothers bring their "flyer" to Europe seeking government contracts and become the toast of the continent.

Two South American earthquakes reach 8.6 on the Richter scale, killing well over 20,000 people. The same year, Mt. Vesuvius erupts, laying waste to the city of Naples. And at 5:12 am on April 18, 1906, the earth begins to move along the San Andres Fault and 3,000 people die from building collapses and fires in San Francisco. It is in the chaos that follows that 14-year-old Thomas Moran begins his pickpocketing career.

The Prince of Pickpockets – 1906

Thomas B. Moran, a boy of 14, is caught in San Francisco's 7.8 magnitude earthquake. The quake leaves the city in ruins and half the city's inhabitants without housing.[1] What is a boy to do? Moran decides he will use the natural disaster to become a thief. He picks his first pocket, but even in the chaos following the earthquake, the police quickly arrest the novice.

Despite the setback, the boy realizes that he has a knack for the trade. When the overwhelmed police release the young Moran, he continues to work the ruined city. "You just do it . . . . You don't need anybody to show you." According to his own account, Moran finds himself at home in other peoples' pockets, and resolves to turn his passion for petty theft into a career.

The chaos of the quake fades, normal life resumes, and Moran decides it is unwise to hang around San Francisco where the police have become well aware of his doings.

DOI: 10.4324/9781003258025-3

He is off to see the world. As an old man looking back, he recalls that he loved his trade in part because "It gives you a chance to travel."[2] Moran's passion takes him to "every big city in the country."[3] Moran often dines in fine restaurants and stays in luxurious lodgings. He lives in an America that few others ever know, filled with the nicest hotels and the crummiest jails.

Moran usually works in "subways, racetracks, buses and one of his favorite places, union meetings – where, of course, no one would suspect a union brother of theft."[4] Moran recalls that he always "loved animals, especially horses,"[5] so racetracks are high in his list. Moran prefers to spend his winters in Miami, and he heads north when the weather warms again. His job offers no paid sick days but plenty of paid vacations.

As his skills improve, he adopts a thieves' code of honor: he will never again snatch a woman's purse, because "purse snatching [is] for amateurs."[6] Moran is definitely not an amateur: the "king of pickpockets" estimates that he has stolen upward of 50,000 wallets.[7] Another source of pride is that he works without a "framer" (someone to distract the victim).[8]

Despite his romantic view of his life's work, Moran is tight-lipped about the specifics of his exploits. He doesn't "like to talk about the places he has visited or the jails he has stayed in because . . . I may visit there again someday."[9] He also rarely divulges the methods he has developed for pickpocketing, except to say that "the secret of successful purse picking is in the fingers alone."

As he travels, Moran's arrests pile up. On his 58th arrest, a Miami newspaper refers to Moran as "Butterfingers."[10] By his last arrest in January of 1970, the 5'6" Moran has been arrested at least 64 times "in every state on the continent" and "in Canada

Figure 2.1 Thomas "Butterfingers" Moran died a free man in 1971

Chapter 2: Punishment Theory

too," according to Miami Police Sgt. Edward MacDermott.[11] He never uses violence and is something of a fatherly figure. "Just about every officer on the Miami police force [knows] him by name," according to one report.[12]

Moran has spent "a total of eight years behind bars, including countless nights in the Dade County Stockade"[13] – roughly 45 days per arrest. However, he is never convicted of any serious offense, and he never spends significant time behind bars for any of his offenses.[14]

Punishment Theory and Alternative Distributive Principles

How should the criminal law deal with such incorrigible repeat offenders as Moran? Indeed, the more important question – perhaps the most important question in criminal law – is the general issue of: how should the criminal law decide who should be punished and how much? The classic *retributivist* view would set liability and punishment proportionate to the extent of the wrongdoing and the offender's blameworthiness. It sees such just punishment as a value in itself that requires no further *utilitarian justification*. The "crime-control utilitarian" view, in contrast, sees the value of liability and punishment as residing in avoiding future crime. There is some overlap between punishment designed to be just and punishment designed to avoid future crime, but there are also, as we shall see, many points of conflict.

The retributivist view, in crude form, is an ancient one. The Athenians saw wrongdoing as giving rise to an anger by the victim that could be assuaged only by proportionate punishment. But it was not just the personal sense of wrong by the victim but also the sense of wrong by the community generally needed attention. As Demosthenes argues in a public prosecution in the 360s: "It's not right that Meidias' behavior should arouse my indignation alone and slip by, overlooked by the rest of you. Not at all. Really, it's necessary for everyone to be equally angry!"[15] More modern retributivists would reject the anger focus altogether and instead press for a calm and thoughtful determination of the amount of punishment that would be proportionate to the extent of the offender's wrongdoing and blameworthiness. See, for example, the proportionality requirement given dominance in the Model Penal Code's 2007 amendment, which is reproduced in the appendix to this chapter.

Justifying punishment upon its potential to avoid future crime gained prominence in the 18th century. English philosopher Jeremy Bentham promoted utilitarianism with his philosophy that "it is the greatest happiness of the greatest number that is the measure of right and wrong." In the context of justifying punishment, this utilitarian view was expressed in William Blackstone's *Commentaries on the Laws of England* (1749). (England had a long string of criminal law treatise writers, but Blackstone was the authority of the day when the United States declared independence in 1776. While American criminal law shared this common heritage with English criminal law, American lawyers understandably ignored subsequent English treatise writers, thereby making Blackstone a foundation of American criminal law more by historical accident than by scholarly excellence.) Blackstone carries forward Bentham's utilitarian view:

> This is not by way of atonement or expiation for the crime committed; for that must be left to the just determination of the supreme being: but as a precaution

19

against future offenses of the same kind. This is effected three ways: either by the amendment of the offender himself . . . or, by deterring others by the dread of his example from offending in the like way . . . or, lastly, by depriving the party injuring of the power to do future mischief.[16]

Modern crime-control utilitarians include these same three mechanisms by which punishment can avoid future crime: *rehabilitation* of the offender, *general deterrence* of others, or *incapacitation of the dangerous* offender.

The most fundamental question facing today's criminal lawmaker is this: what purpose should the criminal law rules seek to achieve? The easy and obvious answer would seem to be that criminal law rules should be formulated to do justice (as the Athenians and modern retributivists demand) and avoid future crime (as Bentham and Blackstone would insist). However, as noted, these two laudable objectives often conflict.[17]

For example, imagine somebody who is seriously mentally ill to the point of being *blameless* for his or her offense conduct but who continues to be extremely dangerous. Should the criminal law ignore a defendant's potential for future criminality and provide an insanity defense in order to do justice (perhaps leaving the problem of future criminality to a civil commitment system)? Or should the criminal law refuse to recognize any defense for mental illness in order to take and keep control of this dangerous person? The classic crime-control utilitarian would impose criminal liability and take control of this dangerous person, while the retributivist would provide an insanity defense based upon the offender's blamelessness.

The same conflict in *distributive principles* can arise in the opposite direction: as in cases where a person is blameworthy for an offense but, perhaps because of its unique circumstances, there is little or no possibility of the person committing another offense in the future. Imagine a person who has been law-abiding all his life but who ends up intentionally killing his father who abused him as a child, where everyone agrees that the crime was a product of that unique circumstance that will never again arise. Should the criminal law focus on justice and impose criminal liability and punishment (perhaps somewhat reduced to reflect the special circumstances arising from the former abuse), or should the criminal law focus on the absence of any future dangerousness and refrain from imposing any criminal liability?

Ultimately, the issue presented is whether the criminal law's focus should be on the past – doing justice for past wrongdoing – or on the future – avoiding future crime. This recurring tension between doing justice and preventing crime appears in a wide variety of situations that criminal law makers must deal with, including the issue of how best to deal with habitual offenders like Thomas Moran.

He commits a number of offenses that are minor in character. Each of which on its own would normally deserve an equally minor punishment. Repeat offenders might be given a slight bump for what some scholars have called "nose-thumbing" – showing open contempt for society's norms by committing another offense after already having been convicted and punished for it. Such nose-thumbing seems to increase the seriousness of the crime, but the empirical evidence suggests that people see this only as a minor aggravating factor, which might justify increasing the *deserved punishment* for an offense by some proportion, but the nose-thumbing is certainly not more important than the offense itself. And yet, *habitual offender statutes*, which began appearing very shortly after Moran died, increase punishment exponentially when there is a prior criminal record – at times more than quadrupling the sentence. They do this in order to better control persons whom authorities think are dangerous, but in the process they seriously deviate from justice notions of *proportionality* between *blameworthiness* and punishment.

Consider the treatment of another habitual offender after the advent of such habitual offender statutes.

William James Rummel – 1973

William J. Rummel has trouble holding down a job. It's not that he can't work – he is simply lazy and does not find it enjoyable. His educational background consists of a few Dale Carnegie courses. At the age of 30, he has no wife, no children, and no friends. His parents are both alive, but their health is poor and Rummel rarely sees them.[18]

Rummel has a series of run-ins with the law. In 1959 in San Antonio, he is convicted of misdemeanor theft and unlawful possession of alcoholic beverages. After being convicted on these charges at the Bexar County Courthouse, he is arrested again the same day, this time for unlawfully carrying a Bowie knife. A year later he is convicted of the weapons charge and fined $100. Later that year he is given three years of probation on a burglary charge. Three years later, as soon as his probation is over, he passes a bad check for $10 at a Holiday Inn, and later that year passes another bad check, this time for $30. The following year Rummel is convicted of two counts of swindling and sentenced to 30 days in jail. Later that year he is convicted of credit card fraud after he uses a company credit card to buy two new tires for his car. The tires are worth a total of $80, and Rummel is sentenced to three years in prison. After being paroled, he violates his parole and is returned to the Department of Corrections in 1966. Two years later Rummel is convicted of assault arising from a domestic disturbance and is sentenced to 30 days in jail. On the day of his conviction, he passes a bad check for $5.61 at a Gulf service station and is again convicted of swindling by check. He is sentenced to 30 days. The next year, 1969, Rummel is convicted of forging a $28.36 check and is sentenced to two-to-four years in prison, of which he serves 28 months.

With this criminal history of ten mostly minor offenses spread over ten years, with the last offense four and a half years ago, Rummel walks into Captain Hook's Lounge in San Antonio. It is a hot day and the bar's air conditioning is not working. Rummel gets an idea. He approaches the bar's owner, David Shaw, and offers to fix the air conditioner. Shaw agrees and Rummel begins his inspection. After a few minutes and a little tinkering, Rummel announces the unit needs a new compressor. Cost: $129.75, labor free. Shaw quickly agrees and writes Rummel a check for the amount. Rummel, who has no intention of ever making the promised repair, leaves, cashes the check, and never returns. Shaw files a complaint with the police, who easily trace Rummel.

Rummel's offense, theft by false pretext, would normally render him liable under Texas law for a maximum sentence of between two and ten years, although violators typically receive a sentence of months, not years. However, Rummel's earlier criminal record changes things. Instead of months, Rummel gets life.

After a jury convicts Rummel of the theft, a felony in this instance because the value of the fraud is over $50, the state presents evidence of two prior felony convictions and asks the judge to declare Rummel a habitual criminal eligible for a life sentence under the Texas' *three-strike statute*.

A habitual criminal classification authorizes the dramatic increase in the available prison term under the theory that such is the only effective way of preventing habitual offenders from committing more offenses in the future. The declared purpose of the

Recidivist Statute.
 Whoever shall have been three times convicted of a felony less than capital shall on such third conviction be imprisoned for life in the penitentiary.
Texas Penal Code Art. 63 (1973)

Figure 2.2

Texas statute is to deal "with those who by repeated criminal acts have shown that they are simply incapable of conforming to the norms of society as established by its criminal law." The prior felony offenses that qualify Rummel as a habitual offender include the 1964 credit card fraud and the 1969 forgery, nine years earlier and four years earlier, respectively. All totaled, the three felonies netted Rummel $233.11. Following the statute, the judge sentences 30-year-old Rummel to life in prison.

Rummel makes something of his time in prison awaiting the appeal. He earns 67 hours of college credit, spends 350 hours teaching other inmates, and takes training in construction maintenance. He appeals his case to the U.S. Court of Appeals for the Fifth Circuit in New Orleans. Helping to craft his own motions and arguments from the prison library, he contends that the state's habitual offender law violates the Eighth Amendment prohibition against cruel and unusual punishment.

Three years after his conviction, on March 6, 1978, a three-judge panel of the Fifth Circuit reverses his sentence finding it cruel and unusual. However, on December 20, 1978, the Fifth Circuit sitting as a whole – lawyers call it sitting *en banc* – reinstates the sentence by an 8 to 5 vote and upholds the constitutionality of the *habitual offender statute*. Rummel appeals to the U.S. Supreme Court, pushing his claim that a life sentence for his $130 air-conditioning fraud is cruel and unusual punishment. The high court agrees to hear his case. His attorney argues, "No jurisdiction in the United States or the free world punishes habitual offenders as harshly as Texas."

Rummel's case attracts national attention from newspapers and television stations. The television news program "60 Minutes" airs a segment on his case in the winter of 1980. "I'm not saying I should not be punished, but why give me a life sentence?" Rummel asks an interviewer as he awaits his appeal.

> If I had murdered 75 people or raped five women, something of that nature, I could see where I could become a potential threat to society. But who do I threaten? I don't threaten anybody. I don't use narcotics. I don't use alcohol to any extent.

The local prosecutor's office begins to bristle under the spotlight, angered by the portrayal of Rummel as having committed a mere petty theft that ignores his long history

Figure 2.3 Rummel serving his life sentence, 1980

of offenses. Ultimately, the Supreme Court sides with the prosecutor: on March 19, the Court rejects Rummel's claim that his life sentence violates the Eighth Amendment.

Habitual Offender Treatment in the States

By the time of *Rummel*, many jurisdictions have adopted so-called *three-strikes statutes* that provide automatic life imprisonment for anyone who commits a third felony offense. Such statutes represent an explicit shift from a focus upon what the offender deserves for his past offense to a crime-control focus that looks instead at future dangerousness. As noted, in *Rummel*, the United States Supreme Court ruled that there is no constitutional violation when a legislature enacts such a shift; Rummel's life sentence for the $130 air-conditioning fraud was upheld.

However, while three-strikes statutes became so popular that every U.S. jurisdiction adopted one, over time many people came to be increasingly uncomfortable with the enormous disproportionality between the punishment the current offense *deserved*, even taking into account "nose-thumbing." Many people saw a serious injustice being done in cases like *Rummel*, and the last few decades have seen a series of limitations on three-strikes statutes.

> The mandatory life sentence imposed upon petitioner does not constitute cruel and unusual punishment under the Eighth and Fourteenth Amendments.
>
> Texas' interest here is not simply that of making criminal the unlawful acquisition of another person's property, but is in addition the interest, expressed in all recidivist statutes, in dealing in a harsher manner with those who by repeated criminal acts have shown that they are incapable of conforming to the norms of society as established by its criminal law. The Texas recidivist statute thus is nothing more than a societal decision that when a person, such as petitioner, commits yet another felony, he should be subjected to the serious penalty of life imprisonment, . . .

RUMMEL v. ESTELLE, United States Supreme Court (1980)

Figure 2.4

States are narrowing their *habitual offender statutes* in a variety of ways, such as by limiting the kinds of offenses that will qualify for three-strikes treatment or by increasing the seriousness of the prior offenses required by the three-strikes rule. The most common means of limiting the application of the statute is to require that the offense at hand, and perhaps the past offenses as well, involves the use of violence. These kinds of reforms are likely to reduce the disparity between the *punishment deserved* and the punishment imposed because the more serious the current and previous offenses, the greater the punishment deserved and therefore the less the disparity with the long sentence imposed.

The map nearby indicates the approach to this issue that each state takes.[19] The darker the shading, the broader the reach of the habitual offender statute.

Six jurisdictions, those with the lightest shading, do not punish habitual offenders with mandatory or discretionary life sentences or sentences of life without parole, except for crimes of violence. Sixteen jurisdictions, those with medium shading on the map, do not punish habitual offenders with such sentences unless the offender has committed at least one felony that the legislature has enumerated as being particularly serious. Thus, instead of requiring the use or threat of physical force against another person, these specifically enumerated crimes can include such offenses as burglary, arson, extortion, online enticement of a minor, or drug offenses, many

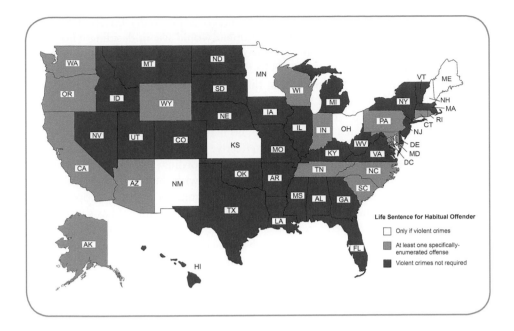

Figure 2.5

of which may be seen as creating a significant risk of injury to innocent people. Twenty-nine jurisdictions, those in black on the map, punish habitual offenders with such extended sentences even if none of the offenses were violent or even likely to result in injury. Note that Texas, the state in which the *Rummel* case arose, is among this group containing the least demanding requirements for application of three-strikes.

Can the Natural Tension between Fighting Crime and Doing Justice Be Minimized?

The narrowing of the three-strikes rule that one sees in the first and even the second groups on the map above is certainly a welcome development for those who focus on doing justice, for the narrowing would seem to avoid application of the rule in cases of greatest disproportionality between the *punishment deserved* and the punishment imposed.[20]

But for those who believe that the criminal law ought to be strictly focused on the future and not the past and ought not be distracted by notions of justice and injustice, this narrowing of the *three-strikes statutes* may not seem a good thing. Doing justice may be a laudable principle but it is a luxury that we cannot afford if we are to effectively fight crime, they may argue. As unfortunate as it may be, perhaps there is a natural and irresolvable conflict between doing justice and fighting crime, and the demands of practical necessity require a focus on reducing crime even if it means deviating from just punishment.

Or does it? It is true that for more than a century the classic view has been that the aims of justice and crime control are necessarily, inevitably, and unavoidably in conflict in many cases. The *distributive principle* that the utilitarian crime fighters would use in deciding who should be punished how much is markedly different from the distributive principle that the moral philosopher would use in deciding who should be punished how much.[21] But the last two decades have seen increasing empirical evidence that doing justice may indeed be the most effective crime-control strategy.[22]

The most important development in this regard is the growing appreciation that ordinary people feel strongly that justice should be done and injustice should be avoided and, further, the evidence suggests that ordinary people have a relatively nuanced and sophisticated sense of justice, no matter their educational level (or any other demographic). What this means for effective crime control is that each time the criminal law deviates from deserved punishment, as ordinary people perceive it, such deviation undermines the system's moral credibility with the community and that, in turn, can seriously undermine the community's willingness to assist, cooperate, and defer to the system and their willingness to internalize the criminal law's norms.[23]

A system that has earned a reputation with the community as one that regularly does injustice or fails to do justice loses that power of social influence that it might otherwise have. Rather than assistance, cooperation, and deference, it provokes resistance, subversion, and defiance. Will people report crimes? Will witnesses assist investigators? Will they testify at trial? Will jurors follow their legal instructions? Will people defer to the criminal law in those gray areas where the condemnability of conduct is unsettled? Will the enormous power of stigmatization that inheres in a criminal conviction be lost? That is, will people conclude that this or that criminal conviction is just one more example of the criminal law being out of step with the community's judgments of condemnability? Most importantly, if the criminal law is seen as regularly and intentionally deviating from just punishment, will people be less inclined to internalize the societal norms that the criminal law promotes?

Ultimately, criminal law's most effective crime-control strategy may be to harness the powerful forces of social influence and internalized norms by always trying to do justice and avoid injustice. That is, the justice system ought to be devoted to doing justice not to please the moral philosophers – the retributivists – but as a strategy of effective utilitarian crime control.

This may be part of the rationale for the American Law Institute's 2007 amendment of the Model Penal Code, the first amendment of the Model Code since its promulgation in 1962. The amendment, reproduced in the chapter appendix, sets desert – punishment in proportion to the offender's *blameworthiness*, taking into account both the seriousness of the offense and the culpability of the offender – as the dominant principal for the distribution of criminal punishment, which is never to be violated.

In this light, the narrowing of the three-strikes statutes to diminish the disproportionality between deserved punishment and imposed punishment is a reform that is likely to reduce damage to the system's moral credibility and thus ultimately increase its crime-control effectiveness.

Aftermaths

Moran dies quietly in his sleep on September 15, 1971 at the age of 79 in the Miami Rescue Mission. His last words are, "I've never forgiven that smart-alecky reporter who named me Butterfingers. To me, it's not funny." According to the headline on one local newspaper, "Even Policemen Mourn the Death of Pickpocket." In 2005, Alan Parker publishes his novel *The Sucker's Kiss*, an adaptation of Moran's life.

After the Supreme Court ruled that Rummel's sentence was not unconstitutional, Rummel files an appeal based on a theory of ineffective assistance of counsel. In 1980 the United States District Court for the Western District of Texas grants Rummel's petition. With the old conviction behind him, Rummel now pleads guilty to theft by false pretenses and is sentenced to time served under the terms of a plea-bargain agreement. Before his release, he repeatedly promises that if he gains his freedom again he would never re-offend. It would appear that he has kept his promise.[24]

Appendix: Model Penal Code "Purposes" Section Amendment

(Adopted May 16, 2007) (emphasis added)
Section 1.02(2). Purposes . . .

2. The general purposes of the provisions on sentencing, applicable to all official actors in the sentencing system, are:

    a. in decisions affecting the sentencing of individual offenders:

        i.   to render sentences in all cases within a range of severity *proportionate to the gravity of offenses, the harms done to crime victims, and the blameworthiness of offenders*;
        ii. when reasonably feasible, to achieve offender rehabilitation, general deterrence, incapacitation of dangerous offenders, restoration of crime victims and communities, and reintegration of offenders into the law-abiding community, provided these goals are pursued *within the boundaries of proportionality in subsection (a)(i)*; and
        iii. to render sentences no more severe than necessary to achieve the applicable purposes in subsections (a)(i) and (a)(ii); . . .

Chapter Glossary

Blameworthiness Proportionality: Under a desert distributive principle, blameworthiness proportionality requires imposition of the amount of punishment that is proportionate to the degree of blameworthiness of the offender, which must take into account the seriousness of the offense, the offender's culpability at the time the offense, as well as the offender's mental and emotional capacities.[25]

Desert/Deserved: Imposing deserved punishment means imposing punishment if and only if a person is blameworthy and imposing the amount of punishment corresponds to the person's degree of blameworthiness, no more, no less.[26]

Distributive Principle: The criterion used to decide who should be punished and how much punishment the individual should receive.[27]

General Deterrence: It refers to the practice of using criminal liability and punishment to instill fear in people in the hopes that such fear will prevent them from committing crimes in the future. This is done by making an example of offenders through their punishments. The focus is not on the offender individually; rather, the offender is punished publicly to prevent others who may have similar ideas from committing similar crimes in the future.[28]

Habitual Offender Statute: A statute prescribing an enhanced sentence, especially life imprisonment, for an offender's repeat offenses. "Three-strikes" statutes are a form of such offenses.[29]

Incapacitation of the Dangerous: It refers to the practice of using criminal liability and punishment to take physical control over an offender through some means.[30]

Punishment Theories: The principles used to decide who should be punished and how much punishment should be imposed.[31]

Rehabilitation: It refers to the practice of using criminal liability and punishment to improve a criminal's character and outlook so that he or she can function in society without committing other crimes.[32]

Retributivist Punishment Theory: A theory that justifies criminal punishment in terms of the ill-desert of the offender, regardless of whether deterrence or other good consequences would result.[33]

Three-Strike Statutes: These are a form of habitual offender statute that gives a significantly enhanced sentence, such as life imprisonment, upon commission of a third felony.[34]

Utilitarian (Crime-Control) Punishment Theories: These include those distributive principles, such as general deterrence, incapacitation of the dangerous, and rehabilitation, that have as their primary goal to reduce future crime, commonly in tension with retributivists (desert) distributive principle that has as its primary goal of to do justice.[35]

Notes

1. Moran was born in Boston. It might be that he is related to another famous pickpocket, Thomas Moran, who was active enough to show up in the New York case records in the late 1800s. This narrative is drawn from the following sources: *People v. Moran* 123 N.Y. 254, 25 N.E. 412 (1890); Timothy J. Gilfoyle, *A Pickpocket's Tale: The Underworld of Nineteenth-Century New York* (New York: W.W. Norton Publishing, 2006), p. 362.
2. 'Arrested 64 Times,' *Spokesman Review*, 16 September 1971.
3. "Butterfingers' Moran King of Pickpockets,' *Evening Independent*, 9 June 1967.
4. Thomas Philbin and Michael Philbin, *The Killer Book of True Crime* (Naperville: Sourcebooks Inc., 2007), p. 15.
5. 'Arrested 64 Times.'
6. 'Arrested 64 Times.'
7. Philbin and Philbin, *Killer Book*, p. 15.
8. Philbin and Philbin, *Killer Book*, p. 15.
9. 'Arrested 64 Times.'
10. Jay Robert Nash, *Bloodletters and Badmen* (New York: M. Evans & Company, 1995), p. 381.
11. Nash, *Bloodletters*, p. 381.
12. Nash, *Bloodletters*, p. 381.
13. 'Arrested 64 Times.'
14. Moran became enough of a curiosity that a novel, *The Suckers Kiss* by Allan Parker, was published in 2005 based on his life.
15. Danielle S. Allen, 'Demosthenes 21.123,' in 'Punishment in Ancient Athens' from Dēmos: Classical Athenian Democracy electronic publication, 23 March 2003, http://www.stoa.org/demos/article_punishment@page=all&greekEncoding=UnicodeC.html.

16. William Blackstone, *Commentaries on the Law of England* (1753), bk. 4, ch. I, https://www.nationallibertyalliance.org/files/docs/Books/Blackstone%20vol%202.pdf.

17. *See* Paul H. Robinson and Michael T. Cahill, *Criminal Law*, 2nd ed. (New York: Wolters Kluwer, 2016), pp. 20–26.

18. This narrative was drawn from the following sources: *Rummel v. Estelle, Federal Supplement 498* (1980), 793; Tom Nelson, 'Rummel Ordered Released for Appeal,' *San Antonio Express*, 4 October 1980; 'S.A. Man Gets Life,' *San Antonio Express*, 13 April 1973; 'Appeals Court Upholds Life Sentence for San Antonian,' *San Antonio Express*, 13 January 1979.

19. The map is taken from Paul H. Robinson and Tyler Scot Williams, *Mapping American Criminal Law: Variations across the 50 States* (Westport: Prager, 2018), ch. 2. All supporting authorities are available from that source.

20. For evidence that three-strikes statutes, as popular as they may be with politicians, conflict with ordinary people's judgments of justice, see Paul H. Robinson, *Intuitions of Justice and Utility of Desert* (Oxford: Oxford University Press, 2013), pp. 120–128.

21. For a complete discussion of these alternative distributive principles, see Paul H. Robinson, *Distributive Principles of Criminal Law: Who Should Be Punished How Much?* (Oxford: Oxford University Press, 2008).

22. Paul H. Robinson, *Intuitions of Justice and Utility of Desert* (Oxford: Oxford University Press, 2013), chs. 8–10.

23. Paul H. Robinson, *Intuitions of Justice and Utility of Desert* (Oxford: Oxford University Press, 2013), chs. 8–10.

24. Rummel's case remains in the national media spotlight. Less than two months after the Supreme Court upholds Rummel's sentence, U.S. District Judge D. W. Suttle orders the state to release Rummel or give him a new trial. Suttle rules that Rummel's trial attorney, William B. Chenault III, provided ineffective counsel in 1973 when Rummel received the life sentence. Noting that Chenault attempted virtually no investigation of the case before it went to trial, Judge Suttle orders Rummel released and sent back to criminal court for a new trial. The district attorney, still weary from the nationwide publicity around at Rummel's case, offers Rummel a deal: if Rummel pleads guilty to felony theft over $50, the state will recommend an eight-year prison sentence. Such a deal would allow Rummel, who has already served almost eight years, to go free immediately. On November 15, surrounded in court by national news media, Rummel pleads guilty to the theft offense and receives a seven-year sentence backdated to 1973. He is released from custody five hours later. "I am ready to go out and work. And I intend to stay free for the rest of my life." As of this writing, he has.

25. Robinson and Cahill, *Criminal Law*, §1.2.1.

26. Paul H. Robinson and Michael T. Cahill, *Criminal Law*, 2nd ed. (New York: Wolters Kluwer, 2012) §1.2; Robinson, *Distributive Principles of Criminal Law*, p. 11.

27. Robinson, *Distributive Principles of Criminal Law*, p. 2; Robinson and Cahill, *Criminal Law*, §1.2.1.

28. *Deterrence*, Legal Dictionary, https://legaldictionary.net/general-deterrence/

29. *Habitual Offender Statutes*, Black's.

30. Robinson, *Distributive Principles*, p. 109; Robinson and Cahill, *Criminal Law*, §1.2.1.

31. Robinson, *Distributive Principles*, pp. 1–3; Robinson and Cahill, *Criminal Law*, §1.2.

32. *Rehabilitation*, Black's.

33. *Retributivist Punishment Theory*, Black's.

34. *Three-Strike Statutes*, Black's.

35. Robinson, *Distributive Principles*, p. 1; Robinson and Cahill, *Criminal Law*, §1.2.1.

Chapter 3

Culpability

Homer Simpson's Felony Murder

1929. The Academy Awards, popularly known as the Oscars, begin, giving *Wings*, a World War I aviation action flick, top honors. American comic book hero Popeye the Sailor begins his long spinach-eating career. The world population reaches two billion people, 120 million of whom live in the United States.

Over four bleak days in October, Wall Street sees the value of the stock market drop by an amount equivalent to $396 billion today. The loss is more than the total cost of World War I. With the end of Prohibition still four years off, crime rates are up in the U.S. and American life is commonly chaotic.

Homer Simpson – 1929

The Homer Simpson of television fame has been arrested too many times to count since his creation almost 30 years ago.[1] Fortunately for him, he has spent little time in jail for his crimes, always managing to get off scot-free. However, there is another Homer Simpson who was not so lucky.

Homer Caswell Simpson is serving as the police chief of the town of Cleveland, Tennessee when America enters World War I in 1917 and he joins the Army. After his discharge, Simpson stays in contact with Malcolm Morrow, a somewhat shady southerner. Morrow resumes a life of bootlegging alcohol between Kentucky and Florida. Simpson returns to Cleveland for a second term as police chief.

When Simpson loses election for a third term, Morrow steps in and offers to send "jobs" Simpson's way and the unemployed police chief now occasionally joins his friend in the bootlegging business. But Simpson and Morrow live in different states and their contact is infrequent.

Morrow decides to up his game from bootlegging, and develops a plan to rob a bank, his "Kingsland Bank Proposition." Morrow and a friend spend several months

DOI: 10.4324/9781003258025-4

developing their scheme. The friend is to pose as a rich landowner interested in a piece of farmland owned by Kingsland banker Carl Perry. Once they have Perry isolated and alone on the farm, they will force from him the combination of the bank vault.

As they are about to set the plan in motion, the would-be robbers begin to worry that Perry will recognize the friend, who is a local man, and realize that he is no rich land buyer from Tennessee. Morrow calls and asks Simpson to come to Georgia. Simpson has only ferried alcohol for Morrow and has no reason to believe this request will be anything different. Simpson arrives in town, hears the plan, and is eventually persuaded to pose as the rich land buyer. The idea is to put banker Perry in a situation where he is so clearly out-numbered that he will cooperate without fighting or bloodshed.

Morrow prepares several bags that include all they will need to pull off the robbery, including rubber gloves, chloroform, a change of clothing, shovels, and a sawed-off shotgun. As per the plan, Banker Perry gets into a car with Simpson and they drive to Perry's farm. The other men are said to be friends of Simpson and follow behind in a separate car.

At the property, Perry, who has been facing threats from the KKK, gets suspicious that he is in danger. Assuming he is being ambushed by the KKK, when Morrow approaches him Perry draws a knife to defend himself. Morrow shoots Perry in the leg. Simpson tells Morrow not to shoot but as Perry continues to advance, Morrow shoots again, this time hitting Perry's right hand, causing him to lose his grip on the knife. Perry runs. Morrow raises his gun and Simpson yells "Don't shoot!"[2] but Morrow fires a third bullet that hits Perry's hip and enters his lower abdomen.

The three men are at a loss. Simpson wants them to take Perry to the hospital. Morrow agrees to do so but only after they stop at the bank to get the money they have planned on. As they load the bleeding Perry into the car, he asks whether they plan to kill him. Morrow replies that all they want him to do is open the bank safe. Perry only now grasps that they are not KKK members. "Oh my God, I wish I had known what you wanted," he says. "If I had, I would never have given you a second of trouble."[3]

From there the scheme unravels completely. On their way to the bank, they accidentally drive their car off the road. When passersby stop to help, the incriminating evidence of the planned bank robbery and the bleeding hostage is apparent. Less than 24 hours later, the police find and arrest Simpson and Morrow. Two days later, Perry dies in hospital from his wounds. Please eventually capture the third man and all three are indicted on homicide charges.

During Simpson's trial, there is little disagreement about the facts. Normally, to convict someone of murder, prosecutors must prove both that an offender's actions caused someone's death *and* that the offender intended this result. There is no evidence to suggest Simpson intended Perry's death, and yet the prosecutors charge him with murder under Florida's *felony-murder rule*.

The rule has two effects. First, it elevates to murder any killing, no matter how accidental, if it occurred in the course of a felony. Second, it applies this *aggravation* of liability to all persons who are accomplices in the underlying felony. Because Simpson was an accomplice to the bank robbery, under the felony-murder rule he is automatically an accomplice to Morrow's killing of Perry and that killing is murder for all the defendants because it occurred in the course of the robbery.

The defense focuses on Simpson's intentions at the time of the killing. He believably testifies that he had "no intention of hurting anyone at all."[4] Indeed, Simpson pulled Perry from the car wreck and carried him away from the leaking gasoline to an area where other cars could see him and transport him to a hospital faster than the robbers could. He is also shown to be a reluctant accomplice in the plan robbery. Most importantly, defense counsel argue, Simpson did not cause the death or even know that Morrow would cause it and, in fact, told Morrow *not* to shoot.

The trial lasts a day and a half. After being instructed on the felony-murder rule, the jury finds Simpson guilty of first-degree murder, which carries a mandatory death sentence. On September 11, 1929, all three men are executed in Georgia's electric chair.

Culpability Requirements

Before society can label anyone a criminal, the law requires proof of two elements: first, a criminal act or omission, often referred to as the "offense *objective requirements*" (*actus reus* in the old common-law vernacular); and second, a criminal state of mind, often referred to as the "offense *culpability* requirements" (*mens rea* in common-law terminology). In place of the plethora of judge-made common-law terms describing culpability requirements – wantonly, heedlessly, maliciously, and so on – modern American criminal codes commonly define four levels of culpability: *purposely*, *knowingly*, *recklessly*, and *negligently*. The codes provide a detailed definition of each of the four.[5]

Modern criminal codes typically recognize three kinds of objective elements: *conduct*, circumstance, and result elements. Most offenses are made up of certain conduct performed under certain circumstances but some offenses, such as homicide or property destruction, also require that the conduct cause a particular result. The Model Code requires that to be liable for an offense a person must have some level of culpability as to each objective element.[6]

A person acts purposely with respect to a result if his conscious object is to cause such a result. This is a demanding requirement that often is difficult to prove. In contrast, a person acts knowingly with respect to a result if causing the result is not his conscious object but he is practically certain of the result. The essence of the narrow distinction between these two culpability levels is the presence or absence of a positive desire or hope to cause the result. In a broader sense, this distinction divides the vague notion of "callousness" – acting even though one knows harmful result – from the more offensive "maliciousness" or "viciousness" – acting with desire to cause the harmful result.

A person acts knowingly with respect to a result if she is nearly certain that her conduct will cause the result. If she is aware only of a substantial risk, she acts "recklessly" with respect to the result. The narrow distinction between knowledge and recklessness lies in the degree of risk – "practically certain" versus "substantial risk" – of which the actor is aware. The distinction between recklessness (and lower levels of culpability) and the two higher levels of culpability (purposely and knowingly) is that we tend to scold a reckless actor for being "careless," while we condemn an offender who falls within one of the higher culpability categories for "intentional" conduct.

A person acts "recklessly" with respect to a result if she consciously disregards a substantial risk that her conduct will cause the result; she acts only "negligently" if she is unaware of a substantial risk but should have been aware of it. Recklessness focuses not on whether she *should* have been aware of the risk, but instead on whether she in fact *was aware* (and whether it was culpable for her to disregard such a risk). Thus, the narrow distinction between recklessness and *negligence* lies in the actor's awareness of risk.

The distinction between negligence and the three higher levels of culpability is one of the most critical to criminal law. A person who acts purposely, knowingly, or recklessly is aware of the circumstances that make his or her conduct criminal or is aware that harmful consequences may result, and is therefore both blameworthy and deterrable. A person who acts negligently, in contrast, is unaware of the circumstances or consequences of his actions and therefore, some might *argue*, is neither blameworthy nor deterrable. While writers disagree over whether negligence ought to support criminal liability, it is agreed that negligence represents a lower level of culpability than, and is qualitatively different from, recklessness, in that the negligent actor fails to recognize, rather than consciously disregards, the risk. For this reason, recklessness is typically considered sufficient for criminal culpability, while negligence is punished only in exceptional situations, as where a death is caused.

Liability imposed for faultless conduct is termed "absolute" or *strict liability*. The narrow distinction between negligence and strict liability focuses on whether a reasonable person would have been aware of the risk of which the defendant was unaware. The broader distinction between the four categories of culpability and faultlessness is the distinction between a blameworthy and a blameless actor.

The Felony-Murder Rule

The original conception of the *felony-murder rule* arose in the early 18th century. Liability for murder required proof that the person causing the death had *malice*, a rather loosely defined concept. Where a killing was entirely accidental, no malice was present and the killing could not be murder. But in 1716, William Hawkins, in his *Treatise of Pleas of the Crown*, reasoned that an accidental killing ought not necessarily escape murder liability if it came about while the actor was engaged in a crime, especially a felony, which at the time included such offenses as burglary, arson, robbery, theft, and mayhem. As Hawkins explained, a crime "necessarily tends to raise Tumults and Quarrels, and consequently cannot but be attended with the danger of personal hurt."[7] Thus, murder liability "should extend to killings in the course of felonies à fortiori." In other words, the intention to commit the underlying felony was thought to satisfy the malice requirement for murder.

As noted in the discussion of the Simpson case, the modern version of the felony-murder rule has two distinct features. First, it serves to *aggravate culpability* by treating an offender as if he has the culpability required for murder – typically *purposely* or *knowingly* causing death – regardless of what his actual culpability is, if the death occurs in the course of a felony. Second, it imposes such liability for murder not just on the actual murderer but also on all who were *complicit* in the commission of the underlying felony.

As to the *aggravation* of culpability aspect, assume the defendant plans to rob a liquor store by brandishing a pen knife to the clerk. If the sight of the knife does not induce the clerk to cooperate, the defendant plans to immediately flee, on assumption that the clerk probably has a gun. When he enters the store, the clerk is not in fact intimidated and the defendant turns to leave but the clerk quickly grabs his gun and leaps over the counter, but as he leaps the clerk ends up shooting himself in the leg. Because the bullet hits an artery, he bleeds to death before medical personnel can stop the bleeding. How would this case be resolved today?

Under most modern criminal codes, homicide is graded – and punishment varies – according to a defendant's culpability as to causing the death: murder requires purposeful or knowing, manslaughter requires *recklessness*, and negligent homicide requires *negligence*. On these facts, when the defendant robs the liquor store brandishing his pen knife, he might have been at most reckless or negligent as to causing the clerk's death. That is, a jury might conclude that he was at most aware of a substantial risk that his conduct in entering the store with the pen knife would cause the death or, if he was not aware of this (which seems more likely), that a reasonable person would have been aware. (Alternatively, a jury might conclude that even a reasonable person would not have thought that such conduct created a substantial risk of causing death.) Depending on the conclusion the jury reaches, the defendant would be held liable for manslaughter or negligent homicide, respectively (or no form of homicide, and liable only for the attempted robbery).[8]

Under the felony-murder rule, however, the defendant will be liable for murder on these facts, because he caused the death in the course of committing a felony. His culpability level as to causing the death becomes irrelevant. In its strictest form, the rule essentially imputes to the defendant the standard culpability required for murder – typically intentionally or knowingly causing the death – based upon his commission of the underlying felony.[9]

The felony-murder rule lives on today in many jurisdictions but has been the subject of increasing criticism, which has led to serious legal limitations and increasingly restrictive use in many jurisdictions. Consider a more modern famous English case, the country from which we take the felony-murder rule.

Moors Child Murderers – 1964

Ian Duncan Brady is 22, recently out of jail, and working as a stock clerk when he meets typist Myra Hindley.[10] The 18-year-old Hindley is immediately attracted to Brady and within a few months, in early 1962, the two are a couple.

Brady, who has a troubled past that includes torturing animals and violence toward his schoolmates. He reads a good deal but usually about subjects such as Hitler, the Nazi movement, the works of the Marquis de Sade, and Friedrich Nietzsche. He introduces Hindley to these philosophies and the couple spends time reading books about Nazi atrocities out loud to each other while on their lunch break. Hindley now bleaches her hair to match the Aryan ideal.

Brady talks openly with Hindley about his belief that murder, rape, and other serious crimes are not wrong, and the pair debate which crimes they should commit. Becoming rich off a life of burglaries and robberies is appealing – Brady has already been convicted of burglary on three occasions – but they ultimately settle on murder, opting for thrills over wealth.

On July 12, 1963, Hindley is driving alone in a van, with Brady close behind on a motorbike. They are looking for their first victim when they spot eight-year-old Marie Ruck. Brady signals that he wants to get her but Hindley does not stop. It turns out little Marie is a close neighbor of Hindley.

Soon thereafter, they spot Pauline Reade, a school-friend of Hindley's younger sister. The 16-year-old is on her way to a dance. Hindley stops her and asks for help in locating an expensive missing glove, in the process of their chat she lures Pauline into the car. With their victim secured, they drive to the moors, where Pauline is beaten, raped, and her throat sliced open. The couple buries the body. As Brady and Hindley drive back to town, they pass the mother and brother of the dead girl, who are already out looking for her.

When they begin to plan the next killing, it is decided that Pauline fought too hard, so the next victim should be younger. Their next victim is a 12-year-old boy. That killing is followed by several others in which the children are tortured, raped, murdered, and buried on the wind-swept moors. Some of the atrocities are recorded by the couple on audiotape.

Myra Hindley has a younger sister, Maureen, who is dating 17-year-old David Smith. Smith begins to hang out with the older couple. He finds Brady and his fascination with the dark side of life very compelling. In August, Maureen and Smith marry. The newlyweds honeymoon with Myra Hindley and Brady.

Smith and Maureen have a child, Angela, who lives for six months and dies suddenly. Smith takes the death of his infant daughter very hard. Brady, who as a practical matter is Smith's brother-in-law, reaches out to the grieving father, befriending the younger man. He shares his intimate fantasies, introducing him to the works of the Marquis de Sade, Nazi ideology, and romantic notions of power. Smith craves the rebel-without-a-cause persona that he senses in Brady.

Brady spends long hours talking to Smith and drinking the night away. Brady brags on more than one occasion that he has killed people but Smith does not take the claim seriously. Smith feels "it was all said in drink." Brady offers Smith a chance at some adventure. He suggests that they "roll a queer."[11] The two plot to pick up someone at a homosexual club, entice him to Brady's home, and then rob him.

After some discussion, Brady brings up the idea of killing their victim. Smith says "no" to that. He makes clear that the robbery something he is keen to do but he will not be part of hurting anyone.

Brady does not bring up killing again and the pair resume planning the robbery. Brady selects 17-year-old Edward Evans as his victim. He lures Evans to his place, shortly after which Hindley and Smith arrive together. The group talks for a time in the living room. When Hindley and Smith go into the kitchen, and Brady and Evan are alone in the living room, Brady drives an axe into Evan's skull. Hearing the commotion, Smith and Hindley return to the living room in time to see Brady repeatedly strike Evans with the axe. When he is done, Brady hands the bloody axe to Smith, and suggests that he see how it feels.

Smith refuses. He is certain that he is next. Brady shares that this is the messiest murder to date. He tells Smith to help with the cleanup and Smith does everything he is asked to do. Evans is wrapped up in a plastic sheet. It is agreed that Smith will come by in the morning with a baby pram to move the body into the car so it can be taken to join the other bodies in the moors. Smith, maintaining an outward calm, says goodnight and leaves.

Once out of view, Smith breaks into a run, arriving home covered in blood, shaking and violently ill. Smith tells his wife everything. The couple is terrified that they will be the next victims. They grab some kitchen knives and go out into the night to hide. Finding a phone booth, they use it as a hide-away until morning, when Smith goes to police and relates the whole affair.

While the story sounds fantastic, the police find Evans exactly where Smith told them they would. When arrested, Brady and Hindley implicate Smith as being part of all of the murders. When the audio tapes are found under the floorboards of Brady's house, only three voices are heard: Hindley, Brady, and the agonized child.

The killing of Evans occurred in the course of a felony, specifically robbery, to which Smith was an accomplice. If Smith were charged under the felony-murder rule applied in the *Simpson* case above, he would be liable for murder. However, the UK abolished the *felony-murder rule* in 1957 (although it retained some more limited aspects of it under a different doctrine). Smith is not prosecuted.

> **Figure 3.1** The police search for the dead (left); Hindley and Brady with their victims, 1965 (right)

For two days Smith testifies at the trial of Brady and Hindley, both of whom are found guilty. Brady is sentenced to three concurrent life sentences and Hindley is given two, plus a concurrent seven-year term for harboring Brady knowing that he had murdered.

Felony-Murder Liability in the States

The states take different views on the felony-murder rule today, and may be divided into five categories, as presented in the map below.[12] The darker the shading, the broader the felony-murder liability.

The first group, represented on the map without shading, has effectively rejected the *felony-murder rule*. These seven jurisdictions either do not have such a rule or if they do have such a rule, the *culpability* required under it is the same as that required for murder. In other words, their felony-murder rule does not expand murder liability to actors other than those normally liable for murder. The effect of this approach is consistent with that offered in the Model Penal Code, quoted in the margin, which as a practical matter rejects the felony-murder rule.

Notice that the last sentence of subsection (1)(b) of the Model Code seems to provide something like a felony-murder rule: it allows the *recklessness* and indifference that would constitute murder under subsection (1)(b) to be presumed under felony-murder-like conditions. On its own, the presumption of recklessness and indifference codified in subsection (1)(b) would eliminate the need to prove a defendant actually had such a state of mind. However, the practical effect of this apparent presumption is severely curtailed by Model Code section 1.12(5)(b),[13] which defines the effect of presumptions in such a way as to render them of little practical effect: the jury is still instructed that they must find the recklessness and extreme indifference required for murder beyond a reasonable doubt.

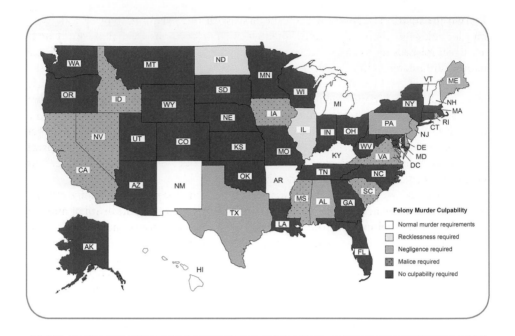

Figure 3.2

Murder.
      (1) [C]riminal homicide constitutes murder when:
      (a) it is committed purposely or knowingly; or
      (b) it is committed recklessly under circumstances manifesting extreme indifference to the value of human life. Such recklessness and indifference are presumed if the actor is engaged or is an accomplice in the commission of, or an attempt to commit, or flight after committing or attempting to commit robbery, rape or deviate sexual intercourse by force or threat of force, arson, burglary, kidnapping or felonious escape.

Model Penal Code §210.2

Figure 3.3

Two jurisdictions, represented on the map with light shading, have true felony-murder rules but their rules are formulated in such a way as to require proof of at least recklessness as to causing the death of another in the course of committing a felony. Without the felony-murder rule, such actors would commonly be liable for the lesser offense of reckless homicide (manslaughter). Neither Simpson nor Smith is likely to be held liable for murder in these jurisdictions or those in the previous group because neither offender at the time of his *complicity* in the robbery seems to be aware of a substantial risk that his *conduct* would help cause the death of the victim. Whether Simpson or Smith would be liable for murder in either of the next two groups of jurisdictions depends upon the jury's conclusions about whether their conduct was negligent as to causing the victim's death.

Six jurisdictions, those with medium shading on the map, impose felony-murder liability but only on actors who are at least negligent as to causing the death of another in the course of a felony. Without a felony-murder rule, an actor in these jurisdictions might otherwise be liable for negligent homicide or involuntary manslaughter. The eight jurisdictions shown on the map with medium shading plus dots impose felony-murder liability but nonetheless require that the government prove *malice*. Malice is generally presumed when the actor should have foreseen the danger in his conduct – that is, when the actor was *negligent* in causing a death, perhaps by engaging in inherently dangerous conduct or conduct dangerous under the circumstances.[14]

A final group of 28 states, appearing in black on the map, impose felony-murder liability on actors who unlawfully cause a death in the course of committing a felony even if the actor was not even negligent in causing a death, including actors who reasonably believe that their participation in a felony does not create a risk of death.

Simpson and Smith would likely be liable for felony murder in these jurisdictions. Notice that, in order to convict Simpson and Smith under the felony-murder rule, the prosecution must rely upon both aspects of the felony-murder rule: the *aggravation* of culpability aspect, which imputes to both men the culpability required for murder, and the complicity aspect of the rule, which holds both men liable for the lethal conduct of the perpetrator.

The trend over time has been to eliminate the felony-murder rule or at least to limit its scope to the more blameworthy offenders. To a large extent, that explains the dramatic difference in treatment between the 1929 *Simpson* case, which resulted in a conviction for murder, and the 1964 *Smith* case, which did not. As noted, the UK Homicide Act of 1957 abolished the felony-murder rule (referred to in that country as the doctrine of "constructive malice"). Nonetheless, as the map suggests, the felony-murder rule remains strong in a large number of American jurisdictions today.

Does the Disproportionality of Punishment to Blameworthiness under the Felony-Murder Rule Help or Hurt the Criminal Law's Goals?

What accounts for the relatively high level of disagreement among the states regarding the *felony-murder rule*? Each of the many sides in the debate has a plausible argument to offer. On the one hand, many will find a certain appeal in the argument that the person who undertakes a serious crime, a felony, is someone who has already demonstrated their willingness to disregard societal norms and to put their interests ahead of others. Why shouldn't they be criminally liable for everything that follows?

On the other hand, the criminal law has increasingly tried to capture the nuanced blameworthiness of each distinct criminal offense. The degree of an offender's blameworthiness ought to determine the degree of his criminal liability and punishment. The liquor store robber who goes into the store with the intention of stabbing the clerk to death and the robber in our hypothetical above who goes in with his pen knife ready to run away rather than use it are people of two very different degrees of moral blameworthiness. A just criminal law is one that will distinguish the two cases and give greater punishment, as deserved, to the robber who plans the death. The jurisdictions that reject the felony-murder rule may do so on this reasoning.

Notice that the Model Penal Code formulation of the murder offense recognizes that one can have the blameworthiness of an intentional murderer if one creates a substantial risk of causing death "under circumstances manifesting an extreme indifference the value of human life" and recognizes that such *recklessness* and indifference might exist in some felony-murder situations. In other words, there is a kernel of truth to the fact that the felony-murder situation can, under some circumstances, raise a reckless killing to the same level of blameworthiness as an intentional or knowing killing. This kernel may have helped sustain the felony-murder rule even in those jurisdictions committed to following a principle of strict proportionality between blameworthiness and punishment.

The moral complexity in these kinds of cases may help explain why many jurisdictions seek some middle ground between the felony-murder abolitionists and those who strictly adhere to the classic felony-murder rule. That is, many jurisdictions keep the rule but limit it by requiring some minimum *culpability* as to causing the death – recklessness, malice, or at least *negligence*. Perhaps these jurisdictions see the limitation that they have added as excluding from the rule's operation the most egregious instances of blameworthiness disproportionality.

The analysis above has been one that focuses exclusively on desert as a principle for distributing punishment, but it seems likely that many of the jurisdictions have been influenced by alternative distributive principles, especially general deterrence.[15] (Generally speaking, desert punishes an offender to the degree that he is blameworthy, whereas deterrence punishes an offender to the degree necessary to prevent others from committing the same offense. Recall the discussion of these alternative distributive principles in Chapter 2.[16])

A traditional felony-murder rule may be attractive under a general deterrence program because the threat of greater punishment may be thought to induce felons to be more careful, and indeed may provide some additional disincentive for the commission of the underlying felony itself. However, as has been detailed in the previous chapter,[17] it may be unrealistic to think that such nuanced deterrence calculations in rule formulation by lawmakers can have any real-world effect. For example, given the diversity among the states demonstrated by the map, how likely is it that the potential liquor store robber deciding whether to go in to rob the store will even know whether his jurisdiction has a felony-murder rule or not and, if it has a rule, what formulation it adopts?[18]

The trend appears to be to move away from distributive principles that conflict with desert: as discussed in the previous chapter,[19] 45 years after its promulgation by the American Law Institute, the first amendment to the Model Code was a 2007 revision that prioritized desert over other distributive principles by stating that "[t]he general purposes of the provisions governing sentencing" are "to render punishment within a range of severity proportionate to the gravity of offenses, the harms done to crime victims, and the blameworthiness of offenders."[20] This blameworthiness proportionality requirement is never to be violated. If this is the trend, then one might expect the number of felony-murder abolition states to grow, or at least one might expect more states following the traditional rule to narrow its scope. Of course, this assumes that legislatures actively re-examine the appropriateness of their criminal law rules, when the truth may be that the force of inertia is often greater than the desire to be just.[21]

Aftermaths

Homer Simpson's friends and family try for years to advance the argument that Simpson was not a murderer and had worked hard to save the life of Perry. Two books are written about the crime that led to his execution. (To avoid comic confusion, one of the books is entitled *The Real Homer Simpson*.) His gravestone, erected by his family, reads: "Homer Simpson, Executed for a Crime he did not Commit."

For David Smith, he is never charged as an accomplice to the child murders but after the trials of Hindley and Brady, he is subjected to extensive harassment. His windows are constantly smashed by bricks, he is roughed up in the street, and his home is covered with graffiti reading "Child Killers Live Here." He is unable to hold a job due to workplace harassment, his wife leaves him, and he attempts suicide. Smith marries again in 1975, this time to Mary Flaherty. Together the couple have a daughter. Hindley continues to assert Smith's involvement in the killings, until she retracts her "pack of lies" in 1987. Hindley dies in 2002; Brady in 2017. Smith devotes himself to finding the bodies of the children buried in the Moors until his death in 2012. The body of Keith Bennett has never been found.

Chapter Glossary

Complicity: The acts of actively planning a crime, but not being present at the time of the commission, or of assisting the criminal at the time of commission of the crime.[22]

Conduct Requirement: The conduct element of an offense defining the physical acts that a person must perform to satisfy the offense requirements.

Culpability: In the context of criminal law, it refers to the culpable state of mind of an offender at the time of committing an offense. In modern American criminal codes, typically based upon the Model Penal Code, the alternative culpability levels include purposely, knowingly, recklessly, and negligently, and all offenses are defined to specify which of these levels of culpability is required as to each of the objective elements of the offense definition. The term is also sometimes used in a broader sense to mean the same as the term "blameworthiness."[23]

Culpability Aggravation: Any fact or circumstance that increases the culpability of a criminal act. Aggravating factors include an increased culpability level (e.g., such as "purpose" or "knowing" rather than just "reckless") and lack of remorse, among many others.[24]

Culpability Requirement: The culpability elements of an offense defining the mental culpability requirements that a person must satisfy in order to be liable for the offense. Under the Model Penal Code, some culpability requirement exists as to each objective offense element and may be either purpose, knowing, reckless, or negligent.[25]

Felony-Murder Rule: It authorizes a court to convict a defendant of murder if they caused a death in the course of committing a felony, even if the killing was unintentional.[26]

Knowingly: Under the Model Penal Code, "knowingly" describes the mental state in which a person knows that his conduct will cause a prohibited result, for example, but does not necessarily desire or hope for the result (purpose).[27]

Malice: The common-law culpability requirement for murder that may roughly correspond to the Model Penal Code requirements for murder (causing a death purposely, knowingly, or recklessly with extreme indifference the value of human life) but include much more complex and commonly unspecific requirements.

Negligence: The failure to exercise the standard of care that a reasonably prudent person would have exercised in a similar situation. Under the Model Penal Code, the failure to be aware of a substantial risk of which a reasonable person would have been aware in the same situation.[28]

Objective Requirements: The elements of an offense defining the conduct, circumstances, or results that must be satisfied if a person is to be liable for the offense. The Model Penal Code requires that to be liable for an offense a person must have some level of culpability as to each objective element.[29]

Purposely: Under the Model Penal Code, a person acts purposely with respect to causing a result or existing circumstances if they want or hope the result to occur or the circumstance to exist.[30]

Recklessness: Under the Model Penal Code, a person acts recklessly with respect to causing a result or as to the existence of a circumstance if they are aware of a substantial risk that the result will occur or that the circumstance exists and choose to go ahead with their conduct anyway.[31]

Strict Liability: Non-negligence. Strict liability is said to be imposed whenever criminal liability is imposed in the absence of a person's culpability. A strict liability offense is an offense for which the action alone is enough to warrant a conviction, with no need to prove a mental state, as is often the case with traffic offenses and illegal sales of intoxicating liquor.[32]

Notes

1. This narrative is drawn from the following sources: '1929: Homer Simpson,' *Executed Today*, 11 September 2014, http://www.executedtoday.com/2014/09/11/1929-homer-simpson/; Tara D. Fields, *The Grave: Murder in the Deep South*, eBook 2011, http://www.camdencounty.org; Randall Higgins, 'Seeking the truth on an 83-year-old murder,' *Times Free Press*, 10 January 2011, http://www.timesfreepress.com/news/news/story/2011/jan/10/seeking-truth-83-year-old-murder/38978/; William Wright, '"The Real Homer Simpson" Is a Haunting Search for Justice,' *Cleveland Daily Banner*, 15 February 2015, http://clevelandbanner.com/stories/the-real-homer-simpson-is-a-haunting-search-for-justice,2566.
2. Randall Higgins, 'Seeking the truth on an 83-year-old murder,' *Times Free Press*, 10 January 2011, https://www.timesfreepress.com/news/news/story/2011/jan/10/seeking-truth-83-year-old-murder/38978/
3. Fields, *The Grave.*
4. Fields, *The Grave.*
5. Paul H. Robinson and Michael T. Cahill, *Criminal Law*, 2nd ed. (New York: Wolters Kluwer, 2016), pp. 156–157.
6. MPC §2.02.
7. William Hawkins, *Treatise of Pleas of the Crown* 86–87 (1716). *See* Guyora Binder, 'Making the Best of Felony Murder,' *Boston University Law Review* 91 (2011):

pp. 403, 414; Guyora Binder, 'The Origins of American Felony Murder Rules,' *Stanford Law Review 57* (2004): pp. 59, 88–92.

8. Robinson, *Criminal Law*, 15.1, 15.2.

9. What is described here might be called the "aggravation of culpability" aspect of felony-murder rule. The traditional role also has a "complicity aspect," which applies the same imputation of murder culpability to all accomplices in the underlying felony. There exists significant diversity among the states on how they deal with this aspect of the felony-murder rule as well. Robinson and Cahill, *Criminal Law*.

10. 'Ian Brady and Myra Hindley,' *Criminal Minds*, http://criminalminds.wikia.com/wiki/Ian_Brady_and_Myra_Hindley; 'Galway Man Who Turned in the Moors Murderers,' *Google Groups,* originally retrieved from *Ireland on Sunday*, 26 November 2002, https://groups.google.com/forum/#!topic/alt.true-crime/7NeAEIgw4zY; Amisha Padnani, 'The Moors Murders: A Notorious Couple and Their Young Prey,' *The New York Times,* 17 May 2017, https://www.nytimes.com/2017/05/17/world/europe/moors-murders-ian-brady-myra-hindley-victims.html; Elisabeth Sherman, 'The Strange Story of Myra Hindley and The Moors Murders,' *All That Is Interesting,* 20 July 2017, http://all-that-is-interesting.com/myra-hindley-moors-murders; David Smith and Carol A. Lee, *Witness: The Story of David Smith Chief Prosecution Witness in the Moors Murders Case* (Edinburgh: Mainstream Publishing, 2011).

11. Padnani, 'Moors Murders.'

12. The map is taken from Paul H. Robinson and Tyler Scot Williams, *Mapping American Criminal Law: Variations across the 50 States*, Chapter 6 (Westport: Prager, 2018). All supporting authorities are available from that source.

13. Model Penal Code § 1.12(5): When the Code establishes a presumption with respect to any fact which is an element of an offense, it has the following consequences:
    (a) when there is evidence of the facts which give rise to the presumption, the issue of the existence of the presumed fact must be submitted to the jury, unless the Court is satisfied that the evidence as a whole clearly negatives the presumed fact; and
    (b) when the issue of the existence of the presumed fact is submitted to the jury, the Court shall charge that while the presumed fact must, on all the evidence, be proved beyond a reasonable doubt, the law declares that the jury may regard the facts giving rise to the presumption as sufficient evidence of the presumed fact.

14. Possibly, in some jurisdictions, malice may be imputed to the actor even when the actor could not have foreseen the danger. In such cases, felony murder per se is a strict-liability offense. In other words, these "malice" jurisdictions end up requiring something in the nature of negligence or less, although without the clear and specific definitions typically found in modern American criminal codes using the Model Penal Code's culpability definitions.

15. *See, e.g.*, Model Penal Code §1.02 (2007) (defining the general purposes of the Model Code's provisions governing the sentencing and correction of individual offenders to include goals of rehabilitation, general deterrence, incapacitation, and restorative justice, "provided that these goals are pursued within the boundaries" of what is required by desert).

16. Chapter 2.

17. Chapter 2.

18. Paul H. Robinson, 'Does Criminal Law Deter?' and 'Deterrence as a Distributive Principle,' in *Distributive Principles of Criminal Law: Who Should Be Punished How Much* (Oxford: Oxford University Press, 2008), (discussing general deterrence), pp. 21–98.

19. Chapter 2.

20. *See id.* At 240–246; *see generally* Paul H. Robinson, 'The A.L.I.'s Proposed Distributive Principle of "Limiting Retributivism": Does It Mean in Practice Anything Other Than Pure Desert?,' *Buffalo Criminal Law Review* 7 (2003): p. 3.

21. Paul H. Robinson, 'The Rise and Fall and Resurrection of American Criminal Codes, Conference Keynote Address,' *University of Louisville Law Review* 53 (2015): pp. 173–191; Paul H. Robinson and Michael T. Cahill, 'The Accelerating Degradation of American Criminal Codes,' *Hastings Law Journal* 56 (2005): pp. 633–655.

22. *Complicity*, The Law Dictionary, 2002 Anderson Publishing Co.

23. *Culpability*, Black's; MPC §2.02.

24. *Aggravating Factor*, Cornell Law School.

25. Model Penal Code section 2.02.

26. *Felony Murder*, Legal Information Institute, https://www.law.cornell.edu/wex/felony_murder_doctrine.

27. *Knowingly*, Black's; MPC §2.02.

28. Negligence, Black's; MPC §2.02.

29. MPC §2.02.

30. MPC §2.02.

31. MPC §2.02.

32. *Strict Liability*, Black's.

Chapter 4

Homicide Provocation

A Webster Murder at Harvard

1849. The Communist Manifesto by Karl Marx and Frederic Engels has just been published in London. The opening line of the work reads, "A spectre is haunting Europe – the spectre of communism." The population of the U.S. reaches 23 million. (It is more than 329 million today.) French physicist Armand Fizeau calculates the speed of light (and is only off by 5%). The first successful appendectomy has recently been performed. Not all medical professionals, however, are advancing the interests of humankind.

Dr. John Webster – 1849

In the mid-1800s, sensational, highly publicized crimes are few and far between.[1] Yet in 1849, a crime takes place in Boston, Massachusetts that remains unrivaled in fame for decades to come. The public follows the trial of John White Webster intently.

Dr. Webster has always known prestige and success. In 1824, at age 31, he has top academic credentials, is happily married, and is seen as an important man when he joins the Harvard Medical School faculty as a lecturer in chemistry. In his new position, his reputation grows, as does his standing in the community. Unfortunately, his salary does not, and he is always in debt.

Webster is constantly borrowing money from other people. One of those is Dr. George Parkman, one of the wealthiest men in Boston. Parkman received his medical degree from Harvard but finds his true calling to be business. Accruing wealth is important to Parkman but he is also a charitable citizen. He donates a significant plot of land to the new Medical College at Harvard and endows the Parkman Chair of Anatomy.

As collateral for a loan from Parkman, Webster pledges some furniture, books, and – most valuably – his personal collection of minerals. Unaware that the mineral collection is already serving as collateral for other loans, Parkman lends Webster $2,432. When he learns of the prior liens on the collection, Parkman is not pleased and when Webster fails to correct the situation Parkman begins to harangue Webster in public. On several occasions, Parkman enters the lecture hall while Webster is lecturing and berates him in front of his students. Parkman also tells Webster's colleagues that he is a scoundrel. Holding a position on Harvard's board, Parkman begins threatening to have Webster fired.

The situation comes to a head on November 23, 1849 when Webster invites Parkman to his lab to discuss the situation. As an argument ensues, Parkman explodes with anger, calling Webster a liar and a scoundrel and demanding return of his money. In a later confession, Webster describes how he reacted:

> I felt nothing but the sting of his words . . . and in my fury I seized whatever thing was handiest – it was a stick of wood – and dealt him an instantaneous blow with all the force that passion could give it.[2]

That one blow to the skull is enough; Parkman slumps to the ground, dead. In a spectacular show of bad judgment Webster sets to work hiding the crime. After dismembering Parkman, he places the body parts in a furnace.

Parkman's disappearance is immediately noted, and a full-scale search is launched. The janitor who works in Webster's building remembers Webster's office being locked while he was in it and that the furnace was burning at a great rate. The janitor does

THIS TIME PROFESSOR WEBSTER WAS READY FOR DOCTOR PARKMAN.

[Contemporary Print.]

Figure 4.1 This drawing, done after the trial, depicts the death of Parkman, 1849

his own investigation of the contents of the furnace and finds the charred remains of Parkman's false teeth. Webster is arrested.

The next day, the city and its press are hysterical with excitement. "Horrible Suspicions!!! Arrest of Professor J.W. Webster"[3] screams the headlines of the *Evening Transcript*. After recounting the arrest, the story adds a colorful but ominous description:

> In the streets, in the market-place, at every turn, men greet each other with pale, eager looks, and the inquiry, "Can it be true?" And the terrible reply, "The circumstances begin to gather weight against him," is wrung forth; the agitated listener can only vent his sickening sense of horror, in some such expression as that of Hamlet – *O, horrible! O, horrible! most horrible!*[4]

When the highly anticipated trial begins, tens of thousands of people come to witness the proceedings. Police estimate that 55,000–60,000 people wait outside the courthouse throughout the trial. To accommodate as many people as possible, spectators are admitted to the courthouse in ten-minute shifts.

After a ten-day trial, the judge delivers his charge to the jury. Under the law at that time – drawn primarily from the "common law" developed by English judges before American Independence – most deliberate killings constitute *murder* for which the penalty is death. However, the court explains, there is a difference between *manslaughter* and murder: "when death ensues from sudden transport of passion, or heat of blood, if on reasonable *provocation* and without malice, or upon sudden combat, it will be manslaughter," which "is punished severely, ignominiously, – but still, not with death."[5]

Webster claims that killing occurred upon such "sudden passion" with "reasonable provocation." However, the law sets limitations on what will qualify as "reasonable provocation." His plea is helped by the fact that he had not planned to kill Parkman, had killed only impulsively in a spasm of anger at Parkman's threats of continuing public humiliation, and had simply grabbed a piece of firewood at hand.

After the judge instructs the jury on the law, he also offers an opinion on the facts of the case. The jurors deliberate and return in three hours with their verdict: John White Webster is guilty of murder and sentenced to hang.[6]

Provocation

The requirements for *murder* are satisfied when a person intentionally kills another human being. Yet, one can imagine very different kinds of intentional killings. When one person shoots another because the person does not want a competitor vying for a business deal or for a woman's affections, it would seem to be a classic case of the worst kind of wrongdoing, deserving the highest levels of punishment. The person is simply putting his or her interests above those of others and even above the value of another's life.

But imagine a different kind of intentional killing. While the defendant is helplessly drunk, another person sodomizes him and then, over the next several weeks, publicly brags about his victimization of the defendant in the hopes of humiliating him among their close-knit community. The defendant is angry and upset but holds himself in check. His appeals to the legal authorities go nowhere because his victimizer has friends on the police force. As he is increasingly publicly mocked and humiliated by his victimizer, his anger begins to rise to the point that it consumes him. After a round of public taunting by a friend of the victimizer, the defendant goes back to his apartment, gets his gun, goes to the house of his victimizer, and in a fit of rage shoots him dead. (These facts are drawn from a real case, *Gounagias*.[7])

Clearly, this is an intentional killing, but it is generally agreed that, compared to the unprovoked killing of the commercial or romantic competitor, it is less blameworthy due to the mitigating circumstances of the *provocation* and sudden (perhaps understandable) rage. The criminal law typically accounts for the difference between these two cases by recognizing that a *provoked killing in "heat of passion"* (or a broader version thereof referred to in modern codes as a killing during an *extreme emotional disturbance*) can mitigate murder to a lesser form of *homicide*, such as *manslaughter*.

> Experts characterize the emergence of provocation principles in fifteenth-century England as a response to the harshness of the extant murder liability and sentencing regime. At that time, nearly all killings were punishable as murders, and murder convictions necessitated the death penalty. By the seventeenth century, courts solidified the legal doctrine of provocation, and defendants claimed provocation as a matter of course to rebut the presumption that they acted with malice and evade execution. Consequently, history shows that the primary purpose of the doctrine was literally to mitigate the harsh effects of an unforgiving legislative regime.
>
> According to experts, the doctrine continued to function as a counterweight to popular penal tendencies well into the nineteenth century: Reflection on this period suggests that while Parliament continued to increase the number of capital offenses, and political rhetoric required the toughest approach to crime, the judiciary sought to mitigate the severity of legislation. The emergence of the doctrine of provocation is. . . one example of this tendency.[8]

The provocation mitigation had its limits, however. Courts created several rules about the situations that could and could not constitute "reasonable provocation." Catching one's spouse in bed with another could constitute reasonable provocation at common law but, as we see in the *Webster* case, being humiliated about a debt lawfully owed would not. Further, under the strict common-law rules, a provocation mitigation would be denied if some time had passed between the provocation and the killing, so that the defendant could have cooled off. Indeed, in the *Gounagias* case described above, in which the sodomy rape victim kills his victimizer, he is denied the mitigation and convicted of murder,[9] because there was a cooling time between the offense and the killing (and because being publicly mocked about his victimization, which was the immediate trigger to the killing, was not on the common-law list of acceptable provocations).

Over time, however, the significant common-law limitations on the provocation mitigation are relaxed. The American Law Institute's Model Penal Code, citing the result in the *Gounagias* case as an example of the improper narrowness of the common-law provocation rule, adopts a significantly broader mitigation of murder to manslaughter. It provides a mitigation for killings:

> committed under the influence of extreme mental or emotional disturbance for which there is reasonable explanation or excuse. The reasonableness of such explanation or excuse shall be determined from the viewpoint of a person in the actor's situation under the circumstances as he believes them to be.[10]

Some Model Penal Code-based jurisdictions adopt this formulation and many non-Model Penal Code jurisdictions adopt other doctrines, such as California's *diminished capacity* mitigation, that can provide a similar effect. Overall, the possibility of mitigating an intentional killing to manslaughter has significantly increased in modern American criminal law.

Consider the application of the more modern doctrines in this famous case.

Dan White – 1978

Election night on November 8, 1977 marks an extraordinary day for the cause of gay rights in America.[11] Harvey Milk, a 40-year-old gay-rights activist, wins a seat on the San Francisco Board of Supervisors and becomes one of the first openly gay Americans elected to public office. Representing a district that includes the growing Castro Village area where the city's gay community is flourishing, Milk wins by making his sexual orientation a central issue of the campaign, arguing that gays should represent gays. His election earns him widespread national media coverage and is hailed as an important step forward for gay rights.

Dan White, a former San Francisco firefighter and police officer, is also celebrating. He has just won his first election, earning him a seat on the board of supervisors. White, who is elected with strong support from unions across the city, represents District 8, a predominantly white, middle-class district that is hostile toward the city's growing gay community. He promises to stand up for "the home, the family, and religious life."[12]

Given their clear differences, Milk and White make unlikely political allies. However, both men arrive early each day to their City Hall offices, both served in the Navy, and both see themselves as idealists, even if they are each animated by a different set of principles. Soon after their swearing-in ceremony, White convinces Board of Supervisors President Dianne Feinstein to make Milk Chairman of the Streets and Transportation Committee, a position Milk wants badly. White also backs Milk on several other initiatives. However, their early cordiality is upended in April 1978, when Milk does not return White's political favors.

As the months wear on, White grows increasingly frustrated by what he sees as rampant corruption and political grandstanding by his fellow supervisors. For example, White is aghast when a colleague spends an hour on a tax measure targeting the San Francisco Giants because he is unhappy with the free seats that the team gave him.

Work, financial, and family pressures all start stacking up on White. Everyone notices the change in the once-steady man: he is now often irate, his moods are erratic, and he suffers periodic states of depression, holing up in his room for days at a time eating only candy bars and potato chips. To the surprise of almost everyone, on November 10, 1978, White announces his resignation from the San Francisco Board of Supervisors.

His resignation sends shockwaves through the city's political class and many people rally around him to get him to re-join the council and to continue his fight against corruption and political shenanigans. Milk is not one of the people who want White to return: he uses the opportunity to secure a guarantee from Mayor George Moscone that White's appointed successor will support his plan to build a gay community center.

Four days after resigning, White has reconsidered his decision and meets with Moscone to ask for his letter of resignation back. Moscone is inclined to give it to

Figure 4.2 Milk's reputation as a reformer lives on

him, understanding that everyone makes mistakes. Moscone tells White that he wants time to think about it. Soon thereafter, Moscone is persuaded to appoint someone else to the seat, but fails to inform White, who is spending his time collecting over 1,000 signatures on a petition that calls for him to be reinstated. White only learns his fate when a reporter calls asking for comment on the appointment that has replaced him.

The following morning, White paces the floor of his home, glancing over newspaper articles from the past year detailing what he sees as repeated betrayals and public humiliation. He thinks about the people who have done this to him, most importantly Milk and Moscone. White takes his .38 caliber pistol and a box of ammunition and asks his aide to drive him to City Hall to galvanize the crowd that has gathered to protest on his behalf.

White arrives at City Hall but instead of greeting his supporters he enters the building through a window in the back of the building in order to avoid the metal detector at the main entrance. He makes his way upstairs to Moscone's office. Moscone invites him in to talk, pours White a drink, and suggests they discuss what White should do next. White begins shouting at Moscone, pulls out his gun, and fires four shots into Moscone's head and chest.

White then runs downstairs to the Supervisors' Chambers, where he runs into Milk. Milk warmly greets White, and they step into White's old office. White begins screaming at Milk, and fires three rounds into his abdomen and two into his head. White runs out of the building into his aide's car, then drives to a nearby Catholic church to pray. His wife Mary Ann finds him at the church. White goes to the police station and turns himself in.

His trial begins in May 1979. Prosecutors believe that White's confession coupled with the overwhelming factual evidence makes a clear case of first-degree *murder*. The defense argues that White had *diminished capacity*[13] at the time of the killings, meaning he was unable to deliberate, premeditate, or understand the gravity of his actions. In his opening statement, defense counsel says that "Good people, fine people, with fine backgrounds, simply don't kill people in cold blood."[14] Then the defense brings a series of mental health professionals to the stand to make the case for White's diminished capacity, detailing his struggle with anxiety and depression.

One of them, Dr. Martin Binder, explains that White dramatically altered his eating habits during these periods, consuming far more junk food, candy, and sodas. In other words, White's eating habits are a symptom of his depression. National media misinterpret the argument, reporting that the defense is arguing that White has diminished capacity *because* he ate junk food, which becomes nationally vilified as the "Twinkie Defense." The prosecution, confident that this argument will fall apart under scrutiny, counters the defense's case for mitigation with only one psychiatrist who did only a cursory evaluation of White a few hours after the killings.

After deliberations, the jury accepts White's argument for a diminished capacity mitigation and finds him guilty of two counts of voluntary *manslaughter*. The judge sentences White to the maximum of seven years and eight months in prison.

Though jurors insist that Twinkies "played no part"[15] in their decision, the national media decry White's "Twinkie Defense." Harvey Milk becomes a martyr for the gay community. A Broadway show and a Hollywood movie are made about his life.

Murder Mitigation in the States

While most jurisdictions recognize a *murder* mitigation for *provocation* under "heat of passion" or something broader, there are a number of important differences in their approach. The map below identifies five different legal approaches to the subject.[16] The lighter the shading, the broader the mitigation.

The broadest mitigation is provided by the ten states with no shading on the map. These jurisdictions follow the Model Penal Code in providing a mitigation from murder to *manslaughter* where the defendant acted under extreme mental or emotional disturbance for which there was a reasonable explanation or excuse, under the Model Code provision quoted in the margin. Typically, the explanation or excuse for the emotional disturbance must be objectively reasonable – more specifically, it must be determined from the perspective of an objectively reasonable person in the actor's situation under circumstances as the actor believed them to be.

The alternative approach, taken by the next three groups of states, retains the common-law provocation rule, which permits a mitigation in a narrower set of circumstances. For example, while the Model Penal Code's formulation allows a mitigation for any killing during *extreme emotional disturbance* for which there is a reasonable explanation or excuse, the narrower common-law provocation approach permits the mitigation only when the actor is responding *immediately* to the provocation. That is, the defendant must be sufficiently provoked such that he acted in the sudden "heat of passion" and without time to cool off.

In the *Gounagias* case discussed above, while the original sodomy rape might qualify as a sufficiently provocative act, enough time had passed for the defendant to cool off, so his subsequent killing would be legally ineligible for the common-law provocation mitigation.

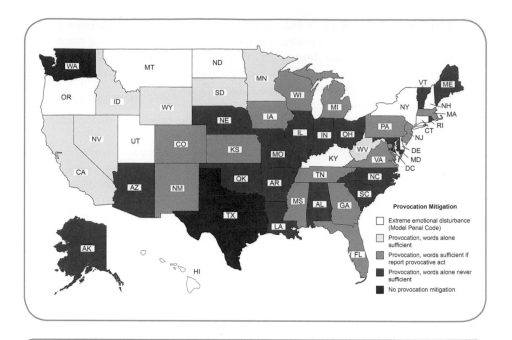

Figure 4.3

For another example of the narrower nature of common-law provocation, the doctrine allows mitigation only if force is used against *the person who is responsible for the immediate provocation*, such as the person doing the taunting that finally sets off the defendant. Thus, Gounagias is again excluded from the mitigation because the earlier sodomizer was not the provoker on the immediate occasion.

Still further, the common-law provocation mitigation recognized only certain events as adequate under the law to qualify as the basis for a mitigation. The map presents the three approaches that common-law provocation jurisdictions commonly take on this matter: in the broadest formulation, words alone are allowed to be sufficient provocation; in the second group, words alone are sufficient to provide a mitigation only if they report an act that is itself legally recognized as adequate provocation (such as a man having just been told that another man raped his wife); and in the third group words alone are never sufficient, only seeing or suffering the provocative act is legally sufficient to trigger a mitigation.[17]

In the 1849 Professor Webster case, strict common-law rules were applied and it is perhaps no surprise that a provocation mitigation was rejected. An angry creditor screaming to be repaid is not on the list of acts legally sufficient to provide a common-law provocation mitigation. In contrast, Webster might well have received a mitigation under the Model Code's *extreme emotional disturbance* formulation.

The steady trend to broaden the scope of *homicide* mitigations is illustrated by the 1978 California case of Daniel White. His mental and emotional disturbance might well have qualified him for a mitigation under the Model Code's extreme emotional disturbance formulation. While California (not a model Penal Code jurisdiction) has only slightly broadened its common-law provocation mitigation, as shown on the map, it has recognized a unique mitigation of *diminished capacity* that can apply to

Manslaughter.
        (1) Criminal homicide constitutes manslaughter when: …
        (b) a homicide which would otherwise be murder is committed under the influence of extreme mental or emotional disturbance for which there is reasonable explanation or excuse. The reasonableness of such explanation or excuse shall be determined from the viewpoint of a person in the actor's situation under the circumstances as he believes them to be.
                                        Model Penal Code §210.3

Figure 4.4

killings under mental or emotional disturbance, which may include some of the cases covered by the Model Code's extreme mental or emotional disturbance mitigation.

Should Provocation or Extreme Emotional Disturbance Be Dealt with Simply as a Sentencing Factor?

The wide diversity among the states on this issue may reflect the awkward nature of the mitigation. It is easy enough to see that many cases of *provocation* or *extreme emotional disturbance* are meaningfully different in degree of blameworthiness from the case of unprovoked clear-eyed killing for advantage. But the provocation and extreme emotional disturbance mitigations must answer the perhaps unanswerable question: how much less blameworthy must the provoked or emotionally disturbed offender be to be different enough from other offenders to merit a mitigation from *murder* to a lesser form of *homicide*?

Ideally, the extent of the offender's mitigation should match the extent of his or her reduced blameworthiness – the principle of blameworthiness proportionality. Adherence to such a principle might be easy to achieve in the context of sentencing, with its large number of incremental punishment options. But in the grading context, which is where provocation and extreme emotional disturbance operate, there is no such possibility. Murder is punished at a very high level, typically death, life imprisonment, or 30 years or so, while the next lower grade, such as *manslaughter*, is commonly punished at a maximum in the neighborhood of 12–15 years. All that can be done in the grading context is to sort intentional killing cases into one of two categories: the mitigated and the unmitigated. There is inevitably a certain fuzziness in deciding exactly where the line between the two categories is to be drawn.

One might be tempted to discard the grading distinction altogether and to leave the matter to sentencing, as some of the states in solid black on the map do, such as Texas. However, this would be bucking the trend of giving more authority to juries – who are responsible for deciding whether an offender is guilty of murder or some lesser form of homicide – and less to judges – who are responsible for imposing a sentence limited by the *offense-grade* verdict returned by the jury.[18]

Broad sentencing discretion is thought to be problematic in part because it creates unjustified disparity in the punishment of similarly situated offenders who are convicted of the same crimes but sentenced by different judges. Part of the notion of just punishment is that similar offenders ought to be treated similarly. Broad judicial sentencing discretion often means that an offender's punishment depends in some significant part on good or bad luck in the sentencing judge the offender is assigned rather than on the seriousness of the offense and the culpability with which it was committed.

Still further, there is a growing sense that for democratic reasons the basic decisions that shape the criminal liability and punishment rules ought to be made by the more representative legislative branch rather than left to the discretion of individual sentencing judges. Finally, there is an increasing sense that the factual determinations upon which criminal liability and punishment are based in a given case ought to be made by a group, juries, rather than by an individual sentencing judge. For all these reasons, jurisdictions will continue to struggle with the challenge of justly distinguishing more serious intentional killings from less serious intentional killings through the formulation of a provocation or extreme emotional disturbance mitigation to murder.

Indeed, one may go further and ask why the same mitigating circumstances given voice in grading homicide ought not be available in grading other offenses. In the case where provocation or extreme emotional disturbance would mitigate murder to manslaughter, but thankfully the injury does not result in death, why shouldn't the same mitigating circumstances be taken into account in determining the grade of the aggravated assault or attempted murder offense?

Aftermaths

The possibility of mitigation to *manslaughter* based upon provoked heat of passion was never presented as an option for the Webster jury. One may wonder, however, whether the killing is, because of the *extreme emotional disturbance*, meaningfully less blameworthy than an unprovoked *murder* for personal advantage. To this day, the Webster trial remains one of American history's most famous. Webster is buried near Boston's Old North Church, in an unmarked grave so as to discourage body snatchers.

In Dan White's case, he serves just over five years in prison for the killings of Harvey Milk and George Moscone. Universally detested in the Bay Area, he tries fleeing to Ireland with hopes of starting a new life but soon returns with nothing more than empty pockets and disappointment. Twenty-two months after his release from prison, with photos of his family arrayed on his lap, he kills himself. Having rigged a rubber hose from his car exhaust, he dies of carbon monoxide poisoning. His trial becomes part of the popular culture, mocked in late-night comedy sketches as the press' "Twinkie Defense" misunderstanding lives on. To White's supporters, his suicide clearly demonstrates the *diminished capacity* of a man suffering from mental health issues.

The public reaction to White's mitigated punishment is largely one of outrage, which leads to political action. In 1982, Proposition 8 becomes California law and rejects the term diminished capacity in favor of the term "diminished *actuality*,"[19] a term designed to focus on an offender's actual intent rather than the offender's capacity. White clearly had the intention of killing Milk, and the new legislation is designed so that in future cases, the reasons behind that intention cannot be a basis for acquittal. At the same time, the state drops the statutory meanings of malice and premeditation,[20] in favor of the historic meanings under the common-law cases.[21] California remains one of the few major jurisdictions that has never adopted a modern criminal code.

Chapter Glossary

Diminished Capacity: A mitigation doctrine sometimes available, commonly in non-Model Penal Code jurisdictions, that allows an impaired mental condition short of insanity – such as that caused by intoxication, trauma, or disease – to provide a mitigation of liability. Sometimes the phrase is used (confusingly) to refer to a mitigation or defense that comes about because the actor lacks the culpability required by the offense definition.[22]

Extreme Emotional Disturbance: A highly disturbed mental state that, under the Model Penal Code, can reduce murder liability demands one. The concept expands and replaces the common-law defense of heat of passion or adequate provocation.[23]

Homicide: The killing of one person by another. Not all homicide is murder, as some killings are manslaughter, and some are lawful, such as when justified by self-defense or excused by insanity.[24]

Manslaughter: Under the Model Penal Code, manslaughter is the reckless killing of a human being or an intentional killing under extreme emotional disturbance. At common law, manslaughter was killing without malice.[25]

Murder: Under the Model Penal Code, murder is the purposeful or knowing killing of a human being or the reckless killing of a human being in the circumstances that manifest extreme indifference in the value of human life. Under common law, murder was the killing of a human being with malice.[26]

Offense Grade: In modern criminal codes, rather than specifying a particular maximum sentence for each offense, offenses are classified into one of many defined offense grades, commonly labeled something like First-Degree Felony, Second-Degree Felony, etc. Modern American criminal codes commonly have five or six grades of felonies and five or six grades of misdemeanors, or more.

Provocation: A common-law doctrine of mitigation that allows an intentional killing that would otherwise be murder to be mitigated to the lesser offense of manslaughter. Such mitigation is available where the killing is provoked by the victim by some act, such as raping the actor's spouse. The Model Penal Code provides a broader mitigation that can apply when the actor kills under extreme mental or emotional disturbance.[27]

Notes

1. This section is drawn from the following sources: Bernard Cohen, 'Some Early Tools of American Science,' *American Journal of Physics 18*, no. 9 (1950): p. 583; Robert L. Gale, 'Webster, John White (1793–1850), University Professor and Murderer,'

American National Biography Online, 1 February 2000, http://www.anb.org/articles/20/20-01097.html; Stewart Holbrook, 'Murder at Harvard,' *The American Scholar 14*, no. 4 (1945): pp. 425–434, http://www.jstor.org/stable/pdf/41204736.pdf?_=1465153104217; Kevin R. Loughlin, 'The Notorious John White Webster: Guilty or Innocent?,' *Journal of the American College of Surgeons 195*, no. 2 (2002): pp. 234–240, http://www.sciencedirect.com/science/article/pii/S1072751502011936; 'Professor John White Webster,' *Christian Register*, 7 September 1850; Tom Quirk, 'The Judge Dragged to the Bar: Melville, Shaw, and the Webster Murder Trial,' *Melville Society Extracts 84* (February 1991): pp. 1–8; Robert Wilhelm, 'Dr. George Parkman-'The Pedestrian',' *Murder by Gaslight Compendium*, 13 March 2010, http://www.murderbygaslight.com/2010/02/murder-at-harvard.html; George Bemis, *Report of the Case of John W. Webster* (Boston: Charles C. Little and James Brown, 1850), https://babcl.hathitrust.org/cgi/pt?id=nyp.33433075956288&view=1up&seq=11.

2. Holbrook, 'Murder at Harvard.'
3. Holbrook, 'Murder at Harvard.'
4. Holbrook, 'Murder at Harvard.'
5. Bemis, *Report*, pp. 216–218.
6. 'Professor John White Webster.'
7. *State v. Gounagias* 88 Wash. 304 (1915).
8. Aya Gruber, 'A Provocative Defense,' *California Law Review* 103 (2015): pp. 273–333 http://scholar.law.colorado.edu/articles/43.
9. *State v. Gounagias* 88 Wash. 304 (1915).
10. Model Penal Code § 210.3(1)(b).
11. Cindi Ernst, 'The Dan White (Harvey Milk Murder) Trial (1979): Selected Links & Bibliography,' *Famous Trials Blog*, http://www.famous-trials.com/danwhite/587-bibliography; Charles P. Ewing and Joseph T. McCann, *Minds on Trial: Great Cases in Law and Psychology* (Oxford: Oxford University Press, 2006), http://site.ebrary.com/lib/upenn/reader.action?docID=10215782; John Geluardi, 'Dan White's Motive More About Betrayal Than Homophobia,' *San Francisco Weekly*, 30 January 2008, https://archives.sfweekly.com/sanfrancisco/dan-whites-motive-more-about-betrayal-than-homophobia/Content?oid=2166110; Carol Pogash, 'Myth of the 'Twinkie Defense' / The Verdict in the Dan White Case Wasn't Based on His Ingestion of Junk Food,' *San Francisco Gate*, 23 November 2003, http://www.sfgate.com/health/article/Myth-of-the-Twinkie-defense-The-verdict-in-2511152.php; Nancy Skelton and Mark Stein, 'For Dan White, Death Ended 2 Years of Fear and Haunted Dreams,' *Los Angeles Times*, 23 October 1985, http://articles.latimes.com/1985-10-23/news/mn-13835_1_friends; Wallace Turner, 'Suspect Sought Job,' *New York Times*, 28 November 1978, http://www.nytimes.com/1978/11/28/archives/suspect-sought-job-moscone-had-been-asked-to-reappoint-him-as-a.html?_r=0; Mike Weiss, *Double Play: The San Francisco City Hall Killings* (London: Macmillan Publishing, 1984).
12. Turner, 'Suspect Sought Job.'
13. Pogash, 'Twinkie Defense.'
14. Ernst, 'Dan White (Harvey Milk Murder) Trial.'
15. Pogash, 'Twinkie Defense.'
16. The map is taken from: Paul H. Robinson and Tyler Scot Williams, *Mapping American Criminal Law: Variations across the 50 States* (Westport: Prager, 2018), ch. 5. All supporting authorities are available from that source.
17. Two states, Texas and Washington – shaded black on the map – do not offer a mitigation for extreme emotional disturbance or for provocation triggering a killing in the heat of passion. In these jurisdictions, provocation or emotional disturbance is relevant only if it negates an offense culpability requirement – such as the requirement

that a killing be purposeful – which normally it would not. Texas, however, does allow provocation to be raised as a mitigating factor at sentencing, when determining the proper amount of punishment for the person convicted of murder.

18. Note, for example, the dramatic increase in the use of sentencing guidelines, together with the recently clarified constitutional requirement that the jury rather than the judge must determine any facts that increase a penalty beyond the maximum permitted by the facts established by a guilty plea or jury verdict. *See United States v. Booker* 543 U.S. 220 (2005). For another example, note the dramatic increase in the grading nuance that legislatures now routinely add to existing offenses. *See, e.g.*, Paul H. Robinson, Matthey Kussmaul, and Ilya Rudyak, 'Report of the Delaware Criminal Law Recodification Project,' *University of Pennsylvania Public Law and Legal Theory Research Paper Series 1*, no. 17–19 (2017): pp. 1–565, https://ssrn.com/abstract=2950728.

19. *See, e.g.,* Robert Weinstock, Gregory Leong, and Arturo Silva, 'California Is Diminished Capacity Defense: Evolution and Transformation,' *Journal of the American Academy of Psychiatry and the Law Online 24*, no. 3 (September 1996): pp. 347–366.

20. *People v. Whitfield* 7 Cal. 4th 437 (1994).

21. Philip Hager, "Diminished Capacity' Abolition Upheld: Crime: State Supreme Court Rules that Such a Defense, Outlawed by Voters in 1982, Cannot Be Presented to Evade a Murder Charge,' *Los Angeles Times*, 13 December 1991, https://www.latimes.com/archives/la-xpm-1991-12-13-mn-137-story.html.

22. *Diminished Capacity*, Black's.

23. MPC §210.3.1; *Extreme Emotional Disturbance*, Black's.

24. *Homicide*, Black's; *Homicide,* Legal Information Institute, https://www.law.cornell.edu/wex/homicide.

25. MPC §210.3; *Manslaughter*, Black's.

26. MPC §210.2; *Murder*, Black's.

27. *Provocation*, Black's; MPC §210.3.

Chapter 5

Causation

The Grand Wizard Causes a Suicide

1925. Over the past eight years, Russia has become a one-party communist state under the leadership of Vladimir Lenin. With Lenin's death in 1924, a power struggle ensues from which Joseph Stalin emerges as victor. Political turmoil does not stop at the Soviet border. In January, Benito Mussolini dissolves the Italian parliament and becomes dictator. Six weeks later, Adolf Hitler resurrects the Nationalsozialistische Deutsche Arbeiterpartei, also known as the Nazi Party, in Berlin. The first volume of his *Mein Kampf* is published. By November, the Nazis have gained enough power to put the SS police in place, and opposition becomes too scary for most people to contemplate. On August 8, the first KKK march in Washington D.C. occurs with 200,000 in attendance. The KKK's Grand Dragon of Indiana is at the height of his power.

D.C. Stephenson – 1925

David Curtis (D.C.) Stephenson is born into a sharecropping family in 1891 in Houston, Texas. He has a history of failure: drunkenness, spouse abuse, and an inability to hold a job. But when he arrives in Evansville, Indiana in 1920 things improve when he makes a bid for a congressional seat. He loses the election but his skills as a candidate pique the interest of KKK leader Joseph M. Huffington, who recruits Stephenson into the organization.

Stephenson proves to be a brilliant organizer: under his leadership, the Klan signs up nearly 104,000 new members between July 1922 and July 1923. Because of his successful recruitment efforts, on July 4, 1923 he is appointed Grand Dragon of Indiana by "Imperial Wizard" William Simmons. Now at the helm of a prosperous and powerful organization, Stephenson commands a large political voting bloc – and the dues that the KKK members pay. He relishes it all, considering himself infallible

DOI: 10.4324/9781003258025-6

and declaring "I am the law in Indiana."[1] When he tries to rape a hotel manicurist, everyone tells the frightened woman that "He is a good fellow . . . You go downstairs and don't bother about it."[2]

Stephenson is attending a banquet in honor of the Indiana Governor in January 1925 when he meets the next object of his fancy, 19-year-old Madge Oberholtzer. At the banquet, Stephenson repeatedly implores Oberholtzer to go on a date with him. She refuses, but later agrees to attend a party at Stephenson's house where several prominent people are present. She is not interested in dating Stephenson but she does accept a clerical position in his office. Her duties are mainly delivering inter-office notes and assisting him in writing a nutrition book, "One Hundred Years of Health."

Stephenson makes it clear that he wants a sexual relationship, but Oberholtzer is insistent that she is not willing to have anything more than a professional relationship. Unwilling to take "no" for an answer, Stephenson, with the aid of two other men, kidnaps Oberholtzer with plans to take her by train to Chicago. Once on the train, he repeatedly rapes her. Oberholtzer eventually passes out. The next morning upon awakening and seeing Stephenson fiddling with his revolver, she asks him to kill her. Stephenson points the gun at her but then holsters it. They all disembark and move to a hotel while they wait for the train that will take them the rest of the way to Chicago.

Oberholtzer is overwhelmed with shame and grief and sees her situation as hopeless against this powerful man. She decides to kill herself. Feigning some measure of normalcy, she asks Stephenson for money to buy a new hat. Stephenson agrees but has one of his associates, Shorty, accompany her to the shop. Without Shorty noticing, Oberholtzer buys tablets of bichloride of mercury.[3] The tablets, frequently sold as a treatment for syphilis, are known to be dangerous. Back at the hotel, Oberholtzer takes six tablets; it is six hours before anyone discovers that she is now sick and perhaps dying.

After Oberholtzer admits that she has poisoned herself, Stephenson gives her some milk and declares that he will take her to the hospital if she agrees to marry him. She refuses. Instead of taking her to the hospital, the group puts her in a car and heads back across the state line to Oberholtzer's home. She is in agony the entire ride, repeatedly vomiting in the vehicle and repeatedly asking for a doctor to kill her with a lethal injection. Stephenson's two helpers are terrified; he reassures them with his familiar refrain: "You must forget this, what is done has been done, I am the law and the power."[4]

Upon arriving at Oberholtzer's house, her parents do what they can but the doctor who is called explains that she will not survive. With the little life left in her, she writes down a full account of what happened, knowing that it will be hard to bring down a powerful man like Stephenson without overwhelming direct evidence. Stephenson is confident that the incident will blow over; virtually every important official in Indiana is someone he knows. However, the one official that matters is no friend: Marion County prosecutor William Remy. Stephenson is indicted for kidnapping and assault.

Oberholtzer continues to deteriorate but it takes two agonizing weeks for her to die. The prolonged suffering brings national attention. The *New York Times* runs an update on the case almost daily through the month of April. Stephenson's political allies quickly abandon him. The grand jury issues another indictment, this time charging him with first-degree murder. He is taken into custody, denied bail, and pleads not guilty.

The prosecution calls Oberholtzer's doctors to the stand, who testify to the toxicity of the mercury she ingested.[5] Prosecutors also submit Oberholtzer's testimony from

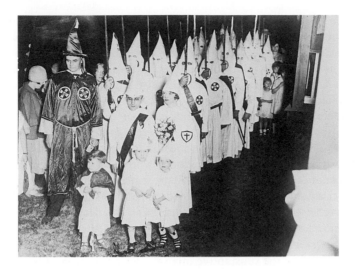

Figure 5.1 A KKK wedding in the 1920s

her deathbed, which gives her account of the entire incident. They portray Stephenson as a "hideous monster . . . who should be put away for the protection of the daughters of the future."[6]

The defense argues that Oberholtzer committed suicide: she bought the poison herself and took it voluntarily; therefore, Stephenson is not responsible for the death. "If this so-called dying declaration declares anything, it is a dying declaration of suicide, not homicide," defense attorney Ephraim Inman says.[7]

The jury, composed mostly of farmers, is handed the case and given their instructions. The judge explains that "A person cannot be held criminally responsible for a homicide unless his act be said to be the cause of death."[8] However, the judge offers several caveats: the defendant is still guilty even if a death is "an indirect result of his unlawful acts," and multiple causes of death do not relieve a person responsible for only one of those causes from criminal liability. The jury convicts Stephenson of second-degree murder and he is sentenced to life in prison.

Causation Requirements

To convict a person of murder, the prosecution must prove that at the time of the killing the person had the required offense culpability – typically that the person intended or knew his conduct would cause the death. But that alone is not enough. Liability for murder also requires proof beyond a reasonable doubt that the person's conduct actually *caused* the death – that there was a legally sufficient causal connection between the defendant's conduct and the death. (This causation requirement exists even in cases of felony murder, the subject of Chapter 3, the doctrine in which no culpability as to causing death need be shown. Nonetheless, the prosecution still must prove the causal connection between the actor's conduct and the death.[9])

Indeed, the legal requirements for causation must be shown not only for murder and other homicide offenses but for every offense that is defined as requiring a particular result. Assault offenses, for instance, commonly require that the defendant's conduct resulted in bodily injury of a particular severity. Property damage offenses require that a defendant's conduct caused physical damage or destruction of property. Even minor offenses such as obstructing a public highway require proof of an adequate causal connection between the defendant's conduct and the prohibited obstruction. (Not all offenses have a result element, however; in fact, the majority of offenses do not. They require only proof of conduct under certain circumstances, such as intercourse without consent or taking another's property without permission.[10])

Empirical studies confirm that people share a strong intuition that, in the absence of an adequate causal connection, an offender's liability should be markedly reduced from what it otherwise would be if there had been an adequate causal connection.[11] Where causation does not exist or cannot be proven, the defendant's conduct amounts to at most an *attempt* to commit the offense. Attempts are typically punished at one offense grade less than the substantive offense, and a reduction of one offense grade commonly results in half the maximum punishment.

There are two independent legal requirements for establishing causation: the *factual cause requirement* (sometimes called the "but-for cause" requirement) and the *proximate cause requirement* (sometimes called the "legal cause" requirement). There is almost universal agreement on some aspects of these requirements but some noticeable differences regarding other aspects.

Regarding the factual cause requirement, it is commonly agreed that an actor's conduct cannot be a factual cause of a result unless the result would not have occurred "but for" the actor's conduct. That is, the actor's conduct must have been *necessary* for the result to occur when it did. If the same result would have occurred when it did even without the defendant's conduct, then the defendant's conduct was not necessary for that result and cannot be a factual cause of that result.

The but-for cause rule seems pretty simple, and ordinarily it is. Things only get complicated in situations where there are multiple causes by different actors contributing to a particular result. Even these situations can be simplified into a clear rule: if the actors are accomplices of one another, which is commonly the case, then each accomplice is accountable for the conduct of all other accomplices and, for the purposes of the factual causation requirement, all of the acts and all of the causal contributions by all of the accomplices can be lumped together as if they were performed by a single person. The question then becomes: was the combined effect of the conduct of all of these accomplices together a *but-for* cause – a necessary cause – of the result? If so, then all accomplices will be said to have satisfied the but-for causation requirement.

The remaining factual-cause issue is how to handle cases of multiple causes from independent actors who are *not* accomplices of one another. When Actor A attacks a victim and later Actor B independently attacks the same victim, who subsequently dies, is the first attacker or the second attacker, or are both, causally accountable for the resulting death? In most instances, the standard but-for test gives a clear answer: if an actor's conduct was *necessary* for the death – if the victim would not have died *but for* the actor's conduct – then the actor factually caused the death.

There is, however, a quirk in the operation of the but-for test in the unusual independent-actors situation in which two independent actors each *simultaneously* inflict an independently lethal wound. Each actor can accurately say that the victim would have died when he did *even without that actor's lethal wounding*, thus there is no causal accountability – a result that seems clearly intuitively wrong. For example, imagine that two people acting independently shoot a victim at the same time, each inflicting a lethal wound. Even though either actor's conduct was *sufficient* to cause the death, neither actor's conduct was *necessary* for the death, given the other concurrent lethal wound. But clearly it would be absurd to hold that neither actor is liable for causing the death.

Everyone seems to agree that both of these actors ought to be held causally accountable for the death. But to reach that result, a jurisdiction must adopt some kind of special rule that compensates for this quirk in the but-for test in cases of concurrent sufficient causes. As will become apparent from the map and the analysis below, there is no universal agreement among the jurisdictions on how to best compensate for the quirk.

Why should we concern ourselves with this particular quirk of the but-for causation requirement? Cases of concurrent sufficient causes are not common. But it is worth understanding this peculiarity of the but-for test because it nicely illustrates how criminal law rules commonly track people's shared intuitions of justice even though the resulting rules are not clean and simple. One could dramatically simplify the factual cause requirement by simply requiring a sufficient cause – that is, requiring that the actor's conduct was sufficient to bring about the prohibited result (rather than by requiring a necessary cause, as the law more commonly does – requiring that the actor's conduct necessary to bring about the prohibited result). But we know from empirical studies that people's intuitions of justice generally track the necessary cause requirement rather than the sufficient cause requirement, and thus the law tends to do the same.

In addition to this factual cause requirement, the law imposes an independent proximate cause requirement, which is conceptually quite distinct. The factual cause requirement asks a hypothetical scientific question: would the prohibited result have occurred without the defendant's conduct? In contrast, the proximate cause requirement asks a more judgmental, normative question – a question that may not be answered strictly according to scientific calculation. Specifically, even if an actor's conduct is *necessary* to bring about the prohibited result, is the nature of the causal connection between the actor's conduct and the result so remote or bizarre or accidental in its occurrence that the actor should not properly be held accountable for the result?

For example, assume the defendant shoots at a victim, intending to kill him, but misses. The victim runs away and 20 blocks later just happens to be running under a piano that is being hauled up to the fourth floor when the rope breaks. The piano falls and kills the victim. The victim would not have died when he did *but for* the actor's conduct in shooting at him earlier, so the factual cause (but-for) requirement is satisfied. However, there is general agreement that the case does not satisfy the proximate cause requirement; it ought not be a case of murder but rather a case of attempted murder, because the death-by-falling-piano is simply too remote from the defendant's original conduct to have that original conduct count as the legal cause of the death.

To give another example, imagine the defendant intentionally attacks another person with a knife but ends up only inflicting a minor cut. The victim is taken to the hospital. The cut is not serious but the doctor on duty is both incompetent and intoxicated and his treatment of the wound is so bad that the victim in fact dies. Again, while the defendant's original conduct of attacking the victim is a necessary factual cause of the death – the death would not have occurred *but for* the initial cutting that sent the victim to the hospital – most people would think that the defendant ought not be causally accountable for the death; the defendant's liability ought to be something less than murder, perhaps attempted murder or, depending upon his intention, assault or aggravated assault.

In the *Stephenson* case above, Madge Oberholtzer would not have died but for her mistreatment by Stephenson. His conduct is a but-for (factual) cause of her death. However, to be criminally liable for the death, it must also be shown that his conduct is a proximate (legal) cause. Yet this may be problematic, or at least debatable, because Oberholtzer is the one who actually did the immediate killing of herself, and if she is a volitional actor, she would break the causal chain, as did the intoxicated doctor. However, one might conclude that she was not an independent volitional actor because her mistreatment by Stephenson so overwhelmed her as to compel her to commit the deed. As you recall, the jury did find that Stephenson had causal accountability for the suicide and was held criminally liable for the death.

Compare Stephenson to a similar but different case of causing a suicide.

Lori Drew – 2006

Megan Meier and Sarah Drew are neighbors and friends in elementary school. After elementary school, Megan's family elects to send Megan to a Catholic middle school. As the girls are no longer going to school together, the friendship fades. Lori Drew, Sarah's mother, is enraged by the cooled friendship and feels her daughter is seriously harmed by the loss.

To get back at seventh-grader Megan, Lori teams up with an 18-year-old employee of hers to create a MySpace account under the name Josh Evans. According to the profile, "Josh" is 16 years old, prefers Coke to Pepsi, and recently moved nearby from Florida. Using a picture of a random teenage boy, shirtless with brown wavy hair, fictitious "Josh" (controlled by Lori Drew) reaches out to Megan and begins a flirtatious relationship. For example, two days after the two are connected over MySpace, "Josh" tells Megan she is "sexi."[12] "Josh" begins to make sexually suggestive remarks, such as inviting Megan to touch the "snake."[13] "Josh" easily wins Megan over with his charm, and induces her to confess her love for him.

Now that Megan is totally smitten, the group begins the attack. "Josh" reveals that he is no longer interested in Megan and begins to say horrible things to her. "Josh's" fictional friends join in the attack. Megan fights back and the insults fly across cyberspace. One fictional girl calls Megan "fat" and a "slut."[14] During the back-and-forth, "Josh" tells Megan that "the world would be a better place without you."[15] Megan writes to "Josh," "You are the kind of boy a girl would kill herself over."[16]

When Megan's mother, Tina, hears of the verbal attacks and sees how upset Megan has become, she insists that Megan log off. When she arrives home, she finds her daughter deeply distraught and still glued to the computer screen. Her mother lectures her about her deep disappointment for the vulgar language Megan has used and for blatantly defying Tina's directions to disconnect from the interactions. Megan jumps out of her chair and screams, "You're supposed to be my mom! You're supposed to be on my side!"[17] Then runs upstairs to her room.

An exasperated Tina discusses with her husband Ron what to do about the situation. About 20 minutes into their discussion, Tina freezes mid-sentence. She runs upstairs to her daughter's room, and finds the lifeless girl hanging from a closet organizer.

Figure 5.2 Megan Meier while a student at Immaculate
Conception Middle School in Missouri, circa 2006

When the emergency vehicles begin arriving at the Meiers' house, Lori Drew goes into action. Drew understands that the cyber-attacks are the cause of the suicide; her first step is to call Megan's immediate neighbor, a girl who had knowledge of the scheme and had posted a single line of text; the child is instructed to erase the messages. Shortly thereafter, Drew deletes the MySpace account of "Josh Evans." She instructs all her confederates to keep silent and actively works to hide her connection to the suicide.

All the message exchanges are on Megan's computer and her grieving family now reads them. That night, Tina tries to contact "Josh" to tell him of the impact of his words, but he does not respond. Lori Drew is erasing him.

The girl whom Drew called while the ambulances were still at the Meiers' is deeply upset by her tiny part in the hoax and she reveals to Megan's family the truth. The parents of the dead girl come to understand that it was no teenage boy but their own neighbor, Lori Drew, who had orchestrated their daughter's despair. Filled with rage, the Meiers smash a foosball table that they were storing for the Drews and throw the remains in the Drews' yard. The box that holds the damaged table is spray painted "Merry Christmas."

The next day, Lori Drew calls the police to inform them of the destruction of the table. When the Meiersare called in for questioning, the plot is revealed to police.

Lori Drew's role in Megan's death sparks outrage across the country. She becomes a subject of intense harassment: her address and phone number are posted online, and she receives hundreds of angry phone calls, emails, and letters. Bloggers, columnists, and talk show hosts castigate Lori Drew, demanding that she be brought to justice.

Lori Drew's scheme with fictitious "Josh" trying to emotionally hurt Megan is clearly a factual cause of Megan's death: the death would not have occurred "but for" the scheme. Whether the scheme is a *proximate (legal) cause* of the death is less clear. Megan may well be seen as an independent volitional actor who independently made the choice to kill herself, thereby breaking the causal chain. On the one hand, Megan's motivation for killing herself was her emotional despair intentionally created by Lori Drew's scheme. On the other hand, can the suicide be attributed in part to pre-existing emotional instability in Megan?

Causing or Aiding Suicide.

  (1) Causing Suicide as Criminal Homicide. A person may be convicted of criminal homicide for causing another to commit suicide only if he purposely causes such suicide by force, duress or deception.

  (2) Aiding or Soliciting Suicide as an Independent Offense. A person who purposely aids or solicits another to commit suicide is guilty of a felony of the second degree if his conduct causes such suicide or an attempted suicide, and otherwise of a misdemeanor.

Model Penal Code §210.5

Figure 5.3

(Even if causal accountability for the death is found, Lori Drew's homicide liability would be limited by her culpability level as to causing the death, as discussed in Chapter 3. If she hoped or knew her conduct would cause the death, she could be liable for murder. If she was only aware of a substantial risk it would cause death, she could be liable for reckless homicide, that is, manslaughter. If she was only negligent, then she could only be held liable for negligent homicide. If nonnegligent – the reasonable person in her situation would not have been aware of a substantial risk that her scheme would cause death – then no criminal liability for homicide.)

Causation in the States

As the previous discussion has revealed, while the notion of causation may initially seem quite simple, in fact it embodies some complex issues. It may be no surprise then to see that, as the map below illustrates, jurisdictions have adopted several different formulations of the causation requirement.[18]

Recall from the discussion above the quirk in the but-for factual cause test that would seem to allow two independent actors simultaneously inflicting a lethal wound to escape causal accountability for the resulting death because each can accurately claim that their lethal wound was not necessary for the death. That is, each can correctly claim that the victim would have died when he did even without this actor's conduct.

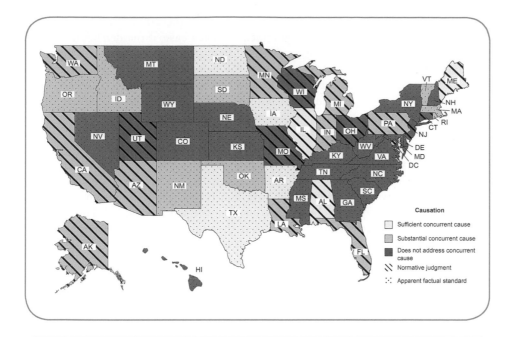

Figure 5.4

A common way of adjusting for this quirk in the otherwise useful but-for test is to simply adopt a special rule. If each of two independent concurrent causes is sufficient to cause the result, then they will be deemed legally adequate to be a factual cause. This is the approach taken in the seven jurisdictions shown with light shading on the map.

Other jurisdictions adopt a different rule to deal with this quirky case: instead of requiring that each actor's conduct itself be sufficient to cause the result, they require only that each actor's conduct make a "substantial" contribution to the result. This is the approach taken in the 19 jurisdictions shown with medium shading on the map.

Twenty-five jurisdictions, shown with the darkest shading on the map, have simply failed to address the problem. In these states, either actors who can show an independent concurrent cause will get off from murder because their conduct does not technically satisfy the but-for test, or a state court will have to recognize the problem and step in on their own to adopt one of the solutions used by states in the two groups above.

One might normally criticize these states for failing to adopt a codified rule fully defining the factual-cause requirement. Why should this criminalization authority be left to the determination of the courts? Like all other aspects of criminal law, why isn't the definition of causation requirements more appropriately determined by the legislature and spelled out in the criminal code? (These were the issues discussed in Chapter 1, concerning the legality principle.) In this instance, however, the states may be forgiven their lapse. The American Law Institute's Model Penal Code, which served as the model for three-quarters of the criminal codes in the United States, failed badly in its attempt to draft a model causation provision.[19] Faced with a model provision that made little sense to them, many states apparently chose not to codify any causation provision at all.

The defendants in the 1925 Stephenson case and the 2006 Drew case seem to clearly satisfy the but-for cause requirement. In each case, if the defendant had not engaged in the conduct that he or she did, the victim would not have committed suicide. The issue, then, becomes whether the defendant in each case satisfies the second causation requirement: the *proximate-cause requirement.*

Regarding this second causation requirement, 20 jurisdictions, shown with a diagonal-lines overlay on the map, adopt a proximate cause requirement that asks jurors to make essentially a normative judgment. For example, many jurisdictions use the phrase from the Model Penal Code that proximate cause is established only if the actual result is "not too remote or accidental to have a *just* bearing on the actor's liability." In the same vein, some jurisdictions provide that proximate cause is not established if it would be "*unfair* to hold him responsible" for the result or "the defendant may *fairly* be held responsible for the actual result." The common denominator of these formulations is that they understand the proximate cause judgment to be a jury's intuitive judgment of what is fair and just to the defendant. The issue is not a factual one but a normative one.

A different approach, taken by the 31 jurisdictions shown with a dots overlay on the map, presents the proximate cause issue as if it were a factual one. The defendant's conduct is the proximate cause of a result if the result was a "natural and probable consequence" or the result was "reasonably foreseeable" or the result was "a substantial and currently operative factor in bringing about the result" or the result "falls within the scope of the risk" or the conduct "directly" caused the result.

In reality, these standards are so broad as to ultimately require the same kind of normative judgment of a jury that one sees in the diagonal-lines category above. How is a jury to decide whether the defendant's conduct was a "substantial" factor? Whether the result was "reasonably" foreseeable? Ultimately, despite the attempt to clothe the standard in apparent factual terms, the jury will have to make some kind of normative judgment in deciding the issue. Nonetheless, this approach is noticeably different from that of the group above because these jurisdictions wish to hide or at least downplay the normative nature of the judgment.

Whenever people are induced to kill themselves, as in the *Stephenson* and *Drew* cases, there exists a serious issue about whether the inducement satisfies the proximate-cause requirement. If the person committing suicide seems to be making a free and voluntary choice, the proximate cause requirement may not be satisfied. In the words of some state codes, the killing may be "too dependent upon another's volitional act."

However, in the *Stephenson* case, one can reasonably argue that the defendant had created by his horrendous treatment of the victim the conditions that made her suicide something quite less than a voluntary choice. His depraved mistreatment was the dominant factor in pushing her to suicide. Indeed, even under the apparently more objective "reasonably foreseeable" tests, he could well be judged the proximate cause of Madge Oberholtzer's death.

The *Drew* case is a little less clear. While the victimization of the seventh grader by the defendant obviously played an important role in inducing the suicide, the suffering and torment the defendant inflicted might arguably be something that doesn't fully explain the suicide. The defendant here could argue that there were other mental or emotional forces at work to produce the death and that the suicide was not a reasonably foreseeable result of her inducing conduct; they could argue that the suicide was "too remote or accidental" or "too dependent upon another's volitional act."

The difference between the two cases, then, may be less a matter of a shift in the law governing proximate cause between 1925 and 2006, and more a product of the factual difference between the two situations. In fact, the proximate cause determination is essentially an intuitive one and ordinary people's intuitions on the issue probably rarely shift over time.

Criminal Law's Reliance upon Ordinary People's Intuitive Judgments of Causation

Causation is an area that nicely illustrates the criminal law's common reliance upon people's shared intuitions of justice. With regard to the factual cause test, for example, one can identify all sorts of technical criticisms of the factual cause but-for test. As discussed above, the but-for test gives apparently erroneous results in the case of concurrent wounds from independent actors, requiring a special rule to fix the problem. But the but-for test can be criticized on a broader level than that because, even in the common cases of consecutive (rather than concurrent) causes, its operation makes an actor's causal accountability depend upon the lethality *of another actor's conduct*, not on the lethality of his own conduct! If the *other person's* conduct by itself is nonlethal, then the actor's conduct is necessary to cause the death and therefore is a factual cause of the death. If the *other person's* conduct is lethal, then the actor's conduct is not necessary for the death and is not a factual cause of the death. Doesn't it seem a bit odd that one person's causal accountability for a death depends upon the lethality of the other person's conduct?

Yet, despite these problems, the but-for test is almost universally relied upon in determining factual causation. Why would this be so? We tolerate its technical and logical limitations because it accurately captures how ordinary people normally think about causation, as has been revealed by variety of empirical studies.[20]

The issue of *proximate cause* teaches the same lesson. The reliance upon people's shared intuitions of justice is obvious when the legal formulation openly calls for open-ended jury determinations, such as the Model Penal Code's formulation that asked the jury to decide whether the result is "not too remote or accidental to have a just bearing on the actor's liability." We have also seen that the legal formulations often rely upon people's intuitions of justice in a less open way, for example, by asking a jury if a result was "reasonably" foreseeable or if a defendant's conduct was a "substantial" factor. In the end, it is clear that proximate cause judgments necessarily depend upon people's intuitive judgments of justice.

However, there are some aspects of the causation legal doctrine that do not track community views. To give one example, the empirical studies make clear that people's judgments of justice on causation would have the degree of an actor's criminal liability reflect *the extent* of the actor's causal contribution to the prohibited result. People don't think of causation in purely binary terms, where causation triggers liability for the full substantive offense and no-causation triggers liability only for an attempt (at typically half the punishment). Instead, people see a continuum of causal contribution and accountability, and believe that an offender's liability ought to shift incrementally depending upon the strength of the causal connection.

In a study of proximate cause cases, for example, the study's subjects assigned varying degrees of liability to different proximate cause cases involving a variety of situations that tend to weaken the original attacker's causal accountability (the victim's unexpected allergy to a medication at the hospital, an incompetent nurse, unexpected causal paths such as the "falling piano," etc.).[21] The stronger the causal connection, the greater the liability people impose. The legal doctrine, in contrast, asks in each case whether the causation requirements are satisfied, thus full liability, or not satisfied, thus only attempt liability. The test subjects, in contrast, see a continuous curve rather than the law's step function; they impose liability along a continuous curve that runs between attempt liability and full substantive liability, depending upon the strength of the causal connection.

If the law were to track people's shared intuitions of justice, it would forgo the binary approach that it currently takes in favor of a mechanism that allows judgments about the strength of the causal connection and then varies the extent of liability with the strength of that connection. Thus, for example, in cases of existing but weak causal connections, the law might allow punishment in between that for an attempt and that for a completed offense.

The situation with causation is just one example of where the criminal law takes a binary yes-no approach where people's share intuitions in fact see a continuous curve. We will see the same situation in the context of complicity. Under the law, either a person is an accomplice and thus fully liable for the substantive offense, or a person is not an accomplice and thus has no liability for the offense. People's shared intuitions of justice, however, see a continuum of assistance in the commission of the offense, and the person who is an accomplice but has contributed very little ought to be punished significantly less than full liability for the substantive offense. It is certainly within the ability of modern criminal codes (and sentencing guidelines) to have the legal rules better approximate community views.

Aftermaths

Stephenson's conviction spells the end of the Indiana Ku Klux Klan. The ties between state officials and the Klan are brought to light and earn widespread condemnation. Politicians seek to distance themselves from the Klan, and by 1928 membership dwindles from a previous high of 500,000 (approximately 50% of the adult white males in the state) to just 4,000. Stephenson is paroled in 1950 but soon violates the conditions of his parole and finds himself back in prison. He is released again six years later. He marries an Indiana woman, but she leaves him after he is arrested for attempting to force a 16-year-old girl into his car. He moves to Tennessee and marries again. However, he never divorces his earlier wife, so when he dies from a heart attack in 1966 at age 74, he is married to two women.

In the *Drew* case, after an investigation into Megan's suicide, Missouri prosecutors announce that there is not sufficient evidence to bring charges against Lori Drew. Without more proof, Drew cannot be held causally accountable for Megan's death. Nor can Drew be held liable for criminal harassment or any other Internet-related offense because at the time of the offense in 2006 no such statutes exist in Missouri.

However, on May 15, 2008, a U.S. Grand Jury in California indicts Drew on three counts of violating the Computer Fraud and Abuse Act and breaching MySpace's Terms of Service. Federal prosecutor Thomas O'Brien argues that he has jurisdiction over the case since MySpace's servers and corporate headquarters are in Beverly Hills. Drew pleads not guilty, and the case goes to trial in November of 2008. Prosecutors bring Drew's young helper to the stand to testify against Drew in an immunity agreement. They show that Drew bragged about the fake scheme to family and friends, and harassed Megan even though she knew Megan was on medication for depression. The defense reminds the jury that the case is really not about Megan's death: it is about whether Drew's violated an internet fraud statute.

On November 26, 2008, the jury finds Drew guilty on three counts of computer fraud. Many legal and computer fraud experts are stunned – Drew is prosecuted for illegally accessing a computer – and the case opens up a wide variety of common internet behaviors to felony charges that carry years in prison and hundreds of thousands of dollars in fines. The federal judge presiding over the case, George H. Wu, eventually throws out the conviction in July of 2009, explaining that under the precedent set by the conviction, "one could literally prosecute anyone who violates a terms of service agreement."[22] Though Drew walks out of the courtroom beaming at her exoneration, the case sparks widespread debate about cyberbullying and leads to several new laws, including one in Missouri. Tina Meier goes on to found the Megan Meier Foundation, which works to prevent bullying and suicide.

Chapter Glossary

Factual Cause Requirement: Conduct is the factual cause of a result if the result would not have occurred but for the conduct. That is, the conduct is the factual cause of a result if it was necessary for the result to occur.[23]

Proximate (Legal) Cause Requirement: In contrast to the scientific inquiry of the factual cause requirement, the proximate (legal) cause requirement presents an essentially normative inquiry: was the result "too remote or accidental in its occurrence" or "too dependent upon another's volitional act" to have a "just bearing" on the defendant's criminal liability. To hold that an act proximately caused a harm is to say that it seems fair and just to hold the actor responsible for that harm.[24]

Notes

1. Karen Abbott, '"Murder Wasn't Very Pretty": The Rise and Fall of D.C. Stephenson,' *Smithsonian Magazine*, 30 August 2012, http://www.smithsonianmag.com/history/murder-wasnt-very-pretty-the-rise-and-fall-of-dc-stephenson-18935042/
2. Abbott, 'Murder Wasn't Very Pretty.'
3. Douglas O. Linder, 'The Dying Declaration of Madge Oberholtzer,' *Famous Trials*, http://www.famous-trials.com/stephenson/86-dyingdeclaration
4. Linder, 'Dying Declaration.'
5. 'Doctor Says Poison Could Not Kill Girl,' *The New York Times*, 3 November 1925, https://search.proquest.com/docview/103487173/fulltextPDF/FB7D0289A155416EPQ/6?accountid=14707
6. NY Times, 'Finds Ex-Clan Head Murdered Woman; Indiana Jury Convicts Stephenson in Second Degree – Penalty Is 20 Years,' *The New York Times*, 15 November 1925, https://www.nytimes.com/1925/11/15/archives/finds-exklan-head-murdered-woman-indiana-jury-convicts-stephenson.html.
7. Abbott, 'Murder Wasn't Very Pretty.'
8. 'Finds Ex-Clan Head Murdered Woman.'
9. Paul H. Robinson and Michael T. Cahill, *Criminal Law*, 2nd ed. (New York: Wolters Kluwer, 2012), p. 123.
10. Paul H. Robinson and Michael T. Cahill, *Criminal Law*, 2nd ed. (New York: Wolters Kluwer, 2016), p. 28.

11. Paul H. Robinson, *Intuitions of Justice and Utility of Desert* (Oxford: Oxford University Press, 2013).
12. *United States of America v. Lori Drew.*
13. *United States of America v. Lori Drew.*
14. Steve Pokin, *St. Louis Post-Dispatch*, 11 November 2007, https://www.stltoday.com/suburban-journals/stcharles/news/stevepokin/my-space-hoax-ends-with-suicide-of-dardenne-prairie-teen/article_0304c09a-ab32-5931-9bb3-210a5d5dbd58.html.
15. Collins, 'Friend Games.'
16. Kim Zetter, 'Government's Star Witness Stumbles.' *Wired*, 20 November 2008, https://www.wired.com/2008/11/lori-drew-pla-3/
17. Pokin, *St. Louis Post-Dispatch.*
18. The map is taken from Paul H. Robinson and Tyler Scot Williams, *Mapping American Criminal Law: Variations Across the 50 States*, Chapter 7 (Westport: Prager, 2018). All supporting authorities are available from that source.
19. *See, e.g.,* Paul H. Robinson, 'The Model Penal Code's Conceptual Error on the Nature of Proximate Cause, and How to Fix It,' *Criminal Law Bulletin 51* (2015): pp. 1311–1326.
20. Robinson, *Intuitions of Justice*, p. 385.
21. Robinson, *Intuitions of Justice.*
22. Rebecca Cathcart, 'Judge Throws Out Conviction in Cyberbullying Case,' *New York Times*, 2 July 2002, https://www.nytimes.com/2009/07/03/us/03bully.html.
23. Robinson and Cahill, *Criminal Law*, §3.2.
24. Robinson and Cahill, *Criminal Law*, §3.2.

Chapter 6

Consent

Marquis de Sade's Sadomasochism

1768. Catherine the Great is Czarina of Russia. Henry Cavendish, a British scientist and natural philosopher, has just discovered that hydrogen is less dense than air. In Westminster, London, the first paved sidewalk is laid. King Prithvi Narayan Shah unifies several small kingdoms into modern-day Nepal. In Scotland, the First Edition of *Encyclopedia Britannica* is published. James Cook sails from England on his first circumnavigation of the globe. The expedition crosses the Atlantic, rounds Cape Horn, and reaches Tahiti in time to observe the transit of Venus. Cook then sails into the largely uncharted ocean to the south, stopping to claim the Pacific islands of Huahine, Bora Bora, and Raiatea for Great Britain. A 28-year-old French aristocrat is first imprisoned for his scandalous sexual adventures, and what will eventually make his name part of the standard lexicon.

The Marquis de Sade – 1768

Born in France on June 2, 1740, Donatien Alphonse François de Sade, better known as the Marquis de Sade, is an 18th-century writer, aristocrat, and enlightenment philosopher.[1] But he is perhaps best known for his debauchery. Sade's mythic nature lives on in a word that derives from his name and is said to describe his sexual proclivities – *sadism*.

   Sade's family, whose wealth comes from textiles, has enough social cache that they live at the Parisian palace of Prince de Conde. Sade's home life is dysfunctional, so he was sent to live with an uncle who was a priest. "Priest though he be, he always keeps a few whores at his place."[2]

   By 1755, Sade has joined the military and the 16-year-old is commended for his bravery in a battle of the Seven Years' War.[3] His impulsive behavior seems to make him a good soldier, but also excessive in his spending and imprudent in his sexual

DOI: 10.4324/9781003258025-7

adventures. Men and women, old and young, virtuous and professional – the chosen partners of the young man are many. Unsurprisingly, the Marquis becomes infected with venereal disease, a fact widely known.

His family resolves to marry him off. Renee-Pelagie Cordier is none-too-attractive but rich. Sade has a bad reputation, incurable venereal disease, and insufficient money but has noble blood. So the match is seen as a good arrangement both for families and for the sum of 10,000 lives, they are married on May 17, 1763.

Within a month of his marriage, Sade is having to explain himself to the police. The prostitute he hired complains because Sade asked her to have sex with him in a "manner contrary to nature,"[4] and also whipped her and asked her to whip him with a red-hot iron whip. But the activities in question are not entirely unusual, so the authorities have little interest in pursuing the matter. However, police do pay attention when the woman swears that the Marquis asked her to renounce her belief in God and admitted to taking a prostitute to church and encouraging her to take communion. She expands further saying that he got her to step on a statue of Jesus and had her bear witness to his masturbating on a religious image. Sade is arrested and charged with religious *heresy*. He pays a fine and does nothing to alter his behavior.

Sade prefers to be hurt by his lovers more than he desires to hurt them, but it does go both ways. His wild orgiastic parties, at which people inflict pain on themselves and others, are a source of annoyance to his neighbors. His affairs are notorious for their drama.

In 1768, charges are brought by a prostitute when during Easter, the most sacred day on the Christian calendar, Sade engages in another round of sex that involves both physical torture and the use of religious items. The woman takes a cash settlement and withdraws her complaint, but this entanglement is one instance too many. The authorities are growing uneasy that Sade is out of control. He is arrested and for the first time spends several weeks in jail. With some exerted effort, and his family's pocketbook, he eventually obtains release.

By the spring of 1772, Sade is running out the clock against his creditors. At the end of the spring, he is ten days from bankruptcy, so he leaves for Marseilles to try to find money. In Marseilles, he gets together an orgy that involves a wide range of activities, including whipping. He counts that he receives 859 strokes at the hands of the participants. He also has one of the women eat anise candies in an effort to get her to pass gas.

The Marquis returns home and the woman who ate the candy gets sick. The French authorities are less than thrilled by Sade's latest deeds. A week after the orgy, an arrest warrant is issued that would have him hanged for his many misdeeds. Sade evades arrest and his wife, Renee, works to repair the damage. She begins bribing the right officials to make sure Sade is not caught and hanged. The bribery works and by agreement Sade is imprisoned rather than hanged. But the agreement does not hold as he escapes from jail after five months.

In 1774, the Sades are back in their own castle. Renee and Sade's valet go about hiring a group of young women from the surrounding area, ostensibly to be household servants but really for the sexual satisfaction of the Marquis. The girls are all between 14 and 16 years old.

Sade and his wife seal themselves up in their fortress with the servant girls and various other guests for two months of orgies and extreme sexual behavior. Inevitably, rumors begin to circulate about what is going on. Mortified families demand to have their children back. One of the girls leaves the fortress and goes to plead with Sade's powerful uncle for help. The uncle, after all, is a man of the church. Instead of offering aid, he keeps the girl prisoner at Sade's behest.

Figure 6.1 An engraved illustration from the Marquis novel, *Justine (or the Misfortune of Virtue)*, 1791

In 1777, Sade is again arrested and sentenced to jail and again escapes and returns to La Coste, his fortress home, hoping that the authorities will forget about him. Humiliated by another escape, the police pursue him aggressively and take him back into custody.

He is imprisoned at Vincennes, where he remains from the age of 36–50. During this time, he begins "to construct a world of his own within the confines of his cell, a world of literature and thought."[5] Now a man of middle age who has known both success and failure, the Marquis makes it clear to all that he has no intention of repenting. "Either kill me or take me like this, for I will not change," writes the imprisoned Sade in 1783. It is now that Sade steps into fame. His writings with fictional characters, which tell mostly of his own real-life exploits, are wildly popular in Paris and beyond. Sade's literary popularity is unstoppable. He spends 29 years in prison, and even behind bars he never ceases to outrage the authorities.

Consent to Injury

In the context of *civil* rather than criminal liability, it makes sense that the valid consent of the "victim" should be a defense to liability. It would seem unfair for a fully consenting adult to permit or even request another person to engage in certain conduct, then turn around, and sue the person for doing what was requested.

But while the civil law aims to provide fair compensation for unconsented to harm, the criminal law serves a very different purpose. The rationale for criminal punishment is to reinforce societal norms through the imposition of deserved punishment in the hopes that it will strengthen the norm and avoid future wrongdoing. In the criminal context, then, the consent of the victim to injury is of little relevance unless the lack of consent puts the conduct outside the bounds of societal norms. Thus, consent to intercourse is a defense to rape and consent to taking property is a defense to theft, because the offenses of rape and theft embody within them the notion of nonconsensual conduct. But consent to be killed is still murder because the criminal law norm against causing death does not depend upon lack of consent. Indeed, most offenses do not have lack of consent is an element. It is still bribery or counterfeiting or incest even if there is consent by the parties involved.

Of course, as societal norms shift, so too must criminal law. In his day, the Marquis de Sade's assault and injury of others was largely ignored because it was perceived (rightly or wrongly) as consensual. What got him into trouble was his apparent blasphemy. Today, many instances of consensual assault are prosecuted because the criminal law commonly sees causing serious bodily injury as sufficiently morally condemnable that even consent cannot provide a defense to it.

This limitation on consent as a defense reflects a fundamental shift in the relationship between the state and the individual.

> Historically, the special rule of consent to physical harm originated in Anglo-American jurisprudence in the 17th century. Prior to that, an individual was free to acquiesce practically to anything, and consent was viewed as a complete ban on prosecution. As the famous maxim goes, *volenti non fit injuria*: "a person is not wrong[ed] by that to which he consents." Changes came as a result of monopolization of the system of punishment by the state. While in the early ages of criminal justice the victim was the central figure in the prosecution and settlement of any nonpublic offense, in the normative and centralized judicial structure the victim became almost entirely excluded from the criminal process.

"In contrast to the understanding of crime as a violation of the victim's interests, the emergence of the state developed another interpretation: the disturbance of the society." An increasing number of historically "private" offenses were reconceptualized as "public." The state (or king) became the ultimate victim and the sole prosecutor of a criminal act. Consequently, an individual lost the power to consent to what the state regarded as harm to itself. . . .

Today, American law continues to maintain that one's life and body do not quite belong to him. Courts habitually disregard the voluntary nature of private harmful actions, citing various public policies. Among those are concerns that private violence may disturb peace; that the injured person may become a public charge; and that harmful conduct has no social utility, is immoral, and expresses the parties' disrespect to law and social order. Accordingly, the individual's power to authorize an act that may affect his physical well-being remain strictly limited.[6]

Sade's sexual *sadism* (and underage sexual partners) seems to be of little interest to the authorities of the era;[7] it is his religious irreverence (and unconsented to assaults) that enrages authorities. Compare this to the treatment of sexual sadism in more modern times.

Marvin Samuels – 1964

Marvin Samuels is a respected ophthalmologist living in Sunnyvale, California.[8] For several years, Samuels, who freely admits to having sadistic sexual tendencies, has been making movies that capture sadomasochistic encounters. In his view, the making of the films is a safe way for him to express his unconventional urges. His movies are cast only with volunteers. The films depict various types of sadistic encounters, including scenes of Samuels whipping bound men.

One evening Samuels meets Kenneth Anger at a bar. The two become friendly and discover they share common interests in sadomasochism and in film. Anger has directed several films, the two best known of which are *Scorpio Rising* and *Fireworks*. Both films include sadomasochistic encounters. Samuels and Anger also share an interest in the greater psychological investigation that surrounds sadomasochistic leanings.

In addition to his role as a director, Anger is employed as a film buyer for the Kinsey Institute, a well-respected research institution with a mission of "investigating the science of love, its connection to sexuality, and their collective impact on our humanity."[9] The Institute is known around the world for its ground-breaking research. At the moment, the Kinsey Institute is working on a comprehensive study of *sadism* and masochism. Anger is interested in obtaining copies of Samuels' films because they are widely believed to be authentic rather than staged depictions of sadism. Over the course of several years, Samuels sells some of his sadomasochistic films to Anger for the Institute.

In 1964, Anger brings a new movie of Samuels' to be developed at a private camera shop. He has previously relied upon the Kinsey Institute to do the film processing. The developer is mortified by the images and calls the police. The police arrest Anger but since he does not actually have anything to do with the production of the movie and holds an academic license to purchase and transport obscene materials for the Kinsey Institute, he is quickly released.

The police turn their attention to Samuels, who directs and participates in the films and has no formal academic credentials. The authorities arrive at Samuels' home and

Figure 6.2 Anger some years before meeting Samuels, 1954

find the living room set-up for movie viewing. They take the movie off the projector. The film obtained earlier from the camera store becomes known as the "horizontal film" and this second movie the "vertical film" because the persons being whipped in the films are standing and lying down, respectively.[10] Both movies show two naked, bound men being whipped by Samuels. White material, remnants of adhesive tape, is clearly visible around their mouths. The two movies become the basis for a criminal prosecution of Samuels.[11] He is indicted on, among other things, two counts of assault by means of force likely to cause great bodily injury. He pleads not guilty to all charges.

The men in the film, according to Samuels, came to him because of Samuels' talents as a sadist; he has a reputation as being "one of the best in the business."[12] He testifies that the men approached him at a gay bar and asked to participate in Samuels' films. They fully consented to every step of the process. At no time does Samuels deny making the films. He explains that the movies took about four hours to make. The men were strung up with hospital restraints, had adhesive tape applied to their mouths, and were hit with a whip and a riding crop. The jury finds Samuels guilty of assault, one count of aggravated assault and one of simple assault.

Consent to Injury in the States

An examination of the criminal laws in American jurisdictions today suggests some continuing disagreement about the kinds of conduct for which a victim's consent is adequate to provide a defense, as the map below illustrates.[13] The darker the shading, the broader the defense.

Four states, those with the darkest shading, permit a defense to assault where the victim consents to the conduct, even if the resulting harm is serious. Typically, serious injury includes protracted or extreme pain, permanent disfigurement, loss or impaired functioning of bodily organs or members, reduced mental capacity, or injury creating

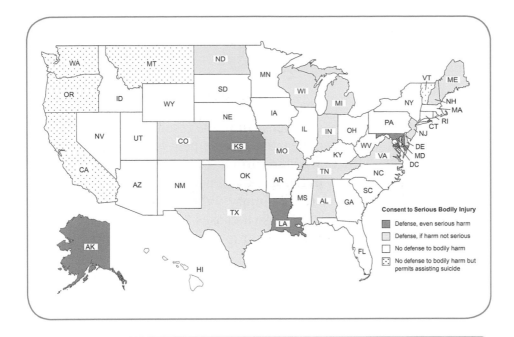

Figure 6.3

a substantial risk of death. The Marquis de Sade and Samuels presumably would have a defense today in these four jurisdictions, and only in these jurisdictions.

Fourteen states, those with light shading, permit a defense to assault or battery where the victim consents to the conduct but where the harm or threatened harm is not serious. (This is the position of the Model Penal Code, quoted in the margin.) Typically, such conduct includes consensual choking, whipping, or slapping, as might occur in hazing or in the context of a BDSM relationship (bondage, discipline, dominance and submission, masochism, and other related activity). Where the harm is serious, the consent defense is generally not available in these states (although other defenses might be available, such as a physician's lawful practice of medicine or participation in a lawful athletic competition).

The 33 jurisdictions with no shading on the map (or no shading but with dots) do not permit a defense to assault or battery for any conduct that threatens or causes bodily harm, even if the harm is not serious. For instance, people who agree to participate in a "choking game" with the goal of inducing temporary loss of consciousness and euphoria. Where no serious harm is threatened, those who play the game may be liable for assault notwithstanding the consent of all parties. Notice that California, where the *Samuels* case occurred, is one of these states, which helps explain why he was held criminally liable.

Five of the jurisdictions in the group above, marked with an overlay of dots on the map, deny a consent defense for any bodily injury but nonetheless permit assisting a suicide. One might expect that the jurisdictions that permit consent to serious bodily injury are the jurisdictions most likely to permit assisting suicide, because they seem to place greater value on personal autonomy. But it might seem that the reverse relationship is the case: all the jurisdictions that allow assisting suicide are jurisdictions that purport to forbid the infliction of bodily injury, even that which is not serious. Upon closer

Consent.

      (1) In General. The consent of the victim to conduct charged to constitute an offense or to the result thereof is a defense if such consent negatives an element of the offense or precludes the infliction of the harm or evil sought to be prevented by the law defining the offense.

      (2) Consent to Bodily Injury. When conduct is charged to constitute an offense because it causes or threatens bodily injury, consent to such conduct or to the infliction of such injury is a defense if:

      (a) the bodily injury consented to or threatened by the conduct consented to is not serious; or

      (b) the conduct and the injury are reasonably foreseeable hazards of joint participation in a lawful athletic contest or competitive sport or other concerted activity not forbidden by law; …

Model Penal Code §2.11

Figure 6.4

examination, however, the two positions are not really in such great conflict. All five jurisdictions that allow assisting suicide provide this exemption only to physicians; thus, the legal rule may simply be a move to protect doctors from criminal liability.

Should a Society Avoid Gaps between the Criminal Law Rules and Its Societal Norms?

Two-thirds of the states, those in the third group above, purport to prohibit a consent defense to any bodily injury even if it is not serious, unless it is the result of a medical treatment or an authorized sport. What may seem puzzling about this is that such a rule seems to bear little resemblance to how the criminal law is actually applied. For instance, tattoo artists are not prosecuted for hurting their patrons and salons are not convicted of assault for piercing a client's ears. Perhaps even more striking is the rise of and increasing tolerance for – if not mainstream – acceptance of S-M (sado-masochism) as a lifestyle choice.

It seems that criminal law in this instance is being used to express a societal preference rather than to announce a genuine criminal prohibition that will be punished. That is, it may be similar to the adultery or seduction offenses that continue to linger in some jurisdictions but are rarely if ever enforced.[14] But using criminal law to signal preferences rather than prohibitions can be both dangerous and damaging.

It is dangerous because it leaves the application of the offense to the unfettered discretion of the local prosecutor. One person holding the office might choose to enforce the rule vigorously while another might choose to treat it only as a symbolic preference. Clearly it would be more appropriate for the legislature to decide the criminal law of the land, rather than the local prosecutor. And one must worry about what sort of fair notice citizens are given when the meaning and effect of a criminal prohibition can change each time a new prosecutor is hired. (Recall some of the virtues of the legality principle discussed in a previous chapter: fair notice, uniformity in application, and reservation of the criminalization decision to the legislature.[15])

But even if the rule applied by prosecutors in practice is publicly announced and consistently applied, it would still produce immediate damage to the criminal law's reputation as a reliable moral authority if the prosecutor's practice conflicts with the legislature's announced legal rule. The existence of a gap between what the law says and what it actually does breeds mistrust and invites speculation as to whether other gaps exist with regard to other rules. Thus, the consent-in-law versus consent-in-practice gap may leave citizens with less reason to take seriously generally the criminal law as written.

This phenomenon was part of the social-legal disaster that occurred with American Prohibition in the 1920s. Prohibition banned the sale of alcohol, but it was obvious that many if not most people, including political leaders, were simply ignoring the legal prohibition. The effect was not only rampant violation of the statutes criminalizing the sale of alcohol but also an increase in non-alcohol–related offenses generally. Once the criminal law's reputation as a reliable legal and moral authority is undermined, it loses some part of its ability to gain deference and compliance from the community.[16]

Today we grapple with the propriety of some drug laws. Marijuana use is prohibited under the Federal law but most states permit its use for medicinal purposes,[17] and 11 jurisdictions, and counting, allow its recreational use.[18] As more people come to see marijuana usage as a personal choice rather than a crime, the disconnect may create some of the same problems that plagued Prohibition.

Whether the issue is the consumption of alcohol or sadomasochistic sexual conduct, jurisdictions would be better off setting their criminal law rules to accurately reflect the conduct that the society sees as sufficiently condemnable to merit criminal conviction and punishment. And once a legal prohibition is set, it ought to be taken seriously. Gaps between the legal rules and existing societal norms serve only to undermine the law's moral credibility.

Consent as a Defense: Sexual Offenses

So far in this chapter our focus has been on the criminalization of consensual conduct, the complexities that it raises and the insights that it provides on the role of criminal law in society. But consent is also at the heart of another central criminal law issue: some crimes, such as theft and many sexual offenses, for example, exist only because the conduct is nonconsensual. Taking property of another becomes criminal only if it is done without the consent of the owner. Sexual intercourse or contact with another may be a quite pleasant and valuable human activity for both parties but becomes criminal if done without consent. In these instances, the consent of the victim becomes an exculpating defense to criminal liability.

An examination of the history of consent to sexual intercourse is a particularly useful example to use in reviewing the role of consent as a defense because it also provides a compelling example of one of this volume's main themes: societal norms change and criminal law must change along with them. Originally, sexual intercourse was criminalized only when it was induced by force or threat of force – commonly referred to as "rape" – or by some form of highly inappropriate coercion or implicit coercion, or intercourse with an underage partner. In all of these cases, the lack of valid consent by the victim was readily apparent. The victim's immaturity vitiated any consent actually given, and the threat of force vitiated the consensual nature of any compliance with a request for sex.

Historically, however, the formulation of sexual assault offenses commonly did not include the simple offense of conduct without consent. This is true even of the Model Penal Code, which was promulgated in 1962 and heavily influenced the codification of sexual offenses in many states. More recently, however, it has been strongly argued that criminal liability ought to stretch to include unconsented to intercourse even in cases where there is no force, threat of force, or improper coercion. This proposed broadening of criminal liability would most commonly take in cases where the defendant is insufficiently attentive to whether their partner is consenting and goes ahead with intercourse or sexual contact without a clear view that it is consensual. That is, the view here is that any ambiguity about consent ought to be resolved before going ahead. Thus, a simple "no" or "don't" by a partner ought to immediately stop any further conduct, unless by subsequent action the partner clearly indicates otherwise.

There is probably little debate that this is how partners in a sexual encounter should behave. The question debated is whether failure to follow this rule is an adequate basis for criminal liability and punishment where no force, threat of force, or coercion is used. In 2022, the American Law Institute officially promulgated a revised set of provisions governing sexual offenses, which expressly criminalize unconsented to sexual conduct. The new offense reads as follows. (Other relevant provisions are reproduced in the Appendix to this chapter.)

Section 213.6. Sexual Assault in the Absence of Consent

1. An actor is guilty of Sexual Assault in the Absence of Consent [a felony of the fourth or fifth degree, depending on specified circumstances] when:

    a. the actor causes another person to submit to or perform an act of sexual penetration or oral sex and:
    b. the other person does not consent to that act; and
    c. the actor is reckless in respect to paragraphs (a) and (b).

As is apparent, the offense is a serious one – it is created as a felony, so the maximum term of imprisonment would be at least several years. But it is also apparent that an important safeguard has been included: it is not enough that the partner was not consenting. To become criminally liable the defendant would have to be reckless as to this. Recall our discussion of culpability requirements in Chapter 3. The recklessness requirement requires here proof that the defendant was aware of a substantial risk that their partner was not consenting yet goes ahead with intercourse anyway.

No doubt there will remain debate about this new offense in state legislatures. Some will argue that it imposes serious felony liability on a defendant who may actually genuinely believe that there is consent, although admittedly is aware of a

Consent.

 (ii) Consent may be express or it may be inferred from behavior—both action and inaction—in the context of all the circumstances.

 (iii) Neither verbal nor physical resistance is required to establish that consent is lacking, but their absence may be considered, in the context of all the circumstances, in determining the issue of consent.

 (iv) Notwithstanding subsection (2)(e)(ii) of this Section, consent is ineffective when given by a person incompetent to consent or under circumstances precluding the free exercise of consent, as provided in Sections ***.

 (v) Consent may be revoked or withdrawn any time before or during the act of sexual penetration, oral sex, or sexual contact. A clear verbal refusal—such as "No," "Stop," or "Don't"—establishes the lack of consent or the revocation or withdrawal of previous consent. Lack of consent or revocation or withdrawal of consent may be overridden by subsequent consent given prior to the act of sexual penetration, oral sex, or sexual contact. .

Model Penal Code, Revised §213.0(2)(e) (May 2021)

Figure 6.5

substantial risk that there may not be. The complexity and subtlety of human interaction, especially in situations of near intimacy, may very commonly produce ambiguity. A partner rarely says, "Please have intercourse with me now."

 The situation becomes all the more complicated by the fact that these cases also commonly arise where both parties are voluntarily intoxicated to some extent; thus, the possibility of misunderstanding on the one side or poor communication on the other may play a significant role in bringing about the ultimate offense. However, presumably the defendant knew at the time of voluntarily intoxicating themselves that such a state would leave them in a poor position to make reliable judgments about their partner's consent. (The voluntary intoxication of the victim may also contribute to the offense conduct, but that hardly reduces the defendant's culpability. On the contrary, contemplating intercourse with an intoxicated partner ought itself raise red flags about assuring the presence of valid consent.)

Because the victim's lack of consent is at the core of the new offense, it becomes critical to clearly define what constitutes valid consent. Therefore, the drafters provide a definition of consent to sexual intimacy that has a good deal of detail (reproduced in the margin).[19]

These new sexual assault formulations are an ambitious attempt to provide the precision that the legality principle calls for in defining criminal conduct, even that involving complex human interactions and in the midst of shifting societal norms.

Aftermaths

In 1790, Sade is freed during the tumult of the French Revolution, and even given a job in the new government. It does not take long, however, for him to be on the wrong side of the revolutionary officials and he is soon re-arrested and imprisoned. The revolutionary government orders his execution, but Robespierre dies before the order can be carried out. The royalists are back in power and while they do not kill Sade, neither do they free him. Confined, Sade continues to evolve into an influential and outspoken writer.

For Marvin Samuels, the quiet life and thriving medical practice he enjoyed before his arrest fades away during the trial. He is convicted of aggravated assault, and the court imposes a suspended prison sentence, fines Samuels $3,000, and places him on probation for a period of ten years.

Samuels continues to believe that his movies do not contain "victims," nor do they depict any type of criminal behavior. He appeals his conviction. The court rejects his appeal, explaining:

> It is a matter of common knowledge that a normal person in full possession of his mental faculties does not freely consent to the use, upon himself, of force likely to produce great bodily injury. Even if it be assumed that the victim in the "vertical" film did in fact suffer from some form of mental aberration which compelled him to submit to a beating which was so severe as to constitute an aggravated assault, defendant's conduct in inflicting that beating was no less violative of a penal statute obviously designed to prohibit one human being from severely or mortally injuring another. It follows that the trial court was correct in instructing the jury that consent was not a defense to the aggravated assault charge.

Appendix: Revised Model Penal Code Article 213. Sexual Offenses

(as of May 2021, following the ALI annual meeting, but not final until approved by the Council)

Section 213.0. General Principles; Definitions

1. This Article is governed by Part I of the 1962 Model Penal Code, including the definitions given in Section 210.0, except that:

   a. Section 2.11 (the definition of "consent") does not apply to this article.

b.   Subsection (2) of Section 2.08 (Intoxication) does not apply to this article. Instead, the general provisions of the criminal law and rules of evidence of the jurisdiction govern the materiality of the actor's intoxication in determining the actor's culpability for an offense.

2.   *Definitions*

In this Article, unless a different definition is plainly required:

* * *

e.   "Consent"

i.   "Consent" for purposes of Article 213 means a person's willingness to engage in a specific act of sexual penetration, oral sex, or sexual contact.
ii.   Consent may be express or it may be inferred from behavior—both action and inaction—in the context of all the circumstances.
iii.   Neither verbal nor physical resistance is required to establish that consent is lacking, but their absence may be considered, in the context of all the circumstances, in determining the issue of consent.
iv.   Notwithstanding subsection (2)(e)(ii) of this Section, consent is ineffective when given by a person incompetent to consent or under circumstances precluding the free exercise of consent, as provided in Sections * * *.
v.   Consent may be revoked or withdrawn any time before or during the act of sexual penetration, oral sex, or sexual contact. A clear verbal refusal—such as "No," "Stop," or "Don't"—establishes the lack of consent or the revocation or withdrawal of previous consent. Lack of consent or revocation or withdrawal of consent may be overridden by subsequent consent given prior to the act of sexual penetration, oral sex, or sexual contact.

* * *

Section 213.6. Sexual Assault in the Absence of Consent

1.   An actor is guilty of Sexual Assault in the Absence of Consent [a felony of the fourth or fifth degree, depending on specified circumstances omitted here] when:

a.   the actor causes another person to submit to or perform an act of sexual penetration or oral sex and:
b.   the other person does not consent to that act; and
c.   the actor is reckless in respect to paragraphs (a) and (b).

* * *

3.   If applicable, the actor may raise an affirmative defense of Explicit Prior Permission under Section 213.10.

* * *

Section 213.10. Affirmative Defense of Explicit Prior Permission

1.   Except as provided in subsection (3), it is an affirmative defense to a charge under this Article that the actor reasonably believed that, in connection with the charged

act of sexual penetration, oral sex, or sexual contact the other party personally gave the actor explicit prior permission to use or threaten to use physical force or restraint, or to inflict or threaten to inflict any harm otherwise proscribed by Sections * * *, or to ignore the absence of consent otherwise proscribed by Section 213.6.

2. Permission is "explicit" under subsection (1) when it is given orally or by written agreement:

   a. specifying that the actor may ignore the other party's expressions of unwillingness or other absence of consent;
   b. identifying the specific forms and extent of force, restraint, or threats that are permitted; and
   c. stipulating the specific words or gestures that will withdraw the permission.

Permission given by gestures or other nonverbal conduct signaling assent is not "explicit" under subsection (1).

3. The defense provided by this Section is unavailable when:

   a. the act of sexual penetration, oral sex, or sexual contact occurs after the explicit permission was withdrawn, and the actor is aware of, yet recklessly disregards, the risk that the permission was withdrawn;
   b. the actor relies on permission to use force or restraint or ignore the absence of consent at a time when the other party will be unconscious, asleep, or otherwise unable to withdraw that permission;
   c. the actor engages in conduct that causes or risks serious bodily injury and in so doing is aware of, yet recklessly disregards, the risk of such injury; or
   d. at the time explicit permission is given, the other party is, and the actor is aware of, yet recklessly disregards, the risk that the other party is:

      i. younger than 18;
      ii. giving that permission while subjected to physical force or restraint;
      iii. giving that permission because of the use or threat to use physical force or restraint, or extortion as defined by Section 213.4, if that person does not give the permission;
      iv. lacking substantial capacity to appraise or control his or her conduct as a result of intoxication, whether voluntary or involuntary, and regardless of the identity of the person who administered the intoxicants;
      v. incapacitated, vulnerable, or legally restricted as defined by Section 213.3;
      vi. subject to prohibited deception, as defined by Section 213.5; or
      vii. subject to trafficking, as defined by Section 213.9.

Chapter Glossary

Civil Liability: A legal obligation that requires a party to pay for damages or to follow other court enforcements in a civil lawsuit. Different from criminal liability, which is often brought by the state to redress a public wrong, civil liability is usually brought by a private party to sue for damages or injunctions. For example, in a car crash case, the injured party can sue the driver and ask for monetary damages.[20]

Heresy: In common-law England, heresy was an offense against religion, consisting not in totally denying Christianity but in publicly denying some of its essential doctrines. The offense is now subject only to ecclesiastical correction and is no longer punishable by the secular law.[21]

Sadism: It is a desire to inflict pain on others, especially for sexual gratification.[22]

Notes

1. This narrative is drawn from the following sources: Neil Schaeffer, *The Marquis de Sade: A Life* (Cambridge: Harvard University Press, 2001); Donald Thomas, *The Marquis de Sade: A New Biography* (Chicago: Citadel, 1998).
2. Schaeffer, 'Son and Heir,' in *The Marquis de Sade*, p. 16.
3. Schaeffer, 'Son and Heir,' in *The Marquis de Sade*, p. 25.
4. Schaeffer, 'Scandalous Debauch,' in *The Marquis de Sade*, p. 62.
5. Schaeffer, 'The Arcueil Affair,' in *The Marquis de Sade*, p. 96.
6. Vera Bergelson, 'Consent to Harm,' in *The Ethics of Consent: Theory and Practice*, edited by Franklin G. Miller and Alan Wertheimer (2009), pp. 165–166.
7. Stephen Robertson, 'Age of Consent Laws,' Children and Youth in History teaching module, accessed 16 July 2020, http://chnm.gmu.edu/cyh/teaching-modules/230?section=primarysources&source=24.
8. This narrative is drawn from the following source: *People v. Samuels*, 250 Cal. App. 2d 501 (1967).
9. 'Home Page,' Kinsey Institute: Indiana University, last modified 2019, accessed 17 June 2019, https://www.kinseyinstitute.org/
10. *People v. Samuels.*
11. *People v. Samuels.*
12. *People v. Samuels.*
13. The map is taken from Paul H. Robinson and Tyler Scot Williams, 'Consent to Injury,' in *Mapping American Criminal Law: Variations across the 50 States* (Westport: Prager, 2018), p. 86. All supporting authorities are available from that source.
14. *See* Chapter 22.
15. Chapter 1.
16. *See* Paul H. Robinson and Sarah M. Robinson, 'Credibility: America's Prohibition,' in *Pirates, Prisoners, and Lepers: Lessons from Life Outside the Law* (Lincoln: Potomac Books, 2015), p. 143.
17. 'Federal Marijuana Law,' Americans for Safe Access, updated 8 May 2018, https://www.safeaccessnow.org/federal_marijuana_law.
18. 'Marijuana Overview,' National Conference of State Legislatures, accessed 16 July 2020, http://www.ncsl.org/research/civil-and-criminal-justice/marijuana-overview.aspx.
19. Model Penal Code: Sexual Assault and Related Offenses Tentative Draft No. 4, Section 213.0 General Principles of Liability; Definitions (18 August 2020).
20. *Civil Liability*, Legal Information Institute, https://www.law.cornell.edu/wex/civil_liability.
21. *Heresy*, Black's.
22. *Sadism*, Your Dictionary, https://www.yourdictionary.com/sadism.

Chapter 7

Attempt

From Child Rape to Cannibal Cop

1916. World War I, sparked by the assassination of the Archduke Francis Ferdinand, brings to an abrupt end the relative peace and prosperity of Europe's Victorian era. Now in its third year, the conflict introduces the world to mechanized warfare and mass killings. In the next year, America will join the hostilities, and by its conclusion three great empires – the Austro-Hungarian, the Russian, and the Ottoman – will have ceased to exist. The war also helps transform science, medicine, and technology. The practicality of blood transfusions makes a huge advance now that blood is refrigerated for the first time. Margaret Sanger opens the world's first birth control clinic. Alaska will not become a state for almost another half-century.

H.M. Wooldridge – 1916

H.M. Wooldridge is at a small gathering hosted by a local Fairbanks, Alaska councilman. The party, which is nearly over, is being held at Rose Machine Repair Shop, a local hang-out where liquor is sold. The councilman host sends word for 14-year-old Laura Herrington to come to the shop. Laura's father knows the councilman, and sees no danger in his daughter accepting the invitation. But when she arrives, with two other men standing by, the councilman rapes the girl. Wooldridge and the other man are also planning on having intercourse with the child, but her screams attract help and she is rescued.[1]

Having been caught in the act, the three are indicted and face charges: rape for the host councilman and attempted rape for Wooldridge and the other man.

Worried that the evidence against Wooldridge may be insufficient because he did not go far enough toward committing rape, he looks for a way to bolster the case. They conclude that Wooldridge appears to have a special interest in Laura, and they speculate that he might contact her again, providing an opportunity to catch him in

DOI: 10.4324/9781003258025-8

Figure 7.1 Street scene in Fairbanks, circa 1916

less ambiguous circumstances. They tell Laura that if Wooldridge ever approaches her, she should agree to meet with him and tell them of the planned meeting.

Wooldridge eventually does contact Laura and it is agreed that the two will meet at the repair shop. After Wooldridge and Laura meet at the shop, they go into the back room and Wooldridge tells Laura to lie on the bed and that he will return shortly. He goes back into the shop, gets a drink, and returns. He tells Laura to turn off the light so nobody will be able to see her in the room. When the marshals break in, Wooldridge has not yet touched Laura. He is charged with attempted statutory rape, among other things.

The two attempted rape incidents are consolidated into a single trial, at which Wooldridge is acquitted for the first attempt, where Laura was raped by the councilman host, but convicted for attempt in the second case, where he arranged the meeting and was alone with Laura. He is sentenced to 18 months to ten years in prison, but in his appeal to the Court of Appeals, the verdict is overturned. The Court finds that though Wooldridge may have wanted to engage in sexual intercourse with Laura Herrington, he did not actually go far enough toward commission of the offense to be held liable for a criminal attempt.

Attempt

Criminal law typically prohibits the harmful or evil conduct that it defines as a criminal offense, but it also punishes attempts to engage in such conduct. Attempts to commit crimes can themselves be destabilizing and damaging to a society but, perhaps more importantly, they also demonstrate the personal blameworthiness and dangerousness of the actor by showing his willingness to commit the offense. Such demonstrated willingness arguably deserves criminal liability and punishment.

George Fletcher speaks to the history of *attempt liability*:

> Though some arguably inchoate offenses, such as vagrancy and conspiracy, have long been part of the common law, the formal doctrine of attempts did not emerge until the late eighteenth century. English law lagged in this process of development. Continental systems had recognized as early as the sixteenth century that an independent crime of attempting could be derived from an offense-in-chief. Professor Sayre argues persuasively that the common-law doctrine stems from *Rex v Scofield*, decided in 1784; in his opinion, Lord Mansfield noted explicitly that the "completion of an act, criminal in itself, [was not] necessary to constitute criminality." The defendant Scofield was charged with having put a lighted candle among combustible material in a house that was then in his possession, with an intent to burn it. The intended arson was apparently unconsummated, but Lord Mansfield reasoned that a derivative crime of attempting covered the case.
>
> . . . The intent to commit the offense-in-chief would be the core of the offense, and the function of the act of partial execution would be to demonstrate the firmness of the actor's resolve and perhaps to provide evidence of his intent. Even the opinion in Scofield contains the comment: "The *intent* may make an act, innocent in itself, criminal. . ." The pattern of subjective criminality eventually did gain the upper hand in the theory of attempts, both in Continental as well as Anglo-American jurisdictions. Yet in the course of the nineteenth century, and to some extent in our own time, judges and theorists have been deeply concerned about the potentially unlimited scope of liability of those who intend to commit recognized crimes.[2]

The appropriate place to draw the line between what constitutes a criminal attempt and the earlier conduct that cannot be the basis for criminal liability has been and continues to be debated. Some jurisdictions require that the person actually come close to committing the offense, using some kind of "proximity" test for how close the person must come, such as comes within "dangerous proximity" of commission. Thus, a person who decides to rob a bank but has only collected the required equipment in the trunk of his car and backed out of his driveway may not yet have come close enough to actual commission to be held liable for attempted bank robbery. It was on this basis that Wooldridge was able to escape liability for attempted statutory rape. In the view of the court, he had not yet come close enough to committing the offense.

Other jurisdictions, typically those with more modern criminal codes based upon the American Law Institute's Model Penal Code, commonly require something less than "proximity" to satisfy the objective conduct element for attempt. They essentially shift the inquiry from asking whether the person has *come close enough* to commission of the offense, to asking whether the person has *gone far enough* from the starting point to demonstrate his intention to offend.[3] (See the MPC attempt provision in the margin.) Thus, the bank robbery suspect who has collected the necessary equipment and begun his drive to the bank may satisfy the conduct requirement for attempt even though he is not yet close to commission, if it is judged that he has taken a "substantial-step" toward commission. Under this Model Penal Code attempt formulation, a substantial-step can include reconnoitering the location of a planned crime, possessing materials that may be used in the commission of an offense, and other steps commonly taken in the path toward commission of a crime, as long as it is "strongly corroborative of the actor's criminal purpose."[4] (Of course, satisfying this objective conduct requirement is not enough for attempt liability; the culpability requirement for attempt must also be satisfied.)

Criminal Attempt.

(1) Definition of Attempt. A person is guilty of an attempt to commit a crime if, acting with the kind of culpability otherwise required for commission of the crime, he:

(a) purposely engages in conduct which would constitute the crime if the attendant circumstances were as he believes them to be; or

(b) when causing a particular result is an element of the crime, does or omits to do anything with the purpose of causing or with the belief that it will cause such result without further conduct on his part; or

(c) purposely does or omits to do anything which, under the circumstances as he believes them to be, is an act or omission constituting a substantial step in a course of conduct planned to culminate in his commission of the crime.

(2) Conduct Which May Be Held Substantial Step Under Subsection (1)(c). Conduct shall not be held to constitute a substantial step under Subsection (1)(c) of this Section unless it is strongly corroborative of the actor's criminal purpose. . . .

Model Penal Code §5.01

Figure 7.2

See how the difference in these two approaches – the objectivist "proximity" test versus the subjectivist *substantial-step test* – works out in the following case compared to the *Wooldridge* case above.

Blaec Lammers – 2012

Blaec James Lammers lives at home with his parents and sister just south of Bolivar, Missouri.[5] For the most part, the four are a happy family. As a child, Lammers has his fair share of age-appropriate misbehavior, but it sometimes creeps past normal. Lammers is not mentally ill but nor is he an ordinary kid. As he grows into his teen years, it becomes clear to everyone that he has an anti-social personality disorder, is on the autism spectrum, and is dyslexic. Due to his psychological conditions, Lammers has a hard time fitting in at school and is frequently bullied. Lammers sees those around him developing friendships and engaging in fun activities, while he feels himself to be alone and something of a hopeless case.

In 2009, in the throes of profound depression, Lammers wanders around the local Walmart with a Halloween clown mask in his hand and wielding a butcher's knife. His goal, which he does not share with anyone at the time, is to get the police to shoot him. Instead, the sheriff escorts the teenager out of the store. Several such bizarre episodes occur but Lammers never makes any attempt to physically harm anyone but himself. At one point he takes what he hopes will be an overdose of medication. His family is well aware of their son's struggles and does what they can to get him help but nothing seems to make much difference.

On July 20, 2012, James Eagan Holmes walks into a Century 16 movie theater in Aurora, Colorado during a midnight showing of the popular film *The Dark Knight Rises* and opens fire, and in what becomes one of the worst mass shootings in the country, he kills 12 and wounds 58.

Lammers is now 20 years old, living with his parents, and has no meaningful direction. Not long after the Colorado shooting, Lammers watches a video about the 1999 Columbine High School shooting during which two students kill 13 and injure an additional 24. Lammers, fascinated by the idea of the mass shootings, decides he will follow the path of Holmes and carry out a mass shooting in a movie theater. But after further consideration, he changes his mind and decides the shooting should take place at the local Walmart, the same store of the 2009 incident. The plan is to walk in and just start shooting until the police arrive to kill him. The crux of the plan is to end his own suffering through suicide by cop.

On November 12 and 13, Lammers purchases two rifles, a .22 caliber and a .223 caliber, along with 400 rounds of ammunition from the same Walmart he is planning to use for his shooting spree. The day after his purchases, Lammers brings the guns to the apartment of a friend who is experienced with rifles. He tells the friend that he wants to learn to shoot so that he can go hunting. Lammers does not have a hunting license, but his friend teaches him how to sight and load the gun and they begin to practice shooting targets.

Lammers knows that his mother will not allow the guns in her house, so he arranges to store the guns at the home of his girlfriend's father. The father makes it clear to Lammers that if the guns are to stay in his home, he must be satisfied that everything is on the up-and-up. He cautions the young man that if he finds anything suspicious, he intends to hand the weapons over to the police. Lammers tells the father everything about the purchase of the guns and the father agrees to store them, then takes control of the weapons.

The father also contacts Lammers' mother and tells her about the weapons. She calls her husband to discuss the matter and both parents worry that their depressed son may have bought the guns to commit suicide. Worried, Lammers' mother drives to the sheriff's office to report her son's recently purchased, and asks them to keep an eye on him. The sheriff, having been involved with the family multiple times, sets off to check on Lammers and finds him at the local Sonic Drive-In with his girlfriend.

As the deputy begins to question him about the guns purchase, Lammers tells him he is planning on going hunting, but the deputy knows Lammers does not have a hunting license and that the rifles purchased are not suitable for hunting. The deputy asks Lammers to accompany him to the sheriff's office to talk further. Lammers fully cooperates.

Figure 7.3 Blaec Lammers as a young man, circa 2011

At the station, a detective questions Lammers further. Each time Lammers is asked, he comes up with a different reason for the guns purchase. The detective now offers Lammers his own thoughts: in his view, Lammers shares multiple characteristics with mass shooters. Lammers picks up the detective's narrative and tells the detective that he has envisioned committing a mass shooting, inspired by Columbine, but also explains that when he was target shooting, he completely abandoned the idea: "But then I realized when I went shooting . . . I was like this, this isn't me. I don't know why I did this."[6] And, he further explains that the prospect of life in prison was scary enough to also dissuade him from emulating famous mass shooters, which is why he gave control of the guns over to his girlfriend's father.

Based on the interview, Lammers is arrested and charged at the Polk County Circuit Court with attempted first-degree assault and related charges and held on a $500,000 bond.

Missouri follows the substantial-step test rather than the proximity test for attempt, so the state must prove beyond a reasonable doubt that the defendant intended to commit the crime *and* that he took a substantial-step toward the commission of the offense. To prove those two elements, the state submits the recorded interview as evidence of Lammers' criminal intent and his purchase of the rifles as evidence of a substantial-step toward commission. At the end of the trial, the judge acquits him on one of the related charges but finds him guilty of attempted first-degree assault. Lammers is sentenced to a 15-year term of imprisonment.

It seems clear that Lammers could not have been held liable for attempted assault under the demanding proximity test used in the *Wooldridge* case in Alaska. (As the map below indicates, Alaska has since shifted to the Model Penal Code's substantial-step formulation.) In contrast, the substantial-step test applied in Missouri was seen as broad enough to criminalize Lammers' preparatory conduct, even though he may have subsequently changed his mind on his own.

Current Diversity in Attempt Liability Requirements

The discussion above has touched on both the objective requirements for attempt and the culpability requirements. The map below shows the diversity among the states on both these issues. The shadings in the map indicate the position of each state with regard to whether the state adopts a *proximity test* (lighter shading) or a substantial-step test (darker shading).[7] The dots overlay shows the position of the states with regard to the culpability level required for an attempt, intention (no dots) or something less (dots).

The Model Penal Code shift to the substantial-step test has had a significant effect on the states. Thirty-five of the 51 jurisdictions, those in dark shading, adopt the test, while 16, in light shading, stay with the older common-law proximity test. Thus, in the latter states, Lammers would have a significant chance of escaping *attempt liability* because his conduct had not yet come in sufficiently close proximity to commission.

The vast majority of the jurisdictions – 45 out of 51 – require proof that the defendant intended to commit the offense, while the remaining six jurisdictions, those with a dots overlay, require that the offender intentionally engaged in the conduct constituting the offense but do not require that the defendant have intended the prohibited result or intended the circumstances that made the conduct criminal.

To illustrate the significance of this difference, consider the case of the antiwar activist who plants a bomb to blow up the local military recruiting office after business hours when there are not likely to be people present. When he triggers his bomb, it malfunctions and never explodes. While he cannot be liable for the offense of destroying the building by explosive, he can be liable for an *attempt* to commit that

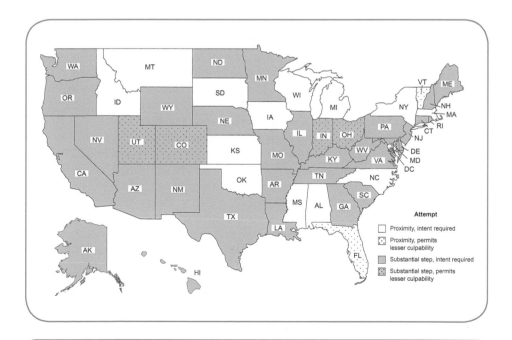

Figure 7.4

offense. His conduct has come close to committing the offense – indeed he has completed all the conduct necessary for commission of the offense – and it was his purpose to destroy the building.

Now assume that just before he triggers his bomb, he sees that the night watchman is in the building, which he was not expecting. He would prefer not to kill the watchman, but he also believes that his antiwar protest is more important. He decides to trigger the bomb anyway, aware that the explosion creates a substantial risk of killing the watchman, but he has no intention or hope or desire that it will. If his bomb explodes and kills the watchman, he would be liable for the homicide, probably manslaughter because of his recklessness as to causing death. But because his bomb does not go off and no one is killed, he cannot be liable for homicide. Can he be held liable for attempted homicide? In most jurisdictions, probably not. To convict an offender of an attempt typically requires proving the offender's *purpose* – intention – to cause the death, which this actor did not have. Even though he was aware of a substantial risk that his bomb might kill the watchman (reckless) and even though this would be adequate culpability for manslaughter liability if the bomb did kill the watchman, the elevation of offense culpability requirements for attempt means that he cannot be held liable for attempted manslaughter in most jurisdictions.

As noted, the vast majority of jurisdictions – 45 in total, those without a dots overlay on the map – take this elevate-to-purpose approach. There are some jurisdictions, however, that do not elevate the attempt culpability requirement to purpose, and thereby allow *attempt liability* for some lesser culpability level, such as knowing or reckless. In these jurisdictions – those with a dots overlay – the antiwar activist could be held liable for attempted homicide.[8]

What Should Be the Objective and Culpability Requirements for Attempt?

In drafting the requirements for *attempt liability*, one can understand why drafters might want to increase the culpability requirement for attempt above those required for the substantive offense, as a way of compensating for the decreased conduct requirements. But the 14 states that adopt the *proximity test* and also elevate all culpability requirements to intent (lighter shading and no dots) seem to go too far. Their adoption of the more-demanding proximity test suggests that they hardly need the dramatic elevation to intent to avoid too broad an offense.

One could argue that the two states that adopt the proximity test and also do not require elevation to intent (lighter shading plus dots) have struck a compromise of sorts. They do allow lesser culpability levels than purpose but only because they keep the objective conduct requirement relatively high by using the more-demanding proximity test.

And one might be tempted to say the same thing about the 31 states that adopt the more narrow *substantial-step test* and keep the demanding elevation-to-intent requirement (darker shading and no dots). They have struck a compromise of sorts. But one can wonder whether their elevation requirement goes too far. The case of the antiwar activist who triggers a bomb that he knows will kill the night watchman makes the point. Engaging in conduct by which a person believes he will cause the death of another human is classic murder. But for the malfunction of the bomb, the antiwar activist would be liable for murder of the watchman. On what moral basis would we say that he should not be liable for attempted murder when, against all his hopes and desires, his bomb does not explode?

A better approach for those jurisdictions adopting the lower objective requirement of "substantial-step" (dark shading) might be to impose a purpose requirement that more accurately judges the moral blameworthiness of the attempter. For example, it ought to indeed be required that it was the attempter's *purpose to engage in the conduct* that would constitute the substantive offense. In other words, it needs to be shown that the actor took the "substantial-step" intentionally, not accidentally. Further, it ought to be shown that it was the actor's true and committed *purpose to complete the conduct* constituting the substantive offense. In other words, it ought to be shown that his intention to engage in the offense conduct was indeed *fully resolute*, rather than just being a daydream or a fantasy. In the bank robbery case above, then, it would need to be proven beyond a reasonable doubt that the person really did intend to drive to the bank and rob it – that this was his resolute purpose – and not that he was just some Walter Mitty flirting with but never really willing to act upon his fantasy.

These are better interpretations of the special "purpose" requirement for *attempt liability*. There is little reason to go further than these requirements, to apply the purpose requirement in a way that also elevates to purpose the culpability requirements relating to other offense elements, such as the result of causing a death. With these two demanding aspects of the purpose requirement in place – assuring that the attempter's conduct toward the offense was not accidental and that his intention to complete that conduct was resolute – a jurisdiction can fairly impose attempt liability on a person who satisfies the normal culpability requirements for the substantive offense. In other words, the jurisdiction can impose attempted murder liability on the antiwar activist who attempts to knowingly kill the night watchman.

This may be the position taken by the four states who adopt the substantial-step test and who also allow culpability less than intention (darker shading and dots overlay). This group can argue that it is a morally justifiable position that probably more closely tracks the community's judgments of justice.

One final issue regarding attempt culpability deserves attention. Whenever intention is required, it necessarily includes a requirement that the intention is real not just fantastical. This can sometimes be a complex issue. Recall the Lammers case in which the actor did at one time had the intention, but then soon dropped it when shooting the rifle brought him to reality of what he was planning. Would we say that his original intention was or was not sufficiently resolute to be sufficient for *attempt liability*? Consider this issue in a somewhat more extreme case that made the tabloid headlines.

Cannibal Cop – 2012

Gilberto Valle joins the New York City Police Department in 2006, and is assigned to the 26th Precinct in Morningside Heights, Manhattan.[9] Three years later, he meets Kathleen Mangan through OKCupid.com, an online dating site. A year into their relationship, Kathleen becomes pregnant and, though Gilberto is annoyed, he relents and marries her to "do the right thing."[10]

Unhappy with his marriage, he begins to spend more and more time online, sometimes until 5:00 in the morning looking at what Kathleen discovers is bondage pornography. On one occasion, she finds him staring at a page on a bondage site that depicts a dead woman. As his marriage crumbles, Valle creates his own fictional online identity on fetish websites under the screen name Girlmeat Hunter and begins posting narratives of his plans for torturing and killing women. The anonymity allows him to fantasize freely, with each storyline becoming more depraved.

Valle's job calls for detailed investigations into many people's lives, allowing Valle to find people's date of birth, height, weight, and more. Valle uses this access to gather information about particular women – both women known and unknown to him – who are the focus of his plans to abduct, cook, and then eat the women.

His elaborate schemes are not orchestrated in solitude. Hiding behind his fictional online identity, Valle frequents fetish websites where he contacts more than 20 other people with similar fantasies, where their conversations often revolve around the exchange of violent sexual fantasies. The loosely formed group begins to settle on a single plan. Valle obtains information about one particular victim, and proposes "tying her body onto some kind of apparatus . . . Cook[ing] her over a low heat, [and] keep[ing] her alive as long as possible."[11]

As a police officer, Valle has resources at his disposal that he uses to advance his schemes. Beyond using the internet for online searches, on multiple occasions he conducts surveillance of women using his police car. He surveils them and then writes about ways that he might capture and harm them. Valle also uses the federal National Crime Information Center to obtain private information.

In 2011, Valle writes to a female college friend with whom he has kept in touch and, using the ruse that he would like to send her a police union card so she might get out of traffic tickets, asks for her address, which she provides. In February of 2012, he offers to kidnap a woman for a New Jersey man, saying "$5,000 and she is all yours,"[12] though he does not actually follow through on the offer.

When Kathleen Valle installs spyware on her husband's computer, she finds all the torture-murder-cannibal plots. According to Valle's writings, Kathleen herself is to be tied by her feet and her throat is to be slit while Valle and his friends watch the blood rush down her body. Horrified, Kathleen immediately reports her husband to the FBI, then flees to a friend's home with their one-year-old daughter. The FBI takes Valle into custody and his computer reveals files on more than 100 women. The computer also contains a history of Google searches on how to abduct women, what the best kind of rope is to tie people up, and which chemicals render a person unconscious. Valle is charged with conspiracy to commit kidnapping and accessing the federal database without authorization. He faces a life sentence for the first charge and a maximum of five years for the second. At trial he is found guilty on both charges.

However, 16 months later, the conspiracy to kidnap conviction is overturned on appeal to the Second Circuit Court of Appeals. The court explains, "fantasizing about committing a crime, even a crime of violence against a real person whom you know, is not a crime."[13] (It also reverses his conviction on the charges of illegal access to databases because he is normally authorized to use the databases as part of his work. There is no federal law at the time that specifically prohibits officers from using the databases for their own purposes.)

Thus, after serving 21 months in prison for his plans to rape, kill, and eat up to a hundred women, the Cannibal Cop is freed.

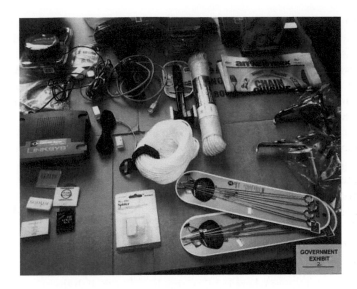

Figure 7.5 The paraphernalia which a co-conspirator brought to a meeting with an undercover FBI agent, 2014

Fantasy and Irresolute Intention

In judging whether a defendant had the required culpability for attempt (or any other *inchoate offense*, such as conspiracy), it must be shown that his actions do not represent simply an acting out of a fantasy of committing the offense; it must be proven beyond a reasonable doubt that it really was his intention *to go through with the commission of the offense*. In other words, his apparent intention to commit the offense must be shown to have been sufficiently resolute.

People can disagree about whether the Cannibal Cop really intended to go through with the offense or whether he was simply fantasizing, with no genuine intention of committing any of the imagined atrocities. But the reversal of his conviction shows how seriously the appellate court took the requirement of showing an intention beyond fantasy. Perhaps Lammers might have been able to make a similar argument, that while at one point he may have "intended" to engage in a mass shooting, in reality it was mere fantasy, not a truly *resolute intention*?

Aftermaths

After the reversal of his conviction, Wooldridge disappears back into the Alaskan territory and never again finds his way to court. The councilman who had intercourse with 14-year-old Laura Herrington serves five years of his 12-year sentence for rape before being released for good behavior. After his release, he successfully runs for office and serves as a representative in the Alaska Territorial House of Representatives.

Blaec Lammers appeals his conviction for attempted mass shooting to the Missouri Supreme Court on the grounds that there is no evidence that he would have harmed anyone. His appeal is unsuccessful, and he remains in prison today.

Cannibal Cop Valle is released in 2014 when his case is overturned on appeal. He then writes a book entitled *Raw Deal: The Untold Story of NYPD's 'Cannibal Cop'*. He makes no secret of the fact that he continues to visit internet sites that explore the topic of cannibalism and the torture of women.[14]

Chapter Glossary

Attempt Liability: An overt act that is done with the intent to commit a crime but that falls short of completing the crime. Under the Model Penal Code, an attempt includes any act that is a substantial-step toward commission of a crime, such as enticing, lying in wait for, or following the intended victim, or unlawfully entering a building where the actor expects to commit a crime.[15]

Inchoate Offense: Crimes where liability attaches even though the crime may not have been completed. They generally involve at least taking a substantial-step toward committing a crime, preparing to commit a crime, enlisting others to commit a crime, or agreeing to commit a crime with another. Three common examples are the offenses of attempt, conspiracy, and solicitation.[16]

Proximity Test: A common-law test for the crime of attempt, focusing on whether the defendant is dangerously close to completing the offense. Factors include the gravity of the potential crime, the apprehension of the victim, and the certainty of the crime's occurrence.[17]

Resolute Intention: An existing intention to which the actor is firmly committed to carry out.

"Substantial Step" Test: The Model Penal Code's conduct requirement for attempt liability. A "substantial-step" is an act or omission toward commission of an offense, after forming an intention to commit the offense, that objectively manifests the actor's willingness to translate their criminal intention into criminal commission.[18]

Notes

1. This narrative is drawn from the following sources: Lael Morga, *Good Time Girls of the Alaska-Yukon Gold Rush* (Fairbanks: Epicenter Press, Inc., 1998), pp. 241–250; *Wooldridge v. United States*, 237 F. 775 (9th ed. 1916).
2. George Fletcher: Rethinking Criminal Law §3.3, Attempts (2000) (footnotes omitted).
3. Paul H. Robinson and Michael T. Cahill, *Criminal Law*, 2nd ed. (New York: Wolters Kluwer, 2016), p. 449.
4. Model Penal Code §5.01(2).
5. This narrative is drawn from the following sources: Todd C. Frankel, 'No Good Option: Parents Called Police on Mentally Ill Son, But He Got Prison, Not Help,' *The Washington Post*, 28 May 2014, https://www.washingtonpost.com/business/economy/no-good-option-parents-called-police-on-mentally-ill-son-but-he-got-prison-not-help/2014/05/28/d15e6fba-e6a7-11e3-a86b-362fd5443d19_story.html?utm_term=.1880aed841f7; 'Police: Mo. Man Planned Aurora-Type Attack,' *UPI*, 16 November 2012, http://www.upi.com/Top_News/US/2012/11/16/Police-Mo-man-planned-Aurora-type-attack/UPI-87411353105804/?spt=su; *State v. Lammers*. No. SC94977 (2016).

6. *State v. Lammers.*
7. Paul H. Robinson and Tyler Scot Williams, *Mapping American Criminal Law: Variations across the 50 States*, Chapter 11 (Westport: Prager, 2018). All supporting authorities are available from that source.
8. Robinson and Cahill, *Criminal Law*, pp. 455–460.
9. This narrative is drawn from the following sources: Joseph Goldstein, 'Officer Plotted to Abduct, Cook and Eat Women, Authorities Say,' *The New York Times*, 25 October 2012, http://www.nytimes.com/2012/10/26/nyregion/gilberto-valle-accused-in-plot-to-kidnap-women-and-cook-them.html; Robert Gearty, "Cannibal Cops' Wife Testifies on NYPD Officer's Sick Bondage Fetish,' *New York Daily News*, 26 February 2013, http://www.nytimes.com/2012/10/26/nyregion/gilberto-valle-accused-in-plot-to-kidnap-women-and-cook-them.html; Benjamin Weiser, 'Ex-Officer's Conviction in Cannibal Case Shouldn't Be Reinstated, Appeals Court Rules,' *The New York Times*, 3 December 2015, https://www.nytimes.com/2015/12/04/nyregion/appeals-court-gilberto-valle-cannibal-case.html?_r=0
10. Robert Gearty, "Cannibal Cop's' Wife Takes the Stand as Horrific Details of Former NYPD officer's Twisted Bondage Fetish Emerge in First Day of Trial', *New York Daily News*, 26 February 2013, https://www.nydailynews.com/new-york/cannibal-case-begins-article-1.1272996.
11. Goldstein, 'Officer Plotted to Abduct, Cook.'
12. Goldstein, 'Officer Plotted to Abduct, Cook.'
13. Weiser, 'Ex-Officer's Conviction in Cannibal Case.'
14. Larry McShane, "Cannibal Cop' Still Visits Websites Dedicated to Eating Human Flesh: 'There's Nothing Illegal',' *New York Daily News*, 9 February 2017, http://www.nydailynews.com/new-york/cannibal-visits-websites-dedicated-eating-humans-article-1.2967342.
15. MPC §5.01; *Attempt Liability*, Black's.
16. MPC art 5.
17. *Proximity Test*, Black's.
18. MPC §5.01.

Chapter 8

Complicity

The Haymarket Riots

1886. Sigmund Freud, a Moravian Jew whose radical notions of the workings of the inner mind will soon shock the world, opens his first psychotherapy practice in Vienna. Karl Benz patents the first gas-powered vehicle. The first production of aluminum occurs. Classified ads appear for the first time, in the *London Times*. And Coca-Cola (which did contain cocaine) is first sold in the United States. The year brings a new tide of immigrants to the United States. As boats enter New York Harbor, a brand-new Statue of Liberty welcomes them, standing on an island owned by New Jersey. The stream of immigrants serves to intensify the ongoing battles inspired by the growing American labor movement.

August Spies – 1886

August Spies comes to America from Germany as a teenager in the 1870s.[1] By 1883, he has become involved in the International Working People's Association (IWPA), whose mission is to engineer a social revolution to empower the working class. He and his associates criticize current societal institutions as promoting suffering and exploitation and argue for aggressive action against them. Spies often refers to dynamite as a "peacemaker."[2] It becomes a central topic in his speeches and articles, mostly as a means to frighten enemies and inspire action among supporters.

During the first half of 1886, union agitation and unemployment increase. New federal legislation will take effect that limits the workday to eight hours, but the Chicago factory owners are particularly vocal in their opposition to the new law and suggest that they will not adhere to it. To protest, large-scale work stoppages are being called for. The newspapers single out Spies and his group as the agitators organizing the protests and urge that they be held responsible if things turn ugly. All over the

DOI: 10.4324/9781003258025-9

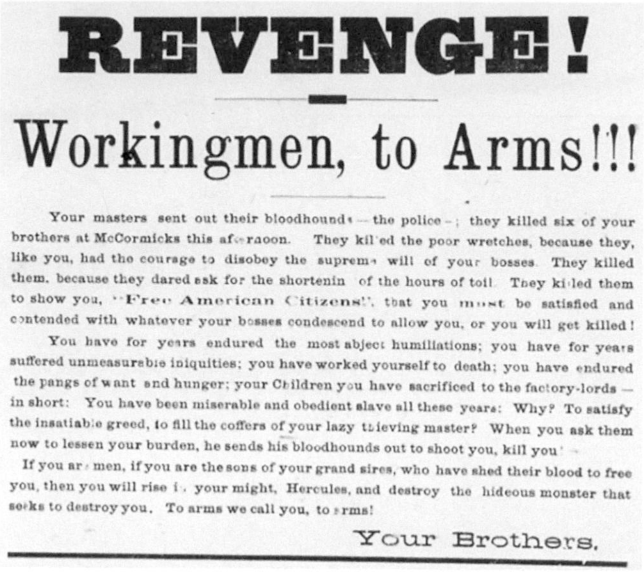

REVENGE!

Workingmen, to Arms!!!

Your masters sent out their bloodhounds — the police—; they killed six of your brothers at McCormicks this afternoon. They killed the poor wretches, because they, like you, had the courage to disobey the supreme will of your bosses. They killed them, because they dared ask for the shortening of the hours of toil. They killed them to show you, "Free American Citizens", that you must be satisfied and contended with whatever your bosses condescend to allow you, or you will get killed!

You have for years endured the most abject humiliations; you have for years suffered unmeasurable iniquities; you have worked yourself to death; you have endured the pangs of want and hunger; your Children you have sacrificed to the factory-lords — in short: You have been miserable and obedient slave all these years: Why? To satisfy the insatiable greed, to fill the coffers of your lazy thieving master? When you ask them now to lessen your burden, he sends his bloodhounds out to shoot you, kill you!

If you are men, if you are the sons of your grand sires, who have shed their blood to free you, then you will rise in your might, Hercules, and destroy the hideous monster that seeks to destroy you. To arms we call you, to arms!

Your Brothers.

Figure 8.1 A flyer written by Spies in advance of the rally, 1886

country, on May 1 hundreds of thousands of workers refuse to work, including 80,000 in Chicago.

The Chicago owners bring in "scabs" (nonunion workers) to do the work. On Monday, May 3, Spies is speaking at a rally for the Lumber Shovers Union outside the McCormick Reaper Works. A large group of "scabs" are leaving the factory after their day's shift and come within range of the rally. The strikers attack and a melee breaks out. Police led by Captain John Bonfield push into the crowd. The mass of workers jeer and throw stones at the outnumbered officers. Police swing their truncheons. Some officers, feeling under lethal attack, fire their revolvers, killing two workers.

Spies and many others are irate at seeing unarmed people being struck and fired upon. He returns to his office and writes an inflammatory article calling upon laborers to take a stand against their murderous oppressors. A public protest of the police attack is planned for the following evening. The protest is to be held at Haymarket Square on Randolph Street. Spies agrees to speak at the rally and produces some flyers to promote the view of many workers that the police violence of the previous night must be answered with violence. "If you are men, if you are the sons of your grand sires, who have shed their blood to free you, then you will rise in your might."

Spies arrives at 8:00 p.m. and discovers that none of the other speakers are not there yet. The crowd of 2,000–3,000 people is much smaller than anticipated.[3] Spies takes over the management of the event and hustles around to round up speakers. Chicago's mayor and a heavy police presence are on hand guarding against trouble. Rain begins to fall, and the crowd begins to move on. In order to salvage the event, Spies climbs onto a wagon and begins an impromptu speech. Other speakers are found.

When another speaker climbs up onto the wagon and begins to address the crowd, the mayor decides to head home and tells Captain Bonfield that "nothing has occurred yet or look[s] likely to occur to require interference."[4] Cold winds and rain return, so many from the rally start toward a popular bar called Zepf's Hall.

At 10:30 p.m., the rally has not yet fully wound down. Police Captain Bonfield assembles his force of 175 men and marches them through the crowd and up to the wagon that is being used to elevate the speakers. The police demand that the meeting disperse. The last speaker replies that they are simply having a peaceful meeting. Nonetheless, when the police repeat their demands, the speaker starts to climb down.

Suddenly, a bomb flies above the crowd, landing among the police who are standing by the speaker's wagon. Shrapnel flies outward and severs an artery in the left leg of Officer Matthias J. Degan, killing him. Chaos ensues, and policemen fire their revolvers in every direction. Police begin to use their clubs and the crowd scatters. Ultimately, seven policemen and at least four workers die. Sixty officers are injured, along with an unknown number of civilians. Many officers have limbs amputated.

Within a day, Spies and several others are arrested. A grand jury is assembled, and a 69-count indictment is issued against several dozen men for complicity in murder.[5] They are also indicted for conspiracy, riot, and unlawful assembly.

The defense provides evidence that Spies never left the wagon after his speech. Defense attorneys acknowledge that the defendant preached the use of dynamite and revolution, but that this was legal under the doctrine of free speech. The defense reminds everyone that no one knows who threw the bomb and therefore it is not possible to hold Spies guilty of complicity in doing so.

Figure 8.2 The explosion as portrayed in the news, 1886

Assistant State Attorney George Ingham closes the prosecution's argument by saying that "the great question which you are to answer by your verdict is whether the law of the State of Illinois is strong enough to protect itself."[6] After three hours of deliberation, the jury finds Spies and the other defendants guilty of complicity in the murder. Spies and most of the men are sentenced to death.

Complicity

If a person does not commit an offense him- or herself but helps another to do so, the person may be held liable for the offense under the doctrine of complicity (in earlier times called "aiding and abetting"). The person who serves as a lookout while his friend robs a bank does not satisfy the conduct requirements for bank robbery – he did not take money from a bank by force or threat – but his assistance to the perpetrator will make him legally accountable for the bank robber's conduct.

The law applied legal accountability for the criminal conduct of another even before it recognized a formal doctrine to do so in either tort or criminal law. As Sayre explains, "Such a doctrine rests upon natural reason and elementary principles of causation than upon any fiction of law."[7] When the defendant causes the death of another by hiring another to do the killing, one might conceive of the case as similar to the defendant who kills by planting a bomb. In the latter case, the causal chain includes the bomb; in the former case, the causal chain includes another person. Upon a causation analysis (recall Chapter 5), in both cases the defendant's own conduct is a but-for cause of the resulting death. The difference between the two cases might be seen as simply a proximate cause issue: whether the existence of a human actor in the causal chain somehow attenuates the defendant's causal accountability for the death. Thus, one could conceive of a legal system in which complicity cases were simply dealt with as an aspect of the causation issue.

But complicity did become a separate and distinct doctrine in criminal law by the 16th century or earlier.[8] First, the complicity rules usefully provide more specific guidance for adjudication than the more open-ended proximate cause assessment. Further, *complicity liability* was broadened to include more than cases where the defendant directed the offense conduct to include cases where the defendant assisted in it. Finally, a specific complicity doctrine was needed to sort out the specific culpability requirements that should be applied (an issue on which there continues to be difficulty and confusion even today).

At early common law, complicity liability was seen as derivative from and dependent upon the liability of the principal actor.

> For instance, until the eighteenth century no accessory could be convicted if his principal had died, had obtained benefit of clergy, or for any reason whatsoever had not been convicted; it was not until 1848 that in England it was made possible to indict, try, convict, and punish an accessory before the fact 'in all respects as if he were a principal felon.'[9]

The modern view assesses the liability of an accomplice based upon what he himself did and with what culpability he did it. The shift to this view can be seen as early as 1730.

> It is a point not to be disputed but that in criminal cases the principal is not answerable for the act of the deputy, as he is in civil cases; they must each answer for their own acts, and stand or fall by their own behaviour.[10]

Under current law, to be held liable for an offense as an accomplice – to have the perpetrator's offense conduct imputed to the aider – the person must aid or encourage the perpetrator in the commission of the offense (or, in some jurisdictions, the person must at least attempt to aid or agree to aid the perpetrator).[11] Further, at the time of aiding the perpetrator, the accomplice must have some culpable state of mind as to the fact that his conduct will aid the commission of the offense. In other words, it is not enough that the accomplice's conduct accidentally aided the perpetrator. At the time of aiding the perpetrator, he must intend to or know that his conduct is assisting.[12]

States disagree as to whether purpose or knowledge should be required. Some states require that the accomplice purposely aid the offense.[13] These states require that the accomplice wanted or hoped that his conduct would aid the perpetrator in the offense. Other states require only that the accomplice knowingly aid the offense.[14]

In addition to this special culpability requirement as to aiding commission, the accomplice must satisfy the culpability requirements included in the offense definition itself. The complicity doctrine imputes to the accomplice only the perpetrator's *conduct* constituting the offense, not the perpetrator's *culpable state of mind*. For example, one cannot be an accomplice to manslaughter (reckless homicide) unless, at the time of

Liability for Conduct of Another; Complicity.

    (1) A person is guilty of an offense if it is committed by his own conduct or by the conduct of another person for which he is legally accountable, or both.

    (2) A person is legally accountable for the conduct of another person when: …

  (c) he is an accomplice of such other person in the commission of the offense.

    (3) A person is an accomplice of another person in the commission of an offense if:

    (a) with the purpose of promoting or facilitating the commission of the offense, he

    (i) solicits such other person to commit it; or

    (ii) aids or agrees or attempts to aid such other person in planning or committing it; or

    (iii) having a legal duty to prevent the commission of the offense, fails to make proper effort so to do; …

Model Penal Code §2.06

Figure 8.3

providing the assistance, one is at least reckless as to causing the death. In other words, to be held liable as an accomplice, the person must purposely (or, depending upon the jurisdiction, knowingly) aid the perpetrator and at the time he provides such aid he must also be aware that such conduct creates a substantial risk of causing death (the traditional culpability requirements for manslaughter). For instance, a person may be held liable as an accomplice to manslaughter if he gives his car keys to his drunk friend intentionally aiding him in the conduct of driving drunk and, at the same time, is reckless – i.e., aware of a substantial risk – that the drunk driving creates a substantial risk of causing death. When his drunken friend in fact kills someone, the person may be held liable for manslaughter as an accomplice in causing the death.[15]

Did Spies satisfy the requirements for complicity in the murder of the police officers? His conduct in organizing the rally certainly was a but-for cause of the death – no rally, no death – which is a stronger causal connection than the complicity doctrine requires: one can be liable for complicity even if the assistance one provides is not actually necessary for commission. And Spies' flyer calling for "Revenge!" and urging people to "destroy the hideous monster" and pleading "To arms we call you, to arms!" could easily be seen as calling for just the kind of lethal attack on police that occurred and at the time and place Spies was calling for it.

However, the prosecution did not have specific evidence of Spies giving directions to the person who actually threw the bomb. Perhaps his only communication with that person was his flyer. Typically, encouragement is enough to satisfy the assistance requirement for complicity. But is it clear that Spies satisfies the culpability requirement for complicity to murder? Did he intend (hope or desire) to encourage the killings? As noted, the law at the time found the requirements for complicity to murder satisfied.

Compare this to the rules applied in a more modern case.

Cardinal Bernard Law – 2003

Father John Geoghan is ordained as a Catholic priest in 1962 and assigned to the Blessed Sacrament Parish in a working-class community outside Boston.[16] It soon becomes clear that Father Geoghan has a dark side – he begins sexually abusing young boys and girls in his parish. After enough allegations surface, the archdiocese in 1967 removes Geoghan from Blessed Sacrament and transfers him to St. Paul's, another parish outside Boston. The cycle of abuse, removal, and re-assignment continues for several decades.

In March of 1984, Bernard Francis Law becomes the Archbishop of Boston, and later that year Margaret Gallant writes to Law to inform him of Geoghan's history of molestation. On October 31, Law assigns Geoghan to St. Julia's Parish in Weston, a wealthy Boston suburb. He informs the parish priest, Monsignor Rossiter, of Geoghan's history. Under the watch of Law and Rossiter, Geoghan continues to supervise altar boys and two youth groups. Law allows this in part because of his Christian values of forgiveness and the possibility of redemption.

In 1985, Law is presented with research on the prevalence of sexual abuse by clergy members. The report states that the rate of repeat offenders among pedophiles is high, and controlled studies conclude that "traditional outpatient psychiatric or psychological treatment DOES NOT WORK." In addition, they observe that pedophilia is "a lifelong disease with NO HOPE AT THIS TIME FOR A CURE."[17]

More and more victims approach the Boston Archdiocese with allegations of abuse, and the church begins paying out settlements on claims against more than 70 priests.

Figure 8.4 Cardinal Bernard Law around the time of his appointment as Archbishop of Boston, circa 1984–1985

In 1986, the Department of Social Services and Boston Police receive complaints about Geoghan from parishioners at yet another church. Cardinal Law pulls Geoghan from service and Geoghan is sent to a program that attempts to reform sex-offending priests. Despite clear information that this type of offender cannot be reformed, upon completion of the program Law allows Geoghan to return to active service and access to children. A 1995 sexual assault leads to additional charges against Geoghan. On August 4, 1996, Law places Geoghan on sick leave for a time, but eventually Geoghan is allowed back in service.

In 1998 Geoghan is forced from the priesthood. The archdiocese headed by Cardinal Law is aware of at least 130 victims. Geoghan blames the children, saying that they were from disturbed homes and, as a result, were ready to accuse anyone. "I don't think they were able to distinguish between normal and abnormal, good or bad, right or wrong."[18]

Law understands that the crimes are not limited to Geoghan. When another victim files suit, the Archdiocese is compelled to make public their confidential files on other priests. The records contain allegations dating back to 1967 and include the names of 90 priests accused of abuse. In 2002 Law writes of the events in his Good Friday letter:

> Betrayal hangs like a heavy cloud over the church today. . . While we do not presume to judge anyone's relationship with God, there is no doubt that a betrayal of trust is at the heart of the evil in the sexual abuse of children by clergy. Priests should be trustworthy beyond any shadow of a doubt. When some have broken that trust, all of us suffer the consequences.[19]

In the first four months of 2002, more than 500 people in the Boston Archdiocese retain counsel for alleged abuse incidents.

Law is named as a defendant in a lawsuit of 14 plaintiffs brought against another Boston priest accused of sexual abuse. On April 10, Law addresses churchgoers before a Mass, saying

> I acknowledge my own responsibility for decisions which led to intense suffering. While that suffering was never intended, it could have been avoided had I acted differently. I see this now with a clarity that has been heightened through the experience of these past 10 months.[20]

On July 23, an official report details its findings of abuse by Roman Catholic priests in the archdiocese. It concludes that for six decades, at least 237 priests and 13 other church employees molested more than 789 children. There is evidence to suggest that the real figure is probably more than 1,000 children.[21]

Attorney General Reilly convenes a grand jury to determine if there is enough evidence to bring criminal charges against Law and other leaders of the Archdiocese. They conclude that the law in Massachusetts requires that an accomplice share the intent of the person committing the offense, making it unlikely that criminal charges will be brought against any member of the administration. After all, while Law knew of the abuse and his facilitation of it, he did not intend (hope or desire) for the abuse to occur.

Attorney General Reilly concludes that the cover-up that allowed the abuse to continue was deliberate. "They knew they were under no obligation to report. These were deliberate choices." He asserts that church officials saw their primary mission as "safeguarding the well-being of priests and the institution." Despite that deliberateness, he concludes that the state of the law precludes prosecution. (As is shown on the map below, Massachusetts still requires purpose/intention for complicity liability.)

Current Diversity in Complicity Liability Rules

One could conclude that both Spies and Cardinal Law did assist in the offense, the killing and the sexual abuse, respectively. The killing would not have occurred but for Spies' organizing the second rally and encouraging the workers to come armed and ready for a fight. His "Revenge!" flyer is the kind of evidence the government is likely to present on this point. Similarly, the sexual abuse of the children would not have occurred but for Cardinal Law placing the offending priests in a new parish in contact with children without always warning anyone of the danger.

As noted, however, assisting by itself is not enough for *complicity liability*. Both Spies and Cardinal Law did intentionally engage in the conduct that aided the offense – they didn't accidentally make up the flyer or accidentally transfer the priest without warning. But that is not enough to establish complicity: it must also be shown that it was their purpose (or in some jurisdictions, they knew) that their conduct would aid the perpetrator's offense.

Was it Spies' purpose to aid the bombing? As noted above, he might argue that he did not want or hope for the bombing to occur; thus, the purpose requirement is not satisfied and no complicity liability would be possible. (If the jurisdiction required only knowingly aiding, as some do, this would be easier for the prosecution to prove. But on the facts of Spies' case, it is possible that the prosecution could prove only that

Spies was aware of a risk that his conduct in organizing the rally and encouraging "revenge" might aid the bombing – in other words, that he was reckless but not purposeful or knowing. Such recklessness would normally not be enough for complicity liability.)

In the case of Cardinal Law, it is probably clear that the Cardinal did not want or hope to assist in the sexual abuse. Indeed, he might even argue that he did not even know that his conduct would assist sexual abuse. (Under many modern codes, knowledge commonly requires that one be "practically certain" that a result will occur.) It is probably the case that the Cardinal was at most reckless as to assisting sexual abuse. That is, he probably knew that his conduct in assisting the pedophile priest created a substantial risk that sexual abuse might occur. If that were the situation, then he could not be liable in a jurisdiction that required purpose, or even knowledge. (He could be liable only if a jurisdiction allowed complicity liability for recklessly assisting an offense.) Recall that Cardinal Law was not prosecuted. The high culpability requirement for complicity probably explains why he was not.

Some states go beyond these standard requirements for complicity liability and significantly expand the potential for complicity liability by adopting what is commonly called the *natural and probable consequence* rule. In these jurisdictions, once a person is held liable for an offense as an accomplice, the person is deemed to also be liable for any offense committed by another that is the "natural and probable consequence" of the offense for which the person is an accomplice. Thus, an actor who is liable as an accomplice to a bank robbery may be held liable for a homicide committed by the perpetrator during the robbery if the perpetrator's killing is judged to be *a* natural and probable consequence of the robbery plan, even where the state cannot prove that the robbery accomplice was purposeful or knowing as to assisting the death.

The natural and probable consequence rule has a significant effect in undercutting the traditional heightened culpability requirements for complicity for any offense beyond the original offense for which the person is an accomplice. That is, the standard requirements for complicity must still be proven in relation to the bank robbery but not in relation to the subsequent killing during the robbery. As the map below suggests, while some states have adopted the natural and probable consequence rule,[22] others have rejected it.[23]

The natural and probable consequence rule would make it easier to hold Spies liable for the police deaths. If Spies was an accomplice to an unlawful assembly where violence was urged, for example, the prosecution could argue that the killing of the officer was the natural and probable consequence of the unlawful violence-prone assembly Spies helped organize. Note in the map below that Illinois adopts a purpose requirement for complicity but also adopts the natural and probable consequence rule (while Massachusetts, where the Cardinal Law case arose, rejects the natural and probable consequence rule).

The map below shows the position of each state regarding each of these two central issues: the culpability requirements for complicity liability (light and dark shading) and the adoption of the natural and probable consequence rule (dots overlay).[24]

Thirty-eight states, those without shading, require purpose, while only 13, those with shading, require only knowledge. Purpose is also required by the Model Penal Code, quoted in the margin above. Thirty states, without a dots overlay, and the Model Penal Code reject the natural and probable consequence rule. Twenty-one states retain it from common law.

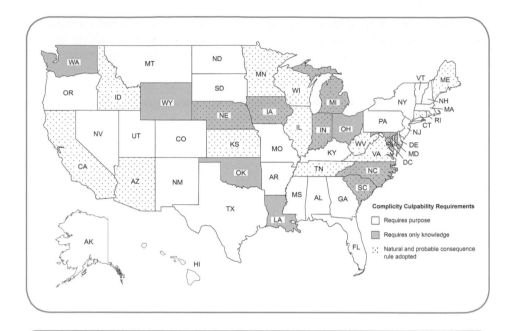

Complicity Culpability Requirements

☐ Requires purpose

☐ Requires only knowledge

∴ Natural and probable consequence rule adopted

Figure 8.5

What Should Be the Culpability Requirements for Complicity?

The culpability requirements for *complicity liability* have created enormous confusion and disagreement. Even the American Law Institute, which drafted the Model Penal Code upon which three-quarters of the state penal codes are based, hotly debated the issue and ended up adopting a rule different from that recommended by its drafting committee. After many years of work, that committee recommended the Model Code require only knowing as to aiding the offense but at the end of the floor debates the Institute membership voted to adopt a purpose requirement.

But the greater source of disagreement, to some extent still unresolved today, is the question of what that culpability requirement actually means. To what does it apply? Does it require the actor to be purposeful (or knowing, jurisdictions that allow this) *as to his conduct* – i.e., his conduct was not accidental – and purposeful (or knowing) as to the fact that his conduct *will aid the perpetrator's offense conduct*? There seems to be a general agreement that it does require at least these two things.

Does it also require that the actor be purposeful (or knowing) as to *all the elements of the offense*, which includes not only the perpetrator's conduct but also the circumstances and results of his conduct that make it criminal.[25] (Recall that this is how the purpose requirement is interpreted in the context of attempt liability, discussed in the previous chapter.) For example, to be an accomplice to a homicide, must the prosecution prove only that the accomplice was purposeful as to aiding the perpetrator's conduct causing death? (Perhaps he intentionally gave him a ride to the crime scene.) Or, must the accomplice also be purposeful as to the perpetrator causing the death itself? (When he gave the perpetrator a ride, did he do so because he wanted to help kill the victim?)

The Model Penal Code drafters provide some clarity on this issue in Section 2.06(4) by explicitly providing that the actor need *not* be purposeful as to a *result element* of the substantive offense: one can be an accomplice to murder, for example, by purposely aiding the perpetrator's conduct even without desiring the resulting death. (The extent of the accomplice's liability will be based upon whatever his level of culpability as to causing the death. If he purposely aided the perpetrator while being only reckless as to whether that assistance would bring about the death, then he can only be liable for complicity in reckless homicide.)

However, the Model Code's official commentary openly concedes that it is unclear whether the "purpose" requirement in complicity should be interpreted to apply to other kinds of offense elements, such as *circumstance* elements. For example, to be an accomplice to statutory rape, must the accomplice intend the partner to be underage or is it enough that he was purposeful as to assisting – that is, for example, he gave a ride to the assignation site and was only aware of a substantial risk that the partner was underage? This unresolved issue is a significant practical problem because the vast majority of offenses are defined by circumstance elements. (Result elements appear in homicide, assault, property destruction offenses, and a few others, but those offenses represent a relatively small proportion of a criminal code's offense definitions.)

On policy grounds, the ALI was probably wrong to have adopted the more demanding purpose requirement instead of a knowing requirement,[26] but at least they, and the 24 states without shading or dots on the map above, are being internally consistent when they then reject the dramatic broadening of liability that comes with adopting a *natural and probable consequence rule*. Both of these positions make the complicity requirements more demanding.

One might think that a better position is the balance struck by the six states with shading and no dots on the map, who adopt the lower knowing requirement, as recommended by the original Model Penal Code drafting group, but reject the *natural probable consequence rule*.

The seven states with shading and dots can also claim at least a rational and internally consistent position when they adopt the lower knowing requirement and also adopt the natural and probable consequence rule. Just as the first group is trying to maximize the requirements for complicity liability, this group of states is consistent in trying to minimize those requirements.

What seems odd, however, is the position taken by the 14 states with no shading but with dots. They reject the knowing requirement in favor of the more demanding purpose requirement, but then dramatically subvert the culpability requirements for complicity by adopting the natural and probable consequence rule. It is hard to imagine a rational explanation for these two seemingly contradictory positions. One can only assume that this is an unfortunate result of the confusion that reigned at common law and that to some extent has carried over into American criminal codes of today.

Aftermaths

In the Haymarket riot case, the Amnesty Association sets to work collecting tens of thousands of signatures for a petition asking Illinois Governor Richard Oglesby to grant clemency for Spies and others convicted in the Haymarket Affair. The anarchists themselves are resistant to this because they fear accepting clemency will be seen both as an admission of guilt and as recognition of an authority that they view as illegitimate.

Just before noon on November 11, 1887, the condemned men process in a single-file line to the gallows at the north end of the jail. More than 150 reporters and witnesses are in attendance. The anarchists have their legs and arms bound and their bodies draped in white shrouds. The executioner covers their heads with a hood and ties a noose around their necks. Spies declares "the time will come when our silence will be more powerful than the voices you are throttling today." Another of the convicts yells "let me speak, Sheriff Matson. Let the voice of the people be heard." However, before he can continue, the executioner pulls the lever. The floor drops out from under them, and all the defendants drop to their death. The dead men are taken through the streets to Waldheim Cemetery. An estimated 200,000 people watch the procession.

In 1893, the famous attorney Clarence Darrow renews efforts to obtain clemency for the men convicted in the affair who have not been executed. The new Governor, John Altgeld, pardons several of them.

In the Cardinal Law case, former priest Geoghan, while housed at the Souza-Baranowski maximum security prison, is beaten and strangled to death by another inmate. Though he is held in a protective-confinement ward, the killer is able to jam the door to Geoghan's cell, preventing guards from entering the cell while the murder is committed. The killer takes action because he overhears Geoghan on the phone making plans to regain access to children upon his release by moving to South America.

In May 2004, Pope John Paul II appoints Law to a ceremonial position overseeing one of the four major basilicas of Rome. The appointment infuriates many critics, but the Vatican offers no explanation. Over the objections from clergy-abuse victims, Law is chosen to say a Mass of Mourning for Pope John Paul II on April 11, 2005. Law remains a cardinal, serves on eight important Vatican congregations and councils, and participates in the 2005 election of Pope Benedict XVI. He dies from diabetes at a hospital in Rome on December 20, 2017.

Chapter Glossary

Complicity Liability: A basis of liability under which one person (the accomplice) is held accountable for the conduct of another (the principal). An accomplice commonly faces the same degree of guilt and punishment as the individual who commits the crime. The key consideration is whether the individual intentionally and voluntarily encouraged or assisted in the commission of the offense or, in special cases, failed to prevent it.[27]

Natural and Probable Consequence Rule: This common-law rule extended accomplice liability to include offences beyond those for which the accomplice satisfies the normal requirements for complicity, imposing liability for any offense that was a reasonably foreseeable result of the offense for which the defendant was an accomplice.[28]

Result Element: A result element within an offense definition is a consequence – a change in the existing physical state of the world – caused by the actor's conduct. A required result will not be satisfied unless the actor's offense conduct caused the result in such a way as to satisfy the criminal law's causation requirements. Most offense definitions do not contain a result element but instead require only of certain conduct under certain circumstances. However, some important offenses, most notably homicide and property destruction offenses, do include a result element.

Notes

1. This narrative is drawn from the following sources: Carl Smith, 'Act I: Subterranean Fire,' *Chicago History Resources: The Dramas of Haymarket*, Chicago Historical Society, 2000, http://chicagohistoryresources.org/dramas/act1/act1.htm; Carl Smith, 'Act II: Let Your Tragedy Be Enacted Here,' *Chicago History Resources: The Dramas of Haymarket*, Chicago Historical Society, 2000, http://chicagohistoryresources.org/dramas/act2/act2.htm; Carl Smith, 'Act III: Toils of the Law,' *Chicago History Resources: The Dramas of Haymarket*, Chicago Historical Society, 2000, http://chicagohistoryresources.org/dramas/act3/act3.htm; Carl Smith, 'Act IV: Let the Voice of the People Be Heard,' *Chicago History Resources: The Dramas of Haymarket*, http://www.chicagohistoryresources.org/dramas/act4/act4.htm; August Spies, 'An Auto-Biographical Sketch by A. Spies,' *UMKC School of Law*, 1886, http://law2.umkc.edu/faculty/projects/ftrials/haymarket/autobiographies.html; 'Blood on the Square: The Haymarket Riot and Trial,' *Haymarket Affair Blog*, accessed 16 July 2020, http://haymarketaffair.blogspot.ca/; James Green, *Death in the Haymarket: A Story of Chicago, the First Labor Movement, and the Bombing that Divided Gilded Age America* (New York: Anchor, 2007); 'Eight Anarchists,' *PBS: American Experience*, accessed 16 July 2020, https://www.pbs.org/wgbh/americanexperience/features/-chicago-eight-anarchists/; Albert Parsons, 'An Appeal to the People of America,' *Chicago History Resources*, 1887, http://www.chicagohistoryresources.org/dramas/act4/fromTheArchive/toThePeopleOfAmerica_f.htm; 'Remembering the Haymarket Riot,' *History*, 4 May 2016, https://www.history.com/news/remembering-the-haymarket-riot; 'Illinois Supreme Court Decision in the Haymarket Case (1887),' *Famous Trials*, 14 September 1887, https://famous-trials.com/haymarket/1176-courtdecision; 'Autobiography of August Spies,' *Anarchy Archives*, accessed 16 July 2020, http://dwardmac.pitzer.edu/Anarchist_Archives/haymarket/spiesauto.html;
2. Smith, 'Act I: Subterranean Fire.'
3. They hoped for 20,000 people to attend. *See* 'Haymarket Square Riot,' *United States History*, accessed 16 July 2020, http://www.u-s-history.com/pages/h750.html.
4. 'Blood on the Square.'
5. The men are charged with only one homicide. No official explanation is given for this, but speculation is that it is because Degan's death was the only one attributable to just the bomb and not the ensuing gunfire.
6. Smith, 'Act III: Toils of the Law.'
7. Francis Bowes Sayre, 'Criminal Responsibility for the Acts of Another,' *Harvard Law Review 43*, no. 5 (1930): pp. 689–723, https://www.jstor.org/stable/1330727.
8. *See, e.g.,* William Staunford, 'Pleas of the Crown' (1557), as discussed in Pollock and Maitland, *History of English Law 2* (1898): p. 509.
9. Francis Bowes Sayre, 'Development of the Criminal Law Concerning Vicarious Responsibility,' *Harvard Law Review 43* (1930): p. 689.
10. Sayre, 'Development of the Criminal Law,' p. 701, quoting C.J. Raymond.
11. Paul H. Robinson and Michael T. Cahill, *Criminal Law*, 2nd ed. (New York: Wolters Kluwer, 2016), §4.1.2.
12. Robinson and Cahill, *Criminal Law*.
13. Ala. Code § 13A-2-23; Alaska Stat. Ann. § 11.16.110; Ariz. Rev. Stat. Ann. § 13-301; Ark. Code Ann. § 5-2-403; *People v. Beeman* 35 Cal. 3d 547 (1984); Colo. Rev. Stat. Ann. § 18-1-603; Conn. Gen. Stat. Ann. § 53a-8; *State v. Fruean* 63 Conn. App. 466 (2001); Del. Code Ann. tit. 11, § 271; *Fulford v. State* 311 So.2d 203 (1975); Ga. Code Ann. § 16-2-20; Haw. Rev. Stat. Ann. § 702-222; *State v. Reid* 253 P.3d 754 (2010);

State v. Mitchell 146 Idaho 378 (2008); 720 Ill. Comp. Stat. Ann. 5/5-2; Kan. Stat. Ann. § 21-5210; Ky. Rev. Stat. Ann. § 502.020; Me. Rev. Stat. tit. 17-A, § 57; *Commonwealth v. Filos* 420 Mass. 348 (1995); *Robinson v. Cook* 863 F. Supp. 2d 49, 67 (D. Mass. 2012), aff'd, 706 F.3d 25 (1st Cir. 2013) (applying Massachusetts law); Minn. Stat. Ann. § 609.05; *Milano v. State* 790 So. 2d 179 (2001); Mo. Ann. Stat. § 562.041; Mont. Code Ann. § 45-2-302; *Tanksley v. State* 944 P.2d 240 (1997); *Bolden v. State* 124 P.3d 191 (2005); N.H. Rev. Stat. Ann. § 626:8; *State v. Anthony* 151 N.H. 492 (2004); N.J. Stat. Ann. § 2C:2-6; *State v. Torres* 183 N.J. 554 (2005); *State v. Vigil* 2010-NMSC-003, 147 N.M. 537, 540, 226 P.3d 636, 639; *State v. Bankert* 1994-NMSC-052, 117 N.M. 614, 618, 875 P.2d 370, 374; *State v. Carrasco* 1997-NMSC-047, 124 N.M. 64, 68, 946 P.2d 1075, 1079; N.Y. Penal Law § 20.00 ("intentionally aids"); *People v. Johnson* 238 A.D.2d 267, 267, 657 N.Y.S.2d 27, 28 (1997); N.D. Cent. Code Ann. § 12.1-03-01; Or. Rev. Stat. Ann. § 161.155; 18 Pa. Stat. and Cons. Stat. Ann. § 306; *State v. Delestre* 35 A.3d 886 (2012); S.D. Codified Laws § 22-3-3; Tenn. Code Ann. § 39-11-402; Tex. Penal Code Ann. § 7.02; Utah Code Ann. § 76-2-202; *McGill v. Commonwealth* 24 Va. App. 728 (1997); *Taylor v. Commonwealth* 31 Va. App. 54 (1999); *State v. Mullins* 193 W. Va. 315, 319, 456 S.E.2d 42, 46 (1995); *State v. Hoselton* 371 S.E.2d 366 (1988); *State v. West* 153 W. Va. 325 (1969); Wis. Stat. Ann. § 939.05.

14. *Byrd v. United States* 364 A.2d 1215, 1219 (1976); *Murchison v. United States* 486 A.2d 77, 81 (1984); *Johnson v. United States* 883 A.2d 135, 142 (2005); Ind. Code Ann. § 35-41-2-4; Iowa Code Ann. § 703.2; *State v. Lott* 255 N.W.2d 105, 109 (1977); *State v. Neal* 796 So. 2d 649 (2001); *State v. Knowles* 392 So. 2d 651, 657 (1980); *State v. Wright* 834 So. 2d 974 (2002); *State v. Fernandez* 50 So. 3d 219 (2010); *State v. Anderson* 691 So. 2d 336 (1997); *State v. Carpenter* 772 So. 2d 200 (2000); *Davis v. State* 207 Md. App. 298, 303, 52 A.3d 148 (2012); *State v. Williams* 397 Md. 172, 195, 916 A.2d 294, 308 (2007); *People v. King* 210 Mich. App. 425, 431, 534 N.W.2d 534, 537 (1995); Monica Lyn Schroth, 'Reckless Aiding and Abetting: Sealing the Cracks That Publishers of Instructional Materials Fall Through,' *Southwestern University Law Review* 29 (2000): p. 567 ("The state of Michigan dispensed with the intent requirement and sets the mens rea at mere knowledge of the perpetrator's criminal purpose. Michigan allows for . . . complicity liability . . . where the aider and abettor knows that the principal has the requisite intent."); *State v. Barfield* 272 Neb. 502, 520, 723 N.W.2d 303, 317–318 (2006); *State v. Mantich* 249 Neb. 311, 324, 543 N.W.2d 181, 191 (1996) (Accomplice liability attaches where defendant "either personally intended" the offense commission or "aided another person whom the [defendant] knew had such an intent."); *State v. Bass* 255 N.C. 42, 51, 120 S.E.2d 580, 587 (1961); *State v. Sauls* 291 N.C. 253, 257, 230 S.E.2d 390, 393 (1976); *State v. Williams* 28 N.C. App. 320, 322–323, 220 S.E.2d 856, 858 (1976); *State v. Sutton* 41 N.C. App. 603, 605, 255 S.E.2d 331, 333 (1979); *State v. Bond* 345 N.C. 1, 24, 478 S.E.2d 163, 175 (1996); *State v. Allen* 127 N.C. App. 182, 185, 488 S.E.2d 294, 296 (1997); *State v. Smith* 1-05-39 (2006) (stating that knowledge is required for complicity); *Conover v. State* OK CR 6 933 P.2d 904 (1997); *Yetter v. State* OK CR 193 528 P.2d 345 (1974); *Bowie v. State* OK CR 4 906 P.2d 759 (1995); *Postelle v. State* 2011 OK CR 30, ¶ 15, 267 P.3d 114, 126–127 (2011); Vernon's Okla. Forms 2d, OUJI-CR 2-6 (pattern jury instruction permitting liability where defendant "knowingly did what he/she did either with criminal intent or with knowledge of the [perpetrator's] intent"); *State v. Reid* 408 S.C. 461, 473, 758 S.E.2d 904, 910 (2014); *State v. Leonard* 292 S.C. 133, 137, 355 S.E.2d 270, 272 (1987); Wash. Rev. Code Ann. § 9A.08.020; Wyo. Stat. Ann. § 6-1-201.

15. These are similar to the facts in *State v. Etzweiler* 480 A.2d 870 (1984).

16. This narrative is drawn from the following sources: the Investigative Staff of the Boston Globe, *Betrayal: The Crisis in the Catholic Church* (Boston: Back Bay Books, 2003); 'Geoghan's Troubled History,' *The Boston Globe: Spotlight Investigation*, accessed 16 July 2020, http://archive.boston.com/globe/spotlight/abuse/stories/010702_history.htm; Leon J. Podles, 'The Murder of Rev. John J. Geoghan: A Case Study of Sexual Abuse and Murder,' *Crossland Foundation*, 8 November 2008, http://podles.org/case-studies/Rev-John-Geoghan-murder.htm; Denise Noe, 'Pedophile Priest: the Crimes of Father Geoghan,' *Crime Magazine*, 1 December 2003, http://www.bishop-accountability.org/news2003_07_12/2003_12_01_Noe_PedophilePriest.htm.

17. 'Reporting an Explosive Truth: The *Boston Globe* and Sexual Abuse in the Catholic Church,' *The Journalism School: Knight Case Studies Initiative, Columbia University*, http://ccnmtl.columbia.edu/projects/caseconsortium/casestudies/14/casestudy/files/global/14/Boston%20Globe%20and%20Sexual%20Abuse%20in%20the%20Catholic%20Church_wm.pdf.

18. Staff of the Boston Globe, 'Betrayal.'

19. Staff of the Boston Globe, 'Betrayal.'

20. 'The Rupturing of that Sacred Trust,' *The Boston Globe*, 4 November 2002, http://archive.boston.com/globe/spotlight/abuse/stories3/110402_text.htm.

21. Michael Paulson, 'Diocese Gives Abuse Data,' *The Boston Globe*, 27 February 2014, https://archive.boston.com/globe/spotlight/abuse/stories5/022704_data.htm.

22. Ariz. Rev. Stat. Ann. § 13-301; *People v. Durham* 70 Cal.2d 171, 181, 74 Cal. Rptr. 262, 449 P.2d 198, 204 (1969); *People v. Prettyman* 14 Cal.4th 248, 58 Cal.Rptr.2d 827, 926 P.2d 1013 (1996); *State v. Henry* 253 Conn. 354, 362, 752 A.2d 40, 45 (2000); *Chance v. State* 685 A.2d 351, 358 (1996); *State v. Ehrmantrout* 100 Idaho 202, 202, 595 P.2d 1097, 1097 (1979); *People v. Kessler* 57 Ill. 2d 493, 497, 315 N.E.2d 29, 32 (1974); *Richardson v. State* 697 N.E.2d 462, 465 (1998); Iowa Code Ann. § 703.2; Kan. Stat. Ann. § 21-5210; Me. Rev. Stat. tit. 17-A, § 57; *State v. Linscott* 520 A.2d 1067, 1070 (1987); *Sheppard v. State* 312 Md. 118, 123, 538 A.2d 773, 775 (1988); *Watkins v. State* 357 Md. 258, 265, 744 A.2d 1, 4 (2000); *People v. Robinson* 475 Mich. 1, 8–9, 715 N.W.2d 44, 49 (2006); Minn. Stat. Ann. § 609.05; *State v. Leonor* 263 Neb. 86, 97, 638 N.W.2d 798, 807 (2002); *State v. Gorham* 212 N.C. App. 236, 713 S.E.2d 252 (2011); *State v. Delestre* 35 A.3d 886, 892 (2012); *State v. Williams* 189 S.C. 19, 199 S.E. 906, 908 (1938); *State v. Richmond* 90 S.W.3d 648, 656 (2002); *Charlton v. Commonwealth* 32 Va. App. 47, 52, 526 S.E.2d 289, 291 (2000); *State v. Rodoussakis* 204 W. Va. 58, 77, 511 S.E.2d 469, 488 (1998); Wis. Stat. Ann. § 939.05.

23. Among these jurisdictions, many state courts have expressly or impliedly rejected the rule. *See, e.g., Riley v. State* 60 P.3d 204, 214 (2002); *Bogdanov v. People* 941 P.2d 247, 251 (1997); *Wilson-Bey v. United States* 903 A.2d 818, 830 (2006); *Commonwealth v. Richards* 363 Mass. 299, 307–308, 293 N.E.2d 854, 860 (1973); *State v. Ferguson* 20 S.W.3d 485, 497 (2000); State ex rel. Keyes v. Montana Thirteenth Judicial Dist. 955 P.2d 639 (1998); *Sharma v. State* 118 Nev. 648, 654, 56 P.3d 868, 872 (2002); *State v. Carrasco* 1997-NMSC-047, 124 N.M. 64, 68, 946 P.2d 1075, 1079; *State v. Lopez-Minjarez* 350 Or. 576, 583, 260 P.3d 439, 443 (2011); *Commonwealth v. Knox* 629 Pa. 467, 471, 105 A.3d 1194, 1197 (2014); *State v. Bacon* 163 Vt. 279, 289, 658 A.2d 54, 62 (1995); *State v. Stein* 144 Wash. 2d 236, 246, 27 P.3d 184, 189 (2001).

24. The map is taken from Paul H. Robinson and Tyler Scot Williams, *Mapping American Criminal Law: Variations across the 50 States* (Westport: Prager, 2018), ch. 12. All supporting authorities are available from that source.

25. The confusion is the product of an essential weakness of the old judge-made common-law rules that predate the modern codes enacted by legislatures: those who shaped the common-law doctrine made the false assumption that every offense had a single culpable state of mind attached to it, when in fact offenses may be comprised of multiple elements each with a different culpability requirement. *See* Paul H. Robinson and Michael T. Cahill, *Criminal Law*, 2nd ed. (New York: Wolters Kluwer, 2016), §4.1.2.
26. Robinson and Cahill, *Criminal Law*.
27. Robinson and Cahill, *Criminal Law*, §6.1.
28. Robinson and Cahill, *Criminal Law*, §6.1.

Chapter 9

Conspiracy

Lincoln's Non-Assassins

1865. Gregor Mendel is living as a monk in Austria when he works out the basics of the laws of heredity. If monks can be scientists, then mathematicians can be novelists: Lewis Carroll publishes *Alice's Adventures in Wonderland*. In Scotland, successful treatments by Glasgow doctor Joseph Lister support the accuracy of the new germ theory of infection. The advance comes too late for the men still dying on American Civil War battlefields, where two-thirds of the 620,000 deaths are the result of infection or disease. The truth that the South will not prevail is now clear to all. And there are many people who are violently outraged by what they see as the North's treacherous destruction of the South and its way of life.

Samuel Arnold – 1865

In 1852, young Samuel Arnold is sent to St. Timothy's Military Academy in Maryland, where he meets another student named John Wilkes Booth, who becomes a fast friend.[1] Arnold subsequently joins the Confederate Army at the start of the Civil War, but his service is short because of health problems.

In the summer of 1864, Booth reaches out to his old school mate and invites him to meet at the Barnum Hotel in Baltimore. There Arnold is introduced to a childhood friend of Booth's. Over cigars and whiskey, Booth outlines for the two men his plan to kidnap President Lincoln when he visits wounded soldiers at a local hospital. They would seize his carriage and take him to Richmond to be held hostage until the North agrees to release the Southern POWs.

Arnold, who is currently unemployed and bored, has always felt uncomfortable about the shortness of his military service. He does not want to be seen as uncommitted to the cause, so he agrees to help Booth. After the meeting, however, communication between the two men ceases.

DOI: 10.4324/9781003258025-10

Several months later, in January 1865, Booth contacts Arnold again and has a new plan, but again nothing ever comes of it. Arnold and Booth have no further contact until mid-March, when Arnold is stopped by a man on the street who asks him to go to a particular saloon where he finds Booth and four other men. Booth lays out his newest plan. They are to go to Ford's Theater and, as Arnold later tells it, he (Arnold) "was to rush in the box and seize the President."[2] Arnold hears the details of the plan and is struck by its implausibility. Among his other objections, Arnold asks what he is to do if stopped. Booth responds that he should shoot anyone who gets in the way.

Arnold refuses to do any killing. He tells Booth, in front of the whole group, that "he could be the leader of the party, but not an executioner."[3] The tension in the room grows. Booth threatens to shoot Arnold. Arnold says that he is welcome to try but that he plans on defending himself. Before leaving the room, Arnold says that he will join the group in the kidnapping scheme, without any killing, but it must be done promptly with no further delays or he (Arnold) would be dropping out of any further plans and getting on with his life.

The plan was for Lincoln to be grabbed while traveling on the road the next day, but Lincoln's plans change and no attempt to kidnap him can be made. Arnold returns to Baltimore and takes a job as a clerk. Booth summons Arnold on March 25 to settle their affairs, but Arnold refuses to come. On March 27, Arnold writes to Booth to make clear that he is withdrawing from any further plots. The North has opened up a prisoner exchange, and for Arnold the issue is settled. He tells Booth to let the whole matter go.

Arnold becomes worried because Booth has compromising letters from him concerning the earlier kidnapping scheme, so when Booth next summons him to a meeting, Arnold goes and at the meeting Booth agrees to destroy the compromising letters (though in the end he does not). During this last meeting, Booth tells Arnold that he is abandoning all plans to kidnap the President. After this, Arnold and Booth have no further communication.

Arnold returns to Baltimore for his new job, and Booth remains in Washington. On April 9, 1865, General Robert E. Lee surrenders his army of 28,000 to General Ulysses S. Grant at the Court House in Appomattox, Virginia. The Civil War is over, and the Union has survived.

Two days after Lee's surrender, Booth stands in a small crowd on the White House lawn and listens to the President as he explains that the right to vote should belong to all men, even black men. Booth turns to his companion and says coldly, "That's the last speech Lincoln will ever make."[4]

Over the next 72 hours, Booth develops a plan for the simultaneous assassination of four prominent Union men: President Lincoln, General Ulysses Grant, Secretary of State William Seward, and Vice President Andrew Johnson. He and his co-conspirators from the earlier kidnaping plot decide that Booth will handle Lincoln and Grant, Lewis Powell will kill Seward, and George Atzerodt will kill Johnson. Booth hopes that this plot will not just eliminate a number of pro-abolition leaders but also destabilize the American government.

Five days later, on the evening of April 15, Booth rides on horseback to Ford's Theater. President Lincoln and his wife Mary are watching the play *Our American Cousin*. As an actor of renown, no one thinks twice about Booth showing up during a performance.

Booth slips into the President's box and fires a bullet into the back of Lincoln's skull. He then jumps from Lincoln's box onto the stage and shouts "Sic semper

Figure 9.1 The assassination of President Lincoln, lithograph by Currier and Ives, circa 1910

tyrannis" (thus always to tyrants). For a moment, the audience believes this may be part of the production. Although he breaks his left leg in the fall, Booth manages to flee on horseback.[5]

Lincoln dies before dawn. While Booth succeeds in his assassination, none of the other planned attempts are successful.

Booth and a companion find their way to the home of Dr. Samuel Mudd in the early hours of April 16. Some months back, when Booth had been familiarizing himself with an escape route in connection with the kidnapping plot, he made the acquaintance of Dr. Mudd. Under the cover of night, Mudd, who is unaware of the assassination, sets Booth's leg and attempts to find a carriage to transport him.

Later in the day, Mudd is checking on a neighbor when he learns of the assassination. The neighbor asks if it is the same Booth who had recently been in the area. Dr. Mudd claims not to know. Soon investigators come to his door, and Mudd continues to deny knowing anything. He does not mention that the two men spent the night at his home, or that he set Booth's broken leg. He repeatedly insists that Booth is a stranger to him. He also misleads the investigators about the direction Booth went upon his departure.

As the investigation continues, authorities find Arnold's letters to Booth, which lead to Arnold's arrest on April 17. He gives authorities the names of the other men who had been involved in the earlier plans to kidnap the President.

Arnold and others are charged with conspiracy to kill Lincoln. Dr. Mudd is also charged as a conspirator. Arnold tries to show both that he had renounced the original conspiracy and that he had no knowledge of the final plot to kill Lincoln and the other officials. His defense emphasizes that Arnold is "only guilty of being a party to a project to kidnap Lincoln, which died unborn."[6]

It is to no avail. Arnold, Mudd, and others are found guilty of conspiracy to murder the President.[7] Four of the conspirators are hung. Arnold and Mudd are sentenced to life imprisonment at hard labor.

Conspiracy and the Complicity Liability of Co-conspirators

If two or more persons agree that one of them will commit an offense and one of them then performs an overt act toward commission of that offense, they can all be held liable for conspiracy to commit the offense, even if the *substantive offense* is never consummated.[8] Conspiracy is therefore an "inchoate offense" (like attempt in Chapter 7) that makes it a crime itself for a group to plan to commit a crime. Because it is only the planning that has taken place, it commonly carries half the punishment of the completed offense (just as they attempt offense commonly does).

It was not until 1611 in the *Poulterers' Case*, decided in the Court of Star Chamber, that a mere agreement to commit a crime became a substantive offense.

> The Poulterers' Case is a landmark in the history of criminal conspiracy, for it departed from the doctrine that the conspiracy must actually be carried into effect before a writ of conspiracy would lie. The Court of Star Chamber ruled in Poulterers' Case that the agreement was itself indictable though nothing was executed.[9]

If the offense is in fact committed, the perpetrator can be held liable for the full substantive offense. A co-conspirator can also be held liable for the substantive offense if he satisfies the requirements of complicity liability, which typically require that the accomplice actually encourage, assist, or attempt to assist the perpetrator, as discussed in Chapter 8. The mere agreement itself – the conspiracy – is normally insufficient for complicity liability.[10] Thus, one might be held liable for conspiracy to commit an offense based on the agreement alone, but nevertheless not be an accomplice because the person had done nothing to assist in the commission.

Arnold is held liable for conspiracy to murder. Apparently, in the upset of the times, the court interpreted the original conspiratorial agreement broadly as a conspiracy to victimize President Lincoln in some way. Although Arnold only agreed to kidnap the President, the court's broader interpretation of the conspiracy allowed his conviction for conspiracy to murder the President.

Many jurisdictions have adopted what is called the *Pinkerton rule*,[11] which allows the state to treat a conspirator as an accomplice. Under the Pinkerton rule, a conspirator may be held liable as an accomplice to all substantive offenses committed by co-conspirators in furtherance of the conspiracy, even if the defendant did not actually take any action to assist (or even try to assist) any of those offenses. If the Pinkerton rule had been applied to the Arnold case, the prosecution might argue that even though the murder of the President was a surprise to the defendant, he could be held liable as accomplices to it – and therefore held liable as an accomplice to the full substantive offense of murder – if the killing was part of the original conspiracy. Because the penalty for conspiracy to murder was so high at the time, there was little need for the prosecutor or court to take this extra step to hold the Arnold liable for not just conspiracy to murder but also accomplice to the substantive offense to murder under the Pinkerton rule.

Even if Arnold had been charged as an accomplice to murder under the Pinkerton rule, he would have had a defense because of his *withdrawal* from the conspiracy before the murder occurred. In applying the Pinkerton rule, a co-conspirator can only be held liable as an accomplice in the crimes of his co-conspirators committed before his withdrawal. Thus, while withdrawal from the conspiracy does not save the conspirator from *conspiracy liability*, it does have the important and dramatic effect of cutting off his liability as an accomplice for all subsequent offenses committed by his co-conspirators. Thus, because of his withdrawal, Arnold could not be liable as an accomplice for the subsequent murder of the President under the Pinkerton rule. (As noted above, however, he was held liable for the offense of conspiracy to murder by interpreting the original conspiracy to kidnap very broadly, and his withdrawal does not provide a defense to the original conspiracy.)

Consider the application of conspiracy and the Pinkerton rule in a more modern case.

Shellie Marie Schorovsky – 1997

In 1996, Shellie Marie Schorovsky and her husband, both heroin addicts, move into an auto repair shop in Odessa, Texas owned by Sammy Enriquez and his wife Dianna Lujan. In exchange for some heroin and a place to stay, Schorovsky and her husband agree to help their landlords sell heroin from the shop. Schorovsky meets with a customer at a predetermined location and sells him 5.4 grams of heroin. With heroin averaging about \$10–\$15 for 0.1 grams, that one sale makes Enriquez a profit of around \$1,000.

Schorovsky's health begins to deteriorate because of her addiction. Heroin is a depressant, which slows the body's ability to function, impairing the functioning of the brain, the beating of the heart, and the control of breathing. In the long term, heroin addicts may suffer collapsed veins and bacterial infections of the heart and blood.

In March, seeing only one way out of what she sees as her grotesque addiction prison, Schorovsky calls her mother-in-law, Darla Sanders, and explains that she wants to "get away."[12] Sanders comes and picks up Schorovsky and her husband. Lujan trails the car and confronts Schorovsky. Lujan threatens that once they leave, they cannot return. The two have a heated argument, and eventually Schorovsky screams that she is leaving for good and does not want anything to do with the drug dealers. After her departure, Schorovsky enrolls in a drug rehabilitation program and breaks off all communication with Enriquez, Lujan, and their associates.

Enriquez and Lujan continue to deal drugs. What they don't realize is that the government has been conducting an undercover surveillance operation in the area. Soon enough, Enriquez and Lujan are identified as the area dealers and in late fall of 1997 the police seize 221.41 grams of heroin from Enriquez and his co-conspirators.

In January of 1998, Schorovsky is arrested for the heroin sale she made at Enriquez's behest before leaving his employ. She is charged with distribution of heroin and conspiracy to possess heroin with intent to distribute. She pleads guilty to the charges in the U.S. District Court for Western District of Texas. According to law, her sentence depends upon the amount of the drugs sold with which she was involved. Although the court concedes that Schorovsky only sold 5.4 grams herself, she is nonetheless held responsible for the 221 grams that was seized after her departure because she is considered to be part of the conspiracy and therefore liable for all the acts of her

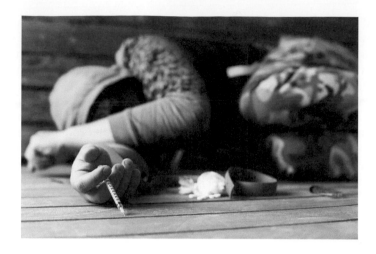

Figure 9.2 Heroin took a toll on Schorovsky's health

co-conspirators. Schorovsky objects, arguing that she withdrew from the conspiracy before the other 221 grams was seized. The district court overrules her objections and sentences her to 60 months in prison.

Schorovsky appeals the sentence to the Fifth Circuit Court of Appeals. The court refers to the United States Sentencing Guidelines, which state in its commentary that "a defendant's relevant conduct does not include the conduct of the members of a conspiracy before the defendant joins the conspiracy, even if the defendant knows of such conduct."[13] The court then infers that the same holds true in the case where the defendant withdraws from the conspiracy – that is to say, the defendant cannot be held responsible for acts of co-conspirators after the defendant's withdrawal from the conspiracy.

Moreover, in the eyes of the court, a conspirator is presumed to be part of a conspiracy until the offender makes a "substantial affirmative showing of withdrawal, abandonment, or defeat of the conspiratorial purpose." Schorovsky bears the burden of proving that she did indeed withdraw and clearly communicated this to the other conspirators. Her parting confrontation with Lujan meets the standard, as she explicitly told Lujan that she would not be involved with any future schemes and enrolled in a drug rehabilitation program. Thus, legally she was no longer part of the conspiracy after her effective withdrawal.

The court rules that the heroin sold by the co-conspirators after Schorovsky's withdrawal cannot be included in the defendant's relevant conduct for the purposes of sentencing. The original sentence is vacated, and the case is remanded for resentencing according to the standard set forth by the Court of Appeals.

So Schorovsky is successful where Arnold is not. Schorovsky's conspiracy liability is limited only to the conspiracy as it existed before her effective withdrawal. Arnold, in contrast, engaged in a conspiracy to kidnap but is ultimately held liable for a much more serious conspiracy to murder that was hatched by his former co-conspirators after his withdrawal.

A defendant is presumed to continue involvement in a conspiracy unless she makes a "substantial affirmative showing of withdrawal, abandonment, or defeat of the conspiratorial purpose." To establish withdrawal a defendant bears the burden of demonstrating affirmative acts inconsistent with the object of the conspiracy that are communicated in a manner reasonably calculated to reach conspirators.

U.S. v. Shellie Marie SCHOROVSKY, 5th Circuit Court of Appeals

Figure 9.3

Diversity among the States Regarding Pinkerton and Withdrawal

As the Arnold and Schorovsky cases illustrate, by withdrawing, a conspirator can try to limit their liability by limiting the scope of the conspiracy for which they are accountable. While the Arnold case shows some uncertainty in the application of this rule, the more modern view is clearly that the scope of the conspiracy ought to be limited to the scope that existed at the time of withdrawal and ought not include any subsequent broadening by others. Thus, under modern rules, Arnold would not have been liable as a conspirator to the murder of the President.

In addition, as discussed above, an analogous effect of withdrawal – and as a practical matter perhaps a more important one – is the effect that withdrawal has in cutting off liability under the *Pinkerton rule* for the full *substantive offenses* (not just *conspiracy liability*) committed by former co-conspirators. In other words, withdrawal would save Arnold from being liable as an accomplice to the substantive offense of murder (not just conspiracy to murder) and would save Schorovsky from being liable as an accomplice to the substantive offense of drug distribution (not just conspiracy to distribute drugs).

However, there is a good deal of diversity among the states on this point, both on whether a jurisdiction adopts the Pinkerton rule and on whether withdrawal extinguishes Pinkerton's effect. The position of each state with regard to the issues is indicated on the map below.[14]

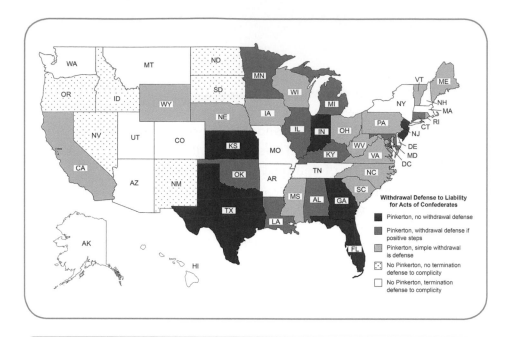

Figure 9.4

The 31 states with some level of shading on the map adopt the Pinkerton rule, which treats conspiracy as sufficient to create complicity liability for the substantive offense. The other 20 American jurisdictions, those with no shading on the map, follow the Model Penal Code in rejecting the Pinkerton rule.

Among the 31 jurisdictions that adopt the Pinkerton rule, six states, those with the darkest shading, do not expressly provide that withdrawal from the conspiracy cuts off Pinkerton liability for subsequent offenses by the co-conspirators. The nine states with medium shading adopt the Pinkerton rule and do allow withdrawal to cut off its effects but only if the withdrawing conspirator takes certain positive steps to rescind the agreement.[15] The remaining 16 jurisdictions, in light shading, adopt Pinkerton but cut off its effects upon a simple withdrawal from the conspiracy.[16]

In the 20 jurisdictions that have rejected the Pinkerton rule, those with no shading on the map, the offender can only be held liable as an accomplice to a substantive offense if they satisfy the requirements for complicity liability – the Pinkerton rule is not available to do this. And even then, some of these jurisdictions that have rejected the Pinkerton rule – the 14 no-shading states with no dots overlay – the offender can escape even complicity liability if they "terminate" their involvement with the accomplices before commission of the offense. Such a termination defense to complicity liability requires that the actor take positive steps against commission of the offense, such as by trying to prevent the offense or by notifying law enforcement or by giving warning to the intended victim. This is the approach taken by the Model Penal Code.[17] Thus, if the original plan to kidnap Lincoln had been carried out, Arnold could have saved himself from liability for complicity and kidnapping if he had "terminated" his complicity in the offense before it occurred, at least in those jurisdictions that follow the Model Code formulation. The remaining six jurisdictions with no shading – but with a dots overlay – provide no such termination defense once a person becomes an accomplice.

Should a State Adopt the Pinkerton Rule? A Withdrawal Defense?

As the previous chapter makes clear, most jurisdictions' complicity provisions take great care in defining the requirements that will allow one person to be held liable for the criminal conduct of another. Having worked out these requirements, why should a jurisdiction ever provide an exception to them? Yet, as this chapter shows, a great number of jurisdictions (31) short-circuit the standard complicity requirements by adopting the *Pinkerton rule*, which essentially substitutes the lesser requirements of conspiracy as sufficient to support complicity liability for the full *substantive offense*.

The fact that there is substantial diversity among the states in the formulation and application of the Pinkerton rule suggests some lack of clarity in its underlying rationale. It is probably fair to say that the rule is based less upon some principled argument of equivalent blameworthiness and more upon a wish to lighten and simplify the prosecutor's burden of proof.

It is probably true that as a practical matter a co-conspirator in a conspiracy that leads to the commission of the substantive offense – *conspiracy liability* requires that the conspirator agree with another person that one of them will commit the offense – will in many cases satisfy the requirements of an accomplice to that substantive offense – complicity liability requires that the accomplice purposely assist in the commission of the offense. That is, many co-conspirators will in fact do enough to become accomplices to a completed offense. In such cases, no harm is done by a Pinkerton rule. But this will not always be the case. There will be instances where the conspirator will not satisfy the requirements of complicity in the substantive offense and does not deserve liability for the full offense, yet such liability will be imposed – analogous to the case of Samuel Arnold.

If an offender really does satisfy the requirements for complicity liability in the substantive offense, then such liability can be established without the use of the Pinkerton rule. The real effect of substituting the lesser requirements of conspiracy under the Pinkerton rule, then, is to extend liability to the cases where the complicity requirements are not satisfied. In other words, the Pinkerton rule, like the use of strict liability, is a device that will regularly generate liability beyond what is deserved.

If one is concerned about avoiding injustice, then the use of Pinkerton is objectionable. The excesses of the rule can be reduced (but not eliminated) by providing as broad a *withdrawal defense* as possible, which will then limit Pinkerton liability. Preferable, however, are those jurisdictions that reject the rule altogether, although even these jurisdictions risk injustice if they deny a termination defense to complicity. For those who care about matching liability and punishment with the defendant's true blameworthiness, the five groups of states listed in the map legend are in rank order from the least just to the most.

Aftermaths

Dry Tortugas, the prison where Arnold and Dr. Mudd and the rest of the convicted men are sent, experiences a serious outbreak of yellow fever in 1867. The disease claims the lives of many people living at the prison, both inmate and soldier. When the prison doctor dies, Dr. Mudd takes over the job. Arnold works alongside to save as many prisoners as possible. Arnold makes it through the outbreak, but he is left sick and weakened.

After seeing the prison through the outbreak, "all the officers of the post united in signing a petition to President [Andrew] Johnson asking for his release on account of the valuable services rendered." President Johnson pardons both Dr. Mudd and Arnold before leaving office in 1869. Mudd is able to go home and resume his practice. He dies at 50 from pneumonia. Arnold returns home and lives a quiet life until his death in his 70s.

In the Schorovsky case, after the sentence is reversed by the appellate court and returned to the trial court for resentencing, the judge reduces her sentence to the length of time already served. Schorovsky is released and put on probation for three years. However, a little more than a year later, she violates the terms of her supervised release and is sent back to prison for a 22-month sentence.

Chapter Glossary

Conspiracy Liability: Conspiracy is an inchoate offense that provides liability and punishment of preparatory conduct; in this respect, it operates in a way analogous to attempt. In older criminal codes, conspiracy can play an additional role, apart from that as an inchoate offense, as a substantive offense that can be charged even after completion of the offense and is designed to provide additional punish for commission of the offense by a group.[18]

Pinkerton Rule: This rule holds a conspirator liable as an accomplice to any other offense committed by co-conspirators in furtherance of the conspiracy. Thus, the rule can expand the imposition of complicity liability by short-circuiting its traditional requirements.[19]

Substantive Offense: The target or object offense of an inchoate offense. It is the offense that the attempter or conspirators are planning to commit.[20]

Withdrawal Defense: A member of a conspiracy may be able to end their on-going liability for the actions of their co-conspirators by withdrawing from the conspiracy. Their withdrawal does not provide a defense to liability for the conspiracy itself. To be effective, the withdrawal commonly must be communicated to all co-conspirators and must be made in time for the others to abandon the conspiracy if they so choose.[21]

Notes

1. This portion of the narrative is drawn from the following sources: Samuel B. Arnold, *Memories of a Lincoln Conspirator*, ed. Michael Kauffman (Bowie: Heritage Books, 1995); William C. Edwards, 'The Confession of Samuel Arnold April 18, 1865,' *The Lincoln Assassination – The Rewards Files* (Edwards, 2012) accessed at *Famous Trials*, https://famous-trials.com/legacyftrials/lincolnconspiracy/Arnoldconfession.html; Christopher Hamner, 'Booth's Reason for Assassination,' *Teaching History*, accessed 13 June 2019, http://teachinghistory.org/history-content/ask-a-historian/24242; Osborn H. Oldroyd, *The Assassination of Abraham Lincoln: Flight, Pursuit, Capture, and Punishment of the Conspirators* (Clark: Lawbook Exchange, Ltd., 2001); Edward Steers Jr., *The Trial: The Assassination of President Lincoln and the Trial of the Conspirators* (Lexington: University Press of Kentucky, 2013),

http://teachinghistory.org/history-content/ask-a-historian/24242; Oldroyd, *The Assassination of Abraham Lincoln*; Steers, *The Trial*.

2. Edwards, 'The Confession.'
3. Edwards, 'The Confession.'
4. Hamner, 'Booth's Reason.'
5. Edwards, 'The Confession.'
6. Steers, *The Trial*, XCV.
7. And in O'Laughlen's case he is not found guilty of "lying in wait" for Ulysses S. Grant.
8. Paul Robinson and Michael Cahill, 'Conspiracy and Solicitation,' in *Criminal Law*, 2nd ed. (Philadelphia: Wolters Kluwer, 2012): p. 466.
9. Albert J. Harno, 'Intent in Criminal Conspiracy,' *University of Pennsylvania Law Review* 624 (1941), p. 624.
10. Robinson and Cahill, 'Conspiracy and Solicitation,' p. 466.
11. *Pinkerton v. United States*, 328 U.S. 640, 647–648, 66 S. Ct. 1180, 1184 (1946).
12. *U.S. v. Schorovsky.*
13. U.S.S.G. § 1B1.3(a)(1)(B).
14. The map is taken from Paul H. Robinson and Tyler Scot Williams, 'Felony Murder,' in *Mapping American Criminal Law: Variations across the 50 States* (Westport: Prager, 2018). All supporting authorities are available from that source.
15. The requirements for an effective withdrawal vary by jurisdiction, with some requiring a specific positive step and others requiring any one of several alternative steps. Positive steps include timely notifying law enforcement, timely notifying a targeted victim, successful efforts to deprive the actor's own involvement of its effectiveness, or efforts of varying degrees to prevent the offense itself.
16. In these jurisdictions, it is sufficient that the actor timely notified his co-conspirators of his intention to withdraw from the agreement. This is still a demanding standard: merely fleeing, leaving the scene, or otherwise withdrawing in silence generally does not suffice. However, notice that this category of states does not require notification of law enforcement authorities; it requires only notification of co-conspirators.
17. *See, e.g.,* Model Penal Code §2.06(6)(c).
18. Robinson and Cahill, *Criminal Law*, §12.1.1.
19. Robinson and Cahill, *Criminal Law*, §12.1.1.
20. Robinson and Cahill, *Criminal Law*, §12.1.1.
21. Robinson and Cahill, *Criminal Law*, §12.2.

Chapter 10

Omissions

The Richest Woman in America Neglects Her Son

1882. The British are involved in the First Boer War in remote South Africa, but the Western World takes little notice. Most countries are at peace. At the Hague a three-mile limit for territorial waters is agreed upon. With peace comes prosperity and innovation, including the technological advances spurring the rapid industrialization and modernization now underway. Before the year is out, the world's first hydroelectric power plant begins operation on the Fox River in Appleton, Wisconsin. With the Transcontinental Railroad completed, the need for immigrant labor has waned and immigration from China to the U.S. is formally banned for ten years. A few days before Christmas, Thomas Edison gives us the world's first electric Christmas lights. The great tide of modernization creates equally great pockets of concentrated wealth.

Hetty Green – 1882

Henrietta (Hetty) Howland Robinson is born in 1834 to a wealthy whaling family. By the time she is six, Hetty is tasked with reading the financial news to her father. The father explains the ins and outs of business as she reads. While still very young, Hetty takes over the household finances, in her words, keeping "a strict account of personal and household expenses."[1] Her father talks her through his various contracts and business transactions. This shared time brings them close and provides her with a deep financial education, as well as her father's economic morality: never "owe anyone anything. Not even kindness."[2]

On several occasions, Hetty is sent to boarding school, which she does not enjoy. She is a beautiful girl but eschews all things feminine. A family member remarks that the girl dresses "like one of the orphans of some sailor lost at sea."[3] In one last attempt

DOI: 10.4324/9781003258025-11

to entice Hetty into an appreciation of gentrified living, she is sent to a finishing school for genteel girls of wealthy families in Boston. Her family's efforts are in vain: she reverts to unfashionable dress and dockyard slang as soon as she returns.

Hetty is sent to a rich relative's home for the social season in New York with the hope that she will return with a prospective husband. They give her $1,200 for expenses. At one New York ball, Hetty is introduced to the Prince of Wales. Showing that she can be a clever socialite, she introduces herself as the Princess of Whales. The Prince is charmed, and the couple dances more than once. Nevertheless, Hetty grows tired of being sociable and asks to come home early. Of her expense allowance, she has spent $200 on clothes and invested the rest in bonds.

Edward Henry Green, an adventurous millionaire who invests in the Far East, meets Hetty and has no problem with her unconventional style. The couple soon marries. As a condition of their marriage, Hetty asks Edward to sign a document protecting her from his debts but requiring him to provide for her. The couple makes an effective business team: Green knows banking and railroads, while Hetty is more knowledgeable about real estate and bonds.

Hetty gives birth to Edward Howland Robinson Green, whom she nicknames "Ned."[4] She loves her son, and he becomes a true source of happiness for her. She also gives birth to a daughter, Sylvia Ann Howland Green. After several years, the couple moves in with Green's mother. Hetty does not approve of her mother-in-law's lavish

Figure 10.1 Hetty Green as a mature woman, 1897

lifestyle and she is repeatedly called upon to rescue Green from a series of imprudent investments. Eventually, the couple grows more distant, and no longer shares a business or a home.

In 1882, when he is about 14, Ned falls from a tree and hurts his leg. A doctor is called to look over the child but when he arrives Hetty sends him away. She has been a competent nurse to her aunt and her father. She will not allow the doctor to get out of his carriage because if he does so, she will be forced to pay him. Over the next several months, Ned continues to exert himself, further compounding the trauma to his leg. Hetty tries every home remedy that she hears of, from poultices of tobacco to packs of hot sand, but she can do nothing to help the boy. As the leg deteriorates, her friends begin suggesting that the leg is beyond hope and must be amputated.

Hetty takes her son to a charity hospital. With Hetty and Ned dressed in costumes of rags, she lies to the staff and claims poverty. Doctor Lewis Sayer of Bellevue Hospital sees the boy and thinks that he can make the leg right again.

Sayer then discovers Hetty's true identity – this is no charity case. Hetty is the richest woman in America. He confronts her, demands that she pay the accrued fees and the cost of the rest of the treatment in advance. By paying first, he hopes, "she would be sure to bring the boy as often as she was told to do so" in order to avoid wasting money.[5] Unfortunately, the doctor underestimates Hetty's thrift. Not only does Hetty not pay up front, she never brings her son back to the doctor. The leg goes untreated.

In 1888, Ned and his father meet for dinner. Green questions his son about his health and Hetty's care of him. Ned knows what people think of his mother but he does not share their contempt. He usually brushes off questions about his leg, but this time his father persists. Ned recounts the many visits to and rejections from free clinics. He talks of the pain that the wounded leg gives him. That same evening, Ned falls down the steps and is unable to get back up. A doctor is called, and he finds traces of gangrene. Seven years after the original injury, the leg is amputated. The doctor is very clear: had Ned received proper care at the time of the accident, his leg would have been fine. Even if the family had brought the boy in two years earlier, a good portion of the leg could have been saved.

While Hetty's failure to provide basic medical care to her injured son may offend our modern sensibilities, no one at the time thinks of her failure as an issue of legal significance. The law of the era generally left such matters purely to parental judgment.

Omission Liability

Liability for a failure to act came to criminal law only sparingly and grudgingly.

> Roman law knew little of criminal liability for omissions. There were only few delicts in omittendo, chief of which were the failure of a slave to defend his master from assault, the failure of a soldier to assist his superior officer when the superior was taken by the enemy, the failure of a husband to prevent his wife from becoming a prostitute and the failure of a son to inform his father of a trap which his brother was laying for the father. . . . Certainly, these fragmentary instances of liability for inaction made no substantial impact on the application of Roman law, and we know of no conceptual difficulties or adjustments to

which they gave rise. The early English institutional writers again show little awareness of criminal omissions as a field of liability of any special significance. Coke, in his Third Institute, seems to regard positive action as an almost inevitable element of guilt. He always insists on the overt deed: even the liability for treason in compassing the death of the monarch has to be excused and explained away as a special case. The only offenses of omission clearly recognized are misprision of treason, misprision of felony, and failure to yield up a treasure trove.[6]

Support for *omission liability* could be found, however, in the Church of the Middle Ages.

> The doctrine of the Church and the canon law brought new problems and viewpoints. St. Thomas helped to lay the foundation for the common argument which has been ever since a dominant motive in the penal treatment of omissions; the assimilation of omissions to positive actions takes place only when there is a duty to act. St. Thomas sees the theoretical foundation for such an assimilation in the volitional element, the spiritual rebellion underlying and accompanying the omission. But if the canon law and its commentators strongly emphasized the duty to act, especially insofar as the duty to prevent criminal acts and the duty to render assistance were concerned, they found little support from other medieval authorities.[7]

Today, most criminal offenses still primarily punish engaging in prohibited conduct, but the criminal law also sometimes requires certain conduct and punishes the failure to so act.[8] Such criminal liability for an omission has two special requirements.

First, as St. Thomas discusses, a person cannot be held criminally liable for an omission unless the person has a duty to act. But criminal liability requires violation of a *legal*, as opposed to a *moral*, duty to act.

Second, an offender cannot be held liable for an omission that he or she could not perform. This provides a defense analogous to the involuntary act defense for commission offenses. Just as it would be unjust to punish a person for an assault they committed while having a seizure, so too would it be unjust to punish a person for a failure to engage in conduct that the person was physically incapable of performing. When an omission results in a death – such as a failure to jump in the water to save a drowning man – by definition it is everyone in the world who has failed to act. However, most people in the world are exempt from criminal liability by this capacity to perform requirement – most people simply had no ability to do so because they were not present.

There may be many people who are present and who are physically capable of saving the man, but who choose not to so. Because of the first requirement, the *duty requirement*, they will not have criminal liability unless they had a legal duty to act to save him. The duty requirement serves as an important shield that limits *omission liability* to those for whom the law has some reason to demand that they act – such as a paid lifeguard or the parent of a young child. The law is typically hesitant to create such legal duties to act. For example, most states have no duty to rescue a stranger, even if the stranger is in deadly peril.[9]

A legal duty to act, which may then give rise to criminal liability for an omission, can arise from a number of sources, including both the civil and the criminal law. Under civil law, a special relationship, such as that of a parent to a child, can create a

Endangering Welfare of Children.
    A parent, guardian, or other person supervising the welfare of a child under 18 commits a misdemeanor if he knowingly endangers the child's welfare by violating a duty of care, protection or support.
                    Model Penal Code §230.4

Figure 10.2

duty to act. A duty may also arise from a contractual obligation, such as the duty of a lifeguard to rescue swimmers in a pool. Beyond these civil law bases for a duty to act, the criminal law creates a legal duty to act whenever it defines an offense in terms of an omission, such as the offense of failure to appear for military induction or the offense of failure to file a required tax return.

One example of a specific omission offense is that of child neglect. While this was not the case at the time of the Hetty Green incident in 1882, today all American jurisdictions have criminal offenses that punish the physical neglect of a child by a parent or guardian who fails to obtain care or treatment for a child's physical injury or disease or for a child suffering physical pain. The Model Penal Code *endangerment offense* is reproduced in the margin. Because the definition of the offense itself criminalizes the failure to act, it thereby creates the needed legal duty to act.

Consider a more modern case of child neglect.

Rebecca and Timothy Wyland – 2010

Rebecca and Timothy Wyland are members of the Followers of Christ, a Christian denomination characterized by its literal interpretation of the Scripture.[10] The sect believes in the power of faith healing and that any and all illnesses can be cured by acts of devotion, such as prayer and the laying on of hands, as done in the Scriptures. To seek outside help is to fault the divine plan of God. Members reject all forms of modern medical care and treatment and those members who ignore this teaching are cast out.

Unsurprisingly, the church has a documented history of deaths from treatable medical conditions. A television exposé reveals that 78 children are buried in the Followers of Christ graveyard just outside their church in Oregon City, Oregon. Of those, at least 21 would have survived had they received medical attention as basic as taking an antibiotic. Even after the exposé, nothing in the church changes and three more children die in 2008.

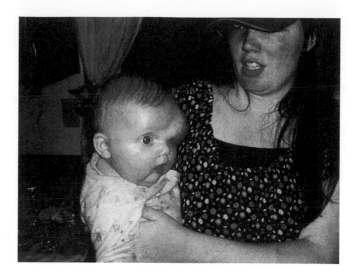

Figure 10.3 Rebecca Wyland holding Alayna with her "strawberry birthmark," 2010

In December of 2009, the Wylands welcome their first child, Alayna Wyland. She is born with a raised growth above her left eye, which her parents call a "strawberry birthmark." Within a few weeks the growth becomes more pronounced. Clearly the growth is not a harmless discoloration of the skin, but is in reality a cavernous hemangioma, a growing mass of blood vessels and fatty tissue. Since it is in its early stages, the abnormal growth could be controlled with medical intervention. This type of benign tumor often spontaneously disappears but also can continue to grow if untreated. Because of their religious beliefs, the Wylands do not consult a doctor.

For six months, the tumor grows, and the parents become concerned. While they do not seek professional medical care, they do consult their relatives and several members of their church. They follow all the advice they are given. Joined by members of their church, they pray, anoint the baby with sacred oil, and perform laying on of hands. Most of the people in the Wylands' social circle share their beliefs and advise that the only way to help the baby is to continue their devotional efforts. They are repeatedly told that the growth poses no serious medical risk.

The tumor is now the size of a baseball that covers most of the left side of Alayna's face, including her entire left eye and is pushing her left eyeball out of its socket. The baby begins to lose her vision. Still, no medical treatment is sought.

Alayna comes to the attention of the authorities and is removed from her parent's care. The tumor is treated but her left eye's function is severely compromised: she has 20/60 vision in her right eye, but 20/1,000 in her left eye.

For failing to provide medical care, the Wylands are charged with first-degree criminal mistreatment, a charge punishable by up to five years in prison. It is clear to everyone that the couple loves their daughter. After an hour of deliberation, the jury finds the couple guilty of first-degree criminal mistreatment, which is defined to criminalize a parent or guardian who "intentionally or knowingly withholds . . . medical attention."[11] Because the couple has no prior conviction, the court sentences them to 90 days in jail and three years of supervision.

Diversity among the States Regarding Child Neglect

Things have changed since the time of Hetty Green in 1882. The conviction of the Wylands in 2009 is no surprise, given the universality of child neglect offenses today. The fact that there was no conviction, or even a thought of prosecution of Green in the 1882 illustrates how much social norms and legal rules have changed in the last century. Government today is more willing to intrude into citizens' private lives in order to promote what it sees as the greater good of child protection.

But beyond the duty to provide appropriate medical care, there is considerable diversity among today's state criminal laws in defining the extent of the legal duty of a parent to a child, as the map below illustrates. The darker the shading on the map, the broader and more demanding the duties contained in the child neglect offense.[12]

Fourteen jurisdictions, those with light shading on the map, commonly criminalize neglect that is harmful to the "health" or "physical health" of the child or criminalize the failure to provide appropriate or necessary "care." These jurisdictions do not specifically criminalize "mental" or "emotional" neglect or neglecting a child's "education." The 2009 Wyland case occurred in Oregon, a state that today requires this lowest duty of care of parents, but still requires more than enough to generate criminal liability for the Wyland parents.

Three states, those with light shading and a dots overlay on the map, also criminalize, in addition to the general health and welfare coverage above, the failure to generally "educate" or to provide "education" necessary for a child's welfare.[13] Twenty-three states, those with medium shading on the map, punish physical neglect but also criminalize omissions that result in harm to a child's mental or emotional welfare.

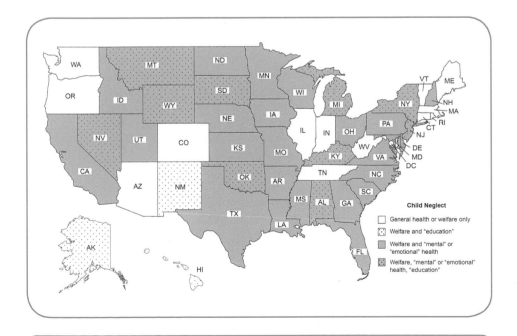

Figure 10.4

Finally, 11 states, those with medium shading and a dots overlay on the map, criminalize everything covered by the three categories above. New York, the jurisdiction in which the 1882 Hetty Green case arose, is in this last group of states with the most demanding duty of care requirements for parents, showing just how far the state has come.

What Duties Should a Parent Have to a Child upon Penalty of Criminal Liability?

It is easy to agree that parents should provide not only the support necessary for physical health and safety but also the support necessary for mental and emotional health and ideally a sound education. But the issue here is not whether parents should feel morally obliged to do so. The question is whether parents should be *criminally liable* for failing to do so.

There should be little surprise that every jurisdiction will criminalize a parent's failure to provide for the health and safety of a child. In many respects, this criminalization logically follows from the criminalization of *endangerment* generally. (Chapter 19 will talk more about the general offense of endangerment.) If the state is going to criminalize the creation of danger to the health or safety of strangers, it obviously will not hesitate to do so for parents who endanger their children, through either commission or *omission*.

That unanimity breaks down, however, as soon as one crosses the line from physical to mental or emotional health, which are brought within the terms of a criminal offense in the darker shaded and dots overlay jurisdictions on the map. The unanimity also breaks down even more with regard to criminal liability for failing to assure minimal educational opportunities. (Notice that most of the jurisdictions that go so far as to criminalize the failure to provide minimal educational opportunity are jurisdictions that already also provide criminal liability for failing to protect mental or emotional health.[14])

Failure to provide adequate educational opportunities – as criminalized in 14 jurisdictions – seems to be the minority view on the more demanding end. Meanwhile, criminalizing only the failure to protect health and welfare – as in 14 other jurisdictions – is the minority view on the less demanding end. Occupying the middle ground are the majority of jurisdictions that protect physical and mental or emotional health.

Why the disagreement among the jurisdictions? Why don't all jurisdictions criminalize child neglect of all types? Aren't these laudable goals that ought to be encouraged in all parents even, if necessary, by criminalizing the neglect? One might speculate that what is spooking some legislatures is the possibility that not all parents have the capacity to provide the support covered by the child neglect offense. For example, a parent's financial limitations, as well as his or her own mental or emotional limitations, might seem to create a significant risk that criminal liability would be imposed in situations that are more tragic than condemnable.

But the truth is that this potential problem can be easily solved and is in fact fully avoided by a well-drafted criminal code that expressly includes the special *capacity requirement* for *omission liability*, discussed above. For example, Model Penal Code sections 2.01(1)&(3) set out a general rule that bars liability for an omission unless the defendant was "*physically* capable" of performing the act required by the omission offense. A better approach would be to require proof that the defendant was "capable" of performing the conduct required by the offense (rather than "*physically* capable"), so as to include in the defense cases of mental or emotional incapacity.

In addition, most modern American criminal codes have a collection of justification defenses that also can play an important role here. A justification defense authorizes people to engage in conduct that otherwise would constitute a criminal offense (as the next chapter will detail). The lesser evils justification defense, as codified in Model Penal Code section 3.02, for example, allows people presented with two bad choices to pick the lesser of the two evils and claim a justification defense on the grounds that they have avoided the worse outcome. Thus, where the parent has money that could be used to promote the child's mental or emotional health or education, but is the same source of funds that is needed to buy food (and thereby to protect the child's physical health), the lesser evils defense would protect the parent from criminal liability for spending the money on food even though he or she was technically "capable" of spending it to promote his child's emotional health or education.

The conclusion, then, is that legislatures could feel more comfortable in expanding their child neglect statutes if they put in place a well-constructed system of principles for omission liability, justification defenses, and excuse defenses. Unfortunately, as the review of state criminal codes in other chapters has made and will continue to make clear, the state of such general liability principles in American criminal codes is quite mixed. A quarter of the American jurisdictions, including some of the largest, such as California and the federal system, have not even adopted a comprehensive modern criminal code that codifies general principles of liability and general defenses.

Aftermaths

Ned and his mother remain on excellent terms for her entire life. She successfully grooms him to take over the family fortune. When Ned is asked by a friend why the leg was amputated, he claims he injured it on a hand cart. Hetty, for her part, justifies the delay in treatment by claiming that Ned, once of age, could make his own choices.

In the *Wyland* case, when the guilty verdict and jail sentence rendered, the family and their supporters are stunned. Conviction in punishment in such cases has been few and far between. But despite the mandated jail time, many doctors and child advocates argue that the courts have not gone far enough. A Rhode Island doctor points out that an intoxicated parent who crashes his car and kills a child is legally accountable. Why should it be different for a parent "stoned on religion?"[15]

Chapter Glossary

Capacity Requirement: Criminal liability based upon an omission commonly requires proof that the actor was physically capable of performing the legal duty without greatly endangering him- or herself or harming other interests.[16]

Duty Requirement: Criminal liability for an omission requires a legal duty to act; a moral duty to act is not sufficient. The duty may arise from the offense definition itself or from some other provision of criminal or civil law, statutory or decisional.[17]

Endangerment Offense: Many modern criminal codes contain an offense of reckless endangerment that punishes an actor who recklessly places or may place another person in danger of death or serious bodily injury.[18]

Omission Liability: It is an exception to the standard requirement that criminal liability must be based upon an act. One can be held criminally liable for an omission if the person had a legal duty to act and the capacity to do so but failed to act.[19]

Notes

1. Charles Slack, *Hetty: The Genius and Madness of America's First Female Tycoon* (New York: HarperCollins Publishers, 2004), p. 17.
2. Janet Wallach, *The Richest Woman in America* (New York: Anchor Books, 2013).
3. Wallach, *The Richest Woman*, p. 31.
4. Wallach, *The Richest Woman*, p. 81.
5. Peter Wykoff, 'Queen Midas: Hetty Robinson Green,' *The New England Quarterly* 23, no. 2 (June 1950): pp. 147–171, https://www.jstor.org/stable/362074?seq=1#page_scan_tab_contents
6. Graham Hughes, 'Criminal Omissions,' *Yale Law Journal* 67, no. 4 (February 1958): pp. 590–637.
7. Otto Kirchheimer, 'Criminal Omissions,' *Harvard Law Review* 55, no. 4 (February 1942): pp. 615–642.
8. Paul H. Robinson and Michael T. Cahill, *Criminal Law*, 2nd ed. (New York: Wolters Kluwer, 2016), §3.4.
9. Robinson and Cahill, *Criminal Law*, p. 141.
10. This narrative is drawn from the following sources: "Faith-Healing' Parents of Alayna May Wyland Sentenced to Prison,' *Patheos Blog*, 24 June 2011, http://www.patheos.com/blogs/friendlyatheist/2011/06/24/faith-healing-parents-of-alayna-may-wyland-sentenced-to-prison/; Steve Mayes, 'Defense in faith-healing trial of Timothy, Rebecca Wyland cites religious prejudice,' *The Oregonian*, 27 May 2011, http://www.oregonlive.com/oregon-city/index.ssf/2011/05/post_19.html; Steve Mayes, 'Timothy, Rebecca Wyland Described as Devoted Parents in Oregon City Faith-Healing Trial,' *The Oregonian*, 3 June 2011, http://www.oregonlive.com/oregon-city/index.ssf/2011/06/timothy_wyland_described_as_a_loving_caring_father_in_oregon_city_faith_healing_trial.html; Steve Mayes, 'Timothy, Rebecca Wyland Guilty of Criminal Mistreatment in Faith-Healing Trial,' *The Oregonian*, 8 June 2011, http://www.oregonlive.com/oregon-city/index.ssf/2011/06/defense_says_state_overreached_in_faith-healing_trial_of_timothy_rebecca_wyland.html
11. Mayes, 'Timothy, Rebecca Wyland Guilty.'
12. The map is taken from Paul H. Robinson and Tyler Scot Williams, *Mapping American Criminal Law: Variations across the 50 States* (Westport: Prager, 2018), ch. 26. All supporting authorities are available from that source.
13. This category does not include laws that criminalize a parent's failure to ensure a child's presence in school, or "education as required by law."
14. Only New Mexico, Alaska, and Hawaii – states with light shading and dots on the map – criminalize the former (failure to provide minimal educational opportunity) but not the latter (failure to protect mental or emotional health). In contrast, 11 jurisdictions – those with dark shading and dots on the map – criminalize both the former and the latter.
15. Wendy Glauser, 'United States Still Too Lenient on "Faith Healing" Parents, Say Children's Rights Advocates,' *Canadian Medical Association Journal 183*, no. 11 (August 2011): pp. E709–E710, https://www.ncbi.nlm.nih.gov/pmc/articles/PMC3153535/

16. MPC §2.01(3)(a); Paul H. Robinson, Criminal Liability for Omissions: A Brief Summary and Critique of the Law in the United States (Conference on Crimes of Omission), *New York Law School Law Review 29* (1984): p. 101.
17. MPC 2.01(3)(b); Robinson and Cahill, *Criminal Law*, §3.4.
18. MPC §211.2; Robinson and Cahill, *Criminal Law*, §15.4.
19. Robinson and Cahill, *Criminal Law*, §3.4.

PART II

General Defenses

This part examines the criminal law's general defenses. These are defenses that will insulate an offender from liability even if he or she satisfies all the elements of an offense definition. For example, a person may satisfy the requirements of murder because he has intentionally killed another person, yet he may escape criminal liability and punishment if he did so out of necessary self-defense.

There are three kinds of general defenses. *Justification defenses* provide a defense because the person has done the right thing. On balance, society tolerates such conduct under such circumstances, such as in a killing in self-defense (Chapter 12) or where a law enforcement officer must use force to make a lawful arrest (Chapter 13). Even if a person's conduct does not satisfy the requirements of any of the many specific justification defenses, the offender in some cases may look to the general justification defense of lesser evils, which provides a defense if his otherwise-criminal conduct is necessary to avoid a greater harm or evil (Chapter 11).

Excuse defenses, such as insanity and immaturity, provide a defense on a quite different basis. In these cases, what the offender did is clearly wrong. The society would not want others to do the same thing in the same situation. Yet excused offenders escape criminal liability because, although their conduct was wrong, they are not blameworthy for performing it – perhaps because they were legally insane (Chapter 14) or immature (Chapter 15) or for any other of the excusing conditions recognized by law. The focus here is on the actor rather than on the actor's conduct. Conduct may be justified; offenders may be excused.

A final group of defenses, called *non-exculpatory defenses*, operate with yet a different rationale. The criminal justice system forgoes imposing criminal liability in these cases even if the offender deserves it, because by forgoing criminal liability the non-exculpatory defense promotes or protects some other societal interest. The statute of limitations defense may bar criminal prosecution after a set amount of time – even if the offense was unjustified and the offender is not excused – in order to promote

DOI: 10.4324/9781003258025-12

societal interests such as ensuring the efficient use of prosecution and adjudication resources (Chapter 16). The diplomatic immunity defense is said to promote effective communication among nations. The entrapment defense (Chapter 17) and the exclusionary rule (Chapter 18) serve to constrain police and prosecutors from overreaching as they fight crime.

Chapter 11

Lesser Evils

Cannibalism at Sea

1884. Conflict between China and France over the Tonkin region of Vietnam ends with a Chinese troop withdraw in exchange for a treaty of trade and commerce. The Washington Monument, the world's tallest stone structure, has been under construction since 1848 but on December 6 of 1884 its 3,300-pound marble capstone is finally installed. The first World Series of baseball is a matchup between the Providence Grays and the New York Metropolitans. Only the first game goes the full nine innings; the others end early because of darkness and extreme cold. Gold discoveries in South Africa bring a surge of European immigration to the country. Another popular immigrant destination is Australia.

Thomas Dudley – 1884

In 1883, Thomas Dudley is hired to sail a 55-foot yacht, the *Mignonette*, from England to Sydney.[1] He takes on the task because he is thinking of emigrating there to find better opportunities. As captain, Dudley is responsible for organizing the voyage and finding a crew. He selects two of his friends: Edwin Stephens to be his mate and Edmund (Ned) Brooks as the able seaman. To round out the crew, he also hires Richard Parker, aged 17, as the ordinary seaman.

The yacht sails from Southampton on May 19, 1884 for a planned voyage of between 14,000 and 16,000 miles. Six weeks after their journey begins and 1,600 miles from the Cape of Good Hope, they are becalmed. Until the weather changes, they cannot advance. Two days later, the weather changes with a vengeance. The *Mignonette* is caught in a violent storm in which an enormous wave, half as tall as the mast, sweeps over the ship, knocking a hole in the side. With the ship sinking, Dudley directs the men to lower the dinghy, as he scrambles to get some supplies, retrieving a

DOI: 10.4324/9781003258025-13

few provisions and the ship's compass. The violence of the storm sinks a cask of water they try to load.

The nearest land is 2,000 nautical miles to the west. Dudley, Stephens, Brooks, and Parker survive the first night, but have no water and no food other than two one-pound tins of turnips. For three days, the four eat nothing but the turnips. On the fourth day, July 9, 1884, Brooks spots and Dudley kills a small turtle. They attempt to catch its blood, but seawater splashes over the side and contaminates it. On that day, they consume the end of the turnips along with some of the turtle.

Thirst is the real issue, all four are drinking their own urine. It does little to alleviate their increasing dehydration. Their lips and tongues become parched and blackened, their feet and legs swell, and their skin develops sores from constant exposure to sea and wind and from the press of the crowded boat.

On July 17, the 12th day since the wreck, the turtle has been entirely consumed, even the bones and the skin. At this time, Dudley first proposes that they draw lots to determine who should be killed and eaten to save the lives of the others. Stephens and Brooks decide that discussion is premature. At the time, cannibalism after a shipwreck is so common that recounting such events is routine among surviving castaways. The tradition is to draw lots to select who will be sacrificed, thereby legitimize the killing.

For the next eight days, the four eat nothing. Despite the fact that he has been explicitly warned that drinking sea water will kill him, young Richard Parker drinks a considerable quantity of it and becomes violently ill. He suffers diarrhea, which further dehydrates him. Parker becomes delirious and then intermittently comatose. Dudley again raises the issue of drawing of lots. The others ignore the suggestion. They say, "We had better die together." Dudley replies, "So let it be, but it's hard for four to die, when perhaps one might save the rest."[2]

Figure 11.1 The survivor's tale became front page news, 1884

The boat drifts on the ocean and remains more than 1,000 nautical miles away from land. On July 25, 1884, Dudley tells Brooks that the boy must be killed. Parker is in and out of consciousness.

If the men do not feed now upon the body of Parker, they will die within a few days. The boy, being in a much weaker condition, will die soon in any case. There is no sail in sight, nor any reasonable prospect of immediate relief. Under the circumstances, it appears to Stephens and Dudley that there is no other chance of saving their lives except by killing one of them to eat.

Dudley goes to the boy and says, "Dick, your time has come, poor boy."[3] Parker asks, "What, me, sir?" and Dudley replies, "Yes, my boy."[4] Parker does not resist but neither does he agree. With Stephens holding the boy, Dudley stabs a two-inch blade into the boy's throat, killing him. The three men, Dudley, Stephens, and Brooks, use the oarlocks of the dinghy to cut the boy into pieces and feed upon his body and blood for four days.

Four days after Parker is killed, with all the survivors still near death, their dinghy is spotted and picked up by a passing vessel, the *Moctezuma*. Dudley's and Stephens' calculations turn out to be right: if they had not killed Parker when they did, the three of them would not be now be alive to be rescued.

When they return to England, the men honestly and completely detail their time on the raft and Parker's death. Dudley answers all questions put to him, even re-enacting his actions in killing Parker. All are sorry that the boy was killed, but none appear to think that they have done anything wrong. However, they are arrested by the Falmouth harbor police and put in jail. All three men are confident that they will be released once the full details of their ordeal are made clear. Upon their arrival in Falmouth, public opinion condemns the men for failing to cast lots. However, by the time they are called before the Falmouth magistrates, the full details of their loss at sea are clear and the magistrates release the men on bail to cheers of approval from the gathered crowd.

When the case goes to trial, four additional judges are added to give the court's decision added weight. After hearing arguments from both sides regarding the existence of a necessity defense, the court rejects the defense of necessity and Dudley and Stephens are convicted of willful murder and sentenced to death.

Lesser Evils Justification

The criminal law defines the conduct that a society prohibits upon pain of criminal sanction, but it also acknowledges that there are some occasions when it may wish to tolerate or even encourage conduct that is normally prohibited. A forest fire is spreading toward an unsuspecting town. While destroying another's property is normally a crime, the community would very much prefer that a person who sees the threat take the initiative and burn a local farmer's field in order to create a firebreak that will save the town. From a societal perspective, the destruction of the field, though an attack on private property, is trivial in comparison to the destruction of the town and the risk to the lives of its inhabitants.

The balance of interests is not always so clear, however. In the *Dudley and Stephens* case, for example, the people adrift at sea are on the brink of death from dehydration and starvation. One more day without food and drink will leave them too weak to survive. Is killing the soon-to-be dead cabin boy in order to save the remaining three the right thing to do? Should they have a *lesser evils defense*, as with burning the cornfield to save the town? By hastening the cabin boy's death just a little, they can save three lives. Perhaps this is a good trade?

But hanging in the balance is more than just the tangible interests of losing all four lives versus losing one and saving three. Part of the balancing requires taking account of important intangible interests, such as the effect of having the law seem to approve taking the life of an innocent non-aggressor. When that important intangible is taken into account, the balance is not so clear. We may save three lives in the case at hand but create a dangerous precedent that may have terrible future costs by seeming to allow in other situations the killing of an innocent. The larger societal interest might be better served in the long run by enforcing an ironclad rule that always prohibits intentionally killing innocent persons.

When the court in *Dudley and Stephens* refuses to recognize a defense of necessity and convicts the two men of willful murder, it explains:

> It is . . . clear . . . that the doctrine contended for receives no support from the great authority of Lord Hale. It is plain that in his view the necessity which justified homicide is that only which has always been and is now considered a justification. . . . Lord Hale regarded the private necessity which justified, and alone justified, the taking the life of another for the safeguard of one's own to be what is commonly called "self defence."[5]

In other words, one might be justified in killing an unlawful aggressor but not in killing an innocent. Saving one's life is important, but not as important as the societal interest in protecting the innocent from aggression.

With the legal verdict of guilty publicly announced and the law seen as officially condemning the custom of cannibalism by those adrift at sea, the sentence is later quietly reduced by royal pardon to six months' imprisonment and a fine. Thus, while the conduct is publicly condemned, the offenders are privately excused.

In most instances, the law gives detailed rules about what prohibited conduct is legally justified under what circumstances, thereby telling people how to conform to the requirements of law. Modern American codes usually contain a range of specific justification defenses, including, for example, those concerning the use of force in self-defense or defense of others or defense of property, the use of force for law enforcement purposes, or by persons with special responsibility for the care, discipline, or safety of others, and for the performance of what otherwise would be criminal conduct when done in the execution of a public duty.[6]

But occasionally a case may arise in which the person's otherwise prohibited conduct is desirable or at least tolerable and is not covered by one of these *specific* justification defenses. This is the case with the firebreak hypothetical and the 1884 *Dudley and Stephens* cannibalism. None of the specific justification defenses covered there kind of situation – there is no unlawful aggressor, there is no exercise of public authority, and so on. To fill the gap, the law typically recognizes what might be called a general justification defense – commonly called the "lesser evils" justification or the "necessity" justification. The Model Penal Code's formulation of the general justification defense is reproduced in the margin.

A person can look to a lesser evils defense if, but only if, his or her situation is not already addressed in one of the specific justification defenses.[7] In other words, one cannot get around the specific rules governing self-defense laid down by the legislature in the definition of the self-defense justification by trying to rely instead upon the more open-ended general justification defense.

Justification Generally: Choice of Evils.

(1) Conduct which the actor believes to be necessary to avoid a harm or evil to himself or to another is justifiable, provided that:

(a) the harm or evil sought to be avoided by such conduct is greater than that sought to be prevented by the law defining the offense charged; and

(b) neither the Code nor other law defining the offense provides exceptions or defenses dealing with the specific situation involved; and

(c) a legislative purpose to exclude the justification claimed does not otherwise plainly appear.

Model Penal Code §3.02

Figure 11.2

Because of its general catchall role, the lesser evils defense can arise in a wide variety of situations, each presenting a different balance of competing societal interests. Consider this modern case.

Wolfgang Daschner – 2002

Jakob Metler, the son of a powerful German banking family, is 11 when he is kidnapped on his way home from school. The kidnapper demands €1,000,000, to be delivered to the Oberschweinstiege bus stop by Sunday night, assuring the family that Jakob will be returned safely if his demands are met. The Metzler family calls the police, and an investigation begins immediately.

The director of the Frankfurt police force is on vacation, leaving Wolfgang Daschner, a long-time police veteran, as the highest-ranking officer in the city. He activates the police emergency plan and orders that a special squad be formed to deal with the kidnapping. The police follow a number of initial leads but none pan out. The ransom is paid and the police observe 27-year-old Magnus Gäfgen take the money from its hiding place.

Gäfgen, it turns out, is no stranger to Jakob von Metzler. Gäfgen's 16-year-old girlfriend attends the same college as Jakob's sister. Gäfgen is a calm and highly intelligent law school student who lacks confidence and social skills. He has a history of trying to impress others with displays of wealth. He is, however, more than €10,000 in debt.

Police follow Gäfgen closely through the rest of the day. The morning after picking up the ransom money, Gäfgen deposits the money at various banks. He then test-drives a Mercedes and buys the car. Next, he picks up his girlfriend and books a vacation for them to the Moroccan Island of Fuerteventura and goes shopping.

Gäfgen does not appear to contact any accomplices, nor does he show any signs of caring for the child. The police worry that he has stashed the boy somewhere and is making no effort to care for him. Feeling that time is running out, they arrest Gäfgen and search his apartment, finding half of the ransom money in addition to a checklist with items such as "Inspect the driving route," "Inspect the boardwalk," "Backpacks," "Letter," "Test delivery of letter," and "Axe."[8] From their investigation, police conclude that Gäfgen does not have accomplices and does have the boy hidden away.

At 6:20 p.m., police begin interrogating Gäfgen. After they tell him what they have found, he admits that he deposited the money at various banks, bought a car, and booked a vacation. He evades all questions regarding the location of the child, and ultimately asks for legal counsel.

When Daschner is advised at 8:00 p.m. of the lack of progress in finding the child, he tells the officers that force can be used to compel Gäfgen to divulge the boy's location before it's too late.[9] The officer in charge of the interrogation does not see this as an order from Daschner, but rather as authorization of an additional tool for interrogators to consider.

A psychologist suggests that the police confront Gäfgen with Jakob's siblings, whom Gäfgen had tried to befriend in the past. The officers agree, and bring in Jakob's siblings and parents, who beg Gäfgen to reveal where Jakob is being held. Gäfgen refuses.

Figure 11.3 Wolfgang Daschner during a court hearing, 2011

After more cajoling, Gäfgen tells the police that Jakob is being held in a shack by a lake in Langen, a small suburb outside Frankfurt. Hours are spent following up on the information, but it turns out to be a lie.

At 8:00 a.m. the next day, Daschner directs that force be used to compel Gäfgen to reveal the child's location. The Frankfurt SWAT commander says that he only knows of one police officer who could administer painful force in a way that would be sure to not cause injury, an instructor in martial arts. A helicopter is sent to collect the officer.

There are no doubts at this point that Gäfgen alone knows where the boy is. Daschner's lieutenant enters the room where Gäfgen is being interrogated and tells Gäfgen that if he continues to lie or to remain silent, "a special officer is on a helicopter on its way here, and he can inflict pain on you which you will never forget."[10] Gäfgen now reveals that he has hidden Jakob below a boardwalk near a lake – approximately 40 miles from Frankfurt. The police take Gäfgen with them as they race toward the boy, and find him just where Gäfgen said they would.

The use of force that causes pain, even if it does not cause injury, is normally a criminal assault. Daschner would argue, however, that he ought to have a lesser evils defense in the situation: he is causing non-injurious temporary pain in order to save the boy's life. And this comparison of the conflicting personal interests of the kidnapper and his victim might well suggest Daschner's balance is an appropriate one.

However, the balance of interests becomes somewhat more complicated when one takes into account society's long-term interest in prohibiting the use of force in police interrogations. It could well be argued that there is value in having a bright red line to guide cases in the future, just as the *Dudley and Stephens* court wanted to establish a bright red line against killing innocent non-aggressors in the lifeboat case. However, rational people can disagree about these calculations.

Diversity among the States for a Lesser Evils Defense

As the map below illustrates, jurisdictions take different approaches in defining the catchall general *justification defense*.[11] The darker the shading, the more narrow the availability of the defense.

In the broadest formulation of the defense, modeled after Model Penal Code Section 3.02, quoted in the margin above, the four states shown in the lightest shading on the map provide the lesser evils justification if the person's conduct is necessary to avoid a greater harm or evil than that threatened. The *necessity requirement* has two aspects to it: necessary in amount and necessary in time. Under the first, the defendant cannot do more harm or evil than is necessary to avoid the threat. A shooting will not be justified if a push would avert the danger. Under the second, the defendant cannot act before it is necessary; he must delay until the last moment in which he can still successfully avoid the threat.

In 24 other jurisdictions, those with light shading and a dots overlay on the map, the same lesser evils formulation is provided: the person is justified if his conduct avoids a greater harm or evil than it causes. In these jurisdictions, however, an *imminence requirement* is added: the defendant cannot get a *lesser evils defense* unless the threatened harm or evil is imminent. This formulation is probably the result of a policy judgment that fails to understand that the necessity requirement already addresses the temporal issue: the person cannot justifiably act until his conduct is necessary; if he can

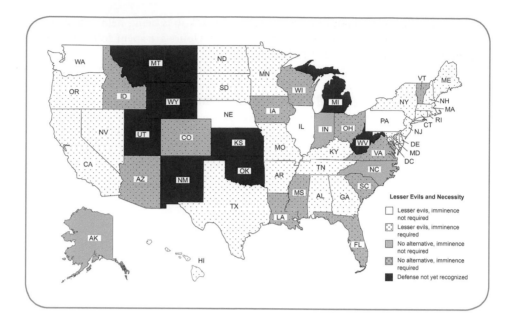

Figure 11.4

as effectively act later, then his conduct is not yet necessary. Adding to this a requirement that the threat be *imminent* may go too far, because it may require that the actor wait until it is too late to successfully avoid the threat. For example, if the law requires that the person wait until the forest fire's threat to the town is literally *imminent*, it may be too late to burn an effective firebreak. If the town is to be saved, the firebreak must be burned well ahead of time, before the destruction of the town is actually imminent. One sees these kinds of limitations on the lesser evils defense because some jurisdictions worry about its potential breadth and they see this as a means of narrowing it.

A minority of jurisdictions, shown in medium shading, adopt a narrower form of the general justification defense. They are similar in that they typically require that the harm caused be less than the harm threatened – although they commonly express this in terms of "proportionality of the harm done compared to the harm avoided." However, they go further and also require that the person had "no alternative" or "no reasonable alternative" means of avoiding the threatened harm or evil. The defendant's course of conduct must be the only course open to him that would avoid the threatened harm or evil.

It is not entirely clear that the additional "no alternative" requirement will in practice narrow the defense in the way that these jurisdictions might expect it to. If there are two different courses of conduct by which a threatened harm or evil can be avoided and both are equally less harmful than what is threatened, the lesser evils formulation described in the first two groups would allow the person a lesser evils defense for either course of conduct. In contrast, the "no alternative" formulation would seem to deny a defense to both alternatives because, whichever course of conduct the person takes, there is *an alternative* course that he could have taken.

It is possible that a jury's intuitions of justice would reject this technical application of the "no alternative" formulation and would simply provide the defense even though the person did have an alternative course of conduct. In other words, in practice, the addition of the "no alternative" requirement might be taken more as a point of emphasis that the conduct must be necessary to avoid the greater harm than as a literal limitation. However, jurors might well follow their instructions as given, as they take an oath to do. Further, different juries may respond differently to the limitation and thus this formulation introduces a degree of unpredictability and arbitrariness in the adjudication process.

Twelve other jurisdictions, those with medium shading and a dots overlay on the map, adopt the "no alternative" formulation and narrow it further by imposing an imminence requirement. Thus, under this formulation, even if the person had no alternative to avoid the threatened harm or evil, he will get no defense if he does not wait until the threat is imminent. For the reasons noted above, this imminence requirement seems a bad policy. It should be enough to require, as the imminence-not-required formulations do, that it was *necessary for the person to act when he did* in order to avoid the threat, even if that means acting before the threat is fully imminent.

Eight other states, those shaded black on the map, have not yet recognized a general justification defense. This is sometimes because they simply have not yet had a case that requires recognizing such a defense in order to do justice. But this simply points to a legislative failure. The criminal law ought to be predictable, and ought to be determined by the legislator rather than left to ad hoc and ex post discretionary lawmaking by the judicial branch. Nor is leaving the issue unresolved until some court decides whether and what lesser evils defense to recognize, consistent with the legality principle.[12]

In some jurisdictions, a lesser evils or necessity defense is not yet recognized because the lawmakers, and frequently the courts, confuse the issue of a justification based upon lesser evils with the issue of an excuse based upon a claim of duress. They mistakenly believe that the justification cases can be fully and adequately dealt with by recognizing a coercion defense. In the two cases examined above, one can see that the sailors adrift at sea might well be able to make a duress of circumstances claim, but that clearly is not true for the good Samaritan passerby who sees the forest fire headed for the unsuspecting town. Nor is it true for officer Daschner trying to find the location of the kidnapping victim. The fire bystander is not personally threatened in the way the dying sailors are, yet, we very much hope he will burn the firebreak, even at some risk to himself, because it will save the town. If only a duress of circumstances excuse is available, he will get no defense and would be criminally liable if he acts to save the town. (It should also be noted that many if not most jurisdictions recognize a duress excuse only when the duress is *applied by another person* and recognize no duress excuse when the coercion is applied by natural circumstances.[13])

This confusion between the categories of justification and excuse defenses creates other serious problems that will become apparent as we look at other general defenses in the coming chapters. Burning the firebreak is not conduct to be excused, as we would excuse somebody who commits an offense because they are insane, under duress, involuntarily intoxicated, or immature. The firebreak burner is blameless *not despite the harmfulness* of his conduct but rather *because his conduct causes no net harm*. Indeed, it creates a net benefit for society. Justified conduct is conduct that we want to signal to others that they too can and perhaps should engage in under similar circumstances in the future. Excused conduct, in contrast, is conduct that we would prefer was never performed, but we are willing to exculpate the actor despite the harmfulness of his conduct because we find him to be blameless for doing it.

Do We Really Need a General Justification (Lesser Evils/Necessity) Defense?

One might conclude that few enough cases arise under the lesser evils justification that perhaps the absence or poor formulation of such a defense ought not be a matter of concern. But the fact is that the defense plays a critical role in a democratic society that cares about justice. First, there inevitably will be cases that raise issues of justification where the situation is not addressed by one of the more specialized *justification defenses* such as self-defense or law enforcement authority. If the society cares about justice, the defendants in those cases ought to have the benefit of a defense where their conduct avoids the greater harm or evil.

Second, the cases in which the *lesser evils defense* arise tend to be important cases with a high profile. The criminal law must be seen as having a clear and just answer in these instances. Sometimes, it may be as important to have the criminal law publicly reject a lesser evils defense as it is in other cases to have the law grant it. But in any case, the law must have a mechanism for providing an answer. Protesters offer a lesser evils defense for damaging an oil pipeline or a nuclear reactor or the Pentagon or an abortion clinic. In each instance, the law's resolution of the case can have far-reaching implications for signaling the propriety of the conduct and the balance of the competing interests.

Finally, the lesser evils defense is unique among justification defenses because it is the one instance in which the criminal law must speak to a justification claim when the legislature has not previously set out a specific rule. What is special about the lesser evils justification, then, is that in the absence of a legislative determination in balancing the competing interests, it is the jury who is called upon to make the judgment, rather than leaving the matter to an individual judge. To the extent that one believes in democratic values and the importance of criminal law reflecting community judgments, it is the lesser evils defense that assures that this deference to community views will prevail.

Aftermaths

In the *Dudley and Stephens* shipwreck case, the public, the courts, and both defendants expect that the Queen will grant a pardon now that the law has officially condemned the custom of cannibalism. They wait in jail for seven days, expecting each day to receive a pardon. On December 11, the sentence is reduced to six months' imprisonment starting from the date of judgment.

The survivors enjoy great notoriety for a short time (including a wax sculpture in Madam Tussaud's). They are formally forgiven by Parker's family. Although their sailing certificates are restored, Dudley finds it difficult to find work in the yachting community and decides to make a new start, moving his family to Australia and becoming a tent and tarpaulin maker. Stephens never quite recovers from the ordeal; he becomes depressed and ultimately turns to alcohol abuse. He dies a poor man at the age of 66. Ned Brooks appears for a while in amusement shows but soon returns to the sea and dies poor and childless 25 years later.

In the *Daschner* case, when the location of the kidnap victim is finally revealed by Gäfgen, police go to the location but find that young Jakob has already suffocated to death.

Later that day, Daschner writes a memo to the local prosecutor's office explaining his reasons for ordering the use of force against a suspect in custody. He explains that "determining the child's location cannot be deferred any longer; it is the duty of the police to rescue the kidnapped child . . . This interrogation of Gäfgen is not done to solve the case, but solely to save the child."

Daschner is relieved of his post a few days after the incident as the press learns of his force-in-interrogation directive. The public reaction is mixed. Interior Minister Otto Schily tells a newspaper, "If we begin to relativize the ban on torture, we are putting ourselves back in the darkest Middle Ages and risk putting all of our values into question." However, Minister Schily goes on to claim that Daschner's actions were "honorable" because he had good intentions. Not all agree: Amnesty International issues a statement condemning Daschner's actions.

In 2003, Gäfgen is convicted of murder, kidnapping, and two counts of false accusations. He receives a life sentence with reduced chances for parole, and his appeal to the German constitutional court is rejected.

In 2005, Daschner is put on trial for ordering the coercion. He is found guilty of persuading a subordinate to commit a crime and sentenced to a year of probation. The presiding judge gives Daschner this minimum sentence because he had the "honorable motive of saving a life." (The lieutenant who actually conveyed the threat to Gäfgen is found guilty of coercion, fined €3,600, and sentenced to a year of probation.)

In 2006, Gäfgen appeals his kidnapping and murder convictions to the European Court of Human Rights, alleging that his trial was unfair because it used evidence obtained after he was coerced to give incriminating statements by agents of the state. In a 2008 ruling, the court holds that Gäfgen cannot claim to have been a victim of a constitutional violation because the evidence obtained via threat was not a coerced confession, rather only an admission of the location of von Metzler's body. Additionally, the trial court barred the prosecution from using any testimony obtained via coercion, thus making the proceeding acceptable to the ECHR. Gäfgen's appeal is dismissed, and as of this writing, he remains in prison.

Chapter Glossary

Imminence Requirement: Many justification defenses require that the threat of harm be imminent before an actor may use force. Underlying this requirement is a presumption that, unless the danger is imminent, action is not yet necessary but this may not always be true. The Model Penal Code does not include requirement that the threat be imminent but only that the use of force be immediately necessary.[14]

Justification Defense: A defense that arises when the defendant's conduct, which would otherwise be an offense, is not prohibited because it promotes or protects a societal interest greater than the harm or evil of the offense. Justification defenses include such defenses as self-defense, defense of others, defense of property, lesser evils defense (necessity/choice of evils), law enforcement authority, and the use of force by public authority.[15]

Lesser Evils Defense: Also called the "choice of evils" defense or the "necessity" defense, a lesser evils defense exculpates an offender when the harm or evil sought to be avoided by his or her conduct is greater than that sought to be prevented by the law defining the offense charged.[16]

Necessity Requirement: All justification defenses have an explicit or implicit necessity requirement that limits the justified conduct to that which is necessary in time and necessary in amount to promote or protect the societal interest at stake. Thus, both a private actor using force in self-defense and a law enforcement officer making an arrest may use force only when it is necessary and only the amount that is necessary.[17]

Notes

1. This narrative is drawn from the following sources: A.W. Brian Simpson, *Cannibalism and the Common Law: The Story of the Tragic Last Voyage of the* Mignonette *and the Strange Legal Proceedings to Which It Gave Rise* (Chicago: The University of Chicago Press, 1984); *Regina v. Dudley and Stephens*, 14 Q.B.D. 273 (1884); see Paul H. Robinson, *Criminal Law Case Studies*, 5th ed. (St. Paul: West, 2015), pp. 29–37.
2. Simpson, 'The Horrid Deed,' in *Cannibalism and the Common Law*, p. 61.
3. Simpson, 'The Horrid Deed,' p. 67.
4. Simpson, 'The Horrid Deed,' p. 67.
5. *Regina v. Dudley and Stephens*, 14 Q.B.D. 273 (1884).
6. *See, e.g.,* Model Penal Code article 3, General Principles of Justification; Paul H. Robinson, Shima Baradaran Baughman, and Michael T. Cahill, *Criminal Law*, 4th ed., '8.1., §4.1.2 (New York: Wolters Kluwer, 2016).
7. Robinson, Baughman, and Cahill, *Criminal Law*.
8. Paul H. Robinson, *Criminal Law Case Studies*, 6th ed. (St. Paul: West Academic, 2020), pp. 139–142.
9. Robinson, *Criminal Law Case Studies*, p. 140.
10. Robinson, *Criminal Law Case Studies*, p. 141.
11. The map is taken from Paul H. Robinson and Tyler Scot Williams, 'Lesser Evils/Necessity Defense,' in *Mapping American Criminal Law: Variations Across the 50 States* (Westport: Prager, 2018), p. 131. All supporting authorities are available from that source.
12. As discussed in Chapter 1.
13. *See, e.g.,* Model Penal Code §2.09(1).
14. Robinson and Cahill, *Criminal Law*, §8.2.
15. MPC art 3; *Justification Defense*, Black's.
16. MPC §3.02(1)(a).
17. Robinson and Cahill, *Criminal Law*, §8.2.2; MPC art 3.

Chapter 12

Self-Defense

Slave Celia Defends against Rape

1855. Florence Nightingale, a British nurse of upper-class birth, cares for those wounded in the Crimean War and champions the improvement of sanitary conditions at military hospitals. As a result of her efforts, which spark worldwide reform in the delivery of healthcare, the death rate among those wounded is reduced by two-thirds and nursing as a true public health profession begins. The reform comes not a moment too soon. In the same year, the third pandemic of the Black Plague strikes. This round of the disease begins in Yunnan, China and kills more than 12 million people in India and China alone. Finding easy mobility on ships, the plague circles the globe for the next 50 years. In the U.S., the first bridge across the Mississippi River is completed in Minnesota. Trains can now reach the American West. The country is expanding and there is fierce debate about whether slavery will also be allowed to expand. As the debate goes on, American slaves continue to suffer the same daily indignity and brutality that they have all their lives.

Slave Celia – 1855

Callaway County in central Missouri is nestled between the state's vast prairies to the north and the green highlands of the Ozarks to the south.[1] In 1818, the lands there draw thousands of settlers from the east. The Missouri wilds pose a hardship for the new arrivals but the abundant natural resources promise prosperity for those who are able to tame the land.

In 1850, Robert Newsom, who arrived in Callaway County decades ago, decides to purchase a sixth slave – a 14-year-old girl named Celia, ostensibly to help his daughters with housework. After purchasing Celia, Newsom and Celia begin the trek to Newsom's farm nine miles south of the Fulton Township, but for Newsom, it seems, the trek is too long to wait. Even before they reach the farm, Newsom violently rapes

DOI: 10.4324/9781003258025-14

Celia. Newsom is 60 years old and recently widowed, and Celia becomes both his property and his concubine.

Newsom sets up a small cabin for Celia separate from the five slave men. The cabin, nestled in a grove of fruit trees, is 150 feet from his house, convenient not only for Celia to work in the house but for Newsom to access to her cabin.

As the years pass, Newsom makes countless trips to Celia's cabin and rapes her routinely. Between 1850 and 1855, Celia gives birth to two children. As is the custom, her children automatically become Newsom's property. Sometime before 1855, Celia begins an emotional relationship with George, another of Newsom's slaves. George begins staying at Celia's cabin at night; the relationship is risky, as Newsom would be unlikely to tolerate it if he found out.

When Celia, now 19 years old, becomes pregnant again in the early spring of 1855, George is hurt and insulted, believing the child to be fathered by Newsom (though the actual father remains unclear). George delivers an ultimatum: "He would have nothing more to do with her if she did not quit the old man."[2] Celia feels trapped, threatened on one side by Newsom's endless sexual exploitation, and on the other by the risk of losing George's affection.

Celia swallows her fear and confronts Newsom directly on June 23, 1855, begging him to leave her alone and threatening to use force otherwise. Newsom shrugs off Celia's pleas, and – perhaps to reinforce his sense of sexual ownership – insists that he is "coming to her cabin that night."[3]

True to his word, Newsom leaves his house at around 10:00 p.m. that night and makes the short trek to Celia's cabin. Celia, however, also stays true to her word; she is prepared to defend herself. Earlier that afternoon, she stashed a heavy stick, "about as large as the upper part of a Windsor chair, but not so long,"[4] in the back corner of her cabin. When Newsom enters the cabin and ignores her demands to leave, Celia hoists the stick in her hands, swings it toward Newsom, and strikes him squarely on his head. Newsom – immediately dazed by the blow – staggers and "[sinks] down on a stool or towards the floor," throwing his hands up toward Celia.[5] Celia acts swiftly; as she would later tell a reporter, "as soon as I struck him the Devil got into me."[6] She clubs Newsom over the head again, killing him.

The cabin is still. After spending an hour thinking about her next steps, she decides to burn Newsom's body. She sneaks outside, gathers wood, and builds a hot fire in her own fireplace. She shoves his body in and lets it burn all night, adding wood constantly.

It is not long before Newsom's absence is noticed by his family. After a fruitless search of the nearby riverbanks and coves, the family decides to get more help. By mid-morning, a search party of family and neighbors fan out across the area. The search yields nothing, and the party's attention turns toward the slaves. Someone – probably a member of the Newsom family who was aware of George's victimization of Celia – suggests that George, Celia's lover, might know where Newsom is. A wave of anger and fear rise in the group; perhaps, they think, George harmed Newsom out of jealousy over Celia.

When George is interrogated, he hesitates at first, perhaps in an attempt to protect Celia, but things change quickly when he ominously suggests that "it was not worthwhile to hunt for him anywhere except close around the house."[7] While it's unknown whether George had actually learned about Newsom's fate by then, the family grows alarmed and suspicious, demanding more information. George is trapped and quickly implicates Celia. Celia is unable to hold up against her interrogators and eventually tells the whole story.

Figure 12.1 Celia not long before her execution, circa 1854

On October 9, 1855, the case of *State of Missouri v. Celia, a Slave*, begins. Celia admits to killing Newsom but adds that "she did not intend to kill him when she struck him, but only wanted to hurt him."[8] Defense counsel's cross-examination immediately fixates on Newsom's repeated raping of Celia over the years, Celia's youth at the time of the first rape, and Celia's intention to injure rather than kill Newsom on the night of June 23. Virginia, Newsom's daughter, admits that Celia had become pregnant in February and had grown too sick to even cook.

While defense counsel presents the case as one of *self-defense*, and Celia's first blow against Newsom might be seen as defending against an imminent threat, her second blow, which killed him, came after he was no longer an immediate threat (although she might argue that he could become a threat again later).

Ultimately, the trial court short-circuits the self-defense issue by ruling that the rape itself could not legally be considered a crime.[9] Thus, the jury is instructed that Celia cannot raise an official claim of self-defense. On October 10, 1855, the jury convicts Celia of first-degree murder. (The notoriety of the case will help galvanize anti-slavery sentiment around the country.)

Self-Defense

The criminal law normally prohibits any use of force against another person, but such use of force is sometimes authorized. Justification defenses define a variety of such authorized use of force situations, one of the most common of which is situations of *self-defense*.[10] A right of self-defense against an unlawful aggressor is probably the earliest recognized exception to the general prohibition against killing. The defense was recognized in the earliest of criminal laws, including the Code of Hammurabi.[11] Fourth century A.D. Roman law similarly codified the defense.

> Roman law was very protective of the individual's right to defend himself and his property from violence, whether offered by a thief on a darkened highway or a soldier in search of plunder. A provision attributed to the late fourth century A.D. reads: We grant to all persons the unrestricted power to defend themselves (Iiberam resistendi cunctis tribuimus facultatem), so that it is proper to subject anyone, whether a private person or a soldier, who trespasses upon fields at night in search of plunder, or lays by busy roads plotting to assault passers-by, to immediate punishment in accordance with the authority granted to all (permissa cuicumque licentia dignus ilico suppliio subiugetur). Let him suffer the death which he threatened and incur that which he intended (CodexJustinianus 3.27.1). The legislator then explains the rationale for this provision, stating, "For it is better to meet the danger at the time, than to obtain legal redress (vindicare) after one's death."[12]

Generally, today a person may use the force that is necessary to defend against the threat of unlawful force by an aggressor. But in addition to this *necessary* force requirement, the self-defense justification has a *proportionality* requirement of sorts: a person may in self-defense use deadly force – that is, force that risks causing death (or, in some jurisdictions risks serious bodily injury) – only when threatened with serious bodily injury (or, in some jurisdictions, with other felonies). See the limitations on the use of force in self-defense provided by the Model Penal Code provision reproduced in the margin.

Clearly, Celia would normally have a right to use force to defend herself against the rape, and indeed would have the right to use deadly force. And because she was attacked in her home, she had no obligation to retreat before the use of such deadly force. If there is a complication for her, it arises in relation to her second blow against Newsom, rather than her first. The prosecution might argue that, after her first blow, Newsom no longer presented a threat, and thus her second blow, which is what killed him, was not justified.

She might argue, however, that once she had struck her first blow, which was justified, it was likely that he would kill her as soon as he was able, whether it was a few minutes later after he had a chance to recover or was the next day. However, the necessary-in-time requirement would require her to wait until the last moment when she could still successfully defend. But she could well argue that her only chance of a successful defense was to act now, while she had the opportunity. If she waited until he chose the moment to new attack, he would pick a time and conditions where she could not successfully defend.

Unfortunately for defenders in Celia's situation, most American jurisdictions have rejected the necessary-in-time requirement of the Model Penal Code, quoted in the margin, and instead allow defensive force only against a threat that is "imminent."[13] Under this approach, once Celia struck Newsom the first blow, there was no longer an "imminent" threat, and Celia's second blow could not be justified.

Even if her second blow was not objectively justified, however, she might be entitled to a defense for having made a *reasonable mistake as to justification*, given how chaotic the situation and how terrified she must have been. (More on the excuse of mistake as to justification later. It will be a primary issue in the following chapter.[14])

Use of Force in Self-Protection.
(1) Use of Force Justifiable for Protection of the Person.
[T]he use of force upon or toward another person is justifiable when the actor believes that such force is immediately necessary for the purpose of protecting himself against the use of unlawful force by such other person on the present occasion.
(2) Limitations on Justifying Necessity for Use of Force.
...
(b) The use of deadly force is not justifiable under this Section unless the actor believes that such force is necessary to protect himself against death, serious bodily harm, kidnapping or sexual intercourse compelled by force or threat; nor is it justifiable if: ...
(ii) the actor knows that he can avoid the necessity of using such force with complete safety by retreating ... , except that:
(1) the actor is not obliged to retreat from his dwelling or place of work, unless he was the initial aggressor or is assailed in his place of work by another person whose place of work the actor knows it to be; ...

Model Penal Code §3.04

Figure 12.2

As noted above, however, these self-defense issues were never reached because the court at the time took the appalling view that rape of a slave was not "unlawful force" and thus did not trigger any right of self-defense.

Consider how these same self-defense issues play out in a more modern case.

Bernhard Goetz – 1984

One night in January, 1981 Bernhard ("Bernie") Goetz is riding the New York City subway.[15] He runs his own electronics repair business from his apartment in Manhattan's Greenwich Village and is carrying a batch of expensive electronic equipment. Suddenly, as the train approaches the Canal Street station, three young men slam Goetz into a glass door, drive the handle into his chest, and then throw him to the ground. With the help of a janitor, Goetz is able to grab hold of the ringleader, Fred Clark, until the police arrive.

The police take Goetz back to the station and question him for more than six hours, while apparently releasing the attackers after less than half that time. His assailants are charged only with criminal mischief – for ripping Goetz's jacket – because authorities conclude that there is insufficient evidence for a successful attempted robbery prosecution. The mugging and the system's inability to protect him disturbs Goetz so much that he spends more than $2,000 trying to obtain a concealed weapon permit. The police turn him down.

Meanwhile, New York City's problems of widespread drug use and rampant crime are only getting worse. By 1984, the city has an annual tally of 600,000 crimes. The steeply escalating rates of street crime and violent crime are linked to the growing epidemic of crack cocaine. The violence hits the subway system in particular: 40 felonies are committed against New York City subway riders every day. Many feel that "the system" has let them down and no longer trust law enforcement to protect them.

The physical and emotional scars of the Goetz's mugging remain; three years on it is clear that his knees are permanently injured and he fears being "beaten to a pulp" by muggers.[16] He likens himself to a caged rat that is continuously poked with red-hot needles. To feel safe, he now leaves his apartment only with a .38 caliber gun in a quick-draw holster.

On December 22, 1984, Goetz leaves his apartment in the early afternoon and catches the train to head downtown. Nearby are four young men, Darrell Cabey, Barry Allen, Troy Canty, and James Ramseur, all high school dropouts with criminal records.[17] Earlier in the year, Cabey had been arrested for armed robbery, accused of robbing three other men at gunpoint. Allen has twice pled guilty to disorderly conduct. Ramseur and Canty have been convicted of petit larceny.

Their aggressive, threatening behavior causes the 15–20 other passengers in the subway car to move to the other end of the car. The men approach Goetz and ask for five dollars. They surround him and are armed with sharpened screwdrivers. Goetz believes that he is being held up for his money but, to be certain, he asks them to repeat their request. One of the group obliges saying, "Give me five dollars."[18]

Goetz pulls his gun and fires rapidly at them. The men scatter. He hits three of the four. A few seconds pass and Goetz registers that Cabey, sprawled near the conductor's cab, is unharmed, so he shoots him. Other passengers pull the emergency cord, jerking the train to a stop. Everyone exits except two terrified women, whom Goetz tries to comfort. When the conductor enters the car and asks Goetz if he is a police officer, Goetz says no and explains that the young men were trying to rob him. Goetz walks off into the subway tunnel.

The men are left lying in pools of blood on the train car's floor. Canty, Allen, and Ramseur all sustain upper body injuries but eventually recover. The shooting paralyzes Cabey and leaves him with permanent brain damage.

Two days later, Goetz walks into the Concord, New Hampshire police station and gives a statement to police. He is interviewed by New Hampshire authorities for two hours and then by New York authorities for two more.

Popular support for Goetz grows. He is dubbed the "subway vigilante" by the New York Post,[19] and the police phone line for the case is called the "avenger hotline." Most of the people who call offer their support and approval of Goetz's actions, and 237 of 240 letters sent to the mayor's office about the case support Goetz's actions. A legal defense fund is set up for Goetz and the "Guardian Angels" group (who patrol the

Figure 12.3 The aftermath of the shooting on the train, 1984

NYC subway system) solicit contributions from passengers. One man who has also been a victim of assault and robbery offers his life savings of $50,000 for bail. Goetz's statement to the police makes clear that he was scared, in some significant part because of prior victimization.

While he has a great deal of grass-roots support, officials are not happy with Goetz.[20] Mayor Ed Koch condemns Goetz's behavior, and President Reagan lectures that while we can all sympathize with "the frustration of people who are constantly threatened by crime and feel that law and order is not particularly protecting them,"[21] *vigilantism* is "a breakdown of civilization."[22] A grand jury returns indictments for Goetz on three counts of illegal gun possession, but not on any of more serious charges such as aggravated assault or attempted murder. In the days that follow, Goetz urges private citizens to arm themselves while the NAACP labels Goetz as a modern version of a KKK "nightrider."[23] Two of the men whom Goetz shot (including Cabey, who is paralyzed for life) file a lawsuit, and their civil rights attorney seeks $50 million in punitive and compensatory damages. The District Attorney's office is criticized for not offering the victims immunity, which would have allowed them to testify before the Grand Jury without fear of prosecution. U.S. Attorney Rudolph Giuliani (subsequently elected NYC mayor) says that the federal government will not prosecute Goetz for depriving the men of their civil rights because there is no evidence of racism.

Shortly after Giuliani's statement, the District Attorney's office releases a report of Goetz's New Hampshire confession, in which he states he went up to Cabey, said something like "You seem to be doing all right; here's another,"[24] and shot him. This disclosure changes public perception. The D.A. presents assault and attempted murder charges to a second grand jury. During the second presentation, the D.A. gives Ramseur and Canty immunity and has them testify. The second grand jury indicts Goetz on multiple counts.

On March 23, 1987, jury selection for the trial begins. Goetz is charged with attempted murder, assault, reckless endangerment, and criminal possession of a gun. The jury is made up of ten Whites and two Blacks. Goetz argues that his use of deadly force was a reasonable response to the men who were clearly trying to rob him, especially given his past experience with such dangerous situations. The Assistant District Attorney argues that Goetz did not act in a reasonable way.

The jury deliberates for 30 hours. Goetz is found not guilty on 12 of 13 counts. He is convicted of a single charge of criminal possession of a weapon in the third degree. A majority of New Yorkers support his acquittal, feeling that it shows that people have the right to stand up and protect themselves when the police fail them in a city overridden with crime and victimization.

Goetz is sentenced to six months in jail, fined $5,075, and given four years of probation. The ruling is appealed and just before Thanksgiving, 1988, New York's appellate court upholds Goetz's conviction. Goetz's sentence is increased to one year in prison, in keeping with the mandatory minimum.

In many ways, the *Celia* case and the *Goetz* case raise similar self-defense issues in some respects. Although the harm threatened to Celia was dramatically greater than that threatened to Goetz, most jurisdictions allow the use of deadly force to prevent a rape or a robbery. Celia's first blow was clearly necessary to protect herself and Goetz can argue that his initial shots were necessary because he was outnumbered and surrounded and had no other means of protecting himself.

However, Celia's second blow was, as a technical matter, unnecessary because the first blow had already neutralized the imminent threat. But Goetz may have greater difficulty justifying his later shot of Cabey, who was no longer presenting a threat, because he was not acting instantly following his first shot, as seems to have been the case with Celia's second blow. Both defendants might argue that if the use of additional force – the second blow and the second shot – was not in fact objectively necessary, they ought to be excused because in the chaos and fear of the moment it would be easy for a reasonable person to *believe* that the later use of force was immediately necessary to defend against an ongoing threat. Celia is certainly in a stronger position to make the argument of a reasonable mistake, because Goetz seems to have had more of an opportunity to collect himself before deciding to shoot Cabey.

How such cases would play out today may depend upon the jurisdiction in which they arise.

Diversity among the States on Self-Defense

As the shadings on map below show,[25] states disagree about exactly what threats should trigger a right to use deadly force in *self-defense*. Should it be permitted only to defend against the threat of serious bodily injury (no shading), or also to defend against rape, robbery, or kidnapping (light shading)? Against other felonies (the two darker shadings)?

Celia is clearly defending against a threat of serious bodily injury, so will satisfy this requirement in all jurisdictions. Goetz can claim that he is defending against robbery, which triggers a right to use deadly defensive force in all but the unshaded jurisdictions. It is more debatable, however, whether he can claim he was defending against serious bodily injury, which is the only thing that would trigger a right to use deadly force in the unshaded jurisdictions.

In the kind of chaotic situations in which self-defense claims typically arise, it is not uncommon for offenders to make a mistake – for example, in perceiving the exact nature of the threat, in judging what kind of force is necessary to effectively defend, or with regard to a wide variety of other legally relevant factors, such as whether safe retreat is possible. Every state will excuse a defender for making a reasonable mistake – that is, a mistake that a reasonable person could have made under the same

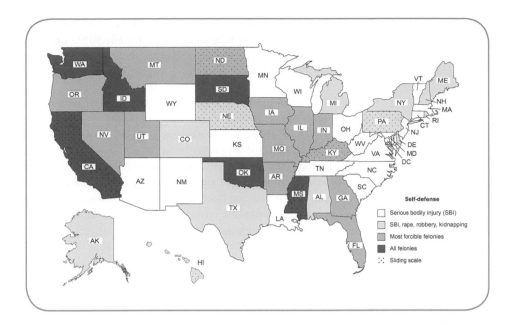

Figure 12.4

circumstances.[26] The person who shoots an attacker pointing a handgun and threatening to kill him or her will have a complete defense in all jurisdictions if it turns out that the attacker's weapon is in reality just a realistic replica of a handgun. Even a reasonable person in the actor's situation could have made the same mistake in assuming the replica posed a threat to his or her life.

However, jurisdictions disagree about what to do if a defender makes an honest but *unreasonable mistake* – that is, a reckless or negligent mistake. An unreasonable, in the sense of negligent, mistake occurs, for example, where the thought never enters the defender's mind that her attacker is threatening only bodily injury (not serious bodily injury) but a reasonable person in her situation would have realized this possibility. In such a case, the defender has made a negligent mistake (as to the seriousness of the threat). Imagine, for instance, that the aggressor verbally threatening death is pointing a replica of a gun but this replica has a yellow plastic tip. Depending upon the exact circumstances – what had happened previously to the intended victim, how obvious it was that the gun was a toy, and what kind of physical threat the aggressor presented beyond the toy gun – a jury might conclude that the mistake was an honest but an unreasonable (negligent) one: the reasonable person would not have made the same mistake in the same situation. In such a case of unreasonable mistake, some jurisdictions will excuse the mistake but most will not.

Most states, 43 (those without a dots overlay on the map), would deny any excuse defense to such an unjustified defender making a negligent mistake, leaving her fully liable for the offense, such as murder. These jurisdictions take what is commonly called the *all-or-nothing approach*, which means that an actor's unreasonable (negligent or reckless) belief that she is justified will not provide any defense or mitigation – she instead incurs full liability. Only a fully reasonable mistake – a non-negligent mistake – provides an excuse and thereby avoids criminal liability.

An alternative to the all-or-nothing *approach* is found in the eight states (with a dots overlay on the map) that follow the Model Penal Code in using a *sliding scale approach*.[27] Under this approach, a defender's reasonable mistake will provide a complete defense, while her negligent mistake will leave her criminally liable but only for a negligent offense. Thus, if she kills in mistaken self-defense and her mistake is negligent, she can be held liable for negligent homicide. If she has made a reckless mistake, she can be held liable for reckless homicide (manslaughter).

Today, Celia's use of deadly force for her second blow might very well be determined to be an entirely reasonable mistake. It seems considerably less likely that Goetz's delayed shooting of Cabey would be seen as a reasonable mistake. If the jury finds that Celia's or Goetz's use of force was not a reasonable mistake, then the defender would be liable in the 43 all-or-nothing jurisdictions for the full offense, Celia for murder and Goetz for aggravated assault. In the eight sliding-scale jurisdictions, however, the mistaken defender would only be liable for a reduced offense, tying the level of liability to the level of culpability of their mistake. If Goetz's mistake is judged to be negligent, then he is liable for negligent assault, and, if judged to be reckless, then he is liable for reckless assault.

To What Threats Should the Right to Use Deadly Defensive Force Be Limited?

There seems to be some considerable disagreement among the states about what kind of threats should give rise to the right to use deadly force in *self-defense*, as noted above. Nineteen states limit deadly force to defending against a threat of death or serious bodily injury; one state adds to that list the threat of rape; four others add the crime of kidnapping; eight more add the offense of robbery; 13 states add miscellaneous other serious felonies, such as arson, aggravated battery, and burglary – in other words, most forcible felonies – while 16 states drop the list approach altogether and authorize the use of deadly force to defend against any felony.

One can imagine criticisms that could be made against each of these approaches, especially those at the extremes of the continuum. Why should the use of deadly force be limited to threats of death or serious bodily injury and not to other serious offenses, such as rape? Isn't it too broad to authorize deadly force against all felonies, including non-forcible felonies? These jurisprudential questions raise interesting points about the relative importance of citizens being able to defend themselves when the police cannot versus the importance of protecting the lives of even criminal offenders. That dispute does not seem easily resolved.

However, the issue is complicated by several real-world concerns that are worth mentioning. As to the latter objection – that authorizing deadly force against all felonies is too broad – it should be noted that the potential for abuse of this breadth of authority is significantly limited by the self-defense requirement that the use of deadly force must be *necessary* to protect oneself. That is, the defender must show that no lesser amount of force, such as non-deadly force, would have been adequate to protect herself and, further, she must show that she had to use the deadly force when she did and could not have waited until some later time. From this perspective, the danger of justifying the use of too much force is significantly reduced. If a defender has no other means to successfully defend herself against a felony other than by the use deadly force, do we really want to insist that she must simply suffer the victimization? If the unlawfully threatened victimization is a felony, many people will feel uncomfortable demanding such sacrifice by the victim in order to minimize risk to the unlawful, felonious aggressor.

As to the former objection – that authorizing deadly force only against the threat of serious bodily injury is too narrow – it is worth noting that the concept of "serious bodily injury" can well be interpreted to include all sorts of conduct, including, for example, rape. Similarly, if one examines the various felonies that other jurisdictions add, such as kidnapping, robbery, and arson, it would not be too difficult to see each one of them as embodying a threat of "serious bodily injury." However, it may well be a clearer and more reliable approach to explicitly list the offenses for which deadly force is authorized rather than depending upon judges to interpret the "serious bodily injury" requirement broadly enough to include these other offenses.

Aftermaths

Celia is sentenced to death. But the nation is fiercely divided on the issue of slavery and Celia's case becomes national news. She is interviewed by reporters and the abolitionist cause publishes several articles on the horrors of her situation. Her execution is delayed so she can give birth. (The child is stillborn.) A new execution date is set. Her defense lawyers, who were initially selected because they would defend her competently but not too well, seem to have been moved by her plight and help her escape from jail. After the scheduled execution date passes, she is captured and returned to jail. Eventually, the Missouri Supreme Court rules against Celia and at 2:30 p.m. on December 21, 1855, she is hanged in a public execution. But the injustice of her desperate plight helped galvanize anti-slavery sentiments around the country.

In the *Bernhard Goetz* case, Goetz serves only six and a half months of his sentence before being released. In a civil action, Cabey is awarded $43 million dollars. Goetz never pays any of this, instead filing for bankruptcy. Goetz becomes a vegetarian and finds new legal troubles. He has become an animal rights activist and is now a protector of New York's squirrel population. In an effort to aid the small rodents, Goetz brings wounded animals to his apartment for rehabilitation, causing his landlord to sue to have the squirrels and Goetz evicted.

At the time of the shooting, crime rates in New York were so high that the *Goetz* case initially served as a lightning rod for public anger over the danger in the subways, but as crime rates fall views on Goetz shift. Today, for many people, the case is seen more as an example of a racially motivated shooting,[28] or at least one in which racial stereotyping played a role in Goetz's assessment of the situation. Did Goetz feel fear because of previous victimization and high crime rates or because he drew unfounded assumptions of danger because the men surrounding him were African-American?

Chapter Glossary

"All or Nothing" Approach: Under this approach to dealing with mistake as to justification, a jurisdiction denies any defense or mitigation to an actor who makes any kind of unreasonable mistake, be it reckless or negligent. Only a reasonable mistake provides a defense. This is in contrast to the Model Penal Code's "sliding-scale" approach.[29]

Reasonable Mistake as to Justification: An actor who reasonably believes their conduct is justified is blameless and is given a complete defense because they could not reasonably have been expected to have avoided the offense.[30]

Self-Defense: The use of force to protect oneself from an unlawful attack is justified if the defensive force is necessary. The use of deadly force in self-defense is commonly limited to situations where serious bodily injury is threatened.[31]

"Sliding Scale" Approach: Under this approach, an actor's honest but negligent mistake would provide a mitigation to an offense of negligence and an actor's honest but reckless mistake would provide a mitigation to an offense of recklessness. This contrasts with the common-law rule that would provide no defense or mitigation for any unreasonable – negligent or reckless – mistake, instead providing a defense only if the actor's mistake was entirely reasonable.[32]

Unreasonable Mistake: A reckless or negligent mistake is an unreasonable mistake. Only a non-negligent mistake is a reasonable mistake.[33]

Vigilantism: The act of a citizen who takes the law into his or her own hands by apprehending and punishing a suspected criminal.[34]

Notes

1. This portion of the narrative is drawn from the following sources: 'Celia, a Slave,' Encyclopedia.com, accessed 17 July 2020, http://www.encyclopedia.com/law/-encyclopedias-almanacs-transcripts-and-maps/celia-slave; Douglas O. Linder, 'Celia, A Slave, Trial (1855): An Account,' Famous Trials, accessed 17 July 2020, http://www.famous-trials.com/celia/180-home; Douglas O. Linder, 'The Trial of Celia: A Chronology,' Famous Trials, accessed 17 July 2020, http://www.famous-trials.com/celia/181-chronology; Melton A. McLaurin, *Celia, a Slave* (New York: Avon Publications, 1999).
2. Linder, 'Celia, A Slave, Trial (1855).'
3. Linder, 'Celia, A Slave, Trial (1855).'
4. Linder, 'Celia, A Slave, Trial (1855).'
5. Linder, 'Celia, A Slave, Trial (1855).'
6. Linder, 'Celia, A Slave, Trial (1855).'
7. Linder, 'Celia, A Slave, Trial (1855).'
8. McLaurin, 'Inquisition,' in *Celia, a Slave*, p. 43.
9. Saidiya Hartman, 'Seduction and the Ruses of Power,' *Callaloo 19*, no. 2 (Spring, 1996): pp. 537–560, http://www.jstor.com/stable/3299219.
10. Paul H. Robinson and Michael T. Cahill, *Criminal Law*, 2nd ed. (New York: Wolters Kluwer, 2016), §8.4.
11. A. H. Godbey, 'The Place of the Code of Hammurabi,' *The Monist 15*, no. 2 (1905): pp. 199–226, www.jstor.org/stable/27899579.
12. Will Tysse, 'The Roman Legal Treatment of Self Defense and the Private Possession of Weapons in the Codex Justinianus,' *Journal on Firearms & Public Policy 16* (2004): p. 163.
13. Paul Robinson, Matthew Kussmaul, Camber Stoddard, Ilya Rudyak, and Andreas Kuersten, The American Criminal Code: General Defenses, *Journal of Legal Analysis, 37* (2015): pp. 6–10.
14. Chapter 13.
15. This portion of the narrative is drawn from the following sources: 'Bernhard Goetz Trial: 1987,' Encyclopedia.com, accessed 17 July 2020, http://www.encyclopedia.com/law/law-magazines/bernhard-goetz-trial-1987; Bob Drogin, 'Prosecutor Calls Goetz 'Vigilante,' Urges His Conviction,' *Los Angeles Times*, 12 June 1987, http://articles.latimes.com/1987-06-12/news/mn-3977_1_subway-gunman; George P. Fletcher, *A*

Crime of Self-Defense: Bernhard Goetz and the Law on Trial (Chicago: University of Chicago Press, 1990); Richard Stengel, 'A Troubled and Troubling Life,' *TIME*, 24 June 2001, http://content.time.com/time/magazine/article/0,9171,141513,00.html.

16. Drogin, 'Prosecutor Calls Goetz 'Vigilante'.'

17. Selwyn Raab, '4 Youths Shot by Goetz Faced Criminal Counts,' *The New York Times*, 10 January 1985, http://www.nytimes.com/1985/01/10/nyregion/4-youths-shot-by-goetz-faced-criminal-counts.html.

18. Stengel, 'A Troubled and Troubling Life.'

19. Stengel, 'A Troubled and Troubling Life.'

20. This subsection is drawn from the following source: 'Asked about Goetz, Reagan Cites the Law,' *The New York Times*, 10 January 1985, http://www.nytimes.com/1985/01/10/nyregion/asked-about-goetz-reagan-cites-the-law.html.

21. 'Asked about Goetz, Reagan Cites the Law.'

22. 'Asked about Goetz, Reagan Cites the Law.'

23. Fletcher, 'A Shooting in the Subway,' in *A Crime of Self-Defense*, p. 4.

24. Stengel, 'A Troubled and Troubling Life.'

25. The map is taken from Paul H. Robinson and Tyler Scot Williams, *Mapping American Criminal Law: Variations across the 50 States* (Westport: Prager, 2018), ch. 15. All supporting authorities are available from that source.

26. *See* Robinson and Cahill, *Criminal Law*, §9.5.

27. The sliding-scale approach was first codified in Model Penal Code §3.09(2).

28. Jennifer Latson, 'Two Shootings: 30 Years Apart – Linked by Fear,' *Time Magazine*, 22 December 2014, https://time.com/3640967/bernhard-goetz-history/.

29. Robinson and Cahill, *Criminal Law*, §8.5.2; MPC §3.09(2).

30. Robinson and Cahill, *Criminal Law*, §8.5.1; MPC art 3.

31. MPC §3.04; *Self-Defense*, Black's.

32. Robinson and Cahill, *Criminal Law*, §8.5.2; MPC §3.09(2).

33. MPC §1.13 (16); Robinson and Cahill, *Criminal Law*, §8.5.2.

34. *Vigilantism*, Black's Law Dictionary.

Chapter 13

Law Enforcement Authority

Gunfight at the OK Corral

1881. On July 4, with $2,000 for teachers' salaries but without a building, Booker T. Washington begins instruction at the Tuskegee Institute in Alabama. Washington sees labor as practical, but also as beautiful and dignified. As part of the school's work-study program, students manufacture their own bricks and construct most of the buildings. The 1876 Battle of Little Big Horn is a major victory for the Sioux Indians who annihilate the troops of General George Armstrong Custer. But with the victory comes renewed efforts by the United States to remove the Sioux from the land. Sitting Bull, who has led his people for years, now crosses over into Canada, but the smaller buffalo herds cannot sustain the Sioux and looming starvation sends Sitting Bull back to the U.S., where he surrenders to federal troops. With the French and Indian War, the Great Sioux War, and the Civil War over, the American West is stumbling toward order but, with little local law enforcement and distant courts, it remains lawless in many towns.

Wyatt Earp – 1881

By 1881, Tombstone, Arizona has several of the Earp brothers working in well-paying positions of authority. Wyatt is the deputy sheriff and a candidate for county sheriff. Virgil is town marshal and holds a post as a federal agent. Morgan is riding shotgun for the Wells-Fargo Company.

While the Earps have a great deal of influence, not everyone loves them. There is a loosely associated group known as the Cowboys who are against the Earps and pretty much against law enforcement generally. One of the prominent members of the group is Ike Clanton, a rancher who has built a reputation and some power because of his success in the cattle business. Ike's business includes cattle rustling and other illegal

DOI: 10.4324/9781003258025-15

activities. A strong law enforcement presence is not good for the Cowboys and Ike has made it clear that he is against the Earp family in general and Virgil in particular.

Ike Clanton also has a reputation for big talk and excessive drinking. In late October, Ike is in town drinking through the night. In violation of local law, he is carrying firearms, a rifle and a pistol. While making his way through town, Ike shouts out threats against the Earps to random townspeople, stating that he is going to harm them. Several townsfolk are sufficiently alarmed by Ike's threats that they warn the Earps. Virgil, the town Marshal, is asleep and when told of Ike's threats, he simply goes back to sleep. Sometime later, he is told of Ike's illegal firearms, which he does not feel that he can ignore. Virgil gets up and in short order locates Ike. He takes the firearms, and takes Ike to court where he is fined $25. When asked by the judge why he was armed, Ike says he was in town to kill Virgil Earp.

After the court session, Ike remains in town. As morning slips into afternoon, he is joined by several of the Cowboys, including his younger brother Billy Clanton, Tom McLowery, Tom's older brother Frank McLowery, and Billy Claiborne. By afternoon, the Clantons and associates are gathered near the OK Corral. The group has a new grudge. They feel that Virgil had been rougher than he needed to be when disarming Ike earlier in the day. By now, everyone in the group has been heard threatening the Earps.

All over town the brewing tension is felt. Ike's very public threats have people on edge. Sheriff John Behan finds the Clantons at the corral and asks for their weapons. They each give Behan a gun, except Frank McLowery who pretends not to have one.

The three Earp brothers are joined by Doc Holliday and as a group they head over to arrest the group for their public threats, carrying of firearms, and other disturbances of the peace. Virgil deputizes Holliday, giving him the legal authority to carry a weapon in town. The Earp group meets Sheriff Behan on the way, who tells them that he has already taken the group's weapons. The sheriff wants to defuse the situation and suggests that he simply persuade the Clantons to leave town. The Earps think the larger conflict will not go away and needs to be confronted.

The two factions are soon standing face to face. Virgil says, "I have come to disarm you."[1] The younger McLowery tells the lawmen that he does not have a weapon and opens his coat to show he has none. However, Frank McLowery, who is armed, begins to draw his weapon. Wyatt shoots at Frank, who is hit in the stomach. Billy Clanton picks up Frank's gun and fires at Wyatt. He misses. Morgan then shoots Billy Clanton. Lying on the ground, Billy Clanton braces the pistol on his arm and returns fire. Tom McLowery, after seeing his brother shot, takes cover behind a horse. Claiborne runs away. Ike Clanton grabs Wyatt's arm. Wyatt shakes free and tells Ike to "Go to fighting or get away."[2] Ike has no gun and runs. No attempt is made by the Earps to stop his escape.

The horse that was shielding Tom McLowery moves, leaving him exposed. Doc Holliday shoots and kills him. Holliday then moves on to Tom's wounded brother Frank. Despite his injuries, Frank fires and hits Holliday in the hip. Holliday fires back and Frank, the first man to go for a weapon, is killed by a bullet to the head. Billy Clanton shoots Virgil in the leg and Morgan in the shoulder. The shoot-out ends as Morgan and Wyatt both shoot and kill Billy Clanton.

The gunfight takes 30 seconds from start to finish. Of the five in the Ike Clanton group, Frank McLowery, Tom McLowery, and Billy Clanton are all dead, and Ike and Billy Claiborne have run off uninjured. Frank and Billy were shot while shooting at the Earps, but Tom was shot by Doc Holliday under a mistaken belief that he too was armed when in fact he was not. Of the four in the Earp group, Virgil, Morgan, and Doc Holliday are all injured.

Upon initial reports that the Clantons were unarmed, there is much resentment about the three killings. The men are put in coffins and placed under a sign that reads:

Figure 13.1 **The remains of the OK Corral, 1882**

"MURDERED IN THE STREETS OF TOMBSTONE." Four days after the shooting, Ike Clanton files a murder complaint against all four in the Earp party. Wyatt and Holliday are arrested and required to post $10,000 bail. Virgil and Morgan are still bedridden from their wounds. Virgil is suspended from his post as town marshal.

As the month-long trial begins, conflicting evidence is offered. In the end, the Earps leave the courtroom acquitted of all charges. The judge decides that Virgil acted within the scope of his duties as marshal, and that his snap judgment to deputize Holliday is within the scope of the law.

Law Enforcement Authority

Every organized society must have some mechanism for the enforcement of its criminal law. Without some such mechanism, there can be no order or safety. In early societies, enforcement mechanisms were provided by the larger kinship group. But as societies became larger, it was typically the monarch who took over the law enforcement role. Rawlings explains how the power of the king replaced the blood feud.

> The Anglo-Saxon codes of law sought to break open the kindred relationship and turn it into a mechanism which supported the state under the king rather than competed with it. The requirement that local communities pursue offenders and deliver them to the Royal courts rearticulated the notion of self-help inherent in the feud into an obligation owed to the king. Placing the obligation to respond to an offense on a community as defined by the law rather than by consanguinity meant that the right of retaliation began to be conceptualized as an aspect of every person's public duty, not as a right of revenge or as a duty owed to the victim through a kindred relationship.[3]

When a police officer of today uses force to make an arrest, his conduct may satisfy the requirements of an assault offense. However, the officer may have a justification defense that protects him from criminal liability.[4] Set out in the margin is the text of the Model Penal Code law enforcement justification defense, which illustrates the many common limitations on the use of force by police officers.

A sometimes more difficult issue is that of mistake as to a law enforcement justification. Suspect-police confrontations are commonly chaotic, requiring split-second decision-making. Is the object the suspect is pulling from his jacket a gun or a cell phone? The officer's duty is to arrest the subject, not run away from the situation, so the officer must deal with the uncertainty and, thus, the confrontation can commonly create risks to officers and to suspects. In other words, jurisdictions must not only set out beforehand clear rules defining when an officer may use force in making an arrest but also must specify the rules by which an officer is to be judged if he or she turns out to be wrong

Use of Force in Law Enforcement.

(1) Use of Force Justifiable to Effect an Arrest. [T]he use of force upon or toward the person of another is justifiable when the actor is making or assisting in making an arrest and the actor believes that such force is immediately necessary to effect a lawful arrest. …

(b) The use of deadly force is not justifiable under this Section unless:

(i) the arrest is for a felony; and

(ii) the person effecting the arrest is authorized to act as a peace officer or is assisting a person whom he believes to be authorized to act as a peace officer; and

(iii) the actor believes that the force employed creates no substantial risk of injury to innocent persons; and

(iv) the actor believes that:

(1) the crime for which the arrest is made involved conduct including the use or threatened use of deadly force; or

(2) there is a substantial risk that the person to be arrested will cause death or serious bodily harm if his apprehension is delayed.

Model Penal Code §3.07

Figure 13.2

in the use of force – if, for example, the suspect's apparent weapon turns out to be a cell phone or a realistic toy gun. How is a court and jury to determine whether the officer should be criminally liable for shooting a suspect who turns out to be unarmed?

At the OK Corral, Clanton's group chose not to acquiesce in their lawful arrest. Instead, Frank McLowery draws his weapon. The Earps, being law enforcement officers, have no obligation to retreat in order to avoid the confrontation but instead have the right to use force to defend themselves. Notice how the self-defense justification, discussed in the previous chapter, reasserts itself here. While the law enforcement justification may not authorize the use of deadly force to arrest, the officer, like any citizen, has a right to use force in self-defense, even deadly force if he is threatened with serious bodily injury.

However, in the OK Corral case, the Earp group, Doc Holliday in particular, ends up shooting not only the two members of the Clanton group who shot at them but also a third member, Tom McLowery, who in fact was not armed. The Earps, having been told that the Clanton group were not armed, but finding that in fact they are – Frank McLowery and then Billy Clanton fire on them – may well have assumed that others in the party were similarly armed. Was their mistake a reasonable one, given the chaos of the situation and their own injuries? Even if it were found to be an unreasonable belief that Frank McLowery was armed, if the honestly and genuinely believed it, should they at least get a reduction in their liability and sentence?

Law Enforcement Authority in the States

Every American jurisdiction has adopted rules governing the treatment of mistakes as to justification in the law enforcement context.[5] The map below indicates the three different approaches that jurisdictions take in formulating such provisions.[6]

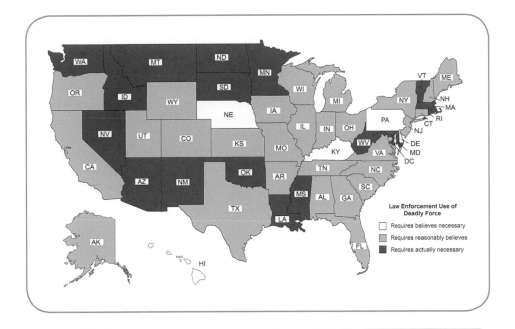

Law Enforcement Use of Deadly Force
☐ Requires believes necessary
▨ Requires reasonably believes
■ Requires actually necessary

Figure 13.3

Five states, those in light shading on the map, provide a justification defense if the officer "believes" that the conditions exist that would justify his use of force. However, the jurisdictions that give a defense purely upon a belief that the force is necessary have an additional provision, typically modeled after Model Penal Code section 3.09(2), which imposes negligent liability for negligent mistake and reckless liability for reckless mistake. Under this sliding-scale approach, as discussed in the previous chapter, when Doc Holliday shoots and kills Tom McLowery mistakenly believing he is armed, Holliday will get a complete defense if his mistake was reasonable, but would be liable for reckless homicide (manslaughter) if his mistake was reckless or liable for negligent homicide if his mistake was negligent.

A more common approach, however, the *all-or-nothing* approach taken by the 29 jurisdictions in medium shading on the map. This approach, as discussed in the previous chapter, gives a complete defense to an officer who mistakenly believes his conduct is justified only if the mistake is completely reasonable. If Doc Holliday's mistake as to whether Tom McLowery was armed is judged to be reckless or negligent, then he gets no defense or *mitigation* and is liable for murder, as if he had simply intended to kill McLowery and no arrest confrontation existed.

Those supporting the all-or-nothing approach in the context of law enforcement authority claim that it can cause officers to be more careful in their use of force, for only a completely reasonable mistake will give them a defense; an honest but unreasonable mistake will leave them fully liable for the offense without even a mitigation. However, this approach has been criticized as violating the blameworthiness proportionality principle. The officer who honestly believes that his force is necessary but turns out to be negligent in his belief clearly does not have the same degree of blameworthiness as the classic murderer who has no claim of being justified at all, yet the all-or-nothing approach equates the two by convicting the negligent officer of the same crime: murder.

Seventeen jurisdictions, marked with the darkest shading on the map, have neither "reasonably believes" nor "believes" language in their statutory formulations of the defense. Instead, in these jurisdictions the law enforcement justification defense is written in purely objective terms: "an actor is justified if his use of force is necessary to. . ."

One might initially think that these jurisdictions are denying a mistake defense to an officer who gets it wrong, even one who "reasonably believes" his conduct is necessary. But this is not the case. These jurisdictions simply take a different approach to drafting their mistake as to a justification defense, by segregating objective *ex ante* rules of what conduct is justified from the subjective *ex post* rules about what kind of mistake will provide what kind of defense or mitigation. That is, they provide a mistake as to justification defense or mitigation but do so in a separate mistake excuse provision apart from their *objective justification* defense.

Whether Doc Holliday would be criminally liable under this approach and, if so, for what, would depend entirely on the terms of the independent mistake as to justification provision, which might take either an all-or-nothing approach or a sliding-scale approach.

There is good reason for this segregation of the objective justification rules from the rules governing mistake as to justification, and some writers have argued that it is to be much preferred over the more common mixing of justification and mistake as to justification seen in the first two groups above.[7] There is an important conceptual difference between objective justification and mistake as to justification. The former doctrine – the objective justification requirements – are part of the ex ante rules of conduct by which the criminal law describes how officers should behave – the circumstances under which we are happy to have, or at least willing to tolerate, the officers' use of force. The latter doctrine – mistake as to justification – are instances where we *disapprove of the conduct* under the actual circumstances and want to signal to others that they should not engage in such conduct under such circumstances in the future. We are giving a defense to the mistaken actor, despite our condemning the conduct, because we hold the actor blameless (or, in the sliding-scale approach, at least less blameworthy).

The jurisdictions that segregate the rules of objective justification from the excuse of mistake as to justification do so because they don't want people to erroneously conclude that the mistaken but excused use of force is actually being approved as an appropriate rule for future conduct. The point is that true objective justification and mistake as to justification send exactly opposite signals about the propriety of the officer's conduct under the actual facts: finding an objective justification approves the officer's conduct, while finding an excuse for a reasonable mistake as to justification condemns conduct.

Is the All-or-Nothing Approach to Mistake as to a Justification to Be Preferred over the Sliding-Scale Approach?

It is easy enough to understand why jurisdictions may be tempted by the all-or-nothing approach. After all, the officer has not only turned out to be wrong – his conduct is not actually objectively justified – but also turned out to be unreasonable in his mistaken belief about the justification. It is also understandable that we would want officers to be particularly careful in their use of force; if they make a mistake, there ought to be entirely reasonable reasons for it, and they should be criminally liable if they have not acted reasonably.

However, the all-or-nothing approach has some serious problems. One of them has already been noted above: it may well be that the actor who makes an honest but unreasonable mistake is blameworthy and deserves some criminal liability, but it is also clear that the extent of the officer's blameworthiness is importantly different from that of the person who acts without any claim of justification whatever. The officer who kills in an honest but mistaken belief that her conduct is necessary and whose mistake is reckless or negligent ought to have some criminal liability, such as liability for manslaughter or negligent homicide, but not liability for murder, for that would equate her blameworthiness with that of the person who kills as an aggressor, without even a claim of acting defensively.

Another serious problem with the all-or-nothing approach is less obvious: while the all-or-nothing approach ignores the blameworthiness proportionality principle, ordinary people, including jurors, do not. The empirical research makes it clear that the proportionality of punishment to blameworthiness is fundamental to ordinary people's judgments of justice.[8]

Consider, then, what happens in all-or-nothing jurisdictions when juries are given their legal instructions in a case where an officer has made an honest but unreasonable mistake in her use of force. The jurisdiction's all-or-nothing approach means that the jury will be given only two options: to convict the officer of murder or to completely acquit the officer. In such cases the jury will find neither option attractive. If they believe her mistake was honest but negligent, they will be reluctant to pretend that it is fully reasonable and to give the officer a complete defense that she does not deserve. However, they are also likely to be reluctant to give the officer no defense or *mitigation* of any kind and to hold her liable as if she was a standard murderer. Faced with these two bad options, it is common for juries to give the officer a complete defense that she does not deserve, rather than to treat her as a murderer when she was thrust into the situation simply because she was doing her job.

Thus, in practice, the all-or-nothing approach has the opposite effect from what was intended. Instead of being an approach that takes a hard line on police use of force, supposedly forcing officers to be more careful and punishing them severely whenever they are not, it turns out that the all-or-nothing approach in practice often gives blameworthy officers a complete defense even when they deserve some punishment.

The previous discussion has focused on those common cases in which police officers are using deadly force in a confrontation in which their own safety is threatened, and they are in fact acting to protect themselves, as in self-defense. But there can also be situations where police use force in other than defensive situations. They may use it to affirmatively promote effective criminal justice, such as a suspect fleeing from police to avoid arrest. What force should police officers be able to use in order to stop the suspect's flight and affect his arrest so he can be brought to justice?

Elton Hymon – 1974

Daisy Bell States is at home when she hears the sound of breaking glass from her next-door neighbor's house. She calls police to report a prowler. Her prudence is understandable: over the last three months, her neighborhood has been plagued by a string of over 120 burglaries and larcenies. She is also right that her neighbor is now being burgled. Moments earlier, 15-year-old Edward Garner broke a window and has let himself into the neighbor's home to steal whatever valuables he can find.

Officers Elton Hymon and Leslie B. Wright soon arrive to investigate the situation. States, a middle-aged woman, is standing on her porch in a housecoat when they

Figure 13.4 Elton Hymon several years later, circa 1999

arrive. She tells the officers that she thinks a person is still inside the house. Using flashlights, the officers head to investigate from opposite sides. As Hymon circles the back of the house with his .38 caliber revolver drawn, he sees the broken window and a light on in the house.[9]

Hearing the officers outside, Garner grabs a small purse that holds ten dollars, heads to the back door, and tries to make a run for it. Hymon hears the screen door slam and sees Garner sprint through a stream of light in the backyard. When Garner reaches a six-foot high chain-link fence, he hears Hymon yell "Police! Halt!"[10] Garner freezes at the foot of the fence.

Training his light on Garner, Hymon sees the face of a young black man, crouching beside the fence. Hymon is about 40 feet away, and despite seeing something unidentifiable in one of Garner's hands, Hymon does not believe that Garner is armed. Wright arrives at the backyard, and Hymon calls out to circle around the chain-link fence. Just as Hymon takes a step toward the fence, Garner leaps up to climb over, almost making it to the top in a single jump. Seeing how fast Garner moves, Hymon is sure that he will escape.

At the time, the Memphis Police Department trains its officers to employ deadly force against suspects fleeing from serious nonviolent crimes. Departmental records show that between October 10, 1966 and September 30, 1974, there were 224 instances in which officers fired at a fleeing suspect. Of those, 113 shootings involved nonviolent property crimes. During this period, the department twice upgraded the quality of its ammunition to increase its velocity, accuracy, and wounding power.

Tennessee law provides that if during an arrest a suspect "either flees or forcibly resists, the officer may use all the necessary means to effect the arrest."[11] Memphis police procedures allow the use of deadly force where it is considered "proper to kill a fleeing felon rather than run the risk of allowing him to escape." About 24 states have similar policies at the time.

Hymon understands the law and remembers his training, so he takes aim at Garner's torso and fires one shot, the first time he has ever fired at a suspect since joining the force. He sees Garner slump over the fence and realizes that the shot hit him in the back of the head.

Wright and Hymon run to get Garner down from the fence and call an ambulance. Garner is rushed to John Gaston Hospital, where he dies on the operating table. Garner's death devastates Hymon, an African-American officer, who hoped Garner would survive. To make matters worse for him, while Hymon knows he followed departmental procedures, he is warned that he may face a murder charge.

As is customary, Officer Hymon is temporarily relieved of duty pending investigation. The Memphis Police Firearms Review Board reviews the incident, and the case is also presented to a grand jury. Both bodies decide that no criminal or disciplinary action should be taken against Officer Hymon.

However, that does not mollify Garner's grieving family. Cleamtee Garner, Edwards' father, brings a civil wrongful death suit against Officer Hymon. He is represented by the NAACP Legal Defense and Education Fund. (Race is not considered a factor in the shooting as both Garner and Hymon are African-American.) The U.S. District Court for the Western District of Tennessee dismisses the case, concluding that, although tragic, the officers were acting within accepted police procedures. Garner's family appeals, and the Sixth Circuit Court of Appeals reverses the district court judgment and orders the lower court to hear the case on the issue of whether police policies are constitutional. Upon remand, once again the district court dismisses the suit against the city and its police officers. On appeal, in January 1983, the Sixth Circuit Court of Appeals reverses the district court's ruling and declares the statute unconstitutional.

The case finally makes its way to the U.S. Supreme Court in 1985. In a 6-3 decision authored by Justice Byron White, the Court determines that the use of deadly force must satisfy the Fourth Amendment's reasonableness requirement, and that deadly force may not be used "unless it is necessary to prevent the escape and the officer has probable cause to believe that the suspect poses a significant threat of death or serious physical injury to the officer or others."[12] The Tennessee statute is held unconstitutional in allowing deadly force against an unarmed, non-dangerous suspect.[13] The Memphis Police Department and police departments across the country are required to conform their use of force policies accordingly.

Aftermaths

After the Supreme Court rules against the use of deadly force in cases such as Garner's, a federal appeals court in 1993 rules that the family should be able to receive compensation for the death. In 1995, 21 years after the shooting, city officials agree to pay the family $440,000 in compensatory damages and lawyer's fees. It comes too late for Garner's father, Cleamtee, who dies in 1994.

Officer Hymon continues working for the Memphis Police Department. In 1983, after 12 years on the force, he receives a promotion to sergeant and takes on the duties of a detective. Upon completing graduate coursework in the administration of criminal justice, he is promoted several years later to lieutenant. He also takes on another job, as pastor of the Botts Chapel Church in Olive Branch, Missouri. In July 2003, Hymon is promoted to captain. He also becomes pastor at New Hickory Hill Church in Memphis.

Reflecting on the incident, Captain Hymon characterizes the department's attitude prior to the shooting as one of "open season," in which officers fired at suspects with little official restraint. Though he believes that his shooting was justified under the then-existing law and circumstances, he is glad that the rules have changed and that lethal force in such situations is no longer allowed. The new policies, he argues, also foster a greater level of compassion for human life and have led to a decline in the use of other potentially lethal weapons such as nightsticks. He has never had to use his weapon since.

As to the shoot-out at the OK Corral, about a month after being acquitted, Virgil Earp is caught in an ambush. Despite receiving multiple wounds, he survives. Ike Clanton is the prime suspect but the case against him does not go far because of lack of evidence. Virgil's brother Morgan is not so lucky – he is ambushed and killed in March 1882. Wyatt Earp and Ike Clanton continue to hunt each other for years. (There have been at least a dozen movies produced about the men and the fight, starting with the 1934 film *Frontier Marshal*.)

Chapter Glossary

Ex Ante: How things appear or exist beforehand, rather than in hindsight. The opposite of ex post.[14]

Ex Post: How things appear or exist after the fact, rather than beforehand. The opposite of ex ante.

Mitigation: A factor tending to show that a criminal defendant, though guilty, is less culpable than the act alone would indicate.[15]

Objective Justification: An act is objectively justified if it actually satisfies the objective requirements of a justification defense. It stands in contrast to subjective justification, in which an actor only believes that his or her conduct is justified.[16]

Subjective Justification: Under criminal codes that define justification defenses subjectively, an actor is justified if they believe that their conduct is justified, even if they are mistaken. It stands in contrast to objective justification, in which an actor's conduct is actually objectively justified.[17]

Notes

1. Carl Sifakis, *The Encyclopedia of American Crime* (New York: Smithmark Pub, 1992), p. 540.
2. Sifakis, *The Encyclopedia of American Crime*, p. 540.
3. Philip Rawlings, *Policing: A Short History* 12 (Devon: Willan Publishing, 2002).
4. For discussion of public authority justifications generally, Paul H. Robinson and Michael T. Cahill, *Criminal Law*, 2nd ed. (New York: Wolters Kluwer, 2016) §4.1.2.
5. For discussion of mistake as to a justification generally, see Robinson and Cahill, *Criminal Law*, §8.5.
6. The map is taken from Paul H. Robinson and Tyler Scot Williams, 'Law Enforcement Authority,' in *Mapping American Criminal Law: Variations across the 50 States* (Westport: Prager, 2018), p. 152. All supporting authorities are available from that source.
7. *See* Paul H. Robinson, *Structure and Function in Criminal Law* (Oxford: Oxford University Press, 1997), chs. 5.C, 7, and 8.
8. Paul H. Robinson, '"Principles of Adjudication: Doctrines of Grading" and "Testing Competing Theories: Justification Defenses",' in *Intuitions of Justice and Utility of Desert* (Oxford: Oxford University Press, 2013), pp. 362–401, 472–493.
9. *Tennessee v. Garner.*
10. *Tennessee v. Garner.*
11. *See* Tennessee Code Annotated §40-808.
12. *Tennessee v. Garner.*
13. *Tennessee v. Garner*, 471 U.S. 1 (1985).
14. *Ex Ante*, Black's.
15. *Mitigation*, Black's.
16. Robinson and Cahill, *Criminal Law*, §8.5.1.
17. Robinson and Cahill, *Criminal Law*, §8.5.1.

Chapter 14

Insanity

The Assassination of President Garfield

1881. The People's Will movement in Russia, after several failed attempts, kill Czar Alexander II on March 13. In Germany, Chancellor Otto von Bismarck is given a petition signed by 250,000 who seek to bar foreign Jews from entering the country and calling for the expulsion of Jews from their positions as judges, teachers, and civil servants. The U.S. Republican national convention of 1880 goes 33 rounds with no winner as competing political machines battle to a standoff. Popular Congressman James Garfield takes to the podium in support of a compromise candidate. When during his remarks he asks "What do we want?" someone in the audience shouts, "We want Garfield!" He insists he is not a candidate but two ballots later he is nominated and later wins the general election.

Charles Guiteau – 1881

Charles Julius Guiteau's childhood is not a happy one: born in Illinois in 1841, his mother dies when he is young and his abusive father psychologically terrorizes the boy for religious reasons.[1] Guiteau tries and fails at an array of endeavors. On June 11, 1880, he is aboard the *SS Stonington*, a passenger ship that collides with the *SS Narragansett*. The *Narragansett* sinks and many die. The *Stonington* is not significantly damaged and returns to port with no casualties. Guiteau sees this as a sign of divine intervention and believes God spared the *Stonington* because he needed Guiteau for a higher purpose: politics.

He writes a speech supporting Ulysses S. Grant, entitled "Grant vs. Hancock."[2] When James Garfield, rather than Grant, receives the nomination, he changes the title to "Garfield vs. Hancock."[3] While he fails to entirely remove Grant's name from the body of the speech, Guiteau nonetheless delivers the speech at several minor political

DOI: 10.4324/9781003258025-16

gatherings and hands out printed copies at the Republican National Committee meeting in New York.

When Garfield narrowly wins the election, Guiteau believes he has been of vital assistance in the victory and therefore is owed a diplomatic post. He decides that Paris would be the appropriate posting for him.

The day after Garfield's inauguration, Guiteau arrives in Washington to arrange his diplomatic post. He visits the White House and drops off a copy of his speech to remind Garfield of his efforts during the campaign.

Guiteau spends the next two months living in boarding houses, always slipping out before the rent is due. He is a regular visitor to the White House – Garfield's secretary reports seeing him at least 15 times. At one White House reception, Guiteau finds Lucretia Garfield, the President's wife, and gives her his calling card. He also instructs her how to pronounce his name. He continues to go to both the White House and the State Department daily, approaching Cabinet members and prominent party members to ask for his Paris appointment. He gives advice on policy matters, too. Finally, he is told by the Secretary of State to "never speak to me again of the Paris Consulship as long as you live."[4] He is banned from the White House.

Guiteau is shocked and furious. From his point of view, he has been working hard to fulfill his calling only to be thwarted at every turn. It is now, in this low moment, that he feels what he understands to be a "divine inspiration": God tells him that he needs to "remove" the President and that he will be rewarded if he does so.[5] Guiteau is uncertain what the command means. He earnestly prays on the subject for weeks to assure himself that the voice talking to him is God and not Satan.

After satisfying himself on that point, he methodically sets a plan in motion to assassinate Garfield. Guiteau borrows $15 from a relative to purchase a revolver. Choosing between two versions of a .442 Webley caliber British Bulldog revolver, he selects the one with an ivory grip, thinking it will look better in a museum after the assassination. He practices his marksmanship and stalks Garfield to learn the President's routine. Guiteau even follows Garfield to church, and on one occasion begins shouting at the minister in the middle of the service. That night, Garfield writes in his diary about the strange young man who was shouting in church.

Guiteau sends a letter to the White House demanding that the man who banned him from the White House be fired or Garfield and the Republican Party "would come to grief."[6] The letter is ignored, along with all his other correspondence. On June 16, 1881, Guiteau drafts an "Address to the American People," explaining the reasons behind the assassination that is to come:

> I conceived the idea of removing the President, because he has proved a traitor to the men that made him. This is not murder, it is a political necessity. This will make my friend Arthur president, and save the Republic.[7]

Guiteau also writes a letter to General William Tecumseh Sherman, to ask for protection from the mob that he assumes will form after the assassination. He goes to the District of Columbia jail and asks for a tour of the facility to see where he will be incarcerated.

Guiteau learns from a newspaper account that Garfield will be boarding a 9:30 train on July 2 for a summer vacation. He decides this is his chance. Garfield enters the station accompanied by two of his sons, James and Harry, and approaches the President from behind, firing two shots from point blank range. One grazes the President's arm and the other hits him in the back, with the bullet lodging itself behind

Figure 14.1 Garfield was shot as he went to board a train, 1881

Garfield's pancreas. Garfield, still alive, falls to the station floor. Guiteau puts his revolver back into his pocket and turns to leave the station but is apprehended. A crowd is beginning to gather and many scream "lynch him."[8] (President Lincoln had been shot by a political assassin 16 years earlier.)

Garfield dies 11 weeks later, after an agonizing battle with infection. Believing that Chester Arthur, who is now President, will grant him a pardon, he writes to Arthur on the day of Garfield's death:

> My inspiration is a godsend to you and I presume that you appreciate it. . . . Never think of Garfield's removal as murder. It was an act of God, resulting from a political necessity for which he was responsible.[9]

Guiteau expects that once the American people understand his motivation, they will thank and celebrate him for ridding the country of Garfield. Instead, he is formally indicted on murder charges on October 14, 1881.[10]

Guiteau believes he can't be convicted of a crime because he carried out God's will. He signs autographs from jail and even sends his jailer a card on New Year's Eve. Guiteau writes to President Arthur, asking him to set him free because he increased Arthur's salary by making him President. Guiteau makes plans to start a lecture tour after his release and plans to run for President in 1884.

At trial, Guiteau is delighted to be the center of attention; he smiles and waves to spectators. He delivers his testimony in the form of epic poems, and asks for legal advice from spectators through passed notes. He harasses witnesses and insults the judge, jury, and lawyers on both sides. He constantly jumps from his seat and shouts objections. The judge threatens to gag him if he does control his outbursts. He sings "John Brown's Body," a marching song from the Civil War, to the court and dictates an autobiography to the *New York Herald*. At the end of the autobiography, he adds a note that he is looking for a nice Christian lady under 30 years of age.

The trial is one of the first high-profile cases in which the *insanity defense* is considered. Guiteau maintains that he is not insane. He instructs his lawyer not to put experts on the stand as "I would rather be hung as a man than acquitted as a fool."[11] He compares himself to Paul the Apostle.

Guiteau himself takes the stand and has the following exchange with the prosecutor:

Q: Who bought the pistol, the Deity or you?
A: I say the Deity inspired the act and the Deity will take care of it.
Q: Were you inspired to buy that British Bull-dog pistol?
A: I do not claim that I was to do the specific act; but I do claim that the Deity inspired me to remove the President, and I had to use my ordinary judgment as to the ways and means to accomplish the Deity's will.[12]
   Later, he is asked:
Q: Did it occur to you that there was a commandment, "Thou shalt not kill?"
A: If it did, the divine authority overcame the written law.

On January 25, 1882, after 72 days of testimony, with less than an hour of deliberation, the jury returns a verdict of guilty. Guiteau screams at the jury: "you are all low, consummate jackasses." He is executed by hanging.

Insanity Defense

The criminal law generally commits itself to imposing criminal liability and punishment only on offenders who are morally blameworthy for their conduct. If the offender's conduct is the result of a serious mental illness, such may undermine that requisite blameworthiness. A person who strangles another to death in a hallucination, believing he is killing an attacking space alien, simply does not have the kind of moral responsibility needed to support criminal liability.

This is not a strictly modern idea. For example:

> The world of the ancient Greeks, long before the classical period and before written law, recognized madness as exculpatory. The most ancient of the generic terms for the grossly distorted mind, *entheos*, refers to "a god within." The victim or vessel of entheos is thereby irresistibly enthralled. The god might speak only to the chosen one, exciting wild and uncoordinated movements; or induce a frenzy as the sign of divine anger; or leave the victim to speak in tongues. The usual treatment for such mind robbing disorders is ritual purification . . . .[13]

But how is the criminal law to define the conditions under which mental disease or defect can exculpate an offender? Certainly, there is a significant portion of the population, some would say a majority, who have mental dysfunction of one kind or another, and many kinds of dysfunction may make it more difficult for a person to remain law-abiding. Yet we expect people to avoid breaking the law even if it is sometimes difficult to do so. How does the criminal law draw the line that distinguishes the small group of people who are so dysfunctional, and dysfunctional in such a way, as to fully exculpate from criminal liability?

The law has come to distinguish two kinds of mental dysfunction. *Cognitive dysfunction* occurs when an offender's mental disease or defect distorts his cognitive ability to understand his surroundings, the consequences of his conduct, or the criminal or wrongful nature of his conduct. An example of a cognitive dysfunction would be the example given above of the person killing another believing him to be an attacking space alien. The offender simply does not accurately perceive what it is that he is doing, and therefore cannot know that it is wrong.

Cognitive dysfunction seems to present in the 1881 *Guiteau* case, above, in which President Garfield's assassin thinks God is directing him. He accurately perceives his surroundings, but his mental illness tricks him into thinking that he is acting at God's direction. Thus, while his assassination of the President is criminal in that it is an intentional killing, it is not wrong in a larger moral sense, in Guiteau's view. (Should it be an excuse if Guiteau knows his conduct is "criminal" under society's laws even though his mental illness leads him to believe that it is not "wrongful" in some larger moral sense because God directs it? As we shall see, jurisdictions disagree about this.)

A second kind of dysfunction, *control dysfunction*, occurs when an offender knows what he is doing is criminal and wrong but his mental disease or defect impairs his ability to control his conduct.[14] More on control dysfunction in a moment.

Insanity Defense Cognitive Dysfunction in the States

The map below shows the five categories into which the states may be classified according to their position on an offender's *cognitive dysfunction*.[15] The lighter the shading, the broader the defense provided. (Each state's position on *control dysfunction* is represented on a second map below.) Five states essentially abolish the *insanity defense*. They are shown in black on the map.

Twenty-eight states, those with the darker shading on the map, follow the traditional common-law rule in providing an insanity defense where a defendant has lost his or her ability to understand the nature of his or her conduct in some very fundamental way. This common formulation is typically referred to as the *M'Naghten test*, from the old English case that allowed an insanity defense if the offender

> was laboring under such a defect of reason, from disease of the mind, as not to know the nature and quality of the act he was doing; or, if he did know it, that he did not know he was doing what was wrong.[16]

(However, some of the 28 jurisdictions in this first group leave a bit of wiggle room by allowing a defense when, as a result of mental disease or defect, the defendant was "unable to appreciate" the nature and quality of his conduct or its wrongfulness. The word "appreciate" here might give a court or jury some ability to stray from the demand that the defendant have a total loss of capacity to "know" or "distinguish" the nature of his conduct.)

The insanity defenses in these jurisdictions stand in contrast to the 16 states in next two groups, which allow the defense even if the defendant's dysfunction at the time of the offense is not a *complete loss* of understanding but rather a *substantial impairment* of his or her cognitive capacity. These 16 lighter shade states follow the formulation of the Model Penal Code (quoted in the margin). Five of the states

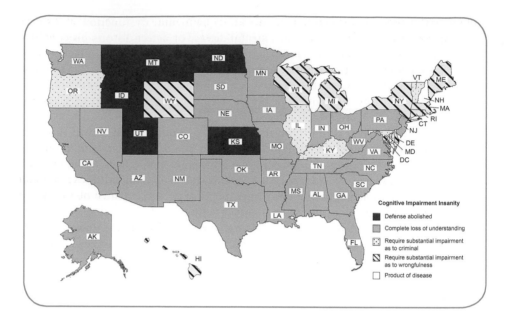

Figure 14.2

Mental Disease or Defect Excluding Responsibility.

(1) A person is not responsible for criminal conduct if at the time of such conduct as a result of mental disease or defect he lacks substantial capacity either to appreciate the criminality [wrongfulness] of his conduct or to conform his conduct to the requirements of law.

(2) As used in this Article, the terms "mental disease or defect" do not include an abnormality manifested only by repeated criminal or otherwise anti-social conduct.

Model Penal Code §4.01

Figure 14.3

adopting this substantial-impairment approach require that the defendant at the time of the offense lacks *substantial capacity* to appreciate "the criminality" of his conduct. The other 11 adopt the Code's bracketed alternative formulation: the defendant must lack the substantial capacity to appreciate the "wrongfulness" of his or her conduct rather than the "criminality" of the conduct.

One can see how these alternative formulations – "wrongfulness" versus "criminality" – might produce different results, as in the *Guiteau* case: the mentally ill defendant believes that God has directed him to commit the offense. He would continue to fully appreciate that his conduct was "criminal" although his mental illness would also lead him to conclude that it was not "wrongful" in some larger moral sense. Thus, he would get a defense under the *wrongfulness* formulation (light shading, overlay of diagonal lines) but not under the *criminality* formulation (light shading, overlay of dots).

As noted above, some jurisdictions recognize a second basis for an insanity defense: a serious control dysfunction, even where there is no cognitive dysfunction. Consider this presidential assassin case arising 100 years after the Garfield killing.

John Hinckley – 1981

In 1955, John Hinckley, Jr. is born into a well-to-do family in Ardmore, Oklahoma. John is a vigorous child who plays on the football team and enjoys life with family and friends in his quaint town.[17] The bright start quickly fades. In the spring of 1976, Hinckley sells his car and uses the money to move to Hollywood, with the goal of becoming a famous musician. A month later, he writes home: "For the past 2 1/2 weeks I have literally been without food, shelter and clothing. On May 14, someone broke into my room and stole almost all of my possessions."[18] His parents send him money.

Over the next few weeks his parents get letters complaining about this city and the people, but reporting that he has a contract with United Artists and a lovely girlfriend. There is no contract and no girlfriend. Around this time, Hinckley watches Martin Scorsese's film *Taxi Driver*. In the film, actor Robert De Niro plays a depressed taxicab driver who attempts to assassinate a presidential candidate and rescue a teen prostitute, played by Jodie Foster, from her pimp. Dejected and disgusted with "the entire weird, phony, impersonal Hollywood scene,"[19] Hinckley soon returns to his parents' home.

The man who returns home is "thin, agitated, and nervous,"[20] according to his parents. Hinckley works a series of low-paying jobs, and uses his money to purchase his first gun, a .38 pistol from a local pawn shop. He expresses racial hatred more and more often. Hinckley starts to educate himself about the American Nazis. After starting on antidepressant medications, he purchases several additional guns. He watches *Taxi Driver* over and over and develops an obsession for the young movie star Jodie Foster, the prostitute needing rescue.

In September of 1980, with help from his parents, Hinckley enrolls in writing classes at Yale. His real reason for doing so is that Foster is there as an undergraduate studying literature. On September 20, he talks to Foster on the phone and tapes the conversation. He talks to her again two days later. She makes it very clear that she is not interested in any type of relationship. Repeatedly rejected, Hinckley becomes increasingly depressed: "I keep getting hit over the head by reality," he writes to his sister. "It doesn't feel very good."[21]

Hinckley decides that, like Robert De Niro in *Taxi Driver*, he can get Jodie Foster's attention and impress her by assassinating the President and thereby becoming a historic figure. In October he attends a speech given by President Jimmy Carter. He has brought two guns and intends to kill Carter, but has a change of heart, stashing the guns in a locker and shaking hands with the President instead.

He tells his psychiatrist that "I have two obsessions in life now: writing, and the person we discussed on November 4,"[22] Jodie Foster. "I care about nothing else!" he insists.[23] Hinckley sends an anonymous letter to the FBI warning them about a plot to kidnap Jodie Foster. "No ransom. She's being taken for romantic reasons," he writes, "This is no joke!"[24]

Ronald Reagan is President elect when Hinckley finds new inspiration in the assassination of John Lennon by Mark David Chapman, who becomes a front-page name. Hinckley begins writing about the power of guns:

> In America, heroes are meant to be killed. Idols are meant to be shot in the back. Guns are neat little things, aren't they? They can kill extraordinary people with very little effort.

The essay is one of despair: "The dream died. I died. You died. Everyone died. America died. The world died. The universe died."[25] In March 1981, he sells several of his guns and boards a Greyhound bus for Washington, DC. He picks up a copy of *The Washington Star* and notes President Reagan's schedule for the day. His mind begins to race, so he takes extra Valium. Shortly after lunch, he puts his loaded .22 pistol in his jacket pocket, writes a letter to Jodie Foster, and takes a cab to the Washington Hilton where Reagan will be speaking.

Hinckley waits outside of the hotel entrance and when Reagan comes out with his entourage Hinckley pulls the pistol from his coat pocket and crouches down, taking careful aim. The President is about to enter the car and, as he turns to give one last wave, Hinckley opens fire with six quick shots. Four of the six shots hit human targets. The President's press secretary, James Brady, is shot in the head; local policeman Thomas Delahanty is shot in the back; secret service agent Tim McCarthy is shot in the abdomen as he spreads his body over the President's. Reagan is shot in the left underarm from a bullet that ricochets off the car, grazing his rib and lodging in his lung, but he survives. The bullet is less than an inch from his heart. Immediately, Alfred Antenucci, a 68-year-old labor official, tackles Hinckley dragging him to the ground. Agent Dennis McCarthy dives on top. The shooting is caught on film by several major news networks and is broadcast across the country.

The trial of John W. Hinckley, Jr. begins a year later.[26] The legal wrangling is not about whether he pulled the trigger; the trial is to establish whether Hinckley due to mental illness is not legally responsible for his conduct.

Hinckley's case is tried under District of Columbia law drawn from *United States v. Brawner*,[27] which allows a defendant to claim the *insanity defense* if he or she, as a result of a mental illness, lacks *substantial capacity*: (1) to understand right from wrong at the time of the crime (the "cognition prong") or (2) to control his or her actions at the time that the crime was committed (the "control prong"). If the defendant meets either one of those standards, he or she may gain an insanity defense under the then-existing law. (As is apparent, the *Brawner* case essentially adopts the Model Penal Code insanity formulation.)

Further, under D.C. law the burden is not on the defendant to prove he was insane, but rather upon the prosecution to prove beyond a reasonable doubt that Hinckley is sane. The defense introduces a number of psychiatric reports that portray Hinckley as insane. Dr. William T. Carpenter testifies that:

Figure 14.4 Hinckley's FBI mugshot, 1981

In my own opinion, I reach the conclusion that he did have a substantial incapacity at that time. The basis for that view deals, of course, with the whole background of psychotic development of his illness that I have described. [B]y the time March 30 had arrived he was so dominated, in my opinion, by the inner state that he had developed over a period of time that his actions and the requirement for his actions were so extensively determined by this inner state that he was, in my opinion, not able to [conform] his conduct to the outside requirements, the legal requirements or social requirements of conduct.[28]

On June 21, 1982, after much deliberation, the jury returns a verdict of "Not Guilty by Reason of Insanity" (NGRI). When such a verdict is returned, the defendant is typically transferred to state civil authorities for evaluation, supervision, and treatment. Hinckley is committed to St. Elizabeth's Hospital in the District of Columbia for an unspecified period of time for treatment.

Insanity Defense Control Dysfunction in the States

In the *Hinckley* case, the would-be assassin knows that his conduct is both criminal and wrongful but seems compelled by his internal fantasies to undertake the assassination in a somewhat bizarre and irrational attempt to impress actress Jodie Foster. He suffers no *cognitive dysfunction* but rather a *control dysfunction*. If

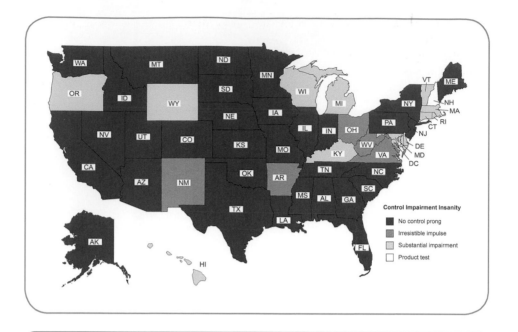

Figure 14.5

Hinckley is to get an *insanity defense*, it can only be in a jurisdiction whose insanity defense includes a "control prong" – that is, where an insanity defense formulation is available not only for cognitive dysfunction but also for control dysfunction: the defendant knew that his conduct was criminal and wrong but was unable to control it. As the map below indicates, however, 32 states – the majority of American jurisdictions – do not recognize any degree of control dysfunction as a basis for an insanity defense.[29] (Again, the lighter the shading on the map, the broader the insanity defense formulation.)

All of the black states on the map have only the cognitive-impairment form of the insanity defense, discussed above, or no insanity defense at all. Thus Hinckley is likely to be ineligible for an insanity defense in any of these jurisdictions (unless he can come up with some means of characterizing effect of his illness as a cognitive dysfunction).

Five jurisdictions, those with medium shading on the second map, adopt what has been called an *irresistible impulse formulation*. This essentially requires that the defendant at the time of the offense no longer had any choice with regard to his engaging in the offense conduct. An irresistible impulse is seen as causing a person to lose all ability to control his conduct.

Compare that formulation with the Model Penal Code's lacks *substantial capacity* formulation, which is adopted by the 13 jurisdictions with light shading. Under this approach, the defendant may gain an insanity defense if the jury concludes that the extent of his impairment of control is sufficient to render him blameless. Under the language of the Model Code quoted above, he "lacks substantial capacity . . . to conform his conduct to the requirements of law."

One jurisdiction, New Hampshire,[30] rejects even the Model Penal Code's "substantial impairment" limitation on the insanity defense. It requires nothing more than the fact that the defendant would not have committed the offense *but for* his or her mental disease or defect. That is, it is enough that the offense was "the product of" mental disease.[31] Hinckley might well get a defense under New Hampshire's *product test.*

Taken together, the five irresistible-impulse jurisdictions plus the 13 substantial-impairment jurisdictions plus New Hampshire's product test mean that only 19 of the 51 American jurisdictions recognize an insanity defense in control dysfunction cases. It is only in these jurisdictions that Hinckley might be eligible for an insanity defense.

How Broad Should the Insanity Defense Be?

The disagreement that we see among the jurisdictions on the breadth of the *insanity defense* moves along two dimensions: first, on whether a control prong should be recognized at all and, second, how powerful must a dysfunction, cognitive or control, be in affecting the offender's conduct in order to entitle the offender to an excuse.

The first dimension of disagreement among the states is whether to recognize a *control dysfunction* (of any sort) as an adequate basis for an insanity defense. It used to be the case that a majority of states had a control prong. The Model Code formulation, which has a control prong, was influential in encouraging states to adopt such a prong in their new codifications in the 1960s and 1970s. But the legal landscape changed after the successful insanity defense of John Hinckley for the attempted assassination of President Reagan, with 36 states reforming their insanity defense in some way.[32]

Again, the split among the states may reflect different degrees of skepticism about whether recognition of a control prong promotes abuse of the insanity defense, a concern highlighted by the Hinckley acquittal. Ironically, Hinckley obtained an insanity defense probably not because the District of Columbia insanity defense had a control prong but rather because the District had an unusual, and probably unwise, rule that put the burden on the prosecution to disprove insanity rather than on the defense to prove it.[33] A more appropriate legislative reform response to the Hinckley acquittal, rather than dropping the control prong altogether, would have been to make clear that the burden of persuasion was on the defendant.

As to the second dimension of disagreement among the states – the extent of dysfunction required – the *M'Naghten test* (of the cognitive prong) and the *irresistible impulse* test (of the control prong) require *complete loss* of cognitive or control capacity. In contrast, the Model Penal Code's insanity formulation requires only a "substantial impairment" of the offender's ability to "appreciate" the criminality or wrongfulness of his conduct or of the offender's ability to conform his conduct to the requirements of law.

Why this disagreement between the complete-loss states and the substantial-impairment states? It may well reflect some general reservation about how easy or hard it is for the insanity defense to be abused. The complete-loss formulation reflects a greater concern about potential abuse than the substantial-impairment formulation. However, studies have shown that while there is a common perception that the insanity defense is frequently given – too frequently given – the reality is that even the substantial-impairment form is a very difficult defense for a defendant to obtain.[34]

Perhaps even more interesting, the evidence suggests that the particular formulation of the defense given to a jury may make little difference and that the academic and legislative skirmishing on the issue may be all for nothing. There is evidence that, no matter which formulation a jury is instructed with, its members tend to look to their own shared intuitions of justice in deciding whether a particular defendant's mental illness in a given case renders him sufficiently blameless to deserve a defense.[35]

Unlike this second disagreement among the states about whether to require a complete loss or substantial impairment – a difference that may have little practical effect on juries – the first disagreement, concerning removal of a control prong from the insanity defense formulation, can have a dramatic effect. Where the dysfunction affects control, even a dramatic loss of control such as an irresistible impulse, the jury may never hear about the mental illness and its effects. Where the insanity defense has no control prong, loss of control is legally irrelevant, leaving no basis to justify its introduction at trial.

Aftermaths

Despite his conviction, Guiteau continues to believe that he will be pardoned and released by President Arthur. He writes to the President:

> I am entitled to a full pardon; but I am willing to wait for the public to be educated up to my views and feelings in the matter. In the meantime I suffer in bonds as a patriot . . . I am willing to DIE for my inspiration, but it will make a terrible reckoning for you and this nation. I made you, and saved the American people great trouble. And the least you can do is let me go; but I appreciate your delicate position, and I am willing to stay here until January, if necessary. I am God's man in this matter. This is dead sure.[36]

Guiteau's court appeal is rejected. On his way to the gallows, the condemned man smiles and waves to spectators and reporters. He dances during his walk and shakes hands with the executioner. As a last request, he recites a poem he wrote during the trial called *I am Going to the Lordy*. He requests orchestra accompaniment during the reading but his request is denied. Modern pathologists have looked at the results of his autopsy and found degeneration of his brain cells suggesting evidence of advanced-stage syphilis.

Regarding Hinckley's case, Reagan makes a full recovery from the assassination attempt and returns to the White House 11 days after the shooting. Hinckley spends the next three decades in a secure mental health facility. In 2016, the court finds that the 61-year-old is no longer a danger to the public, and he is released. He moves to Williamsburg, Virginia and lives with his 90-year-old mother, who dies in 2018.

Chapter Glossary

Cognitive Dysfunction: A phrase used to describe that aspect of insanity defense, and other excuse defenses, a dysfunction in the actor's cognitive abilities, such as their ability to know or appreciate the nature of their conduct or to know whether their conduct is wrong or criminal. Contrast this with a control dysfunction.[37]

Complete-Loss Formulation: The common-law formulations of the insanity defense were commonly understood to require a complete loss of knowledge of the nature or wrongfulness of one's conduct and the total loss of the ability to control one's conduct.[38] Compare this to the substantial-capacity formulation.

Control Dysfunction: A phrase used to describe that aspect of the insanity defense, and other excuse defenses, a dysfunction in the actor's ability to control their conduct. Contrast this with a cognitive dysfunction.[39]

Insanity Defense: Mental illness causing significant cognitive or control dysfunction at the time of an offense may render an offender blameless for his conduct and thereby call for exculpation from criminal liability under an insanity defense.[40]

Irresistible-Impulse Formulation: A supplemental test to the classic M'Naghten insanity test that provides an insanity defense. M'Naghten rests upon a cognitive dysfunction, while the irresistible-impulse test provides an excuse because of a control dysfunction. As one court put it, an actor may qualify for an insanity excuse "if, by reason of the duress of such mental disease, he had so far lost the power to choose between right and wrong, and to avoid doing the act in question, as that his free agency was at the time destroyed."[41]

M'Naghten Test: The common-law test of insanity providing a defense when a disabling cognitive dysfunction prevents the defendant from understanding the nature or the wrongfulness of their conduct.[42]

Product Test: A rarely used test for insanity under which an accused is not criminally responsible if his unlawful act was the product of mental disease or defect. Also called the Durham Test.[43]

Substantial-Capacity Formulation: The MPC formulation of the insanity defense, often referred to as the ALI Test, does not require complete loss of understanding or control but only requires a substantial impairment of an actor's capacity to appreciate the nature or wrongfulness or criminality of the actor's conduct or a substantial impairment of the actor's capacity to control his or her conduct.[44] Compare this to the complete-lost formulation.

Notes

1. This portion of the narrative is drawn from the following sources: Rob Rapley, 'Murder of a President,' Documentary from the PBS American Experience Series, 2016, http://www.pbs.org/wgbh/americanexperience/features/transcript/garfield-transcript/; Charles E. Rosenberg, *The Trial of the Assassin Guiteau* (Chicago: University of Chicago Press, 1968); Carole Bos, 'CHARLES GUITEAU: ERSTWHILE LAWYER,' AwesomeStories Blog, 1 November 2004, http://www.awesomestories.com/asset/view/CHARLES-GUITEAU-ERSTWHILE-LAWYER-Guiteau-and-the-Assassination-of-President-Garfield; Allan Peskin, *Garfield: A Biography* (Kent: Kent State University Press, 1999); Sarah Vowel, *Assassination Vacation* (New York: Simon and Schuster, 2005); Justus Doenecke, 'James A. Garfield: Death of The President,' University of Virginia's Miller Center, accessed 17 July 2020, https://millercenter.org/president/garfield/death-of-the-president; Candice Millard, *Destiny of the Republic* (New York: Random House Publishing, 2012); Jay Bellamy, 'Stalwart of Stalwarts: Garfield's Assassin Sees Deed as a Special Duty,' *Prologue 48*, no. 3 (Fall 2016), accessed online https://www.archives.gov/publications/prologue/2016/fall/guiteau.
2. Charles E. Rosenberg, 'Garfield and Guiteau,' in *The Trial of the Assassin Guiteau: Psychiatry and Law in the Gilded Age* (Chicago & London: University of Chicago Press, 1968), accessed 17 July 2020, https://www.encyclopedia.com/history/news-wires-white-papers-and-books/garfield-and-guiteau.
3. Rosenberg, 'Garfield and Guiteau.'
4. Peskin, *Garfield: A Biography*.
5. Rapley, 'Murder of a President.'
6. Sarah Vowel, *Assassination Vacation* (New York: Simon and Schuster, 2005), p. 168.
7. Bos, 'CHARLES GUITEAU.'

8. Peskin, 'Strangulatus Pro Republica,' in *Garfield: A Biography*, p. 596.

9. Donecke, *James A. Garfield*.

10. He was originally indicted with attempted murder.

11. Rosenberg, 'Garfield and Guiteau.'

12. Bos, 'CHARLES GUITEAU.'

13. Daniel Robinson, 'Furiosi,' in *Wild Beasts and the Idle Humours: The Insanity Defense from Antiquity to the Present* (Cambridge, MA: Harvard University Press, 1996), pp. 10–11.

14. Mental illness can also provide a defense by negating an offense element, MINOE, which is examined in the Advanced Materials at the end of the Educational Supplement for this chapter.

15. The map and supporting authorities are taken from Paul H. Robinson and Tyler Scot Williams, 'Insanity Defense,' in *Mapping American Criminal Law: Variations Across the 50 States* (Westport: Prager, 2018).

16. *R v. M'Naghten* 8 E.R. 718 (1843).

17. This portion of the narrative is drawn from the following sources: Richard Bonnie, John Jeffries Jr. and Peter Low, *A Case Study in the Insanity Defense – The Trial of John W. Hinckley, Jr.* (Eagan: Foundation Press, 2008); Randy Borum and Solomon M. Falero, 'Empirical Research on the Insanity Defense and Attempted Reforms: Evidence Toward Informed Police,' *Law and Human Behavior* 23 (1999): pp. 375–394; Lincoln Caplan, 'The Insanity Defense,' *The New Yorker*, 2 July 1984, http://www.newyorker.com/magazine/1984/07/02/the-insanity-defense; Lincoln Caplan, *The Insanity Defense and the Trial of John W. Hinckley, Jr.* (New York City: Laurel, 1984); Kimberley Collins, Gabe Hinkebein and Staci Schorgl, 'The John Hinckley Trial & Its Effect on the Insanity Defense,' University of Missouri- Kansas City School of Law, accessed 17 July 2020, http://law2.umkc.edu/faculty/projects/ftrials/hinckley/hinckleyinsanity.htm; Emanuel Francone, 'Insanity defense,' Cornell Law School's Legal Information Institute, July 2016, https://www.law.cornell.edu/wex/insanity_defense; Paul L. Montgomery, 'Lennon Murder Suspect Preparing Insanity Defense,' *The New York Times*, 9 February 1981, http://www.nytimes.com/1981/02/09/nyregion/lennon-murder-suspect-preparing-insanity-defense.html; 'Shock and Anger Flash Through the United States,' *The Palm Beach Post*, 31 March 1981.

18. Caplan, *The Insanity Defense*, p. 34.

19. Caplan, *The Insanity Defense*, p. 35.

20. Caplan, *The Insanity Defense*, p. 35.

21. Caplan, *The Insanity Defense*, p. 35.

22. Caplan, *The Insanity Defense*, p. 39.

23. Caplan, *The Insanity Defense*, p. 39.

24. Caplan, *The Insanity Defense*, p. 56.

25. Caplan, *The Insanity Defense*, p. 58.

26. None of the victims shot on 31 March 1981 died, although several were disabled as a result.

27. *United States v. Brawner*, 471 F.2d 969,153 U.S. App. D.C. 1.

28. Douglas O. Linder, 'The John Hinckley Trial: Transcript Excerpts,' University of Missouri- Kansas City School of Law, 2019, http://www.famous-trials.com/johnhinckley/543-excerptshinckley.

29. Robinson and Williams, *Mapping American Criminal Law*, ch. 17B.

30. *State v. Fichera* 153 N.H. 588 (2006).

31. "A defendant asserting an insanity defense must prove two elements: first, that at the time he acted, he was suffering from a mental disease or defect; and, second, that a

mental disease or defect caused his actions." *State v. Fichera* 153 N.H. 588, 593, 903 A.2d 1030, 1034 (2006).

32. Lisa Callahan et al., 'Insanity Defense Reform in the United States-Post Hinckley,' *Mental and Physical Disability Law Reporter 11*, no. 1 (January–February 1987): pp. 54–59.

33. Henry J. Steedman et al., *Before and After Henckley: Before and After Insanity Defense Reform* (New York: The Guilford Press, 1993), pp. 63–64.

34. Lisa A. Callahan et al., 'The Volume and Characteristics of Insanity Defense Pleas: An Eight-State Study,' *Bulletin of the American Academy of Psychiatry and the Law 19* (1991): pp. 331–338.

35. Jennifer L. Skeem and Stephen L. Golding, 'Describing Jurors' Personal Conceptions of Insanity and Their Relationship to Case Judgments,' *Psychology, Public Policy, and Law 7* (2001): p. 561 (cataloguing empirical studies that suggest that jurors "do not apply judicial instruction on legal definitions of insanity," but instead "rely on their own conceptions of insanity to decide whether a defendant is insane").

36. Bos, 'CHARLES GUITEAU.'

37. Robinson and Cahill, *Criminal Law*, §9.3.

38. Robinson and Cahill, *Criminal Law*, §9.3.

39. Robinson and Cahill, *Criminal Law*, §9.3.

40. Robinson and Cahill, *Criminal Law*, §9.3.

41. *Parsons v. State*, 2 So. 854 (ala. 1887); Robinson and Cahill, *Criminal Law*, §9.3.

42. M'Naghten Case, 8 Eng. Rep. 718, 722 (1843); Robinson and Cahill, *Criminal Law*, §9.3.

43. Robinson and Cahill, *Criminal Law*, §9.3.

44. Robinson and Cahill, *Criminal Law*, §9.3.

Chapter 15

Immaturity

Billy the Kid's First Killing

1871. A radical socialist movement, the Paris Commune, rules Paris from March to May, ending in an attack by French regular troops in which 17,000 die. In Pittsburg, a small bible study group forms into the Jehovah's Witnesses, a religion that will grow to include millions of adherents. With a path of destruction four miles long and nearly a mile wide, the Chicago Fire destroys thousands of buildings, kills 300 people, and leads to a massive reconstruction project that spurs both the city's economic development and its population growth. Railways are tying together the country's East and West. After six years of construction, a rail line from Sacramento, California meets a rail line from Omaha, Nebraska at Promontory Point, Utah, opening the American West to a flood of migration. One of the migrant families is that of Henry McCarty.

Henry McCarty – 1871

No record exists of the date or place of Billy the Kid's birth, but he is probably Henry McCarty, born in New York in 1858.[1] By 1871 the 13-year-old is in Silver City, New Mexico where most townspeople remember him with affection. A childhood friend says he was "just an ordinary boy like any other boy and just mischievous."[2] He's small and scrawny, with "girlish looking" features,[3] which makes him a target for bullies. McCarty runs with a group of mischievous, unsupervised band of children who disrupt normal town life and torment citizens.

Out on the streets one day, when a drunk insults his mother, in a fit of rage McCarty attacks the grown man. The 13-year-old soon realizes that he has started a fight he should not have, but luck is on his side and he wrestles free. The drunk pursues him, and just as he is about to catch McCarty, a local man named Ed Moulton steps in to save him. Not long after the rescue, McCarty comes upon Moulton in a fist fight with

DOI: 10.4324/9781003258025-17

two men. McCarty jumps on the back of one of the attackers and stabs him with a pocketknife. Witnesses see his hands literally covered in blood. The man dies from the wounds.

Thirteen-year-old McCarty has killed an unarmed man. Facing murder charges, he takes a gun from his home and with Moulton's aid rides out for Oklahoma. It is this crime that triggers the next steps in the youngster's life, and those in time will blossom into the legend of Billy the Kid.

McCarty hops from ranch to ranch as a laboring hand but by 1876 he strikes up a partnership with John R. Mackie, who has recently been discharged from the army for injuring a man in a gunfight. Skilled in petty theft, Mackie makes McCarty his sidekick. The duo joins the local gang, stealing, trading, and selling livestock all over the Southwest.

A horse theft lands McCarty in jail where he is targeted for abuse by a gruff, burly Irish blacksmith named Francis P. Cahill.[4] On one occasion, when McCarty is shackled, Cahill seizes the opportunity to beat him. McCarty escapes, "shackles and all,"[5] but his bitterness about Cahill's abuse festers.

Later in the year, the Kid, who is now probably just shy of 18 years old, comes back to town and sits in on a poker game at a local cantina. Cahill is also there, and at some point, the two get into an argument. Cahill calls McCarty a "pimp," and McCarty calls Cahill a "son of a bitch."[6] Cahill tackles McCarty, throwing him to the ground and pinning him before slapping his face repeatedly. McCarty manages to get one arm lose, grabs his pistol, and shoots Cahill in the gut. Cahill dies the next day. Some witnesses felt McCarty was without options as the other man was so much larger. Others saw it as murder. Again, Billy does not wait around for the justice system to decide his fate and flees to New Mexico.

Figure 15.1 Billy the Kid, shortly before his death, circa 1880

Almost immediately after crossing into New Mexico, 17-year-old McCarty joins a band who call themselves "The Boys." Notorious for their violence, the band is part of a gang of thieves, murderers, and racketeers that earn a living by rustling cattle, stealing meat, and anything else they can get their hands. When the locals begin to put heat on the gang, they decamp to Lincoln County, New Mexico.

Billy the Kid is no longer a kid. He tries to settle down into a life as a rancher but the cycle of violence keeps coming back into his life. He is jailed several times but always manages to escape.

In April, 1881, the Kid is finally captured and taken to Lincoln under heavily armed escort. The town lacks a suitable jail, so he is confined in the back room of a courthouse. Handcuffed and shackled at all times, two guards watch him. As he is being walked up some stairs on his way back to the holding area, he grabs a gun from one of the guards and shoots his way to freedom. The street is filling with shocked and enthralled townspeople when he hops on a pony, which he promises to return, says "Adios, boys!" and gallops out of town.[7]

His exploits make headlines around the country. Billy claims to have killed 21 people, one for every year of his life, but the historical records suggest that the actual number is probably nine.

Immaturity Excuse

Every American criminal law recognizes in statutes or court opinions a series of *excuse defenses*, such as the insanity defense discussed in the previous chapter. Unlike justification defenses, which exculpate the offender because what he did was something approved or at least tolerated by the law as an acceptable thing to do under the circumstances, excuse defenses condemn the conduct, as something that should not be done by others in a similar situation. Excuse defenses exculpate, despite the wrongness of the defendant's conduct, because the actor is blameless for the wrong done. That blamelessness may flow from a reasonable mistake as to justification, as discussed in previous chapters,[8] or from a variety of disabilities, such as insanity, immaturity, duress, involuntarily intoxication, or some other conditions that undermine the actor's accountability for what was done.

Every jurisdiction recognizes an immaturity excuse. It is hard to blame a seven-year-old for committing a crime when the child is just starting to learn the social rules, let alone the legal rules, and hardly has the kind of foresight of consequences or control of impulses that a normal adult would have. Adolescent brains are not the same as fully mature adults and the differences show up in a young person's judgments and decision-making. Those capacities are predictably different from those of adults in several areas: susceptibility to peer influence, perception of risk, the ability to future orient, and the capacity for self-management.[9] These differences in capacity remain into a person's early 20s. It is also the case that adolescent brains suffer greater mood swings and more intense reactions to fear of abandonment. These differences are a matter of neuropsychological and neurobiological development, not simply matters of social influence.[10]

Long before the modern scientific findings, early criminal law recognized that young children could not be properly blamed for their criminal conduct, and that somewhat older children might be blameless depending upon the extent of their youthfulness and the offense. After reviewing the early common law before the 13th century, one writer concludes:

These cases show two things: 1. That a child under seven years of age might be convicted of felony but would be given a pardon. 2. That a child over that age could be convicted of a felony and sentenced to death if the surrounding circumstances showed that he knew what he was doing. If such a child did not know good from evil, he would be pardoned by the king. It is clear at this stage of the law that the judges were more interested in the mental capacity of the infant than in his chronological age. Indeed, the latter might have been as difficult to prove at that time, when there were no vital statistics, as it would have been to prove criminal capacity.[11]

In modern practice, rather than having the prosecution and defense litigate the extent of a young defendant's immaturity in each case, the criminal law typically adopts a rule that promotes efficiency by presuming that all defendants under a certain age – say, 14 – are immature and thus exempt from criminal liability, while all defendants over a certain age – say, 17 – are presumed mature and thus ineligible for an *immaturity defense*.[12] These age cutoff provisions are often expressed not in the form of an "immaturity defense" available in criminal court, but rather expressed in terms of court jurisdiction, preventing the case from reaching the criminal court or requiring it be handled in juvenile court.[13]

Defendants who fall between the age cutoffs – say, between ages 14 and 17 – may be tried in adult court after a hearing. The factors taken into account often include

Immaturity Excluding Criminal Convictions; Transfer of Proceedings to Juvenile Court.

(1) A person shall not be tried for or convicted of an offense if:

(a) at the time of the conduct charged to constitute the offense he was less than sixteen years of age [, in which case the Juvenile Court shall have exclusive jurisdiction*]; or

(b) at the time of the conduct charged to constitute the offense he was sixteen or seventeen years of age, unless:

(i) the Juvenile Court has no jurisdiction over him, or,

(ii) the Juvenile Court has entered an order waiving jurisdiction and consenting to the institution of criminal proceedings against him.

Model Penal Code §4.10

Figure 15.2

the seriousness of the offense, the defendant's personal history, and the defendant's actual physical and mental maturity.[14] Generally, the more serious the offense, the more likely a young offender will be tried in adult court.

For the most serious offense – murder – states generally adopt a special rule permitting criminal court jurisdiction over some young juveniles. In 1871, it would not have been unusual for 13-year-old Billy the Kid to be subject to prosecution for murder. But a century later, it would have been highly unlikely. In 1962, the Model Penal Code (quoted in the margin) adopted an immaturity defense for persons under 16, and most jurisdictions in the United States followed its lead in recognizing an age cutoff of this sort. (And youthful offenders less than 18 might also be exempt from criminal court prosecution, depending upon the details of the offender and the offense.) Thus, 13-year-old Billy the Kid could not have been prosecuted as an adult for his original homicide under the Model Code.

The most recent trend, however, has tended to reduce the cutoff age for an immaturity defense. Consider this more modern case.

Christopher Pittman – 2001

Christopher Pittman's childhood is wrought with instability.[15] Adults come and go, and he is often shifted to relatives' houses. Christopher's grandparents, Joy and Joe Frank, serve as a source of comfort in the young boy's life. When Christopher stays at his grandparents' house, his grandmother drives him to school every day, and he shares a love of hunting, fishing, and tinkering with his grandfather, whom he idolizes. The Franks move away when Christopher is eight, but they remain involved with their grandson's life and visit often.

When he is 12, Christopher's long-absent mother arrives and reconnects with her children. But she then changes her mind and leaves again in favor of some younger children she has had since abandoning Christopher years earlier.

A few days after his mother's latest rejection, Christopher decides to run away from home. He packs a backpack and heads off to his grandparents' home in South Carolina, 500 miles away. Christopher makes it to the neighboring county before he is picked up by police at an Arby's restaurant. It is clear to all that the boy is not managing well. Upon being returned to his family in Florida, he spends several days at a behavioral health clinic where the doctors diagnose him with depression. The doctors, and his family, feel that Christopher needs more help to manage his life than his parents can provide and arranged for Christopher to live with his grandparents.

As Christopher settles in, he enrolls in Chester Middle School and participates in church activities. While he seems glad to be living with his grandparents, those who know him observe a change in his behavior: he is becoming "withdrawn and mouthy."[16] When visiting his parents during Thanksgiving break, his family finds him to be "happy but hyperactive," and also feels that there has been a fundamental change in him.[17]

At his new school, Christopher becomes aggressive toward other children, a new and worrisome behavior. On one occasion, while riding the bus home, he starts picking on a much younger child in a nearby seat, forcing the boy's head against the window and choking him. The boy begins to cry, and others on the bus pull Christopher away. Before getting off, Christopher tells the other kids that he will kill them if they report the incident. When his grandfather hears the story, he harshly scolds Christopher and makes him write a letter of apology, threatening to send him back to his parents in Florida.

Figure 15.3 Christopher with his parents during family visitation, circa 2008

That evening, Christopher goes with his grandparents to church. At church, it is his grandmother's turn to scold Christopher. Just to be annoying, Christopher repeatedly kicks her chair. Upon returning home, Christopher is sent to his room as punishment. Openly defying his grandparents, he refuses to stay in his room. His grandfather spanks the 12-year-old and sends him back to bed.

Christopher stays in his room until his grandfather goes to bed. He then makes his way to the first floor, removes a .410 pump shotgun from his grandfather's gun cabinet, loads it, enters his grandparents' bedroom, and fires several shots, some into his grandfather's mouth and some into the back of his grandmother's head. Christopher lights several candles and positions them so that the house will catch fire. Before leaving he gets some cash, the family dog, and the keys to his grandfather's truck. He drives off leaving the house ablaze. Neighbors call 911.

When caught, Christopher spins a tale of kidnapping but the physical evidence soon reveals the truth. Christopher confesses and is charged with double homicide and arson.

Due to the level of violence, Christopher is tried as an adult. Prosecutors portray Christopher as a "teenage sociopath" who acts in "absolute cold-bloodedness."[18] They cite Christopher's statements to police in which he said his grandparents deserved to die. The defense does not contest the fact that Christopher killed his grandparents but focuses instead on his troubled past and argue that the depression and the medication that he took for the depression are partly to blame.

The jury convicts Christopher on all counts.[19] Under South Carolina law, judges are forbidden from taking the defendant's age into account for sentencing purposes, and Christopher receives the minimum sentence of 30 years in prison.

Immaturity Defense in the States

The map below displays the minimum age at the time of the offense for which a juvenile charged with murder today may be transferred to adult criminal court over his objection.[20] The darker the shading, the lower the age at which the juvenile can be tried as an adult.

One jurisdiction (with no shading on the map, New York) sets the minimum age for murder prosecution as an adult at 16. Three jurisdictions, those with diagonal lines on the map – the District of Columbia, Connecticut, and New Jersey – set the minimum age for murder prosecution as an adult at 15. Twenty-two states, those designated with the lighter shading, allow prosecution of 14-year-old defendants. This group includes New Mexico, the site of Billy the Kid's first killing. None of these states would today allow the prosecution of 13-year-old Billy the Kid or 12-year-old Christopher Pittman.

Six states, those with medium shading, allow 13-year-olds to be prosecuted for murder as an adult. Thus, Billy the Kid's first killing could be prosecuted in adult court in these states, or in any of the 19 states in the two darker shaded groups. Five states, those with dark shading, allow the prosecution for murder as an adult when the defendant is 12 years old or older at the time of the offense. Fourteen states, those shaded black on the map, allow juveniles of any age to be prosecuted for murder.

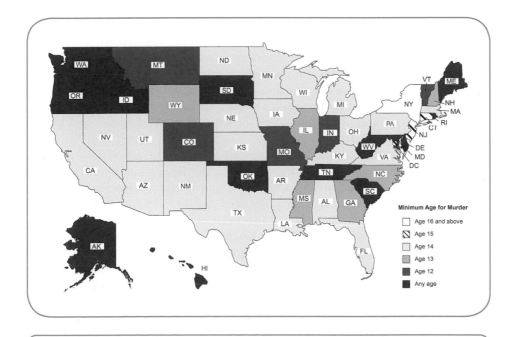

Figure 15.4

Twelve-year-old Christopher Pittman could be tried for murder in any of these 19 states. Note that his home state, South Carolina, is a member of this group.

What Immaturity Defense, If Any, Should Be Available for Murder?

It is easy to understand why the *immaturity defense* has in most instances been converted from a defense into a presumption of jurisdiction in the juvenile court. Most ten-year-old defendants will lack the maturity needed to render them appropriate subjects for adult prosecution; that is, they will lack the blameworthiness needed to deserve criminal liability.

But one of the side effects of converting an immaturity defense into a matter of juvenile court jurisdiction is that, at least in some cases, those defendants who ultimately end up in adult criminal court will have no immaturity defense available to them. An offender over the cutoff age will be conclusively presumed to be sufficiently mature to deserve the blameworthiness of criminal conviction, even if special circumstances suggest that he really did lack the capacity to appreciate the wrongfulness of his conduct or the capacity to control it – a condition that would provide an *excuse defense* if it was caused by mental illness or involuntary intoxication.

One might think that such an offender might have available to him an insanity defense: the immature offender might well, in the words of the Model Penal Code, "lack substantial capacity either to appreciate the criminality or wrongfulness of his conduct or to conform his conduct to the requirements of law."[21] It is well documented, for example, that juveniles frequently do not fully appreciate the nature or consequences of their conduct and commonly lack the impulse control that typically comes with reaching adulthood.[22] Unfortunately, being a normal ten-year-old does not qualify as a "mental disease or defect," as required by the insanity defense.[23]

Where the ten-year-old has limitations on mental or emotional functioning that would fully excuse him if such dysfunction were the result of mental disease or defect, it follows that the immature defendant deserves an excuse defense just as the insane defendant does. To be rational and internally consistent – and, more importantly, to be just – adult criminal courts ought to recognize an immaturity defense that applies whenever a defendant suffers the limitations on cognitive or control functioning that would provide an insanity defense when the excusing conditions required by that defense result from immaturity.

The absence of such an immaturity defense in criminal court reveals a serious failure in all American jurisdictions. However, the failure is dramatically more damaging in those jurisdictions that authorize criminal court prosecution of even very young offenders. Indeed, given the demonstrated cognitive and control limitations of juveniles,[24] it seems hard to understand how so many jurisdictions can justify having such young offenders tried as adults in the first place. If there was ever a rational basis for a conclusive presumption of immaturity, it would certainly apply to offenders aged 13 or younger, for example – yet a majority of jurisdictions, 26, permit such defendants to be transferred to criminal court for murder prosecution as an adult.

It seems particularly odd that many jurisdictions significantly lower their age for criminal court prosecution when the charge is murder. The difference between murder and other offenses against the person is in the extent of the harm caused. There is nothing about the offense of murder that makes the offender necessarily less susceptible to cognitive or control dysfunction. Perhaps the states' different treatment of murder suggests an assumption by policymakers that only criminal prosecution can effectively incapacitate the most dangerous, incorrigible juveniles. But as discussed previously in Chapter 2, a criminal justice system that promotes preventive detention at the expense of being just will ultimately lose moral credibility with the community, which in turn will reduce its ability to reduce crime through the powerful forces of social influence and internalized norms.

It is true that assessing just punishment must take account of the seriousness of the harm or evil, with greater punishment imposed for greater harm caused, all other things being equal. But to be morally credible, criminal punishment must also take account of the offender's circumstances and capabilities. Any offense, including murder, can be tragic yet not an appropriate basis for punishment if the violator lacks sufficient blameworthiness for its commission.

This is the lesson of the insanity defense discussed in the previous chapter, for example, which is available as a defense to all offenses, including murder. The same principle applies to the immaturity defense: it ought to be available in any court and for any offense if the offender's immaturity renders the offender sufficiently blameless.

Aftermaths

Billy the Kid's freedom doesn't last long. In early July 1881, the newly elected Sherriff of Lincoln County, Pat Garrett, hears of the Kid's presence at Fort Sumner. (In 1878 the Kid had participated in an ambush that killed the previous Lincoln County Sheriff.) Garrett and two of his men make the 140-mile trip on horseback, finding Billy soon after arriving. Billy draws his pistol and Garrett fires one time and hits the Kid just above the heart. Within a minute, the 21-year-old outlaw and legend is dead.

In the sensational flurry that follows Billy the Kid's death, the country can't get enough of the Kid's story. Before long, newspapers have made him more myth than real: "How many men he killed, how many deeds of daring deviltry and cruelty he perpetrated will probably never be known until the record books of damnation are opened," one writer concludes.[25] Billy is buried at Fort Sumner.

In the case of Christopher Pittman, his trial as an adult and his sentence of 30 years are both hotly debated, making national news. In spite of the publicity, the South Carolina Supreme Court affirms his sentence. However, the murder conviction is eventually overturned on the grounds of inadequate representation because his lawyers never told Pittman's court-appointed guardian of a possible plea deal (because defense counsel were certain Pittman would be acquitted).

Before a new trial can be held, Pitman takes a new deal, pleading to voluntary manslaughter. The new conviction leads to a new sentence of 25 years. In 2023, Pitman will have served 85% of his new sentence and will be eligible for release, assuming he continues to be the model prisoner he has been. His remaining family supports him.

Chapter Glossary

Excuse Defense: A group of defenses, such as insanity, involuntary intoxication, immaturity, and mistake as to justification, that provide a defense even though the actor's conduct is criminal and objectively unjustified. The basis for granting excuse defenses resides in the fact that the excusing conditions leave the actor blameless for their criminal conduct.[26]

Immaturity Excuse: This defense exculpates immature offenders. Typically, the defense requirements do not examine the actual maturity of the offender but rather assume immaturity if an offender is below a designated cutoff age.[27]

Notes

1. This portion of the narrative is drawn from the following sources: Marcelle Brothers, 'Capture,' *About Billy the Kid*, http://www.aboutbillythekid.com/Capture.htm; Marcelle Brothers, 'Early Life,' *About Billy the Kid*, http://www.aboutbillythekid.com/early_life.htm; Marcelle Brothers, 'The Lincoln County War,' *About Billy the Kid*, http://www.aboutbillythekid.com/Lincoln_County_War.htm; Jay R. Nash, *Bloodletters and Badmen: A Narrative Encyclopedia of American Criminals from the Pilgrims to the Present* (Lanham: M. Evans and Company, 1995), p. 66; Frederick Nolan, *The West of Billy the Kid* (Norman: University of Oklahoma Press, 1999); 'The Death of Billy The Kid, 1881,' Eyewitness to History, 2001, http://www.eyewitnesstohistory.com/billythekid.htm.
2. Nolan, 'Silver City,' pp. 24–25.
3. Nolan, 'Arizona,' p. 55.
4. Nolan, 'Arizona,' p. 55.
5. Nolan, 'Arizona,' p. 55.
6. Nolan, 'Arizona,' p. 59.
7. Nolan, 'Adios Boys,' p. 275.
8. Chapters 12 and 13.
9. Laurence Steinberg and Elizabeth Scott 'Less Guilty by Reason of Adolescence: Developmental Immaturity, Diminished Responsibility, and the Juvenile Death Penalty,' *American Psychologist 58*, no. 12 (2003): pp. 1009–1018. https://doi.org/10.1037/0003-066X.58.12.1009.
10. Steinberg and Scott, 'Less Guilty by Reason of Adolescence.'.
11. Frederick Woodbridge, 'Physical and Mental Infancy in the Criminal Law,' *University of Pennsylvania Law Review 428* (1939): pp. 426–454.
12. The vast majority of jurisdictions permit anyone 18 years of age or older to be prosecuted as an adult for any offense. *See* Paul H. Robinson et al., 'The American Criminal Code: General Defenses,' *Journal of Legal Analysis 7* (2015): pp. 37, 85 (finding that all but six states set the age of majority at 18).
13. *See, e.g.*, Cal. Welf. & Inst. Code § 602 (stating that individuals under 18 years of age at the time of the offense are "within the jurisdiction of the juvenile court"); Cal. Welf. & Inst. Code § 707 (permitting the prosecutor to make a motion to transfer a minor to an adult court where the minor is at least 14 years old and is alleged to have committed enumerated serious felonies, including murder).
14. *See id.*
15. This portion of the narrative is drawn from the following sources: Jason Cato, 'A Family's Tragedy,' *The Herald*, 26 October 2003, accessed from http://www.christopherpittman.org/a_family.htm; Jason Cato, 'Judge Could Send Teen Away from Life,' *The Herald*, 27 October 2003, accessed from http://www.antidepressantsfacts.com/2003-10-27-TheHerald-Pittman-Zoloft-killing.htm; Bill Mears, 'Supreme Court Turns Down Boy Killer's Appeal,' *CNN*, 14 April 2008, http://www.cnn.com/2008/CRIME/04/14/juvenile.killer/index.html?eref=rss_us; Barry Meier, 'Murder Case Entangled in Fight over Antidepressants,' *New York Times*, 23 August 2004, http://www.nytimes.com/2004/08/23/us/drug-trial-justice-science-boy-s-murder-case-entangled-fight-over.html; 'Questions

and Answers on Antidepressant Use in Children, Adolescents, and Adults,' FDA.gov., last updated 2 May 2007, https://www.fda.gov/Drugs/DrugSafety/InformationbyDrugClass/ucm096305.htm; *The STATE v. Christopher Frank PITTMAN*, No. 26339, 14 April 2008, accessed from http://caselaw.findlaw.com/sc-supreme-court/1478531.html.

16. Cato, 'A Family's Tragedy.'
17. Cato, 'A Family's Tragedy.'
18. Cato, 'Judge Could Send.'
19. Mears, 'Supreme Court.'
20. The map is taken from Paul H. Robinson and Tyler Scot Williams, 'Immaturity Defense,' in *Mapping American Criminal Law: Variations across the 50 States* (Westport: Prager, 2018): pp. 171–178. All supporting authorities are available from that source.
21. Model Penal Code §4.01(1), Insanity.
22. Tracy Rightmer, 'Arrested Development: Juveniles' Immature Brains Make Them Less Culpable Than Adults,' *Quinnipiac Health Law Journal 9* (2005): pp. 1, 4–5 (reviewing behavior science research that suggests that juveniles "may not be able to fully understand the consequences of their actions or be able to resist their impulses as adults can," and therefore "may not be fully culpable for their crimes"); Andrew Walkover, 'The Infancy Defense in the New Juvenile Court,' *UCLA Law of Review 31* (1984): pp. 503, 543 (reviewing behavioral sciences research, which suggests that "children under seven generally lack the capacity to be culpable," and that "adolescent children may be generally regarded as possessing the capacity to be culpable, although quite often not at the level . . . of a mature adult").
23. Model Penal Code §4.01(1), Insanity.
24. *See supra* note 5.
25. Nolan, 'The Men Who Made the Myth,' p. 291.
26. Robinson and Cahill, *Criminal Law*, §8.0.1.
27. Robinson and Cahill, *Criminal Law*, §9.4.5; MPC §4.10.

Chapter 16

Statute of Limitation

Hunting Nazi War Criminals

1962. Under a desegregation order from the U.S. Court of Appeals, James Meredith begins classes at the University of Mississippi, prompting riots. As thousands of people flee the Soviet Bloc each month in a divided Berlin, East Germany begins construction of the Berlin Wall. Israeli Mossad locates Nazi war criminal Adolf Eichmann hiding in Argentina and returns him to Israel for a war crimes trial that ends in his conviction and hanging. But Eichmann is not the only Nazi war criminal who sought to escape justice at the end of the war.

Walter Rauff – 1962

Walter Rauff is a trained midshipman when the Nazi Party comes to power in 1933. Adolf Hitler accelerates the process of naval rearmament, over the protests of the Allied Powers, and in the expansion Rauff is promoted to lieutenant and given command of a minesweeper. When war arrives, he takes a job in the SS security service, the Sicherheitsdienst. His success in that position earns him a job as a technical adviser responsible for solving the problems of the execution squads, the SS Einsatzgruppen, in Eastern Europe.

The squads commit mass murder by shooting 15,000 people a day. However, this form of repeated murder takes a psychological toll on the squad members, often leaving them reluctant or in some instance unwilling to continue. Rauff devises a more efficient means that he tries out on the residents of mental hospitals. "Doctors" herd patients who are deemed useless eaters into the sealed compartment at the back of a truck and the vehicle's exhaust is then diverted into the compartment. The screams of the dying are not heard over the revs of the engine. Within 20 minutes, all the unwanted eaters are dead.

DOI: 10.4324/9781003258025-18

Rauff supervises the modification of the vans so that they can accommodate up to 60 people at a time. To make the process more efficient, living people are loaded into the van at the hospital and are gassed as the van drives to a burial site.

The concept is further proven at extermination camps in Chelmno and Nerem, Poland. As the vans are proven efficient, they are deployed elsewhere. The vans are now disguised as mobile homes, or medical facilities with the Red Cross insignia. Without the ruse, the victims would "realize immediately what is going on and get restless, which should be avoided at all costs."[1]

In time, permanent larger-capacity gas chambers are established at extermination camps and the gas vans are no longer necessary. By the time the vans are phased out, Rauff's work has been responsible for approximately 97,000 deaths.

Rauff is transferred to Tunisia (which has recently become Nazi territory) to be the head of the SS's security service there. One of his innovations is to use Jews as human shields against Allied Forces that approach. He also oversees the slave labor performed by various undesirable groups. When it is clear that the Allied Forces are going to take Tunisia, Rauff escapes to Milan, Italy. By the time he leaves, more than 2,500 Tunisians have died at his hands. With this achievement, his superiors recommend him for a high decoration.

When Germany falls, Rauff barricades himself inside the Hotel Regina in Milan with several other SS officers but is eventually taken into custody by the Americans and put in an Allied internment camp in Rimini, Italy. Rauff manages to escape. After working for the Syrians as a military police advisor, and to avoid execution when a new regime takes control in Syria, he sails to South America and obtains permanent residency status in Chile.

As Rauff finds a place to settle permanently, in 1958, another round of Nazi trials commences, this time under West German law instead of international law. The Ulm Einsatzkommando trial against members of an SS killing squad ends with a guilty verdict for all ten defendants. The success of the trial rekindles interest in bringing war criminals to justice, and the West German government establishes the Central Office of the State Justice Administrations for the Investigation of National Socialist Crimes. Nonetheless, the news does concern Rauff. He is confident enough to write to the West German Finance Ministry to ask that his naval pension be paid to him at his new residence.

Adolf Eichmann, a high-level SS officer responsible for deporting millions of Jews to concentration camps during the war, flees to South America, like Rauff, but Israeli intelligence officials track him down in Argentina. His trial sparks additional interest in finding Nazi officials. The Nazi War Crime Office is governed by German law and under German law the *statute of limitation* is 20 years from the date of the murders. Therefore, only four years remain during which Rauff can be tried for his war-time murders.

In 1961, the attorney general in Hanover, West Germany issues an arrest warrant for Rauff and requests his extradition from Chile. Germany cites, among other things, Rauff's own report that "97,000 had been processed"[2] in the vans as evidence of his war crimes. Rauff shows no remorse for his organization of the killings.

In December of 1962, the local police in Chile arrest Rauff in Punta Arenas but Chile's statute of limitation for murder is only 15 years, and it has been almost 18 years since the end of the war. On April 28, 1963, the Chilean Supreme Court issues a ten-page decision refusing the extradition request. The court acknowledges that the "mass slaughter of human beings for racial reasons was a perfidious crime meriting the loathing of the civilized world,"[3] but Rauff had broken no laws since arriving in Chile and the court has a duty to apply its own statute of limitation. Rauff is released and returns to Punta Arenas, where he works as a foreman in a crabmeat-canning factory.

Figure 16.1 Rauff was arrested by the Americans, 1945

Statute of Limitation

Imagine that you are kidnapped and brutally raped by a stranger. You escape but are too traumatized to help police with their inquiries and thus unable to confirm the guilt of their prime suspect. Several years later, after a good deal of counseling and therapy, you realize that your recovery depends upon your coming to terms with this past brutality and you work hard to deal with the painful events. After putting yourself back together and regaining your footing, six years after the offense you go to the police and describe your attacker – a description that just happens to match exactly the man who was their prime suspect. They reopen the investigation and amass compelling evidence against the man, including irrefutable DNA evidence. But the prosecution of your tormentor is barred because the *statute of limitation* has passed, putting him forever beyond the reach of justice.[4]

A defense for this obviously guilty man may seem a gross failure of justice, but the statute of limitation has long been recognized in one form or another as an appropriate defense to crime. While limitation periods did not exist at common law, "ancient Roman law barred prosecution of most offenses after twenty years, and that tradition was adopted by most civil law countries."[5] At the time, criminal and civil actions were not fully distinguished, but one of the primary rationales for the limitation period applied to both: reliability of the evidence would deteriorate with time.

Another argument that can be made in support of having a statute of limitation is that with the passage of time it is quite possible that the offender is now a different person than he was and may no longer need restraint or control. One also might argue that with the passage of time the retributive impulse may have passed, and the community ought not be forever preoccupied with the past but rather should be forward-looking.

For these reasons, the Model Penal Code adopted a statute of limitation, reproduced in the margin, and most American jurisdictions provide such a defense, although commonly with longer terms of limitation than the Model Code.

Notice that the underlying rationale for the statute of limitation is dramatically different from the rationale for justification defenses discussed in earlier chapters on

Time Limitations.

     (1) A prosecution for murder may be commenced at any time.

     (2) Except as otherwise provided in this Section, prosecutions for other offenses are subject to the following periods of limitation:

     (a) a prosecution for a felony of the first degree must be commenced within six years after it is committed;

     (b) a prosecution for any other felony must be commenced within three years after it is committed;

     (c) a prosecution for a misdemeanor must be commenced within two years after it is committed;

     (d) a prosecution for a petty misdemeanor or a violation must be commenced within six months after it is committed.

Model Penal Code §1.06

Figure 16.2

lesser evils, self-defense, and law enforcement authority.[6] Those defenses lay upon the foundation that the offender's conduct causes no net harm – while it violated the terms of a criminal offense, the justifying circumstances mean that the defendant's conduct promotes or protects certain societal interests. The person who burns the firebreak has committed property destruction, but his conduct has also saved the unsuspecting town.

No such dynamic exists for the statute of limitation. There are, admittedly, societal interests that may be promoted by forgoing prosecution, such as the society's interest in reliable adjudications, as well as efficient use of prosecution and punishment resources. But unlike justification defenses, these societal benefits flow not from the defendant's offense conduct, such as burning the firebreak, but rather from forgoing the defendant's prosecution.

Similarly, the rationale underlying the statute of limitation is dramatically different from that of the excuse defenses discussed in Chapter 14, insanity, and Chapter 15, immaturity. Excuse defenses are founded upon the blamelessness of the offender for the criminal conduct. The statute of limitation, which might be best called a *non-exculpatory defense*, provides a defense even if the offender is fully blameworthy, and even if the offense is shockingly serious, as in the *Rauff* case.

Should Statutes of Limitation Be Narrowed?

The long-existing doctrine recognizing a *statute of limitation* continues to be the strong majority rule in the United States. What exactly is it, then, that makes the defense highly debated? Certainly, its *non-exculpatory* nature does not help matters. Offenders escaping punishment that they clearly deserve is commonly frowned upon. However, as noted above, the doctrine has some traditional supporting arguments.

One of the arguments in support of having a statute of limitation, recall, is that with the passage of time it is quite possible that the offender is now a different person than he was and may no longer need restraint or control. But this rationale hardly supports statutes of limitation as they are currently drafted, for the defense never requires any inquiry into the offender's criminal record since the time of the original offense. The offender may have been committing offenses regularly – may have committed a new offense yesterday – yet is still protected by any applicable statute of limitation.

Another argument suggested that with the passage of time the retributive impulse may have passed, and the community ought not be forever preoccupied with the past but rather should be forward-looking. But if the retributive impulse really has passed, then presumably prosecutors would be disinclined to spend their limited resources prosecuting an old case that nobody cares about any longer. The best test of whether the offense has become irrelevant may be whether the system is still driven to prosecute it. If the community does still care enough, why should prosecution be barred? Indeed, the justice system's failure to prosecute an identifiable past offender may leave an open wound that distracts society from focusing on the future. The only way to move ahead in some instances may be to deal with the past so it can be put to rest.

Finally, as to the unreliable evidence argument, there was a time when one could plausibly argue that a long-delayed prosecution increased the chance of wrongful conviction, as evidence degrades and witnesses' memories fade over time. But the modern rules of criminal adjudication and evidence create just the opposite effect of the passage of time: delay that degrades evidence or witnesses' memories makes it increasingly less likely that a prosecution can succeed. The burden of proof is on the prosecution, and the ability of defense counsel to fully cross-examine and challenge the evidence means that the passage of time that degrades evidence works to the defendant's benefit rather than to the prosecution's.

No doubt there remains some kernel of truth in the original arguments in support of the limitation. And perhaps that is why there is less pressure to eliminate statutes of limitation for misdemeanors. It is primarily serious offenses – felonies – for which the bar to doing justice for a clearly guilty offender can undermine the criminal law's moral credibility. And it is the statute of limitation for felonies that has been increasingly narrowed in its length and application.

Criticism over the breadth of the statute of limitation has shown itself in the frustration surrounding the prosecution of war criminals like Rauff. In 1968, the UN adopted the Convention on the Non-Applicability of Statutory Limitation to War Crimes and Crimes against Humanity. The treaty prohibits signatory states from applying statutes of limitation in defense of those who have committed war crimes or crimes against humanity. The German statute of limitation is also extended indefinitely for war crimes.

Consider the treatment of this more modern Nazi war crimes case.

Oskar Groening – 2014

In 1921, Oskar Groening is born in Lower Saxony and raised by his strict and disciplined father, who is a member of the Stahlhelm, a paramilitary organization formed following Germany's defeat in World War I. His nationalistic father becomes a devoted Nazi and teaches his son that the Nazis are "the people who wanted the best for Germany and who did something about it."[7] Groening joins the Hitler Youth in 1933.

Inspired by Germany's early victories in France and Poland, Groening joins the Schutzstaffel, the major paramilitary organization under Hitler and the Nazi Party. He works as a bookkeeper in the paymaster's office until the desk jobs are given to injured veterans. Leaving bookkeeping behind, the 21-year-old is sent to work at Auschwitz.

Due to his background in banking, he is assigned to "Inmate Money Administration," where he is responsible for sorting and counting the different currencies taken from the Jewish deportees as they enter. On his first day, he learns that the Jews are being sent to gas chambers. Through exposure to fellow Nazis and their ideology, he comes to believe that the Germans lost World War I because of the Jews, and therefore it is the Germans' duty to eradicate Judaism from the entire globe. His work for the Nazis is relatively comfortable. He eats well and sleeps well, blanketed by quilts confiscated from the deportees.

Two months after arriving, Groening is assigned to manage the luggage and belongings seized from new arrivals as they disembark. On his first day, he notes a bundle of rags on the platform and from within the bundle he hears a baby crying. The crying child is grabbed by an SS soldier who smashes its head against the iron side of a truck. Horrified, Groening requests to be transferred. His request is denied.

He is subsequently transferred to a fighting position and on his 23rd birthday is captured by the British. Knowing that affiliation with SS combatants would be a dangerous truth to reveal, he tells the British that he worked for SS-Wirtschafts-Verwaltung, a Nazi organization responsible for the country's finances, supply systems, and business projects. He is sent to Britain and serves as a laborer in a prisoner of war camp. From his perspective, he leads a "very comfortable life."[8]

Figure 16.3 Groening at the time of his trial and as a young man

In 1947, Groening is released and returns to Germany. At first unable to get a job at a bank because of his membership in the SS, he later finds employment at a glass factory. There, he works his way up to a management position, eventually becoming the head of personnel and honorary judge of industrial tribunal cases. During this time, he remains quiet about his involvement with the concentration camp.

In 1985, Groening, who is a member of a stamp collectors' club, is at the club's annual meeting when the man next to him says, "It's unbelievable that they're already prosecuting people who deny the Holocaust, even though it really didn't happen."[9] The man hands him a pamphlet, "The Auschwitz Lie," by renowned Holocaust-denier Thies Christophersen. Groening reads the pamphlet and later returns it, with his comments: "I saw everything . . . The gas chambers, the cremations, the selection process. One and a half million Jews were murdered in Auschwitz. I was there."[10] This is his first public acknowledgment of his presence in the camp. These comments are widely circulated among the neo-Nazi community and it isn't long before Groening begins to receive streams of messages from the community attacking him. In the face of the neo-Nazi rhetoric, Groening decides to speak openly about his experiences and becomes an activist combating Holocaust deniers.

In September 2014, Groening is charged by state prosecutors for being an accessory to murder, economically advancing the Nazis, and thereby assisting in the deaths of 300,000 at Auschwitz. Given that the *statute of limitation* is no longer applicable for war crimes or crimes against humanity under German law and by UN Convention, he is tried even though 69 years have passed since the last of the alleged crimes.

His trial takes place on April 20, 2015 in Landgericht, the Luneberg Regional Court. Groening is 94 years old. Though he asks for forgiveness, he still claims his role was merely a "small cog in the gears."[11] For him, "guilt really has to do with actions, and because I believe that I was not an active perpetrator, I don't believe I am guilty."[12]

The court hears over 60 witnesses, many of them Holocaust survivors. For example, Irene Weiss, now an 84-year-old, testifies that after her arrival to Auschwitz at the age of 13, she lost her parents, four siblings, and 13 cousins. She further says that,

> to that 13-year-old, any person who wore that uniform in that place represented terror and the depths to which humanity can sink, regardless of what function they performed. And today, at the age of 84, I still feel the same way.[13]

Many others have the same stories, citing the number of relatives they have lost and the pain and horror they endured.

On July 15, 2015, Groening is convicted of being an accessory to murder of at least 300,000 Jews and, on account of his old age, is sentenced to four years in prison.

Groening, who has worked against Holocaust deniers, is quite repentant but is nonetheless sent to prison at age 96, while unremorseful Nazi Rauff escapes prison altogether under the statute of limitation – illustrating the defense's indifference to whether an offender has become rehabilitated.

Statutes of Limitation in the American States

Every jurisdiction in the United States has a *statute of limitation* of one kind or another. Generally, this means that if the prosecution of a crime has not begun within a certain period of time, it can no longer be prosecuted. (Each state also typically provides specific rules governing when the period-of-limitation clock starts; when it

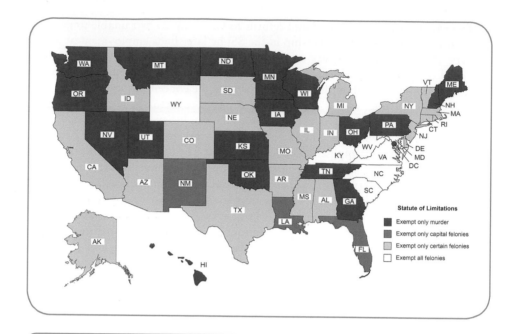

Figure 16.4

may be tolled, or paused, such as when an offender is out of the state; and when it is stopped, that is, what counts as starting a prosecution.[14])

As noted, statutes of limitation are often controversial and there exists a trend toward narrowing the defense by lengthening the limitation period and increasing the number of offenses that are exempt from any limitation period. The controversial nature of the defense may help explain why there is a fair amount of diversity among the states. The map below illustrates four different approaches.[15] The lighter the shading, the broader the category of felonies exempt.

Nineteen jurisdictions, those in black on the map below, exempt from the statute of limitation only cases of murder. This is the approach of the Model Penal Code, quoted in the margin. In other words, every jurisdiction exempts murder but some jurisdictions, such as those in the three lighter-shaded groups, go further to exempt felonies beyond murder.

Three states, those in dark shading on the map, exempt not just murder but any capital offense, defined as an offense so serious as to merit the death penalty. For example, some states authorize the death penalty for rape where the victim is a young child. Twenty-two states, those in light shading on the map, exempt an even broader group of felonies, with different states having somewhat different lists of the felonies exempted.[16] Finally, seven states, those with no shading on the map, exempt all felonies from any statute of limitation.

Because Rauff and Groening are charged as accomplices to murder, they would lose the benefit of any statute of limitation in any American jurisdiction because all states exempt murder. However, as the cases illustrate, some countries have no such rule, including Chile in the *Rauff* case and Germany before 1980 in the *Groening* case.

In the rape case described earlier in this chapter, a statute of limitation would bar prosecution in the 22 states with the black and dark shading on the map, which exempt from the defense only murder or capital offenses.

Aftermaths

Both Germany and Israel work to get Rauff extradited from Chile. In January 1984, the Israeli Foreign Minister travels to Santiago, Chile in an effort to win Rauff's extradition. Again, Chile denies the request. Chilean Foreign Minister Jaime del Valle explains the decision:

> It would be inappropriate to expel a citizen who has lived 20 years in peace here since the Supreme Court ruling [in 1963]. I don't see why a measure should be taken now if it was not taken in 1963.[17]

Nevertheless, the diplomatic pressure continues to mount.[18] The U.S. and the European Parliament join in on the effort to pressure Chile. On May 14, 1984, just as it seems the international community may force Chile's hand, the 77-year-old Rauff suffers a heart attack and dies. Upon his death, he is celebrated by many of the old Nazis, with some yelling "Heil Rauff."[19] During his lifetime, Rauff maintains that he was simply a mid-level "technical administrator."

Regarding the *Groening* case, in 2017 the 96-year-old is legally cleared as physically fit to be imprisoned on the condition that adequate medical care be provided.[20] He appeals the decision, but the appeal is denied. Before he can report to prison, however, Groening dies in March 2018.

Chapter Glossary

Non-Exculpatory Defense: A group of defenses, such as statutes of limitation and diplomatic immunity, that provide a defense in order to promote some societal interest, even though the offender may be fully blameworthy for the offense.[21]

Statute of Limitation: A defense that bars prosecution for an offense after a specific period of time has passed since commission of the offense.[22]

Notes

1. 'Walther Rauff: Letters to the Gas Van Expert,' Holocaust Education & Archive Research Team from the Holocaust Research Project, accessed 20 July 2020, http://www.holocaustresearchproject.org/einsatz/rauff.html.
2. Robert D. McFadden, 'Walter Rauff, 77, Ex-Nazi, Dead; Was an Accused War Criminal,' *The New York Times*, 15 May 1984, http://www.nytimes.com/1984/05/15/obituaries/walter-rauff-77-ex-nazi-dead-was-an-accused-war-criminal.html.
3. 'Chilean Court Bars Extradition of Nazi Who Killed 97,000 Jews,' *Jewish Telegraphic Agency Daily News Bulletin*, 29 April 1963, http://www.jta.org/1963/04/29/archive/chilean-court-bars-extradition-of-nazi-who-killed-97000-jews.
4. The facts are similar to those in the case of Herbert Howard. *See* Paul H. Robinson and Michael T. Cahill, ch. 3, *Law without Justice: Why Criminal Law Doesn't Give People What They Deserve* (Oxford: Oxford University Press, 2005).
5. Lindsey Powell, Unraveling Criminal Statutes of Limitations, *American Criminal Law Review* 45 (2008): p. 115.
6. Chapters 11–13, respectively.

7. Laurence Rees, *Auschwitz: The Nazis & the 'Final Solution'* (London: BBC Books, 2005), p. 140.

8. Rees, *Auschwitz: The Nazis,* p. 287.

9. Matthias Geyer, 'An SS Officer Remembers: The Bookkeeper from Auschwitz,' *Speigel Online,* 9 May 2005, https://www.spiegel.de/international/spiegel/an-ss-officer-remembers-the-bookkeeper-from-auschwitz-a-355188.html.

10. Geyer, 'An SS Officer Remembers.'

11. Geyer, 'An SS Officer Remembers.'

12. Geyer, 'An SS Officer Remembers.'

13. Kate Connolly, '"Accountant of Auschwitz" Trial: Oskar Gröning Admits Guilt,' *The Guardian,* 1 July 2015, https://www.theguardian.com/world/2015/jul/01/accountant-auschwitz-trial-oskar-groening-admits-guilt.

14. Paul H. Robinson and Michael T. Cahill, *Criminal Law,* 2nd ed. (Philadelphia: Wolters Kluwer, 2016), §10.2.1.

15. The map is taken from Paul H. Robinson and Tyler Scot Williams, 'Statute of Limitations,' in *Mapping American Criminal Law: Variations across the 50 States* (Westport: Prager, 2018), p. 182. All supporting authorities are available from that source.

16. Missouri, for example, exempts "murder, rape in the first degree, forcible rape, attempted rape in the first degree, attempted forcible rape, sodomy in the first degree, forcible sodomy, attempted sodomy in the first degree, attempted forcible sodomy, or any class A felony," while Texas exempts murder and manslaughter, certain cases of sexual assault, continuous sexual abuse of a young child or children, indecency with a child, leaving the scene of an accident if the accident resulted in the death of a person, and trafficking of persons.

17. 'Chile Refuses to Push Ex-Nazi into Israeli Trial,' *Chicago Tribune,* 2 February 1984, http://archives.chicagotribune.com/1984/02/02/page/3/article/chile-refuses-to-push-ex-nazi-into-israeli-trial.

18. 'Legislator Seeks to Bar U.S. Aid to Chile While a Nazi Is Harbored There,' *Jewish Telegraphic Agency Daily News Bulletin,* 21 March 1984, http://www.jta.org/1984/03/21/archive/legislator-seeks-to-bar-u-s-aid-to-chile-while-a-nazi-is-harbored-there.

19. Klaus Wiegrefe, 'West German Intelligence Protected Fugitive Nazi,' *Spiegel Online,* 27 September 2011, http://www.spiegel.de/international/germany/ss-colonel-walter-rauff-west-german-intelligence-protected-fugitive-nazi-a-788348.html.

20. 'Former Nazi Guard Oskar Groening Could Be Jailed Aged 96 for Role at Auschwitz,' *Sky News,* 29 November 2017, https://news.sky.com/story/former-nazi-guard-oskar-groening-could-be-jailed-aged-96-for-role-at-auschwitz-11149199.

21. Robinson and Cahill, *Criminal Law,* §8.0.1.

22. *Statute of Limitation,* Black's Law Dictionary.

Chapter 17

Entrapment

Mary Queen of Scots Plots an Overthrow

1587. Pope Gregory XIII gifts the world the Gregorian Calendar, which provides for 12 months of varying lengths and a leap year. After the death of Ivan the Terrible, the first Tsar of Russia, his ineffective son Fedora quickly undoes much of the progress of his father's dynamic rule. Galileo Galilei is busy writing his book explaining planetary movement, which will lead to his conviction for heresy and lifetime house arrest. In England, Elizabeth I is working to bring greater order to her kingdom, in which people of all classes fear the arrival in their towns of gangs of beggars and drifters who, in the absence of any means of controlling them, bring crime, disease, and disorder. Upon her ascension to the throne only one in five English could sign their name, but by the time of her death in 1603, a third of the population will be literate. Nonetheless, some people believe that Elizabeth is a usurper of the throne.

Mary Queen of Scots – 1587

Mary Stuart is six days old when she ascends the throne of Scotland upon the death of her father, King James V.[1] Mary's mother serves as regent for the infant, and baby Mary is betrothed to Dauphin Francois, the French Prince. At age five, young Queen Mary is sent off to France, where she marries Francois II in Notre Dame Cathedral when she is 16.

Because her great uncle is King Henry VIII, she has a claim to the English throne, but her cousin Elizabeth is crowned Queen of England. In less than a year, Mary is crowned Queen of France when her father-in-law King Henry II dies. Over Mary's objections, a treaty is drawn up by which she gives up her claims to rule England. She sees the treaty as an affront and refuses to sign it. For many, this refusal signals that Mary has political ambitions in England. After 17 months in power, King Francois dies. Eighteen-year-old Mary is left a widow, loses her French crown, and is compelled to return to Scotland to rule a country she does not know.

Groomed as a devout Catholic during her time in France, Mary is viewed with suspicion by her majority-Protestant subjects. She attempts to bridge the divide by emphasizing tolerance, most notably by appointing Protestants to her privy council and other high-level posts. However, as a newly arrived outsider, it is difficult for Mary to fully grasp the complex religious dynamics shaping the political landscape of Scotland.

As Queen of France, Mary ruled over a powerful nation and she is not entirely content to rule marginally significant Scotland. She asks Elizabeth to name her as heir to the English throne. Elizabeth agrees that no one else has as solid a claim but makes no promises and declines to name any successor. (Elizabeth sees naming a successor as dangerous because it invites regicide.) In 1565 Mary weds Lord Darnley, her Catholic cousin who also has a claim to the English crown. This consolidation of heirs is seen by Elizabeth and Protestants across England as a direct threat against Elizabeth's Protestant rule. The marriage triggers an uprising by several of Mary's powerful Protestant subjects and Mary's troops are routed on the battlefield.

With few options, Mary abdicates the Scottish throne to her 13-month-old son James. A Protestant lord, James Stewart, is made regent, and Mary is imprisoned. In time, she escapes and unexpectedly services in England. She is hopeful that Elizabeth will give her asylum but this is not easily done from Elizabeth's perspective. If Elizabeth protects her blood relative, she knows her actions will be unpopular among Protestants in England and Scotland. Elizabeth tries to return Mary to Scotland but Regent Stewart refuses to have her back. Elizabeth decides on a middle ground: Mary can stay but is kept far from London and is effectively placed under a plush house arrest.

Figure 17.1 Mary as a young queen, living in France, 1559

Once the queen of two nations, Mary is now stateless, trapped, bored, and confined to a castle. She does little to help her situation when she regularly communicates with many people about the need for a return of Catholic power.

In 1573, Elizabeth appoints Sir Francis Walsingham as her Principal Secretary, and he soon becomes known as the Queen's "spymaster." Walsingham builds an elaborate spy network from the heart of London to the far reaches of the English countryside. Because of Mary's activities, he develops a particularly strong network of informants on Mary's staff. Walsingham is eager to rid England of Mary, but Queen Elizabeth is unwilling to act against her cousin. There are rumors of plots by Mary to take Elizabeth's throne, but they are only rumors and the status quo is maintained for the next ten years.

With designs to end what he sees as a dangerous stalemate, Walsingham forms a plan to further infiltrate Mary's inner circle. First, he hires a famous codemaster to assist him. He then forces Gilbert Gifford, a confidant of Mary's, to switch allegiances and to advise him of all of Mary's correspondence.

The codemaster is then introduced into Mary's small world and spends time at the castle, ingratiating himself with the imprisoned monarch. Soon he is working with Mary on a plan to smuggle secret correspondence. Mary is provided with a secret code in which her letters, to be carried by a confederate, should be written. The codemaster and Mary agree that they will use the castle's weekly beer deliveries to smuggle out her secret correspondence. She devises a waterproof canister and pays the local brewmaster to hide the canister in the beer barrels. The brewmaster then passes the contents back to the Codemaster before sending them on, so Mary's involvement in the plotting can be documented.

Mary is delighted to have what she believes is uncensored contact with the outside world. She begins exchanging letters with Anthony Babington, an energetic young man who is devoted to the Catholic cause and eager to help Mary in any way possible. She does not specifically direct Babington to instigate another Catholic plot, but she indicates she would be grateful for any help in her escape from the castle. Babington is not keen to usurp Elizabeth but is excited at the opportunity to help Mary. Walsingham reads every word and manipulates events to have Mary believe that Babington's commitment is waning and some encouraging words from her are needed. In her next letter, Mary does not hesitate to encourage Babington and his efforts to aggressively promote her cause.

Babington is monitored as he plots with other Catholics who talk of overthrowing the Queen. Babington comes to believe that he has a duty to God to help overthrow Elizabeth and restore England to Catholicism. Walsingham's double agent reassures Babington of the rightness of his plot but advises that he must communicate his plans to Mary and obtain her consent before moving forward.

Babington sends a letter to Mary detailing the plan under which a Spanish army will invade England and free Mary. He says that he will take responsibility for killing Elizabeth, writing "there will be six gentlemen, all my private friends . . . who for the zeal they bear to the Catholic cause and your majesty's service, will undertake that tragic execution."[2] Mary's reply is exactly what Walsingham has been waiting for. Her reply begins by commending Babington for his commitment to the Catholic cause, then launches into the specifics of the plan. She urges Babington to consider how many troops will be required and how they will be paid, recommends three options for her own rescue, and warns him to be wary of Walsingham's spy network.[3]

Walsingham meets with Babington and attempts to persuade him to switch sides but Babington refuses. But now the conspirators realize they have been infiltrated. In his last letter to Mary, Babington warns Mary that they must abandon the plan but still reiterates that "God's cause" will "no doubt succeed happily" in the end.[4] The arrests begin quickly.

Walsingham is directed by Queen Elizabeth "to keep to himself the depth and manner of the discovery." He works to conceal everything he and his agents have done to manipulate Babington and his co-conspirators.[5]

The following month, Mary is tried by a commission of 24 noblemen. Mary initially refuses to participate in her own trial, arguing that she is "a queen, not a subject" and could "never subject herself" to the law under which she is accused without "betraying the dignity and majesty of kings."[6] Less than a day before the trial is set to begin, however, she agrees to attend but continues to argue that the commission has no authority to try her. She knows that her fate is sealed so she sets out to make the trial as uncomfortable and unpredictable as possible for her judges.

Prosecutors present Mary's correspondence with Babington. The most damning passage is in Mary's reply to Babington in which she gives implicit consent to the assassination of the queen:

> The affair being thus prepared and forces in readiness both within and without the realm, then shall it be time to set the six gentlemen to work, taking order, upon the accomplishment of their design, I may suddenly be transported out of this place.[7]

Mary denies the authenticity of the letter and she denies knowing Babington. She accuses the court of fabricating evidence against her. Her denials cannot hold up in the face of the evidence, so Mary shifts her defense. She seeks to appeal to the sympathy of the commissioners: "I have lost my health and . . . through my trials, I have lost the small intellectual gifts bestowed on me by God . . . which might be useful to me in my defense."[8] She retains enough of the intellectual gifts to force the prosecution to admit that the outcome of her case was decided before the trial began. Mary is found guilty of treason.

Entrapment Defense

As a society, we do not want our police and prosecutors or their agents creating crime by inducing citizens to commit it. However, in many situations the only effective means of stopping an ongoing pattern of criminal activity is for the police to go undercover and to act as potential accomplices or as victims. For example, where there has been a serious problem with visitors being robbed in a resort gambling city, where they are particularly attractive targets because they tend to be both cash-laden and intoxicated, the local police might run a "sting" operation in the area where past robberies have occurred, during which they have an officer pretend to be a drunken visitor passed out on the sidewalk with some cash bills slightly protruding from a pocket.[9] Should a person who steals the money from the apparent drunk be entitled to an *entrapment defense*?

The entrapment defense is a uniquely American invention, and a modern one at that. As one writer explains:

> The defense of entrapment does not have roots traceable back to English common law. Rather, the entrapment defense developed in the United States in the early part of the twentieth century. Judges were tentative then, but began to

offer outlines of the defense in a series of cases involving quite egregious overreaching by law enforcement officers. Perhaps the most important early statement concerning entrapment was made by a famous Justice of the Supreme Court, Louis Brandeis, when he commented in the case of *Casey v. US*:

> The Government may set decoys to entrap criminals. But it may not provoke or create a crime and then punish the criminal, its creature. . . . This prosecution should be stopped, not because some right of [the defendants] has been denied, but in order to protect the Government. To protect it from illegal conduct of its officers. To preserve the purity of its courts.[10]

Modern American criminal law now recognizes an entrapment defense, either by statute or by court decision, in all jurisdictions. The formulation of the defense typically takes one of two forms: the *not-predisposed formulation* or the *police-misconduct formulation*.

The not-predisposed formulation, the most common approach, focuses on the offender's predisposition to commit the offense absent the entrapping conduct. If the offender was not predisposed to commit the offense and did so only because of the government's entrapping conduct, then an entrapment defense is appropriate. Tennessee takes this approach, as shown in its provision reproduced in the margin: the defense is available to a person "otherwise unwilling" to commit the offense. Similarly, in Missouri the defense is available if a law enforcement officer or his agent "for the purpose of obtaining evidence of the commission of an offense, solicits, encourages or otherwise induces another person to engage in conduct *when he was not ready and willing to engage in such conduct*." The effect of the "not ready and willing to engage in such conduct" language is to exclude from the defense those persons, such as professional criminals, who would have committed the offense anyway and indeed may well have been actively looking for the opportunity to do so.

Some modern scholars characterize Queen Mary's downfall as an example of entrapment. Andrew Gordon writes that Walsingham supervised the "Queen of Scots' entrapment";[11] Robin Schuster argues that Walsingham's efforts were an "attempt to

Entrapment.

It is a defense to prosecution that law enforcement officials, acting either directly or through an agent, induced or persuaded an otherwise unwilling person to commit an unlawful act when the person was not predisposed to do so.

Tennessee §39-11-505

Figure 17.2

entrap Mary";[12] and Lucy Hinnie argues that Walsingham "fully facilitate(d) the eventual entrapment of Mary."[13] But these claims may be referring to "entrapment" in a conversational rather than a legal sense. As a legal defense to criminal conduct, the entrapment doctrine has very specific demands. Did Walsingham *unlawfully entrap* Mary into committing an offense? Was Mary Queen of Scots an unwilling person not predisposed to commit the offense of conspiring against Elizabeth? A jury might well conclude that Mary was indeed predisposed to commit the offense, that she was not an unwilling person pushed into criminal activity but rather a person who was happy to take the opportunity that presented itself. If that were the jury's conclusion, Mary would not receive an entrapment defense under the not-predisposed formulation.

The other approach to entrapment, what might be called the "police misconduct" formulation, is taken by the Model Penal Code, quoted in the margin. Under this, the characteristics of the particular offender – even his or her criminal history and criminal predisposition – are treated as essentially irrelevant. The focus is only on the police conduct. If the police conduct is improper, then the offender, even if predisposed – even if a career criminal – is entitled to an entrapment defense.

The police conduct is improper – unlawful entrapment – if it "employs methods of persuasion or inducement which create a substantial risk that such an offense will be committed by persons other than those who are ready to commit it." The predisposition *of the offender at hand* is irrelevant; the only question is whether the police conduct created a substantial risk that an offense would be committed by a hypothetical person – a person "other than those who are ready to commit it."

Under this formulation, if the police act improperly, the entrapment defense is available even to those who are predisposed to commit the offense. Thus, the career leg-breaker for an organized crime syndicate who was planning on committing the offense before any interaction with a police agent is nonetheless entitled to the defense under this formulation if the police act improperly.

Did the government agents dealing with Mary Queen of Scots engaged in an unlawful entrapment? That is, did their conduct "create a substantial risk that such an offense will be committed by persons other than those who are ready to commit it"? Walsingham's conduct does seem a bit unsavory. And clearly he was trying to gather evidence that could be used against Mary. But apparently he was doing so because he thought Mary was a threat to his Queen Elizabeth and there were some grounds for reasonable suspicion about this. He no doubt would argue that Mary's private approval of the unlawful escape and assassination plans confirm that he was right to be suspicious.

But none of this really matters under the *police-misconduct formulation*. There, the only question is whether the means of entrapment used were improper, because they created "a substantial risk that such an offense [would] be committed by persons other than those who are ready to commit it." In other words, did he use methods of coercion or temptation that were so great that they created a substantial risk that an ordinary person in the defendant's situation, who otherwise would not be not ready to commit the offense, do so?

Putting the ordinary person in the situation of Mary Queen of Scots may seem a bit awkward. Should we assume that this ordinary person has the same burning ambition to advance the Catholic cause and to take throne of England as Mary had? Probably not. Absent Mary's special ambitions, there seems little reason why the ordinary person would take the opportunity to encourage the escape and assassination, as Mary did. Thus, despite what the historians may claim about Walsingham's

(1) A public law enforcement official or a person acting in cooperation with such an official perpetrates an entrapment if for the purpose of obtaining evidence of the commission of an offense, he induces or encourages another person to engage in conduct constituting such offense by either:

(a) making knowingly false representations designed to induce the belief that such conduct is not prohibited; or

(b) employing methods of persuasion or inducement which create a substantial risk that such an offense will be committed by persons other than those who are ready to commit it.

(2) Except as provided in Subsection (3) of this Section, a person prosecuted for an offense shall be acquitted if he proves by a preponderance of evidence that his conduct occurred in response to an entrapment. The issue of entrapment shall be tried by the Court in the absence of the jury.

(3) The defense afforded by this Section is unavailable when causing or threatening bodily injury is an element of the offense charged and the prosecution is based on conduct causing or threatening such injury to a person other than the person perpetrating the entrapment.

Model Penal Code §2.13

Figure 17.3

entrapment of Mary, she probably would not be entitled to entrapment defense under either of the entrapment formulations.

Because no entrapment defense was recognized at this point in the development of criminal law, the entrapment issue was never raised in Mary Queen of Scots' trial. But consider how the defense might play out in a modern case that involves a similarly ambitious public figure.

John DeLorean – 1982

John Zachary DeLorean's commitment to hard work is clear from an early age.[14] After finishing a master's degree in industrial engineering and business administration, DeLorean follows his father into the car industry, where he is quickly recognized as a brilliant engineer. He becomes one of General Motors' youngest division managers and is subsequently put in charge of the Pontiac brand. In the 1970s, however, DeLorean and GM's top executives increasingly clash over his attitude, the company's structure, and even his style of dress. In 1973, 48-year-old DeLorean marries a 23-year-old as his second wife, and several years later divorces and marries fashion model Christina Ferrare. Fed up with DeLorean's behavior, GM fires him and he loses his $650,000 salary. He is not deterred: he announces he will start his own car company.

DeLorean manages to woo away a team of engineers from GM, form a partnership with Lotus, and get the British government to provide the bulk of the funding. The DeLorean Motor Company sets to work on their first model, the DMC-12. However, the project is plagued with problems from the start. The car sells poorly and suffers significant and costly design flaws. DeLorean himself aggravates the situation by using the company's assets to make private purchases, such as a small Nevada-based snowmobile company and art for his New York office.

When the company runs out of money, the Brits decline to provide more funding. In October 1981, Prime Minister Margaret Thatcher orders a police investigation of the company's finances after a disgruntled former employee provides company documents suggesting mismanagement and revealing DeLorean's personal investment in the company is much less than his deal with the government requires. By February 1982, the company is put in receivership.

The British government announces that it is closing the company's manufacturing plant by the end of May. DeLorean releases a statement that he has new backers who will provide the $37 million necessary to keep the plant open and the company going. He keeps the funding sources a secret, describing them only as "an individual and a bank."[15]

In reality, DeLorean has no idea how he is going to come up with the money. He knows that a former neighbor, James Timothy Hoffman, is involved in drug trafficking

Figure 17.4 John DeLorean with his iconic car

and approaches him about arranging a drug deal. What he does not know is that Hoffman was arrested by the FBI and is anxious for an opportunity to provide information to law enforcement in exchange for a reduced sentence. The day after DeLorean raises the drug deal idea, Hoffman informs his FBI contacts.

Over the course of several surreptitiously video-taped conversations, DeLorean explains to Hoffman that his company has $40 million in cars but no cash, and that he would like to proceed with the drug deal they discussed. An FBI camera hidden underneath the table records DeLorean explaining that his tax man can construct records to make anything look legitimate. Hoffman explains to DeLorean that they can channel the profits from the cocaine sales through Eureka Federal Savings, in San Carlos, California, to make the transactions appear legal. DeLorean comments that he does not really care what the money's source is – drugs, organized crime, anything – so long as it eventually filters through a recognized financial institution so it can be made to look like a legitimate loan or investment.

DeLorean agrees to provide $1.8 million in funding for the drug deal. Hoffman reassures him that he will not be easily connected to the transaction but warns DeLorean that, once they start, he had better not back out without good reason. Hoffman also reminds DeLorean not to take part in anything with which he is uncomfortable. "I won't be mad, I won't be hurt, I won't be anything. If you can get the money somewhere else and it's better circumstances, I'd say do it," Hoffman says.[16] Although he appreciates the option to withdraw, DeLorean tells him, "I want to proceed."[17]

Hoffman introduces DeLorean to the bearded Mafia kingpin, Mr. Vicenza, who is in fact a DEA Agent. While eating lunch, Vicenza discusses rates of return on investment, estimating that DeLorean could have $10 million within 48 hours "from that particular cocaine purchase."[18] Trying to finalize the deal, DeLorean offers Vicenza a 50% ownership stake in his company as collateral if Vicenza will purchase the cocaine with his own money. In a September 29 letter, DeLorean signs over 500 shares of DeLorean Motor Company stock to Vicenza, and 5,000 to Benedict J. Tisa, an undercover FBI agent, which collectively makes up DeLorean's entire voting bloc in the company.

DeLorean flies to Los Angeles to close the deal. The hotel room where the meeting is held is being audio- and videotaped. DeLorean enters the room to see an open suitcase with 60 pounds of cocaine, worth $24 million. Picking up one of the bags, DeLorean says it is better than gold. "Just in the nick of time," he beams.[19] A knock at the door interrupts the celebration. Agent Jerry West enters, announcing, "I'm with the FBI. You are under arrest for narcotics law violations."[20]

DeLorean's main line of defense at the trial is a claim of entrapment. Was John DeLorean an unwilling person not predisposed to commit the drug selling offense? A jury might reach the conclusion that DeLorean was indeed predisposed to commit the offense and was not an unwilling person pushed into criminal activity by the entrapping conduct. If so, then no *entrapment defense* under the not-predisposed formulation.

Did the action of the government agent constitute an unlawful entrapment because it created a substantial risk that a person other than one ready to commit the offense would have been drawn into committing it by the government's conduct? A jury might conclude that the government agent's conduct would have no such effect on a person who is not otherwise ready to commit the offense. If so, no entrapment defense under the *police-misconduct formulation*.

However, DeLorean's attorney argues at trial that the government acted improperly in a variety of ways, although none of them seem to go to creating coercion or temptation so strong as to induce the offense by a person not otherwise ready to commit it. Because DeLorean is being tried in federal court, the federal entrapment defense applies, which follows the not-predisposed formulation. DeLorean is represented by famed trial attorney Howard Weitzman. After 29 hours of deliberation, the jury gives DeLorean the entrapment defense.

The result illustrates how the entrapment defense, probably either formulation, requires the jury to speculate about the internal workings of human behavior. Under the not-predisposed formulation, the jury must determine whether the offender was or was not "predisposed" to commit the offense. Under the police-misconduct formulation, the jury must determine whether there was a substantial risk that an ordinary person in the offender's situation would have committed the offense. The case may also illustrate the advantage of having an exceptional attorney. If Mary Queen of Scots were represented by high-powered counsel today, perhaps she too could win an entrapment defense?

Entrapment Defenses in the States

While the defense of entrapment may not be common in the rest of the world, all American jurisdictions offer it, albeit with some variation in formulation.[21] The map below presents the state alignment for the two major approaches discussed above, together with the competing positions on an important variation regarding availability of the defense for violent offenses.[22]

The most common approach, taken by the 32 light-shaded states, follows the federal courts' *not-predisposed* formulation. The Tennessee formulation has been quoted in the margin. The remaining states, with darker shading on the map, use the

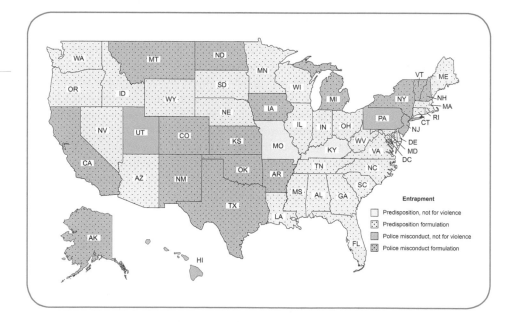

Figure 17.5

police-misconduct formulation. This is also the approach taken by the Model Penal Code, quoted in the margin.

The seven states without a dots overlay – three light-shaded states (Delaware, Kentucky, and Missouri) and four dark-shaded states (Hawaii, New Jersey, Pennsylvania, and Utah) – bar the *entrapment defense* for any offense of violence. To the extent that Mary Queen of Scots' treason offense involved violence, as seems likely, she would be automatically barred from an entrapment defense in these seven jurisdictions. The remaining states have no such absolute bar. However, juries may be less inclined to give the defense when an offender claims entrapment for a crime of violence. How likely is it that the person not predisposed to commit a crime of violence would be induced to do so by government inducement?

Is Entrapment an Excuse or a Non-Exculpatory Defense?

Certainly, the *police-misconduct* formulation of the defense is nothing like an excuse defense, which is based upon an offender's blamelessness. (Recall the other excuses discussed previously in chapters concerning insanity and immaturity.[23]) Excuses are provided where the offender suffers sufficient cognitive or control dysfunction so as to render him or her blameless for their offense conduct. Under the police-misconduct formulation, in contrast, even a career criminal out looking for an opportunity to commit the offense may be entitled to an *entrapment defense*; the focus is only on the police officer's conduct, not the defendant.

However, one might be tempted to think of the *not-predisposed* formulation as a form of an excuse defense, analogous to the duress excuse. One might say, for example, that it is the government's inducement rather than the offender's own selfishness or greed that caused the offense. But this analysis fails to examine whether the entrapment defense requirements actually suggest blamelessness and the offender. Compare them for example to the requirements of the duress excuse: a person is entitled to a defense if he is coerced to commit an offense "by the use of, or a threat to use, unlawful force against his person or the person of another, which a person of reasonable firmness in his situation would have been unable to resist."[24] If the reasonable person could not be expected to have resisted the coercion, then the offender must be seen as blameless, and hence deserving of a duress excuse.

In contrast, the not-predisposed entrapment formulation requires no such overwhelming coercion. A person may not be predisposed to commit an offense yet may be drawn in by pure temptation, and thus entitled to an entrapment defense (if he was not otherwise predisposed to commit the offense). But that is hardly an instance of being coerced to such an extent that a person of reasonable firmness would have been unable to resist.

Further, under the entrapment defense, if an offender is "entrapped" by a nongovernment agent, no defense is available. Imagine a private group that undertakes a sting operation to entrap potential pedophiles using methods that would be illegal for police to use. If the not-predisposed formulation were an excuse based upon the offender's blamelessness for the offense, then it logically ought to provide the defense no matter who was doing the entrapping. The fact that the entrapment defense disappears when the entrapping is by a nongovernment agent makes it clear that the defense – even under the not-predisposed formulation – is a non-exculpatory defense meant to control government officials, not an exculpating defense that excuses blameless offenders.

In other words, the entrapment defense is a non-exculpatory defense much like the statute of limitations and the exclusionary rule.[25] The former provides a defense if the statute of limitation has expired, no matter how blameworthy the offender. The latter excludes even reliable and compelling evidence from admission at trial if gathered in violation of the constitutional limitations on search and seizure: we use the threat of denying a conviction of the offender as a means of controlling police and prosecutors. The entrapment defense – both formulations – performs the same role: by giving an entrapment defense when police have acted improperly, we dis-incentivize such police and prosecutor overreach.

This suggests a different way of looking at the distinction between the two entrapment formulations. In the police-misconduct formulation, any police overreach generates a defense. In the not-predisposed formulation, however, the cost that society is willing to pay in order to deter official overreach is more limited: the predisposed offender, such as the career criminal, will not be given the defense. This may reduce the deterrent effects found in the police-misconduct formulation, but one could argue that it is not an unreasonable trade-off. The same sort of trade-off is found in those jurisdictions that provide an absolute bar to the entrapment defense for crimes of violence. We are willing to suffer some failures of justice in order to discourage overly intrusive sting operations, but we are not willing to release blameworthy offenders who commit crimes of violence.

Those who see substantial costs in allowing blameworthy offenders to go free under the non-exculpatory entrapment defense typically seek to narrow the defense as much as possible or, ideally, to abolish it in favor of some other mechanism for controlling police and prosecutor overreach.[26] For example, they might prefer administrative sanctions of officers, rather than letting guilty offenders go free. If one were really serious about deterring such police misconduct, one might consider abolishing the *entrapment defense* in favor of creating an *entrapment offense* for the police entrapper. If the overreach of entrapment by officials is so intolerable that it should allow blameworthy offenders to go free, why should it not support at least the potential for criminal liability of those who engage in unlawful entrapment?

Aftermaths

Even after Mary has been declared guilty, Queen Elizabeth hesitates, tormented by fears of diplomatic backlash and the moral dilemma of ordering the death of her cousin and fellow Queen. She waits, hoping that the trial and executions of a number of co-conspirators will be enough to satisfy the demands for justice by those around her. But even after the hanging, drawing, and quartering of Babington, her advisors are unrelenting in their pleas for her to sign Mary's death warrant. She does. Mary is beheaded in front of an audience of several hundred at Fotheringhay Castle in 1587.

Mary leaves behind her 21-year-old son Charles James. Upon reaching adulthood, James ascends the Scottish throne as James VI of Scotland. When Elizabeth I dies in 1603, by pre-arrangement, Mary's son becomes James I, King of England, and wears both crowns.

In the *DeLorean* case, the defense argues to the jury that the government did indeed act improperly. It suggests, for example, that a government agent who posed as a drug dealer backdated the forms that authorized the videotaping of DeLorean, that another agent who posed as a dishonest banker rewrote some of his investigative notes, that the government's key witness promised government officials, "I am going to get John DeLorean for you guys."[27] While this evidence does not seem to undermine strong evidence of DeLorean's independent enthusiasm for the drug deal, it could be interpreted to suggest government impropriety of one kind or another.

While DeLorean is not convicted, his reputation is in shambles and his legal troubles are not at an end. After fighting more than 35 additional legal battles resulting from the collapse of his company, in 1999 DeLorean declares personal bankruptcy. He is forced to sell his 434-acre estate in Bedminster, New Jersey. The estate is purchased by then real estate tycoon Donald Trump and converted into a golf course.

At age 75, DeLorean announces plans to build a new sports car.[28] He reports that an overseas investor is interested in building a plant but he "can't disclose more details."[29] The industry is skeptical. DeLorean also moves forward with a plan to start a watchmaking company called "DeLorean Time," selling special-edition watches for $3,495. The watch income is to be used to fund his planned DMC-2 sports car. DeLorean dies in Summit, New Jersey in March 2005 due to complications from a stroke. Neither a DeLorean Time watch nor a DMC-2 car is ever sold.

Chapter Glossary

Entrapment Defense: A defense provided when a law enforcement officer or other government agent induces a person to commit an offense in an attempt to provide the basis for a criminal prosecution against that person.[30]

Not-Predisposed Formulation: A formulation of the entrapment defense in which a defense is provided because the wrongdoing of the officer originates the idea of the crime and then induces the person to commit the offense when the other person is not otherwise predisposed to do so.[31]

Police-Misconduct Formulation: A formulation of the entrapment defense in which a defense is given if the officer has used undue influence, even if the person would have committed the offense even without the undue influence.[32]

Notes

1. This portion of the narrative is drawn from the following sources: Jacquelyn L. Borgeson, 'The Role of Walsingham in the Misnomered Babington Plot of 1586' (student essay, Cumberland College, published in *The Upsilonian* 2, Summer 1990), https://inside.ucumberlands.edu/downloads/academics/history/vol2/Jackie Borgeson90.htm; James Daybell and Andrew Gordon, *Cultures of Correspondence in Early Modern Britain* (Philadelphia: University of Pennsylvania Press, 2016), https://books.google.com/books?id=79I7DAAAQBAJ&printsec=frontcover&source=gbs_ge_summary_r&cad=0#v=onepage&q&f=true; Jane Dunn, *Elizabeth and Mary: Cousins, Rivals, Queens* (New York: Random House, 2004); Lucy Hinnie, 'Mary Queen of Scots: Femme Fatale, Martyr, or Tragic Romantic Heroine?,' University of Edinburgh's Dangerous Women Project, 11 April 2016, http://dangerouswomenproject.org/2016/04/11/mary-queen-of-scots/; Robert Hutchinson, *Elizabeth's Spymaster: Francis Walsingham and the Secret War That Saved England* (London: Weidenfeld & Nicolson, 2006); Paul Johnson, *Elizabeth I: A Biography* (London: Weidenfeld & Nicolson, 1974); 'More Plots against Elizabeth,' The National Archives, accessed 20 July 2020, http://www.nationalarchives.gov.uk/spies/ciphers/mary/ma3.htm; Anka

Muhlstein, *Elizabeth I and Mary Stuart: On the Perils of Marriage* (London: Haus Publishing, 2007); John H. Pollen, *Mary Queen of Scots and The Babington Plot* (Edinburgh: T. and A. Constable Ltd., 1922), https://archive.org/details/mary-queenofscots00polluoft; Edmund Wright and Jonathan Law, 'Ridolfi Plot,' in *A Dictionary of World History*, edited by Edmund Wright (Oxford: Oxford University Press, 2006), https://www.oxfordreference.com/view/10.1093/acref/9780192807007.001.0001/acref-9780192807007; Susan W. Schmid and John A. Wagner, *Encyclopedia of Tudor England* (Santa Barbara: ABC-CLIO, 2011), https://ebookcentral.proquest.com/lib/upenn-ebooks/reader.action?docID=871468; Robin Schuster, 'Mary, Queen of Scots and Plots Against Elizabeth I,' University of Minnesota Online Resource, May 2003, http://www.d.umn.edu/cla/faculty/tbacig/studproj/h3099/maryscots/mary%20site,%20plots%20paper.htm; Edmund Wright and Jonathan Law, 'Throckmorton plot,' in *A Dictionary of World History*, edited by Edmund Wright (Oxford: Oxford University Press, 2006), https://www.oxfordreference.com/view/10.1093/acref/9780192807007.001.0001/acref-9780192807007; Anna Whitelock, 'Deadly Rivals: Elizabeth I and Mary, Queen of Scots,' *BBC History Magazine*, 1 February 2016, https://www.historyextra.com/period/elizabethan/deadly-rivals-elizabeth-i-and-mary-queen-of-scots/; Stefan Zweig, *Mary, Queen of Scotland and the Isles* (New York: Viking Press, 1935).

2. Hutchinson, *Elizabeth's Spymaster*, p. 129.
3. Not quite satisfied, Walsingham has the Codemaster forge a postscript asking Babington to send the names of the six men who are set to kill the Queen. Hutchinson, *Elizabeth's Spymaster*, p. 129.
4. Hutchinson, *Elizabeth's Spymaster*, p. 136.
5. Pollen, 'The Coup de Grace,' August 1586–February 1587, p. 179.
6. Hutchinson, *Elizabeth's Spymaster*, pp. 136, 155.
7. Johnson, *Elizabeth I: A Biography*, p. 285.
8. Hutchinson, *Elizabeth's Spymaster*, p. 163.
9. The facts are similar to those of the Reno, Nevada case of David Kenny Hawkins discussed in: Paul H. Robinson, 'Picking Clean Drunks,' in *Would You Convict? 17 Cases That Challenged the Law* (New York: NYU Press, 2001), pp. 166–177.
10. Paul Markus, 'Entrapment,' in *Encyclopedia of Crime and Justice*, edited by Joshua Dressler (New York: Macmillan Library Reference, 2002), p. 619.
11. James Daybell and Andrew Gordon, 'Material Fictions: Counterfeit Correspondence and the Culture of Copying in Early Modern England,' in *Cultures of Correspondence in Early Modern Britain* (Philadelphia: University of Pennsylvania Press, 2016), p. 100, https://books.google.com/books?id=79I7DAAAQBAJ&printsec=frontcover&source=gbs_ge_summary_r&cad=0#v=onepage&q&f=false.
12. Schuster, 'Mary, Queen of Scots.'
13. Hinnie, 'Mary Queen of Scots: Femme Fatale?'
14. This portion of the narrative is drawn from the following sources: Judith Cummings, 'First Candidates Interviewed for Jury to Hear Trial of John Delorean,' *New York Times*, 14 March 1984, http://www.nytimes.com/1984/03/14/us/first-candidates-interviewed-for-jury-to-hear-drug-trial-of-john-delorean.html; Robin G. Fisher and Bev McCarron, 'Delorean Is Now Cruising Beneath Radar,' *The Times-Picayune*, 17 December 1995; Ken Hoover, 'A Trial of Images; Do the Secret Tapes Show the Real John DeLorean?,' *National Law Journal*, 2 July 1984; 'John Delorean,' Unique Cars and Parts Blog, accessed 20 July 2020, https://www.uniquecarsandparts.com.au/founding_fathers_john_delorean; Dylan Landis, 'Delorean Plant May Close Monday,' *New York Times*, 25 May 1982, http://www.nytimes.com/1982/05/25/business/-delorean-plant-may-close-monday.html; David Margolick, 'A Case for DeLorean,'

New York Times, 17 August 1984, http://www.nytimes.com/1984/08/17/us/a-case-for-delorean.html; Jay Mathews, 'The Trials of John DeLorean,' *The Washington Post*, 4 March 1984, https://www.washingtonpost.com/archive/lifestyle/1984/03/04/the-trials-of-john-delorean/3946af6b-9ca3-4c6f-b205-c23af6ec8ac6/?utm_term=.34d0df6fa923.

15. Landis, 'Delorean Plant.'
16. Mathews, 'The Trials of John DeLorean.'
17. Mathews, 'The Trials of John DeLorean.'
18. Mathews, 'The Trials of John DeLorean.'
19. 'John Delorean.'
20. Hoover, 'A Trial of Images.'
21. *See* generally Paul H. Robinson and Michael T. Cahill, *Criminal Law*, 2nd ed. (New York: Wolters Kluwer, 2016) §10.3.
22. The map is taken from Paul H. Robinson and Tyler Scot Williams, *Mapping American Criminal Law: Variations across the 50 States* (Westport: Prager, 2018), ch. 21. All supporting authorities are available from that source.
23. Chapter 14, Insanity, and Chapter 15, Immaturity.
24. Model Penal Code §2.09(1).
25. Chapters 16 and 17.
26. *See, e.g.,* Paul H. Robinson and Michael T. Cahill, 'Employing Civil Rather Than Criminal Processes,' in *Law Without Justice: Why Criminal Law Doesn't Give People What They Deserve* (London: Oxford University Press, 2005), pp. 218–224, https://ssrn.com/abstract=699842.
27. Margolick, 'A Case for DeLorean.'
28. This subsection is drawn from the following additional source: Dan Jedlicka, 'Ambitious DeLorean Planning a Comeback,' *Chicago Sun-Times*, 3 October 2000.
29. Jedlicka, 'Ambitious DeLorean.'
30. *Entrapment Defense*, Black's Law Dictionary.
31. Robinson and Cahill, *Criminal Law*, §10.3; Del. Code Ann. tit. 11, §432.
32. Robinson and Cahill, *Criminal Law*, §10.3; MPC §2.13.

PART III

Specific Offenses

With the background of Part I's general principles of liability and Part II's general defenses, this part examines different kinds of specific offenses. Most of the cases in this volume so far have concerned crimes against the person, such as homicide, rape, or assault. In practice, however, the vast majority of offenses in a criminal code concern conduct other than physical injury.

There is no attempt in this part to be comprehensive in examining other offenses. Such would be impractical – modern criminal codes define hundreds of crimes – and, perhaps more importantly, such would not serve the purpose of this volume, which is to provide an introduction to the nature of criminal law generally, not a workman's encyclopedia to its practice. Rather than an attempt at comprehensiveness, or even representativeness, the chapters in this part examine a wide sampling of offenses, including offenses that illustrate significant change over time and thereby tell us something about criminal law's process of development.

Modern criminal codes typically include the definition of offenses in the "Special Part" of the code (compared to the "General Part" of the code dealing with general principles of liability and general defenses) grouped according to the societal interest at stake. Thus, endangerment and statutory rape (Chapters 19 and 23) are commonly grouped with other offenses against the person, while adultery, obscenity, and child pornography (Chapters 24–26) are commonly grouped with other public indecency and morals enforcement offenses, and so on.

As will become apparent in this part, as social norms or crime-control demands change, so too do criminal offenses. This includes not only creating new offenses, such as those embodied in the Racketeer Influenced and Corrupt Organizations Act, more commonly known as RICO (Chapter 30), but also abolishing old offenses, such as adultery (Chapter 24). Changing social norms also means changing the level of punishment for some offenses, such as in significantly increasing the penalties associated with domestic violence or child pornography (Chapters 21 and 26).

DOI: 10.4324/9781003258025-20

Chapter 18

Endangerment

Causing the Johnstown Flood

1889. The United States has a growth spurt when North Dakota, South Dakota, Montana, and Washington all become states. The country is suddenly 366,000 square miles larger. Nintendo Koppai, now known simply as Nintendo, is founded to produce hand-made cards for a game called Hanafuda. The company currently has a market value of over US$50 billion. The UK passes legislation to protect children from abuse and neglect; many see the law as an assault on the sanctity of the family. Alexander Gustave Eiffel's 1,056-foot engineering masterpiece is completed, becoming an iconic structure of Paris. While the science of engineering was making great advances, its implementation was sometimes weak.

South Fork Hunting and Fishing Club – 1889

Johnstown, Pennsylvania is an industrial town built on a floodplain at the fork of two rivers. Seasonal rains bring flooding that becomes an ever-greater problem as the town's population grows. To ease the flooding, the South Fork Dam is built in 1853 14 miles upstream to hold back the Little Conemaugh River and gives rise to Lake Conemaugh. The dam is well designed but funding problems lead to several modifications that lessen the strength of the 72-foot earthen structure.

After completion, the dam is neglected. Twenty-six years later, the South Fork Hunting and Fishing Club decides to revive the lake for fishing and other leisure activities. The club is highly exclusive: its 60-odd members include high-profile individuals like Andrew Carnegie and Andrew W. Mellon. The club builds a 40-room clubhouse and a complex of luxury lakeside cottages. Rather than properly repairing the dam, the club simply adds mass where previous building materials have failed. The new materials include brush, tree stumps, hay, manure, old bricks, straw, clay, coal,

DOI: 10.4324/9781003258025-21

Figure 18.1 The Johnstown people were left with a ruined town, 1889

and clay-mining wastes. The inadequacies of the repairs quickly become apparent when the dam's embankment sags, allowing water to spill over the top when the river runs high.

The lovely waterfall created by the poor design is a bonus for the club as it makes for a picturesque view. In 1880, geologist and engineer John Fulton writes to the club, "It did not appear to me that this work was being done in a careful and substantial manner, or with the care demanded in a large structure of this kind."[1] The materials are not only "improperly emplaced but were also the incorrect material to accomplish proper closure."[2] The club is told on many occasions that the dam is not safe.

In the spring of 1889, unusually heavy seasonal rains arrive, weakening the dam's foundation. The soils of the Allegheny Region are already saturated, when yet another heavy rain begins. As the ground can absorb no more rain, the entire deluge goes directly into the Little Conemaugh River and, in turn, into the lake being held back by the dam.

On the morning of May 31, 1889, Lake Conemaugh is rising at a foot per hour. Nearby residents grow concerned about the dam, which is visibly buckling. A group of residents climb onto the dam and do what they can to cut a trench to divert some of the rising water. Using picks, shovels, and a horse-drawn plow they struggle against the rising waters for several hours, but they make very little progress. By noon water is flowing over the dam, and the repair work undertaken by the club is visibly deteriorating. As the failure of the dam becomes ever more likely, on two occasions South Fork Club engineer John Parke makes his way on horseback to the telegraph office in the town of South Fork. He sends warnings to the telegraph offices in the areas below the dam. The collapse of the dam has been a threat for so long that the warnings are dismissed as false alarms. The warnings are not passed on to the town's authorities; Johnstown residents are not alerted to the danger.

At 3:00 p.m., the sides of the dam explode outward with such force that the air blast topples full-grown trees. A 60-foot-high wall of water roars down the valley at 40 miles per hour. It hits the community of South Fork, but most residents survive because the village is situated on relatively high ground. The water engulfs several small communities on its way toward Johnstown. The deadly wall of debris comes to a halt when it collides with the Conemaugh Viaduct, a 78-foot-high railroad bridge. For a few minutes, the viaduct holds back all the accumulated debris and becomes a dam, the pressure builds by the second. The once towering viaduct soon fails and as it does, the pent-up wall surges forward. When the water reaches Johnstown, the compacted debris drives through everything in its path, sweeping entire buildings away. Many who survive the water are crushed beneath wood, metal, and mud. Shortly after the wall of water engulfs Johnstown, the mass of debris catches fire. The fire now becomes the agent of death, killing 80 people.

The area is now stripped bare of vegetation, leaving only rock and mud: 1,600 homes and four square miles of Johnstown are destroyed. Property damage reaches $17 million. And while no accurate count is ever made, it is believed over 2,200 people are dead, including 99 entire families.

The receding waters are clogged with bodies. In the coming days, the bodies begin to decay. Concerns about infectious disease rise. The water supply is contaminated with chemicals and human remains. In cruel irony, the massive flood leaves the town in desperate need of clean water.

The tragedy is considered an Act of God and no criminal charges are ever brought against the Hunt Club or any of its members.

Distinguishing Intentional Killing from Culpable Risk-Taking

The distinction between an intentional killing and an accidental one is of ancient origin. Even by the 4th century B.C.E., Demosthenes reports that unintentional killings, at least certain forms of them, are to be treated differently than intentional.[3] By early common law in the early 13th century, such cases remained criminally liable under the formal law but were routinely subject to royal pardon, but eventually mitigation became formalized. As Perkins explains:

> [I]n 1214 Roger of Stainton, who had killed a girl by accident, was spared only by a royal pardon. Such cases, let it be emphasized, called originally for a special act of grace, for "the king himself must decide in each case whether life and limb shall be spared." And the royal pardon, while it saved the slayer's life, did not shield him from the forfeiture of his goods. "In early days 'there could be little law about this, for all depended upon the king's grace,' " but later the rule changed and such a pardon was granted by the chancellor as a matter of course without referring the matter to the king.[4]

Today, accidental killings are similarly distinguished from intentional killings, but the law makes a more nuanced judgment by making the extent of mitigation dependent on the extent of the offender's culpability in taking the risk of killing, as discussed in Chapter 3 (Culpability). Recklessly taking an unjustified risk that kills another will be punished as reckless homicide (manslaughter); negligently taking such a risk will be punished as negligent homicide; and death resulting from taking a reasonable risk will have no criminal liability.

Criminalizing Risk-Creation Alone

It is a testament to the central role of harm, especially in ancient criminal law, that the harm was at one time seen as an essential prerequisite to criminal liability. "Exodus 21:18f confirms that even if there is both intent and requisite blow, this is immaterial as far as criminal law is concerned unless the victim dies."[5] And as discussed in a previous chapter concerning attempt,[6] even in cases where an actor attempts to cause a harm, criminal liability was not regularly imposed until the 16th century on the continent and the late 18th century in England.[7] Thus, it is no surprise to find that the criminal law for some time resisted the criminalization of creating unreasonable risks that did not come to fruition.

However, the recognition of risk creation as a legitimate basis for criminal liability would seem inevitable as criminal law becomes more nuanced. Where a person knowingly creates a substantial risk of causing death to another, the actor is liable for reckless homicide (manslaughter) when the death comes about. In the lucky case in which the risk of death does not come about, it seems unclear why the risk creator should escape all criminal liability: his own conduct and culpability are the same as in the manslaughter case; the only difference is the simple luck of the victim. While that moral luck might be seen as reducing the offender's blameworthiness – recall that completed-conduct attempts are punished at the usual one grade discount of other attempts – it can hardly support a conclusion on blamelessness.

Recklessly Endangering Another Person.

A person commits a misdemeanor if he recklessly engages in conduct which places or may place another person in danger of death or serious bodily injury. Recklessness and danger shall be presumed when a person knowingly points a firearm at or in the direction of another, whether or not the actor believed the firearm to be loaded.

Model Penal Code §211.2

Figure 18.2

Further, today's criminalization of risk creation is simply one form of punishing conduct beyond the paradigm of injury to persons or property. Modern criminal law offers a wide range of other examples, such as criminalizing risk of undermining the value of the official currency by counterfeiting. In other words, serious risk creation is simply another form of intangible harm or evil. While there may have been no resulting injury in the case at hand, a certain number of cases of this same risky conduct will result in injury. Creating a risk that did not previously exist is a harmful *result* worth criminalizing, even if the harm risked does not occur on this occasion. For this reason, criminalizing unjustified risk creation is common in today's criminal law. The most obvious instance of such is the criminalization of creating a risk of death or serious bodily, which is prohibited and punished by the offense of endangerment. (The Model Penal Code endangerment provision is reproduced in the margin.) Creating a risk of damage to property is also sometimes criminalized.[8]

Causing or Risking Catastrophe.

(1) Causing Catastrophe. A person who causes a catastrophe by explosion, fire, flood, avalanche, collapse of building, release of poison gas, radioactive material or other harmful or destructive force or substance, or by any other means of causing potentially widespread injury or damage, commits a felony of the second degree if he does so purposely or knowingly, or a felony of the third degree if he does so recklessly.

(2) Risking Catastrophe. A person is guilty of a misdemeanor if he recklessly creates a risk of catastrophe in the employment of fire, explosives or other dangerous means listed in Subsection (1).

(3) Failure to Prevent Catastrophe. A person who knowingly or recklessly fails to take reasonable measures to prevent or mitigate a catastrophe commits a misdemeanor if:

(a) he knows that he is under an official, contractual or other legal duty to take such measures; or

(b) he did or assented to the act causing or threatening the catastrophe.

Model Penal Code §220.2

Figure 18.3

In some respects, the proper criminalization of risk creation is more challenging for code drafters than criminalizing causing a harm, tangible or intangible.[9] First, every person's life is full of creating risks. A drive to the local convenience store to get a newspaper creates some degree of risk to persons or property along the way. This is simply the nature of our complex society. These low-level risks are something that we accept as the price we pay for the benefits that flow from our modern lives. And, thus, some such risk creation needs to be excluded from criminal liability.

Further, some risks may be serious but also may be justified. For example, any large construction project is likely to create a substantial risk that someone in the course of the project will be injured or even killed. Nonetheless, even though the project organizers know this beforehand, we don't think them criminally condemnable for moving ahead with the project. Rather, we think that such risk creation, within bounds, is an acceptable price to pay for the societal benefits that the project will bring. Thus, again, such justified risk creation must be excluded from criminal liability.

The Model Penal Code drafters attempt to provide these exclusions by defining criminal recklessness to include only consciously disregarding "a substantial and unjustifiable risk." It adds that,

> The risk must be of such a nature and degree that, considering the nature and purpose of the actor's conduct in the circumstances known to him, its disregard involves a gross deviation from the standard of conduct that a law-abiding person would observe in the actor's situation.[10]

Perhaps because of these complexities, a number of jurisdictions have been hesitant to adopt the Model Code's endangerment offense. However, some jurisdictions do create an offense that punishes particularly serious risks, such as the creation of a risk of widespread property damage, such as the offense of risking catastrophe. The Model Penal Code provision for such an offense is reproduced in the margin. Under such an offense, the Hunt Club may well have been criminally liable even if the flood had not occurred – creating a risk of its possibility be enough. In the case where the unjustified risk does come to fruition, as happened in the Hunt Club case, the Clubs criminal risk creation together with their awareness of it can generate criminal liability for the offense of causing a catastrophe.

In practice, however, the application of such risking catastrophe statutes is not always limited to dramatic cases like the Hunt Club.

Tequilla Newsome – 1990

In June of 1990 19-year-old Tequilla Newsome is living in Pittsburgh, Pennsylvania with her two-year-old son Montelle Thornhill and her three-year-old daughter Charita Thornhill.[11] It is a full house. In addition to Newsome and her children, the household includes Newsome's mother, grandmother, brother, and a German shepherd-bloodhound mix named Fae Lou. Montelle is allergic to Fae Lou, but his great-grandmother, Minnie Bivens, refuses to get rid of the dog.

Newsome decides to take matters into her own hands. She drives Fae Lou downtown and leaves her, hoping the dog will wander off and find another place to live. Unfortunately, Newsome underestimates Fae Lou's spatial reasoning skills – Newsome returns home, only to find that the dog has beaten her back. With the attempt foiled,

Figure 18.4 A German shepherd-hound mix similar to Fae Lou, 2014

Newsome calls upon her friend, 14-year-old Lachan Russell, to help with a more aggressive scheme.

Under the new plan, Newsome will call the dog away from the house, light the animal on fire, and then dispose of the body in a nearby trash bin. Newsome gives Russell a bottle of kerosene. Later in the evening, Newsome tucks her children into bed and tells her grandmother she is going out for cigarettes. Newsome meets Russell outside the house and then douses the dog until she is completely soaked. Newsome lights a match, throws it on Fae Lou, and watches the dog light up in flames.

They suddenly realize, however, that their plot has gone awry. In their haste, Newsome and Russell lit Fae Lou on fire while she was still on the front porch. The two dash toward the street, calling the burning dog to follow, but Fae Lou is tethered to the porch.

Granny Bivens hears the commotion on the front porch and opens the door to find her beloved dog ablaze. She tries to throw water on Fae Lou and unties the leash from the porch. In her frenzy, Fae Lou brushes against a couch on the porch, setting it on fire. She then bounds wildly into the house and up the stairs, leaving a trail of burning kerosene behind with every step. The dog makes it to the third floor and enters the children's bedroom, where she settles under Montelle's bed. The fire from the couch on the porch licks the outside walls of the house as the fire inside spreads. Granny Bivens attempts to douse the fire, but it is no use. Minutes later, the house is engulfed in flames.

Uncle Andre tries to save the children but cannot find them in the thick smoke. To save himself, he is forced to jump out of the third-floor window. Charita wakes during the fire and crawls to a window. The fire department arrived at the scene but it is too late. The house burns almost completely down; the two children are found dead of monoxide poisoning and smoke inhalation, Charita on her knees near the window and Montelle in his bed. Fae Lou's body is found in the bedroom with the children.

Meanwhile, Newsome and Russell walk down Apple Street and look back to see the house aflame behind them. When they hear police sirens, they make a pact to never tell anyone of their role in the incident. Though Newsome is a suspect, no evidence is ever found to link her to the deaths of her two children. How the dog caught on fire remains a mystery to investigators, and the case goes cold for the next 15 years.

Many people are particularly horrified by the fiery death of the children. The case detectives keep pictures of the children on their desks and never quite give up. In April of 2005, the Pittsburgh Police Department re-opens the case. They keep asking questions until they get answers. Under questioning, Newsom's younger friend Lachan Russell eventually reveals the truth about the fire. As one detective explains, "People that were in a fast lifestyle back in the day, they settled down into a more responsible lifestyle and things like this affect them more now. They wanted to get things off their chest."[12] Newsome and Russell are taken into custody. At the conclusion of the 2005 trial, both are found guilty of several arson offenses as well as causing a catastrophe. It is not entirely clear that the Model Code drafters intended the causing catastrophe offense to be applied to such a case. While the case is tragic, it is not the Johnstown Flood.

Endangerment Statutes in the States

The map below shows where each state stands on the enactment of the different sorts of endangerment statutes.[13]

Thirty states, those shown in lighter shading on the map, have adopted a general *reckless endangerment* offense. The offense criminalizes recklessly creating a risk of death or serious bodily injury to another person,[14] even if no harm occurs. These are not statutes of limited applicability, such as those that criminalize a parent placing a child at risk of serious injury, but rather are statutes of general applicability: the risk may be created by any means, and the party at risk may be any other person. The remaining 21 jurisdictions, those with darker shading, have no such general endangerment offense.

If the deaths and injuries had not (yet) come about in the Hunt Club dam case or in the blazing dog house-burning case – that is, if the parties had only created the risk of death or injury – then they could be held liable for their general risk creation in the light-shaded states but probably not in the dark-shaded states (although they might be liable for other more specific offenses).

On the issue of endangering property, six states follow the Model Code in adopting a general offense for risking catastrophe. These states are shown with a dots overlay. They criminalize recklessly creating a risk of catastrophe,[15] widespread damage to property,[16] even if no damage occurs. The statutes commonly require that the risk be created by "widespread dangerous means" – that is, by a means that commonly risks widespread damage, such as fire, flood, or avalanche. (Fourteen states, those shown with diagonal lines, have adopted reckless burning statutes. These statutes criminalize recklessly creating a risk of injury to persons or property.[17] These are statutes of limited applicability, in that the risk must be created by fire.)

The South Fork Hunting and Fishing Club is located in Pennsylvania, which has a risking catastrophe statute. Thus, the Club's risking widespread damage through dangerous means would seem to satisfy the statutory requirements. The risk creation itself is only a misdemeanor but because the risk comes to fruition, the Club is liable for the offense of causing catastrophe, which is a serious felony. In 1879, however, no such statute existed, so the Club is not criminally prosecuted.

The *Newsome* case also occurs in Pennsylvania, in 1990, after the modern causing catastrophe offense is enacted. As noted, one may wonder whether the application of that statute is a bit of an overreach. How "widespread" is the potential injury or

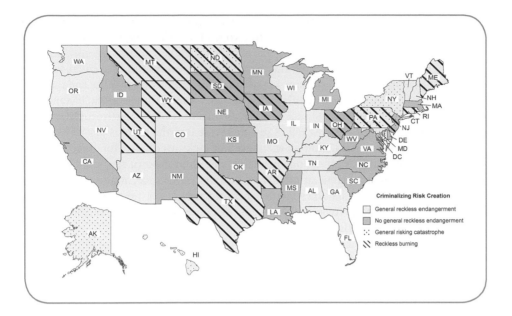

Figure 18.5

damage that arises from lighting up the dog? It is possible that the case could have been as easily and effectively prosecuted under traditional property damage and homicide offenses.

Are General Reckless Endangerment Offenses Necessary?

General offenses that criminalize endangering others or risking widespread property damage would seem to be fairly important for every jurisdiction, yet many have none – as is true of the darker-shaded states on the map. Why should this be so?

For many people, the *Newsome* case illustrates the danger of generalized offenses, such as *reckless endangerment* and risking or causing catastrophe, and such concerns can lead to a preference for narrower offenses. However, jurisdictions that adopt only narrowly defined risk-creation offenses often find themselves unable to prosecute condemnable risk creation that is not sufficiently common to be anticipated by a special offense.

It is true, as noted at the start of the chapter, that risk-creation offenses present challenges in their formulation that ordinary harm-based offenses do not, but the Model Penal Code and the experience of the many states that have adopted its endangerment provisions make clear that those challenges can be met. It is quite feasible to limit such criminal liability to cases of substantial risk of substantial harm.[18] The cases of apparent overreach, as in *Newsome*, could be handled with better judicial oversight to assure the general statures applied only in the cases for which the legislature intended it.

The continuing absence of general risk-creation offenses in many jurisdictions is probably less a principled concern for properly defining the prohibited risks and more a result of the bad habit of state legislatures of responding to a particular lobbying group or newspaper headline without thinking about the larger picture. In every jurisdiction on the map that lacks a general reckless endangerment offense, one can probably find lots of specific crimes that prohibit very specific kinds of endangerment of another person. For instance, many jurisdictions specifically criminalize endangering the welfare of a child or certain vulnerable adults.[19] But if these specific instances of endangerment are to be criminalized, why not all instances of endangerment that create a risk to other groups where the risk is just as severe and the harm is just as likely?

Similarly, in every jurisdiction on the map that lacks an offense for creating a risk of widespread damage or injury, one probably can find a host of specialized offenses that prohibit specific forms of such conduct. For instance, many jurisdictions criminalize risk-creating activities involving motor vehicles or firearms.[20] But if these forms of risk creation are to be punished, why not punish other forms of conduct that create the same kind of risks?

Indeed, for those jurisdictions that have a general reckless burning offense, those shown on the map with horizontal lines, why should it not also be an offense to create an identical risk through some other means, as by explosion or flooding – or a risk of a similar scale through radiation exposure or biological or toxic contamination?

The problem exists in large part because of the nature of the American legislative process as it relates to criminal law: a specific interest group asks for a specific criminal offense to be created that addresses their specific problem. For example, the milk lobby wants the creation of a special offense that criminalizes the taking of the reusable plastic crates that are used to deliver milk containers. Or imagine a newspaper headline tells the story of a particular criminal episode that prompts legislators to want to show their constituents that they are responsive to an apparent problem. For example, car thieves pull a woman from her car and drive off with it. The legislature promptly creates a "carjacking" offense, as if the robbery, assault, and auto theft offenses did not already criminalize and seriously punish such conduct.[21]

This unfortunate legislative dynamic leads to piecemeal criminal code drafting with hundreds, if not thousands, of specialized offenses. Unfortunately, this approach simply makes the criminal code simultaneously too long and complicated and also incomplete, filled with lots of inexplicable holes in coverage. The better approach is, first, to resist creating new offenses if they are already covered by the existing criminal code and, second, when gaps in current coverage are discovered, to look beyond the special case at hand to define an offense that covers the general harm or evil and not just this special version of it.[22]

Aftermaths

In response to the trauma and heartbreak, the disaster at Johnstown prompts a great show of support. Thousands of relief workers flood into the region, peaking at around 7,000. Volunteer physicians and ministers pour out from neighboring communities and a temporary martial government is established over the ruined city.[23]

At the end of town, tents are assembled to provide much-needed temporary shelter for the thousands of survivors. One of the relief workers is a nurse named Clara Barton, the founder and president of the newly created American Red Cross, who works tirelessly for more than five months to help Johnstown recover. This is the first time that the Red Cross has been called to action in the United States. Donations totaling over $3.7 million pour in, including from 18 foreign countries.[24] While

Johnstown digs itself out of the disaster, the Hunt Club members abandon their properties and never return to Lake Conemaugh.[25]

Attention eventually turns to the cause of the disaster and some people start to focus on the hunting club's failure to rebuild and properly maintain the dam. Club members donate thousands of dollars to Johnstown's recovery after the catastrophe but, for its victims, the payments are not enough. In a civil lawsuit against the club, the court holds that, because the dam's collapse was an Act of God, the Johnstown survivors have no right to legal compensation.

In the *Newsome* case, defense counsel at trial argues that, "These girls didn't have a clue about the consequences. They just wanted to get rid of the dog." In counsel's view, the defendants were "horribly overcharged [by prosecutors], perhaps as a result of the exuberance in cracking a 15-year-old case."[26] The detectives who solved the case have a different view. To them, the framed images of the children on their desks seemed to be asking, "Doesn't anybody care how we died? Doesn't anybody care?" As they explain to a reporter, there is no statute of limitations on homicide, adding "nor is there a statute of limitations on a homicide detective's memory."[27]

In addition to the causing catastrophe charge, Newsome faces second-degree murder charges for the death of her children and is given two life sentences. Russell, who was 14 at the time of the offense, is sentenced to 18–60 months in prison.[28]

Chapter Glossary

Reckless Endangerment: The criminal offense of putting another person at substantial risk of death or serious injury.[29]

Notes

1. This narrative is drawn from the following sources: Uldis Kaktins, Carrie Davis Todd, Stephanie Wojno, and Neil Coleman, 'Revisiting the Timing and Events Leading to and Causing the Johnston Flood of 1889,' *Pennsylvania History: A Journal of Mid-Atlantic Studies 80*, no. 3 (2013): pp. 335–363, https://muse.jhu.edu/article/511842/-pdf; Emily Godbey, 'Disaster Tourism and the Melodrama of Authenticity: Revisiting the 1889 Johnstown Flood,' *Pennsylvania History: A Journal of Mid-Atlantic Studies 73*, no. 3 (July 2006): pp. 273–215, https://www.jstor.org/stable/27778765?seq=1# metadata_info_tab_contents; J.J. McIntyre, 'Johnstown Flood (1889),' in *Encyclopedia of Disaster Relief*, edited by K. Bradley Penuel and Matt Statler (Thousand Oaks: SAGE Publications, 2011); Warren Jr. Winkelstein, 'The Johnstown Flood: An Unnatural Disaster,' *Epidemiology 19*, no. 1 (2008): p. 163; Kaktins, Todd, Wojno, and Coleman, 'Revisiting the Timing and Events.'
2. Kaktins, Todd, Wojno, and Coleman, 'Revisiting the Timing and Events.'
3. Bryan C. McCannona, 'Homicide Trials in Classical Athens,' *International Review of Law & Economics 30*, no. 2 (March 2010): p. 46.
4. Rollin M. Perkins, 'A Re-Examination of Malice Aforethought.' *Yale Law Journal* (February, 1934).
5. A. Phillips, Ancient Israel's Criminal Law 87 (1970).
6. Chapter 7.
7. George Fletcher, quoted in the text at Chapter 7 note 9.

8. *See* generally Paul H. Robinson and Michael T. Cahill, *Criminal Law*, 2nd ed. (New York: Wolters Kluwer, 2016) §15.4, §16.1.

9. *See* Robinson, 'Prohibited Risks and Culpable Disregard or Inattentiveness: Challenge and Confusion in the Formulation of Risk-Creation Offenses,' *Theoretical Inquiries in Law 4* (2002): p. 367.

10. Model Penal Code §2.02(2)(c). Some have argued that the Model Penal Code drafters are wrong to think of the issue as strictly one of culpability, which can be addressed in the definition of "recklessness." Rather, it is argued, unjustified risk creation is a harmful result in itself – and intangible result to be sure, but an objective result nonetheless. For example, Robinson, 'Prohibited Risks and Culpable Disregard or Inattentiveness', pp. 367–396 (2005?).

11. This narrative is drawn from the following sources: *Com. V. Newsome.* 2015 Ct. of Common Appeals No. 322 (PCRA 2015); *Com. V. Russell.* 2007 PA Super 376 (Pa. Super. Ct. 2007); Joe Mandak, 'Pennsylvania Woman Charged in 15-Year-Old Pet Arson That Killed Her Children,' *Firehouse*, 16 February 2005, http://www.firehouse.com/news/10511706/pennsylvania-woman-charged-in-15-year-old-pet-arson-that-killed-her-children; Anya Sostek, 'Mom Gets 2 Life Sentences for 1990 Deaths of Son, 2, Daughter, 3,' *The Pittsburgh Post-Gazette*, 20 October 2005, http://www.post-gazette.com/local/city/2005/10/20/Mom-gets-2-life-sentences-for-1990-deaths-of-son-2-daughter-3/stories/200510200455.

12. 'Pennsylvania Woman Charged in 15-Year-Old Pet Arson That Killed Her Children,' *Firehouse*, 6 February 2005, https://www.firehouse.com/home/news/10511706/-pennsylvania-woman-charged-in-15yearold-pet-arson-that-killed-her-children.

13. The map is taken from Paul H. Robinson and Tyler Scot Williams, 'Criminalizing Risk Creation,' in *Mapping American Criminal Law: Variations across the 50 States* (Westport: Prager, 2018), p. 201. All supporting authorities are available from that source.

14. Or in some states, wantonly or negligently, and in some states, only bodily injury.

15. Or in some states, willfully or negligently.

16. Or in New York, simply damage to another's property exceeding $250.

17. Or in some states, negligently.

18. *See* Model Penal Code endangerment and risking catastrophe statutes as well as the recklessness definition.

19. *See, e.g.,* Ala. Code §13A-13-6 (child endangerment); Iowa Code Ann. §726.6 (child endangerment); Alaska Stat. Ann. §11.51.200 (endangerment of a vulnerable adult); Me. Rev. Stat. tit. 17-A, § 555 (endangerment of a dependent person).

20. *See, e.g.,* Fla. Stat. Ann. § 316.192 (reckless driving); N.D. Cent. Code Ann. § 39-08-03 (reckless driving); Tex. Transp. Code Ann. § 545.401 (reckless driving); Cal. Penal Code § 25100 (storage of firearm in a location where a child is likely to gain unsupervised access); Okla. Stat. Ann. tit. 21, §1289.11 (imposing criminal liability for "engaging in reckless conduct while having in . . . possession any [firearm] . . . creating a situation of unreasonable risk . . . of death or great bodily harm"); W. Va. Code Ann. §61-7-12 (criminalizing "wanton[] perform[ance] [of] any act with a firearm which creates a substantial risk of death or serious bodily injury").

21. *See* Paul H. Robinson, 'The Rise and Fall and Resurrection of American Criminal Codes,' *University Louisville Law Review 53* (2015): p. 173; Robinson and Cahill, 'The Accelerating Degradation of American Criminal Codes,' *Hastings Law Journal 56* (2005): pp. 633–655.

22. Paul H. Robinson, Matthew Kussmaul, and Muhammad Sarahne, 'How Criminal Code Drafting Form Can Restrain Prosecutorial and Legislative Excesses: Consolidated Offense Drafting,' *Harvard Journal on Legislation 58*, No. 1 (Winter 2021): pp. 69–102.

23. 'The Desolated Valley,' *New York Times*, 3 June 1889, http://www.johnstownpa. com/History/hist30.html.

24. 'The Johnstown Flood Became the Biggest News Story of the Era,' *Johnstown Area Heritage Association,* http://www.jaha.org/attractions/johnstown-flood-museum/-flood-history/the-relief-effort/.

25. Kaktins, Todd, Wojno, and Coleman, 'Revisiting the Timing and Events.'

26. A. Sostek, 'Mom Gets 2 Life Sentences for 1990 Deaths Caused Fire that Killed Son, 2, Daughter, 3: [Sooner Edition],' *Pittsburgh Post – Gazette*, 20 October 2005, https://-proxy.library.upenn.edu/login?url=https://search-proquest-com.proxy.library.upenn. edu/docview/390739429?accountid=14707.

27. M. A. Fuoco 'City Detectives Crack Cold Case Two Children Died When Burning Dog Set House Ablaze: [Sooner Edition],' *Pittsburgh Post – Gazette*, 17 February 2005, https://proxy.library.upenn.edu/login?url=https://search-proquest-com.proxy.library. upenn.edu/docview/390838667?accountid=14707.

28. Commonwealth of Pennsylvania versus Tequilla Fields, 25 October 2010, http://www. niad.info/page103/files/tequilla-fields.pdf.

29. *Reckless Endangerment*, Black's.

Chapter 19

Extortion

Blackmailing Elvis Presley

1959. Fearing his death at the hands of the occupying army, Tibetans surround the Dalai Lama's palace and smuggle him to India, after which the Chinese slaughter tens of thousands of Tibetans and destroy the major monasteries. Fidel Castro becomes the Premier of Cuba. The U.S. reports a total of 1,250,000 deaths in auto accidents to date, more lives than the country has lost in its all its past wars, prompting Congress to investigate the issue of automobile safety. Buddy Holly, who will be one of the first artists inducted into the Rock and Roll Hall of Fame, dies in a tragic plane crash at age 22. Elvis Presley, for whom Holly had on occasion been the opening act, wrote a letter of condolence to the family, apologizing for being unable to attend the funeral because he was in the Army stationed in Germany.

Dr. Laurenz Griessel-Landau – 1959

Elvis Presley isn't born into stardom – far from it.[1] But, even as a young boy, Elvis' musical abilities attract attention. In 1945, he wins second prize at the Mississippi-Alabama Fair and Diary Show for his singing. The following year, his parents give him a guitar for his birthday. In 1953, having just graduated from high school, he records some of his songs at a local recording studio founded by Sam Phillips.

Phillips encourages him to record more, believing that he has found the performer he has been seeking: "a white man with the Negro sound and the Negro feel."[2] In 1955 Elvis signs on with a new manager, Andreas Cornelis van Kuijk, who goes by the name of "Colonel Tom" Parker. The new manager arranges to get himself a profit share that often reaches 50%. He does much to promote Presley's talent and makes himself rich in the process.

By 1956, Elvis is a national star. His singles, including "Heartbreak Hotel," "Hound Dog," and "Blue Suede Shoes," rocket to the top of the national and

DOI: 10.4324/9781003258025-22

international charts. He also becomes a motion picture star. Elvis calls making his first movie, *Love Me Tender*, "the biggest thrill of my life."[3] The movie premieres in November 1956 just as he is turning 21, the age at which he becomes eligible for the military draft.

The Navy and the Army try to outbid each other with inducements, and both offer him Special Service options whereby he can serve his time while entertaining the troops. Elvis' manager, the Colonel, is none too keen on the idea. Were the young star to sign on, Elvis would be getting a private's pay for super-star work. Probably more to the point, the Colonel would get nothing.

The Colonel decides the best option is regular G.I. service in the Army with no special assignments and no promises to perform. He persuades Elvis that by serving his time as a regular soldier, he can help expand his fan base beyond the teen set. Elvis becomes a tank driver in the Second Armored Division.

His celebrity attracts the attention of the FBI. One former member of the Army Intelligence Services writes to FBI director J. Edgar Hoover that Elvis is a "definite danger to the security of the United States" because his "actions and motions were such as to rouse the sexual passions of teenaged youth."[4]

Behind the handsome face and voice, Elvis is as flawed as anyone. He eats voraciously and struggles with weight gain throughout adulthood, he abuses drugs, and he suffers from an all-too-familiar frustration of youth: acne. In 1959, while serving in Germany, Elvis spots a magazine advertisement for weekly herbal skin treatments offered by Dr. Laurenz Griessel-Landau that promises to erase all skin troubles.

Private Presley has his secretary contact the doctor and the doctor's quick reply is a ten-page letter espousing his enthusiastic agreement to treat Elvis under strict confidentiality ("Boy Scout's honor," the doctor promises). Landau offers to do the treatments at no cost beyond expenses if Elvis isn't satisfied. Elvis is pleased with the

Figure 19.1 Elvis, as an Army sergeant, giving a press conference, 1960

results, even displaying them to his friends and family. (The latter are living with him for a time in Germany.) While Elvis is pleased, nobody else notices any difference.

Over the course of several weeks, Landau spends many hours alone with a partially clothed Elvis. Elvis knows that Landau is bisexual, but he is keenly embarrassed when Landau makes passes at some of his friends who come with him

Theft by Extortion.

   A person is guilty of theft if he purposely obtains property of another by threatening to:

   (1) inflict bodily injury on anyone or commit any other criminal offense; or

   (2) accuse anyone of a criminal offense; or

   (3) expose any secret tending to subject any person to hatred, contempt or ridicule, or to impair his credit or business repute; or

   (4) take or withhold action as an official, or cause an official to take or withhold action; or

   (5) bring about or continue a strike, boycott or other collective unofficial action, if the property is not demanded or received for the benefit of the group in whose interest the actor purports to act; or

   (6) testify or provide information or withhold testimony or information with respect to another's legal claim or defense; or

   (7) inflict any other harm which would not benefit the actor.

   It is an affirmative defense to prosecution based on paragraphs (2), (3) or (4) that the property obtained by threat of accusation, exposure, lawsuit or other invocation of official action was honestly claimed as restitution or indemnification for harm done in the circumstances to which such accusation, exposure, lawsuit or other official action relates, or as compensation for property or lawful services.

Model Penal Code §223.4

Figure 19.2

to the doctor's office. He discontinues the treatments. Now it is Landau who is angry, so he goes to Elvis' home and presents him with a letter that threatens to offer the press photographs, letters, and accounts of "compromising situations" of Elvis with other men.[5]

Elvis says that Landau is mentally disturbed, but he knows that this is a serious problem that requires skills beyond his own. Unsure what to do, Elvis calls the man who orchestrates his life, the Colonel, who in turn phones several high-level army contacts in Washington. On their advice, Elvis enlists the help of the Army's Provost Marshal Division, who contacts the FBI.

The investigators determine that it is not just Elvis who is vulnerable: Landau does not have the appropriate medical certifications. After some back and forth, Landau and Elvis come to an agreement. Elvis agrees to pay Landau $200 for his skin treatments and $315 for a plane ticket for Landau to London, departing on December 25. At the last minute, however, Landau deliberately misses his flight, and demands an additional $250. Elvis agrees to pay. This is followed by an additional demand of $2,000 for the loss of his practice in Johannesburg, which he'd closed to travel to Germany to treat Elvis. According to FBI records, the last contact between the two men occurs on January 5, after which Landau disappears.

Extortion

If you force someone to hand over their money or property upon a threat of immediate physical injury, you have committed a serious offense in all American jurisdictions: robbery. But if you coerce the victim to give you money or property by the threat of some future harm, the offense may be *extortion* or "theft by extortion," or "coercion" or "intimidation." The extortion offense is broader than robbery both in the range of threats it criminalizes and in the broader range of coerced conduct that it covers. The extortion and coercion offenses may criminalize using a threat to obtain property or to compel certain conduct or to reframe from certain conduct. *Blackmail* is a subset of extortion in which the coercion applied is a threat to reveal embarrassing information.

The criminal offense of extortion may have its origins in the First Statute of Westminster, codified in 1275. But the "heyday of blackmail"[6] did not come until the 19th-century Victorian era. The offense became more common and was judged as more serious because of the high value Victorians placed on respectability and reputation – the revelation of embarrassing information, especially of a sexual nature, was feared by anyone whose reputation influenced their place in society, especially members of the upper class.[7] At the same time, blackmail became easier because 18th-century innovations allowed letters to be sent anonymously.[8] In the late 18th-century United States, a few states developed case law that recognized specific forms of the offense, but it was not until the mid-20th century that most states had enacted an anti-blackmail statute.[9]

The Model Penal Code formulation (reproduced in the margin) criminalizes threats made to coerce action or to take property but allows exceptions for those who commit the offense in an attempt to make the victim behave in a reasonable way.[10]

There are important limits on the extortion offense, however. No jurisdiction wants to include within the offense simple "hard bargaining" where, for example, you threaten not to sign a contract unless the other person agrees to provide certain additional compensation.[11]

Figure 19.3 David Letterman in New York, 1982

Perhaps the most interesting aspect of the extortion offense arises in blackmail cases where the law may make criminal a threat to do something that the actor has a lawful right to do, such as reveal certain embarrassing information. This breadth of the offense has made blackmail a favorite puzzle for criminal law theorists. Part of the peculiarity is that the "victim" of blackmail often would very much prefer to buy the embarrassing information himself rather than have it sold to the media. And the "offender" is happy to sell it to the victim rather than to the media. So, what is the basis for making the agreed-upon sale criminal? It would not have been obviously criminal for Landau to sell the photos and recordings to the media,[12] or to tell the stories, so what makes it a crime for him to offer them to Presley instead? Presley preferred to pay the money and avoid the embarrassment, and indeed insisted on doing so.

If the crux of the offense is that blackmail conduct is expressed as a threat rather than an opportunity, consider this more modern case.

Robert "Joe" Halderman – 2009

Robert "Joe" Halderman is a journalist working on domestic shows for CBS. He is married with children, but in 2004, he and his wife divorce. The next year, he becomes the producer of *48 Hours*. His contract with the television show is worth $200,000 annually, with increasing benefits each year. Despite his more than comfortable income, between the divorce settlement, alimony, and child support payments, he receives only about 50% of his paycheck. Critically acclaimed, Halderman's work wins an Alfred I. DuPont-Columbia University Award for broadcast journalism and eight Emmy Awards. Not long after, he meets Stephanie Birkitt and the two soon move in together as a couple.

In 1993, Birkitt had landed a job on the CBS talk show *Late Show with David Letterman* and years later became Letterman's assistant.[13] She worked subsequently on the CBS true crime journalism series *48 Hours*, but later returned to the *Late Show*. In 2002, she began to take on other roles on the show, appearing on the CBS Mailbag segment and conducting on-air reports from the Winter Olympics.

David Letterman, Birkitt's boss, is dating his long-term girlfriend Regina Lasko. Together, they have a son Harry, who in 2005 is the subject of a foiled abduction plot to ransom him for $5 million. It is well known that Letterman regularly engages in flings with staff workers on his show, such as Holly Hester, who claims that she "was madly in love with him at the time" and "would have married him."[14] Another woman he charmed is Birkitt, then 34 years old and a recent graduate of law school. Over the course of their relationship, the two exchange flirtatious emails and Birkitt writes lustful diary entries, which Halderman finds in December 2008. He confronts his unfaithful girlfriend but relents when she promises to end the affair. The two remain together. Similarly, regardless of whether Lasko is cognizant of Letterman's affairs, on March 19, 2009, the couple finally marry.

Just five months into Letterman's marriage, Halderman spots Letterman and Birkitt parked at the end of Halderman's driveway in Norwalk, Connecticut. It is not the fact that the two are in the car that surprises Halderman, as Letterman often drives Birkitt home, but the sight of the two kissing. He is shocked and angry that the affair is continuing. Shortly after, Halderman and Birkitt break up and Birkitt moves to Manhattan, where Letterman also lives.

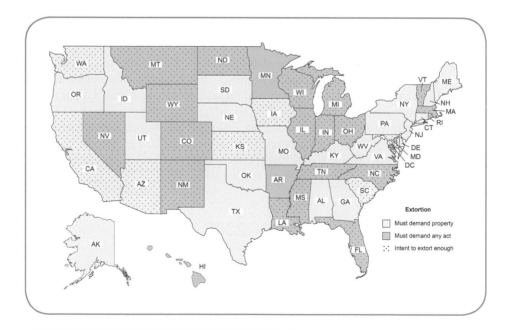

Figure 19.4

Halderman chooses not to ignore the matter. Fueled by rage, his deteriorating financial situation, and his tumultuous family life, especially after his ex-wife and son move to Colorado, on September 9, 2009, Halderman appears at Letterman's Manhattan home at dawn. There, he finds the talk show host's driver and gives him a sealed envelope marked "Privileged and Confidential." Inside the envelope is a letter that reads, "I know that you do some terrible, terrible things and I can prove that you do these terrible things."[15] According to the letter, Letterman's life would soon collapse, both his professional life and his family life. Also included is a one-page "Treatment for a Screenplay," a standard form in the industry, outlining his affair with Birkitt. Unless Letterman accedes to Halderman's request for $2 million, Halderman plans to turn the affair into a movie. The driver is to give the envelope to Letterman.

That morning, Letterman gets the package. After going through the contents, he calls his attorney Jim Jackoway who schedules a meeting with Halderman to confirm the situation. After getting confirmation, the attorney contacts the Special Prosecution Bureau, which deems the act an instance of blackmail. The prosecutor's office advises Letterman and Jackoway to set up another meeting, which is to be secretly recorded, to confirm that the blackmailer is truly serious. In the second meeting, Halderman reveals that he is also planning to write a book on the affair as a companion piece to the film.

Jackoway arranges a third meeting with Halderman, this time for the purpose of giving him the check for $2 million. Unknown to Halderman, the check is a fake and the meeting is recorded. Letterman testifies before a grand jury, admitting the extramarital affair and having sexual relations with his several of his employees. When Halderman goes to a Bank of America branch and attempts to deposit the check, he is arrested.

If Halderman could have made $2 million by selling the screenplay and the book, should it be a criminal offense for him to offer the exclusive rights to these properties to Letterman for this amount? As it happens, Halderman, producer of a crime drama series, knows that his conduct is criminal and actually says so during one of the recorded sessions.

On the day that Halderman is arrested, Letterman announces to a live audience on his show that he was the victim of an extortion attempt over charges of affairs with staff members. He admits to the accusations in unambiguous terms: "I have had sex with women who work on this show."[16] The audience interprets his admission as an act of bravery, and he is applauded.

Extortion Variations among the States

There is a good deal of diversity among the states in formulating the *extortion* offense, especially on the issue of the kinds of threats that will constitute the offense and the effects the threats must bring about, as the map below shows.[17]

Twenty-nine states, those with light shading on the map, require that the actor's demand be for property or something of value, including labor or services. The remaining 22 states, those with darker shading on the map, permit virtually any demand to suffice, such as the demand that the victim "engage in conduct from which [the victim] has a legal right to abstain, or to abstain from engaging in conduct in which the [victim] has a legal right to engage." Both Landau and Halderman meet the demand requirements in all states because both are seeking property (money). However, if the extortionist was asking not for money but for some conduct or forbearance by the victim – a demand that they get a particular role in a television show or certain publicity or a demand that the victim turn down a particular television role or breakup with his girlfriend – then they would be liable only in the dark-shaded states.

Twenty-four states, those *without* a dots overlay, define the offense as containing a result element: these states require that the offender actually obtain or exercise control over the victim's property, or successfully compel, induce, or coerce the victim to act. The remaining 27 states, those *with* a dots overlay, do not contain a result element; they merely require that the actor intends to cause the result if the demands are not met. For instance, in Arizona, it is an offense if the actor "knowingly obtained or *seeked to obtain* property or services by means of a threat."

Notice that Halderman's blackmail of Letterman occurred in New York, which requires that the blackmailer actually obtain what he seeks; it is not enough to show that he intended to obtain it. This explains why in the Halderman case law enforcement authorities had Letterman pay Halderman and waited for Halderman to cash the check, in order to satisfy the statutory requirement that Halderman actually obtained the property demanded.

All jurisdictions require proof that the defendant did indeed intend to coerce the victim to meet his demand. Halderman's attempt to dress up his blackmail as simply an offer to sell the screenplay to Letterman – providing him with an opportunity – was probably an attempt to fuzzy up the evidence of this required "intent to coerce." But given the totality of the circumstances, it seems likely that a jury would conclude that his offered "opportunity" was in practice a simple threat.

What Is the Proper Formulation for a Blackmail Offense?

As noted, *extortion*, and *blackmail* in particular, can be seen as a rather peculiar offense: it criminalizes making a threat to do something that would not itself be a crime. It would not be a crime for John to report his male neighbor's affair to the neighbor's wife, for example, but it is a crime if John gives the neighbor an opportunity to avoid the secret being revealed by asking for something in return, such as the neighbors agreement to move his noisy swimming pool pump away from John's property line. This might seem to both parties a very fair trade. Why should it be criminal? Why should the law care that the "victim" is being given an opportunity that he apparently wants? Notice that the light shaded states on the map above would actually exclude this case from criminality because they require that the blackmail demand must be for some kind of property of value. And the swimming pool pump example may give some indication of why the states adopt this limitation. However, would we feel the same if the blackmailer's demand was that the adulterous neighbor give him a job or educational opportunity that he does not deserve? The dark shaded states might have a number of counterexamples like this to cite.

Indeed, there are a host of issues on which jurisdictions disagree regarding the scope of the extortion offense. Part of the problem may be that even the criminal law theorists cannot agree among themselves about the core nature of extortion and its underlying rationale. As one study has detailed,[18] there are more than half a dozen different theories of why blackmail should be an offense. If the proper underlying theory is this unclear to the scholars, it is perhaps no surprise to see different legislatures disagreeing.

The diversity among the American jurisdictions and among the scholars does provide an interesting opportunity for social psychologists: if empirical researchers test ordinary people's intuitions of justice regarding a variety of different blackmail scenarios, could the research results identify which theories and which statutory formulations best track the shared intuitions of ordinary people?

Such a study was done and came to these conclusions:

> [L]ay intuitions seem to accord with the position that blackmail amounts to extortion because of the blackmailer's bad faith or improper motivations. The blackmailer's central interest is to benefit himself, and his means of pursuing that interest displays his willingness to wrong the other person, either by forcing that person to sacrifice money (or something else) or by subjecting that person to the harm the blackmailer knows the threatened act will cause.
>
> At the same time, however, . . . lay intuitions seem to view some demands as objectively legitimate even if their subjective motivation in a given case is improper. Thus, a person whose demand seeks to vindicate a valid legal or societal interest . . . is not seen as engaging in blackmail even if his underlying motivation is to harm the recipient rather than to advance the legitimate interest.[19]

The study was able to suggest a particular formulation of the blackmail offense that would track community views:

Criminal Coercion

1. A person commits criminal coercion if he demands money or other valuable consideration as a condition of refraining from any act he intends or knows would cause harm to another person.
2. For purposes of subsection (1), "harm" may include physical injury, financial deprivation, or substantial psychological stress.
3. Exception. It is not an offense under subsection (1) if the actor believed his demand to be justified as a means of advancing a legitimate legal or societal interest.[20]

Part of what this demonstrates is that legislatures can look to researchers to determine the shared judgments of justice of their constituents on criminal law liability and punishment issues. As discussed in the chapter concerning punishment theory,[21] there is great practical crime-control value in building the criminal law's moral credibility with the community by having it reflect the community's shared judgments of justice. We see here that criminal law tracking community views is possible, even where the underlying theoretical rationales are disputed.

Aftermaths

While it's understandable that Elvis – who is embarrassed by the allegations of homosexuality – might want Landau out of his life for good, Elvis isn't the only one happy when the case is quickly and quietly closed. As the FBI notes in a February of 1960 report,

Information concerning the subject was furnished to this office by the Provost Marshal Division, Headquarters, U.S. Army, Europe, with the indication that they wished to avoid any publicity in this matter since they did not want to involve Elvis Presley nor put him in an unfavorable light since Presley had been a first-rate soldier and had caused the Army no trouble during his term of service.[22]

True to their word, little additional information regarding the incident has surfaced from a governmental source.

The case represented an odd blotch on a career that in its day generally escaped scandal. By today's standards, however, Presley's career might look somewhat different: as an adult, he has a romantic relationship with a 14-year-old, whom he eventually marries, and uses illicit drugs for several decades. Presley dies a cultural icon in 1977, known thereafter as "The King of Rock and Roll" – a legacy that continues today.

In the *Halderman* case, the blackmailer does not escape notice. Upon his arrest, bail is set at $200,000 and he faces a sentence of up to 15 years. In 2010, he pleads guilty to attempted second-degree grand larceny. In a prepared statement, he admits that he "attempted to extort $2 million from David Letterman by threatening to disclose personal and private information about him, whether true or false."[23] He confesses that his previous defense that the envelope was just an attempt to sell a screenplay was untrue. His goal was to ruin Letterman. He is sentenced to six months in jail on Rikers Island, five years of probation, and 1,000 hours of community service. The judge also signs an order of protection that forbids him from contacting Letterman until 2018 and from going public with any information he previously intended to reveal. While in jail, some of his work is nominated for an Emmy Award. He is released after four months for good behavior, in time to go to the awards ceremony but chooses not to attend. He soon lands a job as a producer on Investigation Discovery's "On the Case with Paula Zahn."

Chapter Glossary

Blackmail: The crime of making one or more threatening demands without justification; the offense of coercing someone by threats of public exposure or criminal prosecution.[24]

Extortion: The practice or an instance of obtaining something or compelling some action by illegal means, as by force or coercion.[25]

Notes

1. This narrative is drawn from the following sources: Phil Arnold, 'FBI Investigates the Strange Elvis Pimple Scam,' *Elvis Blog*, 8 November 2009, http://www.elvisblog.net/2009/11/08/fbi-investigates-the-strange-elvis-pimple-scam/; 'Elvis 1957 … Transitioning from Elvis the Pelvis to Elvis the Movie Star,' *Elvis History Blog*, accessed 20 July 2020, http://www.elvis-history-blog.com/elvis-1957.html; Peter Guralnick, *Careless Love: The Unmaking of Elvis Presley* (New York: Back Bay Books, 2000); Mark Kemp, 'Elvis Presley' *Rolling Stone: Biography*, 2001; Nick Redfern, 'Elvis Presley' *Celebrity Secrets: Official Government Files on the Rich and Famous* (New York: Gallery Books, 2007), pp. 95–102; Stephan Rossner, "Are You Lonesome Tonight?' Elvis Presley 1935–1977,' *Obesity Reviews 11* (2010): pp. 688–689, doi: 10.1111/j.1467-789X.2010.00742.x.

2. Kemp, 'Elvis Presley Biography.'
3. 'Elvis 1957…'.
4. Redfern, 'Elvis Presley,' p. 97.
5. Redfern, 'Elvis Presley,' p. 98.
6. Chen Yehudai, '"Informational Blackmail": Survived by Technicality?,' *Marquette Law Review 92*, no. 4 (Summer 2009): p. 797, http://scholarship.law.marquette.edu/mulr/vol92/iss4/6.
7. Anglus McLaren, 'Sodomy and the Invention of Blackmail,' in *Sexual Blackmail: A Modern History* (Cambridge: Harvard University Press, 2002), p. 11.
8. McLaren, 'Sodomy and the Invention of Blackmail,' p. 12.
9. Yehudai, 'Informational Blackmail,' p. 816.
10. Paul Robinson, Michael Cahill, and David Bartels, 'Competing Theories of Blackmail: An Empirical Research Critique of Criminal Law Theory,' *Texas Law Review 89* (2010): pp. 291–352.
11. Paul H. Robinson and Michael T. Cahill, *Criminal Law*, 2nd ed. (New York: Wolters Kluwer, 2016) §15.7.
12. Today there might be privacy law violations, depending upon the jurisdiction.
13. This narrative is drawn from the following sources: Bill Carter, 'David Letterman Reveals Extortion Attempt,' *The New York Times*, 1 October 2009, http://www.nytimes.com/2009/10/02/business/media/02extort.html; John Eligon, 'Ex-Producer in Letterman Plot Is Off to Jail,' *The New York Times*, 4 May 2010, http://www.nytimes.com/2010/05/05/nyregion/05extortion.html?ref=topics; Samuel Goldsmith and Henrick Karoliszyn, 'Ex-intern Comes Forward to Claim Affair with Letterman,' *New York Daily News*, 3 October 2009, http://www.nydailynews.com/entertainment/tv-movies/david-letterman-ex-intern-holly-hester-woman-alleged-slept-late-host-article-1.379775; *David Letterman Extortion Details*, [online video], CBS, 2 October 2009, https://youtu.be/T9_OfOJYfcE, accessed 20 July 2020; Murray Weiss, 'Suspect Enraged after Seeing Girl with Dave,' *The New York Post,* 8 October 2009, http://nypost.com/2009/10/08/suspect-enraged-after-seeing-girl-with-dave/.
14. Goldsmith and Karoliszyn, 'Ex-intern Comes Forward.'
15. *David Letterman Extortion Details*.
16. *David Letterman Extortion Details*.
17. The map is taken from Paul H. Robinson and Tyler Scot Williams, 'Extortion,' in *Mapping American Criminal Law: Variations across the 50 States* (Westport: Prager, 2018), p. 240. All supporting authorities are available from that source.
18. Robinson, Cahill, and Bartels, 'Competing Theories of Blackmail.'
19. Robinson, Cahill, and Bartels, 'Competing Theories of Blackmail,' p. 348.
20. Robinson, Cahill, and Bartels, 'Competing Theories of Blackmail,' p. 348.
21. Chapter 2.
22. Redfern, 'Marilyn Monroe,' p. 110.
23. Eligon, 'Ex-Producer Off to Jail.'
24. *Blackmail*, Black's.
25. *Extortion*, Black's.

Chapter 20

Domestic Violence

Ike & Tina Turner – What's Love Got to Do with It?

1960. The world's first weather satellite, TIROS 1, is launched. President Eisenhower signs the Civil Rights Act of 1960, which establishes federal inspection of local voter registration polls and penalizes obstructing someone's attempt to register as a voter. Four black students at North Carolina Agricultural and Technical State University ask for coffee at a Woolworth's lunch counter, and the request launches the sit-in movement. The power of TV is demonstrated with the first televised presidential debates, between the robust John Kennedy facing off against the wan Richard Nixon. The first Playboy Club opens in Chicago featuring waitresses in bunny suits. That objectivization of women of the era shows itself in many ways.

Ike Turner – 1960

Ike Turner is one of the seminal figures of early rock and roll who brings a broad new vision to the art form.[1] His band *The Kings of Rhythm* is finding growing popularity. The group is playing a St. Louis nightclub when Turner meets a 16-year-old nurse's assistant, Anna Mae Bullock, who tells Turner that the Kings' music puts her "in a trance." She comes back to see the performance again and again.

Anna makes it clear that she wants to sing with the band but Ike seems uninterested, so uninvited, she walks on the stage, grabs the microphone, and sings so well that Ike signs her up. Anna knows Ike to be an influential performer but also a dangerous man known for his womanizing and enormous ego. Undaunted, she soon moves in with him and by January 1960 is pregnant with his child.

In spring 1960, the band's main vocalist fails to show up for a recording session and Anna, who sings under the name "Little Ann," steps in. The song earns Ike a $20,000 dollar advance and Anna is now a recorded artist. Seeing the financial value of the teenager, Ike drops the name "Little Ann" for "Tina Turner." In Ike's scheme,

DOI: 10.4324/9781003258025-23

Figure 20.1 Ike and Tina Turner, 1974

the name belongs to him and when Anna Mae Bullock leaves his employ, the name will be handed down to the woman who takes her job.

Ike writes the material that Tina performs, and material is male-centric, bordering on misogynistic. "Treat me gentle until we're alone/And scold me after you get me home" from "Don't Play me Cheap." On the first record that Tina records, "A Fool in Love," Ike has her sing, "Without the man, I don't wanna live."[2]

Fans love Tina and with the band's increased stature, Ike leaves St. Louis for Las Vegas. With the success, violence becomes a regular part of Ike and Tina's relationship. Band members corroborate that Ike begins beating Tina regularly. When she tells Ike she is considering leaving the group, Ike beats the pregnant teen with a shoe stretcher, and "after that he made me go to bed, and he had sex with me. My eye was all swollen, God, it was awful."[3] Now Tina is afraid of Ike and will later report that "He kept control of me with fear."[4]

As Tina goes into labor, Ike has Tina get a shot "to freeze [her] muscles to hold off the labor," but the baby arrives on October 27, 1960 despite his father's wishes. Five days later, Tina is on stage performing but having her perform is a serious medical mistake: she bleeds "a lot when [she] hits the high notes."[5] When Ike returns to St. Louis to stand trial on a bank robbery charge, Tina gets two weeks of rest.

Tina becomes increasingly unhappy with her life with Ike. A regular pattern develops. Ike argues with Tina, then over her objections "he would have sex with me. It was torture plain and simple."[6] Ike remains in an active sexual relationship with his common-law wife Lorraine.

Despite their numerous fights, Ike and Tina marry in Tijuana, Mexico in 1962. Ike continues to have sexual relationships with other women. Tina knows about the other women but Ike's volatility keeps her too afraid to act or even to complain, "because you never know what Ike will do." Tina repeatedly goes to local hospitals for medical

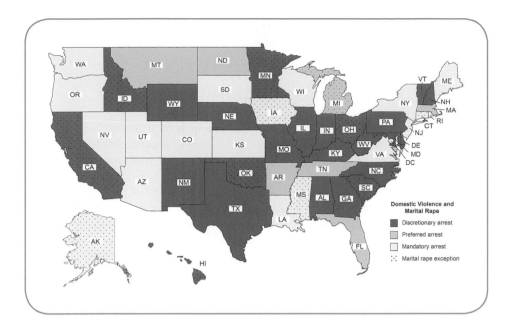

Domestic Violence and Marital Rape

- Discretionary arrest
- Preferred arrest
- Mandatory arrest
- Marital rape exception

Figure 20.2

care. And while the injuries are clearly the result of assaults, she never admits this and no outside authority does anything to intervene.

Tina feels "insanely afraid" of Ike.[7] She closely modulates her interactions with him because of the "mental torture" he puts her through.[8] She is forced to "try to be sweet"[9] to the man torturing her. The appeasement extends to Ike's bed. Ike begins to bring women into bed with Tina, specifically the Turners' housekeeper, Ann. "Tina on one side and Ann on the other."[10] Ike's sexual desires take precedence over any objection that Tina might have. Tina reports that "no one could say anything to Ike."[11]

When cocaine enters Ike's life, his ability to produce creatively begins to fail him. Over the next few years, the popularity of the group wanes and band members leave to avoid Ike's unpredictable behavior. Ike is spinning out of control. His cocaine use burns a hole through his nasal septum, leading to severe nosebleeds, which he treats with more cocaine. He becomes ever more severe in dealing with his band members. The hits are not coming anymore.

On July 2, 1976, an altercation between the couple changes things. As Ike and Tina get off a plane and into a waiting limo to head to the hotel, Ike begins to beat Tina because she refuses to eat chocolate while dressed in her all-white suit. Ike has been awake for five days straight using cocaine. But on this occasion, fear does not hold Tina back. She fights back, jeering and cursing back at him. "Is that your best shot? Can't you do no better than that?"[12] Tina exits the limo with her white Yves Saint Laurent suit splattered red with her own blood and her face swollen by Ike's blows. Tina vows to herself, "You just beat me for the last time, you sucker."[13]

She walks into the hotel and leaves through the back door. Ike has all their money but Tina negotiates with the manager of a local Ramada Inn for a place to sleep. She decides to go somewhere Ike will not be able to find her. Ike tries but fails to track her down. Tina files for divorce and agrees to give everything up but her name, saying "I worked too hard for that."[14]

Both social attitudes and the criminal law on domestic violence change dramatically in the decades that follow.

Changing Views on Domestic Violence

The Pilgrims made laws against domestic violence in 1641.[15] But as their singularly united religiously motivated voice weakened, the issue of domestic violence retreated behind closed doors. Tennessee, in 1850, was the first state to outlaw wife beating and in time all other states followed their lead. Alabama was the first state to hold that spouses were equal before the law and therefore equally entitled to protection under the law. And yet, there remained a vast gap between the law and legal consequences for abusing spouses; arrests were rare and conviction unlikely.

Police, even if they wanted to, often had a limited ability to intervene. They rarely witnessed the abuse and there were no support services to help abuse victims find safety, nor laws that immediately removed the abuser from the home. Society largely saw domestic violence as a private matter. Without strong pressure to do otherwise, even in horrific cases, authorities were unable or unwilling to act. The situation with Ike and Tina Turner was not uncommon.

Then, in 1985, Tracey Thurman, who was stabbed and beaten by her husband in full view of the police, brought suit against the Torrington, Connecticut Township whose officers chose not to protect her. Her lawsuit was successful, and she was awarded nearly $2 million in damages. Her story gained national attention, fueling already-growing concerns about gender equality, and brought police departments nationwide under scrutiny for their handling of domestic violence cases. The public outrage over apparent police indifference prompted widespread reform. Where jurisdictions were slow to respond, insurance companies were no longer willing to underwrite police departments.

Increasing public intolerance combined with the momentum of the women's rights movement to bring a variety of legal reforms.[16] Many states and the federal government responded by passing anti-domestic violence laws. All across the country, police departments, prosecutors' offices, and courthouses changed their policies to better protect abuse victims,[17] including the creation of social support services such as women's shelters, counseling, and emergency hotlines.

Examples of Reform: Marital Rape Exemption and Required Police Intervention

Two common legislative responses have been to abolish the marital exemption to rape and to change police practice so as to encourage or even require arrest in domestic violence cases, even where there is no judicial arrest warrant.

The map below shows how each state deals with each of these issues.[18] The darker the shading, the less aggressive the state has been in promoting reforms on the arrest issue. An overlay of dots indicates that the jurisdiction has retained some form of the limited marital rape exemption.

Regarding marital rape, the traditional rule that existed before the reforms held that a husband could not be convicted of raping his wife. His use of physical force might render him liable for assault or even aggravated assault, but the traditional view barred rape liability under the theory that the sexual intimacy component of the conduct could not be grounds for aggravated liability (through escalation to a rape conviction) if the two people were married. (Recall the discussion in Chapter 6, consent to injury, regarding a wide range of recent revisions to sexual offenses, as for example making all sex offenses gender-neutral and criminalizing unconsented-to intercourse without force or threat. The recently revised Model Penal Code sexual offenses article contained in the Chapter 6 Appendix includes the abolition of the marital rape exemption.)

Today, no state any longer provides such an exemption from rape liability. However, some states – the 15 states with a dots overlay on the map – have retained some kind of limited exemption. For example, while one can be liable for rape of a nonmarital partner by coercing intercourse, some states may limit marital rape to cases where force or threat of force is used.[19] The remaining 36 states, those with no dots on the map, have abolished all forms of the marital rape exemption.[20]

With regard to domestic violence arrest policies, the states are split. Twenty states, those with light shading on the map, have adopted a mandatory arrest policy. In these states, an officer is required to arrest if the officer has probable cause to believe that the individual has recently committed an act of violence toward a member of the household. (The Alaska statute of this sort is reproduced in the margin.)

Another seven states, those with medium shading, have adopted a preferred arrest policy. Where the officer has probable cause to believe that the person has committed domestic violence, the statutes express a preference for an arrest, even in the absence of a judicial arrest warrant. An officer in such circumstances can still lawfully not make an arrest – for example, he or she might be persuaded by a victim's plea that it would be better from the victim's point of view that there be no arrest.

Alaska Criminal Code § 18.65.530. Mandatory Arrest for Crimes Involving Domestic Violence . . .

(a) [A] peace officer, with or without a warrant, ***shall arrest a person if*** the officer has probable cause to believe the person has, either in or outside the presence of the officer, within the previous 12 hours,

   (1) committed domestic violence, . . . whether the crime is a felony or a misdemeanor;

   (2) committed the crime of violating a protective order . . . ;

   (3) violated a condition of release . . . .

Figure 20.3

Figure 20.4 Booking photos of Rando and Latimer

The remaining 24 states, those with the darkest shading on the map, have left their policy as one of discretionary arrest, which is the standard policy for most offenses: if the officer has probable cause to believe the person committed domestic violence, the officer can make an arrest but has the discretion not to do so, perhaps preferring, for example, to perform an arrest at a later time under a judicial warrant.

Most aggressive in addressing the problem of domestic violence, then, are the 15 states that abolish any form of a marital rape exemption and have adopted a rule requiring mandatory arrest (those with light shading and no dots). Least aggressive are the nine states, those with dark shading and dots, that have neither fully abolished a marital rape exemption nor altered their domestic violence arrest rules. California, where Ike Turner perpetrated many of his acts of marital rape and domestic violence, is in this group. Thus, if he had engaged in his conduct today, while he would clearly be criminally liable for the assaults, he might have limited liability for the marital rape, and he would not be subject to mandatory arrest for the domestic violence.

As we have seen with other reforms, however, sometimes the legal changes made in the heat of a popular reform cycle can generate results somewhat different from those that motivated the reform.

Jaimee Rando – 2016

Cody Latimer, born in 1992, grows up in Dayton, Ohio, where he plays football at Jefferson Township High School.[21] He is recruited to play football for Indiana University, and in 2014 is a second-round draft pick for the NFL. He signs with the Denver Broncos as a wide receiver and has many successful seasons with the team. In early 2016, Latimer begins dating Jaimee Rando, a 2014 graduate of Metropolitan State University of Denver who works in real estate. The couple have a son three months into their official relationship. At 23, Latimer is a relatively young player, and he keeps a fairly low profile on the team. But with a family and a growing reputation, life seems to be going well for him.

Duties of peace officers and prosecuting agencies.

(1) When a peace officer determines that there is probable cause to believe that a crime or offense involving domestic violence . . . has been committed, the officer shall, without undue delay, arrest the person suspected of its commission . . . and charge the person with the appropriate crime or offense. . . . . Nothing in this subsection (1) shall be construed to require a peace officer to arrest either party involved in an alleged act of domestic violence when a peace officer determines there is no probable cause to believe that a crime or offense of domestic violence has been committed. . . .

Colorado Statutes § 18-6-803.6

Figure 20.5

On Sunday, May 29, 2016, Latimer is hosting an evening party with friends at a downtown night club called the Epernay Lounge. Latimer and Rando both drink at the party, and soon Rando becomes upset. As the party is winding down, Rando and Latimer get into a "quarrel over jealousy issues,"[22] and Rando reportedly slaps Latimer. Rando characterizes it as a "push in the face."[23]

Several hours later, the couple is back at home. Rando, who by all accounts is drunk, remains upset. She announces to Latimer that she is going to take the couple's baby and drive to her mother's house. Latimer tries to prevent the drunk woman from driving and is adamant that she cannot take the baby. Rando only grows more aggressive and determined to leave. Seeing no other option to prevent his girlfriend from driving away drunk, at about 2:30 a.m., Latimer calls the police and reports the assault.

Latimer makes no attempt to hide his status as a member of the Denver Broncos. "I'm Cody Latimer from the Denver Broncos," he tells the dispatcher. "My girl, my girlfriend put her hands on me. She got too drunk with us out. I hosted a party tonight [and] she got too drunk."[24] On the tape of the 9-1-1 call the dispatcher asks if he is hurt. Latimer responds "No, I'm not at all, heart broke, but no I'm good."[25] He explains that he doesn't "want any drama," but has made the call for help in an attempt to deescalate the situation.[26]

The police arrive and arrest Rando, who is 4′11″ and weighs 115 pounds, on suspicion of simple assault against Latimer, who is listed on the Bronco's roster as being 6′ 2″ and weighing 215 pounds. Thus, the NFL wide-receiver is the victim of domestic violence at the hands of his diminutive girlfriend, who weighs 100 pounds less than he does.

Police run a routine background check on Latimer and discover that he has an outstanding warrant for a failure to appear in court on an unrelated traffic violation – a $311 ticket for improper lighting on his vehicle. Latimer was not aware that the ticket was never paid, and according to the police report, Latimer says "that someone from the Denver Broncos should have taken care of this ticket."[27] Police arrest Latimer as well, and both he and his girlfriend are taken to the police station.

Latimer pays the $311 fine for the improper lighting violation and is released several hours after his arrest. The following day, Latimer pays Rando's bail and she too is released. As it turns out, there is no question that the assault occurred. Latimer was wearing a Go-Pro camera on his shirt the night of the party that captured the entire incident. The Broncos take no disciplinary action against Latimer but he is excused from practice the following day for "a personal issue."[28] He makes it clear that he does not want to press charges against Rando, and the two continue their relationship.

Was Rando's arrest by police the best way to handle the situation? As shown on the map, Colorado is one of the states that has adopted a mandatory arrest policy, so the police really had no choice but to take Rando into custody. (The Colorado statute is reproduced in the margin.)

Is It Important for Criminal Law to Keep Up with the Community's Changing Norms?

The depth and speed of the reforms to the marital rape exemption and to the domestic violence arrest policies demonstrate just how powerful changes in societal norms can be in influencing criminal law policy. There will always be political points of friction on a variety of fronts but when broadly based public attitudes do shift, the criminal justice system is commonly quick to follow.

Which is as it should be. Especially with the loss of influence of other society-wide institutions to educate and communicate societal norms, a function that churches and social organizations once contributed more broadly to. Today criminal law remains as one of the only moral authorities available to describe what society considers to be truly condemnable.

The need for the criminal law to keep up with society's changing norms is not only essential to promote and propagate those norms but also essential for the effective operation of the criminal justice system itself. As empirical studies have shown,[29] people are less likely to assist, support, and defer to a criminal law that they see as out of step, or that seems unreliable as a moral authority of what is and is not condemnable. A system without moral credibility with the community it governs is a system more likely to encourage resistance and subversion, and it loses the ability to harness the powerful forces of social influence.

Perhaps most importantly, a system without moral credibility is one that can have little role in helping a society to change its societal norms. If the criminal law is perceived as being a reliable source in judging what is and is not truly condemnable, then social reformers can harness its norm-influencing power when they seek to shift community norms, be they norms concerning domestic violence, drunk driving, date rape, or downloading music without a license. But where the criminal law has gained a reputation for being out of step with existing societal norms, its announcements that people should think differently about one sort of conduct or another are easily ignored as one more instance in which the criminal law is misguided and outdated.

Ultimately, then, the criminal law must keep up with changing societal norms not only to help propagate those norms today but also to protect its ability to be play a role in changing norms in the future.[30]

Aftermaths

Ike's post-Tina life is tumultuous. His personal recording studio burns to the ground. In 1990, he is convicted of cocaine-related offenses and sentenced to four years in prison and serves 18 months. It is during this time that he and Tina are inducted into the Rock & Roll Hall of Fame. After prison, Ike continues to produce music, and remarries a few more times.

Tina performs solo with a level of success that completely eclipses the success she had with Ike. She releases an autobiography that recounts her life with Ike, published in 1986. In 1993, the book, *I, Tina*, is turned into a film: *What's Love Got to Do with It*, which is titled after Tina's most successful single. Both Ike and Tina agree to the production of the film.

What's Love Got to Do with It focuses a good deal on the domestic violence that raged during their relationship. Ike Turner's reputation as an innovative musician is now eclipsed by his image as an abuser of women. The film portrays a graphic scene in which he rapes Tina. Both parties agree that that particular sequence never occurred but not even Ike denies that he regularly raped his wife. Ike later argues that his agreement to have the film made was given only because at the time he was addicted to crack.

After the movie comes out, Ike continues his struggles with addiction and works on "improving his rotten place in popular history."[31] He publishes his own autobiography in 1999, *Taking Back My Name*, and his 2001 album *Here and Now* receives a Grammy nomination. He dies of a cocaine overdose in 2007.

Tina continues her successful solo career, winning numerous Grammy awards, acting in movies, and eventually remarrying. A month after Ike's death, she comes out of retirement and announces an international tour with 95 shows.

In Cody Latimer's case, he wins a Super Bowl ring as a Denver Bronco months before his arrest, and his career continues on solid footing after he and Rando put the episode behind them. After playing four seasons in Denver, Latimer plays two seasons with the Giants and then signs with Washington. Jaimee Rando becomes a real estate agent in Colorado.

Notes

1. This narrative is drawn from the following sources: Christian J. Wikane, 'The Ike & Tina Turner Story,' *Pop Matters*, 11 October 2007, http://www.popmatters.com/ review/ike-tina-turner-the-ike-tina-turner-story/; Clarence Waldron, 'Tina Turner's Book Tells of Beatings, Sex Abuse and Why She Tried to End Her Life,' *Jet*, 22 September 1986, 54–56, accessed from https://books.google.com/books?id=0bADA AAAMBAJ&pg=PA54&lpg=PA54&dq=after+that+he+made+me+go+to+bed,+and+ he+had+sex+with+me.+My+eye+was+all+swollen,+God,+it+was+awful&source=bl &ots=Z1Z8Yrz3gV&sig=R3fPgUE-MiUVJOY_jK6-PdjmkcE&hl=en&sa= X&ved=0ahUKEwiXoqO2oLbVAhUMcD4KHbPWD84Q6AEIJjAA#v=onepage&q =after%20that%20he%20made%20me%20go%20to%20bed%2C%20and%20 he%20had%20sex%20with%20me.%20My%20eye%20was%20all%20 swollen%2C%20God%2C%20it%20was%20awful&f=false; Elizabeth Christine Thompson, 'Tina Turner: Where to Now?' *Angel Fire*, http://www.angelfire.com/ca2/ spicegirlsfreak/tina.html; Mark Bego, *Tina Turner: Break Every Rule* (Boulder: Taylor Trade Publishing, 2005); Bob Gulla, *Icons of R&B and Soul: An Encyclopedia of the Artists Who Revolutionized Rhythm* (Santa Barbara: Greenwood, 2007), 167–190.

2. Thompson, 'Tina Turner: Where to Now?'
3. Waldron, 'Tina Turner's Book.'
4. Waldron, 'Tina Turner's Book.'
5. Thompson, 'Tina Turner: Where to Now?'
6. Waldron, 'Tina Turner's Book.'
7. Thompson, 'Tina Turner: Where to Now?'
8. Thompson, 'Tina Turner: Where to Now?'
9. Thompson, 'Tina Turner: Where to Now?'
10. Thompson, 'Tina Turner: Where to Now?'
11. Bego, *Tina Turner: Break Every Rule.*
12. Thompson, 'Tina Turner: Where to Now?'
13. Thompson, 'Tina Turner: Where to Now?'
14. Thompson, 'Tina Turner: Where to Now?'
15. Bernadette Dunn Sewell, 'History of Abuse: Societal, Judicial, and Legislative Responses to the Problem of Wife Beating,' *Suffolk University Law Review* 23 (1989): pp. 689, 983.
16. Paul H. Robinson and Sarah M. Robinson, *Tragedy, Outrage & Reform: Crimes that Changed Our World* (Lanham, Maryland: Rowman & Littlefield Publishers, 2018).
17. Paul H. Robinson and Sarah M. Robinson, '1983 Thurman Beatings—Domestic Violence,' in *Crimes That Changed Our World* (Rowman & Littlefield, 2018), pp. 223–233.
18. The map is taken from Paul H. Robinson and Tyler Scot Williams, 'Domestic Violence,' in *Mapping American Criminal Law: Variations across the 50 States* (Westport: Prager, 2018), p. 214. All supporting authorities are available from that source.
19. *See, e.g.,* Ohio Rev. Code Ann. §§2907.02, 2907.03.
20. Indeed, some states have expressly repealed the common-law marital rape exemption. *See, e.g.,* D.C. Code Ann. § 22-3019.
21. This narrative is drawn from the following sources: Janet Oravetz, 'Cody Latimer's 911 Call Released,' *9 News*, 3 June 2016, http://www.9news.com/news/local/cody-latimers-911-call-released/230556780; Jesse Paul, 'Broncos' Cody Latimer Said He Was Wearing GoPro Camera during Fight with Girlfriend,' *The Denver Post*, 2 June 2016, http://www.denverpost.com/2016/06/02/cody-latimer-said-he-was-wearing-gopro-camera-during-fight-with-girlfriend/; Nicole Vap, 'GoPro Caught Broncos Domestic Incident on Tape,' *9 News*, 2 June 2016, http://www.9news.com/news/crime/gopro-caught-broncos-domestic-incident-on-tape/228581042.
22. Paul, 'Broncos' Cody Latimer Said.'
23. Vap, 'GoPro Caught Broncos Domestic Incident.'
24. Oravetz, 'Cody Latimer's 911 Call.'
25. Oravetz, 'Cody Latimer's 911 Call.'
26. Paul, 'Broncos' Cody Latimer Said.'
27. Paul, 'Broncos' Cody Latimer Said.'
28. Paul, 'Broncos' Cody Latimer Said.'
29. Paul H. Robinson, 'Normative Crime Control: The Utility of Desert' and 'Deviations from Empirical Desert,' in *Intuitions of Justice and Utility of Desert* (Oxford: Oxford University Press, 2013), pp. 110–141, 189–208; Paul Robinson and Lindsay Holman, The Criminogenic Effects of Damaging Criminal Law's Moral Credibility, *Southern California Interdisciplinary Law Journal*, 2022.
30. Robinson, 'Deviations from Empirical Desert,' 196–201.
31. *See* 'Ike Turner: On Sex, Drugs and Rock 'n' Roll,' *The Independent*, 26 October 2005, http://www.independent.co.uk/news/people/profiles/ike-turner-on-sex-drugs-and-rocknroll-322628.html.

Chapter 21

Harassment

Wooing Bette Davis

1936. With Berlin cleared of anti-Semitic signage, Adolf Hitler opens the 11th Olympic Games. The world's first superhero appears as *The Phantom* in a newspaper comic strip created by Lee Falk. The Hoover Dam, originally named Boulder Dam, a concrete arch-gravity dam on the Colorado River at the border between Nevada and Arizona, begins generating electricity. At the 8th Academy Awards ceremony, the statues given as awards are called "Oscars" for the first time and Bette Davis wins for her role in *Dangerous*.

Alexander Ross – 1936

Bette Davis, nee Ruth Elizabeth Davis, has always had a strong personality: her magnetic attractiveness and domineering control make her the irresistible center of attention everywhere she goes.[1] When she attempts to break into the New York theater scene, her natural talents are not enough; her career is held back by her refusal to follow the industry practice of trading sex for roles. For all her charisma and beauty, Davis is famously prudish, at least for a theater person. Her absolute rejection of the men who seek to seduce her stokes the resentment of those in power.

When the situation becomes clear, Davis and her mother move across the country for a fresh start in California. In 1932 she signs a contract with Warner Brothers Studio and marries her high school sweetheart Ham Nelson. Their marriage is not very intimate – he is the leader of a band and his music career keeps him on the road most of the time. There are longstanding rumors that Davis only married Nelson to provide herself with a shield against the roving eye of would-be suitors.

Her big show business break arrives when her studio decides to make a movie based on Somerset Maugham's *Of Human Bondage*. No established actress wants to play Mildred Rogers, a beautiful woman who uses her sexual powers to consume

DOI: 10.4324/9781003258025-24

those who fall for her charms. In the story Mildred falls into prostitution and dies an ugly death from syphilis – hardly the romantic Cinderella story that actresses of the day typically dream of. But Davis is excited to play the part. Her brilliant performance earns her wide acclaim and an Academy Award nomination. The man-eating Mildred makes Davis a star.

Ham Nelson is not thrilled with Davis's fame. Though Davis is making a great deal of money, Nelson insists that the couple not buy a home until *he* can pay for it. He also expects Davis to be a more traditional wife, but Davis enjoys being beautiful, rich, and a successful movie star. Tensions in the marriage continue to grow as Nelson fails to find his way into the big time.

Nelson feels like, and probably is, a sidebar in Bette's life. Fiction follows her reality, and her movie roles are commonly women who dominate the men around them. Her stardom continues to grow with her Academy Award for *Dangerous*. She wants to end her marriage, but the morality clause of her studio contract compels her to remain.

The situation grows more complicated when Alexander Ross, an elegant, smooth-talking New York actor, is also signed by Warner Brothers in 1934. Ross is somewhat notorious among gossips because he is said to have lived in New York as a kept man, financially supported by an older man in exchange for physical and emotional intimacy.

Ross, who most likely married to advance his standing with the studio, has a strained marriage. His wife dreams of stardom but cannot land even small roles. Ross, for his part, is becoming busier and busier and often fails to return home. After a dramatic domestic argument, his wife commits suicide with a gun. In the throes of losing his wife and protecting his career, Ross falls madly in love with Bette Davis.

To add to the intrigue, actress Joan Crawford, who is known to be bisexual, comes forth to express her own romantic interest in Davis. Davis is not amused. She makes

Figure 21.1 Studio portrait of Bette Davis, 1937

it clear to Crawford, Ross, and even her husband that she is not interested in romance with any of them.

Ross becomes ever more enchanted with the object of his affection. He writes to Davis many times a day and leaves notes of adoration throughout the studio. Ross enters Davis' dressing room uninvited on several occasions, even when it is empty. He repeatedly begs Warner Brothers executives to be cast in a movie with Davis. He is certain that if he were to once hold her in his arms, the sexually aloof Davis would awaken "like a wildcat."[2] He alone, Ross feels, truly understands the complex Davis. She, in turn, continues to make it clear to Ross that she does not appreciate his attention.

Inevitably, husband Nelson finds one of Ross's love declarations in Davis' dressing room, addressed "To My Beloved One, Bette."[3] The letter clearly implies that the romance is mutual. Enraged, Nelson confronts his wife on the set in front of the entire production crew. She shouts, "That queer is having pipe dreams. He's trying to prove his manhood, or something, and he knows I see right through him."[4] Nelson is not mollified. Upon finding Ross in the men's room, Nelson knocks him to the ground. The movie that Ross is shooting is delayed while his black eye heals.

Neither Davis' public rebuke nor Nelson's assault dissuades Ross. He continues to find new ways to express his love. His infatuation becomes increasingly public, with Ross campaigning even order to be cast with her. Studio executives have little patience for Ross's irrational pleading. Keeping Davis happy is far more important. Ross is demoted to supporting roles.

Somehow, Ross finds it in himself to marry another actress. Even as a newly wed, he spends days at a time drinking and fantasizing about Davis. He writes letters to her, which he leaves around the house for his wife to find. He talks of Davis and writes poetry for her. He talks of ways that he can compel her to see him as the answer to her dreams. Davis responds by publicly humiliating him, mocking his homosexuality, and making a show of throwing away his letters.

One afternoon, Ross picks up a hitchhiker and the two have a sexual encounter. As soon as their tryst ends, the hitchhiker demands money, threatening to go public with the story of their encounter. But Ross is broke, so he goes to studio executives again and pleads for help. Warner Brothers pays off the blackmailer, but the incident is the last straw – his film career is over. Ross is beside himself, for without the studio he will lose all possibility of contact with Davis. He tries to get on to the studio lot but is barred by the guards.

Ross is never prosecuted for any of his repeated unwanted attentions toward Davis. However, *stalking* and *harassment* eventually come to be seen as seriously wrongful conduct and the criminal law is amended accordingly.

Changing Views on Stalking and Harassment

In 1962, the newly promulgated Model Penal Code included a *harassment* offense (quoted in the margin). The offense goes beyond the traditional assault, battery, attempt, and threat offenses to specifically criminalize a wide variety of conduct intended to harass another person.

In the 1970s, a new vocabulary emerged. "Sexual harassment," as currently used, appeared in the writings of the Working Women United Institute and Carroll Brodsky's *The Harassed Worker*.[5] What is and is not sexual harassment in a legal sense becomes

Harassment.

A person commits a petty misdemeanor if, with purpose to harass another, he:

(1) makes a telephone call without purpose of legitimate communication; or

(2) insults, taunts or challenges another in a manner likely to provoke violent or disorderly response; or

(3) makes repeated communications anonymously or at extremely inconvenient hours, or in offensively coarse language; or

(4) subjects another to an offensive touching; or

(5) engages in any other course of alarming conduct serving no legitimate purpose of the actor.

Model Penal Code §250.4

Figure 21.2

widely discussed and Catharine Mackinnon in her book *Feminism Unmodified* does much to connect sexual harassment to sexual discrimination. There is a growing awareness that there are several types of behavior that disproportionately victimize women and seem to be trivialized by people in authority. One of these, the pattern of repeated unwanted contact that is often terrifying, by the 1980s comes to be called *stalking*.[6]

Even after people acknowledge the problem, legal reforms do not immediately follow.

> The legal history of stalking is a testament to the limitations of applying existing statutory law, and the passage of innovative legislation to address a newly conceived crime that extends beyond the boundaries of common-law offences. From the ineffectiveness of civil protection or to the limited utility of a federal antistalking statute, victims are often left with little practical legal recourse.[7]

Some aspects of stalking behavior, such as trespass, are already criminalized but are commonly seen as minor infractions, and the victim may not be able to get the police to take such misconduct seriously. Up until the end of the 1980s, this sort of behavior, which invades a victim's sense of safety and intrudes into their private lives, can only be dealt with civilly. But civil remedies, such as restraining orders and tort claims, are generally ineffective in controlling such conduct.

In the late 1980s, two Hollywood actresses are killed by their stalkers. The high-profile cases spur action and in 1989 California moves past the debate between freedom of speech and protection of the individual when it enacts the first anti-stalking legislation. Other states and the Federal government quickly follow. The statutes are "drafted with an explicit consideration of the behavioral idiosyncrasies that characterize the stalking offences; without the requirement that the stalker has committed a violent act; with less significant mens rea or intentionality provisions; and with increased sanctions."[8] (California's current stalking offense is reproduced in the appendix to this chapter.)

Consider how the law deals with a more modern case.

Joshua Corbett – 2014

Joshua Corbett, age 39, is a huge fan of actress Sandra Bullock.[9] On June 5, 2014, Corbett decides to initiate a face-to-face meeting, and goes to Bullock's home near Los Angeles. But Bullock is attending the American Film Institute's gala that night. Corbett comes back each of the next two days but is still unable to see her.

On June 7, after a third night keeping vigil near Bullock's home, Corbett pens a two-page letter to her, confessing his deeply held love:

> Sandy, you could of had me today however you chose other people over me. [I'll] be around as you know . . . I love you. You are very special to me and without you in my life there is only misery. I've waited and waited and you never come, perhaps this is all suppose to happen some other way. Perhaps Hawaii or a run in on the street who knows. I have no idea . . . You are my girl! I saw you come home after the AFI gala and only wish I was at the entrance to your heart when you came home . . . I will forever be thinking of you and Louie [Bullock's son], my son, as you are my wife by law, the law of God and you belong to me and me to you . . . Always and forever, Love, your husband.[10]

Bullock arrives home later that night. Early the next morning, June 8, 2014, Corbett comes back to Bullock's home carrying a black notebook with the two-page letter he had written the night before and a magazine clipping with four photos of the actress in his pocket captioned "You are so hot and intelligent and lithesome and taut."[11]

Having surveyed the property on several nights, Corbett is now concerned about Bullock's safety and wants to show her that her house is not impervious to danger. He has with him a concealed firearm permit from Utah, no weapon. When at 6:30 a.m. he scales the chain-link fence topped with barb wire and walks up to the house, he has no intention of hurting Bullock. After ringing the doorbell for several minutes, he walks around the house and forces open the locked door to the sunroom. Bullock, asleep alone in her bedroom on the second floor, wakes up to a faint sound coming from her third-floor workout room. At first, she thinks it is the wind but then hears a banging sound that grows louder, so she peeks outside her bedroom door and catches a glimpse of a figure clad in a black sweatshirt and sweatpants. She locks the bedroom door, hides in her closet, and calls police. With panic in her voice, she describes the intruder to the dispatcher.

Hearing Bullock on the phone pleading with the police to come quickly, Corbett knocks on the bedroom door several times but does not enter. Thirteen minutes later, the police arrive at the gate, and Bullock directs them through security from her closet. The police have no trouble finding Corbett, who comes down the stairs and introduces himself as her husband. He is still clutching his love letter. Corbett is arrested. As the police lead him out of the house, he calls out "Sandy!"[12]

Figure 21.3 Joshua Corbett in court, 2017

Corbett presumably would not qualify under the Model Penal Code's harassment provision of 1962 because it was not his "purpose to harass." On the contrary, his purpose was to express his love and admiration, just as was the case with Alexander Ross wooing Bette Davis in 1936 by trespassing in her dressing room and continuing to press unwanted advances.

But the law in Joshua Corbett's 2014 California has changed. He is charged with *stalking* and first-degree burglary. (He is also charged with a variety of weapons offenses for weapons found during an unwarranted search of his home.) He faces over seven years in prison if convicted.

Current State of Harassment and Stalking Offenses

Many states now have an offense that provides a variety of different offense grades to reflect the relative seriousness of different kinds of *harassment* – increasing the offense grade if, for example, the conduct was in violation of a court protective order or if there was a previous conviction for the offense.

The map indicates the position of each state on several other important issues related to the *stalking* offense.[13] In 36 states, the lowest grade of stalking is a misdemeanor (the unshaded states on the map), but in 15 jurisdictions the lowest grade is a felony (shaded states on the map).[14]

State statutes take somewhat different approaches in defining the breadth of the offense. Some states require that the stalking conduct actually cause fear or distress in the victim (appearing on the map *without* an overlay of dots). Generally, any kind of mental or emotional harm will do, including fear, anguish, distress, terror, fright, intimidation, or worry.

Will Ross or Corbett be liable in these jurisdictions? Davis certainly felt annoyed by Ross's unwanted attentions. It is less clear that she felt fear or distress, especially given what a strong personality she was. Sandra Bullock certainly was distressed by Corbett's conduct, as is clear from her panic in conversation with the emergency operator and her hiding in her closet.

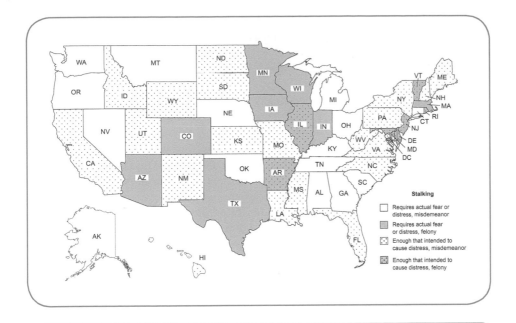

Figure 21.4

Other states (states *with* an overlay of dots on the map) do not require actual fear or distress but only that the defendant intended to cause fear or distress or that he believed that his conduct would cause such or, in some jurisdictions, that a reasonable person in the situation would have believed that it would cause such.

The Model Penal Code's formulation, quoted in the margin above, is similar to the largest group of states, with no shading but with dots. To be convicted of the lowest grade of stalking, which is a misdemeanor, the defendant need not have caused the victim any fear or distress but need only have intended to do so.

As noted, neither Ross nor Corbett is likely to be held liable if the statute requires an intention to cause distress, as the Model Code provision does. However, they may nonetheless be liable in some of the dots-overlay states where negligence rather than purpose as to distress is required – that is, where the state statute only requires that a reasonable person in the actor's situation would have believed that his conduct would cause distress.

Do Today's Stalking Offenses Violate the Proportionality Principle?

The creation of *stalking* and *harassment* offenses recognizes that what might normally be conduct insufficiently serious to warrant the condemnation of criminal conviction – such as staring at a person across the street – can be something quite serious if done repeatedly or continuously under circumstances that are intended to cause fear or distress. Thus, states were right to create new offenses to fill a gap in current law.

As often happens with the recognition of new offenses, however, it is easy to go a bit too far. The public attention and upset that triggers legislative action can often create a momentum toward excess that turns a good idea into a source of future injustice.[15] This is most evident in the dark-shaded states on the map that punish stalking or harassment as a felony.

Every American criminal code already has offenses that punish assault, battery, aggravated assault, and a host of other offenses against the person. Each of these offenses is calibrated to carry a maximum punishment that reflects the seriousness of the offense, typically tied to the extent of the harm caused: for example, the offense grade would be less for causing fear of injury compared to actually causing injury, which in turn would be less serious than actually causing serious bodily injury, and so on. Typically, only the more serious injuries are likely to move an offense out of the category of misdemeanor into the category of felony (typically carrying a potential prison term of more than one year). Yet, the dark-shaded jurisdictions on the map have set their lowest grade of the stalking or harassment offense as a felony even though no physical injury of any sort has occurred.

Perhaps even more objectionable are those dark-shaded jurisdictions with a dots overlay. Not only do they not require any actual physical injury but they provide felony liability even without any actual resulting fear of injury. The victim can be entirely unaffected by the stalking conduct, can suffer no fear or distress of any kind, and yet the offense, even under the jurisdiction's lowest grade of stalking, will carry a felony penalty.

If one believes in the importance of doing justice, one must also believe in the importance of avoiding injustice. The principle of proportionality – between the seriousness of the offense and the seriousness of the penalty – is central to the notion of justice. The creation of stalking offenses was an important and appropriate expansion of criminal liability but, like all other criminal law enactments, it must avoid disproportionality or risk endangering the criminal law's moral credibility with the community.

Aftermaths

On January 3, 1937, after having lost all access to Davis, Alexander climbs up to the loft in the barn behind his house and shoots himself. Studio personnel, under orders from Jack Warner, rush to the Alexander home before police arrive. They comb the house for anything that might damage Davis' reputation, and then take Alexander's body to authorities. His wife of less than a year is not permitted to see her dead husband before the body is taken away.

Alexander's spot on the studio roster is taken by an up-and-coming actor named Ronald Reagan, whose first role is as Davis's gay best friend – a role that might have been well suited for Ross.

In Corbett's case, pending court proceedings he remains in county jail, unable to post the required $2,185,000 bond.[16] During a brief court appearance, he pleads no contest to the charges of *stalking* and residential burglary. (The weapons charges are dropped.) Corbett receives five years of probation and court-mandated mental health treatment. In addition, the court issues a ten-year protective order that requires Corbett to remain at least 200 yards away from Bullock and her children.

When police come to his home in May of 2018 to serve a warrant for parole violations, Corbett barricades himself, producing a stand-off. As SWAT moves in, Corbett cuts himself deeply. By the time the police enter the home, he is dead from his self-inflicted wounds.

The fact that both of these stalkers ended up taking their own lives gives some indication of the potential for violence even when a stalker is motivated by overwhelming love rather than hate.

Appendix: Sample Harassment and Stalking Statute

Cal. Penal Code § 646.9 Stalking (emphasis added)

a. Any person who willfully, maliciously, and repeatedly *follows* or willfully and maliciously harasses another person and who makes a credible threat *with the intent to place that person in reasonable fear for his or her safety,* or the safety of his or her immediate family is guilty of the crime of stalking, punishable by imprisonment in a county jail for not more than one year, or by a fine of not more than one thousand dollars ($1,000), or by both that fine and imprisonment, or by imprisonment in the state prison.

    . . .

e. For the purposes of this section, "harasses" means engages in a knowing and willful course of conduct directed at a specific person that seriously alarms, annoys, torments, or terrorizes the person, and that serves no legitimate purpose.

f. For the purposes of this section, "course of conduct" means two or more acts occurring over a period of time, however short, evidencing a continuity of purpose. Constitutionally protected activity is not included within the meaning of "course of conduct."

g. For the purposes of this section, "credible threat" means a verbal or written threat, including that performed through the use of an electronic communication device, or a threat implied by a pattern of conduct or a combination of verbal, written, or electronically communicated statements and conduct, *made with the intent to place the person that is the target of the threat in reasonable fear for his or her safety or the safety of his or her family,* and made with the apparent ability to carry out the threat so as to cause the person who is the target of the threat to reasonably fear for his or her safety or the safety of his or her family. It is not necessary to prove that the defendant had the intent to actually carry out the threat. The present incarceration of a person making the threat shall not be a bar to prosecution under this section. Constitutionally protected activity is not included within the meaning of "credible threat."

    . . .[17]

Chapter Glossary

Harassment: It is an offense that criminalizes behavior designed to bother or alarm another. Such offenses typically require an identifiable victim rather than causing disruption or harm to the public generally.[18]

Stalking: The offense of following or loitering near another, often surreptitiously, to annoy or harass that person or to commit a further crime such as assault or battery. Some statutory definitions include a requirement that the person being stalked must reasonably feel harassed, alarmed, or distressed about their personal safety or the safety of one or more persons for whom that person is responsible. Some definitions include acts such as telephoning another repeatedly or repeatedly remaining silent during a call.[19]

Notes

1. This narrative is drawn from the following sources: John R. Allen Jr., 'Ross Alexander,' *Classic Images*, 6 November 2006, http://www.classicimages.com/people/-article_2d4ddd12-a04b-5897-a873-7e300e34ed68.html; 'Bette Davis,' *Biography.com*, https://www.biography.com/people/bette-davis-9267626#early-life; Ed Sikov, *Dark Victory: The Life of Bette Davis* (New York, NY: Holt Paperbacks, 2008).
2. Allen, 'Ross Alexander.'
3. Allen, 'Ross Alexander.'
4. Allen, 'Ross Alexander.'
5. Anita Bernstein, 'Law, Culture, and Harassment,' *University of Pennsylvania Law Review 142* (1994): pp. 1227–1311.
6. Ann Burgess, 'Stalking,' in *Encyclopedia of Crime and Justice*, edited by Joshua Dressler (New York: MacMillan Reference, 2002), p. 1500.
7. Burgess, 'Stalking,' p. 1505.
8. Burgess, 'Stalking,' p. 1505.
9. This narrative is drawn from the following sources: 'Man Arrested Inside Bullock's Home Convicted of Stalking,' *USA Today*, 24 May 2017, https://www.usatoday.com/story/life/people/2017/05/24/sandra-bullock-stalker-arrest/102119712/; Andrea Mandell, 'Creepy Letter from Bullock's Stalker Released,' *USA Today*, 10 April 2015, https://www.usatoday.com/story/life/people/2015/04/10/creepy-letter-from-sandra-bullock-stalker-released/25599063/; 'Sandra Bullock Emergency Call as 'Stalker' Breaks into House Played in Court,' *The Telegraph*, 10 April 2015, http://www.telegraph.co.uk/news/worldnews/northamerica/usa/11527375/Sandra-Bullock-emergency-call-as-stalker-breaks-into-house-played-in-court.html; Richard Winton, 'Lack of Search Warrant Damages Case against Man Accused of Stalking Sandra Bullock,' *Los Angeles Times*, 26 July 2016, http://www.latimes.com/local/lanow/la-me-ln-sandra-bullock-lapd-stalker-20160725-snap-story.html; *The People v. Joshua James Corbett* 8 Cal. App. 5th 670 (2017).
10. Mandell, 'Creepy Letter.'
11. 'Sandra Bullock Emergency Call.'
12. *The People v. Joshua James Corbett.*
13. The map is taken from Paul H. Robinson and Tyler Scot Williams, 'Stalking and Harassment,' in *Mapping American Criminal Law: Variations across the 50 States* (Westport: Prager, 2018), p. 222. All supporting authorities are available from that source.
14. Or, more specifically, an offense for which the authorized term of imprisonment is greater than one year.
15. Paul H. Robinson and Sarah M. Robinson, *Tragedy, Outrage & Reform: Crimes That Changed Our World* (Lanham: Rowman & Littlefield, 2017).
16. Corbett was in jail awaiting trial for three years.
17. Emphasis added.
18. Paul H. Robinson and Michael T. Cahill, *Criminal Law*, 2nd ed., §15.4 (New York, NY: Wolters Kluwer, 2012).
19. *Stalking*, Black's.

Chapter 22

Statutory Rape

Oscar Wilde's Sodomy

1895. Empress Myeongseong of Korea is a forward-thinking and influential ruler, so the Japanese, who want to rule the region, have her assassinated. Alfred Nobel, the inventor of dynamite, is dismayed by an obituary mistakenly reporting his death and decides he must change how he will be remembered, prompting the creation of the Nobel Prizes in Chemistry, Literature, Peace, Physics, and Medicine. Gugielmo Marconi advances radio telegraphy to make long-distance ship-to-shore communication possible. Frederick Douglass dies. Born a slave, he became a best-selling author, a skillful orator, a champion for abolition and women's suffrage, and an advisor to President Lincoln. But not every genius who started as an outsider was welcomed in his time.

Oscar Wilde – 1895

Oscar Wilde is born with the bloodline of a great writer.[1] His mother, a lifelong Irish nationalist, writes popular poetry for a well-read Irish newspaper that she frequently reads to Oscar and his brother. Wilde is schooled at home, where languages are emphasized. He becomes fluent in English, German, French, and gains a working knowledge of Italian and Greek. (He speaks no Irish.) His academic star rises as he studies at Trinity College in Dublin and then wins a place at Oxford, where he gains fame for his avid interest in the aesthetic and decadent movements, as well as for his flamboyant, colorful character.

In 1884, he marries Constance Lloyd, the daughter of a wealthy Queen's Counsel. The couple has two sons. Wilde begins writing more seriously in 1886. After the 1890 publication of *The Picture of Dorian Gray*, followed by a series of well-received plays including *The Importance of Being Earnest*, Wilde is established as a preeminent author and playwright.

DOI: 10.4324/9781003258025-25

Figure 22.1 The photograph was published in Lord Douglas' autobiography, 1929

But beneath his stable career and happy marriage, Wilde has a secret: he is a homosexual and has cultivated homosexual relationships since 1886. The first of these is with Robert "Robbie" Ross. At the time of their sexual relationship, Robbie is 17 years old, while Wilde is 32. They quickly form a strong bond that will last a lifetime.

Beyond his stable relationships, Wilde hires boys to be sex partners, some being 14 or younger.[2] In some of his letters, Wilde speaks of a 14-year-old, who he seems to be using for sex, as "a dreadful little ruffian."[3] He and his more stable partners are known to share the young partners.

By 1891 the Wilde family is settled in London and Wilde is reaping the rewards of his burgeoning literary reputation. He attends myriad social events and mingles with both established and emerging writers. At a tea party in mid-1891, Wilde meets a 21-year-old Oxford undergraduate, Lord Alfred Douglas, known to his friends and family as "Bosie." The 17-year age difference does not seem to be a barrier and the two immediately strike up a friendship, which eventually becomes sexual. The

Sexual Abuse of a Minor in the First Degree

(a) An offender commits the crime of sexual abuse of a minor in the first degree if

(1) being 16 years of age or older, the offender engages in sexual penetration with a person who is under 13 years of age or aids, induces, causes, or encourages a person who is under 13 years of age to engage in sexual penetration with another person;

(2) being 18 years of age or older, the offender engages in sexual penetration with a person who is under 18 years of age, and the offender is the victim's natural parent, stepparent, adopted parent, or legal guardian; or

(3) being 18 years of age or older, the offender engages in sexual penetration with a person who is under 16 years of age, and

(A) the victim at the time of the offense is residing in the same household as the offender and the offender has authority over the victim; or

(B) the offender occupies a position of authority in relation to the victim.

Alaska §11.41.434

Figure 22.2

two frequently stay together in each other's houses and in hotels, go on trips together, lunch together, and write poetry and letters to one another. For Wilde, Douglas – with his sweep of brown hair, striking eyes, and handsome face – has an "Adonis-like appearance"[4] for which Wilde is none too shy about expressing his admiration.

Douglas's father, John Sholto Douglas, the Marquess of Queensberry, grows suspicious of the close relationship between his young son and Wilde. Queensberry works to separate the two, threatening restaurant and hotel managers with beatings if Wilde and his son are permitted there. In June, Queensberry, avidly interested in amateur boxing, shows up at Wilde's home in Chelsea with one of his best fighters at his side. A verbal tussle ensues, and Wilde orders Queensberry to leave: "I do not known what the Queensberry rules are, but the Oscar Wilde rule is to shoot on sight."[5] Furious, Queensberry cuts off financial support to his son and writes venomous letters: "You reptile," reads one, "you are no son of mine and I never thought you were." Douglas writes back: "If O.W. was to prosecute you in the criminal courts for libel, you would get seven years' penal servitude for your outrageous libels."[6]

On February 14, 1895, Wilde's new and most famous play, *The Importance of Being Earnest*, opens at the London Saint James Theatre. Wilde hears that Queensberry is planning to ruin the play and tell the audience about Wilde's homosexuality. He hires guards and manages to keep Queensberry prowling outside, but Queensberry refuses to give up. Four days later, Queensberry leaves an inscribed calling card for Wilde with the hall porter at the Albermarle Club that openly accuses Wilde of being a homosexual.

Wilde now faces a difficult decision: ignore Queensberry's calling card and continue to tolerate his attacks or take him to court for libel. The easier path is to ignore Queensberry's provocations; after all, the calling card accusation has only been seen by the porter, and Wilde has managed to keep his homosexual encounters out of the public eye. Further, suing for libel is enormously risky; if Queensberry's allegations are deemed to be true, then not only will Queensberry be found innocent of libel but Wilde's reputation will be ruined. English law, as codified in the 1885 Criminal Law Amendment Act, makes it a crime for any person to commit an act of "gross indecency."[7] (Sodomy was a capital crime in England until 1828.)

Despite the risk, Wilde decides that he must put an end to Queensberry's provocations. He believes, despite warnings from his friends, that his charm and wit will win over a jury no matter what evidence comes out. Wilde approaches a respected barrister named Edward Clark, QC, who tells Wilde that he would only take the case "if you [Wilde] assure me on your honor as an English gentleman that there is not and never has been any foundation for the charges that are made against you."[8] Wilde reassures him the allegations are false, and on March 2, 1895, Queensberry is arrested and charged with criminal libel.

Wilde's closest friends encourage him to drop the case and flee the country, but Wilde, supported by young Douglas, refuses. On April 3, the trial begins. Wilde, dressed in a fashionable coat with a flower in his button-hole, saunters in with his

Figure 22.3 The Andersons start a petition to have the charges dropped, 2015

attorney, confident of victory. Charming or not, the evidence of Wilde's homosexual conduct is compelling, and his own lawyer moves to drop the case but it is too late: a warrant is issued for the arrest of Oscar Wilde in accordance with the 1885 Criminal Law Amendment Act. The judge decides to adjourn the court for an hour and a half, giving Wilde just enough time to flee England on a train bound for the European continent. It's an opportunity that Wilde can't afford to miss but trapped in "a pathetic state of indecision" he does not board the train.[9]

Wilde's criminal trial begins at the Old Bailey, the main courthouse in London, on April 26.[10] Oscar Wilde and Alfred Taylor, "the procurer of young men" for Wilde,[11] are charged with 25 counts of gross indecencies and conspiracy to commit gross indecencies. Several men – including Alfred Wood, Charles Parker, and Edward Shelley – are brought to the stand and all testify to "[acts] of indecency" with Wilde.[12] Twenty-one-year-old Alfred Wood, for example, describes an encounter with Wilde:

> After dinner I went with Mr. Wilde to 16 Tite Street. There was nobody in the house to my knowledge. Mr. Wilde let himself in with a latchkey. We went up to a bedroom where we had hock and seltzer. Here an act of grossest indecency occurred. Mr. Wilde used his influence to induce me to consent.[13]

The trial only goes downhill from there.

Despite the evidence, the jury shuffles back in and announces their decision – or rather, their lack of one, as they are unable to reach a verdict on most of the charges. On May 7, Wilde is released, but only for a short and anxious time. Three weeks later, a second criminal trial begins. Despite the fact that even prior prosecutors, including Queensberry's attorney Carson, urged that the government "let up on" the poor man,[14] the government presses its case and this time the jury finds Wilde guilty on nearly all counts. The courtroom bursts into shouts of joy by some spectators but "Shame!" by others.[15]

Sodomy

Historically, societal views on same-sex intercourse run the gamut from complete acceptance to a capital offense. The word "sodomy" comes to us through the destruction of Sodom due to what was seen as the city's evil ways.[16] While the Bible does not use the word sodomy, it explicitly condemns sexual relations between men.[17] Until the reign of King Henry VIII, the prohibition of same-sex intercourse was a matter of religious law not criminal. Because early American law was taken from English law, England's prohibitions were commonly included in the laws of the new American states. For decades, no one questioned the rational basis for the prohibition but in 1955 the American Law Institute voted to decriminalize consensual sodomy in its Model Penal Code.[18] But of the three-quarters of the states that recodified their criminal law based upon the Model Code, most elected to add the sodomy offense back in.

Some of the resistance at the state level was religiously based. But some was ideological. During the Cold War era, homosexuals were thought to be allies of the communists, which motivated the federal government's "purge of the perverts"[19]; from 1947 until 1975, thousands of suspected gay federal employees were fired. With time, societal norms changed; in 1973 the American Psychological Association ceased to label homosexuality as a mental disorder. By the end of the century, anti-sodomy laws were rarely enforced, but still existed and thus were still exploitable. This changed in 2003, when the Supreme Court ruled anti-sodomy laws unconstitutional in *Lawrence v. Texas*.[20]

While the focus in Oscar Wilde's day was on his sodomy, the fact that his partners were quite young attracted little attention. Partners as young as 15 are confirmed by the written record by name but the evidence is strong that Wilde had partners 14 and younger. Today, the prosecution of Oscar Wilde would be for *statutory rape*, not sodomy.

Statutory Rape

Criminalization of intercourse with a female under a specified age has been a crime in England since the 13th century.

> An age of consent statute first appeared in secular law in 1275 in England as part of the rape law. The statute, Westminster 1, made it a misdemeanor to "ravish" a "maiden within age," whether with or without her consent. The phrase "within age" was interpreted by jurist Sir Edward Coke as meaning the age of marriage, which at the time was 12 years of age.[21]

In 1885, W.T. Stead published an exposé of the traffic in young girls in London, "The Maiden Tribute of Modern Babylon."[22] The publication prompted British legislators to raise the age of consent to 16 years and stirred reforms in the U.S. championed by such groups as the Women's Christian Temperance Union. (Oscar Wilde's liaisons with young boys are occurring during this transitional period.) By 1920, most Anglo-American legislators had responded by increasing the age of consent to 16 years, and even as high as 18 years. (A typical modern statutory rape offense, this one from Alaska, is reproduced in the margin.) Disagreements over the proper "age of consent," which continue today (see the map below), arise in part from conflicting interests in protecting young women from being exploited, especially by older men, versus respecting young women's desires for personal autonomy and control over their own bodies. To many, the danger to vulnerable young women was increasing as more of them followed the modern trend of moving to cities and working in factories, offices, and stores where they were exposed to older men outside of the supervision of family or neighbors. Raising the age of consent was seen as providing needed greater protection.

Add to this protection-versus-personal autonomy mix, especially before the 21st century, a desire by some to use the criminal law to enforce their moral norms against sexual activity by unmarried young women. To these advocates, the more young women's new freedoms led them to a flamboyant, sexually expressive lifestyle, the more obvious the need to raise the age of consent. Of course, as societal norms supporting the sexual freedom of young women have grown in mainstream society, the morality enforcement aspect of the debate has diminished. (More on using the criminal law for morality enforcement in the next chapter, regarding adultery.)

Contrast the criminal law's apparent lack of concern for underage sexual partners on display in Oscar Wilde's case to its views illustrated by this more modern case.

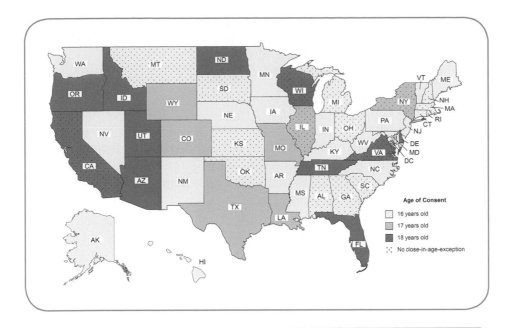

Figure 22.4

Zachery Anderson – 2014

Zachery Anderson, 19 years old, is interested in studying computers.[23] Using an age-restricted over-18 section of the Facebook-hosted site *Hot or Not*, the young man, who will be going to college in a few weeks on a scholarship, communicates with various women. He takes up a correspondence with one woman, who in fact is 17 years old.

Anderson lives in Indiana and the young woman lives about 20 miles away in Michigan. The couple arranges to meet for the purpose of having sex. Anderson drives to her home. As the girl leaves, her mother notices that she has taken a great deal of care with her appearance, and remarks to her daughter, "Dang! Where are you going?"[24] The girl evades the question and heads for the door. She climbs into Anderson's car. They drive off, chat, have sex, and Anderson drives her home. No one would have known anything further about the encounter except that the girl is not 17, she is just shy of 15, and she has epilepsy. While she is off with Anderson, she has missed taking her medication. Her mother, unable to find her, and worried about her health, contacts the police.

The whole encounter has not taken but an hour. As she returns to her home the girl finds the police in her living room. She tells the whole story – including the fact that she had lied about her age. She expresses to everyone that this is a choice that she freely made and will say nothing against Anderson.

Anderson is unaware that trouble is brewing and goes on vacation with his family to Florida. The girl texts him a warning: "Oh, we're in a lot of trouble."[25] The girl confesses that she is actually only 14, just shy of 15. Michigan authorities file charges against Anderson. The judge makes clear his view that current culture encourages such inappropriate behavior:

Sexual Assault

(1) Any actor who knowingly inflicts sexual intrusion or sexual penetration on a victim commits sexual assault if: . . .

(d) At the time of the commission of the act, the victim is less than fifteen years of age and the actor is at least four years older than the victim and is not the spouse of the victim; or

(e) At the time of the commission of the act, the victim is at least fifteen years of age but less than seventeen years of age and the actor is at least ten years older than the victim and is not the spouse of the victim; . . .

Colorado §18-3-402

Figure 22.5

You went online, to use a fisherman's expression, trolling for women to meet and have sex with. That seems to be part of our culture now: meet, hook up, have sex, sayonara. Totally inappropriate behavior. There is no excuse for this whatsoever.[26]

The girl and her family beg the court to dismiss the case. She is distraught over the harm she is doing to Anderson. Anderson does not deny that had sex with her. He is sentenced to 90 days in jail, and five years on probation. During his probation, he will not be allowed to live in a home where there is internet access or a smartphone. Further, he is banned from using the internet under any circumstance, essentially ending his computer studies. Anderson is not allowed to take his final exams or to finish the semester as the judge insists that he start serving his sentence immediately. Anderson can no longer speak to any nonfamily member under the age of 17. He will be listed on the sex offender registry for 25 years.

Statutory Rape Definitions in the States

In Oscar Wilde's day, sexual relations between teenagers and adults were commonly not criminalized while homosexual activity was a serious offense. Today, the situation is reversed. As a result of a Supreme Court decision, same-sex intercourse is not and cannot be made criminal. However, today sexual intercourse with young persons, especially by an adult, is a serious offense, *statutory rape*. In all American jurisdictions today, Wilde could be charged with a criminal offense because 16 years old is the lowest age of consent in the country for intercourse with an adult and Wilde had intercourse with 14-year-olds.

The rationale for the age cutoff is based in part upon the norms and customs of the community but also upon a recognition that young persons below a certain age may not fully appreciate the implications and consequences of their sexual activity. Without this full appreciation, legislators reason, the young person's consent may not be fully informed and therefore ought not be valid. The map below indicates the position of each state with regard to the cutoff age that it adopts.[27] The darker the shading on the map, the higher the age the partner is required to be.

Thirty-three states, those with light shading, ordinarily permit an adult to have intercourse with a consenting person who is 16 years old, provided that the actor does not stand in any relationship of authority to the partner, such as a guardian, teacher, or coach. Wilde having intercourse with a 14-year-old would be criminally liable in these states and, indeed, in all states. Seven states set the age cutoff at 17, and 11 set it at 18.

The cutoff age indicated on the map applies to adults. About two-thirds of the states, those *without* a dots overlay on the map, adopt a special exemption for defendants who are close in age to their underage partner. Thus, in Colorado (whose statute is reproduced in the margin), a much older adult would be liable for the offense if the partner is less than 17. (See that Colorado has medium shading on the map, indicating a 17-year-old cutoff for adults.) But the cutoff age becomes 15 if the offender is less than ten years older than the victim, and the cutoff age may be less than 15 if the offender is less than four years older.

This won't help Wilde, of course, because he is quite a bit older than his partners but could make a difference for Anderson depending on the details. In fact, he would not quite qualify for the exception. He is 19 and his partner is 14, so he is five years older, while the sample Colorado statute would allow an exception if he were only four years older than his partner – in other words, if he were only 18 (rather than 19) or if she were 15 (rather than 14). Different states employ different variations in defining the scope of the exception.

The remaining third of the states, those *with* a dots overlay on the map, provide no close-in-age exception. Even persons the same age (or younger than) the underage partner can be liable. Thus, for example, an 18-year-old boyfriend who wishes to engage in consensual intercourse with his 16-year-old girlfriend would escape liability in a state with a close-in-age exception, like Texas, but not in a state that lacks the exception, such as New York. In New York, a person less than 17 years old is "deemed incapable of consent" by statute. In Texas, however, the 18-year-old boyfriend may assert an affirmative defense, that he "was not more than three years older than the victim."

Zach Anderson lived in Indiana while his 14-year-old partner lived 20 miles away in Michigan. As the map shows, both of these states use 16 as the age cutoff. However, Indiana has a close-in-age exception, so Anderson might escape liability there, depending on the details of the Indiana exception. In contrast, Michigan has no such exception, so Anderson would be criminally liable if the intercourse occurred in that state.

Contemplating the Diversity among the States

As the analysis above indicates, different states take significantly different approaches in defining *statutory rape*. The existence of such diversity is consistent with the idea that the proper age below which sexual intercourse should be criminalized is in some significant part a function of existing community norms and customs. The collection of darker-shaded states in the West, with a line of medium-shaded states separating them from a somewhat lighter-shaded Midwest and East, suggests that some of the cultural differences may be regional. However, it is also possible that a variety of other factors influence the cutoff age. Perhaps some state legislatures are inclined to be influenced by what their neighboring states do. Or perhaps news coverage of some particular case in the state has prompted the legislature to undertake a reform, where their neighboring states may not have had such news coverage or public upset.[28] Interestingly, there seems to be no obvious connection between the baseline age of consent in a state and the recognition of a close-in-age exception; the exception is used with age cutoffs of 16, 17, and 18.

The diversity among the states does create some significant points of contrast, even for neighboring states. Consider two examples of pairs of neighboring states. Alabama provides a cutoff age of 16 while across the state line in Florida the cutoff age is 18. Even more striking, in Alabama, a 16-year-old could be convicted of the statutory rape of his 15-year-old girlfriend, while in Florida, with its permissive close-in-age exception, a 23-year-old may lawfully engage in consensual intercourse with a 16-year-old.

Similarly, Virginia sets the cutoff at 18 and does not provide a close-in-age exception, while neighboring North Carolina sets the cutoff at 16 and does have a close-in-age exception. Thus, an 18-year-old boyfriend is liable for the statutory rape of his 17-year-old girlfriend in Virginia, while the same 18-year-old would be permitted to have sex with a consenting 15-year-old in North Carolina.

These kinds of criminal law differences among the states can have regular and important practical effects. This is particularly true for people who interact with others across the state line, as was the case with Zach Anderson. To promote compliance and to provide fair notice, some serious effort at public education may be needed but such is rarely done today.

Aftermaths

In the aftermath of the trial, Oscar Wilde loses everything, including his family, his reputation, and his wealth. He is sentenced to two years at hard labor, and his books and plays are removed from bookshops and theatres. A wealth of pornographic writing, falsely published illegally under Wilde's name, circulates around England. Emerging from prison, he is hardened, bankrupt, and lonely – lonely except for one man, a devoted friend and confidante throughout Wilde's life: Robbie Ross, who was only 17 years old when they first met. When Wilde is released, Ross is waiting for him with a house in the quiet seaside village of Berneval-le-Grand in northern France.

Living as the mysterious Sebastian Melmoth, Wilde is paid an annual sum, by his wife, to stay away from their children and from Douglas. Despite his promise, he continues to obsess over Douglas, and the two live together for a few months near Naples in 1897. When the affair ends, it is Ross who remains by Wilde's side for the rest of his life. Wilde withers for several years, writing sporadically, before his health declines suddenly in 1900 from cerebral meningitis. Wilde dies on November 30, 1900.

After his death, Ross devotes himself to tending to Wilde's affairs. He secures his legacy by buying back the rights to Wilde's works and stamping out the pornography that is still being published under Wilde's name. He also commissions the work for

Wilde's tomb in a Paris cemetery, to which Wilde's remains are moved from his initial place of burial. He requests that a section of the tomb be reserved for his own remains. Ross himself dies in 1918, and in 1950 – 50 years after Wilde's death – Ross's ashes are laid to rest, alongside his old friend's.

For Zach Anderson, his case makes the national news because many people think the 19-year-old's sentence is too harsh because his mistake as to the age of his younger partner is seen as an easy mistake to make. Jail, probation, a forced end to his computer career plans, and 25 years on the sex offenders' list is thought to be excessive by many. After many trips to court, some minor parole violations (including one for using the internet to obtain directions to build a skateboard ramp), and pleas from the girl's family, Anderson is removed from the sex offender list. His record is cleared, and the case gets people talking about the harshness of the rules. However, the talk does not lead to significant change as it is hard to find a lawmaker who wants to appear to be soft on sexual offenders who target children.

Chapter Glossary

Statutory Rape: Sexual intercourse with a person who has not yet reached the age of consent as determined by state law, whether or not the sexual act is consensual. In many states, "Romeo and Juliet" trysts, in which the male and female are young and there is little difference in age between them, are exempt or punished less severely than when the victim is significantly younger than the perpetrator.[29]

Notes

1. This narrative is drawn from the following sources: 'Biography,' *The Oscar Wilde Society*, http://oscarwildesociety.co.uk/biography/; 'Biography of Oscar Wilde,' *Oscar Wilde Online*, http://www.wilde-online.info/oscar-wilde-biography.htm; Marcus Field, 'Is Oscar Wilde's Reputation Due for Another Reassessment?' *The Independent*, 4 October 2014, http://www.independent.co.uk/arts-entertainment/theatre-dance/features/is-oscar-wilde-facing-a-retrial-9773718.html; Douglas O. Linder, 'The Trials of Oscar Wilde: An Account,' *Famous American Trials, University of Missouri- Kansas City*, http://law2.umkc.edu/faculty/projects/ftrials/wilde/wildeaccount.html; 'Number 2: Oscar Wilde v Marquess of Queensberry, April 1895: The Importance of Being a Colossally Bad Litigator,' *Defamation Watch*, http://defamationwatch.com.au/?page_id=277; 'Oscar Wilde's First Gay Lover,' *The Toronto Dreams Project Historical Ephemera Blog*, 14 September 2010, http://torontodreamsproject.blogspot.com/2010/09/oscar-wildes-first-gay-lover.html; 'Testimony of Alfred Wood,' *Famous American Trials, University of Missouri- Kansas City*, http://law2.umkc.edu/faculty/projects/ftrials/wilde/Crimtranwood.html.
2. William Terpening, 'The Picture of Oscar Wilde: A Brief Life,' *The Victorian Web*, 1998, http://www.victorianweb.org/authors/wilde/wildebio.html; and authorities cited *supra* note 1.
3. Marcus Field, Is Oscar Wilde's reputation due for another reassessment? As a new play and book put the writer back in the dock, his reputation may be set to change once again, *The Independent*, 5 October 2014, https://www.independent.co.uk/arts-entertainment/theatre-dance/features/is-oscar-wilde-facing-a-retrial-9773718.html.
4. Linder, 'Trials of Oscar Wilde.'

5. Linder, 'Trials of Oscar Wilde.'

6. Linder, 'Trials of Oscar Wilde.'

7. Kirby Farrell, 'Wilde on Trial: Psychic Injury, Exhibitionism, and the Law,' in *Processes of Institutionalisation: Case Studies in Law, Prison, and Censorship*, edited by Uwe Boeker and Julie A. Hibbard (Essen: Die Blaue, Eule, 2001), *University of Massachusetts*, http://people.umass.edu/kfarrell/Site/Wilde.html

8. 'Number 2: Oscar Wilde v Marquess of Queensberry.'

9. Linder, 'Trials of Oscar Wilde.'

10. 'Testimony of Alfred Wood'; 'Testimony of Antonio Migge,' *Famous American Trials, University of Missouri-Kansas City,* http://law2.umkc.edu/faculty/projects/ftrials/wilde/Crimmigge.html.

11. Linder, 'Trials of Oscar Wilde.'

12. 'Testimony of Alfred Wood'; 'Testimony of Antonio Migge.'

13. 'Testimony of Alfred Wood'; 'Testimony of Antonio Migge.'

14. Linder, 'Trials of Oscar Wilde.'

15. Linder, 'Trials of Oscar Wilde.'

16. Aimée D. Dayhoff, 'Sodomy Laws: The Government's Vehicle to Impose the Majority's Social Values,' *William Mitchell Law Review* 27, no. 3 (2001) Article 3, http://open.mitchellhamline.edu/wmlr/vol27/iss3/3.

17. Leviticus 20:13.

18. Richard Weinmeyer, The Decriminalization of Sodomy in the United States, *Health Law*, November 2014, https://journalofethics.ama-assn.org/article/decriminalization-sodomy-united-states/2014-11.

19. Eric Berkowitz, 'Homosexuality: From Sin to Sickness,' in *The Boundaries of Desire: A Century of Good Sex, Bad Laws, and Changing Identities* (Berkeley, CA: Counterpoint Press, 2015), p. 91.

20. Berkowitz, 'Homosexuality: From Sin to Sickness,' pp. 60–109.

21. Stephen Robertson, *Youth and Children in History: Age of Consent Laws*, http://chnm.gmu.edu/cyh/teaching-modules/230

22. Stephen Robertson, 'Age of Consent Law and the Making of Modern Childhood in New York City 1886–1921,' *Journal of Social History 35* (Oxford: Oxford University Press, 2002): p. 781.

23. Lenore Skenazy, 'Male Teen Has Consensual Sex with Female Teen. He Gets 25 Years as Sex Offender, Banned from Internet,' *Reason.com*, 16 June 2015, http://reason.com/blog/2015/06/16/male-teen-has-consensual-sex-with-female; Virginia Black, 'Was Justice Served after Teen's Encounter with Girl?' *South Bend Tribune*, 20 May 2015, http://www.southbendtribune.com/news/local/was-justice-served-after-teen-s-encounter-with-girl/article_bede1df7-505d-5d39-b9d8-256719f553d9.html.

24. Black, 'Was Justice Served?'

25. Black, 'Was Justice Served?'

26. Skenazy, 'Male Teen.'

27. The map is taken from Paul H. Robinson and Tyler Scot Williams, 'Death Penalty,' in *Mapping American Criminal Law: Variations across the 50 States* (Westport: Prager, 2018), p. 27. All supporting authorities are available from that source.

28. For a general discussion of this dynamic, see Paul H. Robinson and Sarah M. Robinson, *Tragedy, Outrage & Reform: Crimes That Changed Our World* (Lanham: Rowman & Littlefield, 2017).

29. *Statutory Rape*, Legal Information Institute, https://www.law.cornell.edu/wex/statutory_rape.

Chapter 23

Adultery

Frank Sinatra and a Changing Morality

1938. In Germany, Adolf Hitler gives his first speech to the German Workers' Party. Benito Mussolini launches the Fascist movement in Milan, Italy. The British Parliament enacts a 48-hour work week and sets a minimum wage requirement, the first of its kind by a major country. The Eighteenth Amendment to the United States Constitution is ratified, authorizing Prohibition. In Boston, a large molasses storage tank bursts, releasing a wave of molasses that rushes through the streets at 35 miles per hour, killing 21 and injuring 150. The White Sox throw the World Series playoffs against the Cincinnati Reds in exchange for money from gamblers. Frank Sinatra is eight years away from releasing his first album.

Frank Sinatra – 1938

In the early months of 1938, a young, aspiring musician is looking for love.[1] Frank Sinatra is 23 years old, self-confident, and dashingly handsome, with deep blue eyes and a broad white smile. He has not yet experienced true stardom, but a radio show is starting to build him a fan base in New York.

Antoinette Della Penta Francke, called "Toni" by her friends, goes to hear him sing and by the end of the evening the two are dancing together. She is a pretty brunette, married but separated for some time. Despite the fact that Sinatra is in a long-term relationship with another woman, he and Toni start seeing each other.

Sinatra's mother, Dolly, loathes Toni. To her, Toni Francke and her family seem beneath the Sinatras, a belief founded more on arrogance than on true difference in social status. Dolly openly criticizes the young couple's relationship, claiming they are too young to marry and suggesting that Toni would "keep Frankie from being a big singer."[2]

DOI: 10.4324/9781003258025-26

The couple begins to have sex. Six weeks later, Toni is pregnant. Sinatra promises to take care of her. Three months into her pregnancy, Toni miscarries. Sinatra begins to lose interest in Toni, and at times accuses her of standing in the way of his singing career. He breaks off their relationship when another girlfriend announces that she is pregnant. Toni had not previously known about the other woman and the news devastates her. Furious and humiliated, she swears out a criminal complaint against Sinatra on a charge of seduction. The offense typically requires an inducement to intercourse upon a false promise of marriage. The New Jersey charge states:

> being then and there a single man over the age of eighteen years, under the promise of marriage, did then and there have sexual intercourse with the said complainant who was then and there a single female of good repute for chastity whereby she became pregnant.[3]

It turns out, however, that Toni is not in fact single – she is still just long separated from her husband. So, after 16 hours behind bars, Sinatra is released on a $1,500 bond, and Toni Francke's complaint is eventually withdrawn.[4]

Though Sinatra is out of jail, he's furious about the arrest.

> That broad is crazy. We went out for pasta fagioli, had a good time, went back to her place, and hit the sheets. So what? Next thing I know, this dame is tellin' me she's pregnant, and I'm in the slammer.[5]

But Toni isn't ready to give up. She changes her charge from seduction to *adultery*: it was an offense for Sinatra to have intercourse with her while she was married.

Figure 23.1 Frank Sinatra, mugshot, 1938

On the cold night of December 22, two New Jersey constables wait until Sinatra finishes his midnight radio broadcast before sending him word that they have a Christmas present to give him, courtesy of one of his admirers. Sinatra falls for the ruse and is arrested. He's released after paying a bond of $500. Sinatra is not pleased: "She's got some nerve, that one," he remarks, "She was the one committing adultery! I didn't even know she was married." The story makes the Hoboken headlines the next day: "Songbird held in morals charge."

Toni Francke's father eventually convinces her to drop the adultery charge. Sinatra goes on to marry Nancy Barbato, with whom he has three children. They divorce in 1950 so Sinatra can marry Ava Gardner. Gardner is followed by Mia Farrow. Sinatra's final marriage is to Barbara Ann Blakeley, who previously had been married to one of the Marx Brothers. During most of his marriages, Sinatra continues to have adulterous relationships with other women.

Adultery

During medieval times, the church exercises more power than the state. In the eyes of the church, *adultery* is a serious moral sin. Such morality offenses fall within the penal jurisdiction of ecclesiastical courts.[6] The punishment of both parties often involves prohibitions on future relations, public penance – such as public beatings or a mandated pilgrimage – or the imposition of a fine. (Imprisonment will not become a common penalty until the 18th century.)

In the 13th century, England makes adultery a secular crime subject to civil (but not yet criminal) penalties. Those civil penalties increase in severity over the next several centuries and eventually the wrong is considered sufficiently serious to be recognized as a crime, with the criminal penalties becoming increasingly serious. In 1650 the English Parliament makes adultery a capital offense. The law has the unintended consequence of incentivizing murder of the betrayed spouse because a dead spouse cannot stand as a witness and the murder carries no greater penalty than the adultery.

The newly formed United States adopts adultery as a crime without reference to religious doctrine. As the effects of adultery are felt by all in the community, it is argued, it is not a private failing but a crime against society because "open and notorious"[7] adultery undermines public morality. As one North Dakota court explains:

> It is certainly a monstrous anomaly that the feelings of society should be outraged, and a whole community injured, by the undisputed commission of this offense continued for months and years, and that, under the law, there is no remedy so long as the husband or wife, either from fear of his own or her own degradation, declines or refuses to apply the remedy. But when we go one step further and say that the wife of a guilty husband cannot complain against the wife of another husband, but can only complain of her husband, and that such other wife must escape punishment if her husband does not complain against her, the outrage, to my mind, is still greater.[8]

In the court's view, adultery is a crime that injures all of society and endangers the sanctity of marriage.

Adultery is taken seriously as a criminal offense into the beginning of the 20th century. The case below is probably one of the last cases seriously prosecuted under a belief that adultery is a societal harm deserving criminal sanction (as opposed to a complaint primarily reflecting the personal anger of an aggrieved partner, as in the charges against Frank Sinatra).

Laura and William Geisselman – 1919

On June 22, 1913, Laura and William Geisselman are married in New Jersey. Six months later, Laura leaves to live with her lover and continues with him for the next year and a half. William, it seems, is none too disappointed. Laura is arrested in Camden, New Jersey, for highway robbery along with two male co-conspirators. She is also charged with and convicted of *adultery*. Upon her release from jail, she takes up with another man.

William moves to Maryland, meets a woman, and marries, believing that he is no longer married because his wife has been found guilty of adultery, thereby legally amounting to a divorce. He and his new wife have a child.

When Maryland authorities learn of William's earlier marriage to Laura and his more recent marriage to a Maryland resident, they charge him with bigamy – marrying a person while already married. After being arrested, William stops living with his new wife, and files for divorce from Laura "so that he may again marry the woman whom he married in good faith, and thus make her his legal wife and make her child legitimate."[9]

At this point in the development of divorce law, a court will grant a divorce only if the spouse is committing adultery. William can satisfy this requirement, but because he himself entered into a legally adulterous relationship (with his new wife), albeit by mistake, he too is guilty of adultery and therefore is ineligible to get a divorce.[10] Under the law, apparently, William and Laura must remain married until death ends the union.[11] William is held liable for adultery and bigamy.

Adultery Offenses in the States

As the history of *adultery* makes clear, it was a serious offense, even a capital offense, for many centuries but with changing societal norms it has almost disappeared as a crime. As late as 1919, in the Laura and William Geisselman case, it is still prosecuted but stands out as something of an anomaly. By the time of Frank Sinatra's prosecution of 1938, it has ceased to be a real offense although it is sometimes abused by angry complainants.

The original rationale for the offense was one of morality enforcement and a concern for protecting the institution of marriage. However, a 2003 Supreme Court ruling invalidated anti-sodomy statutes[12] and thereby appeared to put the privacy interests of the individual above the legislative interest in criminalizing violations of societal norms. However, the criminalization of adultery had been previously upheld as constitutional,[13] so the offense was not invalidated as unconstitutional and remained the law in many jurisdictions. Nonetheless, today most Western countries have decriminalized adultery.

As the map below indicates, the same is true of a majority of jurisdictions in the United States. Many states, those with no shading, repealed their adultery statute more than a quarter century ago. (Since New Jersey is in this group, neither Laura Geisselman

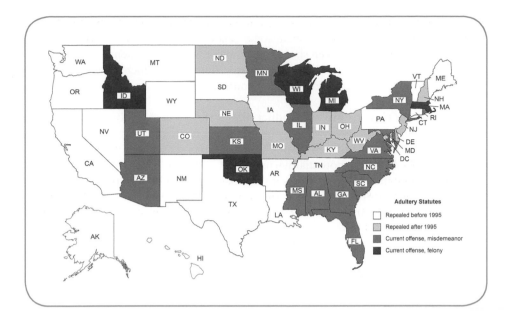

Figure 23.2

nor Frank Sinatra could be charged with adultery in New Jersey today.) Many others, those with light shading, repealed their adultery statute within the last quarter century. Thus, as recently as 1995 the legal landscape of adultery made it an offense in 32 of 51 jurisdictions – about two-thirds of the states.

The 20 states with the two darker shadings, a sizable minority, technically still have the offense.[14] (Maryland is in this group, so William Geisselman could still be convicted of adultery today.) Notice the geographic patterns revealed by the map: the southern states are well represented in this group that have adultery still on their books, joined by a number of other states associated with strong religious norms.

Using the Criminal Law for Morality Enforcement

Adultery is just one of many offenses that has been or still is criminalized in some significant part because it offends existing societal norms. But is offending other people's moral sensibilities an appropriate basis for criminal liability? If there is no tangible harm to those others or to the society or its institutions, then why should the criminal law be used for such morality enforcement?

However, to the extent that the criminal law's reputation – its "moral credibility" (recall the chapter on punishment theory[15]) – will affect its crime-control effectiveness, including people's inclination to defer, acquiesce, assist, and internalize its norms, then perhaps serious conflicts between criminal law rules and the society's existing shared moral norms are something to be avoided. Wouldn't the criminal law lose moral credibility if it decriminalized abuse of a dead body, desecration of sacred objects, bestiality, adult incest, cruelty to animals, and public defecation? (The next two chapters take up the offenses of obscenity and child pornography.) One might be able to construct some claim of harm from some of these activities, but not all, and many of those harm claims have been shown to be make-weight arguments where the true motivating factor for criminalization is simply that the conduct is seen as morally offensive, as was the case when abortion, contraception, adultery, and sodomy were seriously criminalized.

Certainly, not every bit of conduct that offends somebody else should be criminalized. The question is whether conduct that a broad majority of the population considers to be seriously offensive should be put beyond the reach of criminalization because it does not cause potential harm.

Complicating the analysis is the fact that societal norms change over time and can be changed by concerted effort, especially if helped by legal *decriminalization* (or criminalization). A particularly compelling example is same-sex intercourse, once considered a serious offense, yet within the space of one generation lost its stigma with a significant majority of Americans. Similarly, premarital sex was once a crime but is now generally accepted. As this chapter has already shown, adultery was once considered a serious offense but today is, as a practical matter, effectively decriminalized. The same is true of the old offense of seduction (with which Frank Sinatra was initially charged). And probably no one would seriously think to criminalize blasphemy today, although it was once seen as one of the most serious offenses. It can be readily argued that criminal law must keep up with shifts in existing societal norms if it is to maintain its moral credibility with the community.[16] (Does that mean only that it should *decriminalize* conduct when public condemnation of the conduct fades, or does it also mean that it should *criminalize* conduct that is broadly seen as seriously condemnable, such as bestiality, public defecation, and necrophilia?)

Is It Useful or Problematic to Have a Criminal Offense That Is Rarely If Ever Enforced?

As noted, *adultery* remains on the books in many states, but in practice it is rarely prosecuted. The 2003 conviction of one John R. Bushey, Jr. under Virginia's adultery statute generated national attention in part because of the unusualness of such a prosecution. (Bushey was sentenced to community service and the misdemeanor charge was removed upon his completion of the hours.)[17] Many people may see this situation – prohibition without enforcement – as having some practical value. While adultery is rarely prosecuted, its continuing presence in the criminal code provides an official source of moral condemnation of the conduct. Decriminalizing adultery might be seen as approving it, is sending the wrong signal, so *decriminalization* ought to be avoided.

But the prohibition-without-enforcement approach creates several problems. First, it mistakes the proper role of criminal law. There are a number of social institutions in the business of building or reinforcing social norms – churches are a prime example and more recently social movements – but criminal law has a more limited role. It seeks to identify the wrongdoing that is so condemnable as to deserve the label of "criminal" and the punishment that follows. There are many sorts of conduct that may be socially and even morally objectionable, such as lying to a spouse about an important matter or cutting in line to get scarce concert tickets. But just because the conduct is wrong, it does not follow that its wrongfulness rises to the level of criminality.

To criminalize adultery when it is judged insufficiently serious to deserve actual prosecution and punishment is to dilute the power of the "criminal" label. By representing adultery to be a criminal offense, when in practice it really is not seen as meeting those requirements, is to risk having people assume that other offenses in the criminal code are similarly only pretend offenses. Creating that kind of ambiguity tends to undermine the social influence of criminal prohibitions generally.

Further, the criminalization of conduct that is not necessarily meant by the legislature to be prosecuted has the effect of shifting the criminalization power to prosecutors rather than keeping it within the more democratic legislative branch where it belongs. Under a system where criminal law includes a variety of offenses that are only prosecuted depending upon the personal preferences of the current prosecutor, the power to truly criminalize conduct has been passed from the legislature to the prosecutor.

Further, the creation of offenses whose violation are not regularly prosecuted vests prosecutors with an unhealthy discretionary power, for it gives the prosecutor the ability to resurrect the rarely used statute – that is not intended to be enforced and is meant only as a symbolic statement – in order to prosecute an unfavored defendant.

To protect its moral credibility as well as fairness in application, a criminal law ought to say what it means and mean what it says. That is, it ought to be careful to define as criminal only the conduct that deserves the sanction of criminal liability and punishment and, when such conduct occurs, it ought to normally prosecute violations to the extent feasible, unless some special circumstances of the case justify non-prosecution.

Aftermaths

The remainder of Frank Sinatra's life is well-documented. He is tabloid fodder for decades until his death in 1998 at the age of 82.

Laura and William Geisselman appear to have spent the remainder of their lives out of the courtroom and the public eye.

Chapter Glossary

Adultery: This common-law offense, which has been dropped from many modern criminal codes, criminalizes sexual relations between a married person and someone other than their spouse.[18]

Decriminalization: The repeal or amendment of statutes that made certain acts criminal, so that those acts are no longer prohibited or subject to criminal prosecution.[19]

Seduction: Seduction refers to an act by which a person entices another to have sexual intercourse by means of persuasions, promises, flattery, or bribes without threat of physical force.[20]

Notes

1. This narrative is drawn from the following sources: Kitty Kelley, *His Way: The Unauthorized Biography of Frank Sinatra* (New York: Bantam Books, 2015); J. Randy Taraborrelli, *Sinatra: Behind the Legend* (New York: Rose Books, Inc., 1997); Irvin Molotsky, 'F.B.I. Releases Its Sinatra File,' *New York Times*, 9 December 1998; Scott Cronick, 'Sinatra Loved Their Grandma,' *Press of Atlantic City*, 9 October 2010.

2. Kelley, *His Way*, p. 2.
3. Kelley, *His Way*, p. 2.
4. Molotsky, 'F.B.I. Releases Its Sinatra File.'
5. Taraborrelli, *Sinatra: Behind the Legend*, p. 39.
6. This narrative is drawn from the following sources: *Geisselman v. Geisselman* 134 Md. 453 (1919); Erin L. Sheley, 'Adultery, Criminality, and the Myth of English Sovereignty,' *Law, Culture and the Humanities* 11 (2015): pp. 1–44; JoAnne Sweeney, 'History of Adultery and Fornication Criminal Laws,' *University of Louisville School of Law Legal Studies Research Paper*, 21 March 2013; George Poindexter Bagby, ed. *The Annotated Code of the Public Civil Laws of Maryland*, vol. 3 (Baltimore: King Bros. Printers & Publishers, 1914), https://books.google.ca/books?id=Ee hGAQAAIAAJ&dq=editions:STANFORD36105064276707&hl=fr.
7. Sweeny, *History of Adultery Laws*.
8. Sweeny, *History of Adultery Laws*.
9. *Geisselman v. Geisselman*.
10. Laura was convicted in New Jersey which attaches jail time to adultery. Maryland, where William is arrested, imposes a $10 fine. Bagby, *The Annotated Code*.
11. William appeals the case and it reaches the Court of Appeals of Maryland. The appeals judge refers back to an English proviso that reads,

    > Nothing in this act shall extend to any person marrying a second time whose husband or wife shall have been continually absent from such person for the space of seven years last passed, and shall not have been known by such person to be living within that time.

    Geisselman v. Geisselman. Under this, bigamy is only allowed if one spouse is absent for a period of seven years.

    Therefore, the Court decides that William has no right to relief because he had sexual intercourse with a woman other than his real wife. The court acknowledges that the second marriage was a result of a:

    > bona fide mistake of fact which led the husband to marry the other woman and cohabit with her, in the full belief that she was his lawful wife, provided the circumstances were such that he was justified in his belief that the first marriage had ended, and that he had not been negligent or lax in endeavoring to ascertain the actual facts before he entered into the second marriage.

    Geisselman v. Geisselman. Thus, the court affirms the decision of the lower court – William is guilty of bigamy.
12. *Lawrence v. Texas* 539 U.S. 558 (2003).
13. *See, e.g., Commonwealth v. Stowell* 389 Mass. 171 (1983) (upholding a Massachusetts criminal adultery statute as constitutional, challenged by a defendant awaiting trial); *Oliverson v. W. Valley City* 875 F. Supp. 1465 (1995) (upholding Utah's criminal adultery statute as constitutional).
14. The map is taken from Paul H. Robinson and Tyler Scot Williams, *Mapping American Criminal Law: Variations across the 50 States* (Westport: Prager, 2018), ch. 29. All supporting authorities are available from that source.
15. Chapter 2.
16. For a general discussion of using criminal law as morality enforcement, see Kent Greenawalt, 'Legal Enforcement of Morality,' *The Journal of Criminal Law and Criminology* 85, no. 3 (1995): pp. 710–725; Jeremy Bentham, *Introduction to the Principles of Morals and Legislation* (Oxford: Clarendon Press, 1823); Joel Feinberg,

The Moral Limits of the Criminal Law, vol. 2, Offense to Others (Oxford: Oxford University Press, 1988), ch. 9.

17. John F. Kelly, 'Va. Adultery Case Roils Divorce Industry,' *Washington Post*, 1 December 2003, https://www.washingtonpost.com/archive/local/2003/12/01/va-adultery-case-roils-divorce-industry/84ff5ce8-f69b-410e-9a2f-d1bae148993a/.

18. *Adultery*, Britannica, https://www.britannica.com/topic/adultery.

19. *Decriminalization*, Law.com, https://dictionary.law.com/Default.aspx?selected=450.

20. *Seduction*, Legal Information Institute, https://www.law.cornell.edu/wex/seduction.

Chapter 24

Obscenity

Fanny Hill, *the Most Prosecuted Book in History*

1821. Michael Faraday, a book-binding apprentice with no formal education, becomes intrigued when he binds a work about the principles of electricity, and thereafter builds the world's first electrical motor. The population of the United States has grown to 9.6 million, with Irish immigration as the largest source of new Americans. Missouri, acquired through the Louisiana Purchase, now has a sufficiently large population that the territory qualifies for statehood, the first state entirely west of the Mississippi River. President James Monroe takes office for a second term in which he presses the "Munro Doctrine," which essentially declared the Americas as existing independent of the European powers. But while the U.S. may seem big, brash, and independent on the international stage, it continues to share the prudishness of the Puritans.

John Cleland's *Fanny Hill* – 1821

At age 31, John Cleland returns to England from his post as a clerk with the East India Company in Bombay and is at a loss when his mother says she will not support him. Lacking employment, Cleland settles on a plan to revive the Portuguese East India Company, but the scheme requires money and connections, neither of which Cleland has.[1]

He is soon heavily in debt to a friend. By 1748 the size of the debt exceeds the strength of the friendship, and Cleland lands in debtor's prison. He does not have friends or family willing to take over the debt but does have lots of time to sit around and fantasize.

While working in Bombay, Cleland the clerk was also Cleland the would-be novelist. He began a novel rich in fantasy; and now in jail he has endless hours to develop the work. A publisher makes an offer for the completed manuscript, *Memoirs of a Woman of Pleasure*, to be published in two parts. By March 1749, Cleland is a free man.

DOI: 10.4324/9781003258025-27

Memoirs of a Woman of Pleasure is a novel composed in letter form. The letter writer is Fanny Hill, who offers her reader, in one never-ending sentence after another, a full account of herself and her motivations.[2] In the novel, the newly orphaned 15-year-old Fanny goes to London as an innocent. Her first sexual encounters are with women, prostitutes, whom she lives among. She is naively led into a career as a prostitute but does not find the work to be all bad.

Young Fanny finds herself to be a woman who likes sex in many flavors and with lots of spices. She has sex with men and women; she whips patrons; she encourages young men without experience to trust themselves sexually. Heroine Fanny never slides too far down the debauchery ladder, however. Uncared-for offspring, drugs, and disease are not part of the vigorous Fanny Hill world.

Cleland knows his audience and plays to all their common fantasies. When a messenger boy, newly arrived in the city, takes her fancy, Fanny takes time to seduce him. The young messenger is good looking, innocent, being brought into the world of sex by a gentle expert, who is not going to charge him, and of course he is of ample stature. Fanny takes the final step and unbuttons his trousers only to find that this is "not the play thing of a boy, not the weapon of a man, but a Maypole, of so enormous a standard, that had proportions been observed, it must have belonged to a young

FANNY WHIPS Mr. BARVILLE

Figure 24.1 The illustrations printed in *Fanny Hill* were considered scandalous, 1919, Édouard-Henri Avril

giant."[3] The printed book is in the neighborhood of 250 pages and less than 50 do not include sexual acts.

At one point voyeuristic Fanny finally encounters a form of sex that she is not comfortable with. Peeking through a crack, she spies on two men having a homosexual encounter. Buggery, the old term for homosexual contact, is a serious social taboo at the time of the book's publication. Cleland, through the voice of the naïve Fanny, knows that this is not a scene that is going to slip by the authorities unremarked, so he makes certain to convey this type of sex with disapproval. Fanny decides to report the horror to the authorities, but no sooner does she resolve to do this when, overcome with the scene before her, she faints and falls off her seat. The men get clean away before Fanny recovers her senses.

Cleland is a careful writer. Without a single swear word or appearance of vulgarity, Fanny gives her readers wordplay, euphemisms, metaphors, and contextual clues to convey every kind of sexual act that might be imagined by a man trapped in debtor's prison. Every part of the human body is described as a geographical feature somewhere in the book: mountains, valleys, caves, hills, channels, and hidden glens. Anatomical terms are scrupulously avoided. Instead of "penis," for example, Fanny writes of a "wonderful machine," an "engine of love-assaults," or a "stiff staring truncheon."[4] Even the name Fanny Hill is easily to be understood as a more genteel substitution for a region of female anatomy. The use of linguistic substitution is addressed by Fanny near the conclusion of the book. Fanny apologizes "for having too much affected the figurative style."[5] But the character is not actually apologizing. Her apology is another chance for the author to make certain that the authorities do not mistake his writing for pornography.

But the legal sages of the age are not satisfied that "engine of love-assaults"[6] actually comes off as less objectionable than "penis." In November 1749, Cleland is in trouble with the law along with publisher Ralph Griffiths and the book's printer Thomas Parker. All are arrested and brought to trial.

In court, he swears that he is sorry that he wrote the book and that he only did so because he saw no other way out of prison. After being convicted of "corrupting the King's subjects,"[7] he promises to cease publication. Instead of actually ceasing publication, Cleland works to come up with a more sanitized version. What really has people worked up is the homosexual content concerning men. Those portions are now taken out and a new edition is produced. The edit is seen as wanting and he is back in court in 1750. Cleland pays a fine, spends a short time in jail, and puts forth a further edited version of the book, which is accepted.

A scant few hours after the court agrees to allow the new version to be published, London is hit by an earthquake, the second of the year. The Bishop of London immediately sees the connection. He sends a missive to all his clergymen instructing them to make sure all their congregants know that it is the soft treatment of Cleland that has brought this trouble. The Bishop asks, "Have not the histories of the vilest prostitutes been published" right there in London?[8] And as it is the London courts that allowed it, can it be a surprise that it is London that has been hit by the pair of quakes?

The Bishop, it seems, is uniquely informed and is able to tell everyone what God is going to do next: a far more massive quake is soon to follow on April 8. The city experiences epic traffic jams as terrified people flee the coming destruction.

Fanny Hill is a publishing sensation and copies of the original and the abridged circulate around the world. At least one book seller, Isaiah Thomas, is sent to prison for selling the book in London in 1762. Cleland never makes much money off the book, but the publisher does well. Occasionally book sellers are fined for selling copies.

The State of Massachusetts picks up the legal saga of *Fanny Hill* in 1819. After publishing the full original text with accompanying illustrations, Peter Holmes is convicted for publishing a "lewd and obscene"[9] book and sent to jail, fined $300, ordered to pay court costs of $75.53, and required to post a bond of $500 against future misbehavior. This is the first American case that involves a book alleged to be too obscene to be published.

Holmes appeals and upon review the Massachusetts court condemns the book. First, the book by design, according to the published opinion, aims to "debauch and corrupt the morals of youth as well as other good citizens."[10] Second, the scandalous nature of the book and its illustrations are a disruption to the peace. The court views the purpose of the book to be "to raise and create in their minds inordinate and lustful desires."[11] Finally, Massachusetts' Chief Justice Isaac Parker writes in his opinion that publisher Holmes is "an evil and scandalous disposed" individual.[12] In 1821, the state officially bans the book.

Changing Views of Obscenity

Over time, United States Supreme Court cases, in the name of the First Amendment's protection of free speech, reduce the ability of states to criminalize sexually explicit material. The First Amendment does not permit anyone to say or write absolutely anything. However, the process of defining the boundaries of the First Amendment in *obscenity* cases has been in progress in the American courts since 1821 when *Fanny Hill* was banned.

The Comstock Act, a federal statute passed by the U.S. Congress in 1873 as an "Act of the Suppression of Trade in, and Circulation of, Obscene Literature and Articles of Immoral Use,"[13] attempts to put boundaries on sex-related material. In what may seem odd to modern eyes, the Act criminalized not only lewd material but also material concerning "unlawful" abortion or contraception, viewing these issues as closely related. A person convicted under the Comstock Act could receive up to five years of imprisonment with hard labor.

Still, what was or was not obscene remained elusive. For example, in 1894, a popular dancer became the first woman to appear in a film.[14] The 21-second film shows her dancing and her swaying skirt rides up just enough to reveal her stocking-covered ankle. The film was quickly banned.

One might take the laissez-faire view that people ought to be able to have access to anything their personal interests desire. However, it does seem clear that there are some broader societal interests at stake. First, a complete absence of limits could create societal harms beyond simply coarsening sensibilities. To the extent that exposure to certain kinds of images promotes or supports real-world victimizations, one can make a case for prohibiting such images. (The next chapter, concerning child pornography, explores this point further.)

But one can also argue that obscene material can have a societal cost even if its distribution of images does not itself directly prompt real-world victimizations. For example, many feminists have argued that the availability of female depictions in pornography degrades women generally and contributes to the larger societal problem of gender discrimination.[15]

Yet, to criminalize the publication of any text or image also has larger societal costs, in reducing individual liberty and in giving government a dangerous power to intrude in people's lives. Thus is born the difficult balancing act in defining the bounds of criminal obscenity. Consider how more modern American criminal law strikes the balance of interests in defining the crime of obscenity.

Larry Flynt and *Hustler* Magazine – 1976

Magoffin County, Kentucky is among the poorest counties in the nation throughout the Great Depression and things have not improved much by the time Larry Claxton Flynt is born in 1942.[16] But as an adult Flynt is able to dramatically improve his situation when he opens a series of nightclubs featuring scantily clad women dancers. To promote his clubs, he begins publishing racy mailers. In 1972, he expands the newsletter to 16 pages, and by August of the next year to 32 pages. In 1973, however, the nation enters an oil crisis-induced recession, his patrons lose disposable income, and his nightclubs begin losing money.

Flynt notes that the newsletter remains quite popular, however, and concludes that there is a market demand that is going unmet. He envisions a national magazine, and *Hustler* magazine is born. Hugh Hefner's *Playboy* has photographs of flawless women

Figure 24.2 **Larry Flynt, in a golden wheel chair, with his brother Jimmy**

and articles that speak to topics other than sex. *Penthouse* magazine specializes in artistic photography and a fantasy life. Flynt wants something new, more raw, something his blue-collar customers will want. He makes no pretense at art or elitism. Flynt says, "I'd rather have ten truck drivers reading Hustler than one college professor."[17] Already in debt, Flynt gambles on a potentially ruinous funding strategy – he pays the start-up costs for his new *Hustler magazine* by not paying the sales tax that his clubs owe the state of Ohio.

The first issue arrives on newsstands in July 1974. By November, the magazine begins to stake out its bolder stance and publishes "pink shots"[18] (photos of open vulvas), which is a strong indication that *Hustler* is a significant departure from its competitors. But the magazine continues to struggle until a paparazzi offers Flynt pictures of former first-lady Jackie Kennedy Onassis sunbathing nude for $18,000. When the photographs appear in the August 1975 issue, *Hustler* is saved from bankruptcy and launched as a national magazine. One million copies of the Onassis issue are sold within the first few days of its release. Flynt, a newly minted millionaire, buys an expensive mansion.

A *Washington Post* writer explains the *Hustler* difference:

> If dirty-minded teen-age boys were left to commit their nastiest fantasies to four-color paper, the pages they produced would look like the milder passages from Hustler; here was a publication that brought pornography to the liquor store newsstands without benefit of airbrush or gauzy lens.[19]

Flynt's vision for the magazine is more than pornography. Its sensation lies in its discard of social taboos. If the former first-lady is not off-limits, what is? *Hustler* pushes up against every social norm the publisher can conceive of. Disabled women? Sure. Pregnant women? Of course. The elderly? Why not?

Flynt is first prosecuted on *obscenity* charges in 1976. As the date of the trial draws near, Flynt prepares a pamphlet showing graphic photographs of mutilated soldiers in Viet Nam. The pamphlet along with a questionnaire is mailed to 4,000 Cincinnati residents. The recipients are asked to view the photographs and then decide if anything in *Hustler* rivals these images for true obscenity. Flynt promises that if the people of Cincinnati feel that his work is in fact the more obscene, he will plead guilty. New charges are now filed against Flynt and *Hustler* for disseminating material that is harmful to juveniles. Flynt is convicted and sentenced to 7–25 years in jail, but only serves six days because the sentence is overturned, because of prosecutorial misconduct.

Hustler is as political as it is sexual. Political cartoons, which could never appear in ordinary magazines, are ordinary in *Hustler*. Flynt explains that *Hustler* is so often prosecuted because "We are a political journal as well as a sex publication. And believe me, politics is what gets us in trouble, not pornography."[20]

When various press pieces vent their disgust by opining that Flynt might as well depict women hung up like slabs of meat (in fact some of the cartoons in the magazine do just that), Flynt goes one step further. The June 1978 issue depicts the legs of a woman whose torso appears to be being fed into a meat-grinder. The resulting uproar brings *Hustler* a tsunami of publicity, and sales surge.

Flynt, by his own admission, has never actually read the Constitution or the First Amendment before his court cases force him to. Upon doing so, he "discovered that the Founding Fathers did not equivocate when it came to matters of speech and free choice."[21] With ever-increasing focus, Flynt uses *Hustler* as a vehicle to push the public understanding of what is protected under the First Amendment by "treating sacred cows irreverently and contemptuously—in order to make a point."[22] The underlying theme seems to be if someone is not offended, then that issue of the magazine has been a failure.

In 1978, as Flynt leaves the court from yet another lawsuit, he and his attorney are shot by a sniper. Flynt is struck "three times in the stomach with a.44-Magnum rifle, permanently paralyzed and given less than a 1% chance to survive."[23] The trial against him is declared a mistrial and the charges dropped. He beats the odds and survives but the pain is debilitating, and Flynt soon becomes heavily dependent on drugs. It is subsequently determined that the sniper was outraged because Flynt's magazine portrayed interracial couples.

Obscenity Offenses in the States

The contrast between what is criminalized in *Fanny Hill* and what is tolerated in *Hustler* shows the dramatic shift in legal standards, a shift that mirrors dramatic changes in societal norms. The innuendo in *Fanny Hill* produces outrage while the explicit nudity of *Playboy* and *Penthouse* is accepted as near mainstream. Even the intended-to-shock *Hustler* probably produces a limited reaction today, in light of what is available on the internet.

Supreme Court caselaw has long made clear that the free-speech protections of the First Amendment do not apply to *obscenity*.[24] Exactly what "obscenity" is, however, is harder to pin down. The most famous expression of the indeterminacy of the category came from Justice Potter Stewart, who took the view that the Constitution does not protect "hard-core pornography" but was unable to further define that term except to say, "I know it when I see it."[25] In the 1973 case of *Miller v. California*, the Court articulated three criteria for assessing whether material is obscene:

a. whether "the average person, applying contemporary community standards" would find that the work, taken as a whole, appeals to the prurient interest . . . ;
b. whether the work depicts or describes, in a patently offensive way, sexual conduct specifically defined by the applicable state law; and
c. whether the work, taken as a whole, lacks serious literary, artistic, political, or scientific value.[26]

Most states banning promotion or distribution of obscene material define obscenity to include at least the first and third elements of the *Miller* criteria: the material must appeal to people's *prurient interest*, and it must lack "serious literary, artistic, political, or scientific value." States differ, however, in their inclusion of the second criterion: that the material must be "patently offensive." Additionally, a number of states have extended their obscenity offenses to cover so-called obscene "devices."

Under today's standards, there is no possibility that a publisher of *Fanny Hill* could be successfully prosecuted. Based on modern sensibilities, the book is hardly likely to qualify as being "patently offensive" and, even if it does appeal to people's "prurient interest," many will argue that it does have some "literary, artistic, [or] political" value.

The fact that *Playboy* and *Penthouse* make a special effort to include articles of political or artistic interest, as well as a style of photography that seeks to be artistic, serves to at least create some ambiguity as to whether the third factor is satisfied ("lacks serious literary, artistic, political, or scientific value"). By explicitly rejecting the approach of these magazines, *Hustler* left itself more open to a finding of obscenity.

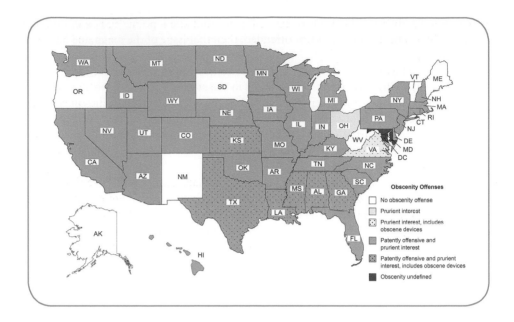

Obscenity Offenses

☐ No obscenity offense
☐ Prurient interest
⣿ Prurient interest, includes obscene devices
▨ Patently offensive and prurient interest
▨ Patently offensive and prurient interest, includes obscene devices
■ Obscenity undefined

Figure 24.3

But notice that Flynt soon rebranded his magazine as having a mission of challenging orthodoxy, giving it a political patina.

The different approaches to obscenity adopted by different states are presented in the map above.[27] Seven jurisdictions, those with no shading on the map, have no obscenity offense – that is, no statute that would criminalize the promotion, distribution, or display of obscene material to consenting adults. The one jurisdiction with light shading on the map, Ohio (the birthplace of *Hustler*), defines obscenity as material that appeals to the *prurient interest* and "lacks serious . . . value," and does not include the other element of *Miller*, requiring that the matter be "patently offensive." This then is the broadest definition of obscenity in the country, which should make it easiest for a successful prosecution. Perhaps it is no surprise then that the sole prosecutorial success against Larry Flynt was in Cincinnati (but recall that it was quickly overturned).

Thirty-four jurisdictions, those shown with medium shading on the map, define obscenity to follow the Supreme Court's language in *Miller*, which includes material that appeals to the "prurient interest" and that portrays sexual conduct in a "patently offensive" way. Six additional states, those with medium shading and dots, take the same approach to defining obscenity but go further to also criminalize the sale of obscene devices.

What may be most interesting about the diversity among the states and their definitions of "obscenity" is that these differences are as a practical matter legally irrelevant. Under the 1973 *Miller* Supreme Court opinion, states may not criminalize obscene speech unless it satisfies all three parts of the *Miller* test.

While societal views on pornography have changed dramatically in recent decades, unlike adultery, discussed in the previous chapter, obscenity laws remain relevant today and are occasionally enforced, despite evidence that a substantial share of Americans consume obscene material in the form of internet pornography.[28] While the prosecution rate is not high, since 2003, federal and state authorities have brought charges in dozens of cases, often resulting in serious penalties.[29] For instance, in 2008, Paul Little was convicted of ten counts of violating federal obscenity statutes, leading to a 46-month prison sentence.[30] In 2006, Ronald Crump was convicted of three counts of promoting obscenity, resulting in a three-year prison sentence (that was ultimately suspended).[31] And Beatrice Villarreal received a six-month prison sentence for violating the state's statute prohibiting the sale of obscene devices, arising out of her 2004 sale of a vibrating dildo to an undercover police officer.[32] In nearly every case where convictions are challenged, courts have upheld the statutes as constitutional.[33]

At a time when Americans' moral views are perhaps more permissive than ever,[34] what accounts for the survival of obscenity statutes? Some argue in favor of continuing criminalization on the view that consumption of obscene material is harmful to individuals and to society.[35] And there are certainly legal academics who argue that adult pornography may be harmful to women or exploitative, and thus a proper subject of the criminal law.[36] However, the continued existence of criminal obscenity statutes, even if only occasionally enforced, may reflect a concern that affirmatively decriminalizing obscenity would be taken as sending the wrong message. Like adultery in the previous chapter, the offense stands as a moral wish rather than a true criminal prohibition, with all the complications that such an unenforced symbolic statute brings.

Should Criminal Law Be in the Morality Enforcement Business?

The attempts to criminalize obscenity and, in the previous chapter, adultery are likely to provoke some people to warn against using the criminal law as a mechanism to enforce morality. And, of course, obscenity and adultery are just two examples in a larger pattern of what we now see as inappropriate criminalizations. Recall the seriousness of blasphemy as an offense in Marquis de Sade case (Chapter 6) and the criminalization of same-sex intercourse in Oscar Wilde's case (Chapter 22).

But a different view of these cases suggests that the lesson to be learned is not that criminal law should avoid being in the norm enforcement business but rather that it should be careful to keep up with changing norms. For example, would we all be happy with a society in which the law decriminalized exhibitionist defecation,[37] sexual intercourse, or masturbation in public? Or what about cruelty to animals, bestiality, abuse of corpse, or necrophilia in private? It seems likely that people would be offended by a criminal law condones or tolerates such conduct.

Those who oppose the notion of criminal law being used for morality enforcement commonly will insist that criminalization be limited to instances of real societal harm (other than norm violation). Where there seems to be broad support for criminalization that might be seen as norm enforcement, they are likely to provide a societal harm explanation for criminalizing the offense. For example, we criminalize consensual adult incest because of the increased chances of genetic defects in offspring. But then why doesn't the incest prohibition exclude cases where a condom is used or where the woman is past child-bearing age? Similarly, exhibitionist public defecation might be justified on public health grounds. But then why isn't the offense formulated to simply require that you pick up your feces, as we require with dog defecation?

Further, what kind of societal harms can one identify in the prohibition against public sexual intercourse? It seems difficult to explain the prohibition in any terms other than by the fact that viewers would find such conduct shocking and offensive, especially because they had not consented to it by entering a sex shop or strip club. In other words, there are a wide variety of offenses for which it is hard to deny that the only apparent justification is the community shared judgment that it is condemnable conduct, a gross violation of existing norms. We are disgusted by cruelty to animals and necrophilia, and that in itself is accepted as adequate for criminalization.

Is there some principled basis on which criminal law can justify being in the morality enforcement business? Recall the discussion in Chapter 2 of punishment theory and alternative distributive principles for criminal liability and punishment. The utilitarian crime-control distributive principles of general deterrence and incapacitation of the dangerous have little or nothing to say about what a society decides what to criminalize. They assume that some other source will provide the criminalization conclusions, which they will then work to avoid. Deontological desert might well generate reasoned justifications for criminalizing conduct that the community found abhorrent.[38] But perhaps most compelling would be empirical desert as a distributive principle, which would set criminalization rules so as to maximize the criminal law's moral credibility with the community. Obviously, failing to criminalize conduct that the community saw as appalling, be it cruelty to animals, exhibitionist public defecation, or necrophilia, could not help but seriously undermine the criminal law's moral credibility, and thereby its crime-control effectiveness.

In other words, if criminal law failed to criminalize such appalling conduct, wouldn't citizens be justifiably suspicious about the criminal law as a reliable moral authority? If the criminal law is so obviously wrong when it fails to condemn these clearly condemnable conducts, isn't it logical to assume that the law is also wrong about other criminalization judgments? This citizen may conclude: I need to make my own judgments about what is and is not condemnable, not internalize the criminal law's judgments. And there is lost one of criminal law's most powerful sources for gaining compliance, acquiescence, assistance, and internalization of norms. The criminal law that loses its reputation as a reliable moral authority is more likely to provoke resistance, subversion, and vigilantism.

Should the criminal law be in the morality enforcement business? Yes. But it also needs to be careful to accurately reflect shared community norms, and to keep up with changing norms. If the community dramatically shifts its views on the propriety of same-sex intercourse, the criminal law must follow that lead, and promptly. To fail to do so is to invite the same kind of damage to its moral credibility that can come from failing to criminalize clearly condemnable conduct.

Aftermaths

John Cleland finds the trouble surrounding *Fanny Hill* too costly to repeat and for the remainder of his career he writes nothing scandalous and nothing good. He dies unmarried and bitter, blaming his mother, who declined to support him, for his troubles.

Larry Flynt remains in litigations for years. In 1976, Bob Guccione, the publisher of *Penthouse* magazine, and his girlfriend, Kathy Keeton, file a libel suit against Flynt for printing cartoons about the pair. Flynt loses to the tune of $39.6 million but the judgment is reversed on appeal. Keeton then attempts to separate her suit from that of Guccione and her case makes it to the Supreme Court in 1983. A drug-addled pain-ridden Flynt is now facing the highest court in the land and he decides he will do it without legal representation.

The court appoints an attorney over Flynt's objections and Flynt himself is not permitted to speak. As the court adjourns, Flynt shouts from the audience: "You're nothing but eight assholes and a token cunt!"[39] He is arrested on the spot for contempt.

Within a few hours, Flynt is arraigned, now wearing a T-shirt that reads "Fuck this Court." He is told to remove the shirt but refuses. Flynt posts bail and returns home. When he makes it known that he will be "subpoenaing all the Supreme Court justices,"[40] the charges are dropped. Again, the media outlets report it all and *Hustler*'s sales grow. Many of his legal battles are against family members. He disinherits his daughter and sues a couple of nephews. A 1996 semi-biographical movie, *The People vs. Larry Flynt*, casts the real-life Flynt as an Ohio judge in the film. Flynt dies in California in 2021.

Chapter Glossary

Obscenity: A comprehensive, legal definition of this offense has been difficult to establish, yet key components of the definition have been provided by the courts. Obscenity is commonly defined by federal and state courts using a tripartite standard established by *Miller v. California*. The *Miller* test for obscenity considers: (1) whether the average person applying contemporary community standards would find that the work, taken as a whole, appeals to prurient interest, (2) whether the work depicts or describes, in a patently offensive way, sexual conduct specifically defined by the applicable state law, and (3) whether the work, taken as a whole, lacks serious literary, artistic, political, or scientific value.[41]

Prurient Interest: A shameful or morbid interest in nudity, sex, or excretion, which goes substantially beyond customary limits of candor in description or representation of such matters.[42]

Notes

1. This portion of the narrative is drawn from the following sources: Wayne C. Bartee and Alice F. Bartee, *Litigating Morality: American Legal thought and Its English Roots* (Santa Barbara: Praeger Publishing, 1992); John Cleland, *Memoirs of Fanny Hill* (Ware: Wordsworth Editions, n.d.); Mike Rendell, 'And Did the Earth Move for Fanny Hill? An Earthquake, February 8th, 1750', *Georgian Gentleman*, 8 February 2012, http://mikerendell.com/and-did-the-earth-move-for-fanny-hill-an-earthquake-february-8th-1750/; John E. Semonche, *Censoring Sex: A Historical Journey through American Media* (Lanham: Roman and Littlefield, 2007); Dawn B. Sova, *Literature Suppressed on Sexual Grounds* (New York: Facts on File, 1998); Sheryl Straight, *Memoirs of a Woman of Pleasure* (London: The Strand, 2003).
2. Cleland, *Memoirs of Fanny Hill*.
3. Cleland, *Memoirs of Fanny Hill*.
4. Cleland, *Memoirs of Fanny Hill*.
5. Cleland, *Memoirs of Fanny Hill*.
6. Cleland, *Memoirs of Fanny Hill*.

7. Straight, *Memoirs of a Woman of Pleasure*.

8. Thomas Sherlock, 'Letter to the Duke of Newcastle', *Secretary of State*, 15 March 1750.

9. Paul E. Pfeifer, 'June 6, 2001: The Trials of Fanny Hill', *The Supreme Court of Ohio & The Ohio Judicial System*, 6 June 2001, https://www.supremecourt.ohio.gov/SCO/justices/pfeifer/column/2001/jp060601.asp

10. Sova, *Literature Suppressed on Sexual Grounds*, p. 68.

11. Sova, *Literature Suppressed on Sexual Grounds*, p. 68.

12. Sova, *Literature Suppressed on Sexual Grounds*, p. 68.

13. The Editors of Encyclopaedia Britannica, Comstock Act, 5 April 2019, https://www.britannica.com/event/Comstock-Act.

14. Olivia Waxman, 'This Is What Americans Used to Consider Obscene', *Time Magazine*, 21 June 2016, https://time.com/4373765/history-obscenity-united-states-films-miller-ulysses-roth/.

15. *See, e.g.,* Catherine MacKinnon, 'Pornography, Civil Rights, and Speech', *Harvard Civil Rights-Civil Liberties Law Review 20* (1985): pp. 1, 18 (arguing that pornography 'sexualizes inequality' and 'institutionalizes the sexuality of male supremacy,' and as such should be carefully regulated through a kind of obscenity statute).

16. This portion of the narrative is drawn from the following sources: Heather Drain, 'Shocking Pink: 'Back Issues: The Hustler Magazine Story," *Dangerous Minds*, 21 May 2014, http://dangerousminds.net/comments/shocking_pink_back_issues_the_hustler_magazine_story; Larry Flynt, *An Unseemly Man: My Life as a Pornographer, Pundit, and Social Outcast* (Los Angeles: Dove Books, 1996); Tonya Flynt-Vega, *Hustled: My Journey from Fear to Faith* (Louisville: Westminster John Knox Press, 1998); Dave Ghose, 'Flynt Family Values', *Morning Cincinnati,* 1 February 2013, http://www.cincinnatimagazine.com/features/flynt-family-values1/; Cynthia Gorney, 'The Brief, Hot Flame of Althea Flynt', *The Washington Post*, 6 July 1987, https://www.washingtonpost.com/archive/lifestyle/1987/07/06/the-brief-hot-flame-of-althea-flynt/-695cf27e-fd49-447b-a019-e420ebffbcb5/?utm_term=.bb08ac2b4d50; *Hustler Magazine, Inc. v. Falwell,* 485 U. S. 46, No. 86-1278, 2 December 1987, https://www.law.cornell.edu/supremecourt/text/485/46; 'Larry Flynt', *Biography.com*, https://www.biography.com/people/larry-flynt-9542114; Douglas O. Linder, 'Plaintiff's Trial Exhibit', *Famous Trial*, http://famous-trials.com/falwell/1781-exhibit.

17. Drain, 'Shocking Pink.'

18. Flynt, *An Unseemly Man*.

19. Gorney, 'The Brief, Hot Flame.'

20. Linder, 'Plaintiff's Trial Exhibit.'

21. Flynt, *An Unseemly Man*.

22. Linder, 'Plaintiff's Trial Exhibit.'

23. Linder, 'Plaintiff's Trial Exhibit.'

24. *See, e.g., Roth v. United States*, 354 U.S. 476 (1957); *Chaplinsky v. New Hampshire*, 315 U.S. 568, 571–572 (1942); see generally Paul H. Robinson and Michael T. Cahill, *Criminal Law*, 2nd ed. (New York: Wolters Kluwer, 2016) pp. 505–507. Note that mere private possession of obscene matters cannot constitutionally be criminalized. *See Stanley v. Georgia*, 394 U.S. 557, 559, 89 S. Ct. 1243, 1245, 22 L. Ed. 2d 542 (1969).

25. *Jacobellis v. Ohio*, 378 U.S. 184, 197 (1964) (Stewart, J., concurring).

26. *Miller v. California*, 413 U.S. 15, 24–25 (1973) (internal citations omitted).

27. The map is taken from Paul H. Robinson and Tyler Scot Williams, 'Criminal Obscenity', in *Mapping American Criminal Law: Variations across the 50 States* (Westport: Prager, 2018), p. 253. All supporting authorities are available from that source.

28. *See* Mark Regnerus et al., 'Documenting Pornography Use in America: A Comparative Analysis of Methodological Approaches'. *Journal of Sex Research 53* (2015): p. 873 (finding that 46% of American men and 16% of American women between the ages of 18 and 39 intentionally viewed pornography in a given week). Cf. Cody Harper and David C. Hodgins, 'Examining Correlates of Problematic Internet Pornography Use among University Students'. *Journal of Behavior Addiction 5* (2016): p. 179 (finding, in a study of university students in Calgary, Canada, that only 5% of male students indicated that they did not "use [Internet pornography] for masturbation at all").

29. In Kinsley, *supra*, the author documents at least 25 state prosecutions of obscenity violations across at least seven jurisdictions since 2003. *See* Kinsley, *supra*, at 615–638. "[O]bscenity prosecutions are still very much occurring on both the federal and state levels." Kinsley at 615.

30. *See United States v. Little*, 365 F. App'x 159, 161 (11th Cir. 2010).

31. *See State v. Crump*, 223 S.W.3d 915, 915 (Mo. Ct. App. 2007).

32. *See Villarreal v. State*, 267 S.W.3d 204, 206 (Tex. App. 2008).

33. *See, e.g.*, Ex parte Dave, 220 S.W.3d 154 (Tex. App. 2007); *Varkonyi v. State*, 276 S.W.3d 27 (Tex. App. 2008); *Williams v. Morgan*, 478 F.3d 1316, 1323 (11th Cir. 2007); *1568 Montgomery Highway, Inc. v. City of Hoover*, 45 So. 3d 319 (Ala. 2010); *United States v. Little*, 365 F. App'x 159, 161 (11th Cir. 2010); *State v. Crump*, 223 S.W.3d 915, 915 (Mo. Ct. App. 2007); *Villarreal v. State*, 267 S.W.3d 204, 206 (Tex. App. 2008).

34. Jeffrey M. Jones, Americans Hold Record Liberal Views on Most Moral Issues, Gallup.com (May 11, 2017), http://www.gallup.com/poll/210542/americans-hold-record-liberal-views-moral-issues.aspx.

35. For instance, in a law review article encouraging prosecution of obscenity, U.S. Senator Orrin G. Hatch argues that obscenity, including hard-core pornography, is damaging to individuals and communities. Citing studies over the last three decades, Hatch argues that some pornography is associated with aggressive behavior toward women as well as other social maladies, such as violence. *See* Orrin G. Hatch, 'Fighting the Pornification of America by Enforcing Obscenity Laws', *Stanford Law & Policy Review 23* (2012): pp. 1, 17.

36. *See supra* note 24.

37. One can imagine cases of public defecation, for example by homeless persons, where a lesser evils defense is available or the conduct is essentially not voluntary. The focus here is on "exhibitionist" cases where people do it to shock or annoy, or just out of indifference to other people's sensibilities.

38. For example, John Rawls' decision-making in the original position under a veil of ignorance might well lead to a principle that criminalizes conduct that the community broadly holds to be outrageous and seriously condemnable.

39. William Turner, 'Larry Flynt', in *Figures of Speech: First Amendment Heroes and Villains* (Oakland: Berrett-Koehler Publishers, 2011), p. 133.

40. Flynt, *An Unseemly Man*, pp. 166, 195.

41. *Obscenity*, Legal Information Institute, https://www.law.cornell.edu/wex/obscenity.

42. *Prurient Interest*, Law Insider, https://www.lawinsider.com/dictionary/prurient-interest.

Chapter 25

Child Pornography

Lewis Carroll Photographs Alice in Wonderland

1859. Construction of the Suez Canal begins, and continues for ten years, shortening the trip between Europe and South Asia by 4,300 miles. In large part a result of his six years of travels as a naturalist on the British ship HMS Beagle, Charles Darwin publishes his book *On the Origin of Species*, which offers compelling evidence in support of the theory of evolution. In Pennsylvania, the world's first oil well is drilled. After several decades of development, photographic technology has finally gotten to a point where it can be a practical hobby and becomes a fashionable pursuit for the artistically inclined.

Lewis Carroll – 1859

Lewis Carroll is born Charles Lutwidge Dodgson on January 27, 1832, in the sprawling fertile hills of Daresbury, Cheshire, England, to a stern but well-respected parish priest and his wife.[1] He displays an uncanny aptitude for math and logic; one esteemed mathematician declares he's "not had a more promising boy" for a student.[2] As a young adult, Dodson enrolls in Christ Church College at Oxford, receiving degrees in classical moderations and mathematics in only two years. Oxford offers him a studentship position, promising him income, residence, and a track to full priesthood. While he accepts the offer and stays for 37 years, he is never ordained.

He becomes a respected mathematician, eventually publishing several books on geometry, algebra, logic, and more. By the mid-1850s, he's establishing himself in the pre-Raphaelite circle, a community of artists and writers. In 1856, he publishes his first work under the pen-name Lewis Carroll, marking the start of a new era in Dodgson's life.

Dodgson's professional life flourishes, and his mind stays playful and young. As an adult, he seeks the company of children, usually those of his peers and admirers. Dodgson feels particularly comfortable with young girls; as he once famously said,

DOI: 10.4324/9781003258025-28

"I am fond of children except boys."[3] His friendships often begin with "chance meeting[s] on the sea-shore, in the street, at some friend's house," which "led to conversation; then followed a call on the parents."[4] From here they progress to "all sorts of kindnesses, presents of books, invitations to stay with him at Oxford" and "visits with him to the theatre."[5] He's particularly fond of the three daughters of one of his colleagues, the Dean of Christ Church, Henry Liddell. Liddell's daughters, named Lorina, Edith, and Alice, are all young brunettes with charming personalities. Dodgson is especially drawn to Alice. She's spunky and opinionated, possessing a self-assurance that Dodgson loves. It's Alice Liddell that inspires *Alice's Adventures in Wonderland,* the work that launches Dodgson's career as a writer.

Dodgson's artistic ability is not confined to writing. In the mid-1850s, he enthusiastically takes up the new art of photography, drawn in particular to its demand for exquisite, almost mathematical precision. Over a 24-year period, he takes thousands of beautiful, haunting photographs. His subjects are most often people, although he also photographs "landscapes, dolls, dogs, statues, paintings, trees, and even skeletons."[6] Fewer than 1,000 of his photographs have survived, as photographs taken during this time period decay significantly over time.

Dodgson's best-liked subjects for photography are, perhaps unsurprisingly, young girls, usually between the ages of 10 and 15, which make up over half of his surviving portfolio. The majority of the photographs depict girls engaged in ordinary activities but many of them depict nude or semi-nude girls – some lying down and some in erotic poses. Dodgson has many of the photographs professionally colored, such that they look more like idyllic paintings than they do photographs. In one, believed to have been taken in 1859, young Alice, at age eight, in Dodgson's lap, crawling, catlike, upward. Her hand lies lightly on his cheek and she is a breath away from kissing his mouth. With modern sensibilities, it is difficult to see such a photograph without concern.

Another photograph – reproduced below – that seems to invite modern concern depicts Alice's eldest sister Lorina, completely nude. She faces the camera directly, such that her entire body is exposed to the viewer. (Some evidence of modern sensibilities is reflected in the fact that, although the untouched version of this photograph was generally available on history, art, and literature websites when we began work on this book, the publisher has chosen to blackout parts of the photo.)

Nude children appear in many photographs from the time and they are often truly innocent. Moreover, Victorian society does not look unfavorably on a man's interest in young girls. As one scholar, Nicholas Shrimpton, explains in the documentary *The Secret World of Lewis Carroll,*

> It seemed fine for a bachelor to spend his time with little girls, but very questionable for him to spend his time with sexually adult young women. And so, [Dodgson's first biographer] slightly twisted the evidence to make them younger, with very odd consequences, of course, for Carroll's subsequent reputation, since we now take precisely the opposite view.[7]

Some evidence reinforces the notion that Dodgson's interest in children might have been less than wholesome. The middle-aged math teacher asks both Alice and other young girls for locks of their hair, and he later writes to one of the girls, "Extra thanks and kisses for the lock of hair. I have kissed it several times – for want of having you to kiss, you know, even hair is better than nothing."[8] He writes to artist Gertrude Thompson, a contemporary who sketches fairy girls, "I confess I do not admire naked

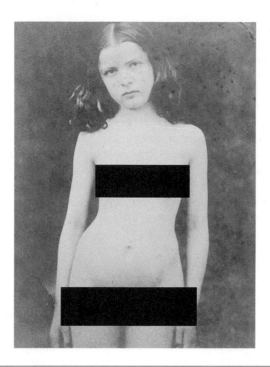

Figure 25.1 Portrait of Lorina Liddell, sister of Alice, circa 1859–1860

boys in pictures. They always seem . . . to need clothes, whereas one hardly sees why the lovely forms of girls should ever be covered up."[9] He meets hundreds of little girls on his outings, and he always carries games and puzzles in his pockets. While there's no evidence that Dodgson does anything more than photograph and befriend little girls, his behavior would certainly raise a few eyebrows today.[10]

Child Pornography

Societal views of creating images of naked children, especially sexually suggestive ones, have changed dramatically. The shift has been the exact opposite of the increasing acceptance of adult pornography. No state is prosecuting *Playboy* centerfolds for their choice to appear naked in a national magazine. The models have the right to participate in business transactions that include nudity. Legally, children do not have the capacity to give meaningful consent, however, which means that a picture of a naked adult is a choice, but a similar picture of a child can be a form of exploitation. Adult pornography is now largely protected by the First Amendment, as discussed in the previous chapter, while images of nude children are increasingly seen as akin to serious offenses such as assault and punished by increasingly harsh sentences.[11]

When all pornography is seen as morally wrong, there is little reason to distinguish adult from child pornography. But as the criminalization of adult pornography recedes, special child pornography offenses must be enacted in order to continue its criminalization, and to enhance it. In 1977, Congress steps in with the Protection of Children against Sexual Exploitation Act. In 1982, in *New York v. Ferber*, the court concludes that children require blanket protection: "the evil to be restricted so overwhelmingly outweighs the expressive interests, if any, at stake, that no process of case-by-case adjudication is required."[12] *Ferber* agrees that to effectively protect children it may be necessary to prohibit the exhibition and dissemination of the pornographic materials that contain images of children.[13] In fulfilling these goals, legislation continues to struggle to keep up with the many ways in which creative offenders and ever-advancing technology can help child pornographers avoid capture and successful prosecution.

However, as we have seen in other instances of legal reform riding the wave of popular indignation, it is often easy for the new legislation to go too far. Consider, for example, this modern case.

Cormega Copening – 2015

Cormega Copening is a junior at Douglas Byrd High School in Fayetteville, North Carolina. Things are going well for Copening. He is well respected as a football player and has a girlfriend, Brianna Denson.[14]

In October 2014, several students at the school come under investigation for sexual interactions between a 14-year-old girl and a group of older teenage boys. Soon the Cumberland County Sheriff's Office takes over what becomes a rape investigation. Police officers question the suspected students, search their lockers, and look through their cell phones.

Figure 25.2 Copening prior to his arrest, circa 2014

Copening is not a suspect in the rape but the police believe he has received photos of the encounter on his phone. With permission from Copening's mother, the police examine his phone. There are no photos of the crime, but police do find consensually taken nude photos of Copening and of his girlfriend, who is his age, 16. There are pictures of genitals and pictures with the teens together without clothing. The police charge the high school junior with five felony counts of sexually exploiting a minor: two for taking nude selfies, two for sending them to his girlfriend, and one for

Disseminating harmful material to minors

(a) Disseminating Harmful Material. - A person commits the offense of disseminating harmful material to minors if, with or without consideration and knowing the character or content of the material, he:

    (1) Sells, furnishes, presents, or distributes to a minor material that is harmful to minors; or

    (2) Allows a minor to review or peruse material that is harmful to minors.

Definitions. Harmful to Minors. - That quality of any material or performance that depicts sexually explicit nudity or sexual activity and that, taken as a whole, has the following characteristics:

    a. The average adult person applying contemporary community standards would find that the material or performance has a predominant tendency to appeal to a prurient interest of minors in sex; and

    b. The average adult person applying contemporary community standards would find that the depiction of sexually explicit nudity or sexual activity in the material or performance is patently offensive to prevailing standards in the adult community concerning what is suitable for minors; and

    c. The material or performance lacks serious literary, artistic, political, or scientific value for minors.

North Carolina Gen. Stat. §§14-190.13, .15

Figure 25.3

possession of an explicit photo of his girlfriend. She is also charged for exchanging nude photos with Copening, though she faces only two felony counts: one for taking a nude selfie and another for sending it to Copening.

Under North Carolina law (reproduced in the margin), copying or distributing any sort of child pornography is a felony. The law is designed primarily to protect children from sexual exploitation by adults but can also by its terms apply to children who consensually make and send nude photos to one another. (Recall from Chapter 15, discussing immaturity, that many states allow the adult prosecution of 16-year-olds for serious offenses.)

Twenty states have enacted legislation, often called Romeo and Juliet laws, to prevent child pornography laws from being used against teenagers who exchange sexually explicit content as a couple or at least with consent. However, 30 states – including North Carolina – have no such exception.[15]

The case makes headlines across the globe, most of them sympathetic to Copening and his girlfriend and critical of America's laws on child pornography as going too far.

Protected-Age Diversity among the States

The *Lewis Carroll* case and the *Copening* case show how dramatically norms can change and how criminal law commonly changes with those norms. As noted, however, in this instance the shift is toward criminalization compared to the shift toward practical decriminalization of adult pornography and adultery.

All 51 American jurisdictions categorize the possession, distribution, or production of child pornography as a serious crime. To qualify for the offense, the material typically must depict a minor engaged in sexual conduct or must contain a "lewd" exhibition or depiction of the genitals or female breasts of the minor "for purposes of

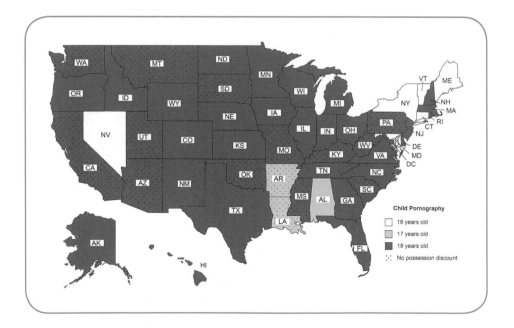

Figure 25.4

sexual stimulation of the viewer."[16] (Note that an image does not have to satisfy the legal definition of obscenity to qualify as child pornography.[17]) It seems possible that Lewis Carroll's 1859 photographs of the Lindell daughters could satisfy this requirement and leave him open to prosecution for producing, distributing, and possessing child pornography.

The most significant distinctions among the states concern two issues. First, states adopt different views on how young the subject child must be to trigger the child pornography offense. As the map below shows, 16, 17, and 18 are all common age cutoffs. The darker the shade on the map, the higher the age and thus the broader the reach of the offense.

A second distinction among the states is whether mere possession of material is to be punished the same as its production or distribution. The states *with* a dots overlay take the more aggressive approach of punishing possession just as seriously as distribution.[18]

The narrowest formulation of the offense exists in the six states with light shading on the map, indicating that they use 16 as the cutoff age. Even under this narrowest formulation, Lewis Carroll is likely to fall within the scope of the offense for his production, distribution, and possession of his nude photographs of the Lindell daughters, all of whom are under 16.

The states with the darkest shading on the map, the vast majority of states, have the broadest offense by including in it any subject who is less than 18. North Carolina, the state in which Cormega Copening and his girlfriend are prosecuted, is in this group and, both youths, being 16, fall within the terms of the statute (reproduced in the margin).[19]

Most states treat mere possession of child pornography as a less serious offense than the offenses of production or distribution. But 15 states, those *with* an overlay of dots, do not make this distinction, so mere possession will result in the same punishment as the lowest level offense for production or distribution.

Does Child Pornography Justify the Serious Treatment It Is Given Today?

Does child pornography justify this serious treatment, especially the serious penalties for mere possession of such material? Multiple rationales can be offered. The most obvious is that producing material is objectionable from the start because the young subjects may not be able to give valid consent, and by accepting distribution of the material the possessor is providing material support to the producer, thus sharing responsibility for the initial wrongdoing. Under this argument, possessors are essentially accomplices of producers because it is their willingness to consume the material that may well motivate its production and, in any case, they are providing material support to the producer. However, possession by itself would not satisfy the usual modern rules of complicity if it comes only after the creation of the materials and lacks the required culpability of purpose to assist.[20]

Another argument for criminalizing the possession of child pornography is that such possession makes the possessor more likely to commit sexual offenses against children. That is, anti-child pornography legislation is a sort of risk-prevention measure akin to an endangerment offense.[21] The federal Child Pornography Prevention Act of 1996, which banned possession of images that even "appear" to be minors engaging in sexual conduct, suggests this rationale.[22] That is, the harm of the offense exists even if there is no real victim but only a CGI (computer-generated image) representation. But the empirical support for the claim that pornography contributes to child sexual abuse is mixed.[23]

Yet another possibility is that such possession is simply immoral or indecent and is properly criminalized on that basis.[24] Of course, as discussed in the previous chapters concerning adultery and obscenity, some people argue that the perceived morality of conduct is insufficient in itself to justify criminalization and punishment. Perhaps they would note the practical decriminalization of adultery and obscenity as evidence in support of their view that criminal law ought not be in the morality enforcement business. The law is on the books but is ignored.

However, it seems likely that the practical decriminalization of adultery and obscenity may be offered as evidence that criminal law is and ought to be in the business of morality enforcement. Adultery and adult obscenity have been effectively decriminalized precisely because they lost the societal condemnation that earlier justify their criminalization. And note that other forms of perceived immoral conduct, such as polygamy, bestiality, adult incest, bigamy, public nudity, and others, remain actively criminalized today because social perceptions of their immorality remain sufficiently strong.

Whatever the rationale – material support of unconsented to depiction, increased risk of sexual victimization of children, or conflict with existing societal norms – the criminalization and punishment of possession of child pornography is today actively pursued and strongly supported. (We actually had difficulty obtaining a copy of the Lindell daughter photograph used above to illustrate what was widely tolerated in an earlier era.)

Aftermaths

Dodgson retires from teaching in 1881. On a trip to see some of his sisters outside London in 1898, he becomes ill. On January 14 of that year, he dies of pneumonia just shy of 66 years old. The country and the world mourn, and many remember his love of children with affection. Even the *London Daily Graphic* notes in his obituary, "Like many bachelors, he was very popular with children and very fond of them."[25] Alice Liddell and other female "child-friends" of Dodgson remember him fondly; later in her life, Alice calls him her "fairy godfather."[26] For the most part, the nation of England – in love with the works of its beloved but mysterious Lewis Carroll – recollect the artistic scholar to be "a sort of child-loving saint."[27]

In the Cormega Copening case, because it makes the national news, there is pressure on the prosecutor and the court to correct what many see as overzealous enforcement. Copening and his girlfriend strike a deal in which they agreed to plead guilty to the lesser offense of disseminating "harmful material" to minors. The felony charges are dropped, they avoid jail time, and the court sentences them to a year of probation. During this probation period, they are ordered to stay in school, take a class on making good decisions, complete 30 hours of community service, not use or possess alcohol or illegal drugs, not possess a cellphone for the entirety of the year, and pay $200 in court costs. Copening also is required to agree to all police searches, regardless of whether they have a warrant. The charges are eventually dropped from their records and they are not required to register as sex offenders. Copening enters junior college and hopes to move on to a bigger school and resume his football career.

Notes

1. This portion of the narrative is drawn from the following sources: 'Lewis Carroll,' Gale: Biography in Context Series, 8 March 2010, https://galeapps.gale.com/apps/auth?userGroupName=auctr_woodruff&origURL=https%3A%2F%2Fgo.gale.com%2Fps%2Fi.do%3Fu%3Dauctr_woodruff%26v%3D2.1%26it%3Dr%26id%3DGALE%257CK2426100062%26p%3DBIC%26xp%3D&prodId=BIC; *The Secret Life of Lewis Carroll* [online video], Director Clare Beavan, Oxford, BBC Documentaries, 2015.
2. Gannon Burgett, 'A Look at the Unknown and Controversial Photography Career of Lewis Carroll,' *Peta Pixel*, 18 April 2014, http://petapixel.com/2014/04/18/look-unknown-controversial-photography-career-lewis-carroll/.
3. 'Just Good Friends?,' *The Guardian*, 29 October 2001, https://www.theguardian.com/world/2001/oct/29/gender.uk
4. Stuart D. Collingwood, *The Life and Letters of Lewis Carroll* (London: T. Fisher Unwin, 1898), p. 369.
5. Collingwood, *The Life and Letters*.
6. Burgett, 'A Look at the Unknown Photography Career.'
7. Kearney, *The Secret Life of Lewis Carroll*.
8. 'Just good friends?'.
9. 'Just good friends?'.
10. Several preeminent Lewis Carroll scholars – particularly Daniel Thomas, Michael Bakewell, and Morton Cohen – note the pedophilic undertones of his behavior, though they tend to believe he never acted on them.
11. James R. Kincaid, 'Is This Child Pornography? American Photo Labs Are Arresting Parents as Child Pornographers for Taking Pictures of Kids in the Bath,' *Salon Magazine*, 31 January 2000.
12. *New York v. Ferber* 458 U.S. 747 (1982).
13. James Kincaid, 'Is This Child Pornography?.'
14. This portion of the narrative is drawn from the following sources: Michael E. Miller, 'N.C. Just Prosecuted a Teenage Couple for Making Child Porn- of Themselves,' *The Washington Post*, 21 September 2015, https://www.washingtonpost.com/news/-morning-mix/wp/2015/09/21/n-c-just-prosecuted-a-teenage-couple-for-making-child-porn-of-themselves/?utm_term=.db3caa4904ac; Joanna Walters, 'Teen Prosecuted as Adult for Having Naked Images- of Himself- on Phone,' *The Guardian*, 20 September 2015, https://www.theguardian.com/us-news/2015/sep/20/teen-prosecuted-nakcd-images-himself-phone-selfies; Danielle Wiener-Bronner, 'Teen's Probation for Nude Selfies Includes Accepting Warrantless Searches,' *Splinter*, 16 September 2015, https://splinternews.com/teens-probation-for-nude-selfies-includes-accepting-war-1793850908; Paul Woolverton, 'Sexting Charges Dismissed for Fayetteville Teenager,' *The Fayetteville Observer*, 7 July 2016, http://www.fayobserver.com/bae7b802-8b76-542b-9cd5-f0671cee3d47.html.
15. Moreover, North Carolina is one of two states that designate 16 as the age of adult criminal responsibility. To disseminate and receive sexually explicit texts, photos, or videos, however, one must be 18. So the penalties for sexting are harshest between the ages of 16 and 18 because on one hand such teens are held to the same criminal standard as adults (making it illegal to make, possess, or share sexually explicit images of anyone under 18) and on the other hand they are barred from engaging in conduct allowed to real adults (exchanging consensual pornography). This means that high

school students like Copening and Denson who consensually send each other nude pictures of themselves and keep the content between themselves can face the same penalties as, say, a 35-year-old man who takes nude pictures with an unwilling eight-year-old girl and posts them on the internet. The only difference is that Copening and Denson are treated as both the defendants (who produced and distributed the pictures) and the victims (who appear in the pictures); they are charged with crimes against each other. Given that each felony count allows for a maximum of two years in jail, Copening, with five felony counts, faces up to ten years in jail. Denson, with two counts, faces four years.

16. *See* authorities collected at Paul H. Robinson and Tyler Scot Williams, 'Child Pornography,' in *Mapping American Criminal Law: Variations across the 50 States* (Westport: Prager, 2018), p. 261.

17. *See New York v. Ferber* 458 U.S. 747 (1982).

18. The map is taken from Robinson and Williams, 'Child Pornography,' p. 262. All supporting authorities are available from that source.

19. Notice that this particular North Carolina offense generally tracks the definition of obscenity discussed in the previous chapter but alters the "prevailing standards" requirement to apply to apply to the "prevailing standards in the adult community concerning what is suitable for minors."

20. For discussion of complicity liability, see Paul H. Robinson and Michael T. Cahill, *Criminal Law*, 2nd ed. (New York: Wolters Kluwer, 2016) § 6.1.

21. For discussion of endangerment offenses, see Robinson and Cahill, *Criminal Law*, §15.4.

22. This federal ban on so-called "virtual" child pornography, which does not in fact involve the use of children in its production, was held unconstitutional by the U.S. Supreme Court in *Ashcroft v. Free Speech Coalition* 535 U.S. 234 (2002).

23. *See, e.g.*, Ian O'Donnell and Claire Milner, *Child Pornography: Crime, Computers and Society* (Milton: Willan, 2007), p. 75 ("There is much debate . . . as to whether the use of child pornography stimulates sexual fantasies of children, relieves impulses to commit offenses, or leads to a desire to act out those fantasies."); Dean D. Knudsen, 'Child Abuse and Pornography: Is There a Relationship?,' *Journal of Family Violence* 3 (1988): p. 253 ("The degree to which child sexual abuse is related to the availability of child pornography is extremely difficult to establish." p. 261).

24. For discussion of offenses against public values, see Chapter 18 of this book.

25. Jenny Woolf, 'Lewis Carroll's Shifting Reputation: Why has Popular Opinion of the Author of Alice's Adventures in Wonderland Undergone Such a Dramatic Reversal?,' *Smithsonian Magazine,* April 2010, http://www.smithsonianmag.com/arts-culture/lewis-carrolls-shifting-reputation-9432378/?no-ist=&page=1.

26. Elizabeth Winkler, 'Who Was the Real Lewis Carroll?,' *New Republic,* 28 January 2015.

27. Woolf, 'Lewis Carroll's Shifting Reputation.'

Chapter 26

Deceptive Business Practices

Collier's Great American Fraud

1907. Desperate to find a way for his hemophiliac son to survive, Czar Nicholas II invites a monk/healer/drunk/mystic named Grigori Rasputin to the Imperial Palace. The monk restores the child to health but also, through his growing exercise of personal power, fans the flames of resentment against the monarchy that are smoldering in the empire. Indiana enacts an involuntary sterilization law directed at "confirmed criminals, idiots, imbeciles, and rapists" as a means of combating social ills. A seemingly kinder, gentler Philadelphia establishes Mother's Day. Under President Theodore Roosevelt, the U.S. solidifies its power as a great nation on the international stage. Roosevelt starts the year celebrating his receipt of the Nobel Peace Prize for helping to end the Russo-Japanese War and ends the year sending the "Great White Fleet" off to tour the world in a display of American naval power. Unfortunately, America is less successful in its performance on some domestic issues.

Anglo-American Drug Company – 1907

Until the 20th century, medical knowledge is tragically rudimentary.[1] Infant mortality is high, and simple cuts regularly become deadly due to infection. Over time an entire industry springs up to exploit this limited understanding. Called patent medicines, or "nostrums," these medicinal products are sold over the counter directly to consumers. Sellers heavily advertise their products, creating an enormous new source of revenue for magazines, newspapers, and almanacs. Some nostrums bear legitimate government issued patents, but this makes the product no more effective or safe. There are no laws that say the products need to be either safe or effective.

By the turn of the 20th century, nostrums are a $250,000,000 industry (more than $600 billion in today's currency).[2] Beyond the name of the product, the consumer often knows little. Some products are harmless, containing nothing more than burnt sugar or corn starch. The packaging on a bottle of Liquozone claims that the syrup is liquefied oxygen which acts as a universal antiseptic. In reality, it is water. (Liquid oxygen only exists at temperatures below –361.82 degrees Fahrenheit.)

Some nostrums are harmful, like Orangine, which is marketed as promoting heart health and relieving headaches. The active ingredient acetanilide does in fact relieve headaches, but also can lead to sudden heart failure. In the years immediately following the introduction of nostrums containing acetanilide, deaths due to sudden heart failure increase dramatically, exceeding deaths from typhoid by six-fold in the New York area.

Other nostrums contain addictive substances. Alcohol is a major ingredient in many potions: "Duffy's Pure Malt Whiskey" is malt whiskey but by labeling it as an elixir the manufacturer is able to market the product in dry states and avoid liquor taxes.[3] "Hostetter's Celebrated Stomach Bitters" are also more than 40% alcohol but, unlike the malt whiskey, the alcohol content is not mentioned in the name or on the label.[4] Nostrums marketed to help a user break an addictive habit may well be the drug from which the buyer is seeking to break dependence. For example, *The Painless Cure*, marketed to cure opioid addiction, is mostly morphine.

Some products are simply poisonous. *Dr. King's New Discovery for Consumption* is a blend of chloroform and morphine. Chloroform stops the coughing and morphine stops the pain associated with consumption (tuberculosis) but the combination also causes respiratory failure.

Mrs. Winslow's Soothing Syrup is unrivaled for its ability to kill consumers. The syrup is first sold in the 1830s by a mid-wife. In time, her son-in-law and his partner build it into an international brand, the Anglo-American Drug Company. For 25 cents the buyer receives a small glass vial wrapped in attractively decorated yellow paper.

Figure 26.1 An advertisement for the lethal elixer, 1887

They run ads for "The Mother's Friend." The ads feature richly colored pictures of beautiful, finely dressed women, holding robust babies. Beneath the image, the ads read:

> ADVICE TO MOTHERS – Are you broken in your rest by a sick child suffering with the pain of cutting teeth? Go at once to a chemist and get a bottle of MRS. WINSLOW'S SOOTHING SYRUP . . . it is perfectly harmless and . . . it soothes the child, it softens the gums, allays all pain, relieves wind.[5]

In addition to artistic ads, the company publishes "testimonials" from druggists and satisfied mothers, gushing that "its effect upon [my son] was like magic" and "every mother who regards the health and life of her children should possess it."[6] Unlike many nostrums, this one is actually very effective. Beyond sugar water and herbs, the syrup contains 12% alcohol and a heavy dose of morphine. One would be hard-pressed to find a formula better for "producing natural, quiet sleep" in an infant.[7]

In 1860 – after the product has been on the market for almost 30 years – the *American Medical Times* publishes a report in New York criticizing Mrs. Winslow's Syrup and the newspapers who run its advertisements. The report states that "thousands of mothers in this city are annually relieved of all further care of their infants through the magically soothing effects of Mrs. Winslow's syrup" when the syrup kills the children.[8]

But how many young mothers are reading the *American Medical Times*? The warning is a lonely unheard voice – the message never reaches the general population. When, a few years later, a California doctor takes up the alarm, he estimates that "thousands of babies might be dying from opium poisoning because of the ignorance of mothers and nurses."[9] By 1870, the dangers of opiate addiction have become clear to medical professionals, and several other medical journals and newspapers raise the issue of opiates and alcohol in soothing syrups. Still, sales of Mrs. Winslow's Syrup hold strong. In an ingenious marketing move, the Kopp's Company, one of Anglo-American's competitors, follows birth notices in newspapers throughout the country and sends free samples of the product to new mothers. In addition to increasing infant deaths, these soothing nostrums produce a generation of morphine addicts.

In 1907, Samuel Hopkins Adams produces a series about the patent medicine industry in *Collier Magazine* titled "The Great American Fraud." Adams offers a blistering expose of these "medicines" with no medical value. The report takes aim at the arrangements between medicine companies and newspapers. Dependent on nostrum manufacturers for advertising revenue, newspapers are willing to ignore the dangers to their readers. As a result, "newspapers of America not only maintain silence, but actually lobby . . . on behalf of patent medicines."[10] When an Illinois lawmaker introduces a bill mandating a warning label, 40 different newspapers attack the legislator, saying that "[he] had to go."[11] In Boston, newspapers refuse to cover a legislative debate about patent medicines.

Controversially, Collier's Adams publishes the names and addresses of "two hundred and sixty-four patent medicines, quack doctors, firms, individuals, institutes and institutions" implicated in their investigation.[12] As the magazine notes, this is just a sampling of the thousands of players who work to sustain this industry.

Adams also decries the "opium-containing soothing syrups, which stunt or kill helpless infants."[13] "The sight of a parent drugging a helpless infant into a semi-comatose condition is not an elevating one for this civilized age."[14] The magazine offers its readers horrific stories of tearful parents whose children become addicted to Mrs. Winslow's Syrup and similar brands. The stories leave no doubt of the dangers:

> The child (after taking four drops) went into a stupor at once, the pupils were pin-pointed, skin cool and clammy, heart and respiration slow. I treated the case as one of opium poisoning, but it took twelve hours before my little patient was out of danger.[15]

After Adams' explosive series, more reports of infant deaths begin to surface. The American Medical Association publishes a 700-page report titled "*Nostrums and Quackery.*"[16]

> Is it possible that we have accidentally heard of all such cases? Is it not more likely that there are hundreds that are never even reported to the coroner? Kopp's Baby Friend is only a sample; it is no worse than hundreds of others that are allowed to be sold for the aggrandizement of the few, but to the injury and death of the many.[17]

The reports keep coming and yet the legal system does not act. One of the first is a 1906 action against T.B. Ganse, a young entrepreneur pushing a nostrum called ROBUSTO. Ganse claims that ROBUSTO is a "cure-all" that alleviates stomach complaints, liver disease, constipation, weak blood, frayed nerves, sexual under-performance, gonorrhea, "sickness, over-work or dissipation," and "brain fag."[18] As Ganse explains in his advertisements, which are filled with medical terms such as spermatorhea, gleet, varicocele, and hydrocele, ROBUSTO builds up a man's strength and causes him to expel damaged tissue. "We firmly believe that there is not a man living, young or old, who is so weak that ROBUSTO will not revive him; none so strong that he will not benefit."[19]

Based on complaints from purchasers, the U.S. Post Office charges Ganse with operating "a scheme to effect the sale at an enormous profit of a combination of drugs palmed off as a wonderful discovery, by falsely representing its curative powers."[20] The government concludes that none of Ganse's ROBUSTO products work.[21] Ganse is barred from sending advertisements through the U.S. Post; however, nothing prevents him from continuing to manufacture the mixtures and using the postal service to ship them.

Congress tries to outlaw opiates in over-the-counter drugs but faces fierce political pushback from the well-funded patent medicine industry. The Pure Food and Drug Act, which takes effect at the start of 1907, gives new but limited powers to the Bureau of Chemistry to investigate dangerous drugs. Under the new law, opiates can still be used in over-the-counter nostrums but the label must clearly state their presence.

The Bureau makes baby-soothing syrups a priority and brings the first suit against a manufacturer for misbranding. The morphine content of the particular brand is stated on the label along with the reassurance: "Mothers need not fear to give this medicine to the youngest babe, as no bad results come from the continued use of it."[22] The Bureau wins the case but on appeal the Supreme Court rules that the provision of the Pure Food and Drug Act against false and misleading branding does not apply to therapeutic claims.

The Bureau also files suit against the Anglo-American Drug Company for alleged misbranding of Mrs. Winslow's Syrup. Prior to the trial, the company pleads guilty and is ordered to pay a fine. The company then drops the word "soothing" from the syrup's name and continues its sales, eventually eliminating morphine from the formula.

The dangers of opiates have been well known since the 1870s, yet various companies continue to legally manufacture products for babies that contain morphine until 1925. In the end, no person from the Anglo-American Drug Company or Kopp's Company is ever indicted for producing a product that causes the deaths of hundreds and leads thousands down a path of drug addiction. The combined legal fines against the two companies total $115.

Consumer Protection

When people think of criminal law, they commonly think of murder, rape, assault, robbery, theft, and other such common crimes, but the kinds of conduct that is sufficiently condemnable to deserve criminal conviction include a wide variety of other behaviors. Indeed, the vast bulk of criminal codes prohibit conduct that falls outside of the traditional core offenses. However, fraud offenses, such as the deceptive business practices examined in this chapter, are closely associated with the core offense of theft.

The core of wrongdoing that all cultures share and that all people intuitively understand certainly includes physical aggression and taking another's property without consent. But social psychologists suggest that there is a third piece of the core of wrongdoing: deception in exchanges.[23] In theft, the person takes your property when you aren't looking. But the criminal intent and the resulting injury are the same in instances where you are essentially tricked out of your property, like the classic case of the butcher who puts his thumb on the scale to exaggerate the weight of the meat you are sold.

In earlier times, there was little distance between a merchant and the consumer. This made it hard for the sellers of goods to engage in some types of deceptive practices. If a supplier sold a customer watered down milk, the buyer knew exactly where to place her wrath. In such a personal economy, there was little need for government to resort to legal action to protect citizens. As the economy of modern life grew ever more complicated, however, where the consumer commonly has little or no continuing personal relationship with the producer or seller, the need for the criminal law to protect citizens became clear.

Unfortunately, even though the need became clearer, little was done. In 1905, Upton Sinclair, in an effort to bring people to see the value of socialism, published *The Jungle*. Sinclair's exposé on the meat-packing industry's horrid conditions prompted widespread outrage (but little interest in his socialist message).[24] City dwellers, who did not live near farms, had no way to know what they were actually buying when they purchased a sausage or a bottle of milk. *The Jungle* made clear what meat packers and others had comfortably kept quiet: business practices that regularly killed people through tainted food.

The outrage led to several pieces of federal legislation, such as the Pure Food and Drug Act.[25] In 1914, the United States Federal Trade Commission (FTC) was created to ensure consumers high-quality products at competitive prices in a marketplace free of deception.[26] Several decades later during the New Deal era, further steps were taken to regulate corporations and protect consumers at the federal, state, and local levels.

Another major wave of consumer protection reform came during the "Great Society" presidency of Lyndon Johnson. During the 1960s and 1970s, consumer advocates like Ralph Nader called attention to the existence of unsafe products on the market that called for greater government oversight of corporations.[27] As the economy enjoyed general postwar growth that gave more Americans disposable income, consumer activism increased with support from traditionally underrepresented groups in the political sphere, such as women and African-Americans.[28] Expansion of consumer protection agencies and laws has continued into the 21st century, especially in the wake of the 2008 financial crisis. For example, in 2009 the Credit Card

Deceptive Business Practices.

A person commits a misdemeanor if in the course of business he:

(1) uses or possesses for use a false weight or measure, or any other device for falsely determining or recording any quality or quantity; or

(2) sells, offers or exposes for sale, or delivers less than the represented quantity of any commodity or service; or

(3) takes or attempts to take more than the represented quantity of any commodity or service when as buyer he furnishes the weight or measure; or

(4) sells, offers or exposes for sale adulterated or mislabeled commodities. "Adulterated" means varying from the standard of composition or quality prescribed by or pursuant to any statute providing criminal penalties for such variance, or set by established commercial usage. "Mislabeled" means varying from the standard of truth or disclosure in labeling prescribed by or pursuant to any statute providing criminal penalties for such variance, or set by established commercial usage; or

(5) makes a false or misleading statement in any advertisement addressed to the public or to a substantial segment thereof for the purpose of promoting the purchase or sale of property or services; ...

Model Penal Code §224.7

Figure 26.2

Accountability and Responsibility Act sought to protect consumers from abusive practices by credit card companies.[29]

One of the most common offenses aimed at fraudulent conduct is the offense of "deceptive business practices." The Model Penal Code offense definition is reproduced in the margin. In summary, it criminalizes:

1. use or possession of false weight or measure,
2. giving less in quantity than what a person represented to the buyer,
3. taking more in quantity than what a person represented to the seller,
4. selling or offering adulterated or mislabeled commodities,
5. making a false statement in an advertisement or communication addressed to the public or some substantial number of people.[30]

Most deceptive business practices could be prosecuted through a broader statute punishing fraud or false pretenses generally. For instance, in Oklahoma, a person is liable for criminal fraud when the person,

> with intent to . . . defraud, . . . obtain[s] from any person . . . any money [or] property . . . , by means . . . of any . . . deception, or false or fraudulent representation or statement . . . .[31]

But as a practical matter, it would take major investigative resources to prove these offense elements in every case of business cheating.

The "deceptive business practices" statutes are designed to make prosecution more feasible.[32] Thus, instead of having to prove that it was the actor's intention – his purpose, his conscious object – to obtain money or property through deception, it is enough to show that the actor knew his conduct was deceiving the victim or was aware of a substantial risk that his conduct was deceiving the victim. Further, the deceptive business practices offense requires only proof of the deceptive conduct, such as using false weights or publishing a misleading advertisement, not proof that any particular person was actually defrauded as a result. In other words, it is the deceptive business practices statute, rather than the general fraud statute, that is the daily workhorse in the battle against defrauding consumers.

However, as we have seen in other areas of criminal law reform, it is not unusual for enthusiastic activism to go too far or at least to extend criminal prosecution beyond the cases that initially inspired the reform. For example, compare the legal enforcement in the following modern case to the abuses of the Great American Fraud era that sparked the modern reforms.

Samuel Girod – 2016

Samuel Girod lives in Bath County, Kentucky with his wife, 12 children, and 25 grandchildren.[33] The Girod family belongs to the Old Order Amish faith. They operate Satterfield Naturals, which sells products for health problems. Girod sells three main products: Chickweed Healing Salve, which is made from rosemary, beeswax, and olive oil and treats skin problems; R.E.P., which serves as a breath freshener and counters sinus infections; and TO-MOR-GONE, a natural herbal remedy to remove abnormal growths like warts, moles, and tumors.

Girod's business, however, does not fit well within the realm of federal law. Girod's Chickweed Healing Salve's label reads "good for all skin disorders. Skin cancer, cuts, burns, draws, and poison ivy."[34] In 2001, this catches the attention of the Food and Drug Administration, and an agent visits Girod to tell him that, under the Fair Packaging and Labeling Act, he cannot claim his products can help skin cancer. Girod agrees to remove that part of the labeling, but the FDA believes his product should be classified as a drug, meaning that Girod must register his farm as a drug facility. Girod contends that he makes herbal remedies, not drugs.

Over the next three years, FDA agents visit Girod several more times. Each time, they seem to find another issue with his products, and each time Girod complies with the FDA regulations. His Chickweed Healing Salve is renamed, at the FDA's direction, Healing Chickweed. The FDA then requires a second change: Healing Chickweed becomes Original Chickweed. He often calls the FDA office itself for suggestions, but most of the time they refuse to answer his questions.

Eight years pass, and the FDA either forgets about Girod or decides that their concerns about his business are not worth pursuing. But in January of 2012, the FDA finds that a store is selling a product with the old objectionable label Chickweed Healing Salve. Having gotten the FDA's attention, the agency launches an investigation. They confiscate the product everywhere it is sold and send it to a lab to identify exactly what it contains. The laboratory analysis reveals that Girod's three products are all-natural and contain no drugs.

The next year, the FDA claims that a consumer in Missouri has made a complaint about skin damage from TO-MOR-GONE. The FDA says that the harm was caused by one of the ingredients, bloodroot extract. The extract is legal and readily available from vendors such as Amazon, and it does have a mildly corrosive effect on skin. The FDA is also interested in another ingredient: comfrey, a plant often used in fertilizers and herbal medicines. In response to the Missouri complaint, armed FDA agents enter Girod's property and demand that he consent to a search. Girod reluctantly agrees on condition that agents not take photos, as he is religious beliefs forbid them. The agents agree, but once they enter, they ignore their agreement and begin taking pictures.

Girod is summoned before a federal judge in the fall of 2013. The victim who issued the complaint against Girod's TO-MOR-GONE is not present, and it comes to light

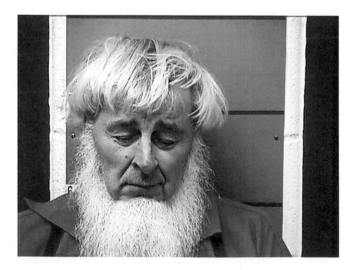

Figure 26.3 Girod at Grayson County Detention Center, 2017

that the product he had used was not Girod's. Nevertheless, the court issues an injunction mandating three things: Girod is not to make or sell any of his products until he clears up the labeling infraction; he is not to sell any products containing bloodroot in any form; and finally he is to allow the FDA to inspect his property for five years. Girod repeats his conviction that since the products he sells are herbal remedies and not drugs, he should not be subject to FDA oversight, but nonetheless initially complies.

But having complied with every request for more than a decade, Girod seems to run out of patience. When in November 2013 two FDA agents come to Satterfield Naturals for an authorized inspection, Girod, out of a conviction that the FDA is violating his religious freedom, brings together a group of family and friends on the day of the inspection and the group blocks the road to his farm. Eventually the agents leave.

The FDA then begins impounding his products from store shelves, hurting Girod's clients. Girod then decides to restart production but to be sold only through a private membership club, where membership requires written confirmation that buyers understand the content and purpose of his products.

Girod is indicted in federal court on 12 counts including conspiring to impede federal officers, obstructing a proceeding before a federal agency, failing to register with the FDA, tampering with a witness, failing to appear for a hearing, and distributing misbranded drugs. He represents himself and is convicted on all counts. He is sentenced to six years in prison followed by three years of supervised release.[35]

It seems clear that Girod's frustration with federal authorities led him to act in ways that constituted criminal offenses beyond the original federal mislabeling complaint. However, one can have some sympathy for Girod's feeling that the federal agency was overreaching. It was shown that his product was entirely natural ingredients. He had agreed to alter the labeling to satisfy the federal demands and was willing to make any other adjustments the FDA wanted in order to fully describe the contents. And the natural ingredients that he used were regularly used in other products without federal intervention. This is hardly a case of surreptitiously selling alcohol and morphine as Mrs. Winslow's Soothing Syrup.

Unfortunately, it is not uncommon that government regulation in an area, once established, moves to expand its jurisdiction and enforcement beyond the limits envisioned by the original legislation.[36] Part of this common pattern is to criminalize conduct that is appropriately sanctioned only as a regulatory violation. Such overcriminalization has become a heavily debated subject in modern America,[37] in part because the criminalization of regulatory violations tends to dilute the condemnatory effect of criminal convictions generally.[38] (Note the parallel dynamic in the previous chapter: the advent of special child pornography statutes, which address what was a serious danger, ended up being applied in the Copening case to prosecute a 16-year-old boyfriend and girlfriend, a use of the statute that was probably beyond what its creators intended.)

Criminalizing Deceptive Business Practices in the States

While almost all states have an offense that criminalizes deceptive business practices, there is some diversity as to the breadth of the offense, as the map below makes clear.[39] The states marked with diagonal lines criminalize false advertising. The states with a dots overlay criminalize false measures. The darker the overall effect of the overlays, the broader the criminalization.

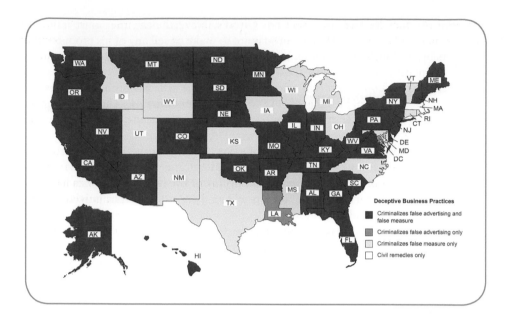

Figure 26.4

Thirty-two states, those with both dots and diagonal lines, specifically criminalize both false advertising and the use in commerce of false or incorrect weights or measures.

The false advertising statutes specifically prohibit making false or misleading statements in advertising or other communications addressed to the public or to a substantial number of people. The false measure statutes specifically prohibit the possession or use of a device that misrepresents the weight or quantity of a commodity. Many of these states have modeled their offense after the Model Penal Code, quoted previously in the margin. In the remaining 19 jurisdictions, the deceptive business practices offense reaches only false advertising or false measures or neither.

Clearly, the companies exposed in *Collier's* Great American Fraud article would be criminally liable under these statutes, like Model Code subsections (4) and (5), for selling adulterated or mislabeled commodities and making a false or misleading statement in advertising, respectively, but in 1907 such statutes were not commonly enacted and enforced. Kentucky, where Amish farmer Samuel Girod lived and did business in 2016, has a comprehensive statute of this type, but it is not entirely clear that he satisfies the requirements of those subsections. Notice that he was prosecuted not by Kentucky but rather by federal authorities under specialized federal statutes.

Why Would a Jurisdiction Fail to Have a Full Deceptive Business Practices Offense?

An obvious question raised by the states without both overlays – that is, states that do not criminalize both false advertising and false measures – is why such a significant number of jurisdictions would fail to criminalize such common deceptive business practices. Given the increasing sensitivity to the need for consumer protection, one would have thought that the criminalization of such practices would be a popular legislative priority. Note for example the recent creation of the new independent federal agency of the Consumer Financial Protection Bureau.[40]

One might initially speculate that in the area of deceptive business practices criminal law has simply not caught up with popular sentiment. That is, one might speculate that some of the states simply don't realize their need to expand their statutes to cover such business practices.

But that explanation does not work well. The Model Code, which is the basis for three-quarter of the state codes, criminalizes a full basket of different forms of deceptive business practices, as noted above. Many of the jurisdictions with narrower deceptive business practice prohibitions have them because they affirmatively rejected pieces of the Model Code's offense.

Presumably, this approach – trimming the breadth of the Model Code offense – was a move pressed by business groups, or legislators with special sympathies for such groups, perhaps on the theory that civil liability was always available to undo cheating or misrepresentation in a business context. However, as a practical matter, that argument has limits. Few noncommercial victims have the financial means to bring a civil lawsuit. More importantly, even if the victim is well financed, such civil litigation would make little economic sense. The butcher would feel free to put his thumb on the scale 100 times a day comforted in the knowledge that no victim would rationally endure the cost of a lawsuit to collect the few dollars he has cheated each of them of.

The point of the deceptive business practices offense – made available even though a more demanding general fraud statute may already cover the conduct – is to make the threat of criminal prosecution sufficiently clear and meaningful that violators cannot hide behind undue burdens for prosecution. The Model Penal Code statute and the statutes of a majority of American jurisdictions typically provide an appropriate balance of interests: the requirements for criminal liability are sufficiently demanding that criminal liability is imposed only on those who engage in clear wrongdoing, yet effective prosecution is feasible, albeit producing liability only in the misdemeanor range.

Aftermaths

After the Collier's exposé series is published, the American Medical Association publishes a pair of reports expressly confirming that Mrs. Winslow's Syrup causes death in children. The reports lead the federal government to take legal action on the grounds that the Anglo-American Company, manufacturer of the syrup, "knowingly and in reckless and wanton disregard of their truth or falsity" marketed a dangerous product.[41] With federal government now pursuing them, the company sees fit to reformulate its product (and remove the word "soothing" from the product name). The new and presumably less dangerous product continues to be sold through the 1940s. An analysis of the product shows that the ingredients of the new mix operate to reduce gas and act as a laxative.[42]

Samuel Girod petitions the U.S. Sixth Circuit Court of Appeals for a new trial based on an argument of bias, but in May 2018 the court rejects his request. In 2020, Girod is released from federal prison due to the Covid-19 pandemic.[43]

Notes

1. This narrative is drawn from the following sources: Samuel H. Adams, *The Great American Fraud* (New York: P.F. Collier & Son, 1906); Samuel H. Adams, 'The Great American Fraud: A Series of Articles on the Patent Medicine Evil,' *Collier's Weekly*, http://www.gutenberg.org/files/44325/44325-h/44325-h.htm; Arden Christen and Joan Christen, 'Sozodont Powder Dentifrice and Mrs. Winslow's Soothing Syrup: Dental Nostrums.' *Journal of the History of Dentistry 48*, no. 3 (November 2000): pp. 99–105; Ferdinand Meyer V., 'Mrs. Winslow's Soothing Syrup – oooh so Soothing,' *Peachridge Class*, 5 January 2013, http://www.peachridgeglass.com/2013/01/mrs-winslows-soothing-syrup-oooh-so-soothing/; 'Mrs. Winslow's Soothing Syrup,' *Herb Museum*, http://www.herbmuseum.ca/content/mrs-winslows-soothing-syrup; 'Patent Medicine,' *Medical Discoveries*, http://www.discoveriesinmedicine.com/Ni-Ra/Patent-Medicine.html; 'Pharmacology.' *Journal of the American Medical Association 45* (1905): pp. 934–936, https://books.google.com/books?id=9fhGAQAAMAAJ&pg=PA936&lpg=PA936&dq=nostrum+hydrozone+positively+prevents+yellow+fever&source=bl&ots=qJHeCqCTFK&sig=e79uFeBAgQGvpNUlXnyHQ4n9B78&hl=en&sa=X&ved=0ahUKEwiqzdT017PVAhVHMz4KHUcFAA0Q6AEIKDAB#v=onepage&q=hydrozone&f=false; 'A Post Office Exposure.' *Journal of the American Medical Association 44*, nos. 9–17 (1905): pp. 1391–1397, https://babel.hathitrust.org/cgi/pt?id=umn.319510027085509;view=1up;seq=747; Marty Stempniak, 'TBT: In the 1800s, One Opium-Laced Drug Helped Moms Soothe the Pains of Teething Children,' *Hospitals & Health Networks*, 31 March 2016, http://www.hhnmag.com/articles/-7085-tbt-in-the--s-one-opium-laced-drug-helped-moms-soothe-the-pains-of-teething-children; James H. Young, *American Health Quackery: Collected Essays of James Harvey Young* (Princeton: Princeton University Press, 2014).
2. Adams, 'The Great American Fraud,' p. 9.
3. Adams, 'The Great American Fraud,' p. 21.
4. Adams, 'The Great American Fraud.'
5. Meyer V., 'Mrs. Winslow's Soothing Syrup,' *Herb Museum*.
6. Meyer V., 'Mrs. Winslow's Soothing Syrup.'
7. Meyer V., 'Mrs. Winslow's Soothing Syrup.'
8. *See* 'The Week,' ed. Stephen Smith, *American Medical Times*, 6 October 1960, 245, https://books.google.com/books?id=Ky4TAAAAYAAJ&pg=PA245&lpg=PA245&dq=%E2%80%9Crelieved+of+all+further+care+of+their+infants%E2%80%9D+and+winslow%27s+soothing+syrup+and+american+medical+times&source=bl&ots=fg3YQA8tdh&sig=bkuCZTGw_AAh6TCeU8pqawO_9pc&hl=en&sa=X&ved=0ahUKEwj8kvuTnenLAhWKnYMKHUTOBP8Q6AEIIzAB#v=onepage&q=%E2%80%9Crelieved%20of%20all%20further%20care%20of%20their%20infants%E2%80%9D%20and%20winslow's%20soothing%20syrup%20and%20american%20medical%20times&f=false.
9. Young, '"Even to a Sucking Infant": Nostrums and Children,' *American Health Quackery*, p. 150.
10. Adams, 'The Great American Fraud,' p. 130.
11. Adams, 'The Great American Fraud,' p. 5.
12. Adams, 'The Great American Fraud,' p. 148.
13. Adams, 'The Great American Fraud.'
14. Adams, 'The Great American Fraud.'
15. Adams, 'The Great American Fraud.'
16. *See* 'Nostrums and Quackery.' *American Medical Association* (1912): pp. 431–435. https://babel.hathitrust.org/cgi/pt?id=uiug.30112113410036;view=1up;seq=437.

17. 'The Slaughter of the Innocents.' *JAMA: The Journal of the American Medical Association, 46,* (University of Michigan, American Medical Association, 1906), p. 666, https://books.google.com/books?id=o5E1AQAAMAAJ&pg=PA666&lpg=PA 666&dq=kopp+baby+friend&source=bl&ots=zgeQzI68uK&sig=Lp8495_ QrdOHYZAUnM-T7c01XX8&hl=en&sa=X&ved=0ahUKEwj1jfSMv5PVAhVk74 MKHX6aDsM4ChDoAQgkMAE#v=onepage&q=kopp%20baby%20 friend&f=false.

18. 'A Post Office Exposure.' *Journal of the American Medical Association No. 9-17 44,* 29 April 1905, p. 1392, https://babel.hathitrust.org/cgi/pt?id=umn.31951002708550 9;view=1up;seq=747.

19. 'A Post Office Exposure.'

20. 'A Post Office Exposure.'

21. 'A Post Office Exposure':

> ROBUSTO cannot possibly have the properties ascribed to them in the advertising circulars of the Chicago Cure Company which you have submitted for examination. In my opinion these remedies are practically inert. The circulars are calculated to excite groundless fears in the minds of those reading them and to develop false hopes of the benefits which are promised.

22. Young, '"Even to a Sucking Infant": Nostrums and Children'.

23. Paul H. Robinson, Robert Kurzban, and Owen D. Jones, 'The Origins of Shared Intuitions of Justice.' *Vanderbilt Law Review 60,* 20 December 2006, p. 1633, https:// ssrn.com/abstract=952726.

24. Spencer Waller, Jillian Brady, R.J. Acosta, Jennifer Fair, and Jacob Morse, 'Consumer Protection in the United States: An Overview.' *European Journal of Consumer Law* (2011): pp. 1–2.

25. Lizabeth Cohen, 'Colston E. Warne Lecture: Is It Time for Another Round of Consumer Protection? The Lessons of Twentieth-Century US History.' *The Journal of Consumer Affairs* (2010): pp. 235–236.

26. Waller et al., 'Consumer Protection in the United States,' p. 2.

27. Waller et al., 'Consumer Protection in the United States,' pp. 1–2.

28. Cohen, 'Colston E. Warne Lecture,' pp. 236–238.

29. Waller et al., 'Consumer Protection in the United States,' pp. 28–29.

30. *See* Model Penal Code §224.7.

31. Okla. Stat. Ann. tit. 21, § 1541.1.

32. They also are intended to reach further by softening the mens rea requirements and by extending attempt liability to earlier acts beyond mere preparation. *See* Model Penal Code Commentary §224.7.

33. This narrative is drawn from the following sources: 'Convicted Amish Farmer Sentenced to Six Years in Prison,' *WKYT,* 30 June 2017, http://www.wkyt.com/content/news/ Convicted-Amish-farmer-to-be-sentenced-Friday-in-Lexington-431745623.html; Bill Estep, 'Amish Man Convicted of Selling Improperly Labeled Health Products,' *Lexington Herald Leader,* 2 March 2017, http://www.kentucky.com/news/state/article135986318. html; Greg Kocher, 'Amish Farmer Sold Herbal Health Products. He's Going to Prison for 6 years,' *Lexington Herald Leader,* 30 June 2017, http://www.kentucky.com/news/ local/crime/article159031869.html; Sally Oh, 'Detailed Story: FDA's Persecution of Samuel Girods,' *Kentucky Free Press,* 1 March 2017, http://www.kyfreepress.com/2017/ 03/fda-v-sam-girod-complete-story-video/; Hillary Thornton, 'WKYT Investigation: Amish Farmer in Jail Awaiting Trial, Facing Time in Federal Prison,' *WKYT,* 26 January 2017, http://www.wkyt.com/content/news/WKYT-Investigation-Amish-farmer-in-jail-awaiting-trial-facing-time-in-federal-prison-411915635.html.

34. Oh, 'Detailed Story: FDA's Persecution.'

35. Kocher, 'Amish Farmer Sold Herbal Health Products.'

36. For examples of this common pattern of regulatory overreach, see Paul H. Robinson and Sarah M. Robinson, 'Conclusion: Trigger Crimes and Social Progress,' in *Tragedy, Outrage & Reform: Crimes That Changed Our World* (Lanham: Rowman & Littlefield, 2017), p. 317.

37. 'Overcriminalization,' *The Heritage Foundation*, 12 June 2019, https://www.heritage.org/crime-and-justice/heritage-explains/overcriminalization.

38. Paul H. Robinson and Michael T. Cahill, *Law without Justice: Why Criminal Law Doesn't Give People What They Deserve*, ch. 10 (Oxford: Oxford University Press, 2005).

39. The map is taken from Paul H. Robinson and Tyler Scot Williams, *Mapping American Criminal Law: Variations across the 50 States*, Chapter 27 (Westport: Prager, 2018). All supporting authorities are available from that source.

40. Ross Colvin, 'Obama Signs Sweeping Wall Street Overhaul into Law,' *Reuters*, 21 July 2010, http://www.reuters.com/article/us-financial-regulation-obama/obama-signs-sweeping-wall-street-overhaul-into-law-idUSTRE66K1QR20100722.

41. Stempniak, 'TBT: In the 1800s.'

42. Joe Nickell, '"Baby Killer" Nostrums,' *Center for Inquiry*, 20 November 2017, http://www.centerforinquiry.net/blogs/entry/baby_killer_nostrums/.

43. Gerry Wagoner, 'Amish Sam Is Coming Home!!,' Fulcrum 7, 19 April 2020, http://www.fulcrum7.com/news/2020/4/19/amish-sam-is-coming-home.

Chapter 27

Rigging Sporting Events

The Dean of Race Fixing

1934. Traveling 5,600 miles over some of the worst terrain in China, the Red Army loses 90% of its soldiers and yet when Mao Zedong takes control of warring internal factions, the newly unified force turns the tide of the war. Seizing largely on economic dissatisfaction, Chancellor Adolf Hitler removes any vestiges of democracy and, taking on dictatorial powers, assures the German people that the Third Reich will last for a thousand years. In the U.S., the grip of the worldwide depression is lessening, and unemployment drops by 22%. Police finally catch up with several famed depression-era outlaws. Bonnie and Clyde are killed in a shootout. John Dillinger escapes from prison using a carved wooden gun only to be killed a few months later. But at least one famous criminal continues his long run.

Peter Barrie – 1934

Peter Barrie is known as the "King of the Ringers" on the British side of the Atlantic and as the "Master Horse Faker" on the American side.[1] According to Barrie, his first attempt at horse faking is in England when he is 16. He buys a gray mare for 16 guineas, paints the horse brown, and sells it back to the very same aristocrat for 300 pounds.

The ability to alter a given horse, a ringer, so that it can be passed off as a different animal can be profitable at the racetrack. When people bet on a horserace, they use information such as the animal's age and past performance to determine the horse's chances in a given field of contestants. By visually altering a horse, a horse faker can distort the odds – by running a better horse than the bettors expect or a worse horse than the bettors expect – thereby creating a situation where his own betting can take advantage of the public's error.

DOI: 10.4324/9781003258025-30

An approach that Barrie sometimes uses is to visually alter beforehand the look of one horse, which may run badly in earlier races, to look like a second horse who unpainted runs well in a race on which Barrie bets heavily. The oddsmakers, unaware of the substitution, set odds based on the previous poor performance. Barrie and his pals clean up on a horse that appears to be a long shot but is actually a good runner. The money can add up quickly: a two-dollar bet on a 70-1 win means a $140 payoff.

Another version of the same scam is to run the weak horse, then run a stronger horse painted to look like the weak one. In one scheme, Barrie and a confederate buy a successful three-year-old named Jazz. The sales contract stipulates that the horse cannot be raced in England. Barrie enters an unimpressive horse, Coat of Mail, in a race and has Jazz put on a train that is heading out of the country. Before many miles pass, Jazz is taken off the outbound train, and put back on an inbound train. Barrie does "all the faking in the box on the journey,"[2] turning Jazz into Coat of Mail between King's Cross Station and Stockton. In this instance, the scheme suffers because the man hired to place the bets boasts about the substitution. Strong horse Jazz, under the name Coat of Mail, wins the race but the profits, which should have been 40,000 pounds, only amount to 5,000 pounds because the secret was no longer a secret and many of the oddsmakers adjusted the odds accordingly.

The police finally begin investigating Barrie and charge him and five others. Barrie pleads guilty and is sentenced to three years in prison for his "gross and scandalous fraud."[3] Barrie gets out of prison in 1923 just in time to witness his wife give birth, although he was not out in time for the conception. With his marriage no longer keeping him in England, he looks for greener pastures. He is ineligible to emigrate to the United States but bribes his way to New York.

The racing climate in America is quite rough-and-tumble compared to the tradition-bound English circuit and has less official scrutiny. The American police finally do catch on to Barrie's schemes, and in 1934 he is brought up on race fixing charges. But

Figure 27.1 Horse racing was a very different sport in the 1930s, circa 1933

upon closer examination there turns out to be no criminal offense covering the particular kind of fraud that Barrie is perpetrating. The authorities try to stretch the evidence to make a case for check fraud and attempted horse theft but the grand jury declines to indict on either charge. During the hearing Barrie admits that he is in the U.S. illegally, so when the prosecution fails, Barrie is deported.

After his scrape with the law, Barrie, always short of money, sells his story to the *New York Daily News*. His pursuit of his place in racing mythology leads to the headline "$6,000,000 Race Horse Ringer." The article claims that Barrie has left the country, leaving behind him "a trail of the most sensational swindles in the annals of racing."[4] In his interview Barrie explains that he "never had any compunction about ringing a horse" because "all racing is crooked."[5]

Attempts to Regulate Gaming

There is a long and checkered history of government attempts to regulate gaming in order to save its citizens from deceitful con-artists, and themselves. As the preamble to England's Gaming Act of 1744 explains:

> Whereas notwithstanding the many good and wholesome laws now in being, for preventing excessive and deceitful gaming, many persons of ill-fame and reputation who have no visible means of subsistence, do keep houses, rooms, and other places for playing, and do permit persons therein to play at cards, dice and other devices for large sums of money, by means whereof divers young and unwary persons and others are drawn in to lose the greatest part and sometimes all their substance; and it frequently happens that they are thereby reduced to the utmost necessities and betake themselves to the most wicked courses, which end in their ruin. . . .[6]

Throughout the 17th and 18th centuries, the English crown and then Parliament attempt to tamp down the growing enthusiasm for gaming of all sorts, gaming that frequently leads to pitiful results for entire families. But the gaming desire is sufficiently strong that people find one way after another of getting around the latest prohibition. When public gaming is prohibited, private gaming dens are created. When specific games are outlawed, new games are created.

> A 'really important landmark' in the history of gaming legislation, section 2 declared the games of ace of hearts, pharaoh, basset, and hazard to be illegal per se, while that and section 1 made it an offence to maintain any place where these games were played. As with much legislation that nominates the particular activities to be prohibited rather than identifying them generically, the affected population invented a new dicing game, passage, which achieved instant popularity. Parliament responded the following year by prohibiting it and, by section 9, 'every other game [save backgammon], invented or to be invented, with one or more die or dice, or with any instrument, engine or device, in the nature of dice, having one or more figures or numbers thereon. The gaming housekeeper's response was the development of roulette (also called roly-poly); Parliament's response was the Gaming Act 1744 . . . .[7]

Ultimately, governments, including state and federal governments in the U.S., came to more frequently seek to regulate and supervise rather than prohibit gaming.

The previous chapter, concerning deceptive business practices, introduces the criminal law's challenge in prosecuting the wide variety of frauds that humans can invent. As we saw, while every state has a general fraud offense, a more specialized offense was needed to effectively punish common fraudulent activities, such as false advertising or false labeling, that may not have a specific identifiable victim.

Fixing public sporting events is another example of the challenge to define and punish fraud. As we see in the *Peter Barrie* case, the victims of Barrie's scams are somewhat diffuse, and include those bettors who lose in part because their bets were based upon erroneous information provided by Barrie (although many of them would have bet on a horse that would not have won anyway).

However, while Barrie seems to be clearly acting improperly, the case can seem a bit awkward as the basis for criminal liability. The rules that are being violated may not be rules promulgated by the government at all but rather rules created by the organizers of the particular sporting event. Why should violation of such private sporting rules be a criminal offense?

Rigging Publicly Exhibited Contest.

(1) A person commits a misdemeanor if, with purpose to prevent a publicly exhibited contest from being conducted in accordance with the rules and usages purporting to govern it, he:

(a) confers or offers or agrees to confer any benefit upon, or threatens any injury to a participant, official or other person associated with the contest or exhibition; or

(b) tampers with any person, animal or thing.

(2) Soliciting or Accepting Benefit for Rigging. A person commits a misdemeanor if he knowingly solicits, accepts or agrees to accept any benefit the giving of which would be criminal under Subsection (1).

(3) Participation in Rigged Contest. A person commits a misdemeanor if he knowingly engages in, sponsors, produces, judges, or otherwise participates in a publicly exhibited contest knowing that the contest is not being conducted in compliance with the rules and usages purporting to govern it, by reason of conduct which would be criminal under this Section.

Model Penal Code §224.9

Figure 27.2

The answer is found in the fact that the criminal law is designed to punish not just harms to individuals but also endangering larger intangible societal interests – in this instance the integrity of public sporting events generally. One can imagine the rawness of social life if public sporting events claiming to follow fixed rules could be lawfully manipulated for the benefit of a few. Such would inspire anger and distrust on a wide scale, feelings that would not only destroy public confidence and interest in the sport but also could easily spill over into distrust in other aspects of public life. The same interests do not exist for purely private sporting events and, accordingly, the existing offenses generally are limited to public sporting or gaming events. As the Model Penal Code offense (reproduced in the margin) makes clear, the gravamen of the offense is violating "the rules and usages purporting to govern" a "publicly exhibited contest."

As broad as the offense seems to be, it may not be a match for the boundless ingenuity of potential cheaters. For example, was Barrie's race fixing in violation of the Model Code offense? When he drugs a horse or uses some improper stimulation, he presumably is in violation of the racing rules. But when he paints a horse in order to mislead bettors, is it as clear that his conduct is a violation of the racing rules – the painting has no effect on how fast or slow the horse will run. It is the betting system rather than the sports event itself that he is manipulating.

Consider the application of *sports fixing* statutes in the following more modern case involving a different kind of sport.

Tulane Basketball – 1985

The Tulane Green Waves men's basketball team is having a decent season in 1985.[8] Clyde Eads is a starter who plays forward. Eads also sells cocaine to fellow students. One of his customers, Gary Kranz, approaches Eads with a proposition. The oddsmakers have said that Tulane is expected to win the game against Southern Mississippi by 10½ points. Kranz and some of his friends have bet $7,000 through various sports-betting organizations that Tulane will win by less than 10½ points. If Eads get them to win by a closer margin than 10½, he will pay Eads. He is not asking Eads to throw the game, only to "shave points."

Eads agrees but cannot do it alone. He enlists the help of three teammates, all starters, which include star player John Williams. Given an opportunity to earn easy money without changing the team's when-loss record, the three agree to the scheme with little hesitation. The game ends with Tulane winning by a single point. The players are paid around $600 each.

After the players collude with Kranz, a pair of convicted bookmakers ask them to shave points in their next game, against Memphis State. Tulane is expected to lose but it is agreed that the players will make sure they lose by at least seven points. This game is expected to be particularly intense as star player Williams and his Memphis State counterpart Keith Lee are fan favorites.

As in the game against Southern Mississippi, the players perform more poorly than usual, but this time their actions are more obvious. Williams gets himself in early foul trouble and is forced to sit on the bench before halftime, which allows Lee to score a pair of layups in the final minute of the first half. Despite this, the Green Waves are still leading 34-28 at the break. The game quickly turns around after halftime, with opposing star Lee quickly scoring six points to tie the game. When Williams returns to the court, he does not show his usual aggression; he needs to ensure his team loses by at least seven. He shoots 0-for-2 from the field and 2-for-4 from the line and gets only one rebound in the second half, finishing the game with only 14 points, below his season average. Tulane loses to Memphis State 60-49. The players couldn't be more thrilled with the result as they collect $16,000.

After this, the team makes no more attempts to shave points and ends the season with 15 wins and 13 losses, the same record they probably would have had whether they shaved points or not, and they each end up with several thousand dollars in extra cash. With the season drawing to a close, most of the players simply forget about the scheme.

However, a Tulane fan and attorney overhears the players talking about the earlier point shaving. Already suspicious because of the team's abnormally poor performance against Southern Mississippi and Memphis State, he investigates further and contacts the district attorney, who, along with many law enforcement officials of the time, is concerned about the growing popularity and potential malfeasance connected with sports betting. The two men approach Eads, who admits to the scheme. For their testimony before a grand jury, Eads and another player receive immunity.

On March 26, Williams and two other players are handcuffed and walked to Central Lockup in New Orleans. Kranz and the other arrangers are also arrested. On April 4, head coach Ned Fowler and assistant coaches Mike Richardson and Max Pfeifer resign after admitting to paying the players in a separate scandal. That same day, Tulane President Dr. Eamon Kelly announces his recommendation to the Board of Administrators to disband the men's basketball program permanently. With a Division I basketball program being shut down in a gambling scandal, reporters flocked to the story and the disgraced Tulane basketball program gains national headlines.

Figure 27.3 Williams went on to a successful career in the NBA

On April 5, eight people, including Williams and Kranz, are indicted on allegations of violating Louisiana's sports bribery law for altering the score of the games against Southern Mississippi and Memphis State. All are charged with either sports bribery (which carries a maximum penalty of five years in prison and a $10,000 fine) and/or conspiracy (which carries a maximum penalty of two years and a $5,000 fine), with Kranz facing additional charges of drug dealing.

Have the Tulane players violated the Model Penal Code offense? Was it their "purpose to prevent a publicly exhibited contest from being conducted in accordance with the rules and usages purporting to govern it"? Probably not, unless the organizers had the foresight in 1985 to include a rule that says something like: all players must try their hardest at all times. But this rule might be difficult to enforce. There are times in a sporting event, including basketball, when a coach or player might have good reason to ease up for a while. The rule will probably have to be something like: all players must try their hardest at all times consistent with the customary conduct of the sport.

The real complication with point shaving is that the intended victims are not the competitors but rather the bettors, just as Barrie's horse painting was designed to mislead and thereby victimize bettors not racers. However, if the concern that drives criminalization is the perceived public integrity of the game, then scamming bettors rather than participants can be as destructive to the game's public reputation.

And, indeed, *sports fixing* statutes have become considerably more sophisticated since Barrie's day, and have been interpreted sufficiently broadly to include manipulations like point shaving.

Sports Fixing Offenses in the States

Sports fixing is essentially a specialized form of *commercial bribery*, which presumably everyone agrees should be criminal as it is simply a form of fraud. Commercial bribery is exerting corrupt influence on private sector employees or agents in relation to the employer's or principal's affairs, such as where a third party induces an employee to violate a fiduciary duty without the employer's knowledge. Thirty-eight states have a general offense criminalizing commercial bribery, the remaining states commonly have a series of more specialized commercial bribery offenses.

The commercial bribery offense will not cover many if not most fences of sports bribery, however, because it requires that the offender knowingly "violate a duty of fidelity." Commercial partners, agents, employees, trustees, guardians, directors, managers, lawyers, doctors, accountants, etc. all have fiduciary duties and breach of those duties by accepting a bribe will constitute the offense. But basketball players probably do not stand in the relationship of fiduciary duty to anyone. In public sporting contests generally, there may be no contractual or fiduciary relationship between the defendant schemer and the public viewers or bettors. Thus, most commercial bribery statutes would not cover bribes intended to cause players or participants to fail to give their "best efforts" in an athletic contest, such as the Tulane point shaving. Arizona's general commercial bribery statute, for example, applies only in the context of an employer-employee relationship, where the corruption results in economic loss to the employer.[9] Arizona's sports bribery statute, in contrast, covers bribes of participants and officials where the intent is to influence [the player] to lose or try to lose or cause to be lost or to limit his or his team's margin of victory or defeat, or in the case of a referee or other official to affect his decisions or the performance of his duties in any way.[10]

Not all sports fixing involves bribery. Much of it falls under a special kind of corruption called sports tampering. Such statutes cover tampering with persons, animals, or things in a manner inconsistent with the rules of the contest, and the conduct need not involve any officials or participants. For instance, a third party may be liable for criminal tampering where he sneaks into a locker room and deflates the game ball below league standards, with the intent that one team's performance be improperly enhanced or another's inhibited. Thus, prosecutors may use the tampering statute to punish conduct that, though not involving bribery, undermines the integrity of high-profile social institutions.

The map below indicates the position of each state with regard to a specific criminal prohibition against sports bribery and sports tampering.[11] The darker the shading on the map, the broader the coverage of the offense.

Thirty-seven states, those with the darkest shading on the map, have adopted criminal statutes specifically prohibiting bribery of both officials and participants in professional and amateur sports as well as other public contests.[12] Bribery of an official is framed in terms of inducing the official to perform her duties improperly. It is not required that the participant or official successfully alter the course or result of the contest.

Ten states, those with light shading on the map, have adopted criminal statutes targeting sports bribery of participants only. The members of the Tulane basketball team who agreed to shave points could be liable in these states and in the dark-shaded states noted above. However, a referee in a Tulane game who agreed to do the same thing would not be liable in these states but would be liable in the group above. (As

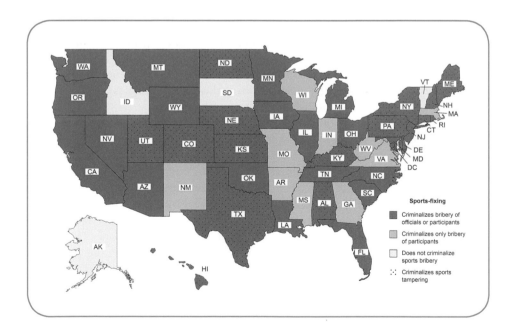

Figure 27.4

the map shows, however, the Louisiana statute criminalizes misconduct by both participants and officials, and thus a Tulane referee would be liable.)

Four states, those with no shading on the map, do not have special criminal statutes targeting bribery of sports participants or officials. In these states, the criminal law can only reach sports bribery if the case happens to fit under the reach of the state's general commercial bribery statute.

Fifteen states, those *with* a dots overlay, have adopted statutes that also criminalize "tampering" with people, animals, or things (such as equipment), with the intent to prevent a public contest to be held according to the rules of play. For instance, these statutes would prohibit deflating footballs or poisoning or drugging a racehorse or dog with the intent to confer an inappropriate advantage or disadvantage.

Peter Barrie's horse drugging would certainly be an offense under these statutes, but his horse-switching trick presents a more complicated issue. It does seem to constitute a form of tampering. However, Barrie might well argue that his "tampering," if that is what it was, was not "with the purpose to prevent a publicly exhibited contest from being conducted in accordance with the rules and usages purporting to govern it," as, for example, subsection (1)(b) of the Model Code tampering provision requires (quoted in the margin earlier). In other words, Barrie's argument that he is not manipulating the race but rather the bettors may still be a winning argument depending upon the exact language used in the jurisdiction's sports tampering statute.

One may wonder why there is such variation in coverage of sports fixing among the states. Setting aside Idaho, which appears to have neither a general commercial bribery statute nor a specific sports bribery or tampering offense, every jurisdiction has some related offense. The differences among the states may come down to how much detail they feel they need to provide in order to assure that the offense definition will cover all possible versions of sports fixing.

It should be no surprise, then, to see that many if not most of the states with the most detailed approach – those with the darkest shading and with dots overlaid, indicating both a sports bribery and a sports tampering offense covering both officials and participants – are states with active sports cultures, such as New York, Pennsylvania, and New Jersey, as well as horseracing Kentucky and football-obsessed Alabama and Texas. There are, however, other states with active sports cultures, professional or amateur, that do not have this full coverage.

Why wouldn't a sports bribery offense be drafted to cover not only corrupt participants but also corrupt officials? Why wouldn't such statutes be drafted to specifically include tampering not just bribery, especially since tampering is the kind of activity the general commercial bribery statute is less likely to capture? In the states with limited coverage, it may be simply a matter of legislative inertia. Until a major scandal breaks, the legislature may not focus on the risk of incomplete coverage or the greater difficulty of having to prosecute under the general commercial bribery statute.

Aftermaths

There seems little doubt that Barrie is a skilled horseman but the criminal streak in him seems to have been too deeply ingrained for honest work. After being deported, Barrie transitions from ringing horses to doping them. The change in specialties comes about because his previous scams have shown the racing community the need for stricter controls.

While his manipulation methods have evolved, very little else about Barrie appears to change. He remains imprudent, broke, and vocal. (He does interviews in the British press on his work as a horse doper.) The talented horseman wanders about various British territories until his death at the age of 85 in Greenwich, England.[13]

In the Tulane basketball point-shaving case, the participants are convicted at trial. As noted, Eads testifies for the prosecution and is given immunity. The players receive relatively mild sentences, including a suspended prison sentence, several years on probation, a community service requirement, a fine, and a required donation of their profits to a charity.

Arranger Kranz's sentence is more harsh. He faces nine counts of distributing cocaine, one count of possession of cocaine, ten counts of sports bribery, and three additional counts of conspiracy, meaning he is eligible for a 332-year prison sentence. However, the drug charges are dropped after he testifies for the prosecution against the players. He gets off with three months in jail, 1,500 hours of community service, and a fine of $45,000.

Star player Williams has the most to lose – he has been selected by the Cavaliers in the 1985 NBA Draft and the criminal charges threaten to derail his career. However, Williams is granted a mistrial because of a prosecution procedural error. In the second trial, the judge again finds prosecutorial error and Williams avoids all punishment. Unfortunately, the NBA refuses Williams permission to play, at least temporarily. The following year his eligibility is restored, and he goes on to have a successful 13-year career.

The University's president, stung by the embarrassment of the scandal, sentences the basketball program to death. He ends the program "forever," which turns out to be for four years. The program is reinstated 1990.

Chapter Glossary

Commercial Bribery: It applies where one accepts payment (or other consideration) in return for violating a fiduciary obligation to an employer or other principal.[14]

Sports Fixing: An intentional arrangement, act or omission aimed at improper alteration of the result or the course of a sports competition in order to remove all or part of the unpredictable nature of the aforementioned sports competition with a view to obtaining an undue advantage for oneself or for others.[15]

Notes

1. This narrative is drawn from the following source: David Ashforth, *Ringers & Rascals: The True Story of Racing's Greatest Con Artists* (Lexington: Eclipse Press, 2004).
2. Ashforth, 'Heating Up,' in *Ringers & Rascals*, p. 28.
3. Ashforth, 'Heating Up,' in *Ringers & Rascals*, p. 42.
4. Ashforth, 'Hot,' in *Ringers & Rascals*, p. 80.
5. Ashforth, 'Heating Up,' *Ringers & Rascals*, p. 80.
6. David Miers, 'Gaming in the Seventeenth and Eighteenth Centuries,' in *Regulating Commercial Gambling: Past, Present, and Future* (Oxford: Oxford University Press, 2004), p. 27.
7. Miers, 'Gaming in the Seventeenth,' p. 27.

8. This narrative is drawn from the following sources: Rob Gloster, 'The Point-Shaving Scandal at Tulane University,' *United Press International*, 5 April 1985, http://www.upi.com/Archives/1985/04/05/The-point-shaving-scandal-at-Tulane-University-that-may-end/7030481525200/; Frances F. Marcus, '8 Indicted in Tulane Scandal; School to Give Up Basketball,' *The New York Times*, 5 April 1985, http://www.nytimes.com/1985/04/05/sports/8-indicted-in-tulane-scandal-school-to-give-up-basketball.html?pagewanted=all; 'Tulane Scandal Hasn't Hit Bottom Yet: A Cocaine Purchase Apparently Led to Point-Shaving Scheme,' *Los Angeles Times*, 6 April 1985, http://articles.latimes.com/1985-04-06/sports/sp-18477_1_point-shaving-scheme; Lenny Vangilder, 'A Sad Anniversary: 25 Years Since Tulane Basketball's Point Shaving Scandal,' *Sports Nola*, 26 March 2010, http://sportsnola.com/a-sad-anniversary-25-years-since-tulane-basketballs-point-shaving-scandal/.

9. Ariz. Rev. Stat. Ann. § 13-2605.

10. Ariz. Rev. Stat. Ann. § 13-2309.

11. The map is taken from Paul H. Robinson and Tyler Scot Williams, 'Fixing Sporting Events,' in *Mapping American Criminal Law: Variations across the 50 States* (Westport: Prager, 2018), p. 298. All supporting authorities are available from that source.

12. A sports participant includes any person whose role is to advance a particular player or team, such as players, coaches, managers, and trainers. Bribery of a participant is nearly always framed in terms of conferring a benefit on the participant in exchange for his agreement to try to lose or diminish his performance, or to fail to put forth his best efforts. A sports official includes any person whose role is to be neutral and whose role would ordinarily permit the person to influence the outcome or result of a competition, such as a judge, referee, or umpire.

13. Liam O'Brien, *Don't Bet the Farm: The Encyclopedia of Betting and Gambling* (New York: eBookPartnership.com, 2014).

14. Paul H. Robinson and Michael T. Cahill, *Criminal Law, 2nd ed.* (New York: Wolters Kluwer, 2012), §16.5.

15. Council of Europe Convention on the Manipulation of Sports Competitions 3 (2014), https://rm.coe.int/16801cdd7e.

Chapter 28

Anti-competition

Vanderbilt's Market Manipulation

1866. Russia and the United States are about to work out a real estate deal: the purchase of Alaska for two cents an acre. With the American Civil War over, the last issue of the last abolitionist magazine, *The Liberator*, is published. Jesse James, who becomes a folk hero, robs his first bank. Alfred Nobel invents dynamite. Andrew Rankin patents the urinal. The laying of the 1,686-mile-long trans-Atlantic telegraph cable shows the growing power of enterprise to change the world. Another larger-than-life personality shows the power of enterprise in other realms.

Cornelius Vanderbilt – 1866

At age 11 Cornelius Vanderbilt quits school and works with his father, ferrying passengers and goods between Staten Island and Manhattan. In 1810, at age 16, the teenager concocts a plan to start his own ferry and freight business, charging 18 cents per trip, which is much lower than other ferry services. Within a year of operation, he earns himself more than $1,000. He branches out from there and his various businesses expand and grow quickly.

Even as a young man his tactics are aggressive and relentless. One of his strategies is to start a new service that undercuts the companies already in business, weakening them. Then, when the moment is right, he buys up the weakened company. He also receives what amounts to ransom payments from other companies by promising not to compete with them. After several decades establishing himself as a Titan in steamships, Vanderbilt is worth half a million dollars.[1]

He decides to expand his empire to include railroads, which he sees as the future of the transportation business. He begins by buying shares of the New York and Harlem Railroad in 1857, a line generally considered worthless and decrepit. He acquires an array of small under-valued railroads that he uses to put pressure on his

DOI: 10.4324/9781003258025-31

real target, a line called the Stonington. He cuts fares on the lines that he has acquired, and he takes control of all the choke points into New York City. Owning the choke points allows him to deny the Stonington trains access to through routes. The Stonington's stockholders see the value of their company evaporating and move to sell their stock before the line goes into bankruptcy. As the price of the shares plummet, Vanderbilt buys. Once he controls a majority of the stock, he installs himself as president and restores the Stonington to full service. The power plays keep coming and his influence keeps growing.

Vanderbilt spends years constructing a railroad empire. Because Wall Street insiders initially see him as a steamship entrepreneur with little railway expertise on the big national stage, they assume he is buying stock in bad railroads out of ignorance or unrealistic grandiosity and generally ignore him. With no one paying much attention, Vanderbilt grows his portfolio, commonly using stock watering, bribery, and stock cornering, tactics that were not illegal at the time.

A group of Wall Street traders, unimpressed by Vanderbilt, begin to sell short one of his rail lines, the Hudson. ("Shorting" a company's stock is essentially betting against the company's success.) Vanderbilt is only too happy for the stock shorting plan to proceed; in fact he helps put their plan into high gear. He concocts a scheme to convince the public that the company does not have the cash to keep the line going. The false rumors cause the stock price to plummet which is just what the short sellers want. But Vanderbilt now sends his agents out to purchase the cheap shares, significantly increasing his stock holdings in the company. In 1864 Vanderbilt is made head of the board and in 1865 he becomes president of the Hudson. When it becomes clear that the company is in fact financially quite healthy, the stock value increases and the short sellers lose their bets. With majority ownership in the company, Vanderbilt is now in the position that his long-term strategy has been seeking.

The Albany Bridge, a 2,000-foot-long span over the Hudson River, accommodates two rail lines – one line belongs to the Stonington and the other to the Hudson. Now, as the owner of both lines, Vanderbilt controls the bridge, which is the sole route for trains servicing New York City.

During 1863 and 1864, Vanderbilt begins buying stock in the New York Central Railroad. For a time, he owns enough stock to dictate how the line is run but in December 1866 a coalition of other stockholders, many of whom lost huge sums in the Hudson deal, decide to combine forces. They gain control of the New York Central's board and push Vanderbilt out. Vanderbilt is 72 years old, and the younger men are confident that he is no longer the strongman he once was.

Vanderbilt is at this point the richest man in the country with a net worth of $65 million,[2] and he puts his considerable resources toward addressing the insult and re-gaining control of the New York Central Railroad. Vanderbilt makes sure that everyone knows that this fight is personal, and he publicly announces that he wants to "watch them bleed."[3] For their part, the coalition is unafraid, as together they own far more of the New York Central than Vanderbilt. They see no options for Vanderbilt.

On January 14, 1867, the river flowing under the Albany Bridge freezes solid, which means that all boat service across the river ceases. Vanderbilt takes this occasion to close the Albany Bridge, which he now controls.

Rail traffic in and out of New York City stops. Passengers can cross the ice on foot or in sleds, but critical supplies are marooned in place. A backlog of freight accumulates outside the city. Millions of dollars of cargo and thousands of passengers are affected.

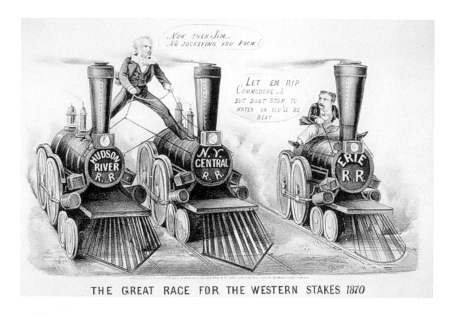

THE GREAT RACE FOR THE WESTERN STAKES 1870

Figure 28.1 The dominance of Vanderbilt was clear to everyone, Currier and Ives, 1870

New York City is the nation's largest port, so the problem caused by the closure of the bridge ripples across the country.

Throughout the railroad industry there is a huge sell-off of stock. If Vanderbilt does not open his bridge, many companies will go bankrupt. Most of the endangered companies are of no interest to Vanderbilt – his target is the New York Central Railroad. As stock in the New York Central plummets,[4] he buys up the cheap shares. The State Assembly holds hearings on the blockade and Vanderbilt successfully defends his rights to use his bridge in any way he sees fit. Vanderbilt makes no attempt to hide his motives, saying that he can use "the power in my own hands to punish."[5]

With no other option, the board of the New York Central Railroad elects Vanderbilt to be president of the company. The Albany Bridge is again open for business.

Responding to the Growing Power of Economic Titans and Their Corporations

The spread of industrialization during this era prompts expansion of federal power to control the growing power of massive private companies, especially those prospering from the development of an interstate railroad system.[6] One significant limitation on the ability to limit corporate power is the view that while corporations could be liable for civil wrongs, criminal liability did not make sense when applied to a nonhuman legal entity. In an 1852 prosecution of a railroad, the court "conceded that a corporation cannot, from its nature, be guilty of treason, felony, or other crime involving malus animus in its commission."[7] More generally, the legal view was that

SEC. 1 Every contract, combination in the form of trust or otherwise, or conspiracy, in restraint of trade or commerce among the several States, or with foreign nations, is hereby declared to be illegal. Every person who shall make any such contract or engage in any such combination or Conspiracy, shall be deemed guilty of a misdemeanor, and, on conviction thereof, shall 'be punished by fine not exceeding five thousand dollars, or by imprisonment not exceeding one year, or by both said punishments, in the discretion of the court.

An Act To Protect Trade And Commerce Against Unlawful Restraints And Monopolies. July 2,1890

Figure 28.2

corporations cannot be held liable for crimes that require intent. In 1903, however, Congress passed the Elkins Act, which allowed criminal intent to be imputed to corporations. Six years later, the Supreme Court cites the danger of increasing corporate power in upholding the constitutionality of the Elkins Act in *New York Central & Hudson River Railroad v. United States*.[8]

And in 1890, Congress enacts the Sherman Antitrust Act, reproduced in the margin, which prohibits conduct "in restraint of trade or commerce." But having this general authority does not automatically translate into being able to effectively police aggressive companies in the complex real world.

Consider the *Swift Meats* case, which came after these initial reforms.

Swift Meats – 1905

Gustavus Franklin Swift never liked school. In 1855, the 14-year-old drops out and takes a job working in his brother's butcher shop. At age 16, Swift sets off on his own, opening his own butchering business.[9] With a loan of $400 from one of his uncles, he begins his venture by purchasing livestock in Brighton, Massachusetts, and driving them to Eastham, Massachusetts, a ten days' journey. He proves to be a wily businessman, denying his herds water during the last miles of the trip so they would drink more when they arrived at the market in Eastham. As cattle are sold by weight, the extra water earns him a fatter profit.

In 1878, Swift and engineer Andrew Chase design the first working refrigerated railcar. He finances the building of the first fleet of refrigerated cars and establishes a contract with the Grand Truck Railway to use his cars on routes from Michigan through Canada to the East Coast. From there, he creates the Swift Refrigerator Line, allowing his company to ship fresh meat to all parts of the country and even to foreign countries. Now that Swift has his own railroad line, he takes control of all aspects of the meat production process, beginning with slaughterhouse and meatpacking plants, moving the meat to market over his transportation line, and ending at the local butcher shop.

In 1893, an entrepreneur purchases the Fort Worth Union Stockyards. He hopes that by offering 50 cents more per animal than the market in Kansas City, he can draw cattlemen into Fort Worth. The strategy is wildly successful: so many cattlemen flood Forth Worth clambering to sell their herd that the entrepreneur does not have enough money to pay them all. Swift proposes a solution to the entrepreneur's problem cash shortage. *Swift & Co.*, and another large meatpacker, *Armour and Co.*, will guarantee purchases of the livestock if in return it receives property on which to build a meatpacking plant as well as a one-third interest in the stockyard company. He and Armour are now in a unique position to control this arm of the industry.

The lessons Swift learns in Fort Worth he now applies to the industry as a whole. At the time, there are six major firms in the meatpacking industry, dubbed the "Big Six." Collectively, they make around $700 million a year in profit. The "Big Six" set to work to eliminate competition between one another by deciding in advance which company will bid on each livestock purchase and pledging to never outbid one another. Without a competitive market in which multiple parties bid for the sale, owners of the cattle are compelled to sell to a single buyer at a low price. The system gives the meatpacking cartel the ability to buy most of the nation's livestock at a price they find advantageous.

In addition to driving down the price of the livestock, the group works to push up the price of the meat they sell to consumers. The companies agree to fix the prices at

Figure 28.3 Gustavus Franklin Swift in the year he died, 1903

which they sell meat throughout the United States in order to avoid competition among the group that would undercut their profits. They also agree to restrict the amount of meat shipped, decreasing supply and thus increasing the price. Further, they establish uniform contract agreements with the dealers to whom they sell so that dealers cannot shop around for the company that sells meat with the best terms. The group creates a single standard for extending credit to dealers and any dealer who does not comply is added to a joint blacklist. All six companies agree to refuse business with any dealer on the blacklist, which usually ends up putting that dealer out of business. By agreement, any member of the group that does not follow the group's rules must pay a penalty.

Aside from the sale and distribution of meats by the companies, the "Big Six" also control transportation. The major railroads, which initially refused to use refrigerated cars, now use them and the "Big Six" set uniform delivery rates for their meat, further leveling out prices and diminishing competition. On rail lines that they do not control, their economic power enables Swift and partners to obtain rebates that effectively reduce their costs below the rates that other customers pay.

In effect, the "Big Six" have formed an oligopoly by which the six firms control the industry. Such cartels are technically illegal because such collusion can undermine competition among them – which was, of course, the primary purpose of the meatpacking cartel. But because the collusion is done in private, while law enforcement authorities have legal authority to intervene, they have no effective means of uncovering and prosecuting such anticompetitive behavior.

Despite the cartel's best efforts at secrecy, regulators do eventually notice the anti-competition problems in the meat industry. In 1902, President Theodore Roosevelt, as part of his efforts to control corporations and protect consumers under the Square Deal, directs that a lawsuit be brought against the beef industry using the Sherman Antitrust Act of 1890. The companies, facing a federal injunction, decide that their best strategy to avoid government legal action is to merge into one big company, called the National Packing Company.

However, in 1905 the Supreme Court finds the reconstituted company to be acting improperly. To the court the problem is not that the consolidated company is seeking to get good credit terms or advantageous cattle prices, because that is what businesses should do. The illegality comes from the overall intent of the National Packing Company, whose very existence is designed to monopolize the fresh meat market. "Even if the separate elements of such a scheme are lawful, when they are bound together by a common intent as parts of an unlawful scheme to monopolize interstate commerce, the plan may make the parts unlawful."[10]

The Court does not require that the combined companies be broken up but only that they limit themselves to doing what is good for them rather than doing what would harm other companies.

> But nothing herein shall be construed to prohibit the said defendants from agreeing upon charges for cartage and delivery, and other incidents connected with local sales, where such charges are not calculated to have any effect upon competition in the sales and delivery of meats; nor from establishing and maintaining rules for the giving of credit to dealers where such rules in good faith are calculated solely to protect the defendants against dishonest or irresponsible dealers . . .[11]

Because of the limited scope of the 1905 decision, the ruling changes little in the operation of the company.

The monopolistic behavior of Vanderbilt and the price-fixing behavior of Swift Meats are now a thing of the past. Federal legislature has increasingly outlawed such conduct and court decisions have interpreted and applied the Sherman Antitrust Act of 1890 in more demanding terms. But today's law must deal with a wider variety of anticompetitive schemes, many of which are somewhat more nuanced than the bald aggressive monopolistic behavior of Vanderbilt and Swift, and were first developed by entrepreneurs like Rockefeller, Carnegie, Gould, and Frick.

Anti-competition Offenses in the States

Federal authorities typically investigate and prosecute anti-competitive practices that have a national or at least a multi-state scope (which is what creates federal jurisdiction). States have the authority to prosecute anti-competitive conduct even if it occurs and has effect only within that state. However, state authorities cannot use federal law but must rely upon their own state anti-competition laws.

One of the most common modern schemes that the state law works to police is what is called *predatory pricing*. While small companies generally must set prices according to the actual costs of goods or services in a particular marketplace, larger companies are able to set prices at whatever level is required to undermine competitors, offsetting their temporary losses with profits from other marketplaces. Modern economic policy seeks to ensure competition and protect long-term price stability by prohibiting such predatory pricing schemes. Thus, a large number of states criminalize the practice. The statutes target two kinds of such anticompetitive practices: sales below cost and *price discrimination*.[12] Both of these kind of violations commonly require that the conduct be performed for the purpose of undermining competition.

While prohibitions on *sales below cost* first appeared in early 15th-century England, such statutes began to be adopted in the United States at the start of the 20th century. As noted, the primary justification for the prohibition is the potential for larger companies to use the practice against smaller companies, thereby eliminating competition and allowing them to subsequently raise their prices above the previously existing market price. Some have cast doubt on the contention that sales below cost can actually eliminate competition. In most cases, such sales are unprofitable even in the long term. "The predator loses money during the period of predation," so the argument goes, and "if he tries to recoup it later by raising his price, new entrants will be attracted," and the predator will be undersold.[13] Nonetheless, such statutes are common, as is shown by the states with a dots overlay on the map below.

In addition to its anticompetitive potential, sales-below-cost practices are also frowned upon as a form of deception of customers. The U.S. Supreme Court notes that selling selected goods at a loss in order to lure customers into the store is not only "a destructive means of competition," but also a deceptive tactic that "plays on the gullibility of customers by leading them to expect what generally is not true, namely, that a store which offers such an amazing bargain is full of other such bargains."[14]

The other kind of predatory pricing is *price discrimination*. In the early 1900s, states began to adopt *territorial* price discrimination statutes, which prohibit selling goods in one area at a lower price in order to eliminate competition in that

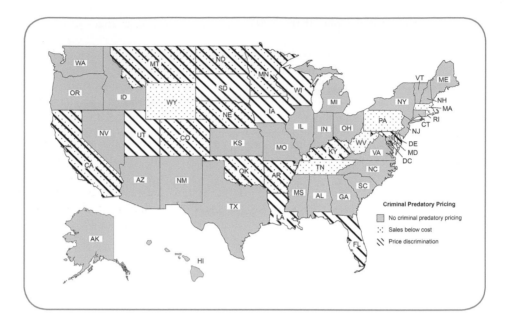

Figure 28.4

area. Generally, firms recoup losses in one area by retaining higher prices where there is little or no competition. Most states that target price discrimination have adopted such *territorial* price discrimination statutes, but a handful of states have adopted statutes modeled on the federal Robinson-Patman Act of 1936, which prohibits

> discriminat[ion] in price between different *purchasers* of commodities of like grade and quality, . . . where the effect of such discrimination may be substantially to lessen competition or tend to create a monopoly in any line of commerce, or to injure, destroy, or prevent competition.[15]

This prohibition on price discrimination at the *purchaser* level is meant to "provide some measure of protection to small independent retailers and their independent suppliers from what was thought to be unfair competition from vertically integrated, multi-location chain stores."[16] Or as the U.S. Supreme Court noted, the Robinson-Patman amendment was "motivated principally by congressional concern over the impact upon secondary line competition of the burgeoning of mammoth purchasers, notably chain stores."[17]

The map below indicates the position of each state with regard to these two kinds of predatory pricing.[18] Twenty-eight states, those with shading on the map, have not adopted criminal statutes prohibiting either species of predatory pricing, sales below cost, or price discrimination with the purpose of injuring competition. (However, some of these states have adopted civil statutes prohibiting predatory pricing.) Of the unshaded states, which do criminalize some kind of predatory pricing, 15, those with a dots overlaid, have adopted criminal statutes specifically prohibiting sales below cost, and 17 states, those with diagonal lines on the map, have adopted criminal statutes specifically prohibiting price discrimination.

How Can There Be Such a Thing as a Price So Low as to Be Criminal?

What is it exactly about *predatory pricing* that merits the condemnation of the criminal sanction? "Low prices" are generally thought to be a *good* thing. A common reaction among laypersons to criminal sales-below-cost statutes is puzzlement: how could there be such a thing as a bargain price so low that it's criminal?

The criminalization of predatory pricing nicely illustrates how criminal law concerns itself not just with tangible harms to people and property but also with intangible harms to institutions and larger societal interests. As noted above, the purpose of predatory pricing statutes is to "safeguard the public" by preventing ruinous competition,[19] which threatens to "drive smaller merchants out of business,"[20] thereby leaving the larger company with less or no price competition. In the 1930s, when new statutes targeted predatory pricing, the societal benefit of criminalizing predatory pricing was apparent to consumers, many of whom loathed the influx of large retailers into their communities that tended to undermine the previously existing personal social order, especially of small communities.

A separate justification for predatory pricing offenses relates to fraud or misdirection of consumers. As the U.S. Supreme Court noted regarding the predatory practice of sales below cost: not only are sales below cost destructive of competition, a harm to the general welfare, but they are *dishonest*, "play[ing] on the gullibility of customers by leading them to expect what . . . is not true, . . . that a store which offers such an amazing bargain is full of other such bargains."[21] Further, it also *hides an agenda* from the consumer, one that may ultimately be against the consumer's interest – namely, the destruction of another businessperson's ability to make an honest living.

Much has changed since the early predatory pricing statutes were adopted, including important shifts in the way that consumers purchase goods and services. Consumers today regularly benefit from the lower prices of the large retailers and many have already adjusted to life no longer dominated by their small town community. Also, nearly all consumers today are able to purchase goods online, allowing quick and easy comparisons of price, and generally forestalling the possibility of territorial *price discrimination*. A few, large, national retailers often control the bulk of a market, but their market share is not deemed illegal. For instance, CVS and Walgreens together control between 50% and 75% of the drugstore market in the nation's largest metropolitan areas.[22]

Despite these changes, the states' predatory pricing statutes largely remain unchanged. As retail habits continue to evolve in the 21st century, it's an open question whether such statutes will continue to be relevant. Indeed, one may wonder about the future of criminal antitrust practices generally. The accelerating rate of marketplace and industry change due to technological advances has made it more difficult to obtain and hold a monopoly long term. A monopoly in rail transportation was not worth nearly so much once the interstate highway system was established. And in more recent times, we have seen an apparent monopoly in some aspect of the marketplace – such as dial-in internet service by AOL – quickly disappears with the next technological advance or clever entrepreneur.

The world today has many enormous multinational corporations, such as J.P. Morgan Chase, Walmart, Amazon, Apple, Samsung, and Alphabet (parent of Google), yet, if history is any gauge, it seems possible, if not likely, that many of them may lose their places over time to more innovative companies. However, the ability of any one government to control large corporations may become increasingly limited as the marketplace becomes increasingly international. We have seen in many other chapters that criminal law commonly changes as societal norms change. In this instance, change again seems likely but here driven by economic, marketplace, innovation, and political forces.

Aftermaths

The young upstarts are wrong about Vanderbilt, who keeps his edge well into old age. And nothing much changes in the way he conducts his business. He dies on January 4, 1877, leaving behind a fortune of $105 million dollars, the equivalent of $2.6 trillion dollars today,[23] more than the value of Apple and Microsoft combined. He leaves $95 million to his eldest son, William, and $500,000 to each of his daughters.

In the meatpacking case, Swift's business continues to do well even after the Court ruling. The impact on business is hardly noticed. But over time, the business steadily shrinks and in 2007 JBS, an American food processing company and a subsidiary of the Brazilian company JBS S.A., purchases Swift & Co. for $1.5 billion. If $1.5 billion is a shadow of the former company, it is easy to imagine how mighty the market leader once had been.

Chapter Glossary

Predatory Pricing: It is a kind of unlawful anti-competitive conduct in which prices are set low in an attempt to eliminate the competition.[24]

Price Discrimination: It is a kind of unlawful anti-competitive conduct, criminalized by the Sherman Antitrust Act, Clayton Antitrust Act, and Robinson-Patman Act, in which different customers are charged different prices for the same good or service with the intent that such discrimination will harm competitors.[25]

Notes

1. 'Cornelius Vanderbilt, The Commodore,' *American-Rails.com*, http://www.american-rails.com/cornelius-vanderbilt.html.
2. 'Cornelius Vanderbilt.' *History.com*, updated on 7 June 2019, accessed on 13 June 2019.
3. 'The Story of Vanderbilt's Hudson River Bridge,' *Compete Smarter Not Harder*, 3 October 2013, https://competesmarternotharder.wordpress.com/2013/10/03/the-story-of-vanderbilts-hudson-river-bridge/.
4. 'The Men Who Built America: A New Bar Begins,' *History Channel*, Episode 1; Joanne Reitano, *New York State: Peoples, Places, and Priorities: A Concise History with Sources* (Abingdon: Routledge, 2015).
5. Reitano, *New York State*.
6. Sara Sun Beale, *The Development and Evolution of the US Law of Corporate Criminal Liability* (German Conference on Comparative Law, 2013), pp. 3–6.
7. Thomas J. Bernard, 'The Historical Development of Corporate Criminal Liability,' *Criminology* 22, no. 1 (1984): pp. 3–18.

8. Sun Beale, *The Development and Evolution of the US Law of Corporate Criminal Liability*, p. 12.

9. This portion of the narrative is drawn from the following sources: Jon Kutner, 'Swift and Company,' *Handbook of Texas Online*, https://www.tshaonline.org/handbook/online/articles/dis02; *Swift & Co. v. United States*, 196 U.S. 375 (1905).

10. *Swift & Co. v. United States*, 196 U.S. 375 (1905).

11. *Swift & Co. v. United States*, 196 U.S. 375 (1905).

12. *See* William J. Haynes, Jr., *State Antitrust Laws* 183 (1989).

13. Richard A. Posner, The Chicago School of Antitrust Analysis, 127 U. Pa. L. Rev. 925, 927 (1979).

14. *Safeway Stores, Inc. v. Oklahoma Retail Grocers Ass'n, Inc.*, 360 U.S. 334, 340 (1959).

15. 15 U.S.C.A. §13 (emphasis added).

16. Donald S. Clark, Secretary of the Fed. Trade Comm'n, The Robinson-Patman Act: Annual Update, The Robinson-Patman Act Committee, Section of Antitrust Law, Forty-Sixth Annual Spring Meeting (2 April 1998), https://www.ftc.gov/es/public-statements/1998/04/robinson-patman-act-annual-update.

17. *F.T.C. v. Anheuser-Busch, Inc.*, 363 U.S. 536, 543–544, 80 S. Ct. 1267, 1271, 4 L. Ed. 2d 1385 (1960).

18. The map is taken from Paul H. Robinson and Tyler Scot Williams, *Mapping American Criminal Law: Variations across the 50 States*, Chapter 34 (Westport: Prager, 2018). All supporting authorities are available from that source.

19. *See, e.g.*, Cal. Bus. & Prof. Code § 17001; Colo. Rev. Stat. Ann. § 6-2-102; Utah Code Ann. § 13-5-17.

20. *Vill. Food & Liquor Mart v. H & S Petroleum, Inc.*, 2002 WI 92, ¶ 28, 254 Wis. 2d 478, 492, 647 N.W.2d 177, 184.

21. *Safeway Stores*, 360 U.S. at 340.

22. Corey Stern, 'CVS and Walgreens Are Completely Dominating the US Drugstore Industry,' *Business Insider*, 29 July 2015, http://www.businessinsider.com/cvs-and-walgreens-us-drugstore-market-share-2015-7.

23. Calculator at https://www.in2013dollars.com/us/inflation/1877.

24. *Predatory Pricing*, Investopedia https://www.investopedia.com/terms/p/predatory-pricing.asp.

25. *Price Discrimination*, Legal Information Institute, https://www.law.cornell.edu/wex/price_discrimination.

Chapter 29

RICO

Joe Bananas Builds a Criminal Empire

1931. New Jersey and New York become a little closer with the completion of the George Washington Bridge. Through a congressional resolution, "The Star-Spangled Banner" officially becomes the national anthem. In Arkansas, Hattie Caraway becomes the first woman ever elected to the U.S. Senate. Cabell "Cab" Calloway, an African-American jazz singer and bandleader, records "Minnie the Moocher," Jazz's first million-disc seller. In an effort to combat the economic woes brought on by the stock market crash, Nevada's state legislature legalizes both gambling and divorce. The old Mafia is transitioning from the traditional Mustache Petes to be run by a new breed of ruthless Young Turks.

Joe Bonanno – 1931

In 1905, Giuseppe (Joseph) Carlo Bonanno is born in Sicily, Italy.[1] Bonanno sees from a young age how "men of the old tradition" function as a "shadow government that exist[s] alongside the official government."[2] "Men of honor" control business, politics, and serve as middlemen in disputes.[3]

Orphaned at age 15, he finds his way to the United States in 1924. Arriving in Brooklyn during the height of Prohibition, he becomes involved with Mafia boss Salvatore Maranzano, working as a bootlegger and then an enforcer. Impressed with Bonanno's acumen, spirit, and ruthlessness, Maranzano mentors the young man, introducing him to his larger organization of criminal enterprises, which include prostitution, narcotics, bootlegging, and bookmaking. In 1930, a civil war erupts between the Maranzano family and a rival clan. The war is good for Bonanno, who, thanks to his ruthlessness, becomes Maranzano's second-in-command.

Maranzano and the rival don are known as "Mustache Petes." These Sicilians are characterized by their refusal to work with non-Sicilians, and their upholding of

DOI: 10.4324/9781003258025-32

"Old-World Principles": honor, tradition, respect, and dignity. In contrast, the "Young Turks" are a diverse group of Italians who began their criminal careers in the states. The Young Turks prefer to adopt a business model that includes Irish and Jewish organizations and want Mafia activity to expand beyond Italian neighborhoods.

The rival don is killed by his own underbosses who are Young Turks, and the war ends. Maranzano survives long enough to reorganize New York City's Italian crime organizations into five families. For a brief moment he is the boss of all bosses, but the Young Turks are quick to assassinate him. Claiming, unconvincingly, to have no prior knowledge of the attack on his boss and mentor, Bonanno, now 26, becomes head of the Maranzano family, which he re-names after himself. By 1931, the new status quo ushers in two decades of peace among the families.

The Bonanno crime family is small but tightly knit and loyal. Something of a hybrid between the old and the new ways of doing business, Bonanno's family emphasizes omertà, the code of silence, and an absolute refusal to cooperate with authorities. After expanding into new businesses, theirs is the most profitable of the families. Bonanno uses his large cash reserves to make numerous real estate investments. He owns three coat factories, a laundromat, cheese factories, and a truck company all of which are used to launder money. Conveniently, Bonanno also owns funeral parlors which are handy when there is a need to dispose of bodies.

Bonanno eschews the spotlight and carefully insulates himself from law enforcement scrutiny. The only outward signs of wealth are his expensive cigars and well-cut suits. Bonanno speaks seven languages, keeps a substantial library, and regularly quotes Dante. Over the decades, he quietly increases his power through clever management, coercion, force, and an array of illicit maneuvers.

In late 1957, in Apalachin, New York, a summit of Mafia leaders is hosted at Bonanno's home. An estimated 100 people attend, with some from Italy and Cuba. Police become suspicious, set up roadblocks, and raid the meeting, causing participants to flee into the woods surrounding the estate. The authorities question 58 men. All have the same explanation: they were visiting their dear sick friend Joseph Bonanno. While the police have no grounds on which to hold the men, no one is deceived by the story and the episode provides the first compelling evidence of a large-scale highly organized criminal enterprise at the root of crime in the United States.

In 1959 investigators indict 27 attendees from the Apalachin meeting, including the supposedly very ill Bonanno, on conspiracy to obstruct justice for refusing to testify before the grand jury. The U.S. Court of Appeals overturns the convictions but Bonanno is no longer flying under the radar. The press celebrates his role as a key player by giving him the nickname "Joe Bananas." *Time* magazine calls him "one of the bloodiest killers in Cosa Nostra's history."[4] ("Cosa Nostra" is Italian for "our thing.") Newspapers tell stories of his ruthlessness, showing his method for eliminating rivals: "Make sure the guy thinks you're his friend until the right time comes, the right setup, and then you make your move like a tiger."[5]

Prosecutions of Bonanno and other bosses fail because the big men are never pulling the trigger. The powerful players operate in the shadows to organize the enterprise and give direction, usually through several layers of buffers.

Beginning in the early 1960s, Bonanno begins the importation and distribution of heroin smuggled from Turkey to France, then to Canada, and finally to the United States. Approximately 2,000–5,000 pounds of heroin enters the United States annually and by 1969 80–90% of American heroin comes via this route.[6]

In 1963, Joseph Valachi, a member of a different Mafia family, is under indictment for murder. He feels betrayed when his Mafia associates fail to care for his family during his imprisonment. Valachi breaks omertà and works with the FBI and the DOJ,

WANTED AS THE ALLEGED VICTIM OF A KIDNAPPING

THE ABOVE PHOTOGRAPH IS ONE "JOSEPH BONANNO" MALE, WHITE, 59 YRS., WANTED AS THE ALLEGED VICTIM OF A KIDNAPPING.

AT APPROXIMATELY 12:20 A.M., OCTOBER 21, 1964, "JOSEPH BONANNO" OF 1847 EAST ELM STREET, TUCSON, ARIZONA, WHILE IN THE COMPANY OF HIS ATTORNEY, WAS REPORTED PHYSICALLY SEIZED IN FRONT OF 35 PARK AVENUE, MANHATTAN BY TWO (2) UNKNOWN WHITE MALES AND FORCED INTO AN AUTOMOBILE WHICH THEN SPED AWAY.

DESCRIPTION OF PERPETRATORS AS FOLLOWS:

#1 - MALE, WHITE, 6'2", 210 LBS., WEARING BLACK RAINCOAT, A DARK FEDORA, ARMED WITH A GUN.

#2 - MALE, WHITE, 6'0", 200 LBS., DARK CLOTHES.

GETAWAY VEHICLE WAS A BEIGE 2-DOOR SEDAN OF RECENT MODEL OF UNKNOWN MAKE, BEARING NEW YORK REGISTRATION PLATES.

ANY INFORMATION ON THE ABOVE, NOTIFY THE 13TH DETECTIVE SQUAD FORTHWITH: OREGON 4-0770 - OREGON 4-0771 - 777 3290.

Figure 29.1 The night before he was to testify to a Grand Jury, Joe Bonanno was reportedly kidnapped, 1964

describing the organizational structure of the Mafia. Now for the first time authorities get to peek behind the curtain that has hidden the workings of the families for so long.

On the night before Bonanno is going to be forced to testify about the workings of organized crime, he disappears. His people maintain that he has been kidnapped but suspicions are high that he is simply on the lam. Upon his return, two years later, Bonanno is again facing charges of obstruction of justice and contempt of court. After five years of legal maneuvering, he is not convicted of anything.

In 1968, Bonanno announces his permanent retirement and moves to Tucson. He may be willing to leave the life behind, but the FBI still wants to hold him accountable for his lifetime of crime. He is repeatedly indicted and always acquitted.

The last prosecution is over a mob-style hit in 1976. His house is put under surveillance, a tracker is planted in his car, wiretaps are conducted, and police search his garbage regularly for three years. Despite the FBI's best efforts, he never serves any jail time for his Mafia-related actions and dies at age 97 in his own home.

RICO

The rise of Joe Bonanno provides just one example of the rise of organized crime in the United States. From 1920 to 1933, when there was a nationwide prohibition on the commercial sale of alcoholic beverages, gangs entered the liquor business and "transformed themselves into sophisticated criminal enterprises, skilled at smuggling, money laundering and bribing police."[7] Chief among them were those gangs that would become the American Mafia, which continued to operate after Prohibition ended. These crime "families" conducted a number of illegal activities alongside legitimate businesses, using tactics such as bribery and criminal threats to increase profits, avoid prosecution, and eliminate business competitors. As Joe Bonanno did, it was common for profits from organized crime to be used to buy and operate legitimate businesses, and while law enforcement was sometimes able to prosecute an individual offender, the operation's economic base permitted the syndicate to go on. By the 1950s, there were 24 known criminal enterprises with thousands of associates.[8]

As the Joe Bonanno case makes clear, for many decades, traditional criminal liability rules proved inadequate to reach the leaders of organized crime. Crime bosses could simply insulate themselves from liability by providing general direction rather than engaging in any specific offense and by giving direction only through a few trusted lieutenants, making it difficult for prosecutors to collect enough evidence to charge the boss even as an accomplice. Bonanno was a Mafia don for almost 40 years but, as noted, the government was never able to convict him of any Mafia-related activity. He retired to Arizona two years before the enactment of the federal *RICO* statute.[9]

The federal RICO Act, enacted in 1970, was designed to eliminate organized crime by "crippling its financial base."[10] (The key provision of the Act is reproduced in the margin.) This it could do by broadly targeting anyone who "has received any income derived, directly or indirectly, from a pattern of racketeering activity" to "use or invest" the proceeds to acquire interest in real property or to establish or operate any enterprise.[11] RICO specifically criminalizes conduct in which a person may "acquire or maintain any interest in or control of an enterprise" to "conduct, or participate in, any enterprise," where the enterprise involves "a pattern of racketeering activity."[12] Under RICO, it is also unlawful to "use or invest proceeds derived from racketeering activity to acquire interest in real property or to establish or operate any enterprise."[13] RICO is not like complicity liability in holding a person liable for a specific offense committed

Prohibited Activities.

(a) It shall be unlawful for any person who has received any income derived, directly or indirectly, from a pattern of racketeering activity or through collection of an unlawful debt in which such person has participated as a principal . . . to use or invest, directly or indirectly, any part of such income, or the proceeds of such income, in acquisition of any interest in, or the establishment or operation of, any enterprise which is engaged in, or the activities of which affect, interstate or foreign commerce. . . .

(c) It shall be unlawful for any person employed by or associated with any enterprise engaged in, or the activities of which affect, interstate or foreign commerce, to conduct or participate, directly or indirectly, in the conduct of such enterprise's affairs through a pattern of racketeering activity or collection of unlawful debt.

18 U.S. Code § 1962

Figure 29.2

by another. Instead, it holds the offender liable for the special offense of being a member or a leader of a racketeer-influenced corrupt organization. The use of RICO was wildly successful, ultimately providing the basis for destroying the American Mafia.[14]

Unfortunately, but perhaps necessarily, the terms of the RICO offense are rather broad and there has been a tendency to use this special form of liability in cases well beyond the organized crime families that prompted its creation. Consider this more recent case.

David Camez – 2010

In 2007, website Carder.su is created as a platform through which hackers can profit from their stolen data and exchange information.[15] The site contains two forums: one for vendors to discuss the trade and sale of illicit goods such as fake IDs, stolen credit card information, and counterfeiting gear; the second is used to vet new members as part of a screening process to keep out law enforcement. The site amounts to an Ebay for cyber-criminals on which hundreds of vendors sell illegal products and services.

Unbeknownst to Carder.su administrators, the site is in the crosshairs of the U.S. Secret Service. The agency has apprehended a Nevada man with a reputation for producing high-quality fake IDs under the pseudo-name "Celtic," and Secret Service Agent Mark Adams has assumed control of Celtic's account as part of an undercover initiative dubbed Operation Open Market. Adams shifts Celtic's operations to Carder.su without a hitch. The scheme is perfect from Adams' perspective because, seeking Celtic's services, criminals send their personal information, including real pictures and addresses, directly to Adams.

Celtic, now Adams, continues to sell fake IDs, expanding the catalog of fake identification from 3 states to 13. In order to maintain his official stamp of approval from Carder.su, Adams calls upon both his acumen as an experienced law enforcement agent and his relationship with Nevada DMV to procure high-quality IDs. Satisfied customers gush about them, saying that they are "flawless" and "guaranteed to work ANYWHERE."[16]

In the summer of 2008, 16-year-old David Ray Camez is living in Phoenix, Arizona and begins exploring Carder.su under the usernames "Bad Man" and "Doctorsex." In May 2009, Camez makes the unfortunate decision to buy a fake Arizona driver's license from Celtic for $330. He continues to communicate with Celtic throughout 2009 and 2010 and purchases other fake IDs and stolen credit cards from Celtic and other vendors. Camez also dabbles in the production of fake credit cards, purchasing from Celtic the equipment and software that will allow him to load stolen magnetic strip data onto counterfeit cards. Because of his contact with Celtic, all of Camez's activities are being tracked by investigators. In 2010, authorities intercept a package containing counterfeit credit and gift cards ordered by Camez.

Celtic's reputation as one of the most reliable sources of forged IDs at Carder.su continues to grow. He moves up the Carder.su ranks from a "general member" to a "reviewed vendor," survives a sweeping user purge in 2009 aimed at tightening security, and is eventually dubbed by moderators as a "VIP member of the

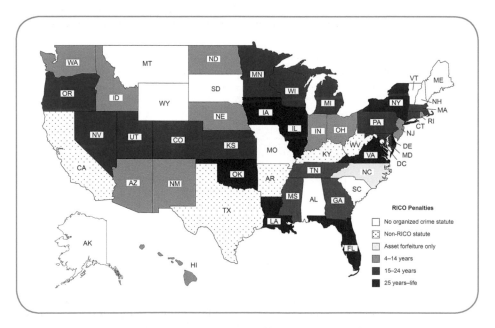

Figure 29.3

organization."[17] Celtic, while controlled by Adams, sells not only fake drivers' licenses but also a number of other secondary IDs, including Carson City voter identification cards and fake AT&T employee cards. At the same time, Carder.su itself expands rapidly, and its user list swells to over 5,500 members.

In May 2010, investigators raid 18-year-old Camez's home, and he is arrested when police find counterfeit cards and stolen identity information in his room. Camez is tried and convicted on fraud charges in Nevada court and receives a seven-year sentence.

Celtic continues to operate on Carder.su, enhancing the understanding of the criminal networks that operate through the site. In the winter of 2012 authorities finally drop the hammer, and the Justice Department issues indictments against over 55 of the individuals with whom Celtic had contact through Carder.su. Those indicted include not only buyers and sellers but also Carder.su site administrators.

Camez, along with 39 other defendants, is charged under the federal *RICO* Act. Among other things, as noted, RICO makes it an offense to be a member of a criminal organization and increases criminal liability even for organizers who themselves commit no crimes. Carder.su is the first case in which RICO is applied to cybercrime.

In total, the government estimates the total financial damage caused by Carder.su to be $50.5 million. Because many of the high-level members of Carder.su are in Russia and other foreign countries that do not have extradition treaties with the United States, only the low-level members of Carder.su, like Camez, are available for prosecution.

Camez is brought from his prison cell to the federal courthouse in Las Vegas and pleads not guilty. He insists that while he did purchase counterfeit cards and equipment on Carder.su, he cannot be held responsible for the actions of the thousands of criminals from around the world who used Carder.su. At trial, prosecutors argue that Carder.su is analogous to a criminal organization like the mob, and as a member of such an organization Camez is criminally liable for more than just the offenses that he himself committed.

The defense maintains that Carder.su should instead be likened to Craigslist, a site on which anyone can sign up to exchange goods and services independently of everyone else on the site. They contend that there is little coordination among the collective members and that no one is in charge or directing Carder.su members in their criminal activities.

In December 2013, Camez is convicted of one count of participating in a racketeer-influenced corrupt organization and another count of conspiracy to participate in a racketeer-influenced corrupt organization. He is sentenced to 20 years in federal prison and ordered to pay $20 million in restitution.

The RICO case against Camez illustrates how the use of the Mafia-busting legislation has expanded in its role since its creation.

RICO in the States

Most states have now adopted their own *RICO* statutes to supplement the federal statute. These state statutes commonly use the same structure as the federal but what constitutes "racketeering activity" differs from state to state.[18] Recall that an organization is a criminal enterprise under RICO only where it is involved in a pattern of "racketeering activity." The term often includes dozens of crimes – from violent crimes, such as murder, kidnapping, or robbery, to property offenses, such as theft or trespass, to certain white collar crimes, such as extortion, bribery, or corruption, to crimes against public health or morality, such as soliciting prostitution, pandering obscenity, or distribution of child pornography.

On the map below, all states with shading have adopted their own RICO statutes.[19] The darker the shading on the map, the more aggressive is the state RICO offense. While 11 states, those with no shading, have no statute targeting organized crime, some have statutes targeting specific kinds of criminal enterprises, such as street gangs or drug syndicates. They also may have civil RICO statute. Five states, those with no shading but with dots on the map, have no statute patterned on federal RICO but have some kind of statute targeting organized crime.[20]

Eleven states, those with medium shading, have adopted statutes patterned on federal RICO and provide a maximum sentence on the first offense (where there are no special circumstances) that ranges from 4 years (Nebraska) to 14 years (Idaho). Fifteen states, those with darker shading, impose a prison sentence of up to between 15 (Massachusetts) and 24 years (Colorado). Eight states, those with black coloring, impose a maximum prison sentence from 25 years (New York) to life (Oklahoma).

Why would a RICO offense all when a federal RICO offense already exists? First, states have an independent interest in prosecuting organized crime, and federal authorities necessarily tend to focus their resources on only the most serious criminal enterprises. Second, state RICO statutes reach more conduct than the federal statute, not only due to textual differences in the statutes but also due to some courts' broader construction of the state statute. In addition, many state statutes target patterns of activity involving state law offenses that are outside the scope of the federal statute, such as computer fraud, environmental offenses, and unfair competition.[21] Finally, as a matter of federal constitutional law, the federal RICO statute is only available to prosecute organized crime cases in which there is a federal interest, such as with a crime group operating across state borders.

Aftermaths

Eleven years after his 1968 retirement as crime boss, Bonanno is indicted for conspiracy to interfere with a grand jury investigation of a scheme to launder money through businesses in California operated by his sons. He is convicted, his first conviction – ironically for conduct unrelated to his organized crime family. The 75-year-old is sentenced to five years in prison but after serving only eight months is released due to poor health. Once freed, Bonanno's health miraculously improves. He dies 12 years later in May 2002 at the age of 97. He is buried in Tucson having had the longest Mafia career of any boss. One of the five New York Italian Mafia families is still working under his name.

On December 21, 1992, Victor J. Orena, the acting boss of the Colombo crime family, is convicted of racketeering, the third time that year that Federal prosecutors obtained a conviction of a Mafia boss in New York City.[22] The conviction marks the last step in the effort to dismantle the traditional organized crime families, a victory that many credit directly to the federal *RICO* statute. "Not one of the nation's twenty-four Mafia families has escaped successful prosecution in recent years, and only a few are left with their leadership intact."[23]

In the David Camez case, the defendant appeals his conviction to the United States Court of Appeals for the Ninth Circuit, claiming, among other things, that he was a juvenile when he started the work and that he was a minor player. The court rejects his claims. He remains in jail.

Roman Seleznev, who first set up the Carder.su website, is apprehended in 2014 while on vacation in the Maldives. Convicted on 38 counts related to a scheme (not connected with Carder.su) to hack into point-of-sale computers to steal and sell credit card numbers to the criminal underworld, he is currently serving a 27-year sentence in a U.S. prison. The Russian government objected to his arrest, calling it a kidnapping. Seleznez's father, Valery, is a member of the Russian Parliament.

Chapter Glossary

Money Laundering: A financial transaction scheme that aims to conceal the identity, source, or destination of illicitly obtained money. The money laundering process can be broken down into three stages. First, the illegal activity that garners the money places it in the launderer's hands. Second, the launderer passes the money through a complex scheme of transactions to obscure who initially received the money from the criminal enterprise. Third, the scheme returns the money to the first party in an obscure and indirect way.[24]

Racketeering Activity: This can be made up of any of a long list of offenses commonly engaged in by organized crime, including bribery and extortion; federal mail or wire fraud can also support RICO liability. Prosecution under RICO typically requires a "pattern" of racketeering activity, which exists when any two acts of racketeering activity occur within ten years of one another.[25]

RICO: Racketeer Influenced and Corrupt Organizations statutes are designed to combat criminal enterprises. They were designed to enable prosecution of organized-crime rings, in part by limiting their ability to cloak themselves in legitimate "front" businesses, and to protect legitimate businesses from being taken over by organized crime.[26]

Notes

1. This narrative is drawn from the following sources: Brad Hunter, 'The Life and Crimes of Joe Bonanno,' *New York Post*, 13 May 2002, http://nypost.com/2002/05/13/the-life-and-crimes-of-joe-bonanno/; 'Joe Bonanno,' *National Crime Syndicate*, 22 July 2020, http://www.nationalcrimesyndicate.com/joe-bonanno-biography/; 'Joseph Bonanno,' *Biography.com*, 19 June 2019, https://www.biography.com/people/joseph-bonanno-438744; 'Legendary Don: Mysterious and Powerful, Joe Bonanno Retreated to Tucson, but Violence Followed,' *The Chicago Syndicate*, 26 June 2015, http://www.thechicagosyndicate.com/2006/03/legendary-don-mysterious-and-powerful.html; Selwyn Raab, *Five Families: The Rise, Decline, and Resurgence of America's Most Powerful Empires* (New York: St. Martin's Press, 2011); Selwyn Raab, 'Joe Bonanno Dies; Mafia Leader, 97, Who Built Empire,' *The New York Times*, 12 May 2002, http://www.nytimes.com/2002/05/12/nyregion/joe-bonanno-dies-mafia-leader-97-who-built-empire.html?pagewanted=all.
2. 'Joseph Bonanno.'
3. 'Joseph Bonanno.'

4. 'Legendary Don.'

5. 'Legendary Don.'

6. 'The DEA Years 1970–1975,' *Drug Enforcement Administration*, 22 July 2020, https://www.dea.gov/sites/default/files/2018-07/1970-1975%20p%2030-39.pdf.

7. 'Mafia in the United States,' *History.com*, 22 October 2009, http://www.history.com/topics/mafia-in-the-united-states.

8. 'Mafia in the United States.' For additional history of federal RICO and the Italian-American Mafia, see Miranda Lievsay, 'Containing the Uncontainable: Drawing Rico's Border with the Presumption against Extraterritoriality,' *Fordham Law Review 84*, no. 4 (2016): p. 1735. *See also* Benjamin Levin, 'American Gangsters: Rico, Criminal Syndicates, and Conspiracy Law as Market Control,' *Harvard Civil Rights-Civil Liberties Law Review 48* (2013): p. 105; Lesley Suzanne Bonney, 'The Prosecution of Sophisticated Urban Street Gangs: A Proper Application of RICO,' *Catholic University Law Review 42* (1993): p. 579.

9. *See* 18 U.S. Code §§ 1961–1968.

10. Bonney, 'The Prosecution Urban Street Gangs,' p. 580.

11. 18 U.S. Code § 1962. Prohibited activities (a).

12. 18 U.S. Code § 1962. Prohibited activities (b).

13. 18 U.S. Code § 1962. Prohibited activities (a).

14. *See* Paul Robinson and Sarah Robinson, '1957 Mafia Commission Apalachin Meeting—Racketeer Influenced and Corrupt Organizations Act (RICO),' in *Crimes That Changed Our World: Tragedy, Outrage, and Reform* (Lanham: Rowman & Littlefield 2018), pp. 88–90.

15. This narrative is drawn from the following sources: Rick Anderson, 'Russian Hacker Went from Poverty to Making Millions in Stolen Credit Cards. Now He's Facing 27 years in Prison,' *Los Angeles Times*, 21 April 2017, http://www.latimes.com/nation/-la-na-russian-hacker-20170421-story.html; Daniel Bogden, 'United States v. Kilobit et al.' (sealed Carder.su indictment, United States District Court, 10 January 2012), https://www.nyccriminallawyer.com/wp-content/uploads/2014/06/carder.su_.kilobit.indictment.pdf; 'Member of Organization That Operated Online Marketplace for Stolen Personal Information Sentenced to 20 Years in Prison,' *Department of Justice Office of Public Affairs*, 15 May 2014, https://www.justice.gov/opa/pr/member-organization-operated-online-marketplace-stolen-personal-information-sentenced-20; Kevin Poulsen, 'Guilty Verdict in First Ever Cybercrime RICO Trial,' *Wired*, 20 November 2013, https://www.wired.com/2013/12/rico/; Kevin Poulsen, 'In Las Vegas Courtroom, First Ever Cybercrime RICO Trial Begins,' *Wired*, 20 November 2013, https://www.wired.com/2013/11/open-market-trial-begins; Kevin Poulsen, 'The Secret Service Agent Who Collared Cybercrooks By Selling Them Fake IDs,' *Wired*, 22 July 2013, https://www.wired.com/2013/07/open-market/; Danika Worthington, 'Phoenix Man Gets 20 Years for Credit Card, ID Scheme,' *The Arizona Republic*, 15 May 2014, http://www.azcentral.com/story/news/local/phoenix/2014/05/15/phoenix-man-gets-years-prison-credit-card-scheme-abrk/9146825/.

16. Poulsen, 'In Las Vegas Courtroom.'

17. Poulsen, 'In Las Vegas Courtroom.'

18. Every RICO statute uses the term racketeering activity, except Minnesota ("criminal activity"), New York ("criminal activity"), Ohio ("corrupt activity"), Utah ("unlawful activity"), and Washington ("criminal profiteering activity"). *See infra* note 19.

19. The map is taken from Paul H. Robinson and Tyler Scot Williams, 'Organized Crime,' in *Mapping American Criminal Law: Variations across the 50 States* (Westport: Prager 2018), p. 291. All supporting authorities are available from that source.

20. One state, North Carolina, shown in light shading on the map, has adopted a statute patterned on the federal RICO statute, but the statute does not create any additional criminal liability. Instead, the statute authorizes the government to initiate a separate civil forfeiture proceeding to show by a preponderance of the evidence that the assets were involved in the criminal enterprise.

21. John E. Floyd, *RICO State by State: A Guide to Litigation under the State Racketeering Statutes*, 2nd ed. (Chicago: ABA Publishing, 2011).

22. Arnold H. Lubasch, 'Acting Crime Boss Is Convicted of Murder and Racketeering,' *The New York Times*, 22 December 1992, http://www.nytimes.com/1992/12/22/nyregion/acting-crime-boss-is-convicted-of-murder-and-racketeering.html.

23. Ron Nordland, 'The "Velcro Don": Wiseguys Finish Last,' *Newsweek*, 12 April 1992, http://www.newsweek.com/velcro-don-wiseguys-finish-last-197190.

24. *Money Laundering*, Legal Information Institute, https://www.law.cornell.edu/wex/money_laundering.

25. Paul H. Robinson and Michael T. Cahill, *Criminal Law*, 2nd ed. (New York: Wolters Kluwer, 2012), §12.4.

26. Robinson and Cahill, *Criminal Law*, §12.4.

PART IV

Supplemental Issues

Two other issues are worth considering even though they are not strictly criminal liability issues. First, a state is not free to prosecute any offense committed by any person anywhere in the world. Typically, the offense must have some specific connection with the state. Criminal codes commonly provide rules governing the offenses over which the state has *jurisdiction*.

Even if a state has jurisdiction over an offense, it cannot prosecute, convict, or punish an offender unless the state also has the offender in hand. Thus, offenders who flee may be immune from criminal liability. However, a system of *extradition* exists by which one state can obtain custody of a fugitive who has fled to another state.

DOI: 10.4324/9781003258025-33

Chapter 30

Jurisdiction

The Aaron Burr-Alexander Hamilton Duel

1804. President Jefferson is facing on-going criticism for his deal with France to purchase the Louisiana Territory. Ludwig von Beethoven composes his No. 3 Symphony, *Eroica*. Western explorers William Lewis, Merriweather Clark, and their diverse group, which includes a newborn baby, are sending back exciting dispatches about their efforts to cross the continent. The Napoleonic Code is adopted in France, stressing the importance of clearly written law. In the United States, state sovereignty and the existence of a different criminal code for each state are starting to show its complications.

Aaron Burr – 1804

On the eve of America's third presidential election, the country is fiercely conflicted about what democracy should look like.[1] Alexander Hamilton, former Secretary of the Treasury, is vocal in his insistence on a structure of government where a ruling elite guides the government – an intellectual aristocracy. Many others, including Aaron Burr, a former U.S. Senator and a political thought leader, see democracy as more inclusive. While these disagreements have been going on for years, they become personal during the presidential election of 1800.

President John Adams is a Federalist vying for his second term in office. Hamilton is also a Federalist but does not want the uncontrollable Adams to be re-elected and secretly works against him. The plan works but when the duplicity becomes public, Hamilton's reputation is damaged among many colleagues, including Aaron Burr.

The race for the presidency is now between Thomas Jefferson who is currently Vice President and former Senator Burr. At this time, only 146 people, the members of the electoral college, elect the president. The man with the most votes gains the presidency and the runner-up becomes vice president. The flexible and less-partisan Burr is seen

DOI: 10.4324/9781003258025-34

as the lesser of two evils by many voters. Hamilton does not agree, he tells everyone that Burr only wants the job for personal gain and is morally "bankrupt beyond redemption."[2]

On election day, after 34 rounds of deadlocked balloting, the representative from Delaware, under pressure from Hamilton, changes his vote for Burr to a blank vote. And so it is that Jefferson becomes President and Burr Vice President. For his efforts, Hamilton has earned the life-long animosity of Adams, Burr, and many others.

Jefferson and Burr never find a way to work together and by the next election, the 12th Amendment is in place allowing presidential candidates to select their own running mate. Jefferson does not select Burr. Burr, still finishing out his term as Vice President, enters the 1804 New York gubernatorial race. Hamilton is not a candidate and does not live in New York but nonetheless runs a vigorous campaign against Burr. Burr is not elected and blames his loss on Hamilton. After the election, Burr obtains a copy of a newspaper article in which a letter quoting Hamilton is reprinted. In it, Hamilton states that Burr is "a dangerous man, who ought not to be trusted with the reins of government."[3]

Burr asks for an apology; Hamilton does not give it. Burr engages a lawyer friend to write to Hamilton and lay out the history of their feud. Within the letter is this line, "There is, on the part of Mr. Hamilton, a settled and implacable malevolence; that he will never cease in his conduct towards Mr. Burr."[4] The letter goes on to say that Burr is incapable of obtaining revenge because he will not stoop to the levels of duplicity that Hamilton will. It is decided that the only honorable solution is a duel.

Dueling is new to neither man. Three years earlier, Hamilton's son was killed in a duel defending his father's honor. Both men write careful letters outlining what they want done to conclude their affairs if they die. Hamilton writes about his hesitation to duel, as it is counter to his religion and his basic good sense. He wonders if maybe he really has wronged Burr, but at this point he feels that he must go forward.

Figure 30.1 Aaron Burr statue in the United States Capitol building

In New York City the night before the duel, each man gathers a party of witnesses who will accompany him to the dueling ground. On the morning of July 11, everyone rows the two and a half miles across the Hudson to Weehawken, New Jersey. Dueling is illegal in both New York and New Jersey, but New York treats dueling as a capital crime, whereas New Jersey takes a much milder view of the offense. Therefore, all local duels are fought across the river in New Jersey.

Just after dawn, Hamilton and Burr meet at the same place at which Hamilton's son died three years earlier. At the signal, Burr fires and the bullet pierces Hamilton's abdomen. Hamilton, either by design or by accident, misses. Hamilton is rowed back to New York and dies the following day.

While most duels do not garner much public interest, this one sets the country abuzz. As one of the nation's founding fathers, in death Hamilton is elevated to martyrdom. Public sentiment turns against Burr. Three separate juries are empaneled and elect not to charge anyone with any crime related to the duel. However, a coroner's jury in New York is convened and considers for a fourth time whether to charge Burr with murder. What is somewhat awkward about the New York prosecution is that the duel occurred in New Jersey and it had been previously understood that New Jersey duels are not prosecutable in New York.

For Burr, the regular rules are no longer in play. He knows that he will not be allowed to post bond if he is arrested, as bail is not permitted on murder charges in New York. He leaves the state before the jury issues its ruling. The New York coroner's jury charges Burr with murder, and soon after New Jersey also indicts Burr for murder. Burr slips into Washington, where, as still the sitting Vice President, he is immune from prosecution.

One senator complains that the man "indicted for the murder of the incomparable Hamilton appeared yesterday and today at the head of the Senate."[5] Back at work as Vice President, Burr runs the impeachment trial of Supreme Court Justice Samuel Chase, whom Jefferson is trying to remove from the bench for some of his particularly partisan rulings as a lower court judge. This is quite galling to many – the press notes the irony in the notion "that a man under *indictment* for MURDER presided at the trial of one of the justices of the Supreme Court of the United States, accused of a petty misdemeanor."[6] By the time the trial ends in February of 1805, Burr has only one month left in his term and the prevailing opinion is that he has done his duty well. Many are sad to see him depart Washington as a private citizen. Some senators openly weep at his departure. As to the duel, in the eyes of many, there is no crime. Burr could as easily have been the victim.

In time, New Jersey quietly drops the murder charges against Burr. The main line of reasoning is that all of the participants were New Yorkers and Hamilton did not die in New Jersey, so there is no murder within the state's *jurisdiction*. The shooting in New Jersey resulted in a live Hamilton being rowed to New York. Burr leaves the country and during his absence, New York decides against pursuing the murder charges. The legal grounds for dismissing the New York case rest on the fact that the duel did not occur within the state.

Jurisdiction

Each state commonly has *jurisdiction* to prosecute offenses committed within its borders. California generally cannot prosecute a murder committed in Nevada, and vice versa. However, sometimes offenses are committed or have effects in more than one state. A California murder is planned and organized in Nevada. The victim of a Nevada attack flees to California before dying. The governor of California is shot while vacationing in Nevada. Does California have jurisdiction in these cases? A state

Territorial Applicability.

(1) Except as otherwise provided in this Section, a person may be convicted under the law of this State of an offense committed by his own conduct or the conduct of another for which he is legally accountable if:

(a) either the conduct which is an element of the offense or the result which is such an element occurs within this State; or

(b) conduct occurring outside the State is sufficient under the law of this State to constitute an attempt to commit an offense within the State; or

(c) conduct occurring outside the State is sufficient under the law of this State to constitute a conspiracy to commit an offense within the State and an overt act in furtherance of such conspiracy occurs within the State; or

(d) conduct occurring within the State establishes complicity in the commission of, or an attempt, solicitation or conspiracy to commit, an offense in another jurisdiction which also is an offense under the law of this State; or

(e) the offense consists of the omission to perform a legal duty imposed by the law of the State with respect to domicile, residence or a relationship to a person, thing or transaction in the State; or

(f) the offense is based on a statute of this State which expressly prohibits conduct outside the State, when the conduct bears a reasonable relation to a legitimate interest of this State and the actor knows or should know that his conduct is likely to affect that interest.

Model Penal Code §1.03

Figure 30.2

might define its criminal jurisdiction so as to allow prosecution in one or another or all of these examples.[7]

Historically, the jurisdiction to prosecute criminal offenses was narrow:

> At the end of the 19th century, it was widely accepted that the principal basis of jurisdiction in common law systems was territoriality. The *locus classicus* for this position was the statement of Lord Halsbury that "[a]ll Crime is local. Jurisdiction over crime belongs to the country where the crime is committed, and, except over her own subjects, Her Majesty and the Imperial Legislature have no power whatsoever."[8]

In other words, in English common law there were no extraterritorial offenses and extraterritorial application was possible only upon statutory extension of the traditionally narrow common-law rule.

This narrow conception of jurisdiction had its origins in a view of crime as essentially a local problem: if a person murdered another in a different county, that was a problem to be solved by that other county. This conception of jurisdiction also reflected practical necessity: the authorities where the offense takes place have access to witnesses and crime scenes that are necessary for an effective prosecution. Given the traditionally narrow view of jurisdiction, the decision by New York in the Burr-Hamilton case that they lacked jurisdiction because the duel did not occur in New York, and the decision by New Jersey that they would not exercise jurisdiction because the participants were all New Yorkers and the death occurred in New York seem like plausible conclusions (although it also seems likely that they may have been driven by other than strictly legal considerations).

Public life and societal affairs are more complicated today and the potential for effective investigation outside a state's territory is greater. Old notions of jurisdiction based strictly upon territoriality have given way to broader conceptions seen as justifying a state's exercise of jurisdiction well beyond its borders. See the significantly increased breadth of jurisdiction reflected in the Model Penal Code (reproduced in the margin).

Thus, state today has become much less reluctant to exercise criminal jurisdiction over offenses committed in whole or in part outside of their territory. Consider the treatment of jurisdiction in this more modern case.

Dannie Gayheart – 2005

Rosemary Reinel is 73 when she moves from Florida to Michigan to care for her mother.[9] She is an active outgoing person who often goes fishing, enjoys singing, and loves passing time with her boyfriend. When a new neighbor, 54-year-old Dannie Gayheart, moves in across the hall, the two become fast friends. In time, Reinel's mother dies, and she decides to move back to Florida. Gayheart asks Reinel to allow him to drive to Florida with her. He wants to try to rekindle his romance with an ex-girlfriend. Reinel agrees; having a friend along will make the long drive easier. They plan to leave on September 20, 2005, driving Reinel's 1994 Buick Riviera.

A few weeks before they leave, Reinel learns that Gayheart is on parole for obtaining money under false pretenses and perjury. In fact, when he moved into the apartment complex, he had just gotten out of jail. The planned drive to Florida,

Figure 30.3 Dannie Gayheart as an adult, circa 2003

leaving the State of Michigan, would be a violation of Gayheart's parole. Reinel disinvites Gayheart. She explains she does not want to be found complicit in Gayheart's parole breach. Gayheart is disappointed but the two remain friends – at least from Reinel's viewpoint. In preparation for what is now to be a solo trip, Reinel withdraws $2,900 from the bank.

On September 20 – the day they were originally scheduled to leave – Gayheart asks Reinel for a ride to pick up some money in Indiana (they live near the state border). She agrees and the two leave early that morning. Before they leave, she calls her boyfriend to tell him where she is going.

When Gayheart meets Reinel, he is carrying a bag that contains a pair of channel-lock pliers stolen from the utility room of the apartment complex, some zip ties, a roll of duct tape, and four lengths of cord tied with slip knots. After they have been driving for some time, Gayheart opened the bag, pulls out the heavy pliers, and strikes Reinel in the head seven times, killing her. He dumps the body in a cornfield in LaGrange County, Indiana.

An Indiana farmer inspecting his field finds a partially buried corpse. Because the corpse is found in Indiana, the Indiana State Police launch a homicide investigation. Dental records identify the body as that of Rosemary Reinel. Investigators eventually assemble a large body of evidence from witnesses and forensic tests, providing overwhelming proof that Gayheart murdered Reinel in her car, but they cannot determine where the couple was when the killing took place.

Under the old territoriality view of *jurisdiction*, prosecution by either Michigan or Indiana would be difficult because neither can clearly establish that the killing occurred within their territory. However, with the broader extraterritoriality jurisdiction adopted by many states today, proof of the killing location may not be necessary. Prosecutors in Michigan can prove that the killing was planned in their state and materials assembled there. Prosecutors in Indiana can show that the body was buried in their state. Whether either or both states have jurisdiction to prosecute the homicide will depend upon the exact reach of the extraterritoriality jurisdiction statute in each state.

Variations in State Jurisdictional Requirements

As the map below makes clear, different states take different approaches to defining the breadth of their criminal *jurisdiction*.[10] In other words, they take different views about how much of an offense, if any, must be committed within a state in order for the state to exercise jurisdiction. The darker the shading on the map, the broader the jurisdiction.

Five states, those with no shading on the map, exercise territorial jurisdiction over a criminal defendant where an "essential" element of the offense "occurred within" the state. As one Maryland court explained, the law "does not permit prosecution . . . in every jurisdiction in which an element of the offense takes place."[11] Rather, courts "generally [focus] on one element, which is deemed 'essential' or 'key' or 'vital' or the 'gravamen' of the offense, and the offense may be prosecuted only in a jurisdiction where that essential or key element takes place." In practice, which elements are deemed "essential," and which nonessential, are matters for the courts of each state to decide.

This notion that certain elements are crucial for jurisdiction is an old idea, one gradually supplanted by modern statutes asserting broader jurisdiction. Under the more limited jurisdiction recognized at common law, discussed above, some courts held that the essential element of homicide is the impact on the victim's body causing the death, not the conduct causing the impact – the bullet striking the victim rather than the offender pulling the trigger. In bigamy prosecutions, this demanding view held that subsequent cohabitation with the second spouse is not enough for jurisdiction, because the "gist" of the offense is the second marriage, thus providing jurisdiction where it was actually solemnized. Under this most narrow approach, probably only New Jersey would have jurisdiction to prosecute Burr for killing Hamilton, since the ultimately lethal conduct occurred in New Jersey. Jurisdiction in the Gayheart case

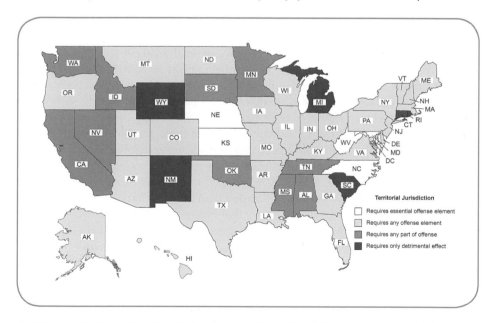

Figure 30.4

would be problematic, since neither Michigan nor Indiana could prove beyond a reasonable doubt that the killing occurred in their state.

Thirty states, those with light shading on the map, exercise territorial jurisdiction where any element of the offense has occurred within the state's boundaries. In these states, the courts do not attempt to distinguish the more and less "essential" or "material" elements of an offense; the occurrence of any element is sufficient.[12] Under this slightly broader approach, requiring proof that some element of the offense occurred within the state, both New Jersey and New York today would have jurisdiction to prosecute Aaron Burr: New Jersey because the duel occurred there, and New York because Hamilton's death occurred there. Even under these standards, however, neither Michigan nor Indiana would not have clear jurisdiction to prosecute Danny Gayheart because neither can prove where either the offense conduct or death occurred. (This is the approach taken by Indiana today.)

Ten states, those with medium shading on the map, authorize territorial jurisdiction where any aspect of the offense has occurred within the state, even where no offense element occurred within the state. For instance, repeated assaults over a period of hours may result in the death of the victim, even though no single assault is alone sufficient to satisfy the conduct element of homicide. A court might find that any single assault is "part" of the homicide offense and would suffice for jurisdiction. Likewise, a defendant's mere preparations for an offense (short of the conduct that constitutes a criminal attempt) do not satisfy any offense element, yet a court may view such preparations as "part" of the offense and are sufficient for jurisdiction. Under this broader approach, both New York and New Jersey could prosecute Burr's killing of Hamilton because some part of the offense and its preparation were performed in their state. And, under this approach, Michigan could prosecute Gayheart's killing of Reinel because it can show that some of the conduct in preparation of the offense occurred in Michigan. Indiana might also have jurisdiction but, if the only conduct they can prove is dumping the body, it will depend upon whether the Indiana courts are willing to see this conduct as part of the offense.

Six states, those shaded black on the map, generally permit jurisdiction over a criminal defendant even where no part of the offense takes place in their state, provided that the offense at least produces some detrimental effect there. For instance, where an Arizona defendant uses a New Mexico victim's personal information without the victim's consent, the defendant may be liable in New Mexico, even where the court does not find that any part of the offense took place there. Or where a diver illegally obtains sponges off the Florida coast and outside its territorial limits, the state nevertheless may exercise jurisdiction because the state "has an interest in the proper maintenance of the sponge fishery."[13] Michigan adopts this broadest formulation, which may explain why it was Michigan, rather than Indiana, that prosecuted Gayheart in 2009 even though they could not prove that either the lethal conduct or the death occurred in the state. Michigan prosecutors can argue that the murder had a detrimental effect within Michigan because both the killer and the victim lived there.[14]

As broad as it is, this last approach – providing jurisdiction whenever the offense has a detrimental effect on a state's interest – has limits. For instance, where a Georgia cocaine dealer agreed to deliver cocaine to a Virginia buyer in Georgia, a South Carolina appellate court held that South Carolina could not exercise jurisdiction over the Georgia dealer, even though the dealer might have inferred that the buyers would transport the cocaine through South Carolina after the transaction. The arrest of the buyers in South Carolina was not enough to meet the detrimental-effect standard, which the court construed as requiring that it must be the defendant's intent to "have a detrimental effect within South Carolina."

Does the Trend toward Broader State Jurisdiction Create More Overlapping Jurisdiction among the States for Which the Criminal Law Diversity among the States Is a Problem?

Over the 20th century, the law of territorial *jurisdiction* decisively shifted from one of narrow jurisdiction to broad. The older view represents the historical "strict territorial" principle, under which "only one state could have jurisdiction over a particular crime."[15] Jurisdiction over an offense was a matter of exclusivity. When only part of an offense occurred within a territory, courts had to decide which portion of the offense should control jurisdiction – only the state with the "essential" element had jurisdiction. Thus, even when the old territorial jurisdiction was broadened, it initially maintained the notion of exclusivity in prosecution of an offense.[16] As U.S. Supreme Court decisions paved the way for expanded jurisdiction,[17] which states were happy to assert, the exclusivity of jurisdiction increasingly broke down.

It remains to be seen whether the trend toward broader jurisdiction will continue. The Model Penal Code drafters understood the trend,[18] and Section 1.03 of the Model Code eventually prompted a majority of states to adopt the "any element" principle.[19] There is certainly room to expand in this direction, for as things stand, only a handful of states have extended territorial jurisdiction to the limits of due process. The Model Penal Code Commentaries acknowledge, for instance, that the provision in Section 1.03 fails to reach certain risk-creation offenses, where the only territorial nexus is that the conduct creates the risk within the state, and the risk does not materialize.[20] If the trend toward broader jurisdiction continues, one would expect a move toward assertion of jurisdiction in such cases.

But even if the trend toward expanded territorial jurisdiction does not continue, even the current state of affairs is one that has potential complications that are not always considered in the jurisdiction debate. Unlike the more limited territoriality of the old view in which there existed exclusivity in jurisdiction, today it is increasingly common that multiple states have jurisdiction to prosecute a given offense. And such overlapping jurisdiction between or among states means overlapping obligations of potential offenders. The illegal sale of drugs in Virginia to a buyer from Georgia is subject to the demands of at least three sovereigns: the states of Virginia and Georgia, and the federal government. And if the person's conduct produces a detrimental effect in South Carolina, that body of criminal law may impose yet further demands.[21]

In other words, the modern expanded view of criminal jurisdiction gives greater practical importance to one of the main themes of this volume: the enormous diversity in criminal law among the states. As the Model Penal Code drafters explain, "Since the commands and the excuses of the penal law may vary with the jurisdiction," which the maps within this volume dramatically confirm, "there is danger of inconsistent obligations if one's conduct is governed by a multiplicity of legal systems."[22] In addition, when multiple states have jurisdiction over an offense, it may be difficult for the ordinary person to fully understand what the criminal law (of the various states) require of him or her. For example, recall from the statutory rape chapter,[23] the complications of boyfriend-girlfriend going on a trip or even living near a state line. Are they likely to know the criminal law's demands if states other than their home state have jurisdiction to prosecute?

Aftermaths

Burr uses his time out of state while the New York charges are pending to bring new troubles on himself. Without informing President Jefferson, Vice President Burr attempts to enlist the aid of the British to prevent Mexico from seizing part of the new Louisiana Purchase. President Jefferson is furious: he suspects Burr made his overtures to the British only to enable the British to seize territory itself – and to ensure Burr's position in any new government the British might create in their new territory.

Burr is charged with treason and tried several times on the charges but acquitted, in large part because, whether his intention was to overthrow the government or not, he had done nothing more than talk about what he thought about doing. Without an overt act, he does not meet the standards of the charge of treason. To President Jefferson, the strict interpretation of the Constitution that allows Burr to remain free is proof that it is a mistake to have an independent judiciary.

Hated by many, but legally convicted of nothing, Burr leaves the United States in disgrace for Europe in 1807. He remains in Europe for four years, where he continues to pursue schemes to earn himself power and money. He tells some of his friends he will make himself the Emperor of Mexico and starts handing out cabinet positions.

By 1812, after the political climate at home changes and his European debts grow large, Burr returns to New York to practice law. He marries a rich widow, who later sues for divorce on the ground that he has taken all her money and is an adulterer. The divorce is granted in 1836 on the same day Burr dies.

In the Danny Gayheart case, as the investigation moves forward, the Indiana State Police join the LaGrange County (Indiana) Sheriff's Department and Sturgis (Michigan) Police Department at the FBI office in Kalamazoo, Michigan to determine which *jurisdiction* should first prosecute Gayheart. As noted in the analysis above, Michigan has the broader jurisdictional statute of the two. Under Michigan law, the state has jurisdiction to prosecute crimes committed outside of the state if the victim is a Michigan resident, if the victim is located inside Michigan at the time of the crime, or if the "conduct constitutes an attempt to commit a criminal offense within this state."[24] Gayheart took substantial steps within Michigan toward the commission of the crime, such as preparing the bag of supplies. So, it is no surprise that it is agreed that Michigan will undertake the prosecution.

Gayheart is convicted of first-degree murder and sentenced to life imprisonment without parole. He appeals, arguing that the Michigan court does not have jurisdiction over the case because there is insufficient evidence to show the murder took place in Michigan, as the body was found in Indiana. The prosecution notes the broadening of the state's jurisdictional statute in 2002, and the court affirms his conviction.

Chapter Glossary

Indictment: An indictment formally charges a person with a criminal offense. The indictment authorizes a government prosecution of a suspected criminal for the offenses charged in the indictment. In order to obtain an indictment, the prosecution must persuade a grand jury that there is adequate basis for bringing criminal charges against a suspected criminal actor.[25]

Jurisdiction: The term "jurisdiction" can be best understood by being compared to "power." Any court possesses jurisdiction over matters only to the extent granted to it by the Constitution or by legislation of the sovereignty on behalf of which it functions.[26]

Notes

1. This portion of the narrative is drawn from the following sources: Ron Chernow, *Alexander Hamilton* (New York: Penguin Books, 2005); Mark O. Hatfield, Donald A. Ritchie, Jo Anne McCormick Quatannens, Richard A. Baker, and William T. Hull, *Vice Presidents of the United States 1789–1993* (Washington, D.C.: U.S. Government Printing Office, 1997); James Parton, *The Life and Times of Aaron Burr* (New York: Houghton Mifflin, 1893).

2. Parton, *The Life and Times of Aaron Burr*, 341.

3. Parton, *The Life and Times of Aaron Burr*, 341.

4. Parton, *The Life and Times of Aaron Burr*, 343.

5. Chernow, *Alexander Hamilton*, 718.

6. Chernow, *Alexander Hamilton*, 719.

7. The law of jurisdiction at first glance is a simple issue: what parts of an offense generally must take place within the state in order for the state to exercise jurisdiction? For instance, the Model Penal Code drafters offer a simple rule in § 1.03(1)(a), that where no more specific rule controls, then there is jurisdiction over an offense where "either the conduct which is an element of the offense or the result which is such an element occurs within th[e] state." No state, however, leaves the matter at that. The issue is made complex by a number of specific rules covering attempts, conspiracies, complicity, and still other specific offenses, such as failure to provide child support. The Model Penal Code does this as well. After the simple rule in § 1.03(1)(a), the remaining provisions under § 1.03 are more specific rules, governing attempts in subsection (1)(b), conspiracies in subsection (1)(c), complicity and inchoate offenses targeting another jurisdiction in subsection (1)(d), omissions in subsection (1)(e), and offenses "which expressly prohibit conduct outside the State" in subsection (1)(f). Further refinements to the rules are provided in subsections (2) through (5). The focus of this chapter, however, is the simple rule in 1.03(1)(a), and the variations on that rule among the states. (Six states do not have any variation of the rule – that is, no part of an offense needs to have occurred within the state in order for the state to exercise territorial jurisdiction. *See infra* note 15.)

8. Lindsay Farmer, 'Territorial Jurisdiction and Criminalization,' *University of Toronto Law Journal 63* (2013): pp. 225, 232.

9. This portion of the narrative is drawn from the following sources: Latisha R. Gray, 'Man's Conviction Is Little Comfort to Victim's Son,' *Herald-Tribune*, 3 November 2007, http://www.heraldtribune.com/news/20071103/mans-conviction-is-little-comfort-to-victims-son; Matt Getts, 'Ex-Rome City Man Accused of Murder, May Face Death Penalty in Michigan,' *KPC News*, 1 April 2007, http://kpcnews.com/-article_74783103-9a43-5559-b7ec-ea21c3680197.html; Lou Mumford, 'Arrest Made in 2005 Slaying,' *South Bend Tribune*, 31 March 2007, http://articles.southbendtribune.com/2007-03-31/news/26768257_1_sturgis-murder-charges-murder-counts; *People v. Gayheart* 285 Mich. App. 202 (776 N.W. 2d 330).

10. The map is taken from Paul H. Robinson and Tyler Scot Williams, *Mapping American Criminal Law: Variations across the 50 States*, Chapter 38 (Westport: Prager, 2018). All supporting authorities are available from that source.

11. Robinson and Williams, *Mapping American Criminal Law*, 310.

12. Twenty-four of these jurisdictions have adopted the Model Penal Code formulation, quoted in the margin above, which permits territorial jurisdiction when "either the conduct that is an element of the offense or the result that is such an element occurs within [the] state." The other six jurisdictions provide that the occurrence of "an[y] element" within the boundaries of the jurisdiction will suffice.

13. Robinson and Williams, *Mapping American Criminal Law*, 313.

14. The very broad rule adopted by this last group of states – shaded black on the map – originated in *Strassheim v. Daily*, a 1911 U.S. Supreme Court decision that held that Michigan could convict an Illinois defendant who unlawfully defrauded the State of Michigan even though the defendant "never had set foot in the state until after the fraud was complete." The Court held that "[a]cts done outside a jurisdiction but intended to produce and actually producing detrimental effects within it, justify a state in punishing the cause of the harm as if [the defendant] had been present at the effect." Though the decision should be read as expressing the outer limits of a state's constitutional exercise of territorial jurisdiction, several states have effectively adopted the Court's statement, or variations of it, as their general rule.

15. *State v. Allen*, 2014-NMCA-111, ¶ 15, 336 P.3d 1007, 1012.

16. *See, e.g., Commonwealth v. Apkins*, 148 Ky. 207, 146 S.W. 431, 433 (1912) (holding that, where poison was administered in Ohio but death resulted in Kentucky, Kentucky had no jurisdiction, because "[t]he wrong was done" in Ohio).

17. *See supra* notes 17 and 18.

18. The Model Penal Code § 1.03 was drafted "[o]n the premise that it is particularly desirable in a federated state to increase jurisdictional options," within the limits of fairness. Model Penal Code and Commentaries § 1.03 at 35 (1985). The code therefore prescribed "broad" jurisdictional bases. *Id.*

19. *See supra* notes 9–11 and accompanying text.

20. Model Penal Code and Commentaries S 1.03 cmt. 4, at 52 (1985).

21. *Cf. State v. Dudley*, 354 S.C. 514, 533 (Ct. App. 2003) (involving a Virginia sale to a buyer in Georgia with detrimental effects in South Carolina).

22. Model Penal Code and Commentaries § 1.03 cmt. 1, at 38 (1985). In contrast, the strict territorial principle "yields some safeguard against the unfair condemnation of conduct that is approved or tolerated by the community in which the acts involved occurred." *Id.*

23. Chapter 23.

24. *People v. Gayheart* 285 Mich. App. 202 (776 N.W. 2d 330).

25. *Indictment*, Legal Information Institute, https://www.law.cornell.edu/wex/indictment.

26. *Jurisdiction*, Legal Information Institute, https://www.law.cornell.edu/wex/jurisdiction.

Chapter 31

Extradition and Rendition

The Hatfields and McCoys Feud

1888. Wilhelm II becomes Emperor of Germany and will remain ruler until the German Revolution of 1918 forces him to abdicate, making him the last German Emperor. Nikola Tesla and other scientists establish that radio waves belong to the same family as light waves. The pneumatic tire is invented by J.D. Dunlop. Vincent Van Gogh works to establish an artists' colony but when his efforts fail, he slices off part of his ear (which he gives to a prostitute for safe keeping). The National Geographic Society is founded in Washington, D.C. for "the increase and diffusion of geographic knowledge," as the world becomes ever more inter-connected. But clear boundaries remain and continue to produce their own special problems.

Devil Anse Hatfield – 1888

The Hatfield and McCoy families live on opposite sides of the Tug River: the Hatfields in West Virginia and the McCoys in Kentucky.[1] The two families tolerate each other until the Civil War, when a McCoy family member, on his way home to Kentucky after serving in the Union army, is killed by a West Virginia Confederate militia group led by William Anderson "Devil Anse" Hatfield, future patriarch of the Hatfields.

Animosity between the families grows. The West Virginia Hatfields are wealthier and more politically connected, leaving the Kentucky McCoys vulnerable. In the late 1870s, Devil Anse Hatfield sues a member of the McCoy family, claiming a large tract of McCoy land. With the help of a rigged jury, Anse is awarded 5,000 acres. In a subsequent dispute over a prized pig, the McCoys again end up losing because of a rigged jury. Then, in a Romeo-and-Juliet affair between Roseanna McCoy and Johnse Hatfield, the McCoys are incited to capture Johnse Hatfield. The idea is to get him out of Roseanna's life by turning him over to Kentucky authorities who want him for

DOI: 10.4324/9781003258025-35

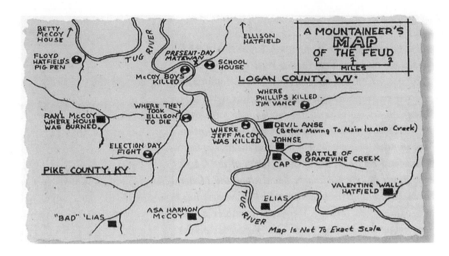

Figure 31.1 The Tug River marks the boundary between Kentucky and West Virginia on this 1898 map showing the locations of some of the feud events

outstanding bootlegging warrants. But before he can be handed over, Devil Anse arrives in Kentucky with a rescue party.

In 1882, the festering hatred explodes into serious violence. Two of Devil Anse's brothers get drunk and wander about on the Kentucky side of the river, crossing paths with three McCoy brothers. Inevitably, a fight breaks out and one of the Hatfield brothers sustains a gunshot wound and is stabbed 26 times. Police arrest the McCoys, but before they are jailed, Anse rounds up a posse, overwhelms the police, and takes the three McCoys back to West Virginia for Hatfield justice. As long as the wounded man lives, the McCoys are not harmed but when the Hatfield brother dies the McCoy captives are stripped, tied to pawpaw trees, and shot 50 times.

Kentucky indicts a score of Hatfields for the murders, but none of the well-connected Hatfields are arrested by West Virginia authorities. The Hatfields know that the McCoys will not drop the matter and they form the Logan County Regulators, a group of about 50 men who will stand guard to prevent the McCoys from transporting any of the accused murderers to Kentucky. Soon, the force takes on more than a defensive role and regularly crosses into Kentucky to commit robberies, threaten businesses, and harass residents. They announce their intention to burn down the Pike County Courthouse if they are provoked. The raids affect the entire region, causing people on both sides of the river to leave their homes in search of safety. It is reported that "Business along the border is practically suspended."[2]

In a speech on December 31, 1887, the governor of Kentucky declares that these Hatfield bad apples are a threat to Kentucky and promises that "the commonwealth [will] take action to weed them out."[3] A formal request for *extradition* is filed with West Virginia but its governor does not reply. The Kentucky governor offers rewards to anyone who seizes any of the wanted men and brings them to Kentucky for trial. Angered that the arrest warrants are being pursued, the Hatfields cross the river in force and surround the McCoy's main homestead, opening fire on the sleeping family and setting fire to Randolph McCoy's cabin to force them out so that they can be shot.

After this "New Year's Massacre," the reward for the arrest of the Hatfields is raised to $2,700 (over $70,000 in today's currency).

Despite the extreme violence, West Virginia refuses to extradite the wanted men. It is the position of the West Virginia governor that the law does not allow him to extradite them. The "Governor could not honor a request for extradition from another state if the defendant could prove by witness that he had not committed a crime in the state that sought his extradition."[4]

The citizens living in the area are becoming increasingly frustrated because no one seems able to hold the Hatfields accountable for their ongoing criminal activities. To keep the peace, they call for "sufficient troops to prevent West Virginians from crossing … on the Kentucky side, and Kentuckians from crossing to the West Virginian side."[5] West Virginia's governor orders two companies of infantry to protect the West Virginia side of the Tug River and requests that the Governor of Kentucky do the same on his side.

In time, Kentucky obtains custody of several members of the Hatfield family but not the leaders. West Virginia's governor demands the men be returned because they have been illegally removed from their home state. He complains that the men "were taken from this State without any legal process whatever."[6] But West Virginia's Attorney General tells his governor that "Kentucky has an exceptionally convincing case, and we have a rather weak one."[7]

The case eventually makes its way to the Supreme Court. As one writer puts it, the "family feud that began in a log cabin with a hog trial is scheduled to go before the highest court in the nation."[8] April 23, 1888 brings "down the curtain on the protracted battle over state's rights." In the case of *Mahon v. Justice*, the Supreme Court rules 7-2 that "The nine West Virginia men will remain in Pikeville Jail [in Kentucky] until their day in court arrives."[9] The Hatfield men are then tried for the murder and seven receive life sentences. Ellison "Cottontop" Mounts, who is mentally impaired, is hanged.

Extradition

After a person commits an offense, especially a serious one to which serious punishment attaches, it is not uncommon for the person to flee the state. Because it is the states, rather than the federal government, that are given the police power under the Constitution, most offenses are crimes for which only the state authorities have jurisdiction to prosecute. (Federal offenses are limited to instances where there is a special federal interest, such as assaulting a federal officer or engaging in interstate criminal activity.) Because each state is an independent sovereign, the officials of the state pursuing the fugitive cannot simply go to the receiving state and arrest the suspect. They must instead request the other state to capture, detain, and return the person. (The term *extradition* is used to describe the process of seeking to obtain the fugitive; the term *rendition* is used to describe the process of turning over the fugitive to another sovereign.[10] However, in common usage the term "extradition" is used to refer to both actions.)

Whether to agree to an extradition request is not left to the discretion of the state to which the fugitive flees. The United States Constitution, in Article IV, Section 2, Clause 2 – the Extradition Clause (reproduced in the margin) – obliges each state to extradite a fugitive upon the request of a state that has jurisdiction to prosecute.

U.S. Constitution, Article IV, Section 2, Clause 2

A person charged in any state with treason, felony, or other crime, who shall flee from justice, and be found in another state, shall on demand of the executive authority of the state from which he fled, be delivered up, to be removed to the state having jurisdiction of the crime.

Figure 31.2

Clearly, the state of West Virginia had a constitutional obligation to extradite the Hatfields to Kentucky, and the West Virginia refusal was a violation of that obligation. However, at the time of the Hatfields and McCoys feud there was little effective means of enforcing this constitutional obligation.

To provide enforcement against recalcitrant states, federal legislation, under 18 U.S.C. §3182, now provides a mechanism for implementing and enforcing the constitutional mandate.[11] Commonly governing the details of the extradition process in many states is the Uniform Criminal Extradition Act (UCEA), which many states have adopted. Federal agents also may get involved in interstate extradition processes through 18 U.S.C. §1073, which creates the federal crime of Unlawful Flight to Avoid Prosecution (UFAP). The offense is used less as a basis for federal prosecution and more as a basis for federal jurisdiction to return a suspect to the site of the crime – the state from which he or she unlawfully fled – without having to use formal extradition procedures.

Fugitive Transfers between the States

The mechanics of locating and returning fleeing felons rely upon a variety of mechanisms, most prominently the FBI's fugitive tracking database, known as the National Crime Information Center (NCIC). Rather than actually chasing after fugitives, states commonly simply register their arrest warrant with the NCIC, then wait for the fugitive to pop up on the system when some law enforcement agency somewhere has contact with the fugitive.

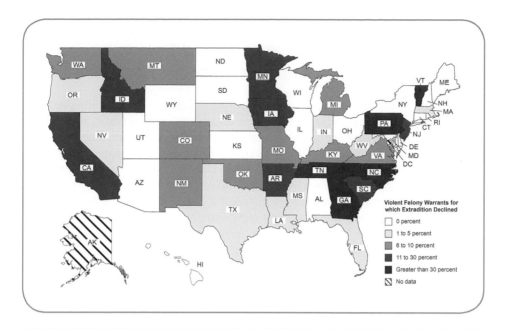

Violent Felony Warrants for which Extradition Declined

- 0 percent
- 1 to 5 percent
- 6 to 10 percent
- 11 to 30 percent
- Greater than 30 percent
- No data

Figure 31.3

Interestingly, some states don't want to bother with the expense or the legal hassle of bringing the fugitive back to the state of his crime, so they will flag their warrant in the NCIC database as "non-extraditable." This happens even in the case of violent felonies, such as murder, non-negligent manslaughter, forcible rape, robbery, and aggravated assault. In one study, for example, certain major cities like Philadelphia and Atlanta indicated that they would not bother to signal *extradition* for as many as 90% or more of their felony suspects. Los Angeles, for example, said they would not extradite 77 people wanted for murder or attempted murder. Among those the police would not pursue are a man accused of attacking his roommate with a machete, a man who allegedly threatened a store manager with a gun in the course of a robbery, and a man identified as one of Pittsburgh's "most wanted" fugitives.[12]

A state's policies in signaling a willingness to extradite a fugitive posted on NCIC can change as the state's administrative authorities change. But to illustrate how diverse these policies can be, the map below presents the data from one available study,[13] showing the percentage of total warrants for violent crimes for which the state has signaled it will not pursue extradition. The darker the shading on the map, the greater the number of violent felons for which extradition is not requested.[14]

Eighteen states, those with no shading on the map, sought extradition for all of their outstanding violent felony warrants while ten states, those with light shading on the map, declined extradition for only 1–5% of their violent felony warrants. In contrast, seven states, with darker shading, declined extradition for between 11% and 30% of their violent felony warrants. And five states, with black shading, declined extradition for more than 30%.

Why Would a State Issue a Warrant for a Violent Felon but Refuse to Extradite Him When Captured by Another State?

The practice of listing violent felony warrants on NCIC as "non-extraditable" does seem like a peculiar practice. Not only are these states not pursuing their violent fugitives themselves; they are not bothering to collect them when someone else detains them. The most obviously troubling aspect of the practice is the apparent indifference to the importance of doing justice that it reveals. If the state has the evidence required to support a felony warrant, why wouldn't it have a moral obligation to pursue the case further? Presumably they would pursue the case if the fugitive happens to be found in their state – if not, they would simply withdraw the warrant altogether – but they can't be bothered if doing justice involves the inconvenience of returning the fugitive from another state? (If the underlying felony offense is really so minor that it does not deserve the pursuit of the fugitive, then perhaps they ought to reform their criminal codes to drop such offenses from the felony classification?)

Also quite unsettling is the message that this practice sends to other states. Apparently, the sending states that are declining *extradition* are happy to have their fugitives remain in other states. The problem, of course, is that these other states have no legal basis for detaining the dangerous fugitive – only the sending state has that authority – so the state to which the felon has fled must simply tolerate having the dangerous fugitive in their midst until he victimizes someone else, which will give that state authority to deal with him. This suggests something of a lack of empathy for the citizens and law enforcement of the receiving state.

If one were cynical, one could see such declined-extradition policies as similar to the old Western sheriff telling the gunfighter to "get out of Dodge." The message is: as long as you get out of our state and stop victimizing our citizens, we won't pursue you. Especially to hardened professional criminals, this may be a message quickly and easily understood. But the selfish states who send this message, and thereby encourage the dangerous to victimize elsewhere, ought to worry about the corollary message: if you want to commit a violent crime and minimize your chances of getting caught and punished, be sure to commit your crime in one of the non-extraditing states, so you can flee with less worry of being pursued. A better approach would be for all states to take seriously their moral and legal obligations to do justice, as well as their moral and ethical obligations to their fellow states to actively pursue the prosecution of all violent felony fugitives.

While the extradition practices of some states may be debatable, there is little doubt that a state can successfully get extradition of a fugitive if it wishes to do so. However, where the fugitive flees the country, no such orderly extradition system exists in international law. Even where foreign countries allow extradition, it commonly can be limited and discretionary. Many countries routinely refuse extradition and there is nothing, other than political pressure or abduction, that the country seeking extradition can do about it. Consider the following case.

Dr. Alvarez Machain and the Torture of DEA Agent Enrique Camarena-Salazar – 1985

Enrique Camarena-Salazar is working in Mexico as an agent for the United States Drug Enforcement Agency (DEA).[15] In 1984, acting on information from Camarena, 450 Mexican soldiers destroy a 2,500-acre marijuana plantation with an estimated annual

Figure 31.4 DEA Agent Enrique "Kiki" Camarena, circa 1983

production worth $8 billion. The facility includes 13 smaller farms, each ranging from 500 to 1,200 acres and containing over one million plants. The operation is the financial heart of the powerful Caro-Quintero drug clan. The DEA announces that 8,000 tons of marijuana is seized in the raid, making it among the largest of all time.

In early 1985, Camarena, known as Kiki, leaves the U.S. Consulate in Guadalajara to meet his wife for lunch. He never makes it – on the way he and his pilot Alfredo Zavala-Avelar are kidnapped. When the American authorities turn to the Mexican government for help in hunting down the kidnappers, they are underwhelmed by the government's response. Taking matters into their own hands, the United States initiates Operation Camarena. They stop and search every vehicle passing from Mexico into the United States, turning the entire 2,000-mile border between the two nations into an epic traffic disaster.

The bodies of both men, still bound and gagged, are found weeks later buried on a ranch north of Guadalajara. The body of Camarena shows that his nose, cheekbones, and windpipe are crushed. His ribs are broken, and there is a hole from a power drill in his skull. According to the autopsy report, Camarena's skull had been "shattered like an egg-shell."[16] Audio tapes of Camarena's violent two-day interrogation are also recovered. The tapes allow authorities to understand exactly how Camarena was beaten and tortured as the cartel tried to extract information about the DEA's surveillance of players in the drug trade.

The discovery of the bodies and the audio tapes sparks Operation Leyenda (Operation Legend), the largest manhunt in DEA history. The authorities know that Camarena and the pilot died at a large estate outside Guadalajara, owned by suspected drug kingpin Ernesto Fonseca. Voices of individual conspirators can be heard clearly on the recording. Among the suspects the DEA pursues is Humberto Alvarez Machain, a 44-year-old gynecologist. Dr. Machain administered drugs during the torture session in order to keep Camarena alive and awake.

Five years later, in 1990, Machain is at his office when he is kidnapped by a pair of bounty hunters seeking to claim a reward offered by the United States. No representative of the American government is at hand during the capture of the doctor, nor did the government assist in any way in planning the kidnapping. Machain is taken from his Guadalajara office to a private plane bound for El Paso, Texas. The bounty-hunting kidnappers notify DEA agents that they've captured Machain. The DEA is on hand to greet the doctor at the airport with handcuffs and a reading of his Miranda rights.

Machain's arrest outrages Mexican officials, who see it as a violation of Mexican sovereignty. The DEA responds by explaining that they did not plan or participate in the kidnapping. However, it is also true that the kidnappers acted in order to obtain a promised $50,000 reward for Machain. The incident quickly precipitates diplomatic fallout but the United States steadfastly refuses to return the doctor to Mexico. Over Mexico's protests, Machain is put on trial with seven others in connection with Camarena's torture and murder (including two other men illicitly abducted from Mexican soil).

In June 1992, the Supreme Court reverses a lower court ruling and holds that Machain's abduction does not preclude criminal prosecution in the United States[17] "The presence of an *extradition* treaty between the United States and another country does not necessarily preclude obtaining a citizen of that nation through abduction," reasons Chief Justice William Rehnquist, writing for the majority. "It has been established that abduction, in and of itself, does not invalidate prosecution against a foreign national."[18] He goes on to argue that customary international law does not apply in this case because it is precluded by the extradition treaty, and that the extradition treaty itself does not explicitly bar abductions like Machain's. The 6-3 decision earns a strong rebuke from some human rights advocates.

Mexico's refusal to extradite Machain illustrates the dramatic difference between intra-country and inter-country transfers. The former is today relatively easy, especially given the variety of mechanisms by which such transfer between American states can be arranged, as discussed above, while inter-country transfers can sometimes be impossible to arrange.

Aftermaths

After the 1888 Supreme Court decision and the trial and conviction of the eight Hatfield men in custody, the focus shifts to the men who participated in the New Year's Massacre and are still at large in West Virginia. Kentucky continues to press that state for the men to answer for their crimes, but with limited success.

Cap Hatfield, who organized the New Year's Massacre, kills three more people in 1896. He is arrested and jailed but is able to escape. He is never brought to trial and dies of old age. Johnse Hatfield, who killed Alifair McCoy during the New Year's Massacre by bashing her skull in with the butt of his rifle, is finally captured in 1900. He is tried and found guilty of the murder and serves 13 years of a life sentence. The trial marks the last law enforcement action related to the feud. All other major players are left unpunished.

Anse Devil Hatfield takes up Christianity, leaves the Tug River, and dies of pneumonia at 81. He remains large in death; his grave is topped by a life-sized marble statue of himself. Randolph McCoy loses most of his family and most of his wealth in the feud but is not killed. He too leaves the river area. He dies at age 88 in a cooking accident.

In the Dr. Alvarez Machain case, the defendant goes to trial in Los Angeles in December 1992. Prosecutors present evidence linking Machain to a number of powerful Mexican cartel leaders and show his bootprints appeared throughout the house where Camarena was tortured. However, after the prosecution wraps up its case, Judge Rafeedie rules that there is not sufficient evidence against Machain to send the case to the jury. He orders the charges dismissed and Machain is freed, returning to Mexico on December 16, 1992.

Chapter Glossary

Extradition: Extradition occurs when one state requests the surrender of a person in another state for the purpose of prosecuting the person for a criminal offense.[19]

Rendition: Rendition occurs when one state sends a person to another state for the purpose of criminal investigation or prosecution in that other state.[20]

Notes

1. This narrative is drawn from the following sources: 'Called Out: An Order for Troops on the Kentucky Border,' *Wheeling Register*, 30 January 1888, accessed from Contemporary Articles on Hatfield-McCoy Feud, http://www.wvculture.org/history/-hatfield/hatfieldmccoyarticles.html; 'From the Frontier: The Commissioner's Report,' *Wheeling Intelligencer*, 1 February 1888, accessed from Contemporary Articles on Hatfield- McCoy Feud, http://www.wvculture.org/history/hatfield/-hatfieldmccoyarticles.html; L.D. Hatfield, *The True Story of the Hatfield and the McCoy Feud* (New York: Cosimo, 2012); 'Kentucky Outlaws,' *Wheeling Register*, 28 January 1888, accessed from Contemporary Articles on Hatfield-McCoy Feud, http://-www.wvculture.org/history/hatfield/hatfieldmccoyarticles.html; Charles G. Mutzenberg, *Kentucky's Famous Feuds and Tragedies: Authentic History of the World Renowned Vendettas of the Dark and Bloody Ground* (New York: R.F. Fenno & Co., 1917), https://archive.org/details/cu31924030316164; 'A Terrible Story of a Family Feud and Murder,' *Wheeling Daily Intelligencer*, 9 January 1888, accessed from Contemporary Articles on Hatfield-McCoy Feud, http://www.wvculture.org/history/-hatfield/hatfieldmccoyarticles.html; Altina L. Waller, *Feud: Hatfields, McCoys, and Social Change in Appalachia 1860–1890* (Chapel Hill: The University of North Carolina Press, 1988).
2. 'Kentucky Outlaws.'
3. 'Kentucky Outlaws.'
4. Hatfield, *The True Story*; 'Kentucky Outlaws.'
5. 'Called Out.'
6. Hatfield, *The True Story*.
7. Hatfield, *The True Story*.
8. Mutzenberg, 'The Tolliver-Martin-Logan Vendetta,' in *Kentucky's Famous Feuds and Tragedies*, p. 140.
9. Mutzenberg, 'The Tolliver-Martin-Logan Vendetta,' in *Kentucky's Famous Feuds and Tragedies*, p. 141.
10. Wikipedia, https://en.m.wikipedia.org/wiki/Rendition_(law)#:~:text=In%20law%2C%20rendition%20is%20a,for%20extradition%20has%20taken%20place.

11. It reads as follows:

> Whenever the executive authority of any State or Territory demands any person as a fugitive from justice, of the executive authority of any State, District, or Territory to which such person has fled, and produces a copy of an indictment found or an affidavit made before a magistrate of any State or Territory, charging the person demanded with having committed treason, felony, or other crime, certified as authentic by the governor or chief magistrate of the State or Territory from whence the person so charged has fled, the executive authority of the State, District, or Territory to which such person has fled shall cause him to be arrested and secured, and notify the executive authority making such demand, or the agent of such authority appointed to receive the fugitive, and shall cause the fugitive to be delivered to such agent when he shall appear. If no such agent appears within thirty days from the time of the arrest, the prisoner may be discharged.

18 U.S. Code § 3182.

12. Brad Heath, 'The Ones That Get Away,' *USA Today*, 11 March 2014, https://www.usatoday.com/story/news/nation/2014/03/11/fugitives-next-door/6262719/.

13. *Id.*

14. The map is taken from Paul H. Robinson and Tyler Scot Williams, 'Extradition,' in *Mapping American Criminal Law: Variations across the 50 States* (Westport: Prager, 2018), p. 306. All supporting authorities are available from that source.

15. This narrative is drawn from the following sources: Peter Gorman, 'Big-time Smuggler's Blues,' *Cannabis Culture*, 16 June 2006, http://www.cannabisculture.com/content/-2006/06/16/4768; Marjorie Miller, 'Mexico Asks U.S. to Extradite Doctor in Camarena Case: Drug murder: But there appears to be little possibility that the suspect, who was abducted and shipped to the United States, will be returned,' *Los Angeles Times*, 24 May 1990, http://articles.latimes.com/1990-05-24/news/mn-268_1_united-states; Kim Murphy, 'Tape of Drug Agent's Torture Is Made Public,' *Los Angeles Times*, 7 June 1988, http://articles.latimes.com/1988-06-07/news/mn-3854_1_made-public; Henry Weinstein, 'Judge Rules DEA Kidnap Violated U.S.-Mexico Pact: Camarena case: In precedent-setting decision, repatriation is ordered for doctor accused in murder,' *Los Angeles Times*, 11 August 1990, http://articles.latimes.com/1990-08-11/-news/mn-197_1_united-states; *United States v. Alvarez-Machain*, 504 U.S. 655 (1992).

16. Murphy, 'Tape of Drug Agent's Torture.'

17. *United States v. Alvarez-Machain* 504 U.S. 655 (1992).

18. *United States v. Alvarez-Machain.*

19. *Extradition*, Legal Information Institute, https://www.law.cornell.edu/wex/extradition.

20. *Rendition*, Dictionary.com, https://www.dictionary.com/browse/rendition.

Chapter 32

Patterns and Themes

The previous 31 chapters have examined a wide range of criminal law principles, rules, and offenses, and every subject has its own unique story. However, stepping back from this mountain of material, one can see some repeating patterns that suggest some larger truths about criminal law and its evolution.

A March toward More Nuanced Blameworthiness Judgments

One particularly strong pattern is a centuries-long trend toward increased sophistication and nuance in judging an offender's blameworthiness. For example, early criminal law, before the 4th century B.C.E., shows the development of the important distinction between an intentional and an accidental killing.[1] Centuries later the criminal law formalizes doctrine that further distinguishes provoked intentional killings from unprovoked intentional killings, mitigating the former.[2]

And that trend toward increasingly nuanced blameworthiness judgments continues in a wide variety of doctrines as criminal law develops, and indeed continues today. Recall the increasing limitations that many states put on the felony-murder rule.[3] Recall similarly the introduction of sliding-scale liability instead of all-or-nothing liability for mistake as to justification, so that the offender's extent of liability will match the level of his or her culpability.[4] Similarly, recall the shift from the fairly narrow common-law provocation doctrine that mitigates murder to manslaughter to the broader modern doctrine of extreme mental or emotional disturbance.[5]

The most obvious expression of this trend may be the 2007 American Law Institute amendment of the Model Penal Code's general purposes section, in which it sets

DOI: 10.4324/9781003258025-36

blameworthiness proportionality as the dominant distributive principle and thereby limits the use of non-desert distributive principles such as deterrence or incapacitation to the extent they conflict with blameworthiness proportionality.[6]

On the other hand, greater blameworthiness proportionality is a trend, not an established state of affairs. Many jurisdictions still have the natural and probable consequence rule in complicity.[7] Recall that this rule helped convict Spies for deaths during the Haymarket riot. Many states still use the Pinkerton Rule in conspiracy.[8] It was this kind of liability rule that allowed persons uninvolved in Booth's assassination to be held liable for President Lincoln's death. Many states still have a three-strikes statute,[9] the doctrine under which William Rummel was given life imprisonment for a $130 air-conditioning fraud. A majority of states at present have no control dysfunction prong of their insanity defense.[10] And most jurisdictions still have some form of the felony-murder rule.[11] Finally, many states have very low age cutoffs for prosecution as an adult.[12] Recall that South Carolina convicted 12-year-old Christopher Pittman for murder. Supporters of these doctrines no doubt can argue that there are crime-control benefits for imposing disproportionate criminal liability and punishment but recall that imposing what the community sees as disproportionate liability and punishment also has significant crime-control costs because it undermines the criminal law's moral credibility.[13]

Increased Governmental Willingness to Intrude in People's Lives

Another common trend that becomes evident in historical perspective is the increased willingness of government to intrude in people's lives, usually in an attempt to make those lives better. Recall the law's disinterest in prosecuting Hetty Green for her failure to get proper medical care for her son, a reluctance to intervene in parental decision-making that eventually disappeared.[14] Even more dramatically, recall the law's initial reluctance to curb domestic violence as with Ike Turner. Thankfully, that apparent tolerance has dissipated – recall the introduction of special domestic violence enforcement rules and the dropping of the spousal rape exemption.[15] Similarly, the law has given up its indifference to consensual physical injury that we saw in the era of Marquis de Sade, and now places real limits on the kinds of injury to which a person can consent.[16] Sometimes, however, the government's intrusion into people's lives can go too far, as we saw in the case of 1920s Prohibition.

At the same time, there are several instances in which criminal law has stepped back from intrusion in private lives. Recall that it has now essentially decriminalized Frank Sinatra's adultery,[17] same-sex intercourse, too late for Oscar Wilde,[18] and Larry Flynt's pornography.[19]

Another form of expanding criminality is the criminalization of criminal risk-taking, as by the Hunt Club in failing to repair their dam.[20] And this trend applies even in instances where no harm comes about, as in the creation of pure endangerment offenses.

Analogous to this trend is the criminal law's expansion to impose criminal liability and punishment on non-human legal entities, such as corporations. We saw such liability in the context of deceptive business practices and anti-competition offenses,[21] but the shift has been applied broadly so that legal entities can be held liable today for essentially any offense.

Criminal Law Tracking Changing Societal Norms

The collected cases in this volume also make clear that criminal law has changed and continues to change as societal norms change. Many examples of this are already illustrated above: criminalizing Ike Turner's domestic violence, criminalizing Hetty Green's failure of parental responsibility, criminalizing Marquis de Sade's consensual assault, decriminalizing Oscar Wilde's same-sex intercourse, decriminalizing Frank Sinatra's adultery, and decriminalizing Larry Flynt's pornography.

But the book provides a host of other examples as well, including decriminalizing Marquis de Sade's blasphemy,[22] criminalizing Lewis Carroll's child pornography,[23] criminalizing Oscar Wilde's statutory rape,[24] criminalizing Vanderbilt's market manipulation,[25] criminalizing Mrs. Winslow's Soothing Syrup,[26] criminalizing Alexander Ross' harassment of Bette Davis,[27] and criminalizing the reckless risk-taking of the South Fork Hunting and Fishing Club.[28]

This continuing connection between existing societal norms and criminal law is of critical importance in understanding criminal law's role in society. The criminal code is not just a collection of dry rules that experts have calculated would be good for society. Rather, the criminal law aspires to be an institution – today perhaps the only institution – that reflects the society's shared views of what conduct is truly condemnable and the factors that make an offender more or less blameworthy.

This pattern of criminal law tracking changing community views is also an important trend to cherish and perpetuate. Only a criminal law that tracks community judgments of justice can earn a reputation with the community as a moral authority – establish its moral credibility – and thereby gain the community's deference, acquiescence, and support and, perhaps most importantly, increase the chance that people will internalize its norms.[29]

Notes

1. Chapter 3.
2. Chapter 4.
3. Chapter 3. Recall that David Smith participated in a robbery and was on hand when the victim was killed yet was not charged with murder because the UK had come to reject the felony-murder rule.
4. Chapter 12. New York's adoption of the all-or-nothing approach probably had a good deal to do with the acquittal of Bernard Goetz after he shot his would-be muggers.
5. Chapter 4. Daniel White obtained a mitigation for his killing of Harvey Milk based upon an analogous murder mitigation rule.
6. Chapter 2.
7. Chapter 8.
8. Chapter 9.
9. Chapter 2.
10. Chapter 14.
11. Chapter 3.
12. Chapter 15.
13. Chapter 2.
14. Chapter 10.

15. Chapter 20.
16. Chapter 6.
17. Chapter 23.
18. Chapter 22.
19. Chapter 24.
20. Chapter 18.
21. Chapters 26 and 28.
22. Chapter 6.
23. Chapter 25.
24. Chapter 22.
25. Chapter 28.
26. Chapter 26.
27. Chapter 21.
28. Chapter 18.
29. As discussed in the chapter on punishment theory, Chapter 2.

Chapter Glossary Terms

Index

Note: *Italic* page numbers refer to figures and page numbers followed by "n" denote endnotes.